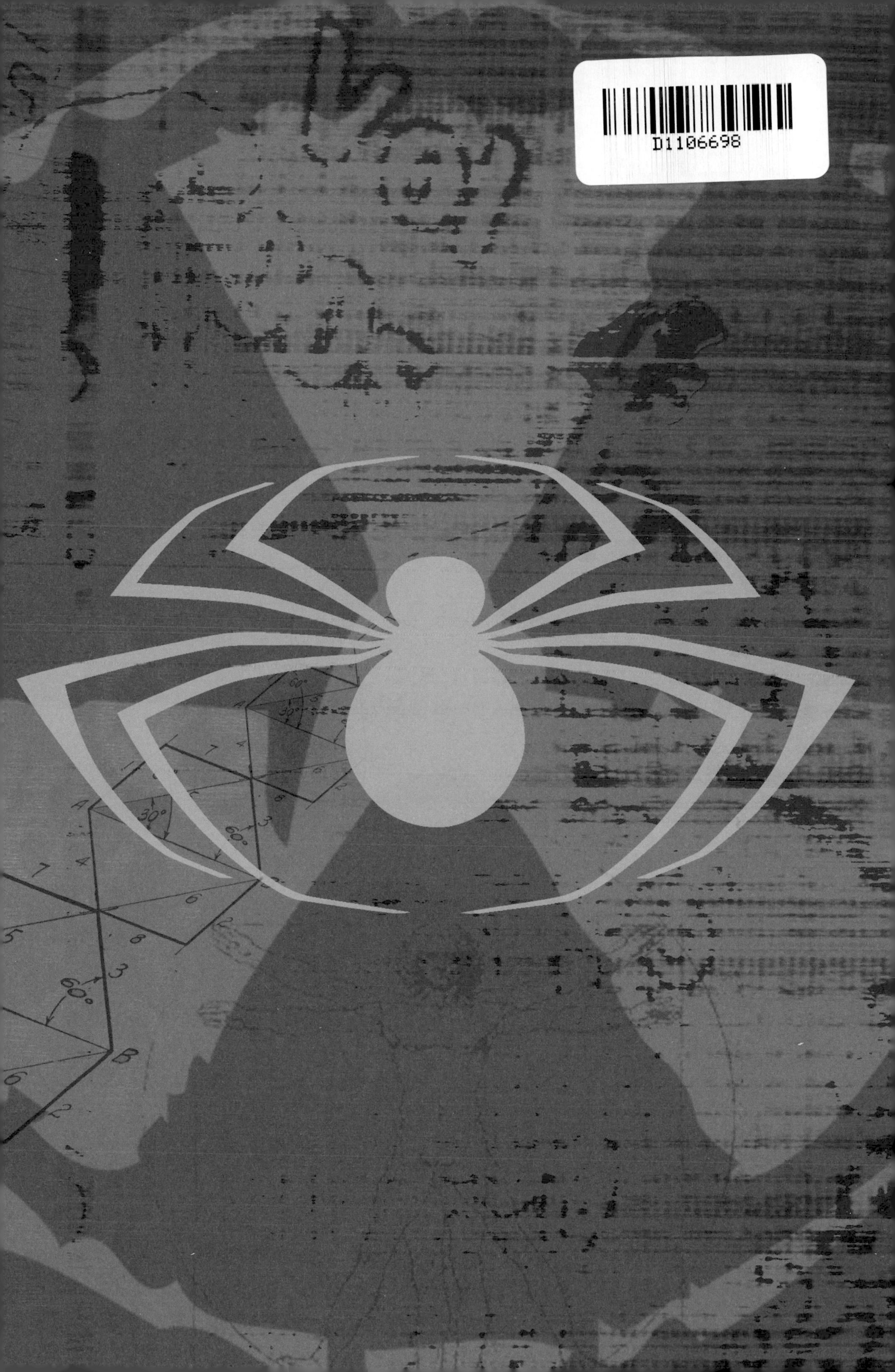

ULTIMATE SPIDER-MAN

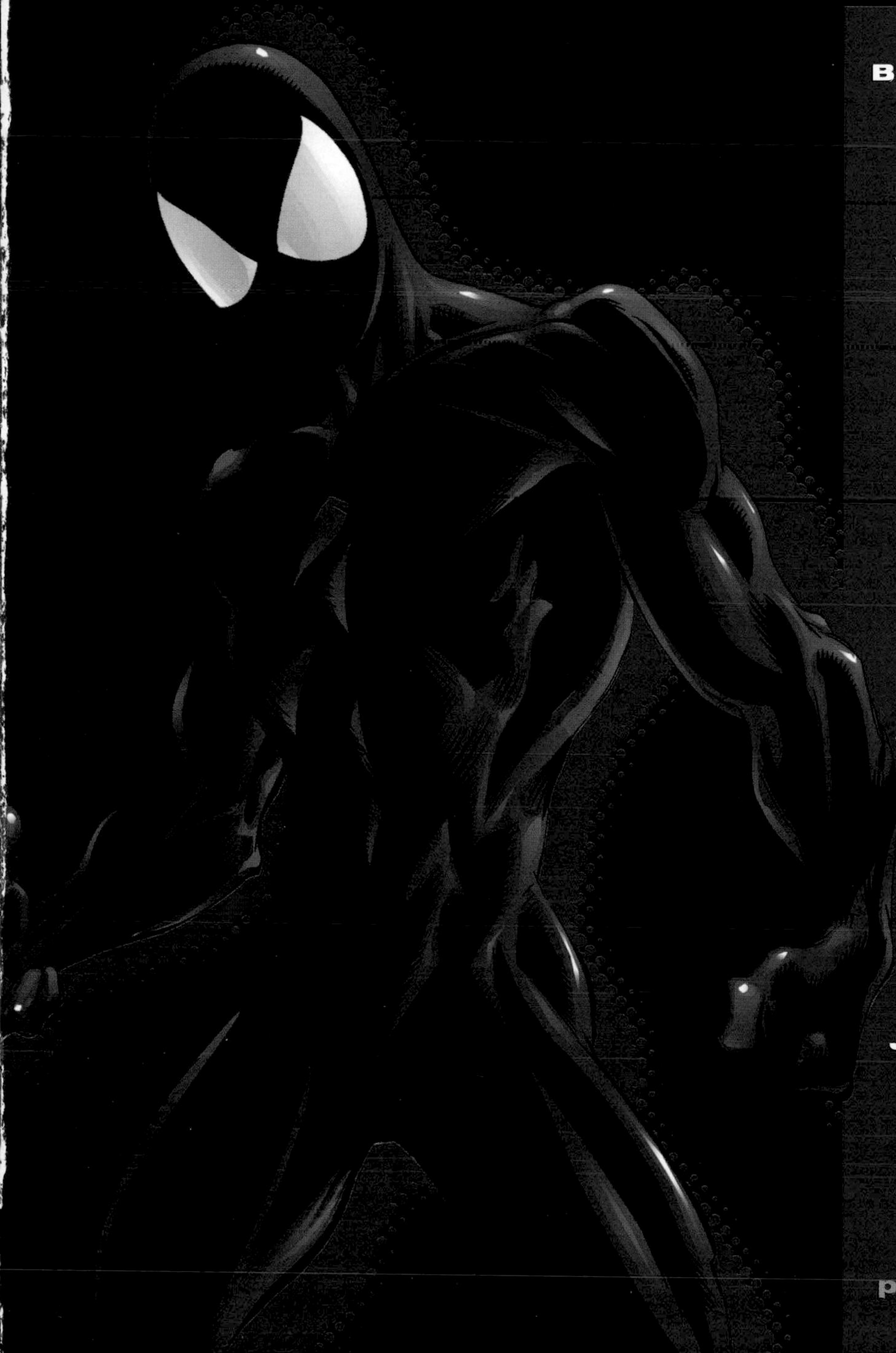

script
BRIAN MICHAEL BENDIS

pencils
MARK BAGLEY

inks
ART THIBERT
with RODNEY RAMOS

colors
TRANSPARENCY DIGITAL

letters
CHRIS ELIOPOULOS
DAVE SHARPE

assistant editors
STEPHANIE MOORE
NICK LOWE

associate editors
BRIAN SMITH
C.B. CEBULSKI

editor
RALPH MACCHIO

collections editor
JEFF YOUNGQUIST

associate editor
CORY SEDLMEIER

assistant editor
JENNIFER GRÜNWALD

book designer
JEOF VITA

editor in chief
JOE QUESADA

president & inspiration
BILL JEMAS

ULTIMATE SPIDER-MAN VOL. 3. Contains material originally published in magazine form as ULTIMATE SPIDER-MAN #28-39 and #1/2. First printing 2003. ISBN# 0-7851-1156-5. Published by MARVEL COMICS, a division of MARVEL ENTERTAINMENT GROUP, INC. OFFICE OF PUBLICATION: 10 East 40th Street, New York, NY 10016. Copyright © 2002 and 2003 Marvel Characters, Inc. All rights reserved. $29.99 per copy in the U.S. and $48.00 in Canada (GST #R127032852); Canadian Agreement #40668537. All characters featured in this issue and the distinctive names and likenesses thereof, and all related indicia are trademarks of Marvel Characters, Inc. No similarity between any of the names, characters, persons, and/or institutions in this magazine with those of any living or dead person or institution is intended, and any such similarity which may exist is purely coincidental. **Printed in the U.S.A.** ALLEN LIPSON, Chief Executive Officer and General Counsel; AVI ARAD, Chief Creative Officer; GUI KARYO, Chief Information Officer; DAVID BOGART, Managing Editor; STAN LEE, Chairman Emeritus. For information regarding advertising in Marvel Comics or on Marvel.com, please contact Russell Brown, Executive Vice President, Consumer Products, Promotions and Media Sales at rbrown@marvel.com or 212-576-8561.

10 9 8 7 6 5 4 3 2 1

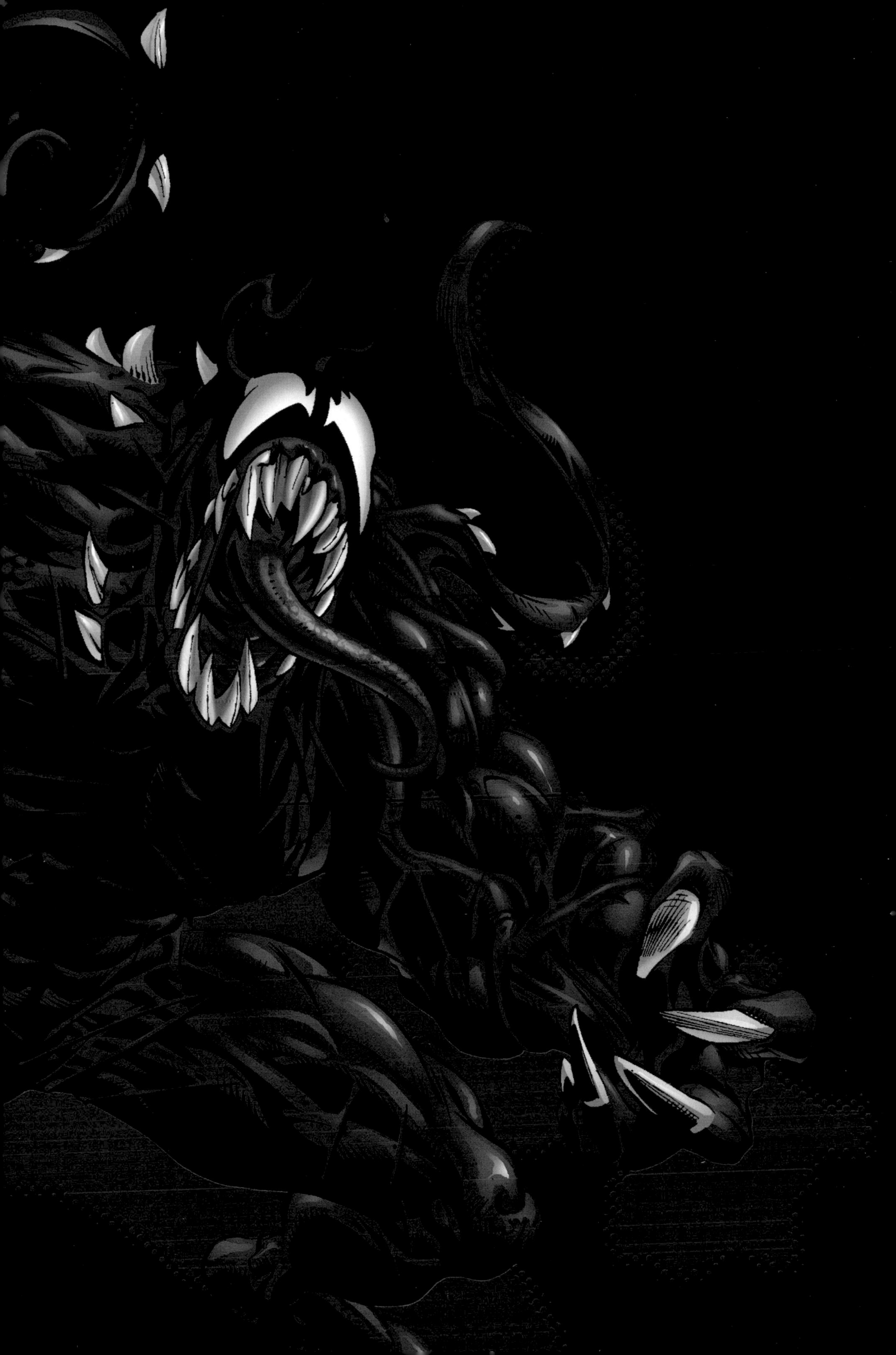

INTRODUCTION
BY BRUCE CAMPBELL

Super heroes have had a great pull on our imagination for as long as I've been alive. These overdeveloped do-gooders are always at the forefront of every medium, from old movie serials to comic books, action figures, and now video games.

As a kid, every time I rode my bike up to Sherman's Drugs in suburban Detroit, I saw the latest incarnation of super heroes lining the shelves. But in all the years of riding my single-gear Huffy bike to the store, did I ever buy a super-hero comic? Nope. Not once. Me? I put my lawn mowing money down on the comic *Sad Sack*. Most of you don't even know who I'm referring to. If your dad doesn't remember, have him call a friend from the late '60s who got better grades.

Sad Sack was my hero because he was just a schlub like me. He wasn't born on another planet, or descended from kings, and he sure as hell didn't seek some magical ring in the Southern Hemisphere. No, Sad Sack was just trying to make it through another day in the regular army (not even Covert Ops).

The reason I never jumped on board the "did you read the new Silver Surfer?" train is because I couldn't relate to how "unreal" those characters were. You folks might groove on Kryptonite (I don't even know if I spelled that right), but me personally, I couldn't give a rat's ass about some phony green rock—I need to care about what's going on.

Along came a spider(man).

This new breed of comic-book character caught my eye because of how different he was. Finally, a super hero that came from a place I could actually find on a map! I remember defending him in junior high school for that very reason.

"But he's a wuss," my friend Mike Ditz insisted. "He hardly has any powers at all."

"Shut up," I said defiantly. "Spider-Man may be a regular guy, but he has enough cool powers to kick your butt."

In this post-9/11 world, I think we all need someone to save us from the reality of everyday life, and Spider-Man might just be that guy. Why? The answer is as simple as Peter Parker. On one hand, he's just a high school kid with dreams, disappointments, and oily skin (check out Pete's zit—page six, lower right panel). But when his radioactive enhancements kick in, pistol Pete morphs into the ultimate hero—yet we know, deep beneath the spandex suit, he's just a punk from Queens trying to do the right thing.

We root for Peter Parker/Spider-Man to succeed, not because he can shoot webs and navigate Fifth Avenue during rush-hour, but because in some basic way, he's just like us.

Bruce Campbell
Oregon

p.s. We hear a lot about which super hero is the strongest. As an actor, I've worked with both Superman and Hercules and let me tell you, neither of them can muscle up a residual check like Spider-Man!

In 1979, with his Detroit friends, Sam Raimi and Rob Tapert, Bruce Cambell raised $350,000 for a low-budget film, Evil Dead. Dubbed "the most ferociously original horror movie of the year" by Stephen King, the film spawned a popular trilogy including, Evil Dead II: Dead By Dawn and Army of Darkness. Campbell has starred in TV's Adventures of Brisco County Jr., Hercules: The Legendary Journey, Xena: Warrior Princess and Jack of All Trades. His film work also includes Serving Sara, Jim Carrey's The Majestic, and Sam Raimi's blockbuster, Spider-Man. Bruce continues to share his experience in independent filmmaking at universities around the country. He recently enjoyed a national book tour to promote his best-selling memoir entitled If Chins Could Kill: Confessions of a B Movie Actor. He currently resides with his wife, Ida Gearon, in Oregon.

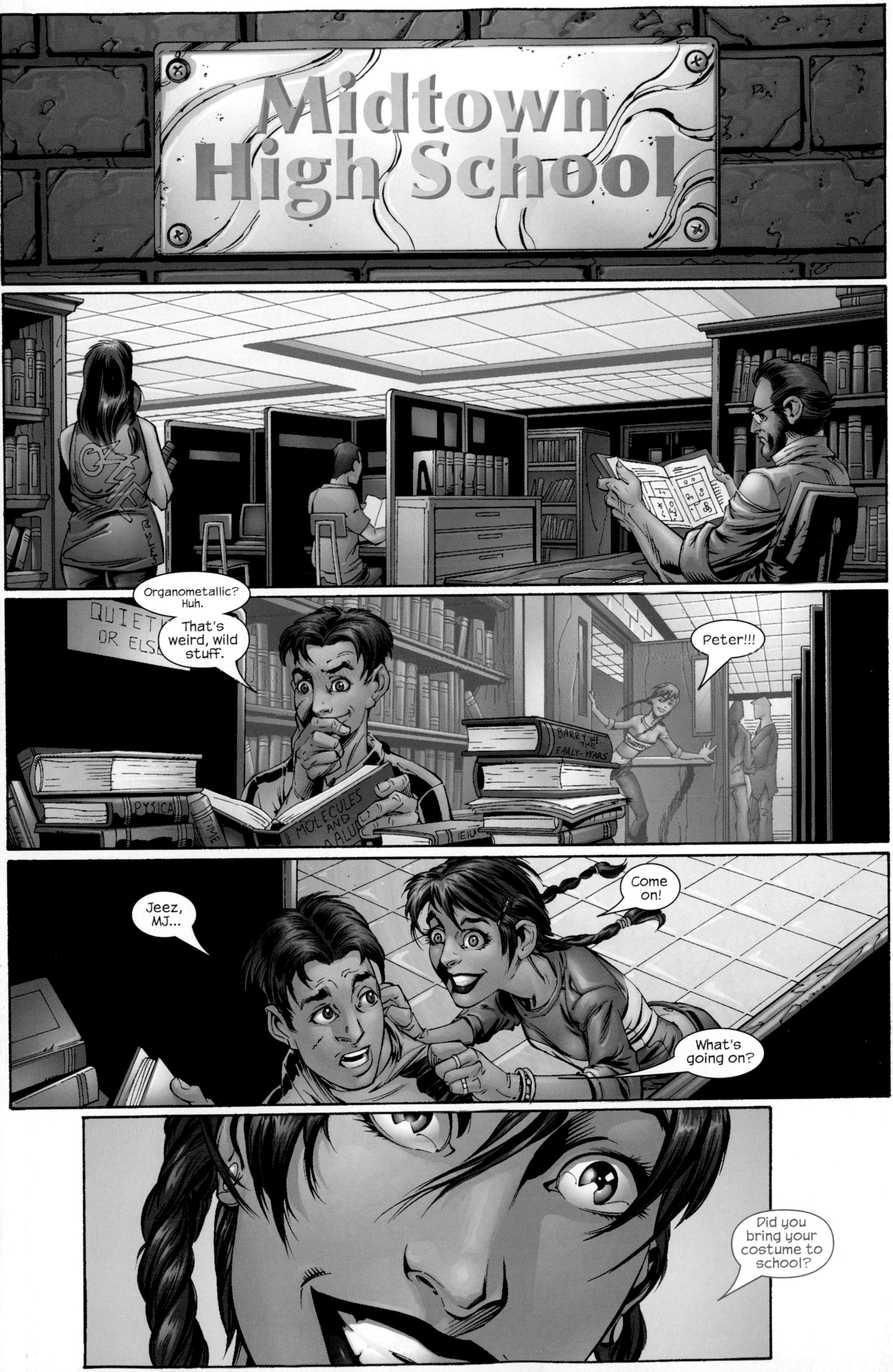
Midtown High School
QUIET OR ELSE
Organometallic? Huh.
That's weird, wild stuff.
MOLECULES AND VALUE
Peter!!!
Jeez, MJ...
Come on!
What's going on?
Did you bring your costume to school?

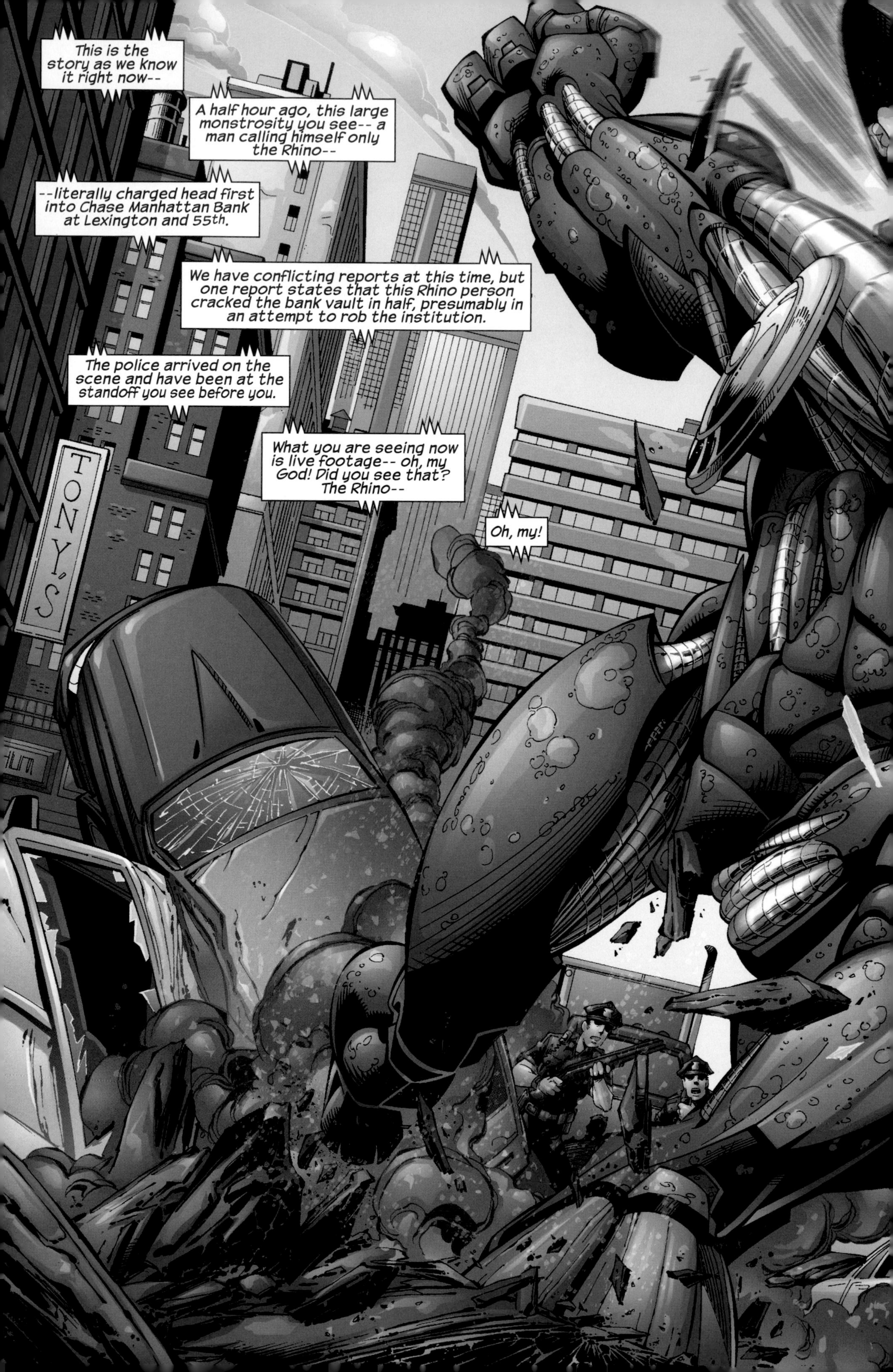
This is the story as we know it right now--
A half hour ago, this large monstrosity you see-- a man calling himself only the Rhino--
--literally charged head first into Chase Manhattan Bank at Lexington and 55th.
We have conflicting reports at this time, but one report states that this Rhino person cracked the bank vault in half, presumably in an attempt to rob the institution.
The police arrived on the scene and have been at the standoff you see before you.
What you are seeing now is live footage-- oh, my God! Did you see that? The Rhino--
Oh, my!
TONY'S

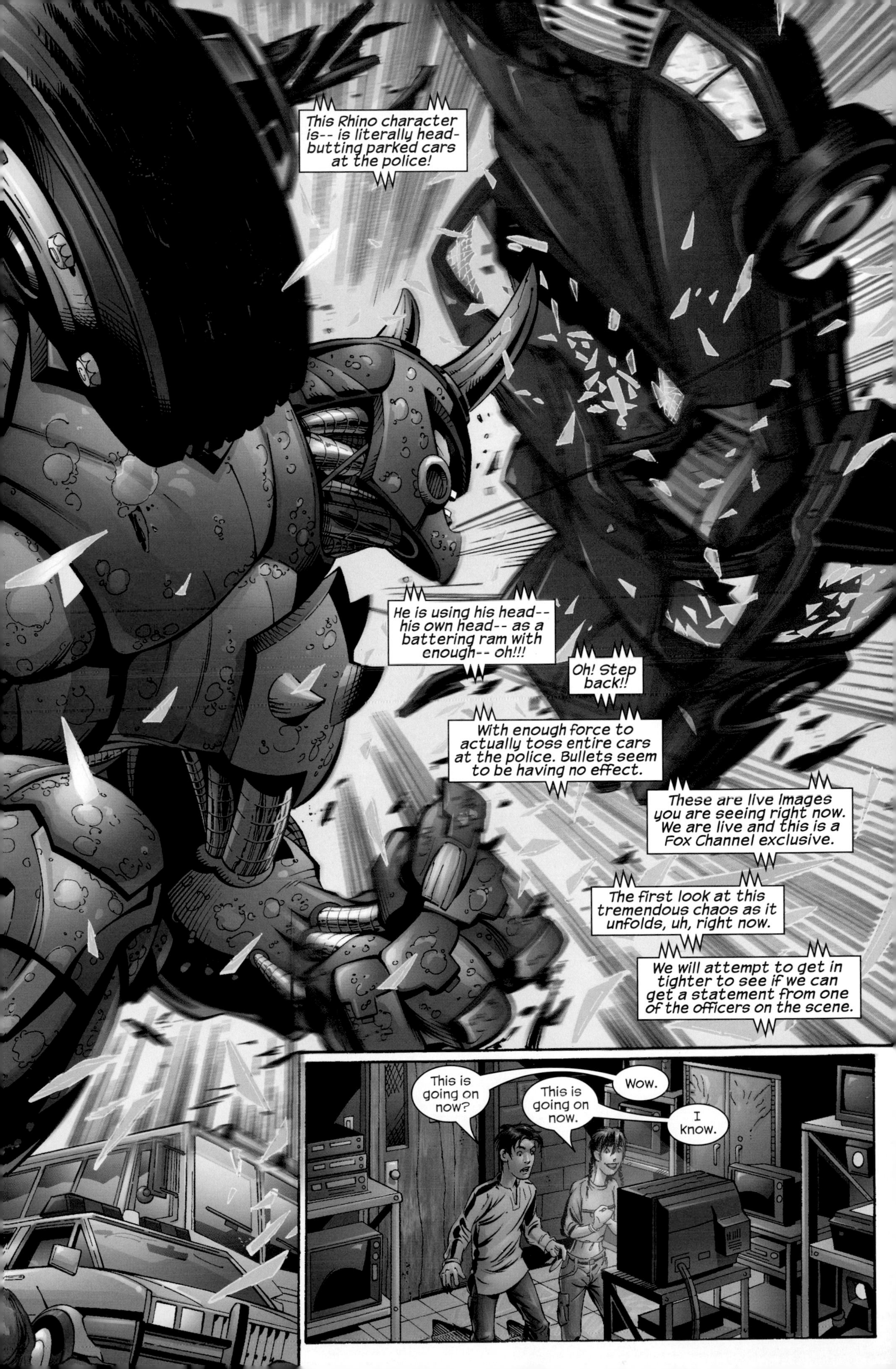
This Rhino character is-- is literally head-butting parked cars at the police!
He is using his head-- his own head-- as a battering ram with enough-- oh!!!
Oh! Step back!!
With enough force to actually toss entire cars at the police. Bullets seem to be having no effect.
These are live images you are seeing right now. We are live and this is a Fox Channel exclusive.
The first look at this tremendous chaos as it unfolds, uh, right now.
We will attempt to get in tighter to see if we can get a statement from one of the officers on the scene.
This is going on now?
Wow.
This is going on now.
I know.

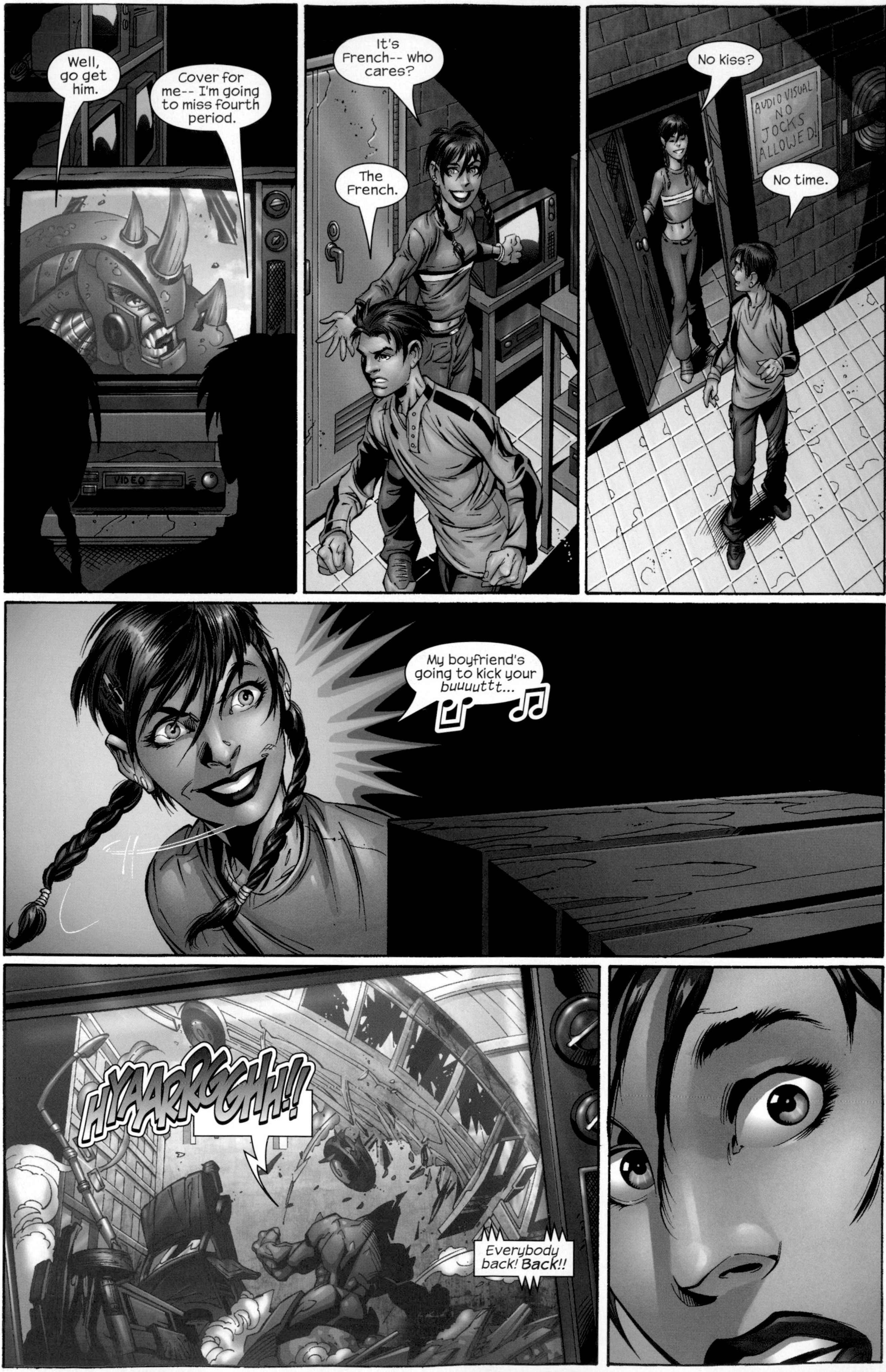

Well, go get him.
Cover for me-- I'm going to miss fourth period.
It's French-- who cares?
The French.
No kiss?
AUDIO VISUAL NO JOCKS ALLOWED!
No time.
VIDEO
My boyfriend's going to kick your buuuuttt...
HYAARRGGHH!!
Everybody back! Back!!

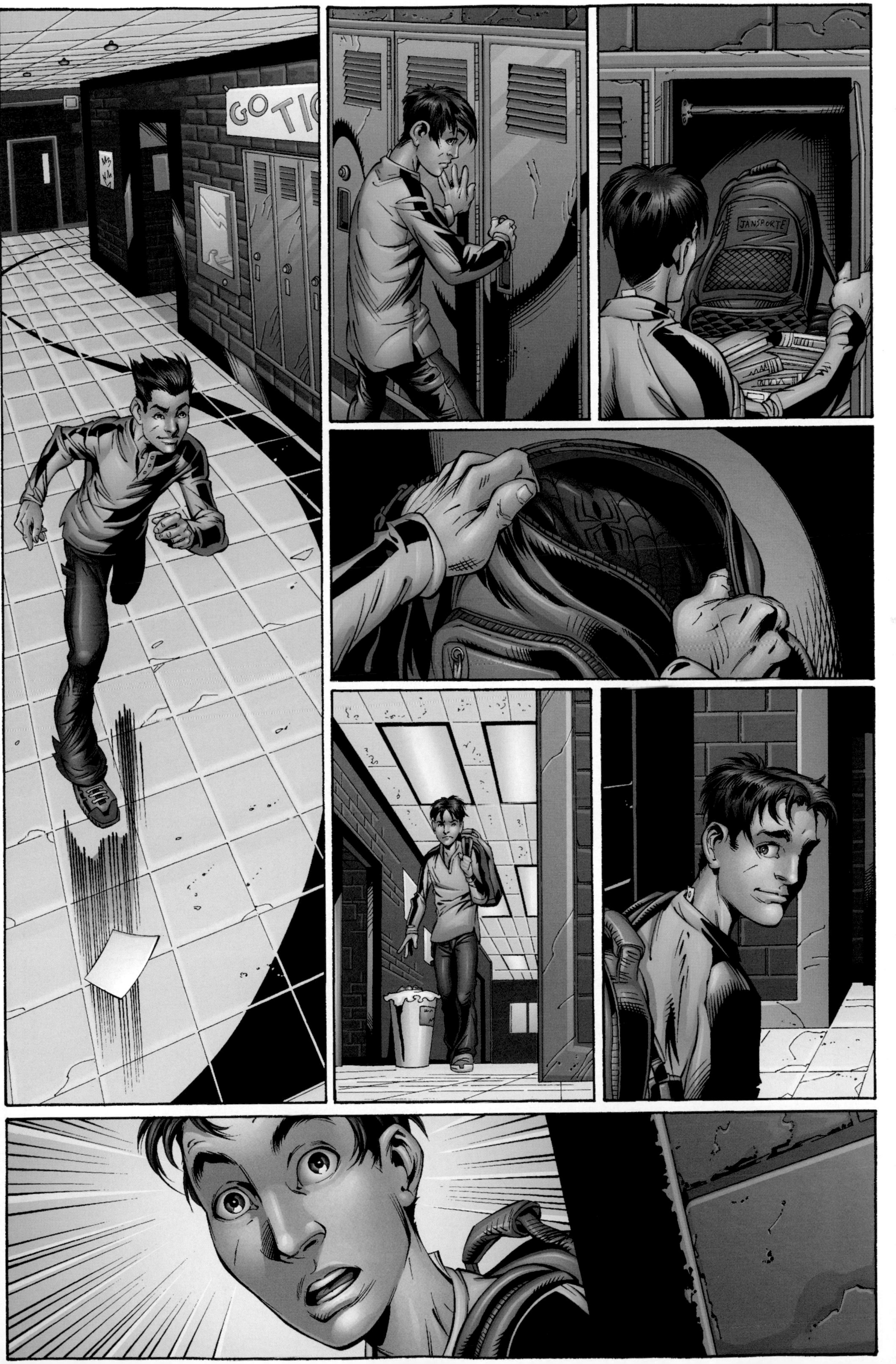
JANSPORTE

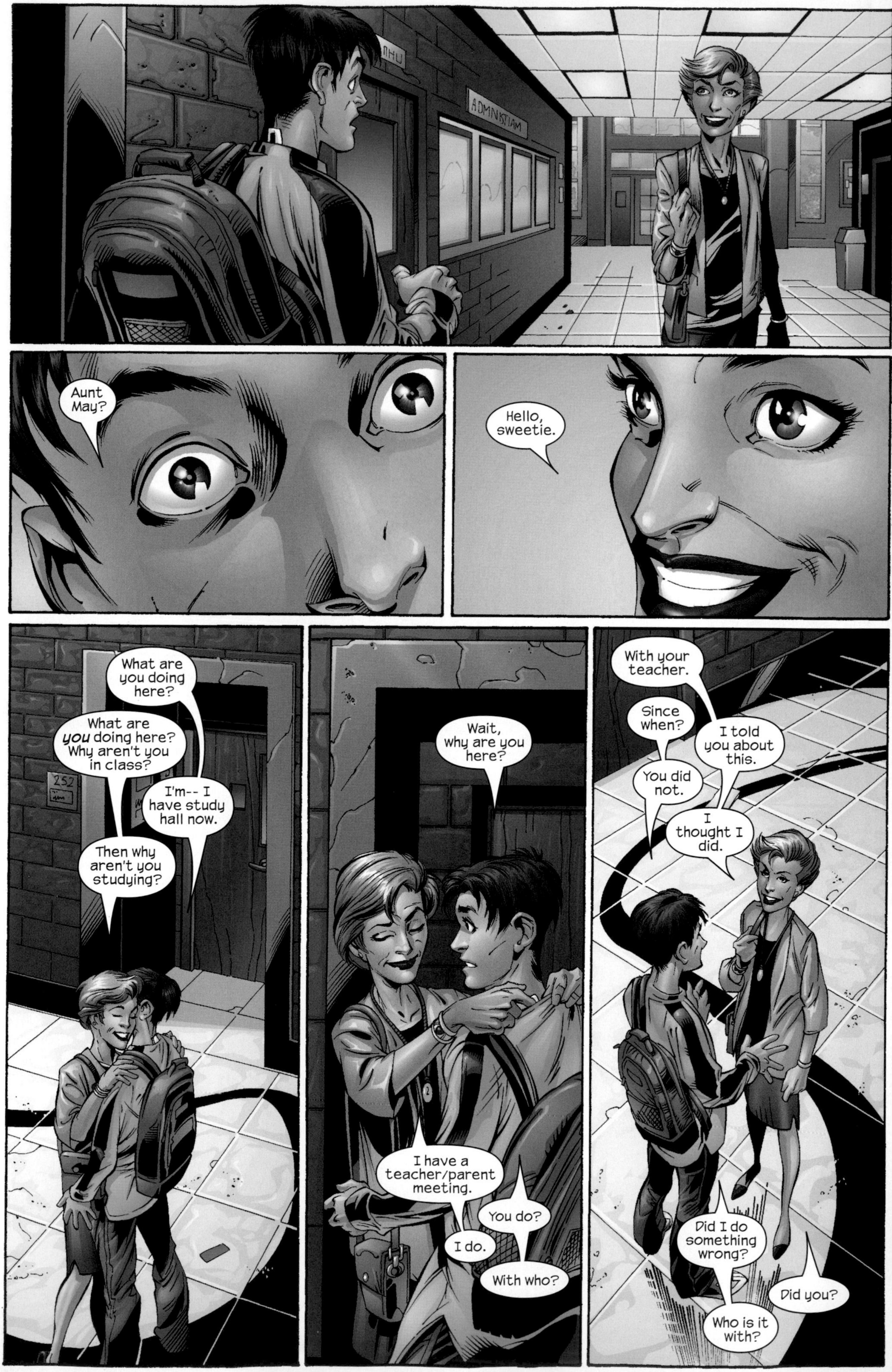
ADMINISTRATION
Aunt May?
Hello, sweetie.
What are you doing here?
What are *you* doing here? Why aren't you in class?
I'm-- I have study hall now.
Then why aren't you studying?
252
Wait, why are you here?
I have a teacher/parent meeting.
You do?
I do.
With who?
With your teacher.
Since when?
I told you about this.
You did not.
I thought I did.
Did I do something wrong?
Did you?
Who is it with?

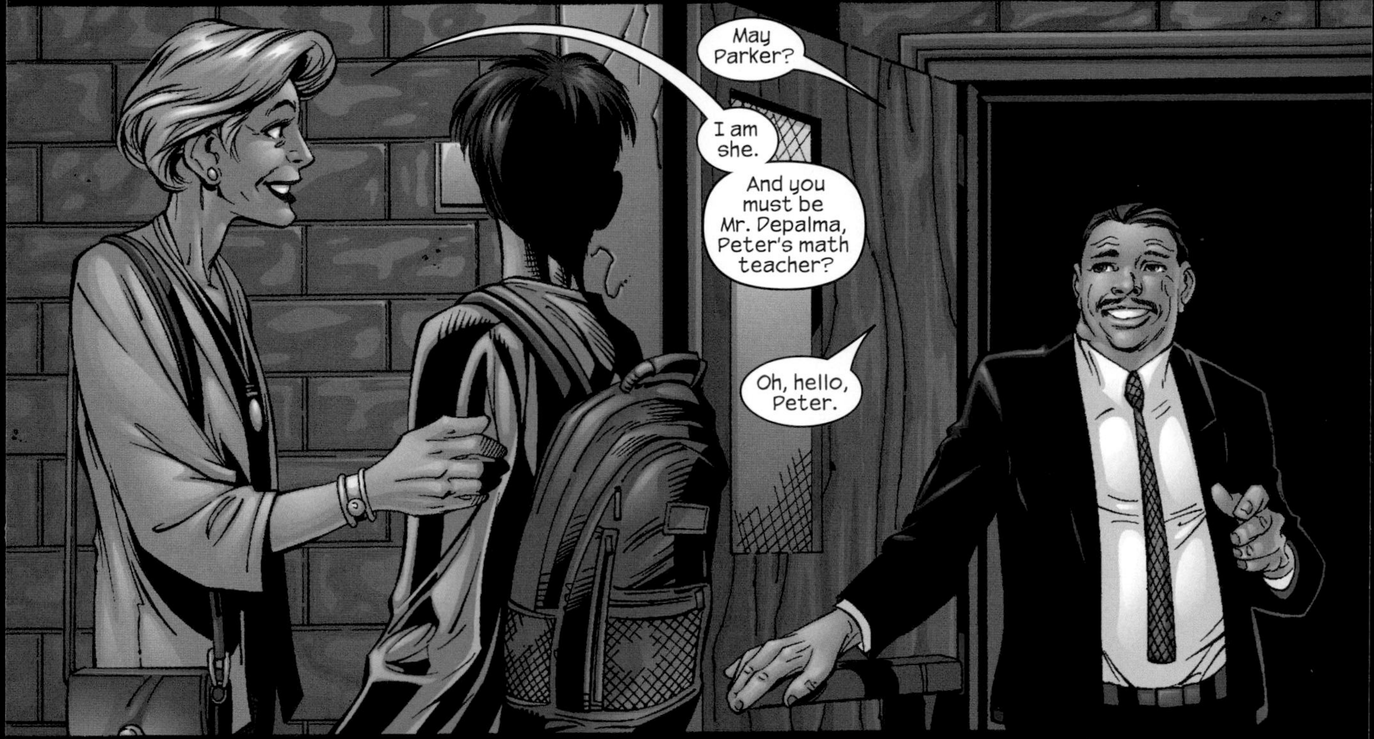
May Parker?
I am she.
And you must be Mr. Depalma, Peter's math teacher?
Oh, hello, Peter.

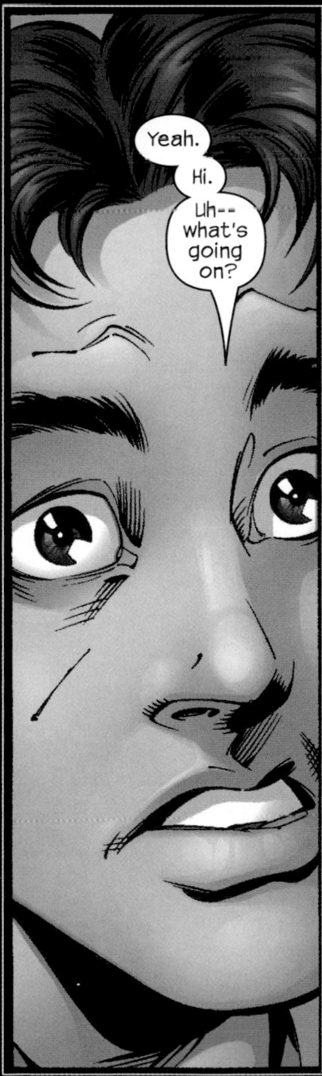
Yeah.
Hi.
Uh-- what's going on?

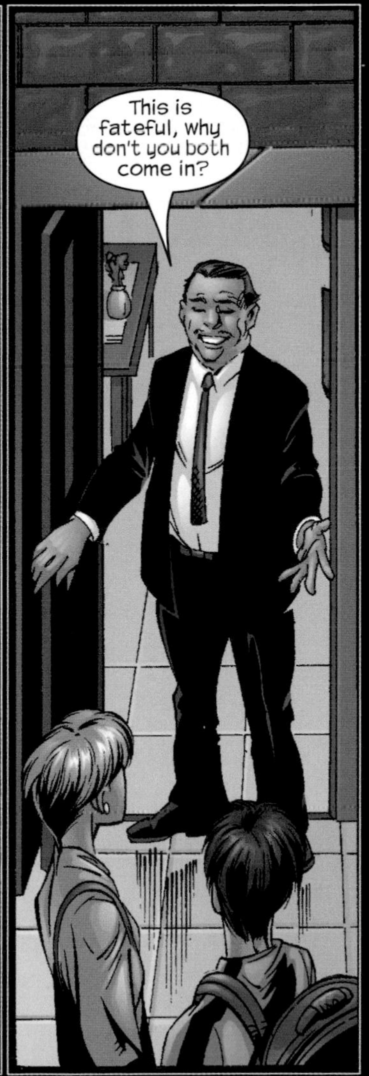
This is fateful, why don't you both come in?

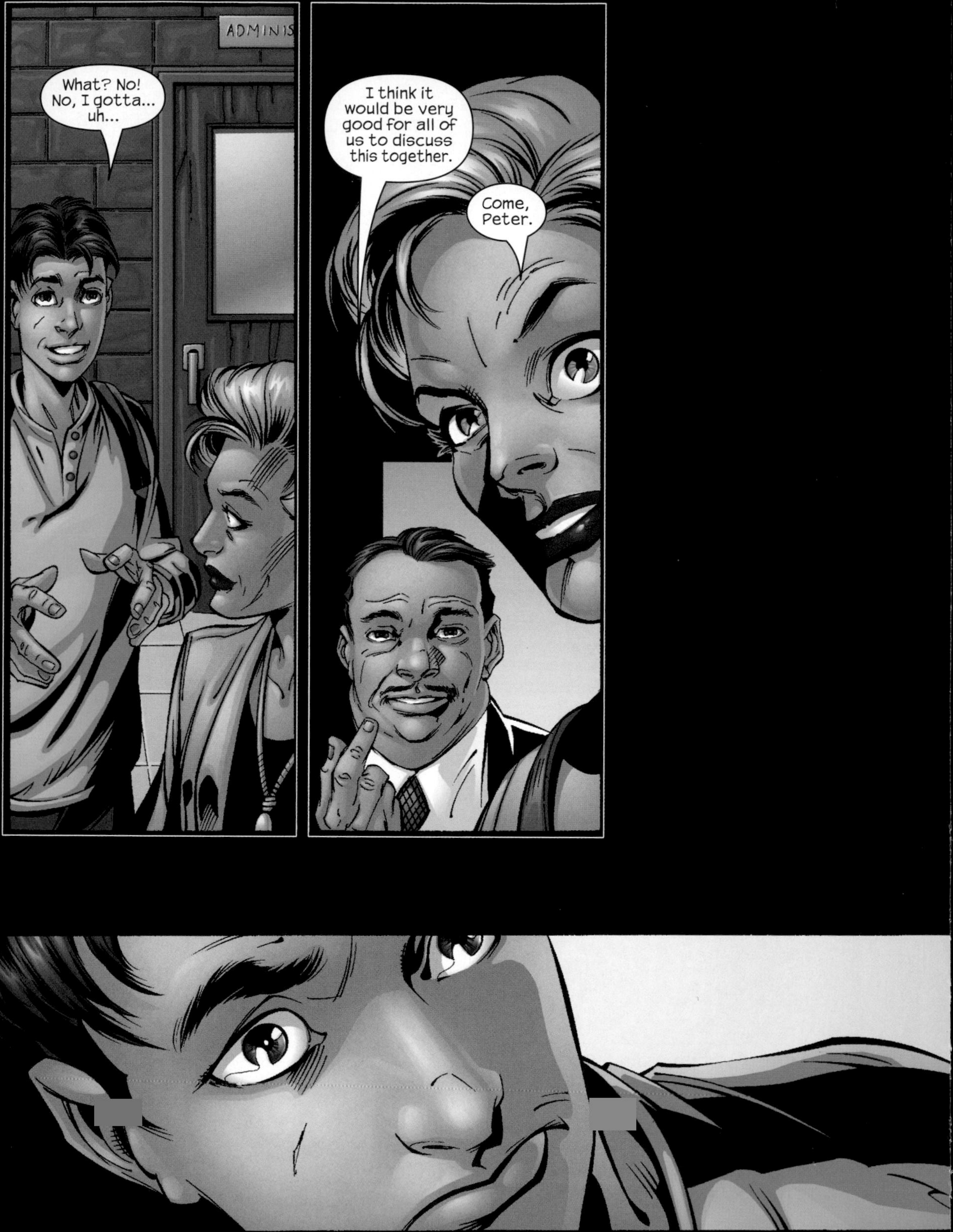
ADMINIS
What? No! No, I gotta... uh...
I think it would be very good for all of us to discuss this together.
Come, Peter.

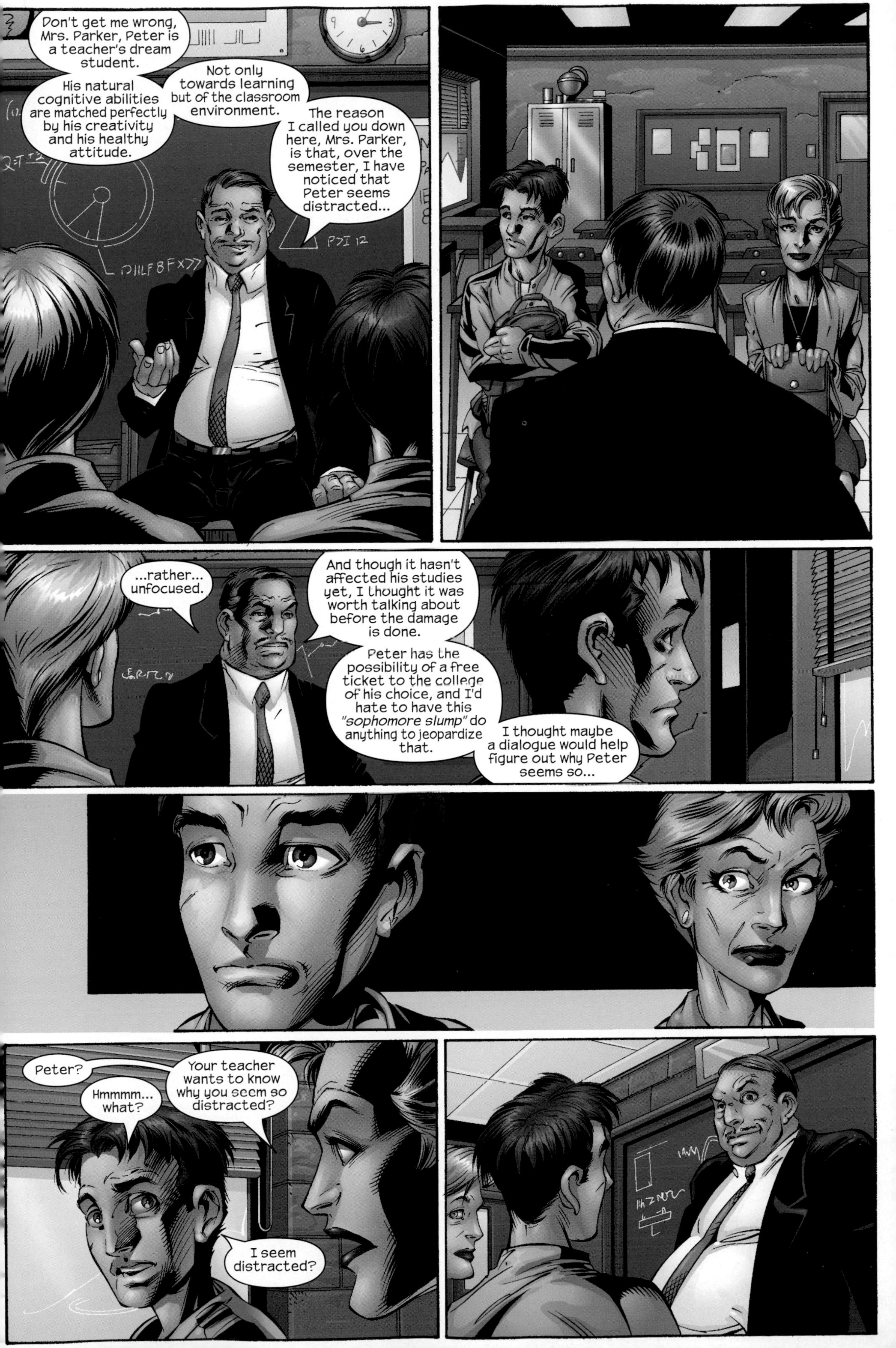

Don't get me wrong, Mrs. Parker, Peter is a teacher's dream student.
His natural cognitive abilities are matched perfectly by his creativity and his healthy attitude.
Not only towards learning but of the classroom environment.
The reason I called you down here, Mrs. Parker, is that, over the semester, I have noticed that Peter seems distracted...
...rather... unfocused.
And though it hasn't affected his studies yet, I thought it was worth talking about before the damage is done.
Peter has the possibility of a free ticket to the college of his choice, and I'd hate to have this "sophomore slump" do anything to jeopardize that.
I thought maybe a dialogue would help figure out why Peter seems so...
Peter?
Hmmmm... what?
Your teacher wants to know why you seem so distracted?
I seem distracted?

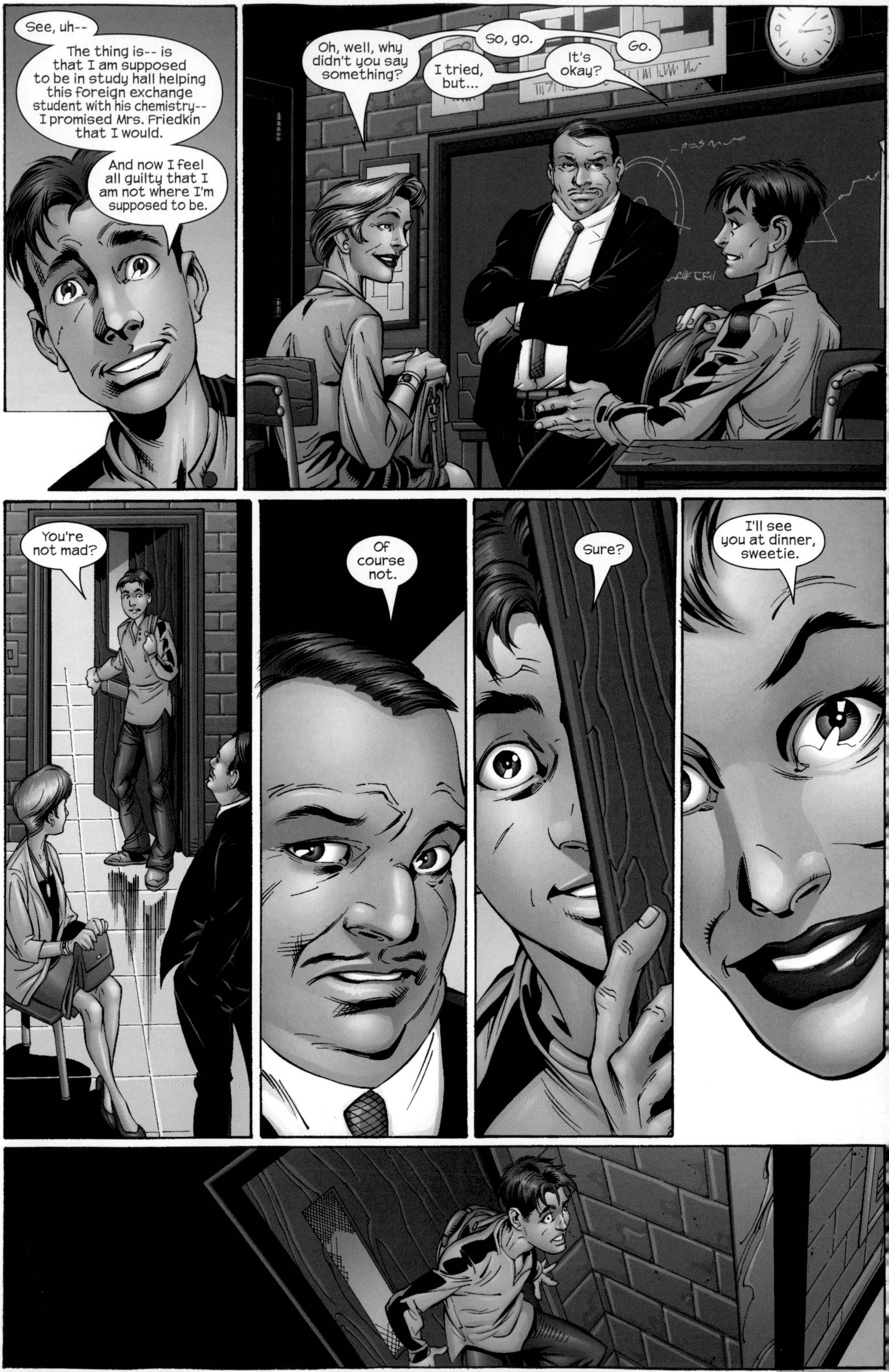
See, uh--
The thing is-- is that I am supposed to be in study hall helping this foreign exchange student with his chemistry-- I promised Mrs. Friedkin that I would.
And now I feel all guilty that I am not where I'm supposed to be.
Oh, well, why didn't you say something?
I tried, but...
So, go.
It's okay?
Go.
You're not mad?
Of course not.
Sure?
I'll see you at dinner, sweetie.

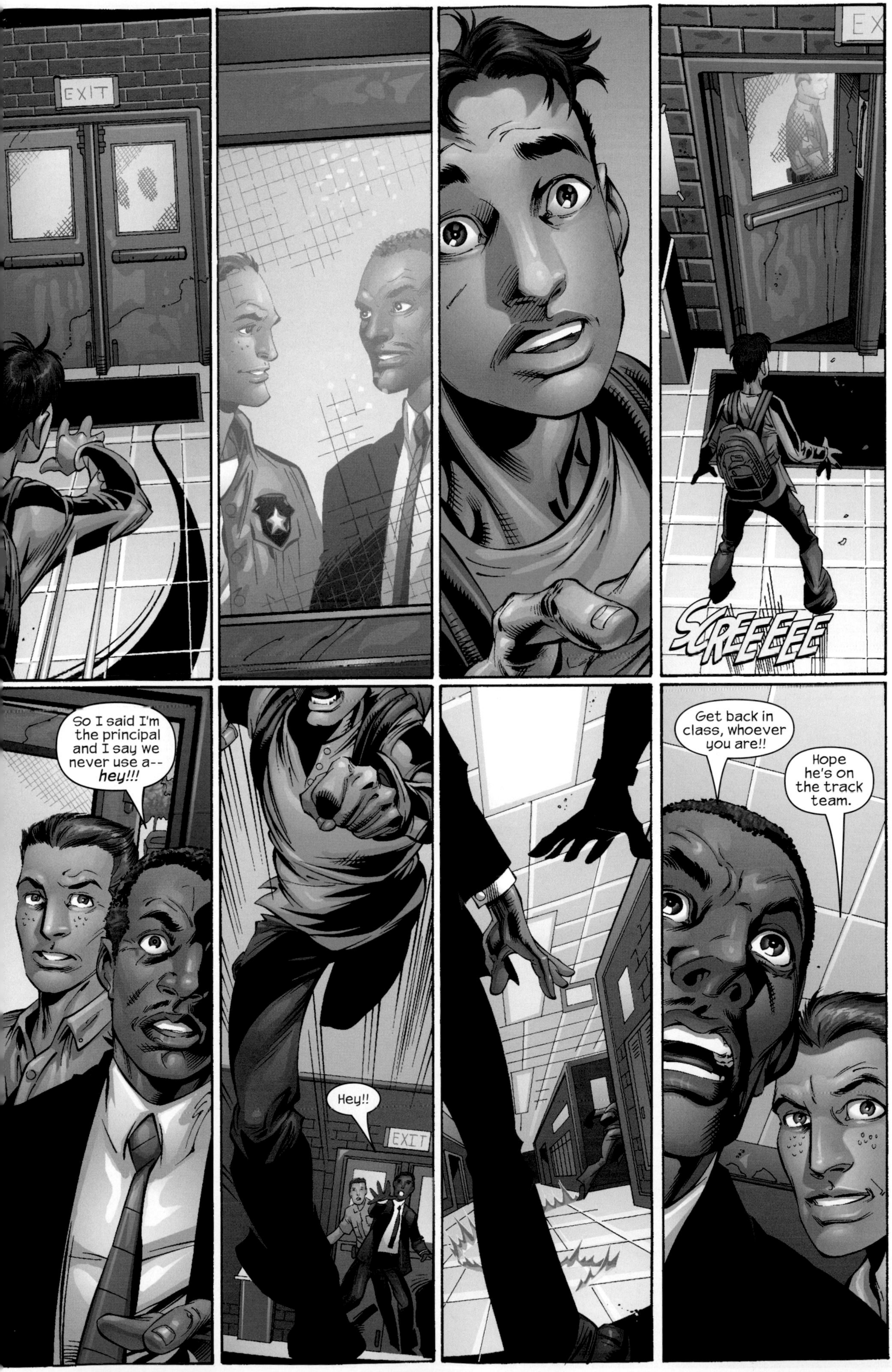
EXIT
SCREEEEE
So I said I'm the principal and I say we never use a-- *hey!!!*
Hey!!
EXIT
Get back in class, whoever you are!!
Hope he's on the track team.

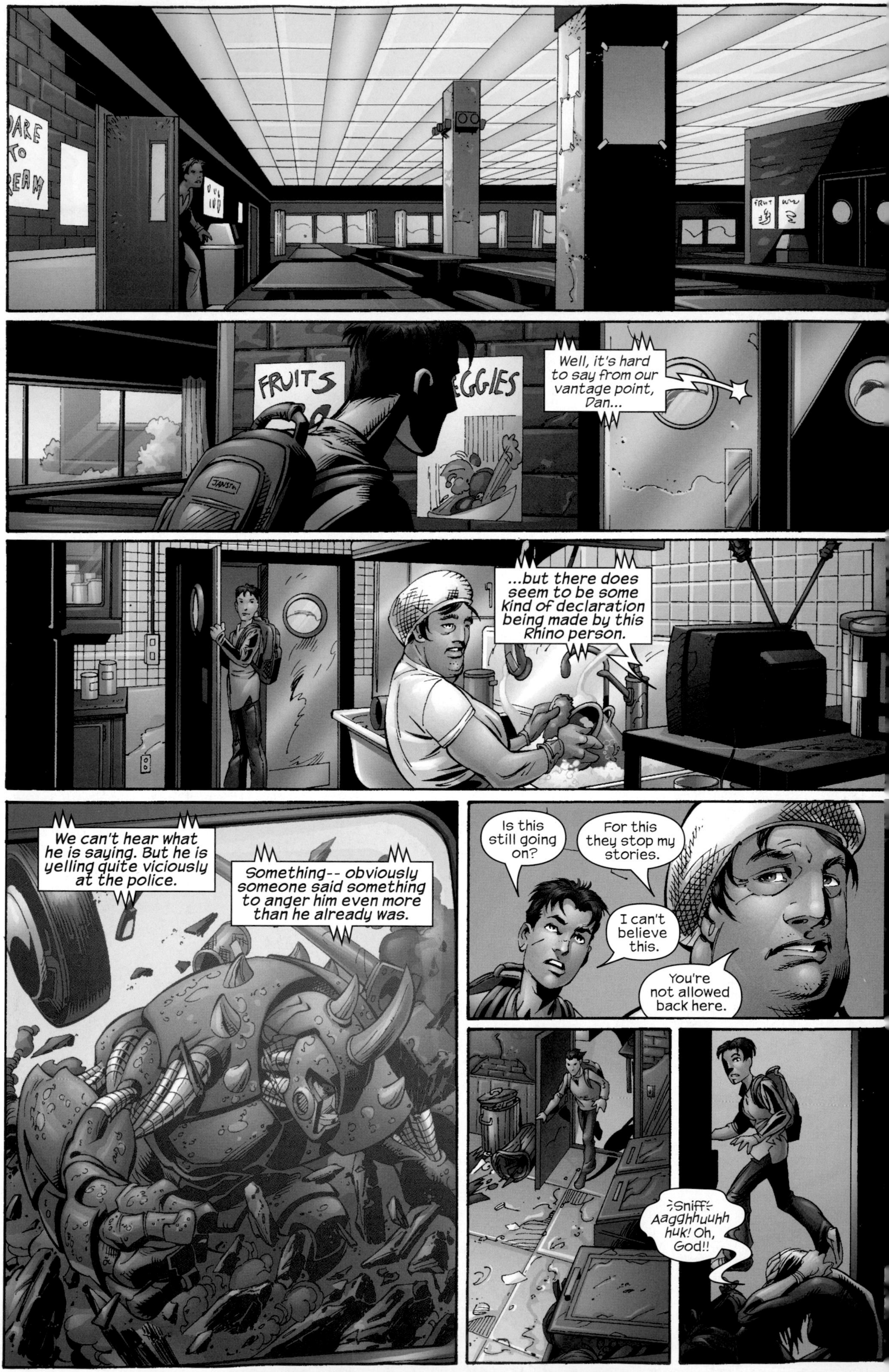
DARE TO DREAM
FRUITS
VEGGIES
Well, it's hard to say from our vantage point, Dan...
...but there does seem to be some kind of declaration being made by this Rhino person.
We can't hear what he is saying. But he is yelling quite viciously at the police.
Something-- obviously someone said something to anger him even more than he already was.
Is this still going on?
For this they stop my stories.
I can't believe this.
You're not allowed back here.
Sniff
Aagghhuuhh huk! Oh, God!!

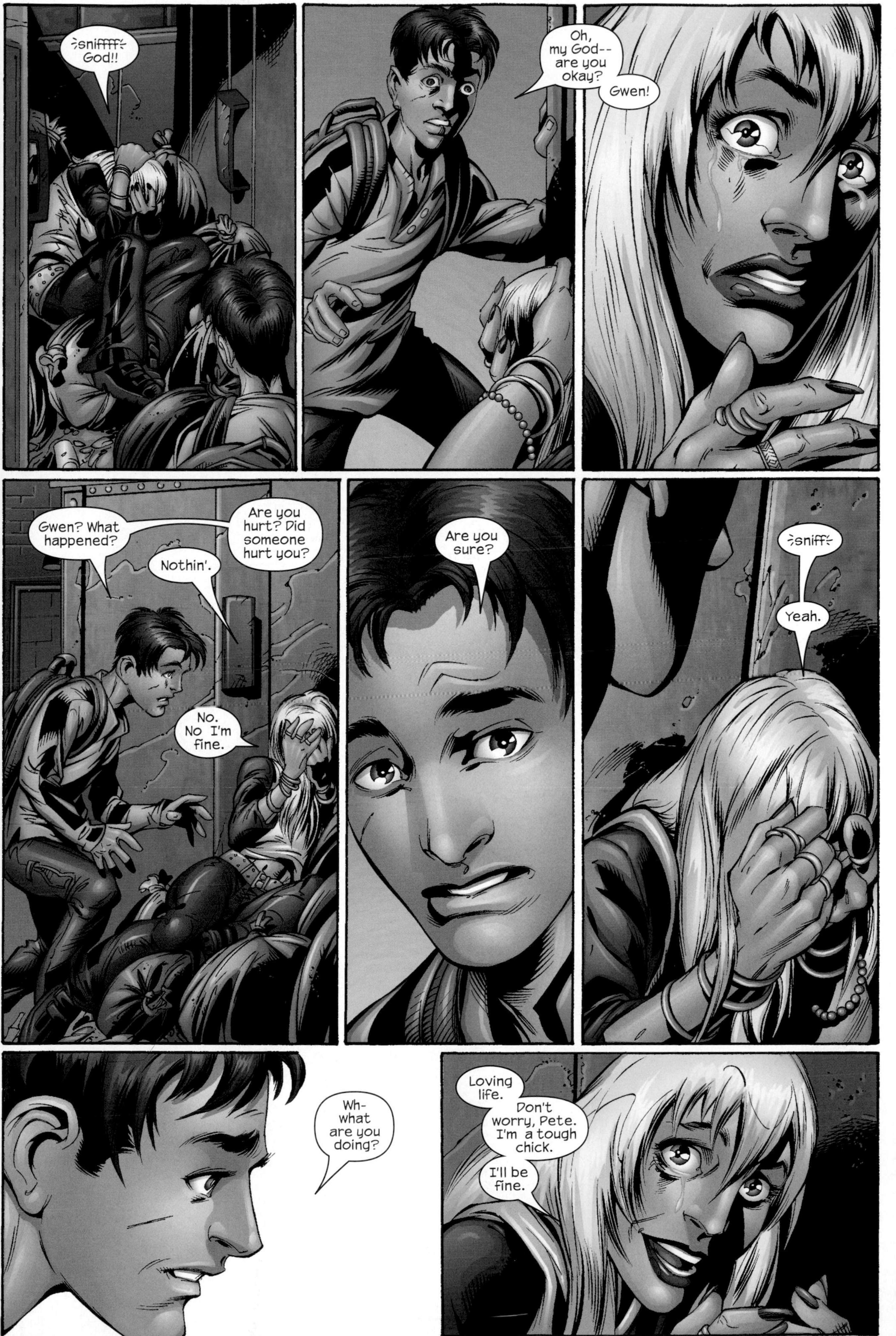

-sniffff- God!!
Oh, my God-- are you okay?
Gwen!
Gwen? What happened?
Are you hurt? Did someone hurt you?
Nothin'.
No. No I'm fine.
Are you sure?
-sniff-
Yeah.
Wh- what are you doing?
Loving life.
Don't worry, Pete. I'm a tough chick.
I'll be fine.

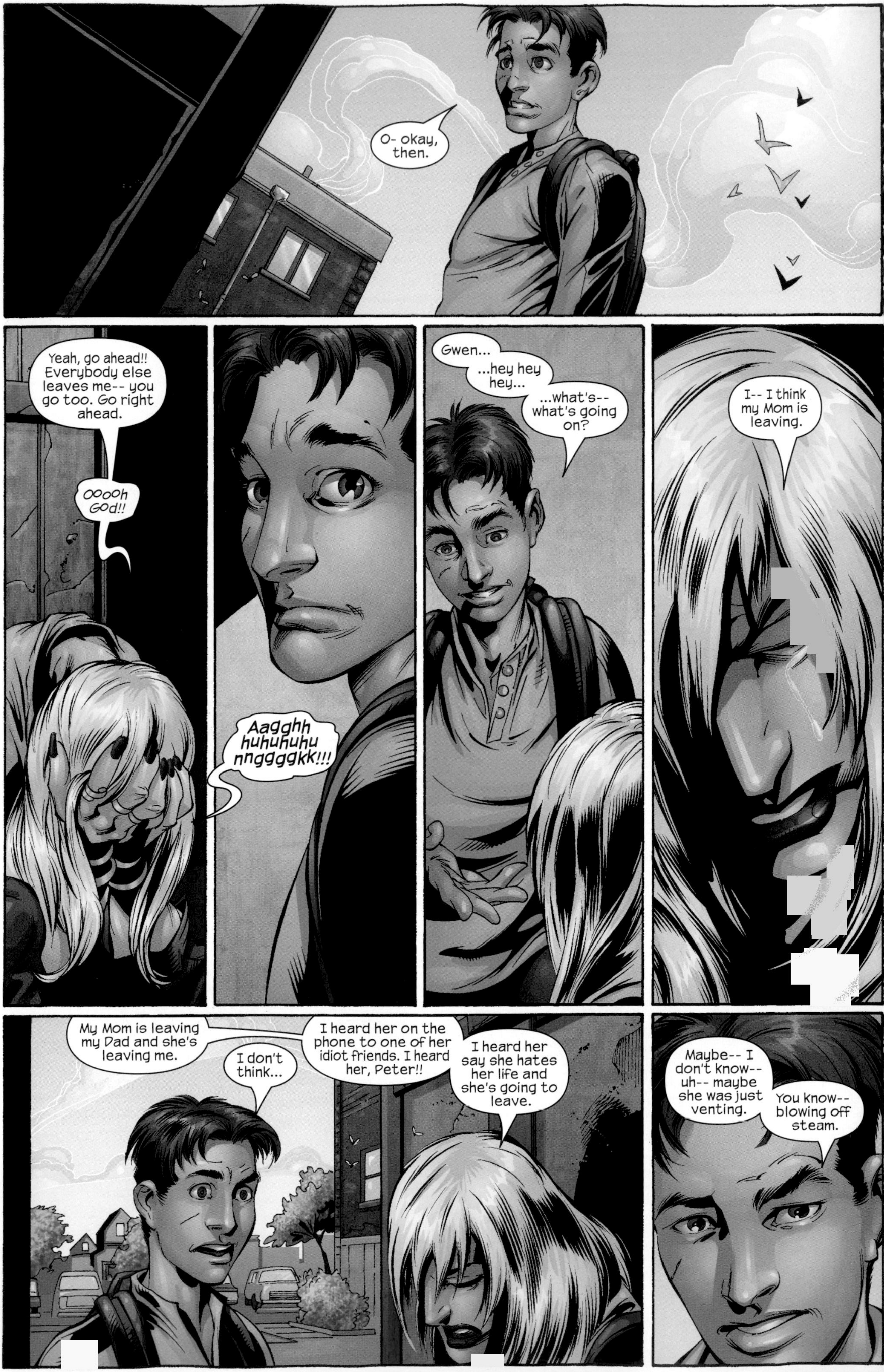
O- okay, then.
Yeah, go ahead!! Everybody else leaves me-- you go too. Go right ahead.
Ooooh God!!
Aagghh huhuhuhu nngggggkk!!!
Gwen...
...hey hey hey...
...what's-- what's going on?
I-- I think my Mom is leaving.
My Mom is leaving my Dad and she's leaving me.
I don't think...
I heard her on the phone to one of her idiot friends. I heard her, Peter!!
I heard her say she hates her life and she's going to leave.
Maybe-- I don't know-- uh-- maybe she was just venting.
You know-- blowing off steam.

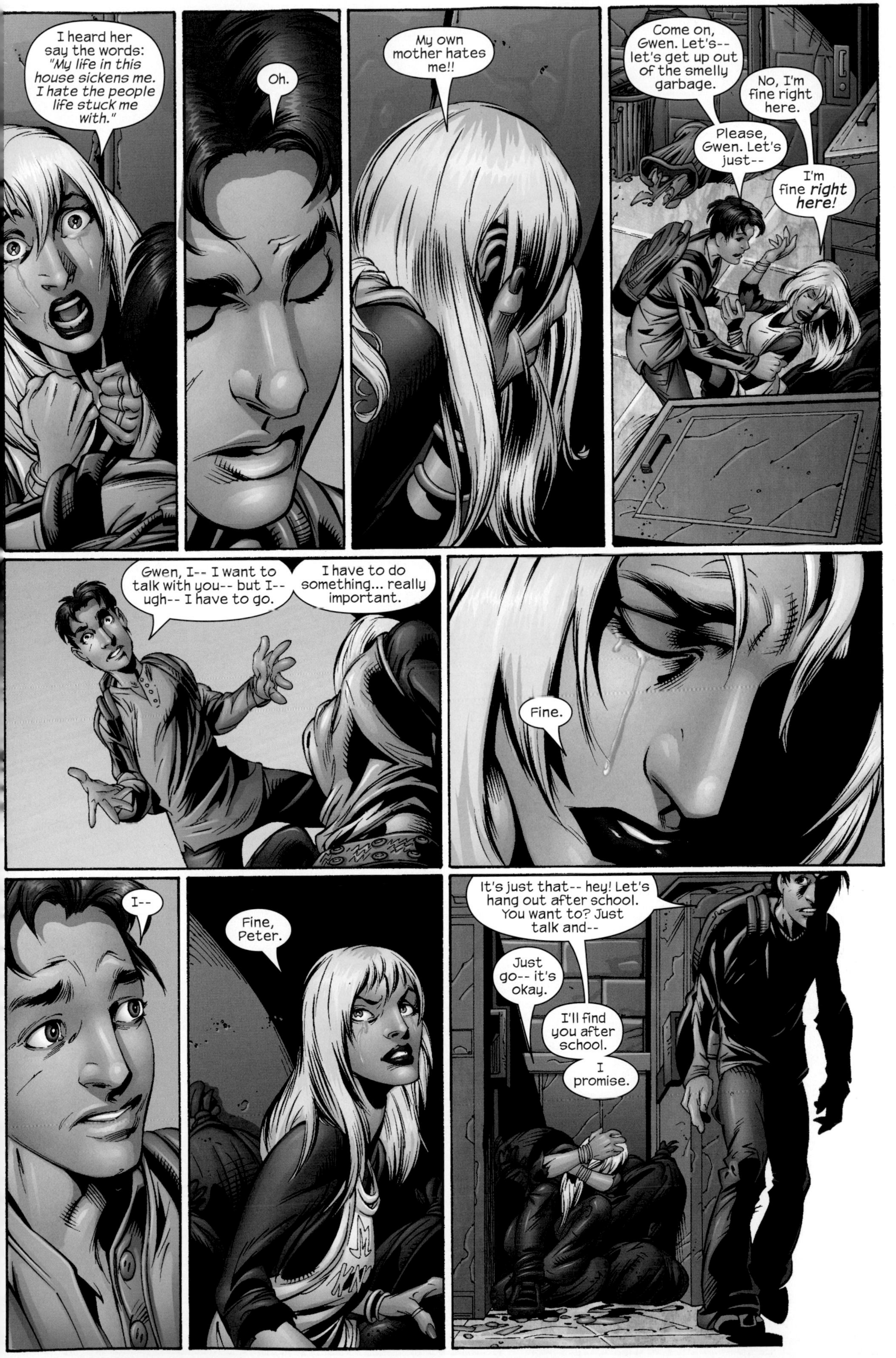

I heard her say the words: *"My life in this house sickens me. I hate the people life stuck me with."*
Oh.
My own mother hates me!!
Come on, Gwen. Let's-- let's get up out of the smelly garbage.
No, I'm fine right here.
Please, Gwen. Let's just--
I'm fine ***right here!***
Gwen, I-- I want to talk with you-- but I-- ugh-- I have to go.
I have to do something... really important.
Fine.
I--
Fine, Peter.
It's just that-- hey! Let's hang out after school. You want to? Just talk and--
Just go-- it's okay.
I'll find you after school.
I promise.

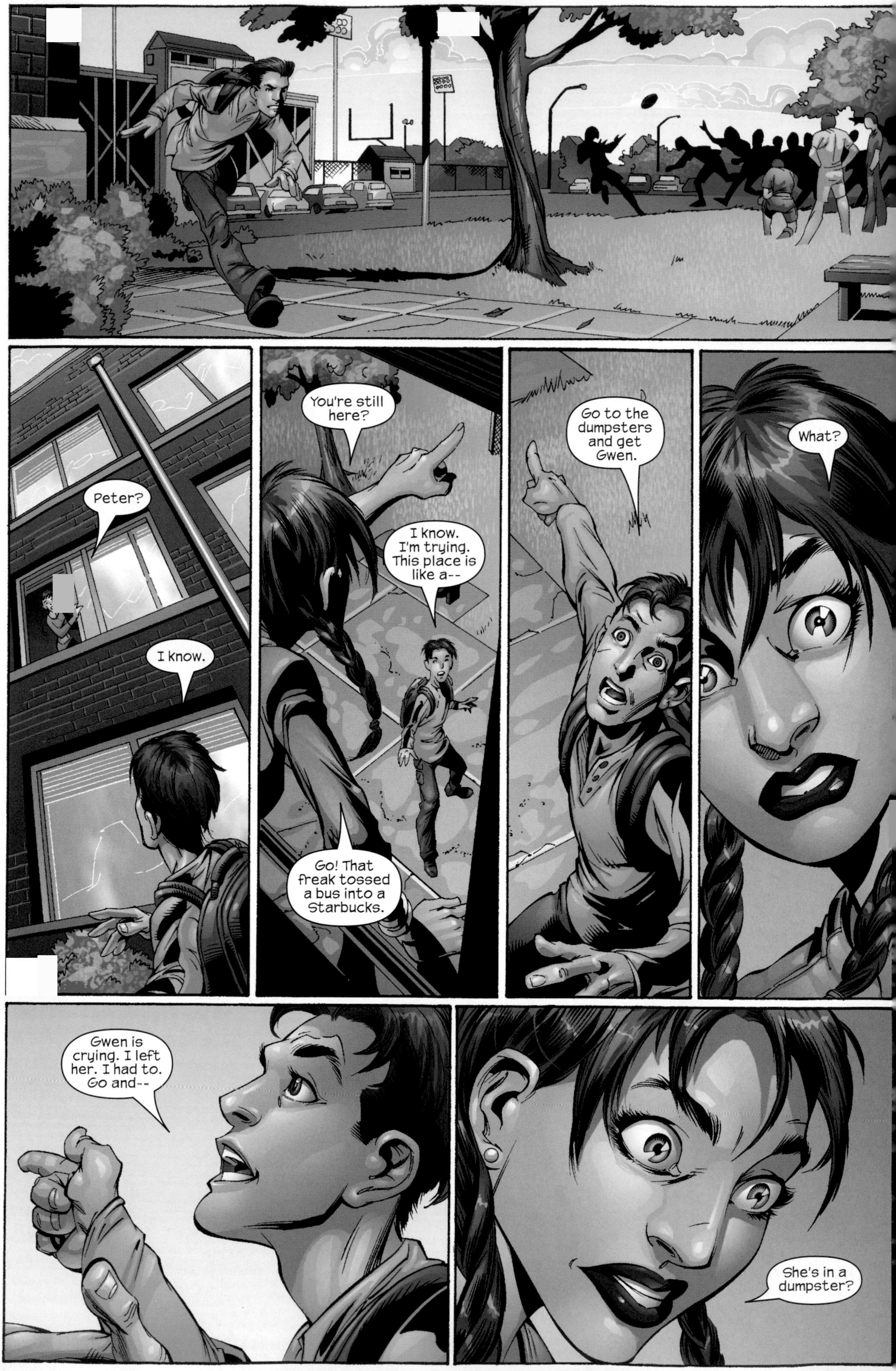
Peter?
I know.
You're still here?
I know. I'm trying. This place is like a--
Go! That freak tossed a bus into a Starbucks.
Go to the dumpsters and get Gwen.
What?
Gwen is crying. I left her. I had to. Go and--
She's in a dumpster?

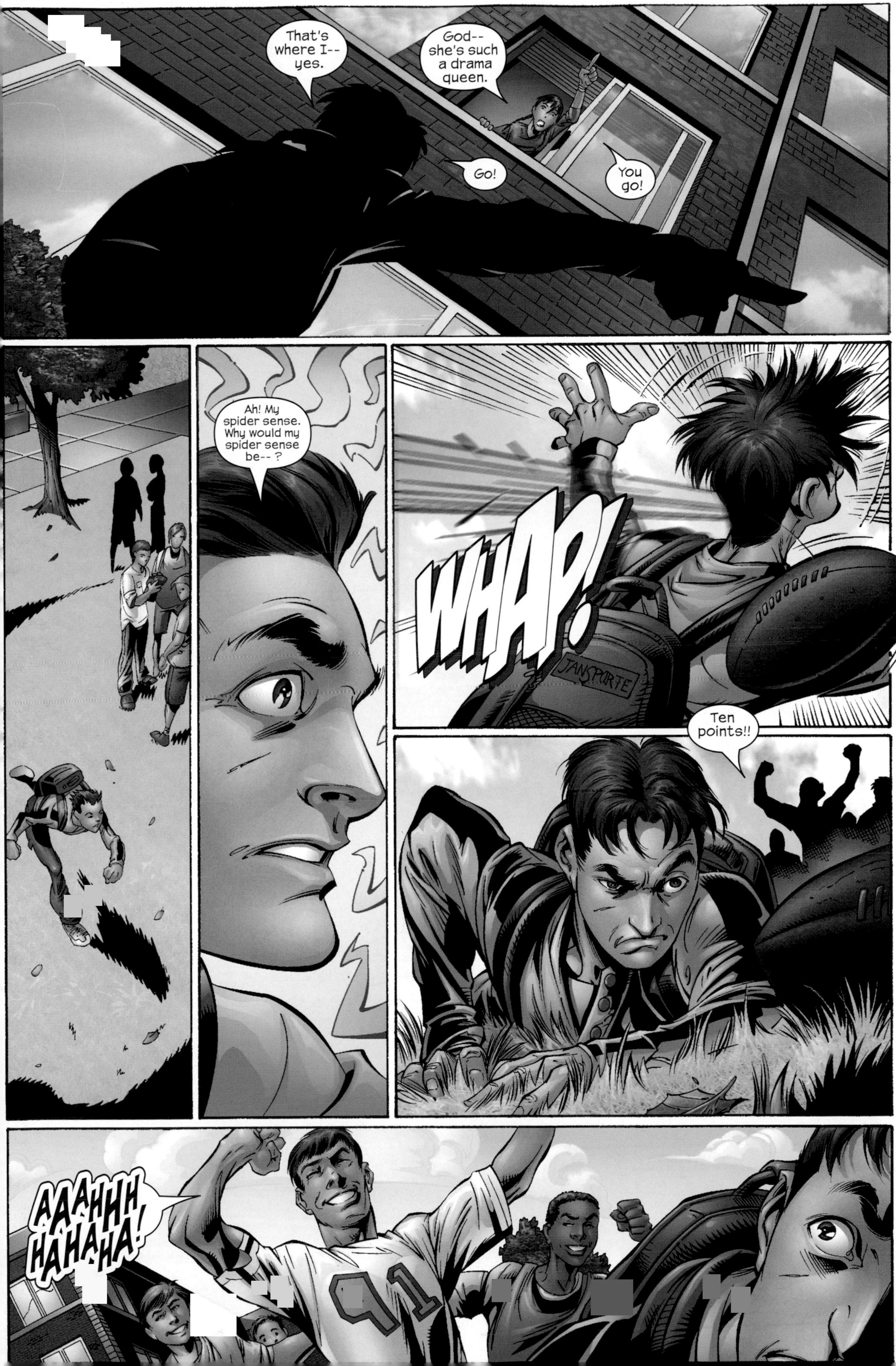
That's where I-- yes.
God-- she's such a drama queen.
Go!
You go!
Ah! My spider sense. Why would my spider sense be-- ?
WHAP!
JANSPORTE
Ten points!!
AAAHHH HAHAHA!

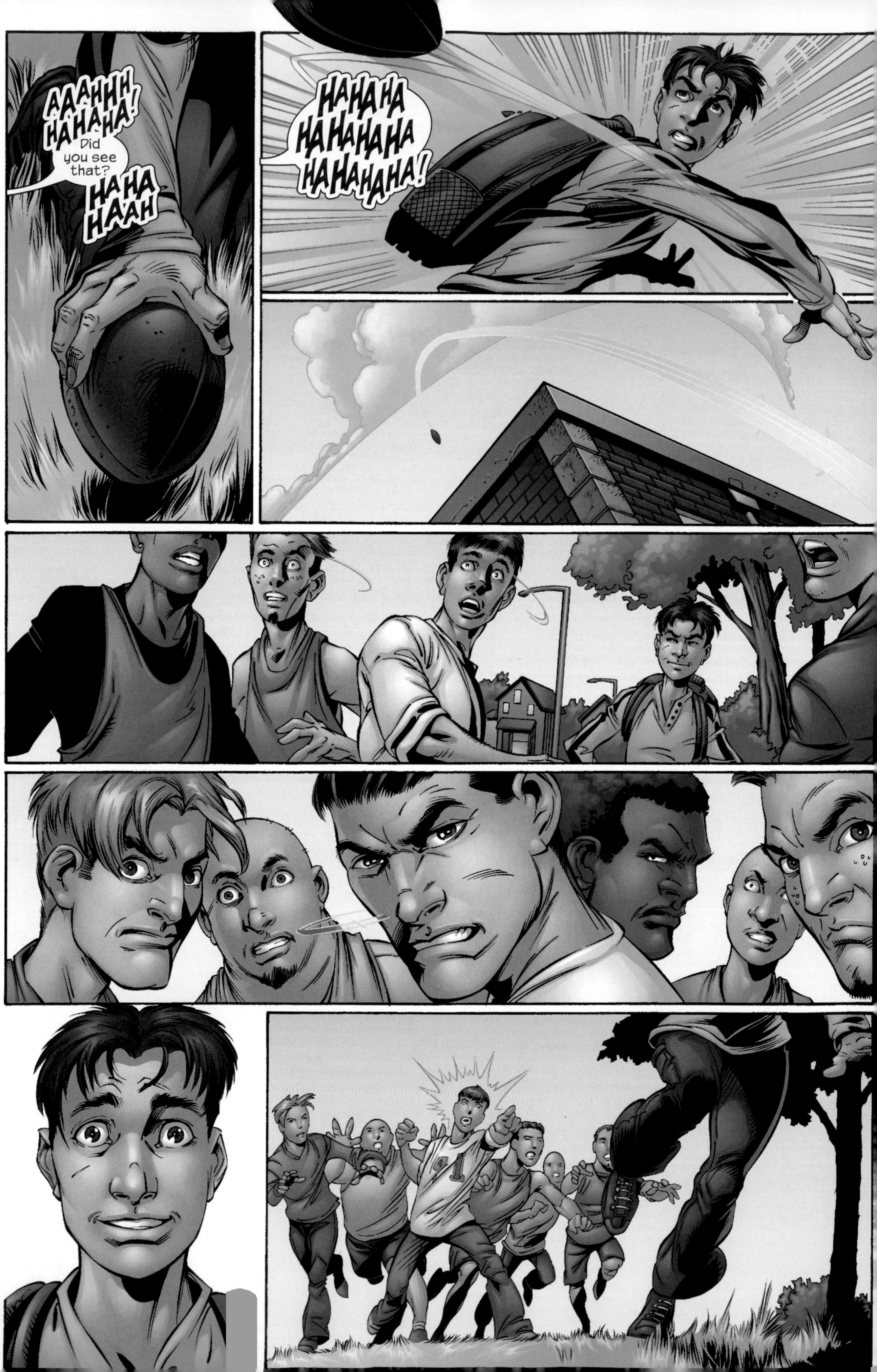

AAAHHH HAHAHA! Did you see that? HAHA HAAH
HAHAHA HAHAHAHA HAHAHAHA!

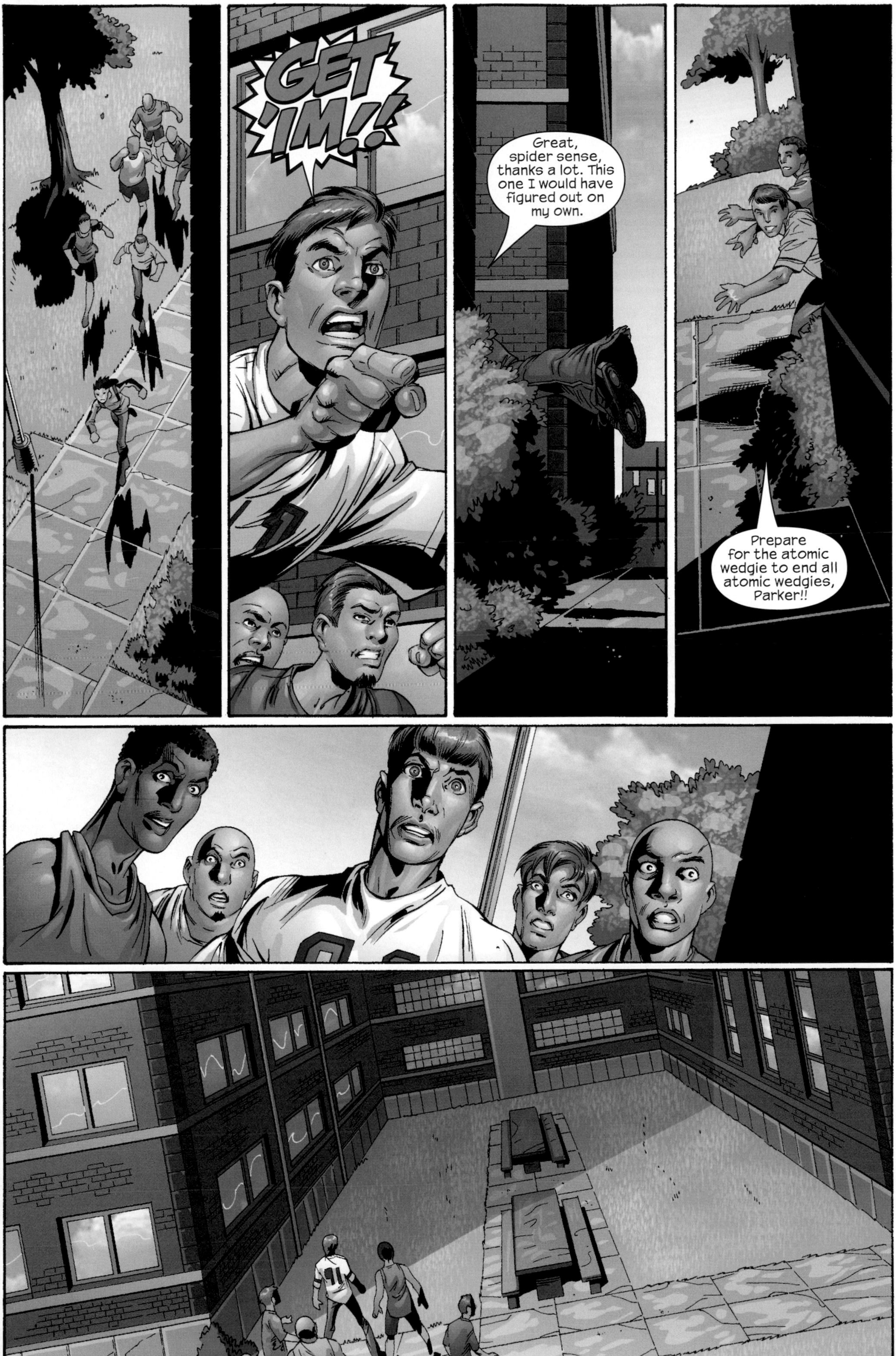
GET 'IM!!
Great, spider sense, thanks a lot. This one I would have figured out on my own.
Prepare for the atomic wedgie to end all atomic wedgies, Parker!!

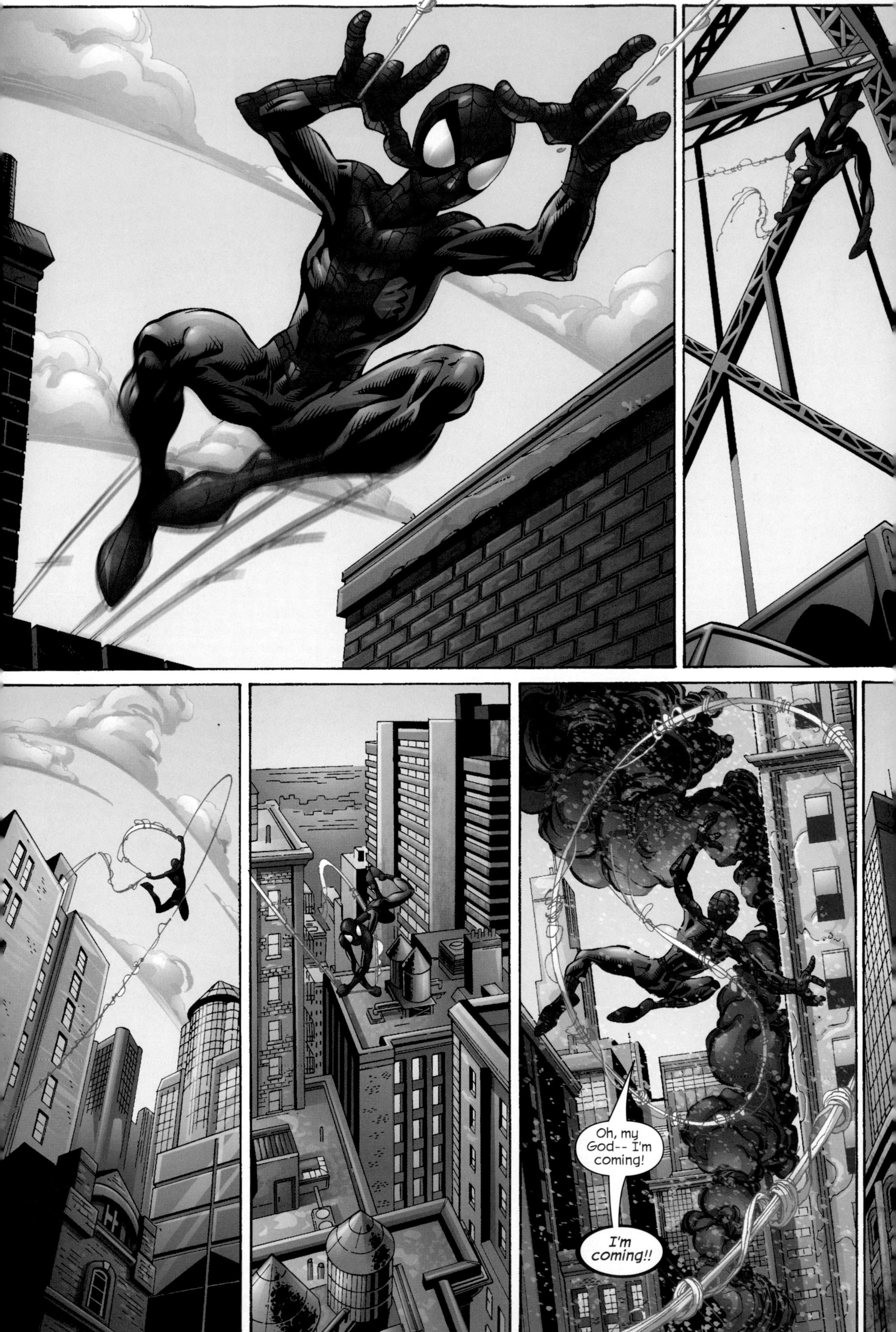

Oh, my God-- I'm coming!
I'm coming!!

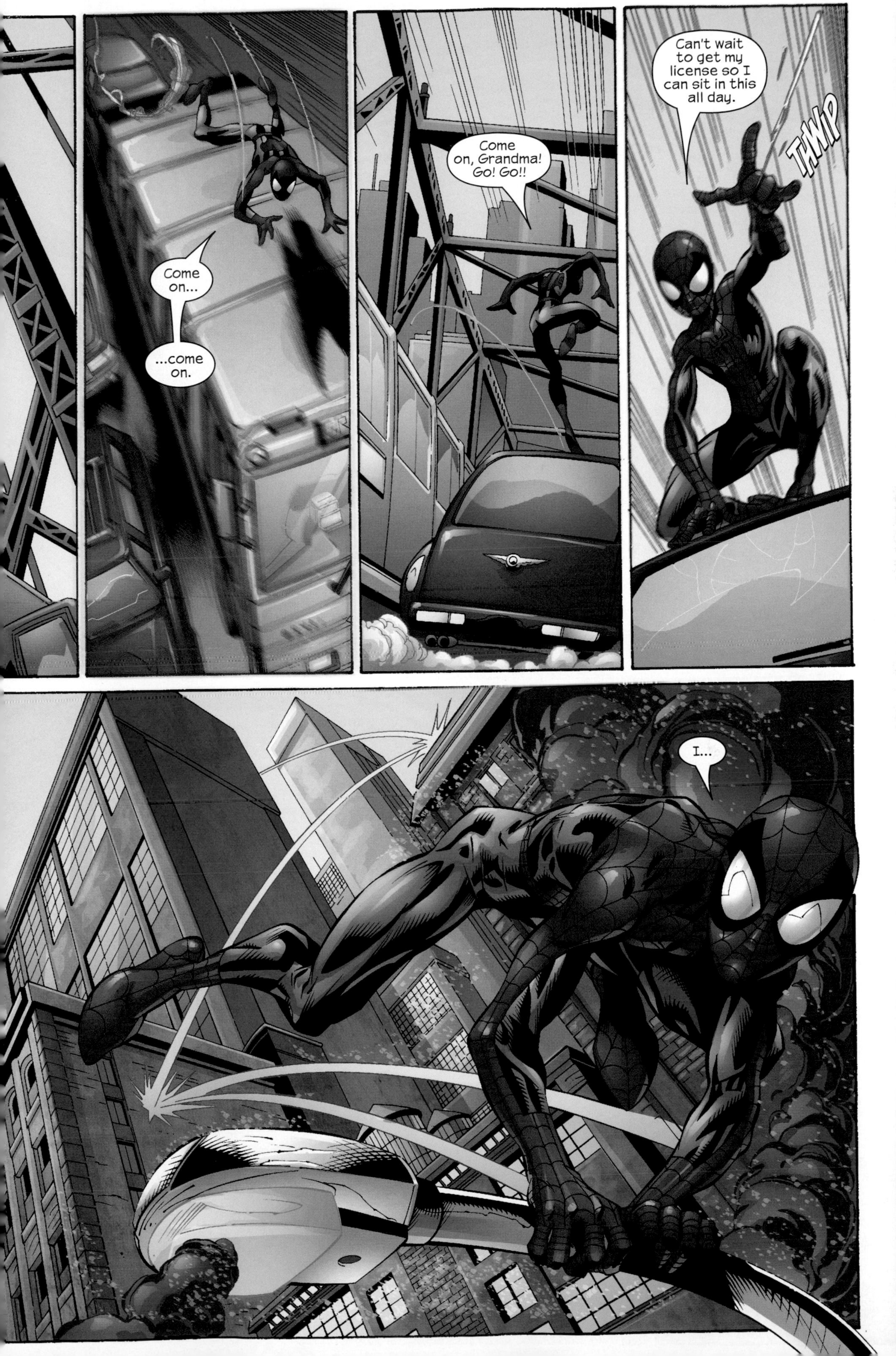

Come on...
...come on.
Come on, Grandma! Go! Go!!
Can't wait to get my license so I can sit in this all day.
THWIP
I...

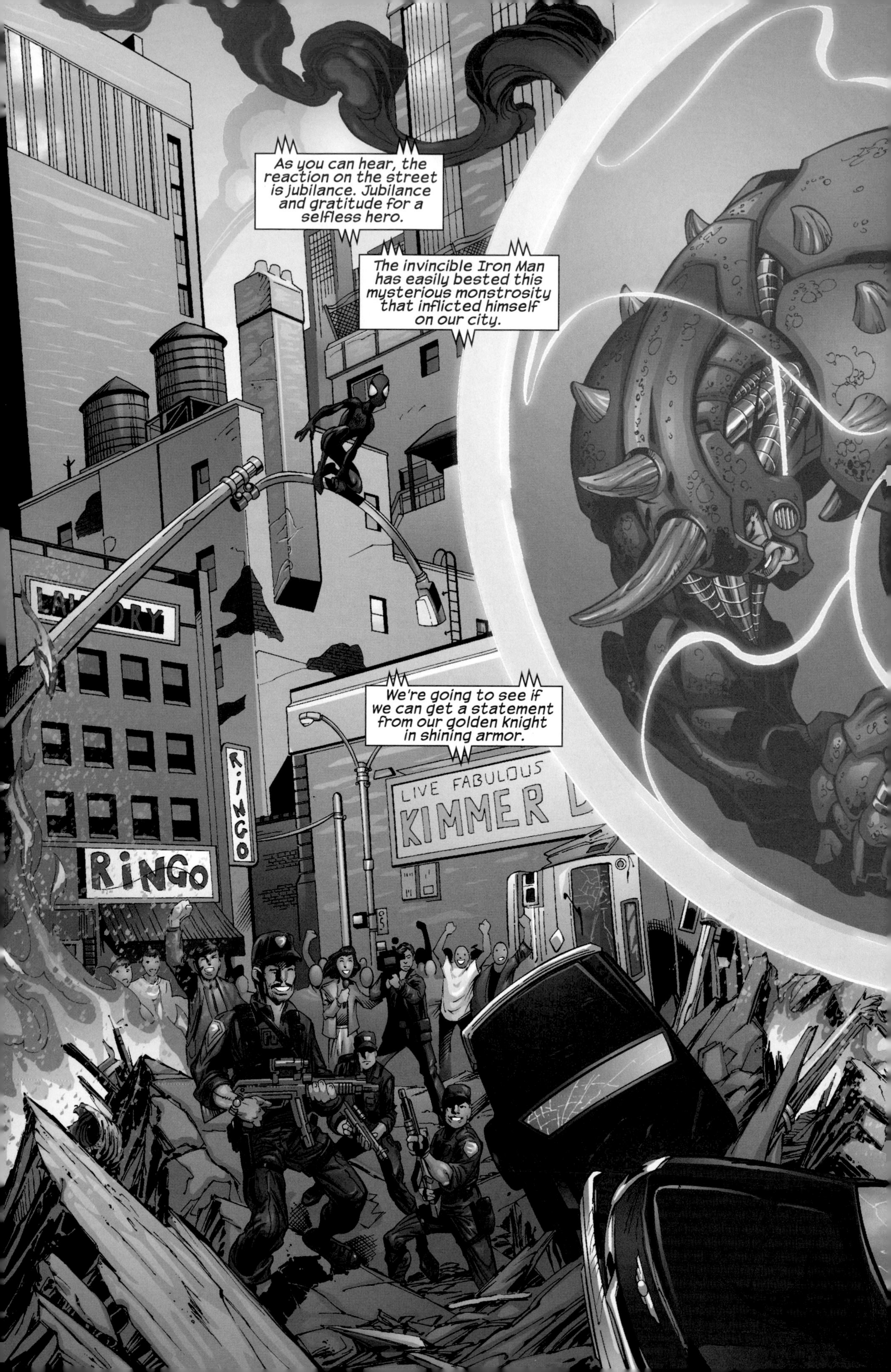
As you can hear, the reaction on the street is jubilance. Jubilance and gratitude for a selfless hero.
The invincible Iron Man has easily bested this mysterious monstrosity that inflicted himself on our city.
We're going to see if we can get a statement from our golden knight in shining armor.
LAUNDRY
RINGO
R-INGO
LIVE FABULOUS
KIMMER

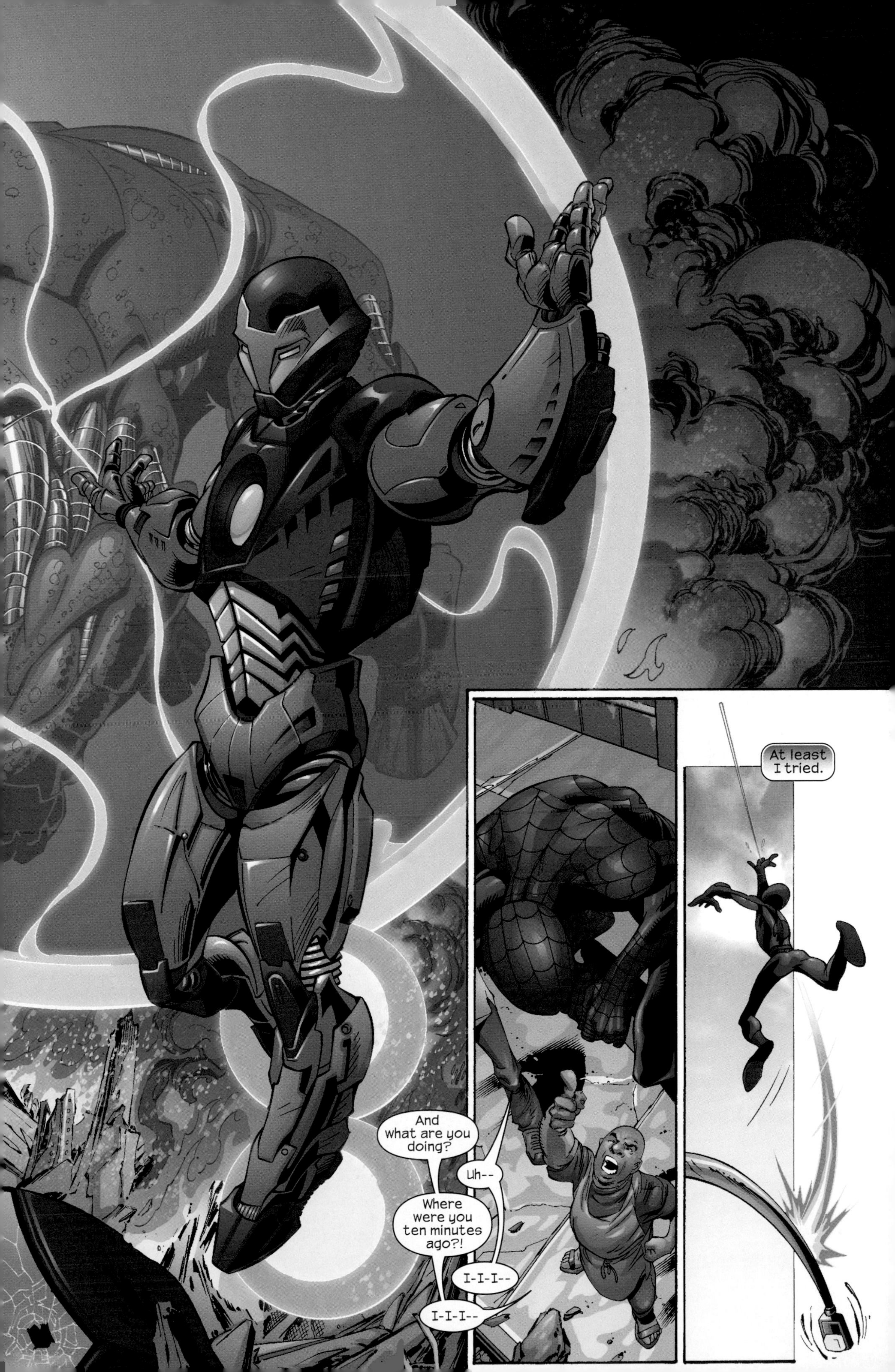
At least I tried.
And what are you doing?
Uh--
Where were you ten minutes ago?!
I-I-I--
I-I-I--

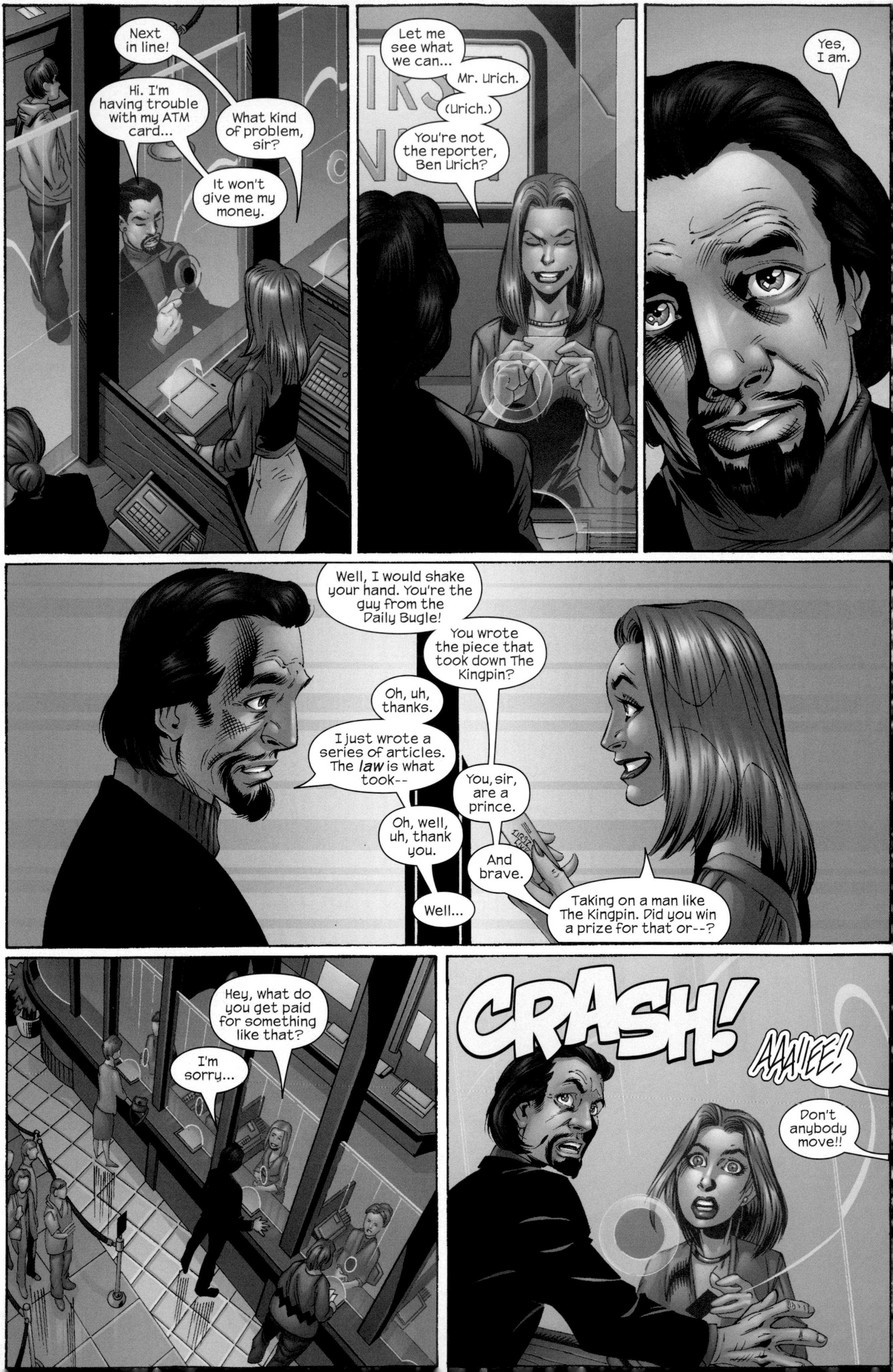
Next in line!
Hi. I'm having trouble with my ATM card...
What kind of problem, sir?
It won't give me my money.
Let me see what we can...
Mr. Urich.
(Urich.)
You're not the reporter, Ben Urich?
Yes, I am.
Well, I would shake your hand. You're the guy from the Daily Bugle!
You wrote the piece that took down The Kingpin?
Oh, uh, thanks.
I just wrote a series of articles. The *law* is what took--
You, sir, are a prince.
Oh, well, uh, thank you.
And brave.
Well...
Taking on a man like The Kingpin. Did you win a prize for that or--?
Hey, what do you get paid for something like that?
I'm sorry...
CRASH!
AAAIEE!
Don't anybody move!!

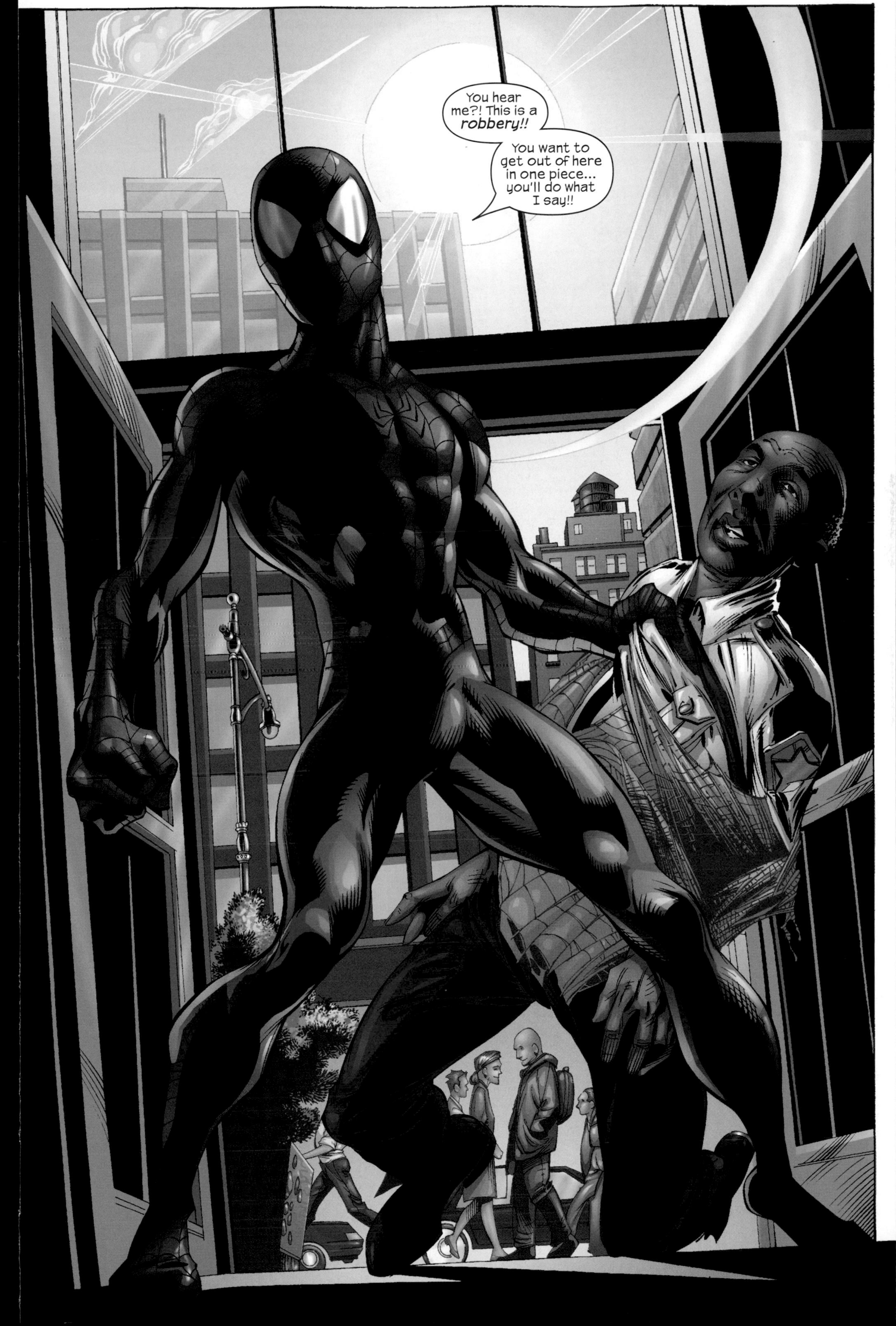
You hear me?! This is a *robbery!!*
You want to get out of here in one piece... you'll do what I say!!

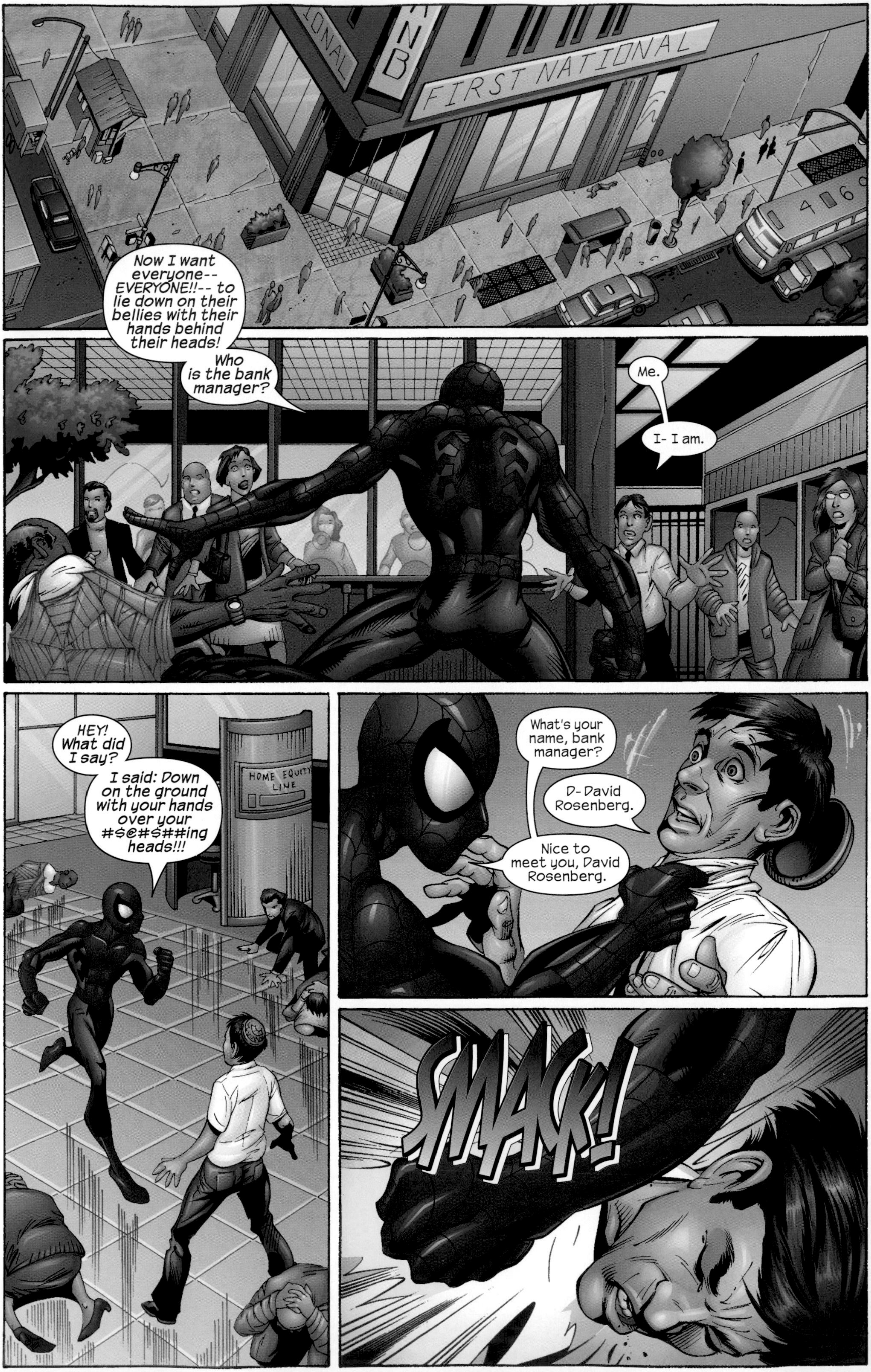
FIRST NATIONAL
FNB
Now I want everyone-- EVERYONE!!-- to lie down on their bellies with their hands behind their heads!
Who is the bank manager?
Me.
I- I am.
HEY! What did I say?
I said: Down on the ground with your hands over your #$@#$##ing heads!!!
HOME EQUITY LINE
What's your name, bank manager?
D- David Rosenberg.
Nice to meet you, David Rosenberg.
SMACK!

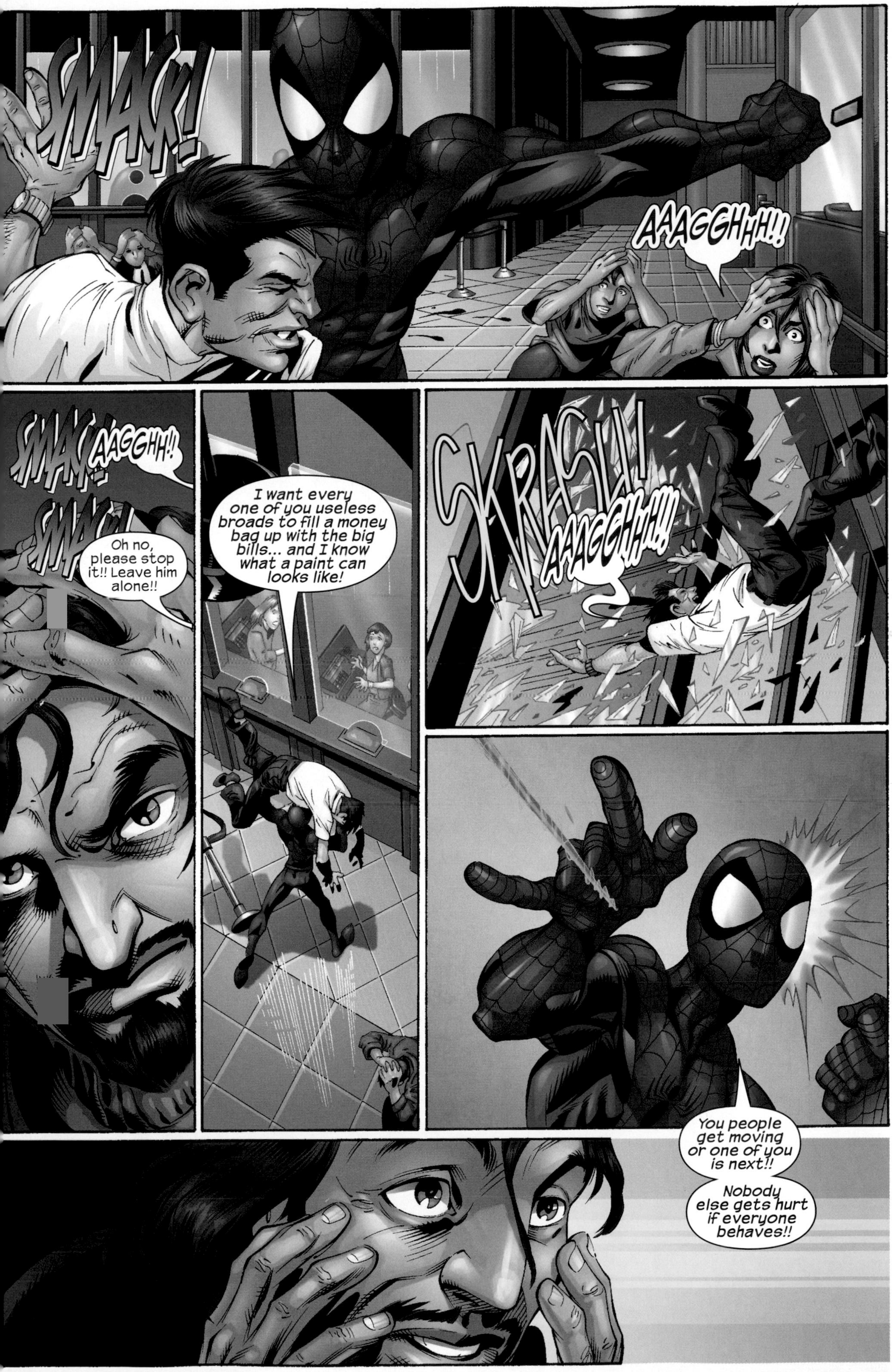
SMACK!
AAAGGHHH!!
SMACK!
AAGGHH!!
SMACK!
Oh no, please stop it!! Leave him alone!!
I want every one of you useless broads to fill a money bag up with the big bills... and I know what a paint can looks like!
SKRASH!
AAAGGHHH!!
You people get moving or one of you is next!!
Nobody else gets hurt if everyone behaves!!

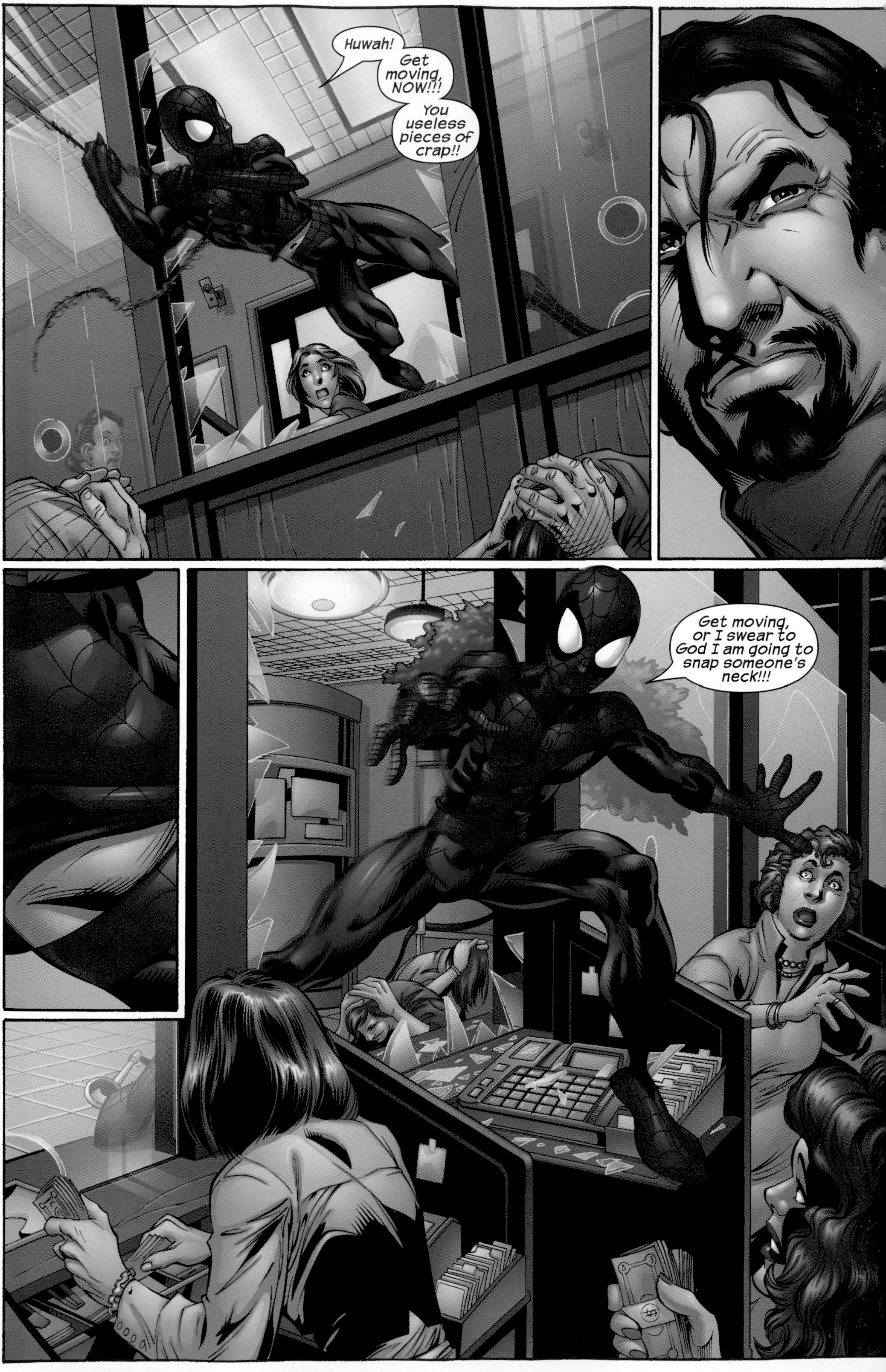
Huwah!
Get moving, NOW!!!
You useless pieces of crap!!
Get moving, or I swear to God I am going to snap someone's neck!!!

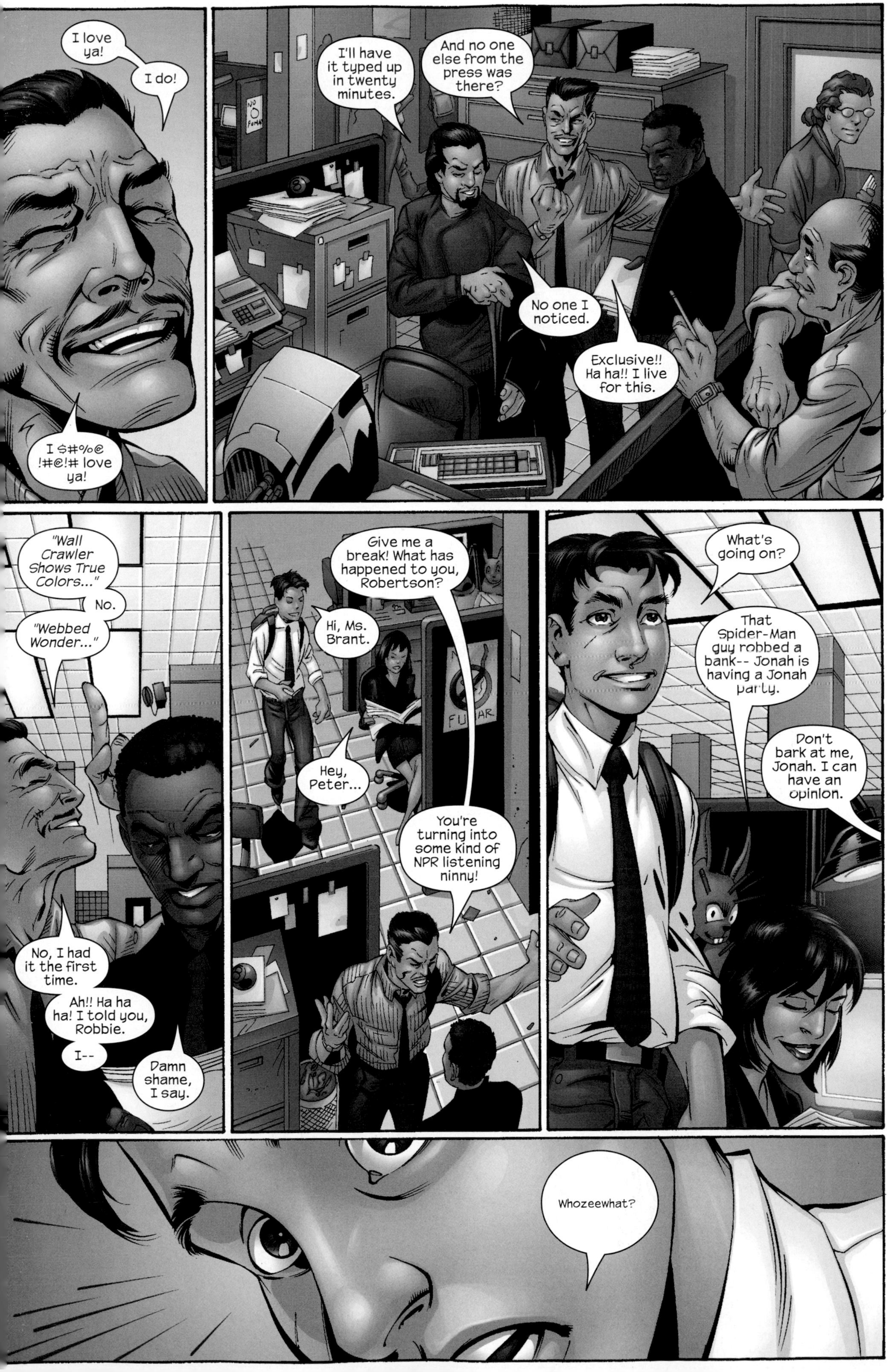
I love ya!
I do!
I $#%@ !#@!# love ya!
I'll have it typed up in twenty minutes.
And no one else from the press was there?
No one I noticed.
Exclusive!! Ha ha!! I live for this.
"Wall Crawler Shows True Colors..."
No.
"Webbed Wonder..."
No, I had it the first time.
Ah!! Ha ha ha! I told you, Robbie.
I--
Damn shame, I say.
Give me a break! What has happened to you, Robertson?
Hi, Ms. Brant.
Hey, Peter...
You're turning into some kind of NPR listening ninny!
What's going on?
That Spider-Man guy robbed a bank-- Jonah is having a Jonah party.
Don't bark at me, Jonah. I can have an opinion.
Whozeewhat?

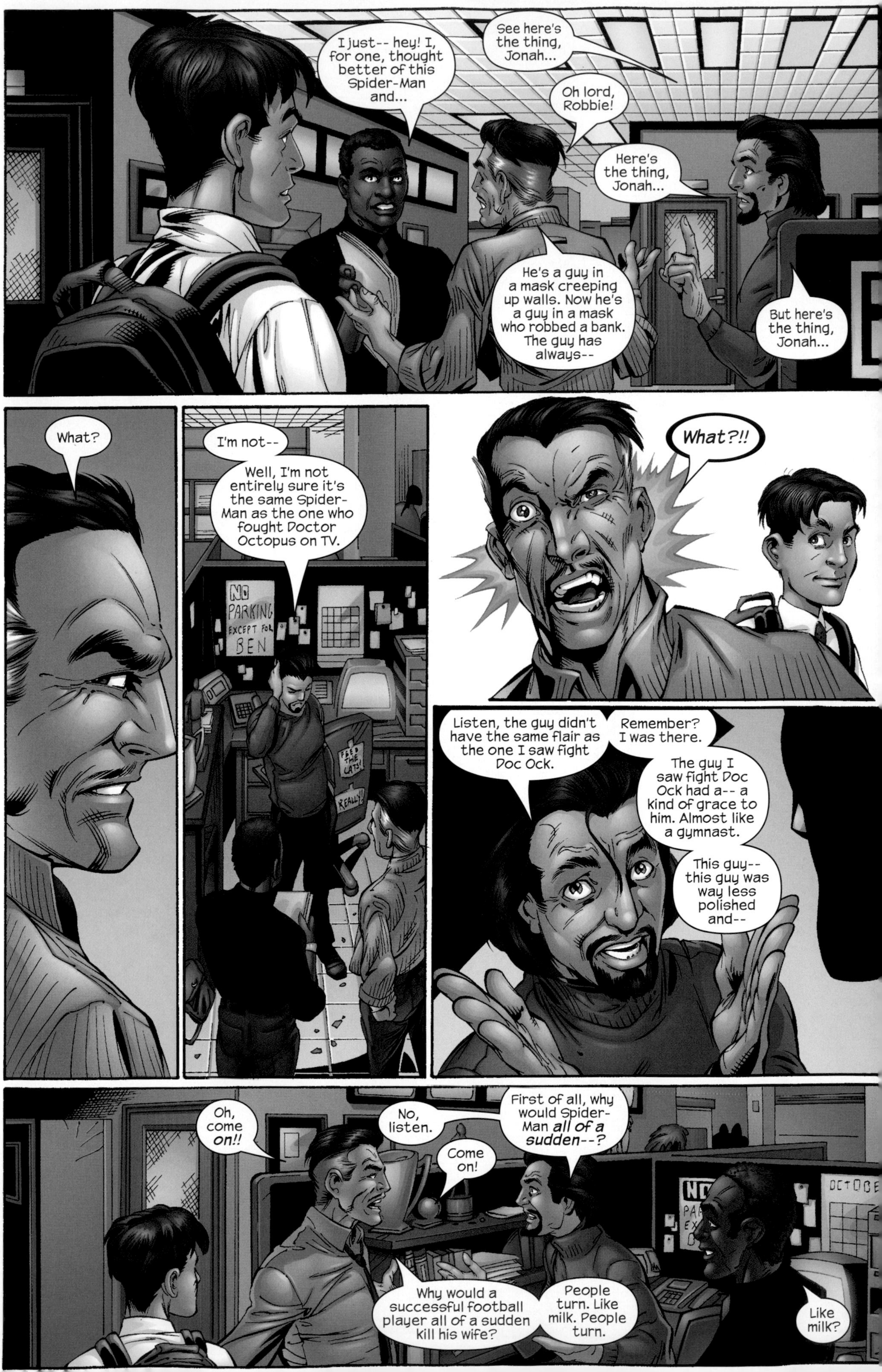

I just-- hey! I, for one, thought better of this Spider-Man and...
See here's the thing, Jonah...
Oh lord, Robbie!
Here's the thing, Jonah...
He's a guy in a mask creeping up walls. Now he's a guy in a mask who robbed a bank. The guy has always--
But here's the thing, Jonah...
What?
I'm not--
Well, I'm not entirely sure it's the same Spider-Man as the one who fought Doctor Octopus on TV.
NO PARKING EXCEPT FOR BEN
FEED THE CATS!
REALLY!
What?!!
Listen, the guy didn't have the same flair as the one I saw fight Doc Ock.
Remember? I was there.
The guy I saw fight Doc Ock had a-- a kind of grace to him. Almost like a gymnast.
This guy-- this guy was way less polished and--
Oh, come on!!
No, listen.
First of all, why would Spider-Man all of a sudden--?
Come on!
Why would a successful football player all of a sudden kill his wife?
People turn. Like milk. People turn.
Like milk?

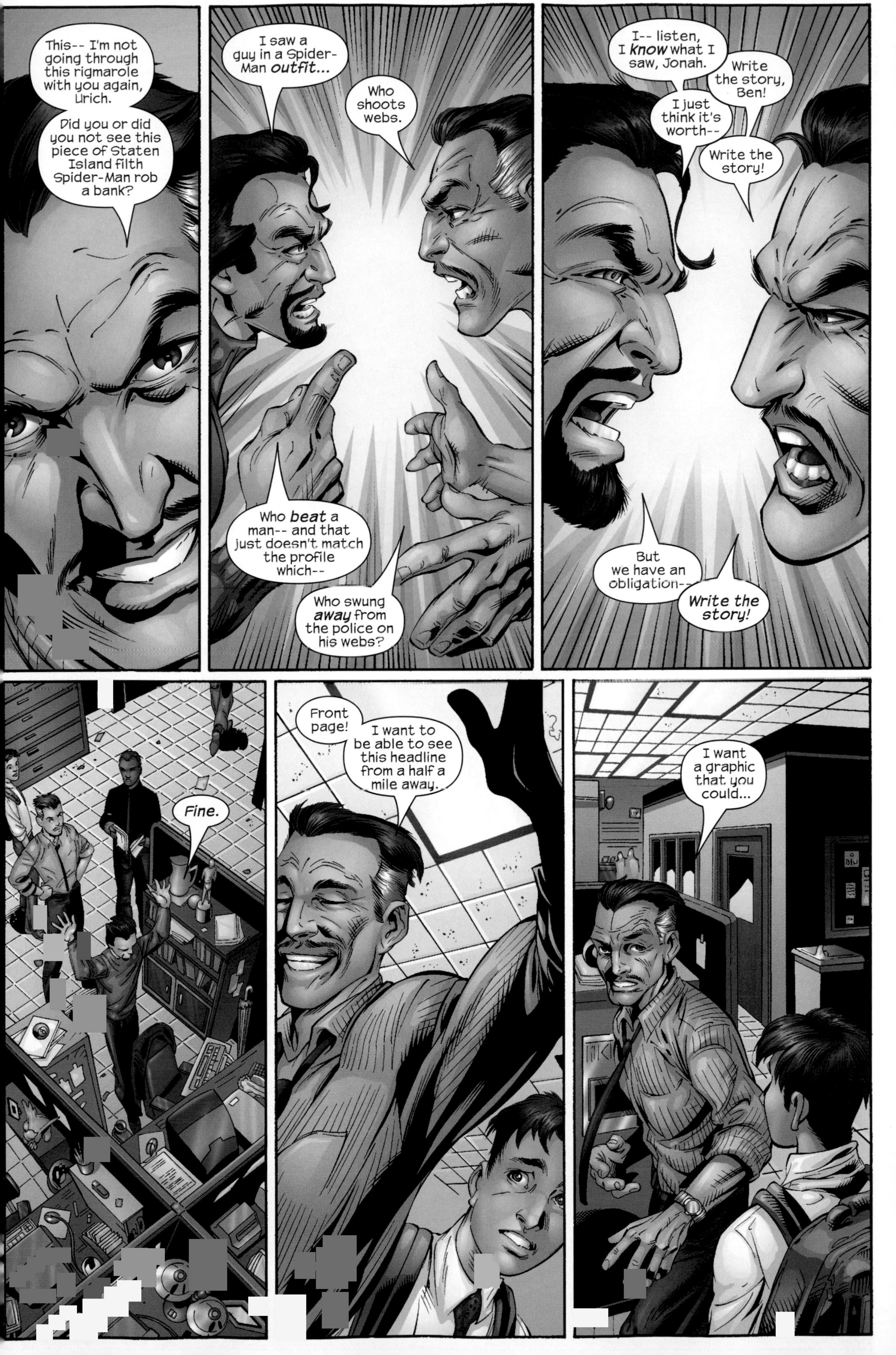
This-- I'm not going through this rigmarole with you again, Urich.
Did you or did you not see this piece of Staten Island filth Spider-Man rob a bank?
I saw a guy in a Spider-Man *outfit*...
Who shoots webs.
Who *beat* a man-- and that just doesn't match the profile which--
Who swung *away* from the police on his webs?
I-- listen, I *know* what I saw, Jonah.
Write the story, Ben!
I just think it's worth--
Write the story!
But we have an obligation--
Write the story!
Fine.
Front page!
I want to be able to see this headline from a half a mile away.
I want a graphic that you could...

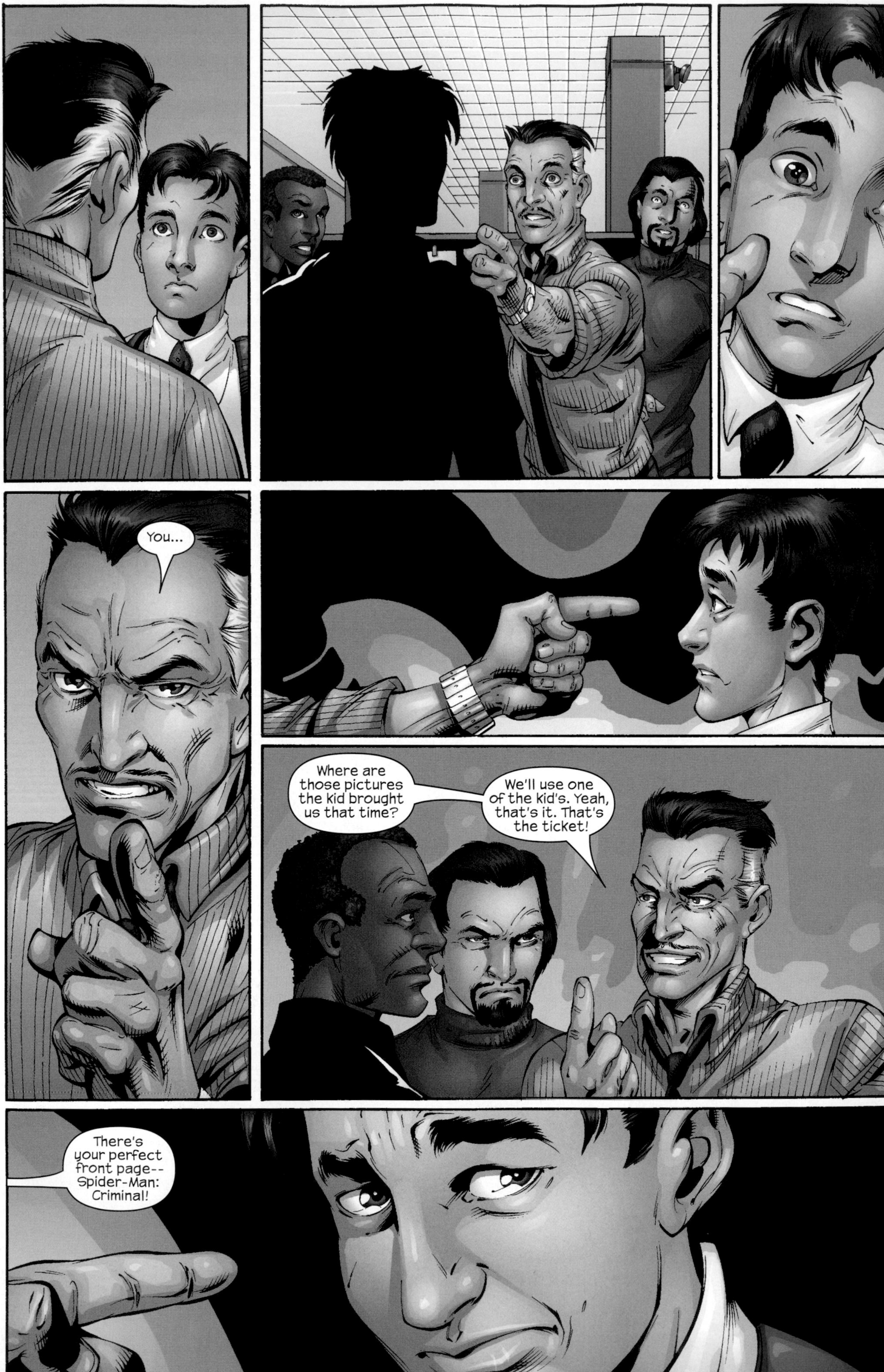
You...
Where are those pictures the kid brought us that time?
We'll use one of the kid's. Yeah, that's it. That's the ticket!
There's your perfect front page-- Spider-Man: Criminal!

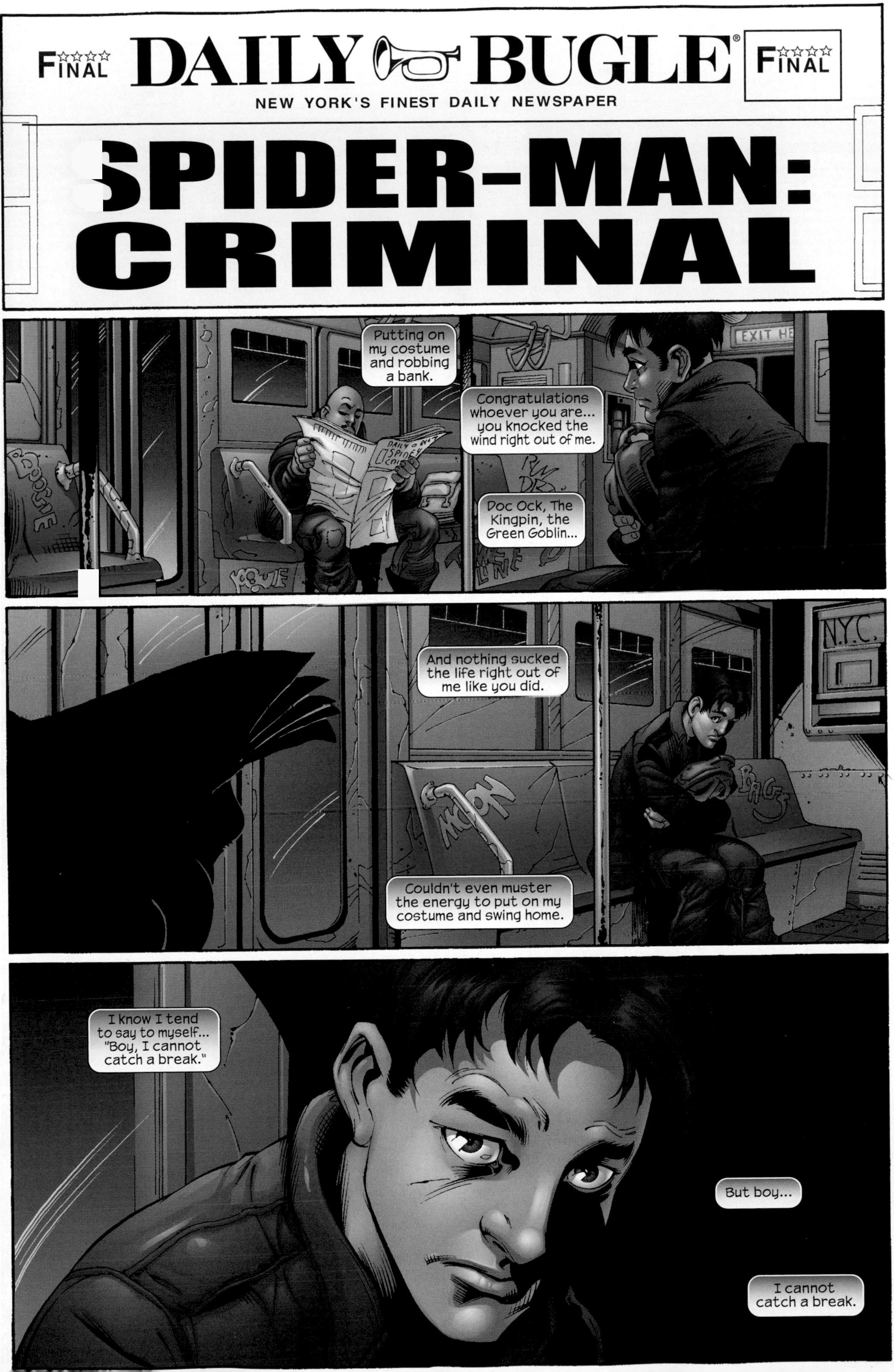
FINAL DAILY BUGLE FINAL
NEW YORK'S FINEST DAILY NEWSPAPER
SPIDER-MAN: CRIMINAL
Putting on my costume and robbing a bank.
Congratulations whoever you are... you knocked the wind right out of me.
Doc Ock, The Kingpin, the Green Goblin...
EXIT
And nothing sucked the life right out of me like you did.
N.Y.C.
Couldn't even muster the energy to put on my costume and swing home.
I know I tend to say to myself... "Boy, I cannot catch a break."
But boy...
I cannot catch a break.

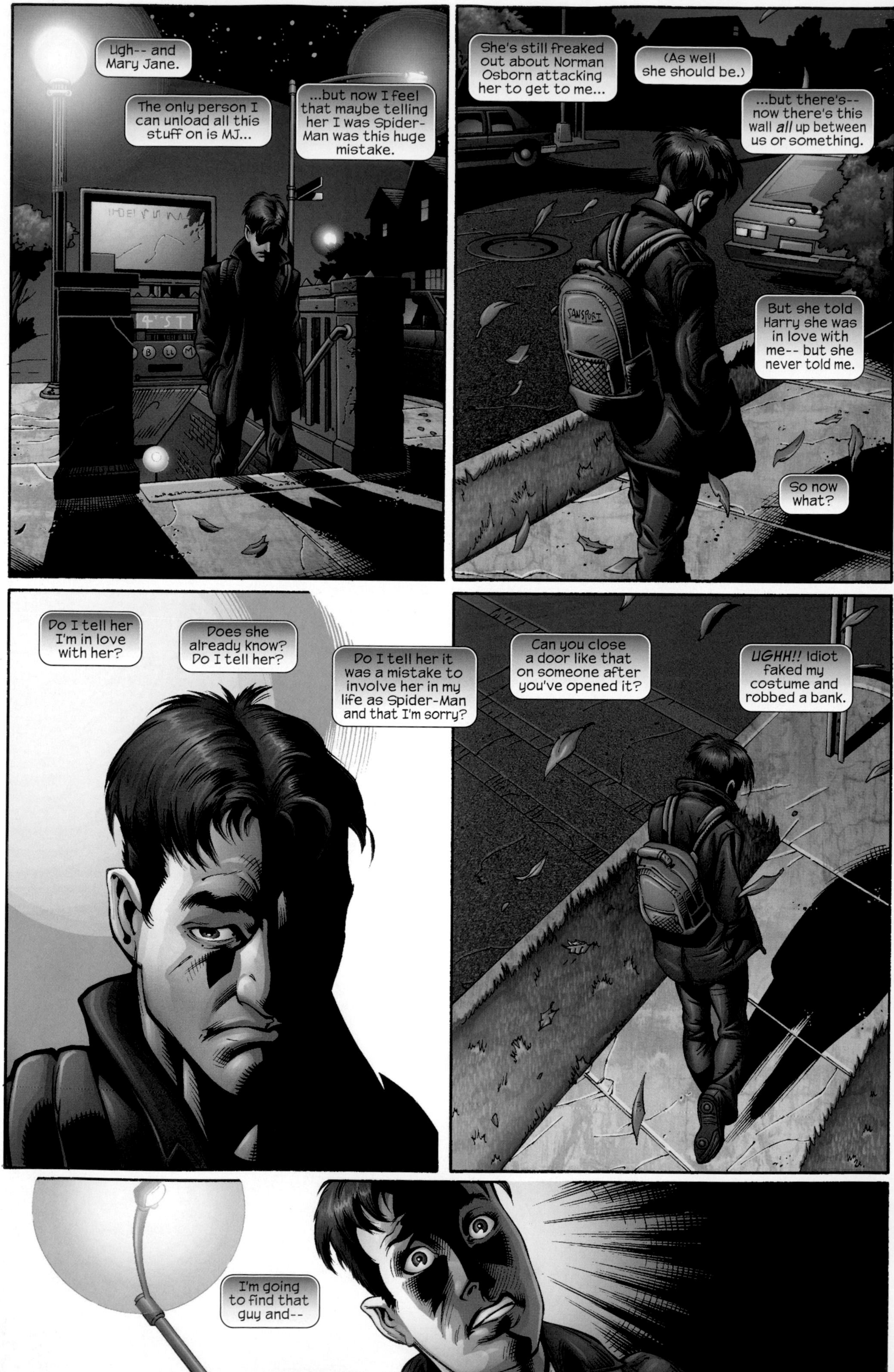
Ugh-- and Mary Jane.
The only person I can unload all this stuff on is MJ...
...but now I feel that maybe telling her I was Spider-Man was this huge mistake.
4TH ST
She's still freaked out about Norman Osborn attacking her to get to me...
(As well she should be.)
...but there's-- now there's this wall *all* up between us or something.
But she told Harry she was in love with me-- but she never told me.
So now what?
Do I tell her I'm in love with her?
Does she already know? Do I tell her?
Do I tell her it was a mistake to involve her in my life as Spider-Man and that I'm sorry?
Can you close a door like that on someone after you've opened it?
UGHH!! Idiot faked my costume and robbed a bank.
I'm going to find that guy and--

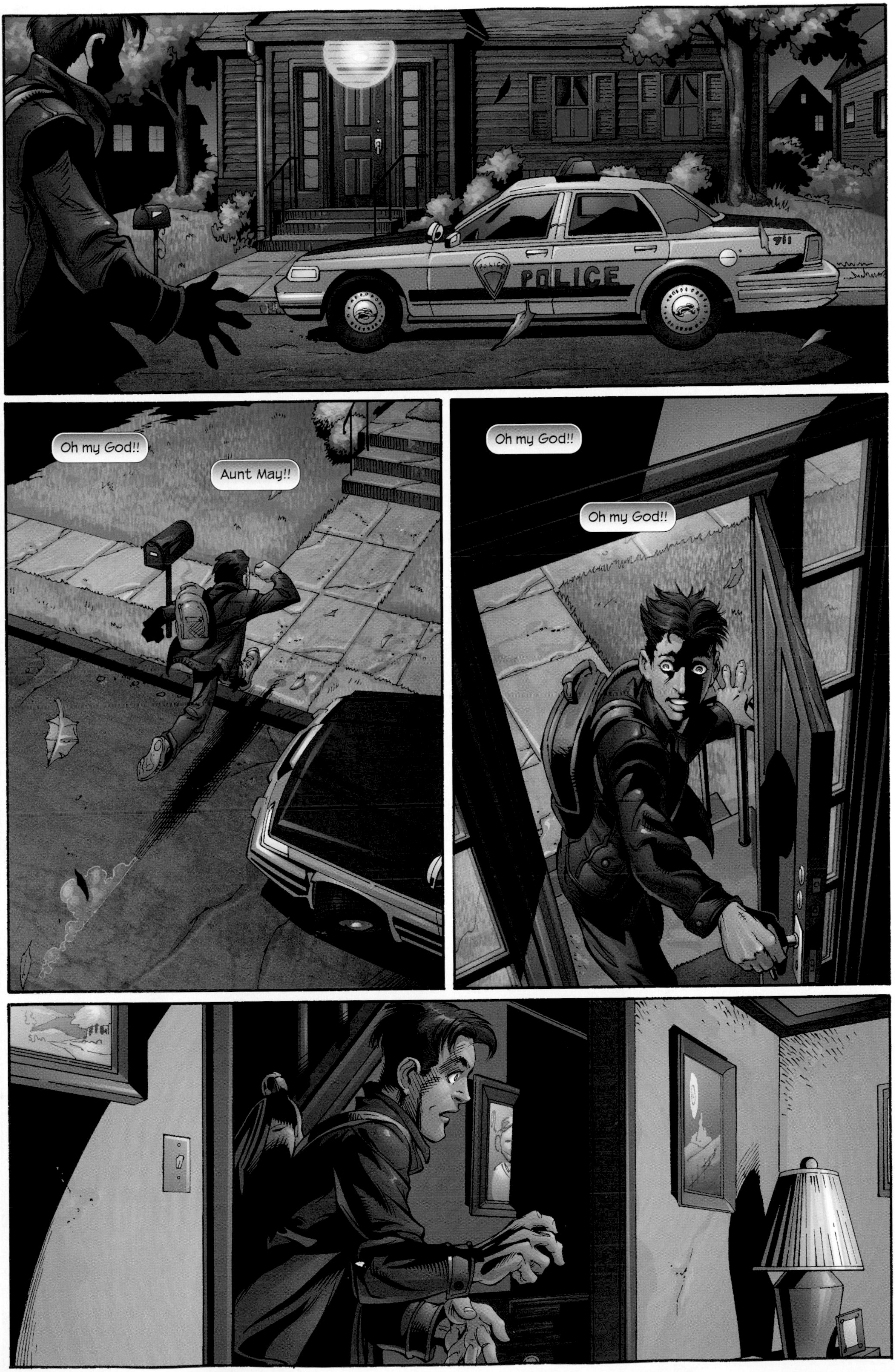
POLICE
Oh my God!!
Aunt May!!
Oh my God!!
Oh my God!!

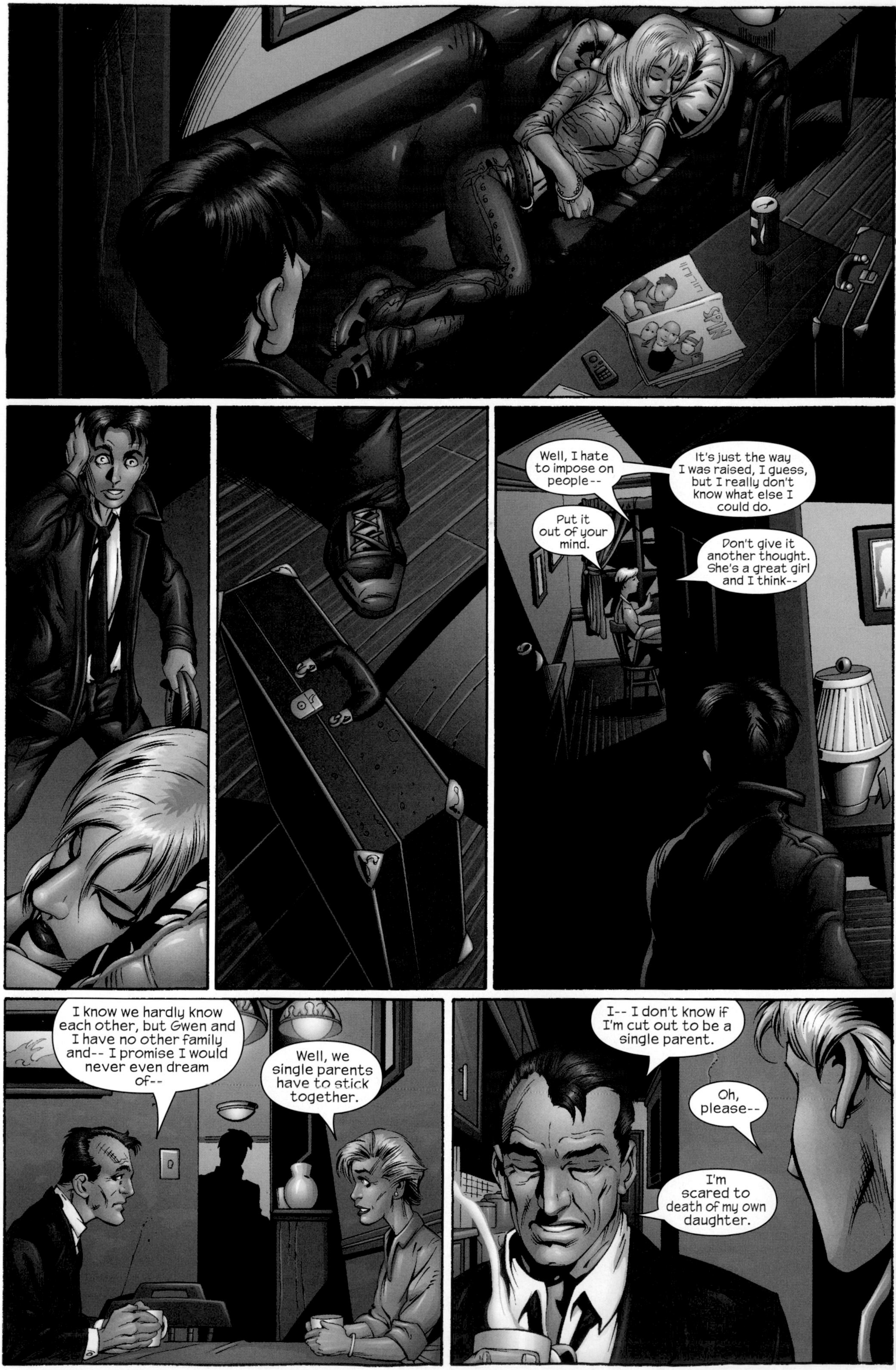

Well, I hate to impose on people--
It's just the way I was raised, I guess, but I really don't know what else I could do.
Put it out of your mind.
Don't give it another thought. She's a great girl and I think--
I know we hardly know each other, but Gwen and I have no other family and-- I promise I would never even dream of--
Well, we single parents have to stick together.
I-- I don't know if I'm cut out to be a single parent.
Oh, please--
I'm scared to death of my own daughter.

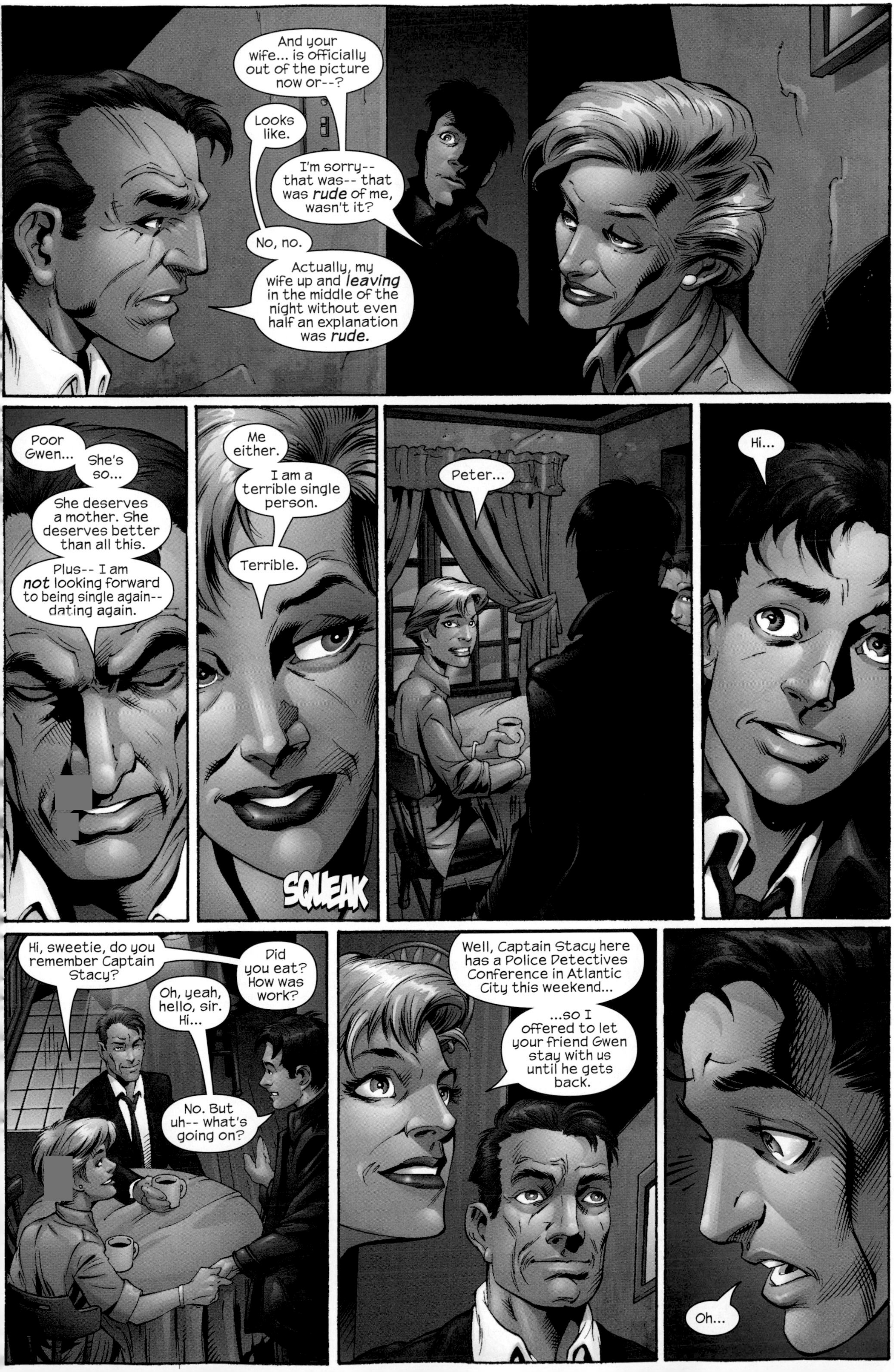
And your wife... is officially out of the picture now or--?
Looks like.
I'm sorry-- that was-- that was *rude* of me, wasn't it?
No, no.
Actually, my wife up and *leaving* in the middle of the night without even half an explanation was *rude.*
Poor Gwen...
She's so...
She deserves a mother. She deserves better than all this.
Plus-- I am *not* looking forward to being single again-- dating again.
Me either.
I am a terrible single person.
Terrible.
SQUEAK
Peter...
Hi...
Hi, sweetie, do you remember Captain Stacy?
Did you eat? How was work?
Oh, yeah, hello, sir. Hi...
No. But uh-- what's going on?
Well, Captain Stacy here has a Police Detectives Conference in Atlantic City this weekend...
...so I offered to let your friend Gwen stay with us until he gets back.
Oh...

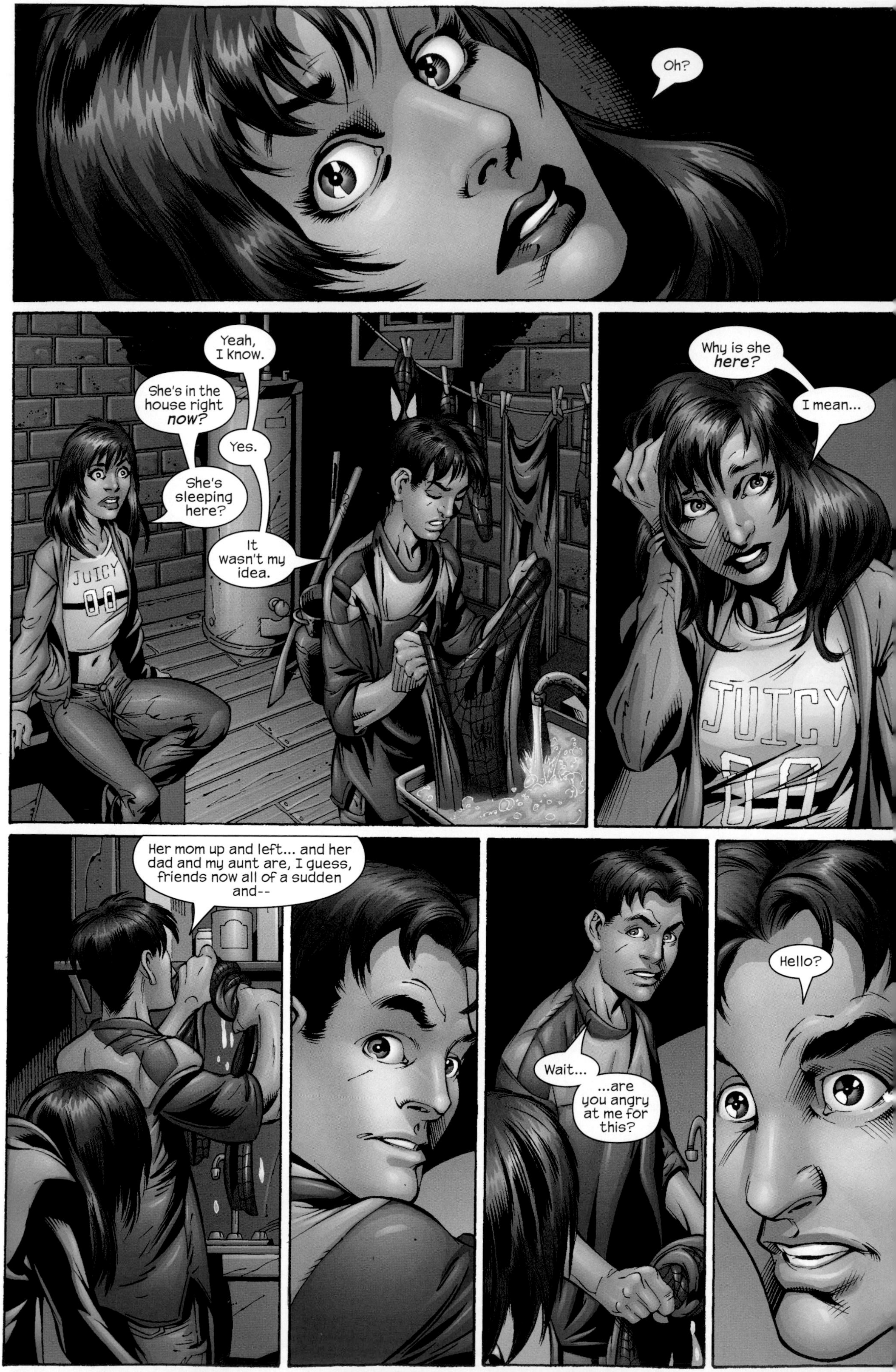
Oh?
She's in the house right *now?*
Yeah, I know.
Yes.
She's sleeping here?
It wasn't my idea.
Why is she *here?*
I mean...
Her mom up and left... and her dad and my aunt are, I guess, friends now all of a sudden and--
Wait...
...are you angry at me for this?
Hello?

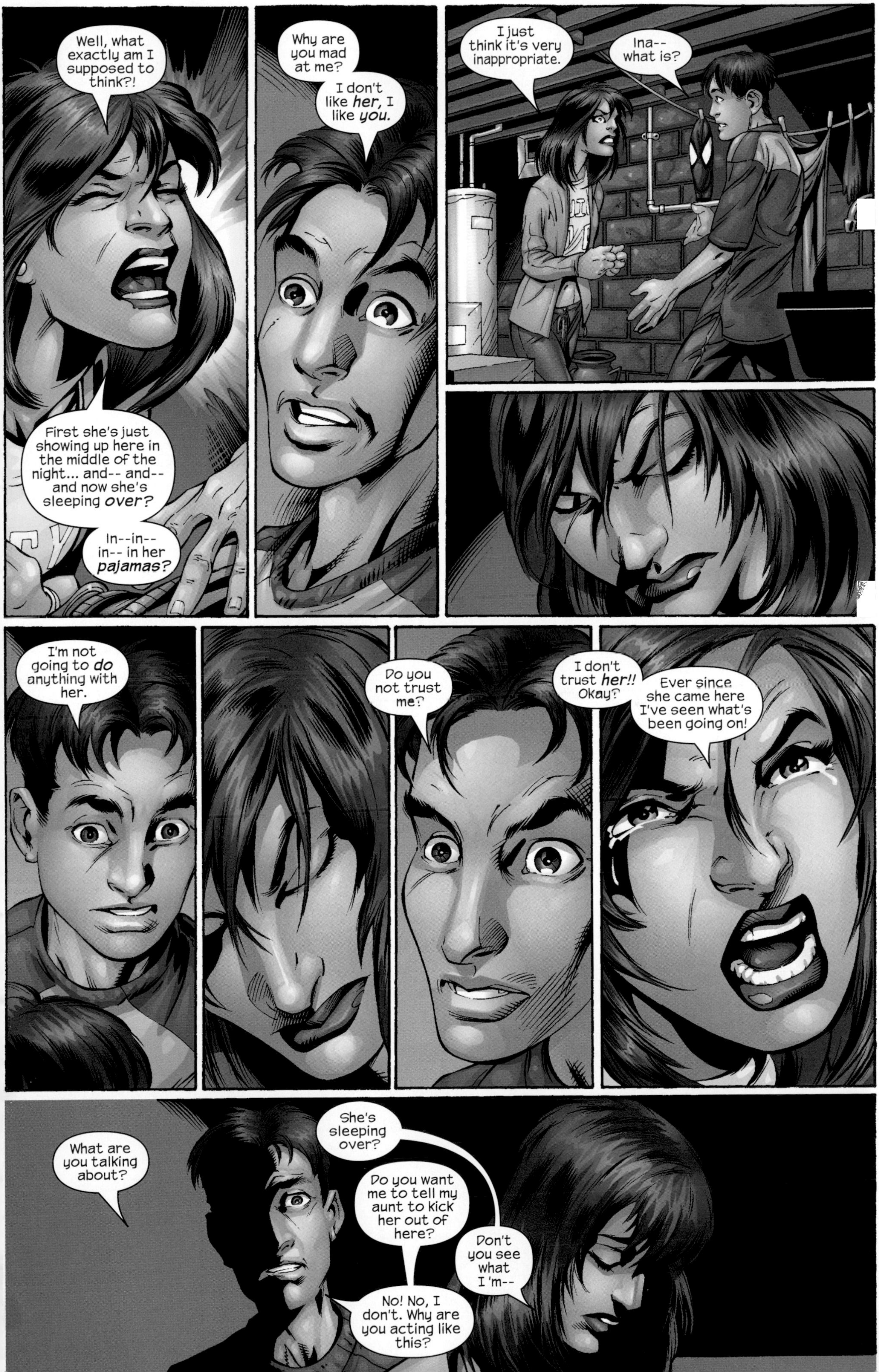
Well, what exactly am I supposed to think?!
First she's just showing up here in the middle of the night... and-- and-- and now she's sleeping *over*?
In--in-- in-- in her *pajamas*?
Why are you mad at me?
I don't like *her*, I like *you*.
I just think it's very inappropriate.
Ina-- what is?
I'm not going to *do* anything with her.
Do you not trust me?
I don't trust *her!!* Okay?
Ever since she came here I've seen what's been going on!
What are you talking about?
She's sleeping over?
Do you want me to tell my aunt to kick her out of here?
Don't you see what I'm--
No! No, I don't. Why are you acting like this?

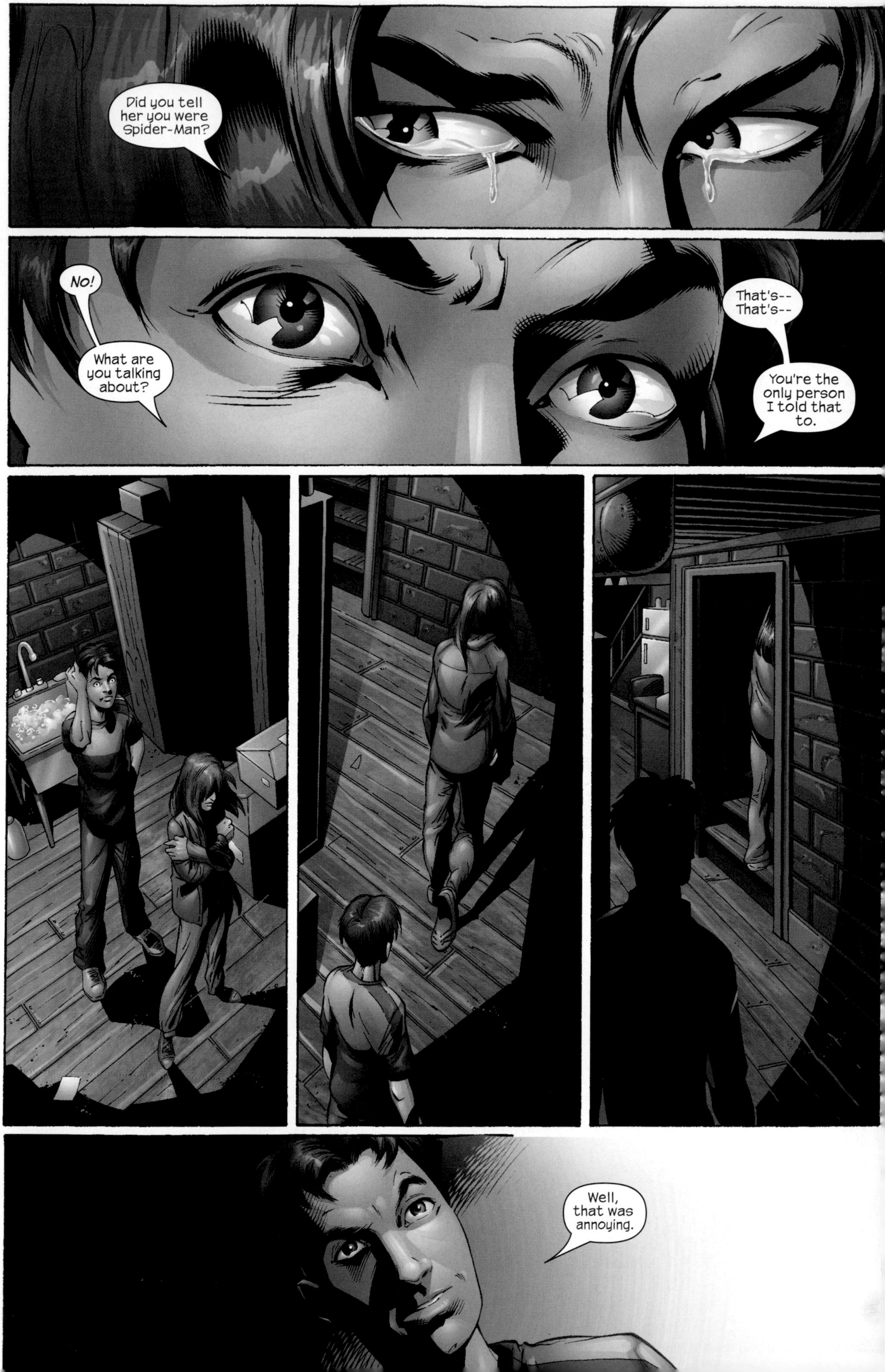
Did you tell her you were Spider-Man?
No!
What are you talking about?
That's-- That's--
You're the only person I told that to.
Well, that was annoying.

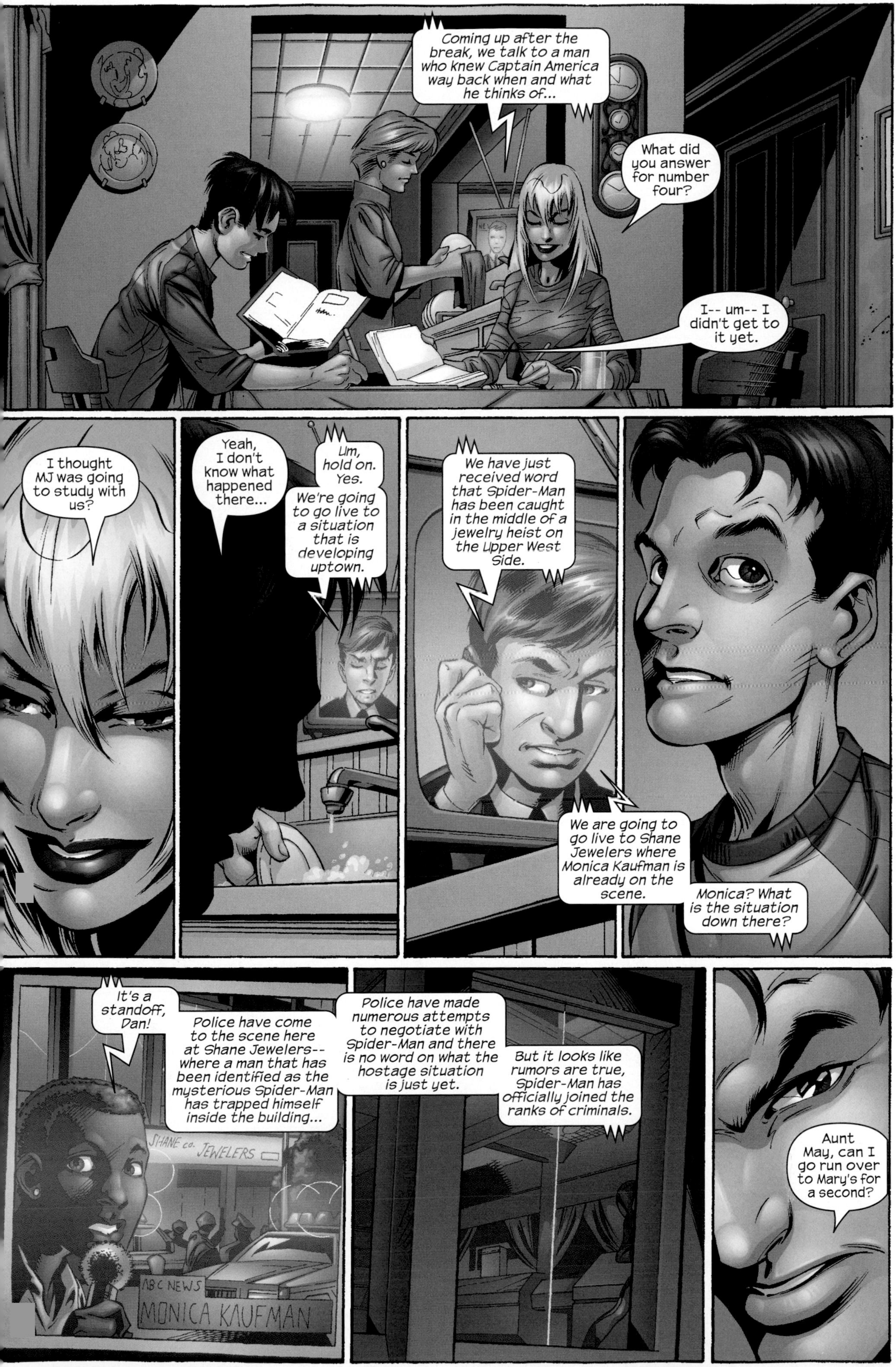
Coming up after the break, we talk to a man who knew Captain America way back when and what he thinks of...
What did you answer for number four?
I-- um-- I didn't get to it yet.
I thought MJ was going to study with us?
Yeah, I don't know what happened there...
Um, hold on. Yes.
We're going to go live to a situation that is developing uptown.
We have just received word that Spider-Man has been caught in the middle of a jewelry heist on the Upper West Side.
We are going to go live to Shane Jewelers where Monica Kaufman is already on the scene.
Monica? What is the situation down there?
It's a standoff, Dan!
Police have come to the scene here at Shane Jewelers-- where a man that has been identified as the mysterious Spider-Man has trapped himself inside the building...
SHANE co. JEWELERS
ABC NEWS
MONICA KAUFMAN
Police have made numerous attempts to negotiate with Spider-Man and there is no word on what the hostage situation is just yet.
But it looks like rumors are true, Spider-Man has officially joined the ranks of criminals.
Aunt May, can I go run over to Mary's for a second?

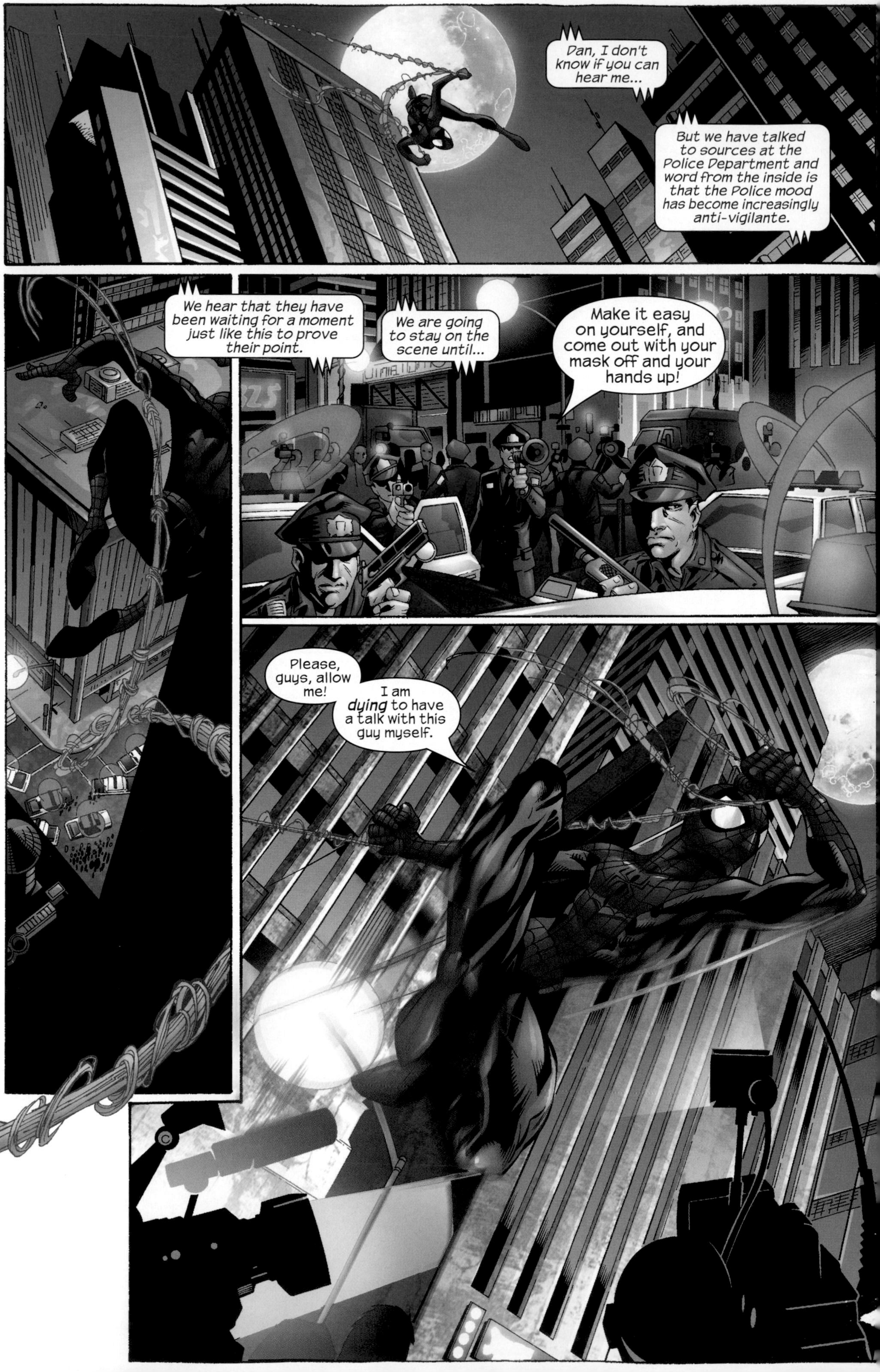
Dan, I don't know if you can hear me...
But we have talked to sources at the Police Department and word from the inside is that the Police mood has become increasingly anti-vigilante.
We hear that they have been waiting for a moment just like this to prove their point.
We are going to stay on the scene until...
Make it easy on yourself, and come out with your mask off and your hands up!
Please, guys, allow me!
I am *dying* to have a talk with this guy myself.

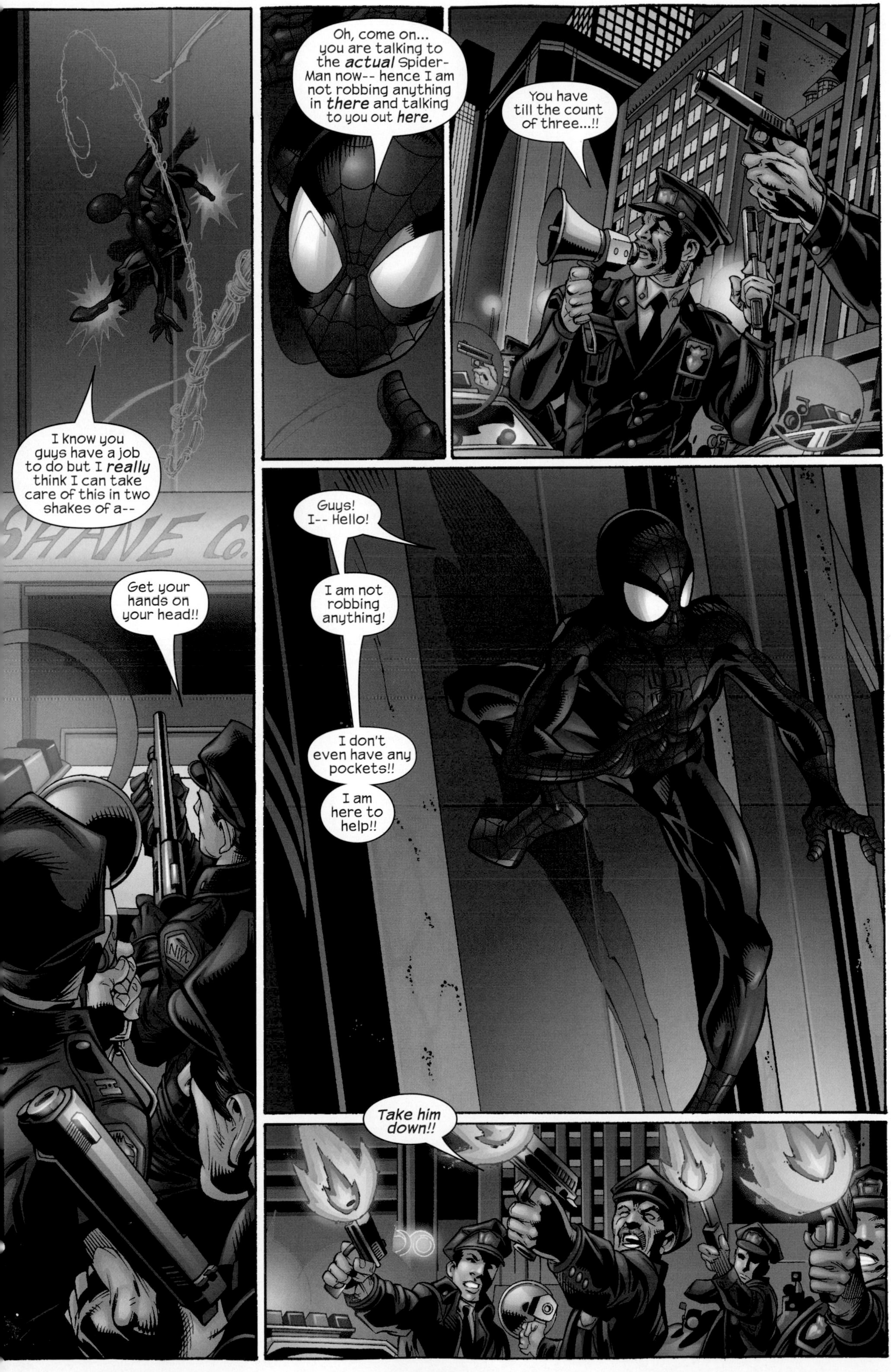
I know you guys have a job to do but I *really* think I can take care of this in two shakes of a--
SHANE Co.
Get your hands on your head!!
Oh, come on... you are talking to the *actual* Spider-Man now-- hence I am not robbing anything in *there* and talking to you out *here*.
You have till the count of three...!!
Guys! I-- Hello!
I am not robbing anything!
I don't even have any pockets!!
I am here to help!!
Take him down!!

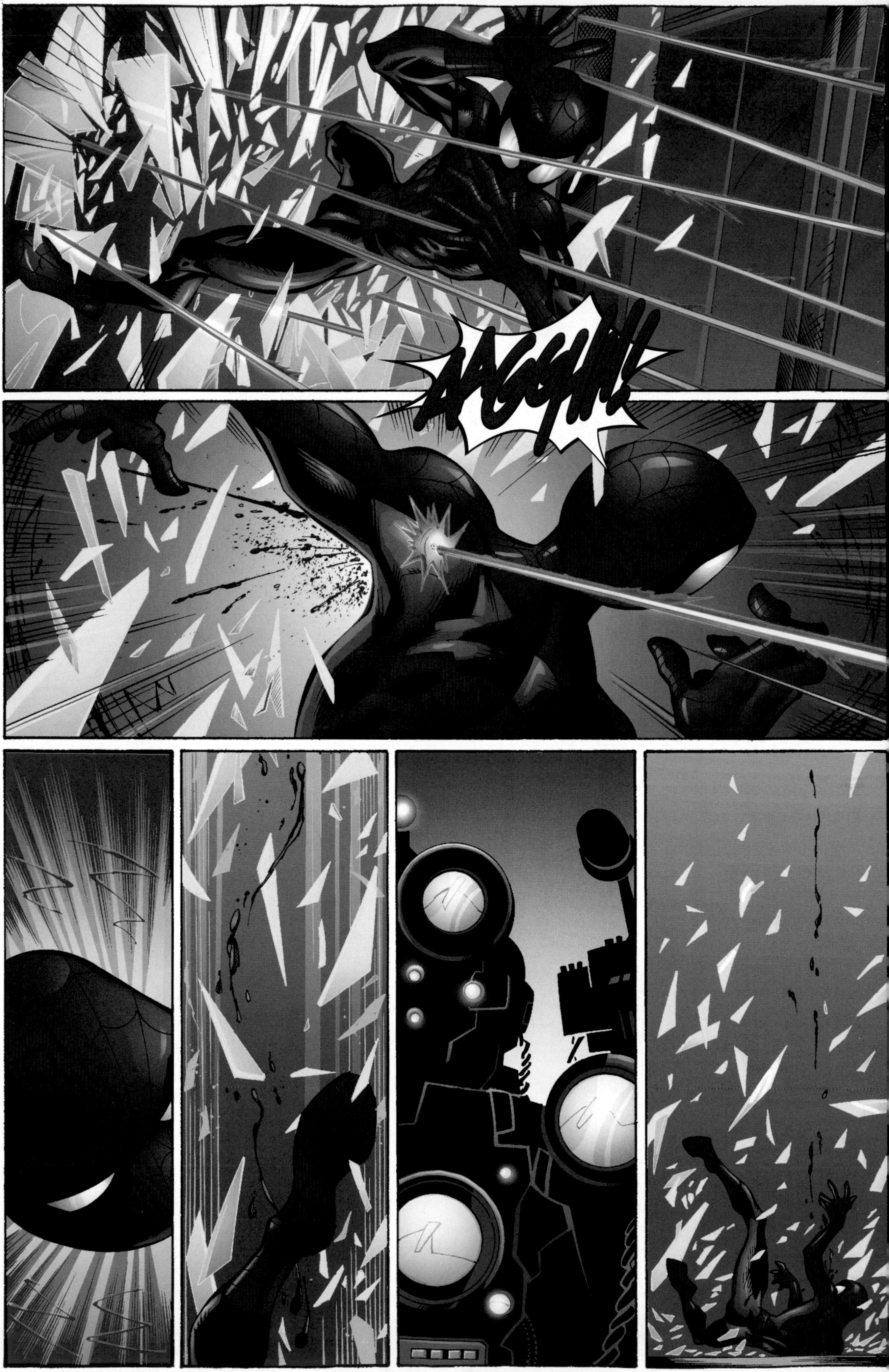
AAGGHH!

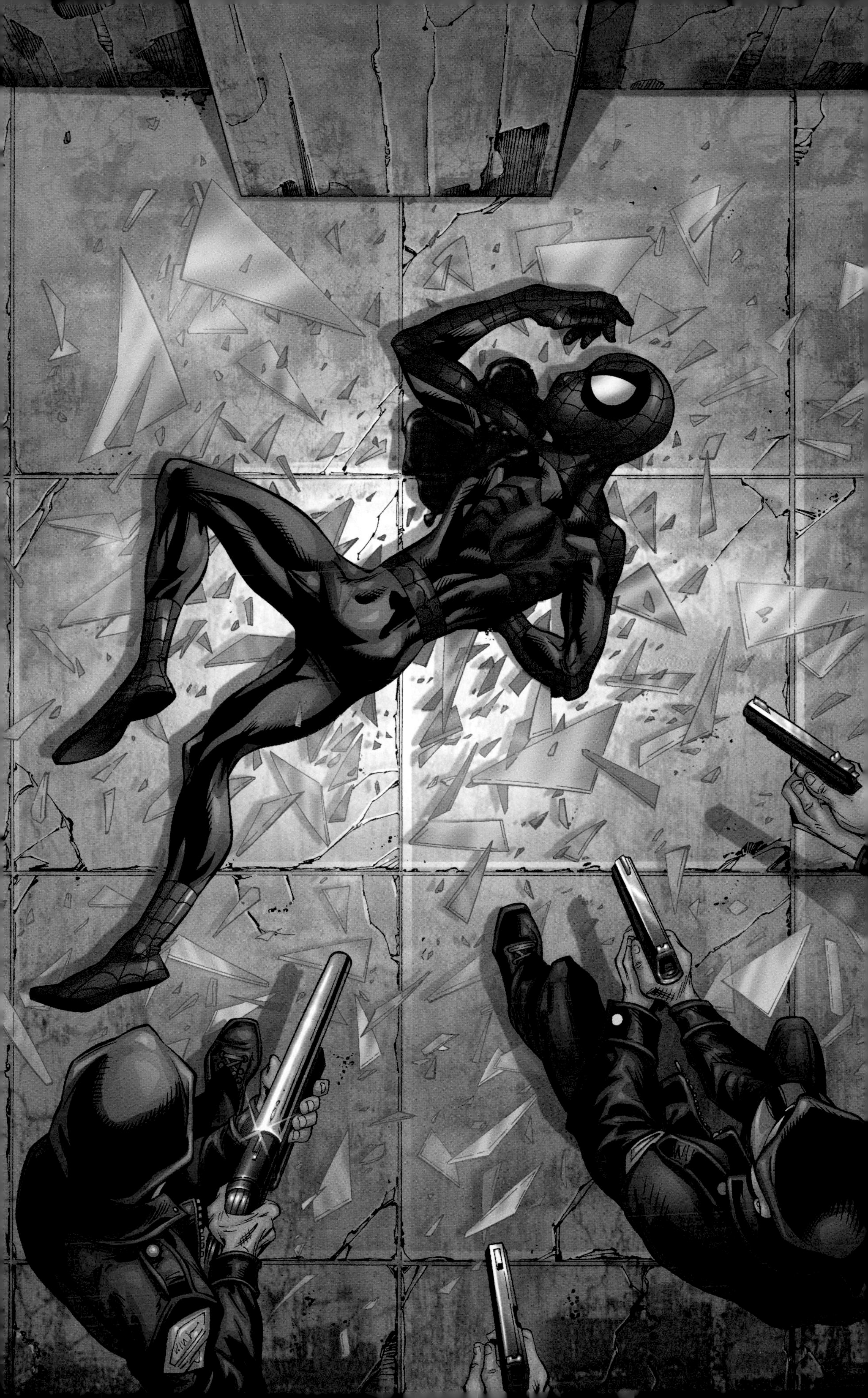

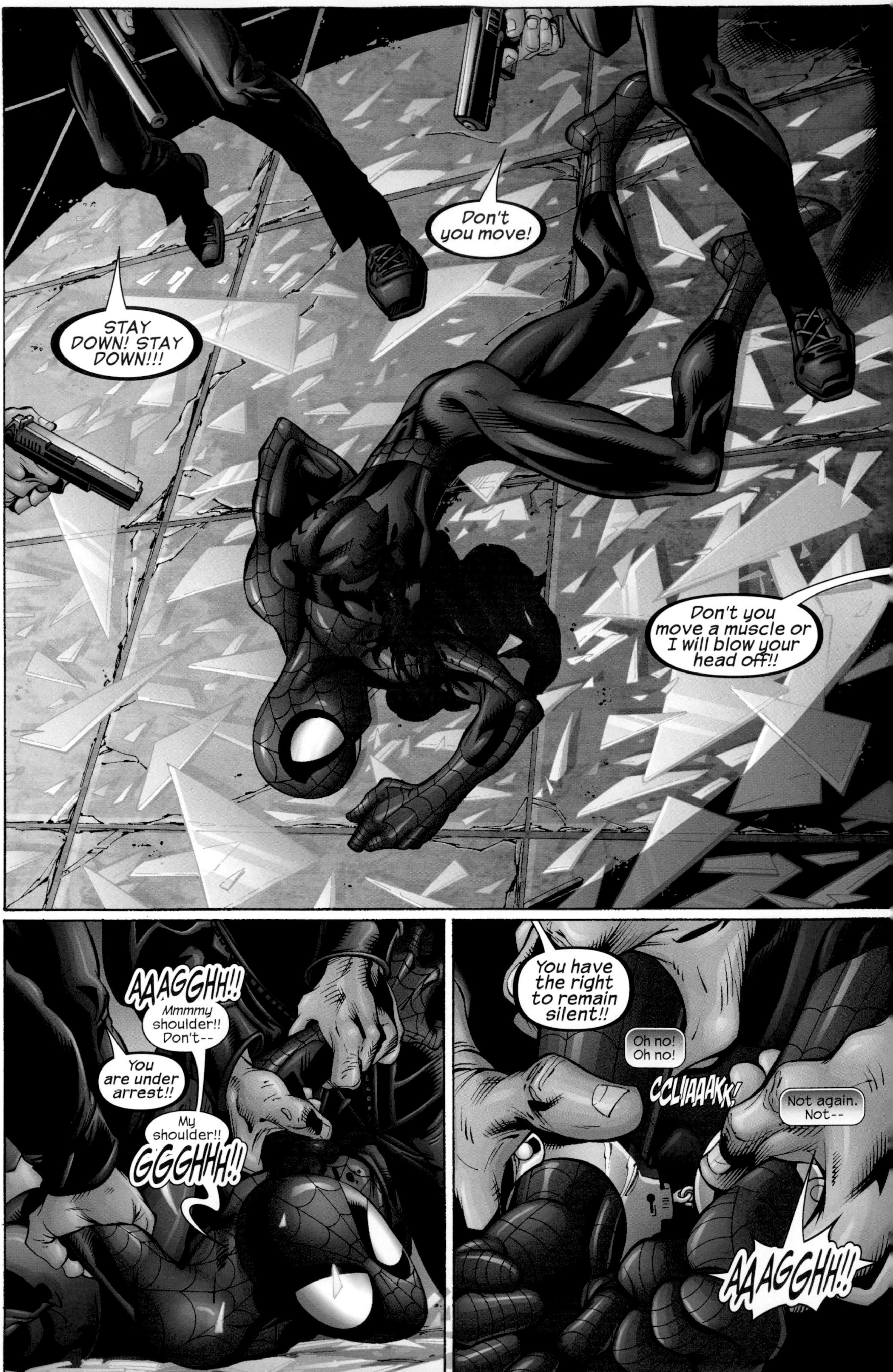
STAY DOWN! STAY DOWN!!!
Don't you move!
Don't you move a muscle or I will blow your head off!!
AAAGGHH!!
Mmmmy shoulder!! Don't--
You are under arrest!!
My shoulder!!
GGGHHH!!
You have the right to remain silent!!
Oh no! Oh no!
CCLIIAAAKK!
Not again. Not--
AAAGGHH!!

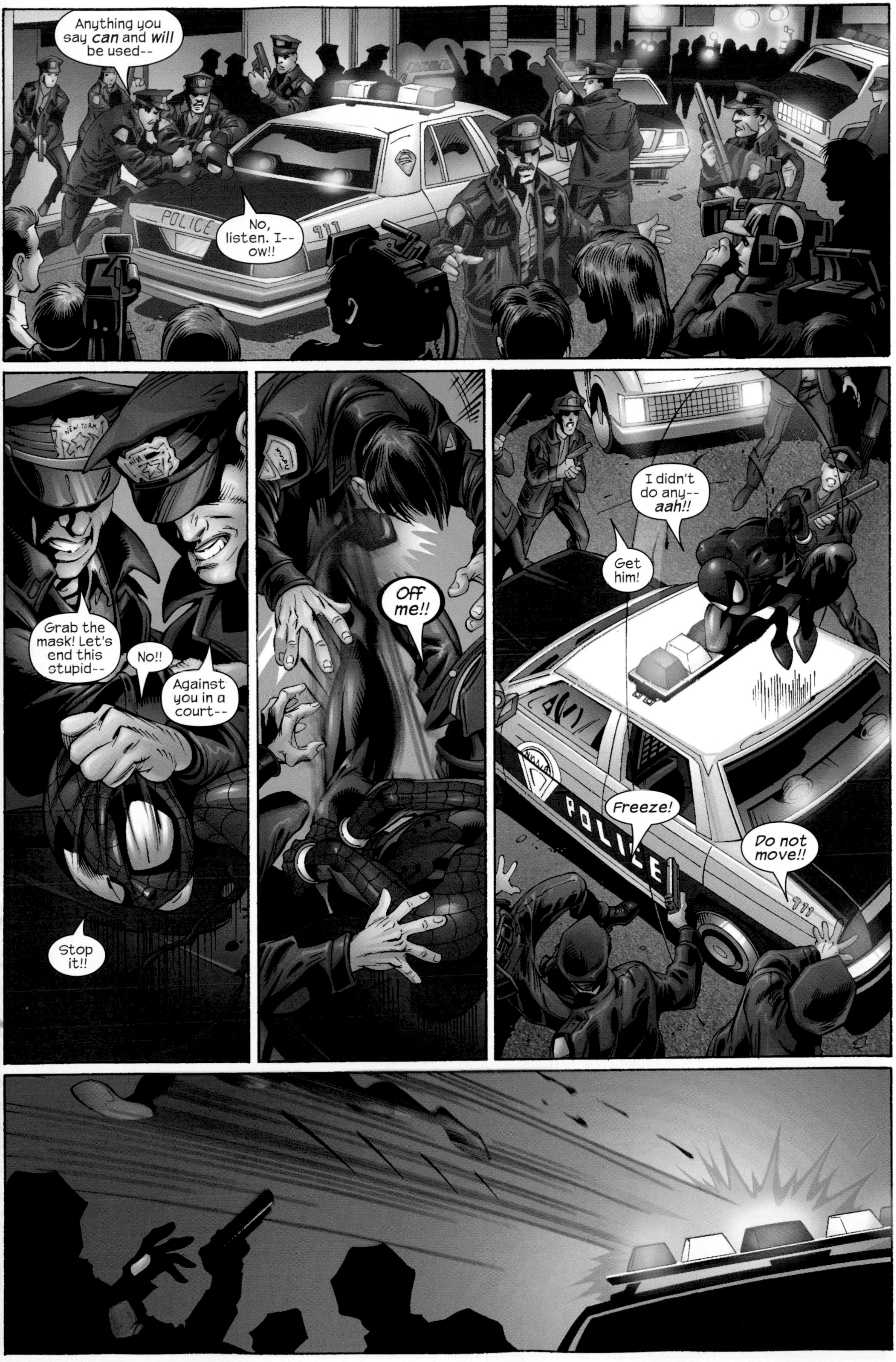

Anything you say can and will be used--
No, listen. I-- ow!!
Grab the mask! Let's end this stupid--
No!!
Against you in a court--
Stop it!!
Off me!!
I didn't do any-- aah!!
Get him!
Freeze!
Do not move!!

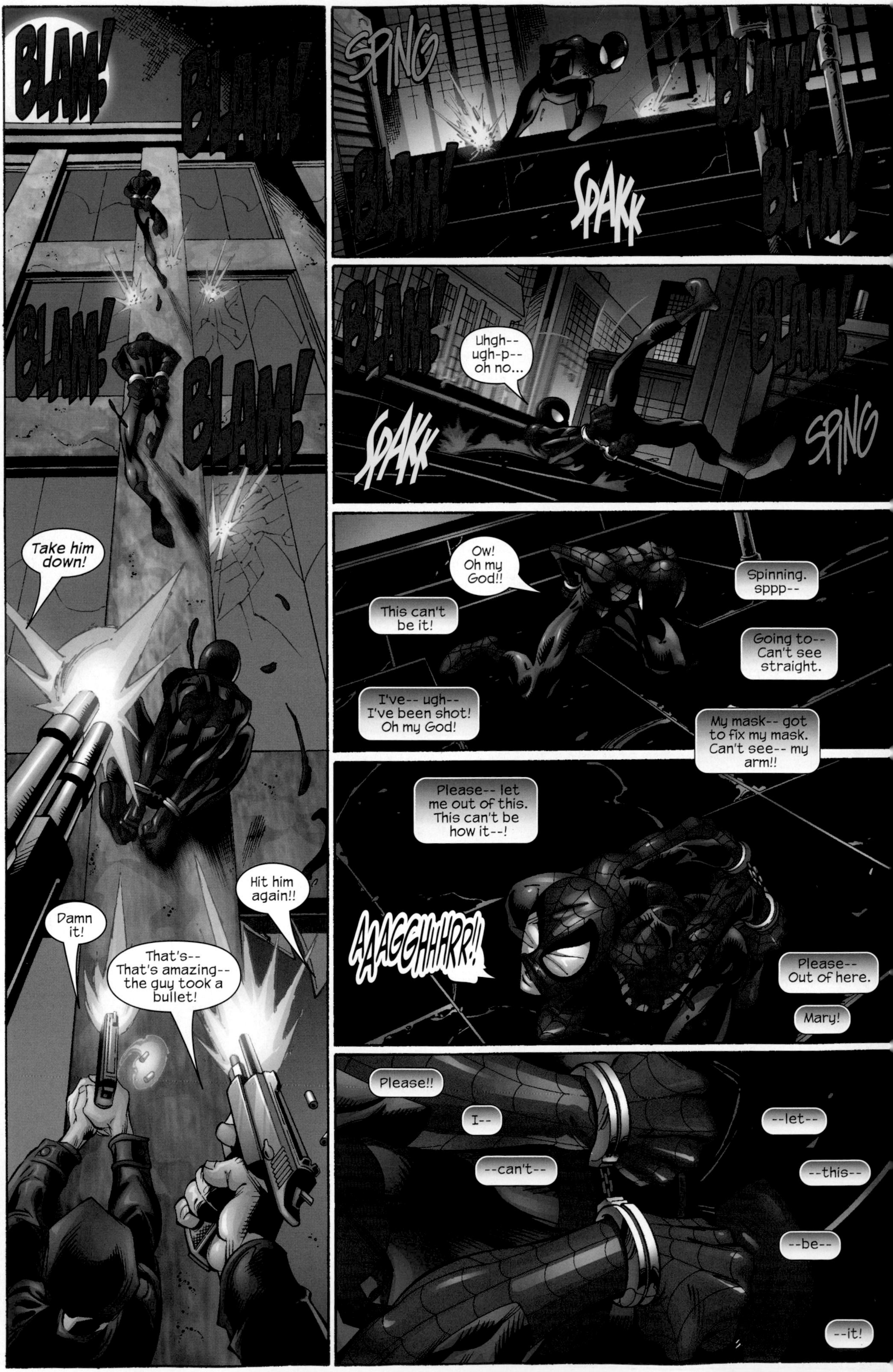
BLAM!
BLAM!
BLAM!
BLAM!
Take him down!
Hit him again!!
Damn it!
That's-- That's amazing-- the guy took a bullet!
SPING
BLAM!
BLAM!
SPAKK
BLAM!
BLAM!
Uhgh-- ugh-p-- oh no...
SPAKK
BLAM!
SPING
Ow! Oh my God!!
This can't be it!
Spinning. sppp--
Going to-- Can't see straight.
I've-- ugh-- I've been shot! Oh my God!
My mask-- got to fix my mask. Can't see-- my arm!!
Please-- let me out of this. This can't be how it--!
AAAGGHHRR!!
Please-- Out of here.
Mary!
Please!!
I--
--can't--
--let--
--this--
--be--
--it!

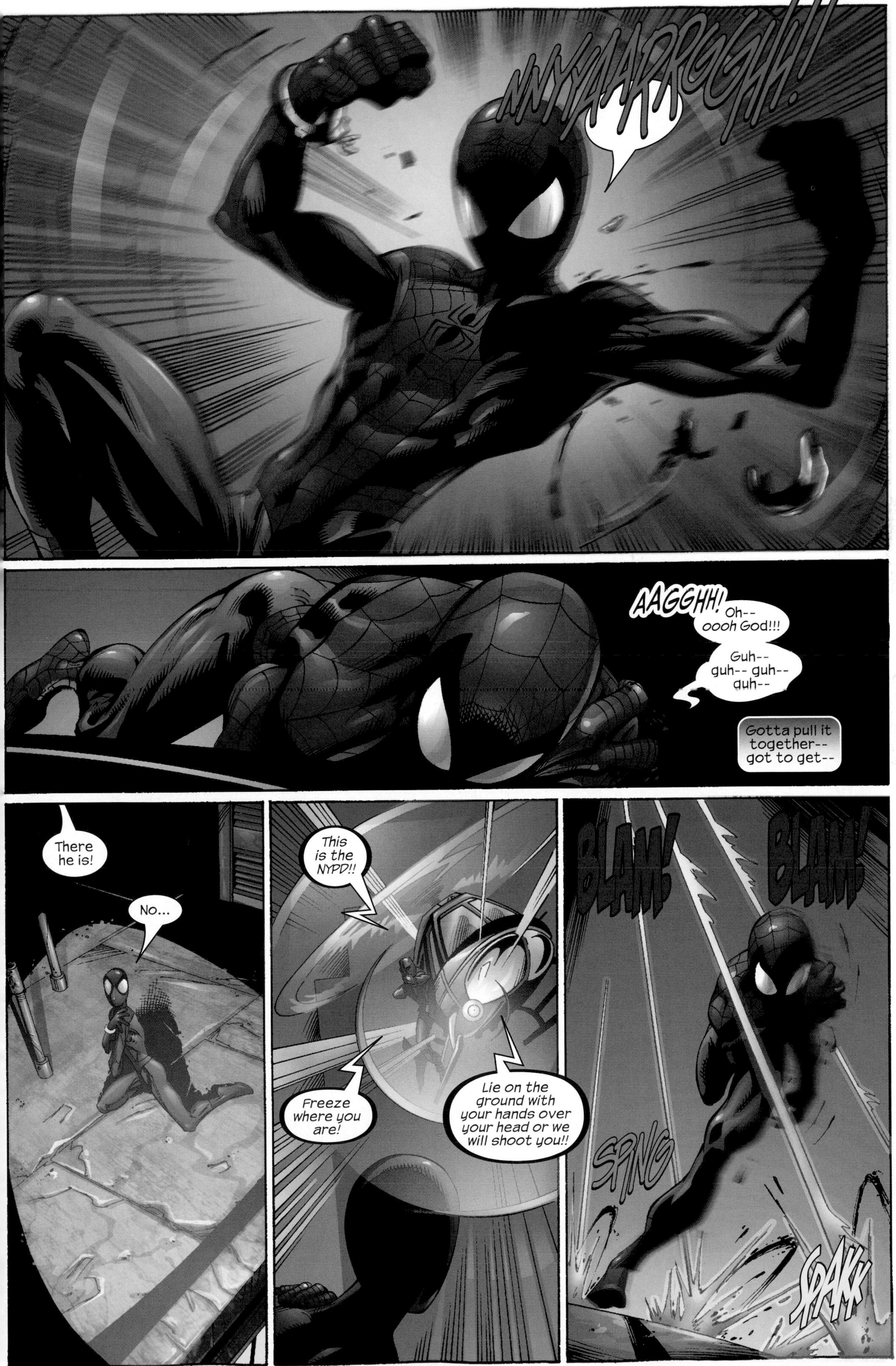
NNYYAARRGGHH!!
AAGGHH!
Oh-- oooh God!!!
Guh-- guh-- guh-- guh--
Gotta pull it together-- got to get--
There he is!
No...
This is the NYPD!!
Freeze where you are!
Lie on the ground with your hands over your head or we will shoot you!!
BLAM!
BLAM!
SPNG
SPAKK

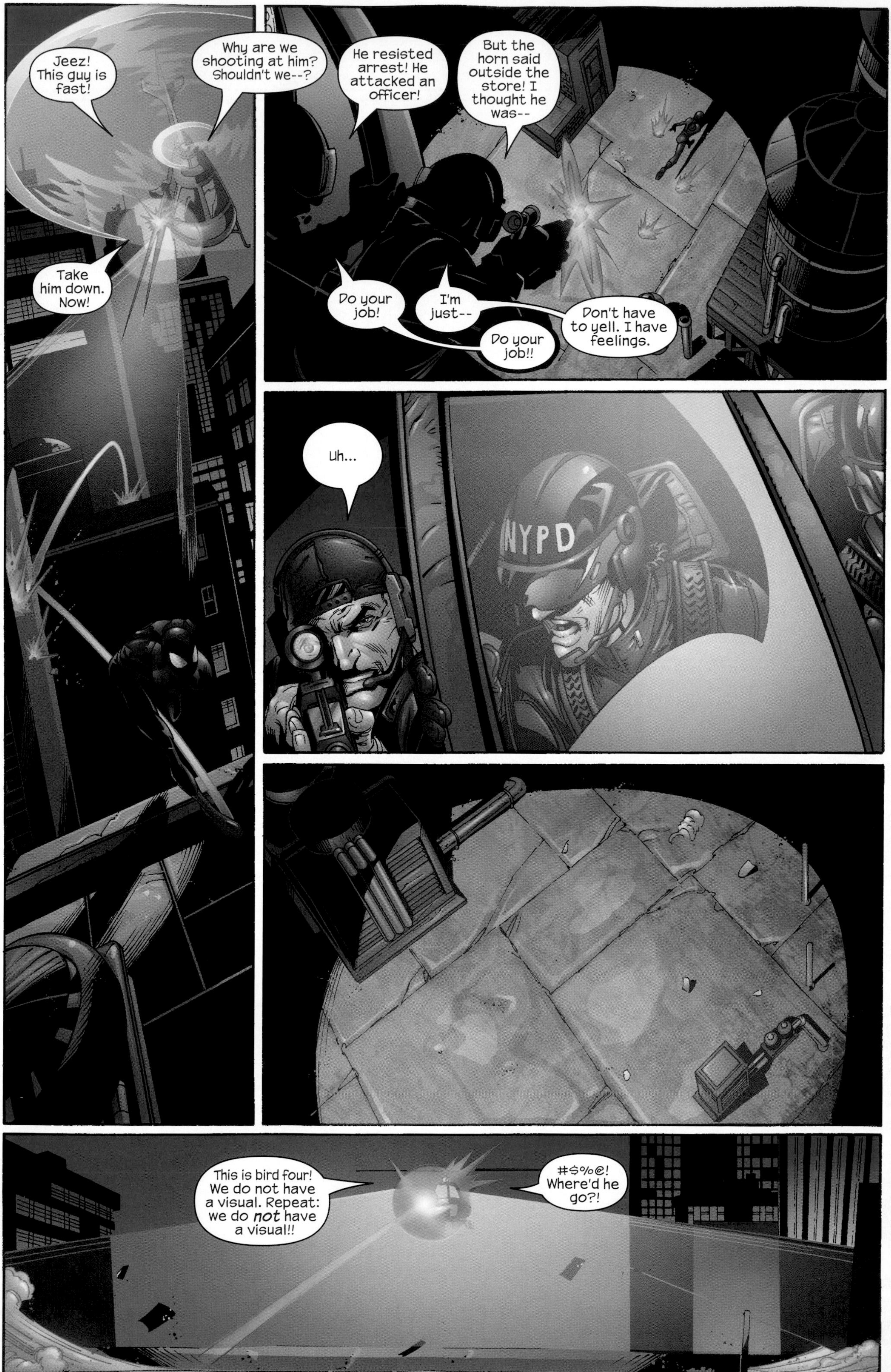
Jeez! This guy is fast!
Why are we shooting at him? Shouldn't we--?
Take him down. Now!
He resisted arrest! He attacked an officer!
But the horn said outside the store! I thought he was--
Do your job!
I'm just--
Do your job!!
Don't have to yell. I have feelings.
Uh...
This is bird four! We do not have a visual. Repeat: we do *not* have a visual!!
#$%@! Where'd he go?!

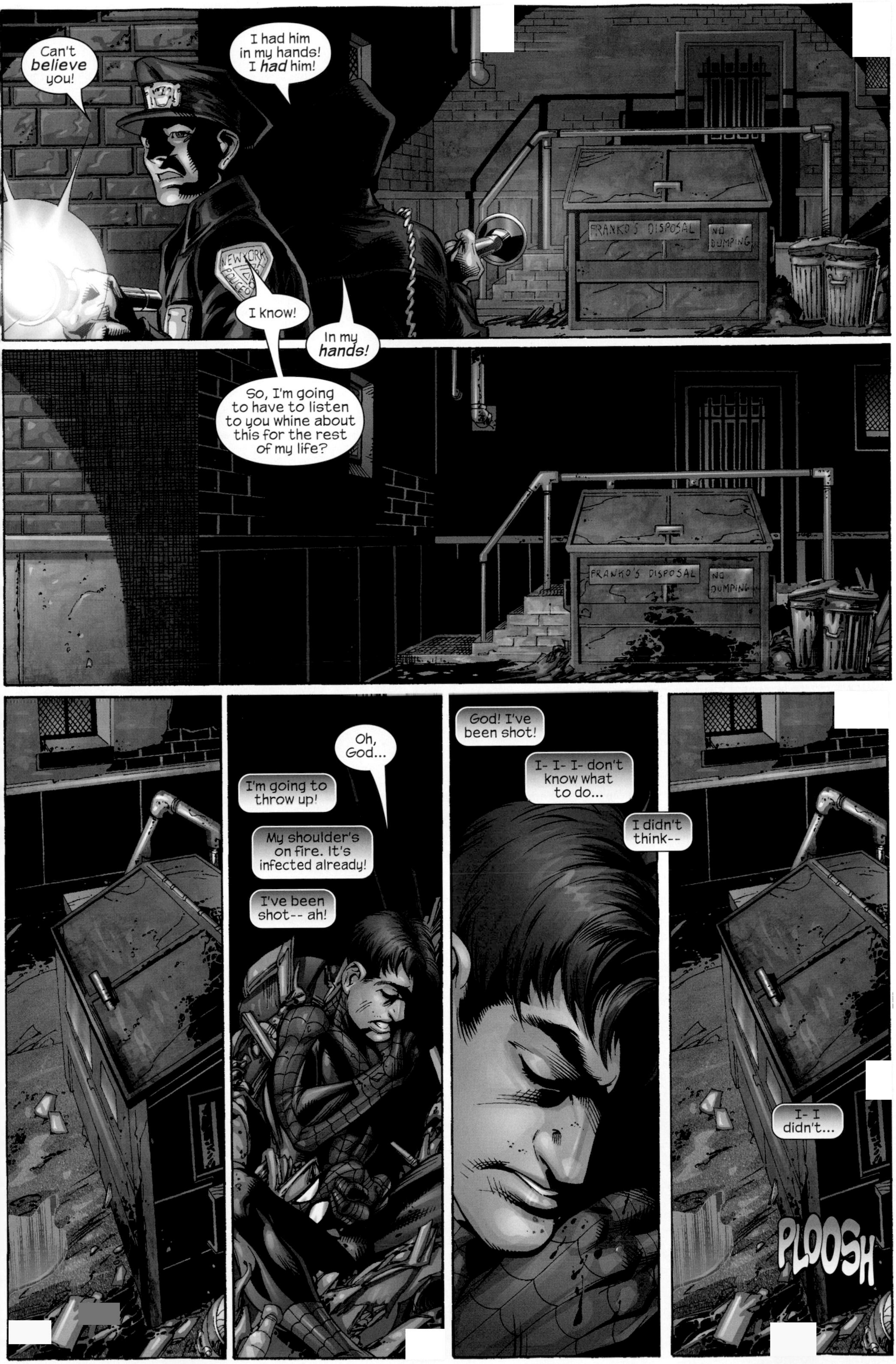

Can't *believe* you!
I had him in my hands! I *had* him!
I know!
In my *hands!*
So, I'm going to have to listen to you whine about this for the rest of my life?
FRANKO'S DISPOSAL
NO DUMPING
Oh, God...
I'm going to throw up!
My shoulder's on fire. It's infected already!
I've been shot-- ah!
God! I've been shot!
I- I- I- don't know what to do...
I didn't think--
I- I didn't...
PLOOSH

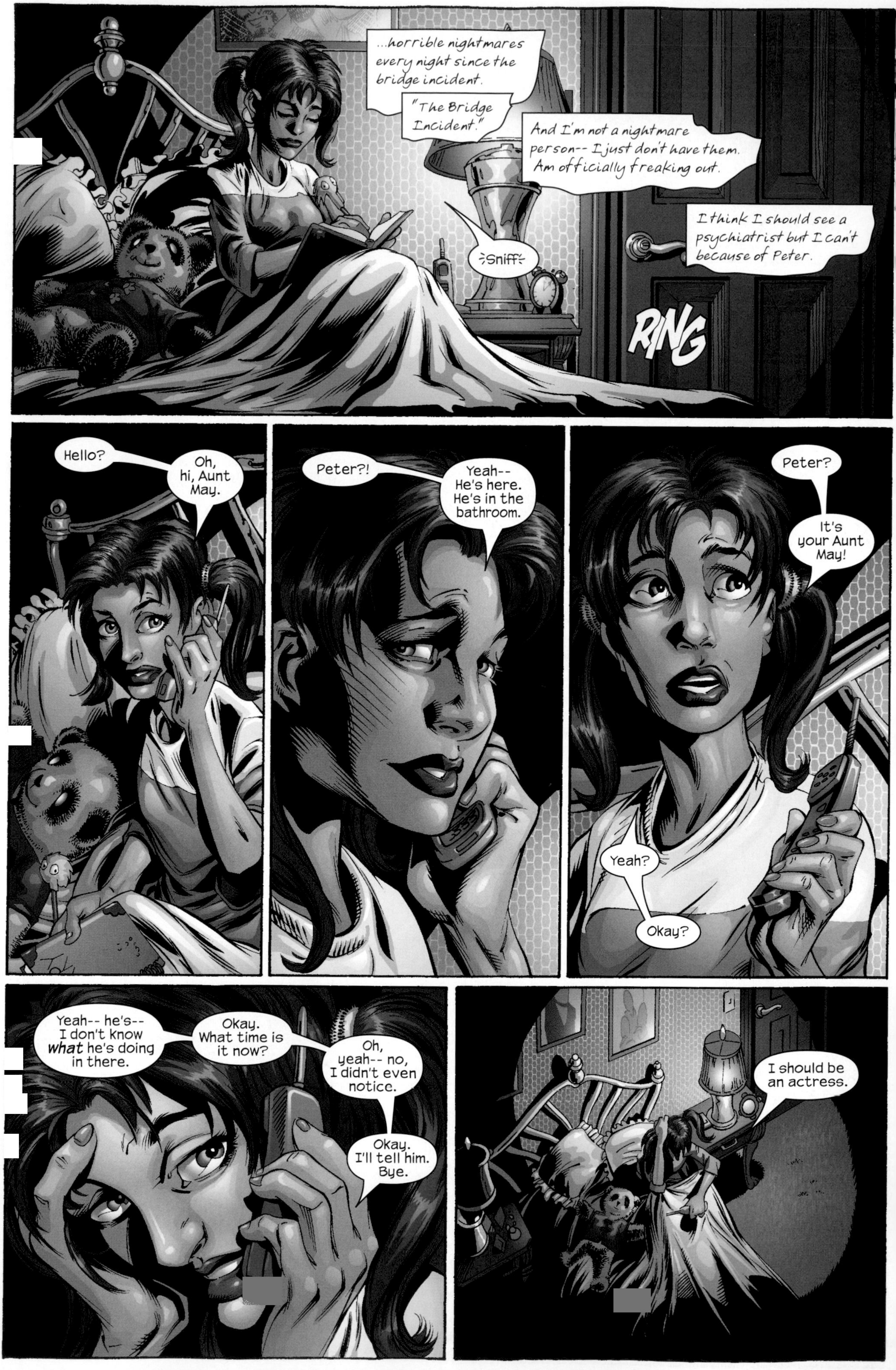
...horrible nightmares every night since the bridge incident.
"The Bridge Incident."
And I'm not a nightmare person-- I just don't have them. Am officially freaking out.
I think I should see a psychiatrist but I can't because of Peter.
Sniff
RING
Hello?
Oh, hi, Aunt May.
Peter?!
Yeah-- He's here. He's in the bathroom.
Peter?
It's your Aunt May!
Yeah?
Okay?
Yeah-- he's-- I don't know *what* he's doing in there.
Okay. What time is it now?
Oh, yeah-- no, I didn't even notice.
Okay. I'll tell him. Bye.
I should be an actress.

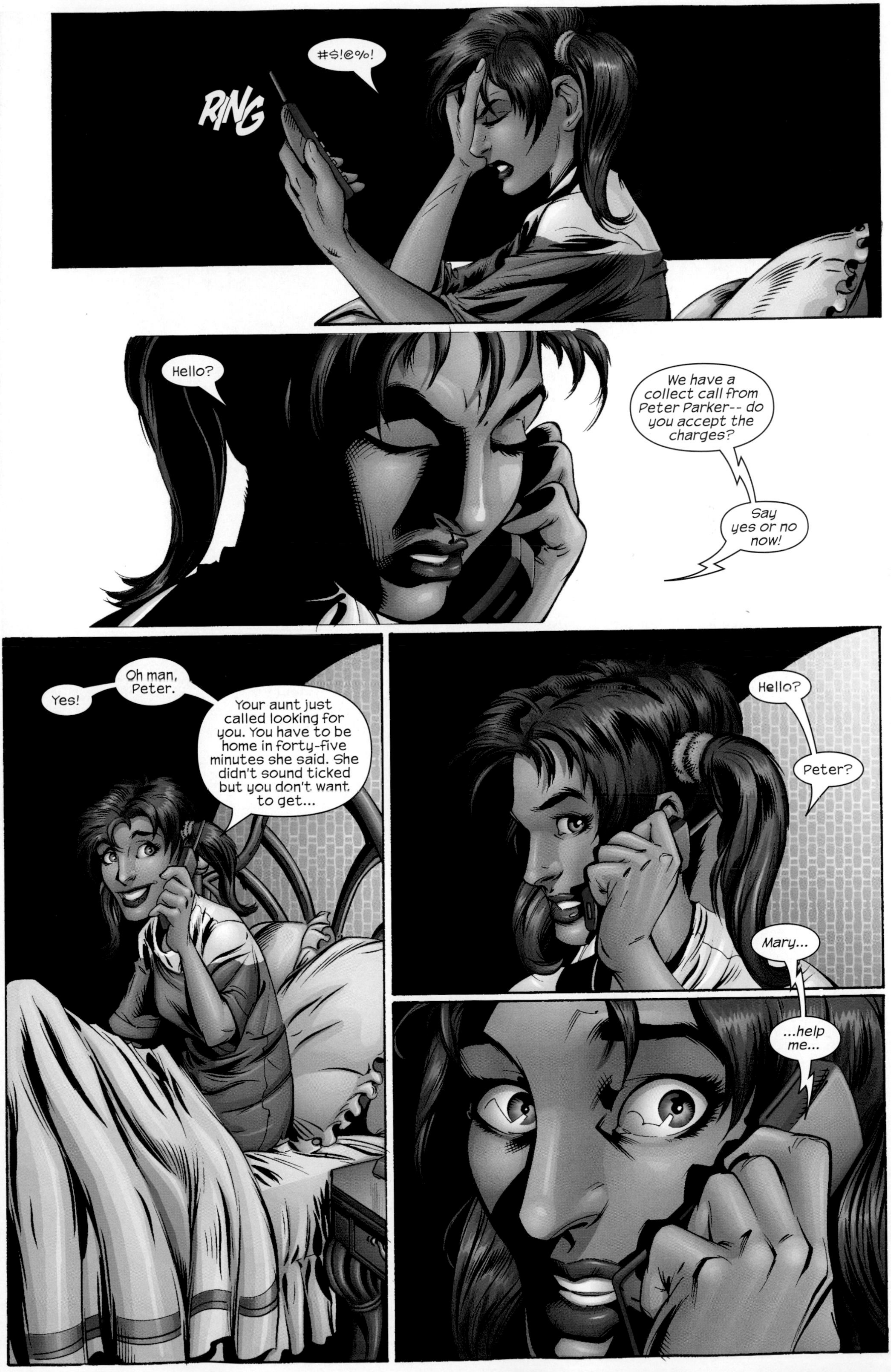
RING
#$!@%!
Hello?
We have a collect call from Peter Parker-- do you accept the charges?
Say yes or no now!
Yes!
Oh man, Peter.
Your aunt just called looking for you. You have to be home in forty-five minutes she said. She didn't sound ticked but you don't want to get...
Hello?
Peter?
Mary...
...help me...

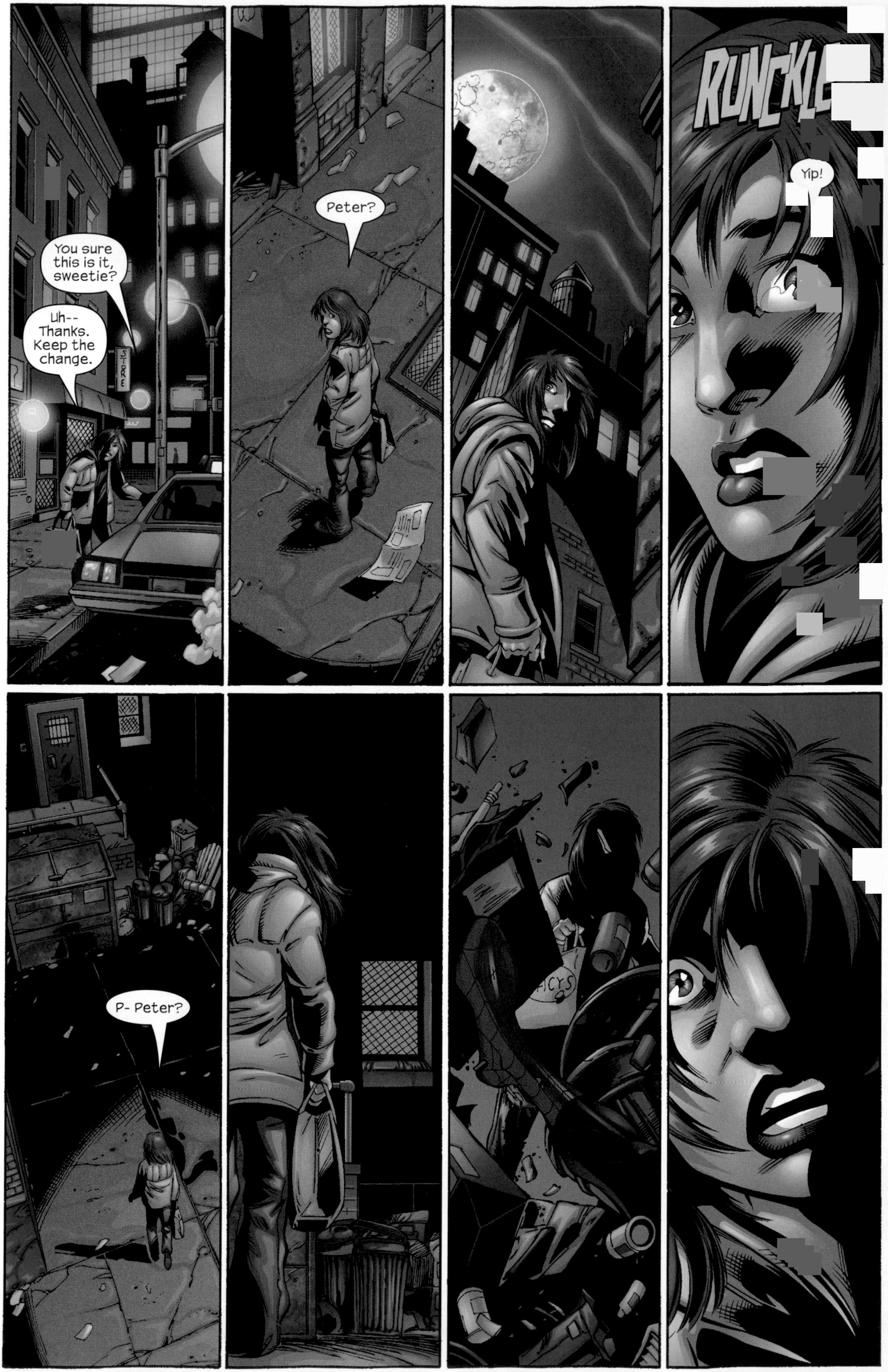
You sure this is it, sweetie?
Uh-- Thanks. Keep the change.
Peter?
RUNCKLE
Yip!
P- Peter?

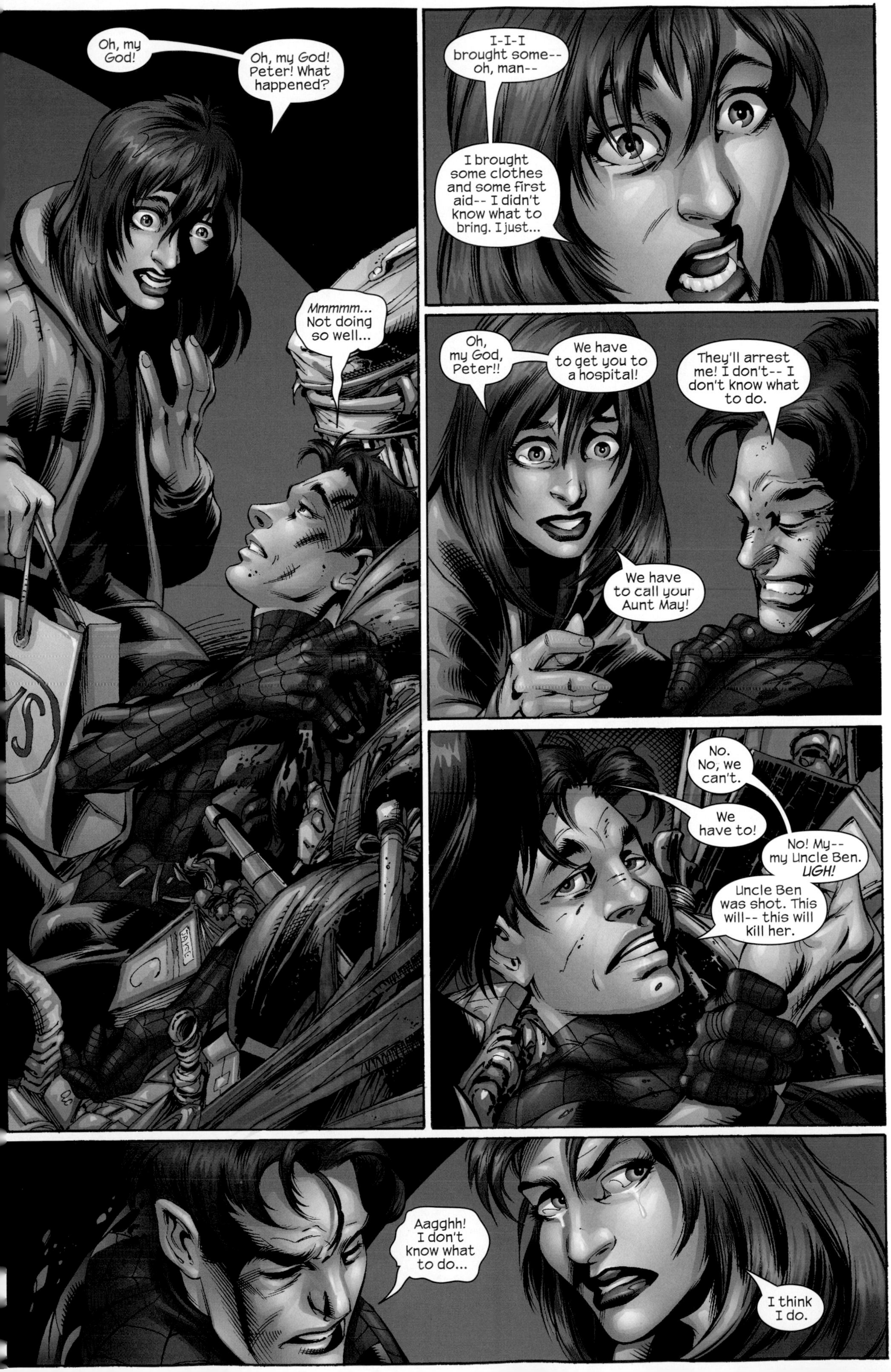
Oh, my God!
Oh, my God! Peter! What happened?
Mmmmm... Not doing so well...
I-I-I brought some-- oh, man--
I brought some clothes and some first aid-- I didn't know what to bring. I just...
Oh, my God, Peter!!
We have to get you to a hospital!
They'll arrest me! I don't-- I don't know what to do.
We have to call your Aunt May!
No. No, we can't.
We have to!
No! My-- my Uncle Ben. UGH!
Uncle Ben was shot. This will-- this will kill her.
Aagghh! I don't know what to do...
I think I do.

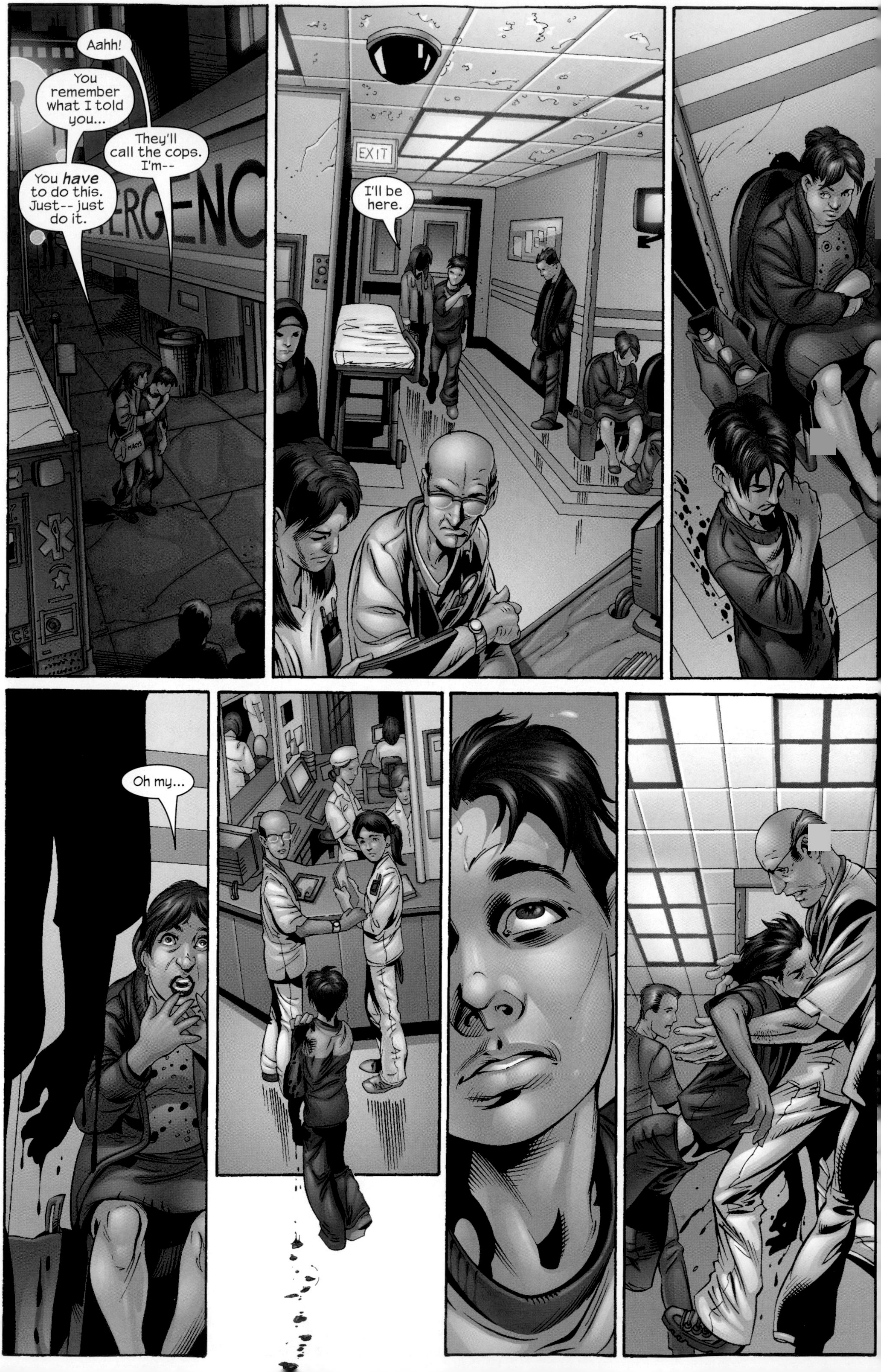
Aahh!
You remember what I told you...
They'll call the cops. I'm--
You have to do this. Just-- just do it.
ERGENC
I'll be here.
EXIT
Oh my...

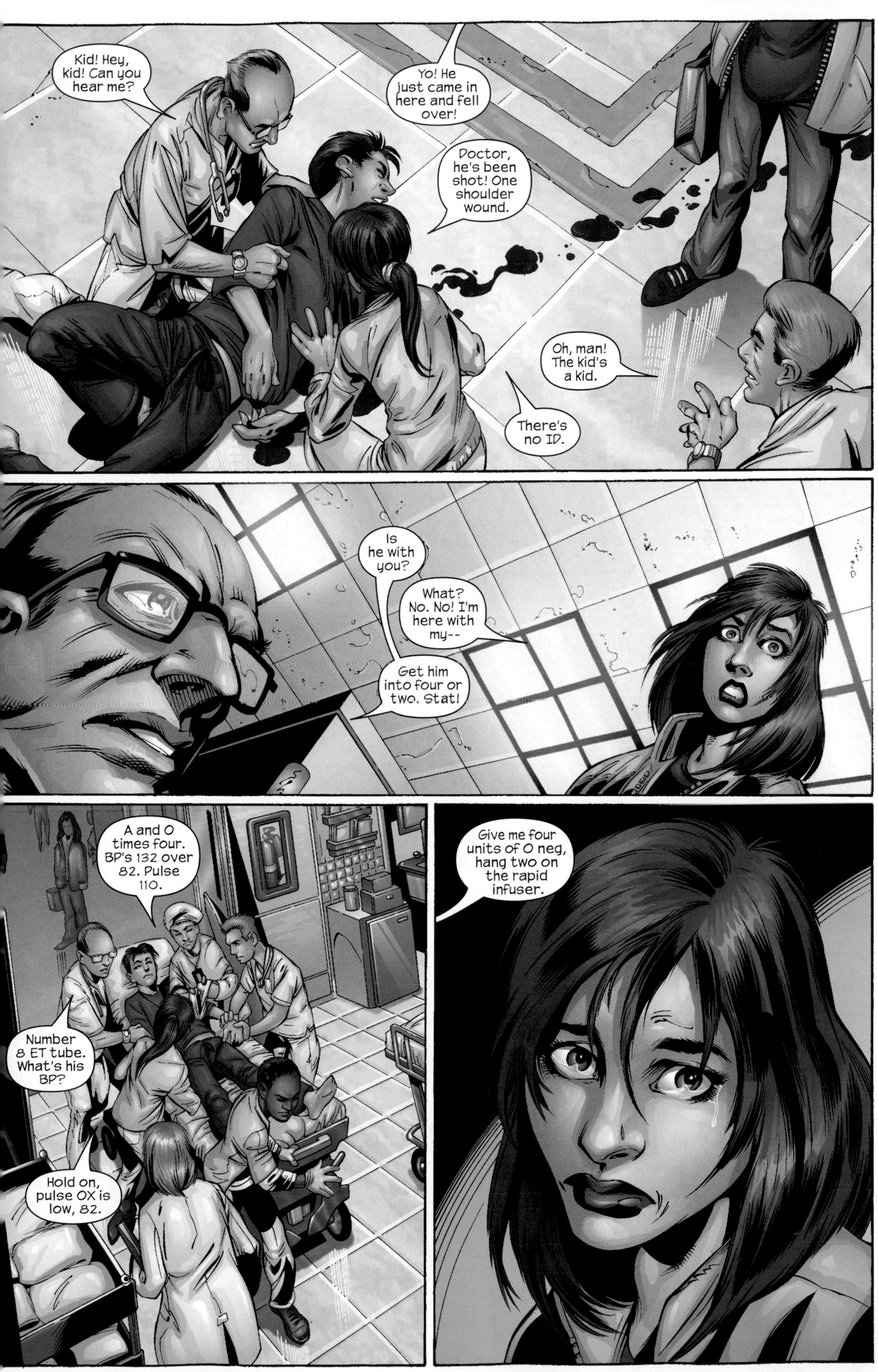
Kid! Hey, kid! Can you hear me?
Yo! He just came in here and fell over!
Doctor, he's been shot! One shoulder wound.
Oh, man! The kid's a kid.
There's no ID.
Is he with you?
What? No. No! I'm here with my--
Get him into four or two. Stat!
A and O times four. BP's 132 over 82. Pulse 110.
Number 8 ET tube. What's his BP?
Hold on, pulse OX is low, 82.
Give me four units of O neg, hang two on the rapid infuser.

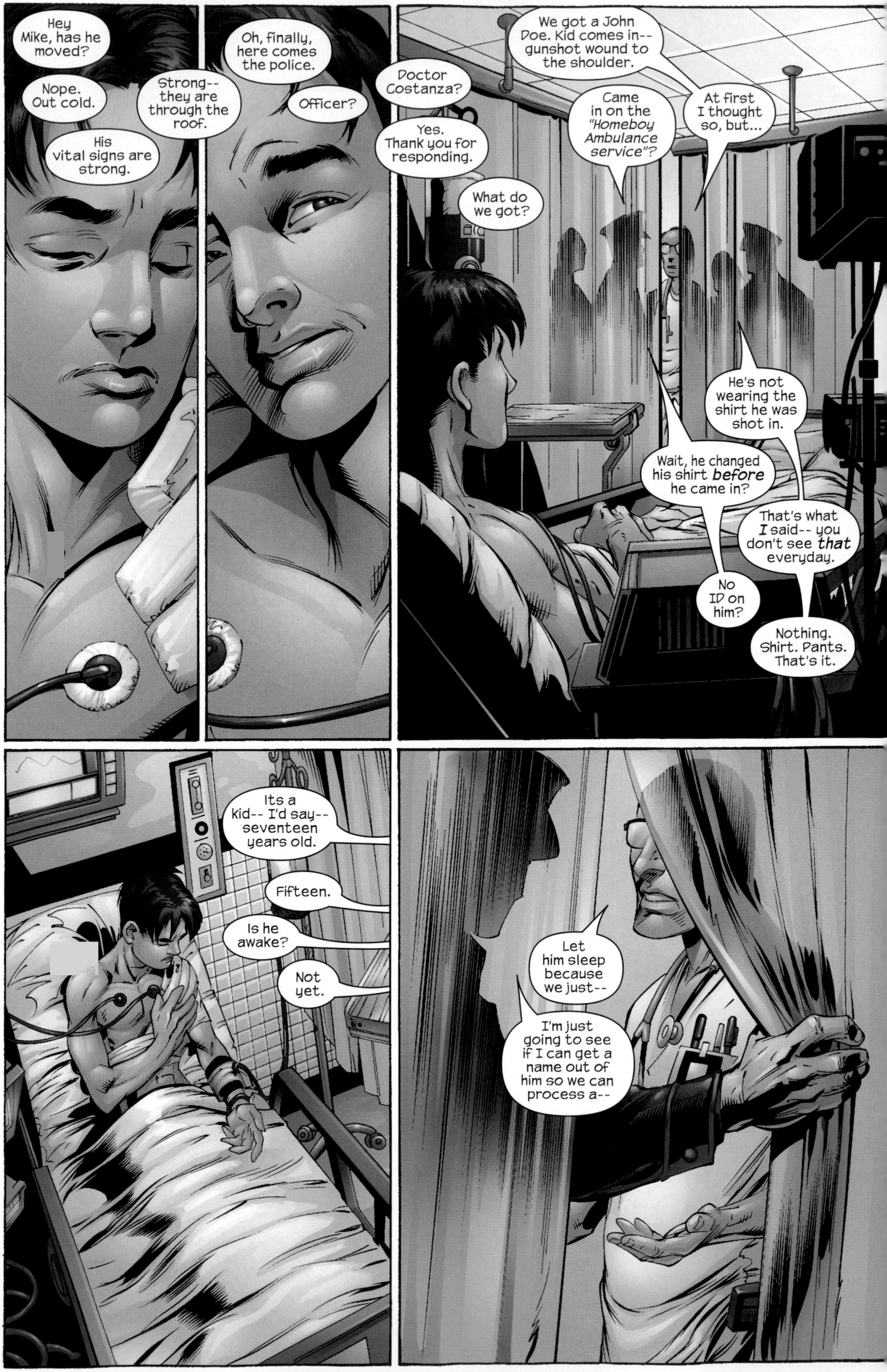
Hey Mike, has he moved?
Nope. Out cold.
His vital signs are strong.
Strong-- they are through the roof.
Oh, finally, here comes the police.
Officer?
Doctor Costanza?
Yes. Thank you for responding.
What do we got?
We got a John Doe. Kid comes in-- gunshot wound to the shoulder.
Came in on the "Homeboy Ambulance service"?
At first I thought so, but...
He's not wearing the shirt he was shot in.
Wait, he changed his shirt before he came in?
That's what I said-- you don't see that everyday.
No ID on him?
Nothing. Shirt. Pants. That's it.
Its a kid-- I'd say-- seventeen years old.
Fifteen.
Is he awake?
Not yet.
Let him sleep because we just--
I'm just going to see if I can get a name out of him so we can process a--

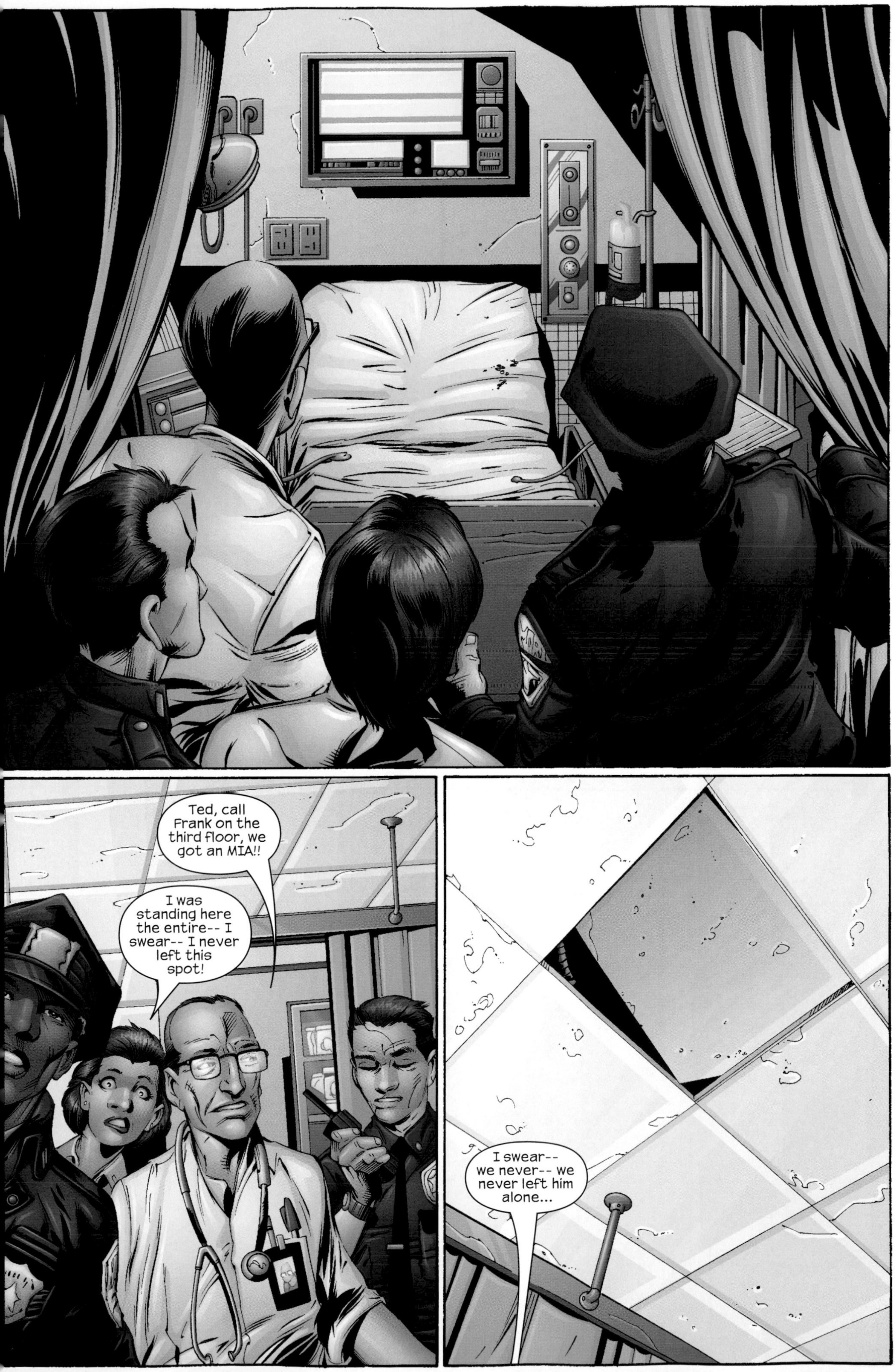
Ted, call Frank on the third floor, we got an MIA!!
I was standing here the entire-- I swear-- I never left this spot!
I swear-- we never-- we never left him alone...

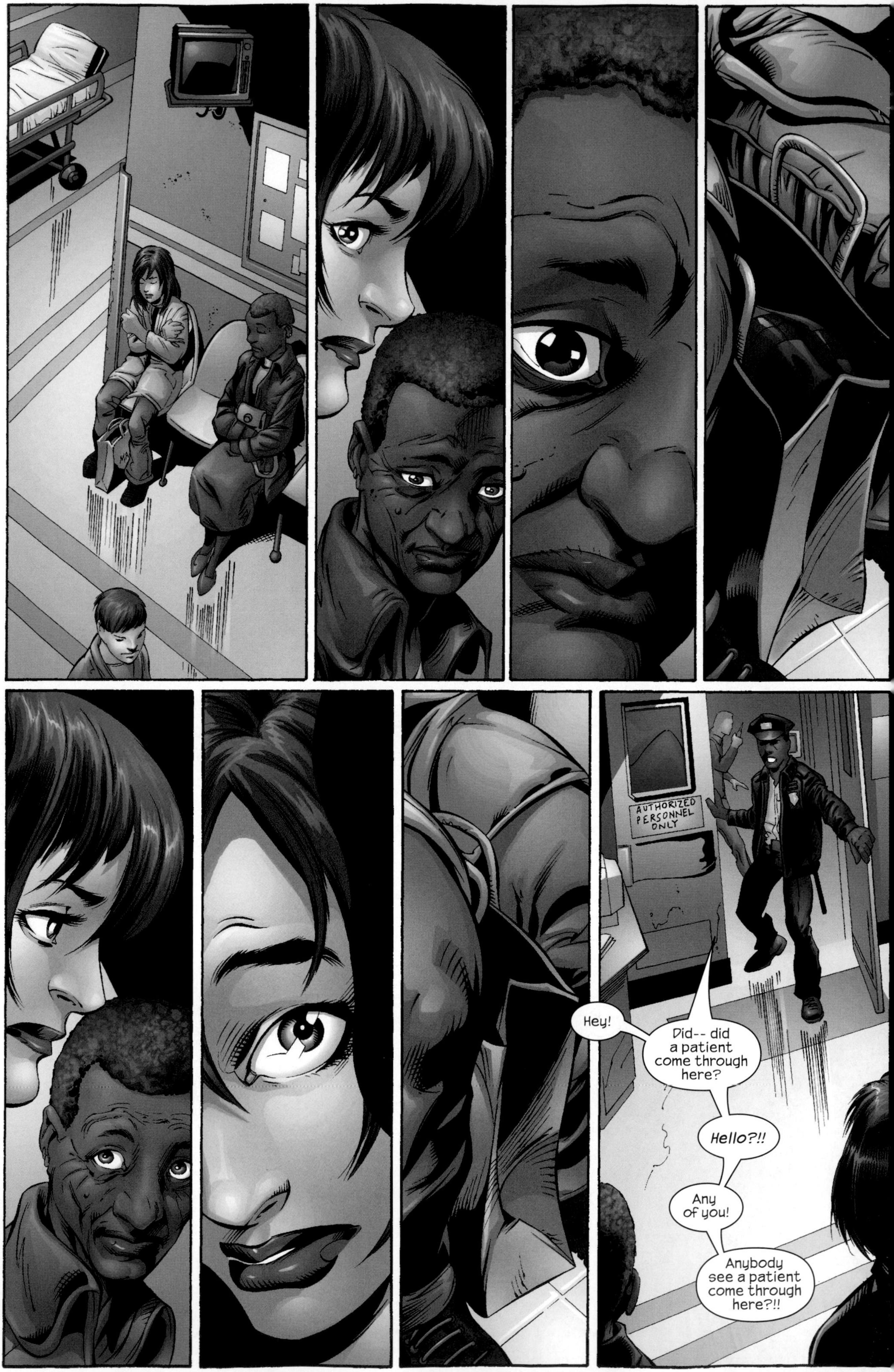

AUTHORIZED PERSONNEL ONLY
Hey!
Did-- did a patient come through here?
Hello?!!
Any of you!
Anybody see a patient come through here?!!

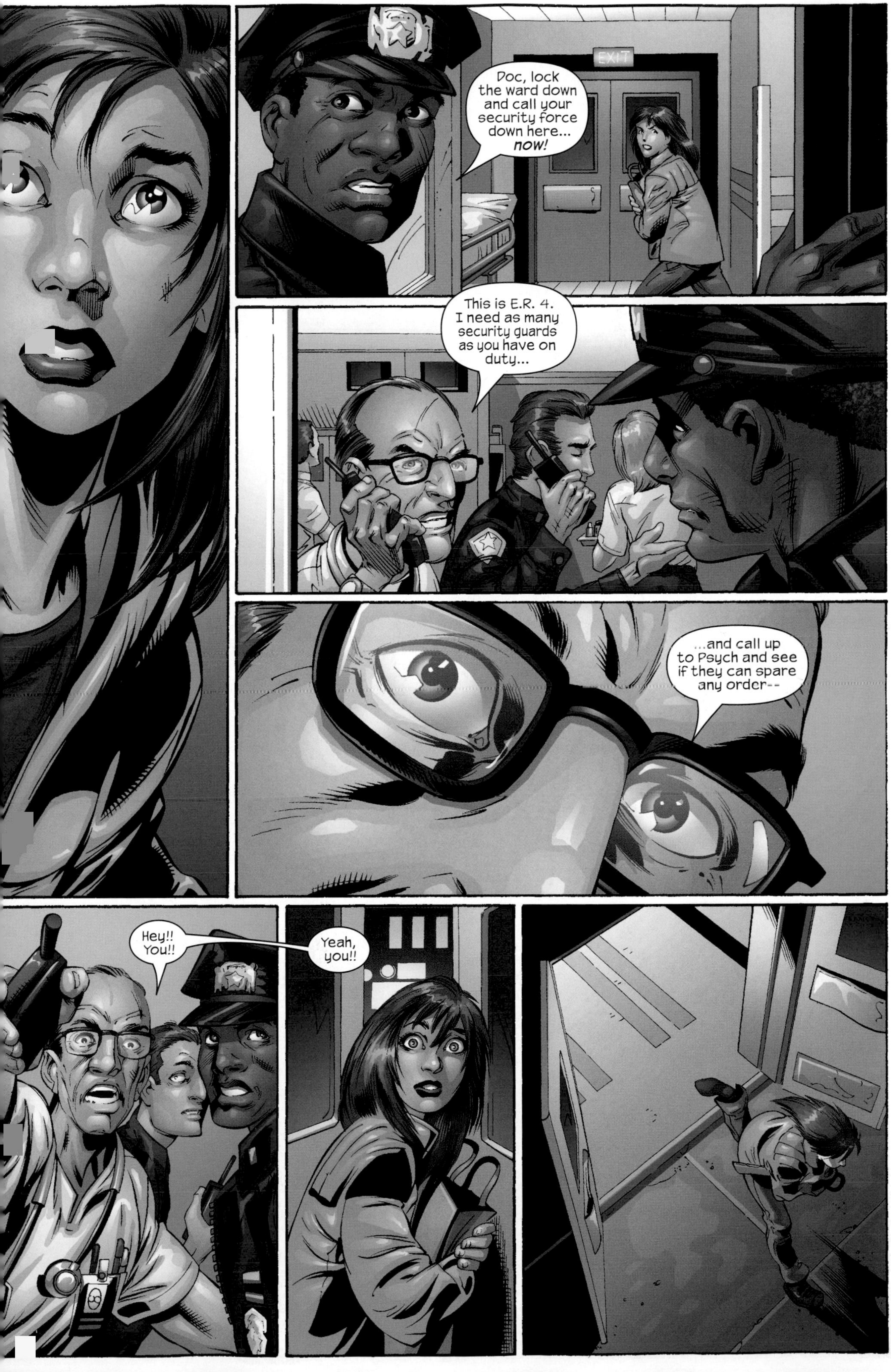

EXIT
Doc, lock the ward down and call your security force down here... *now!*
This is E.R. 4. I need as many security guards as you have on duty...
...and call up to Psych and see if they can spare any order--
Hey!! You!!
Yeah, you!!

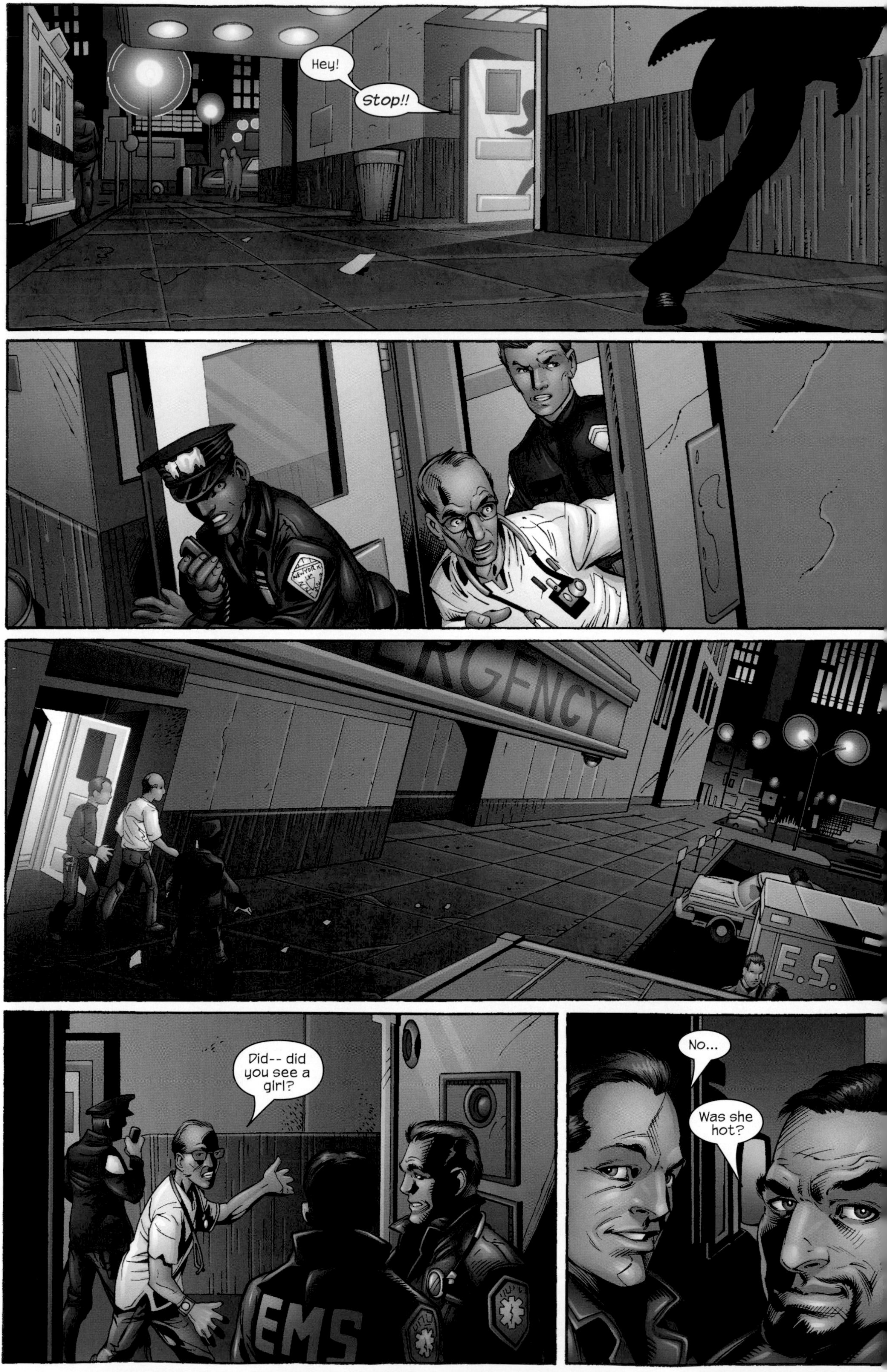
Hey!
Stop!!
ERGENCY
E.S.
Did-- did you see a girl?
EMS
No...
Was she hot?

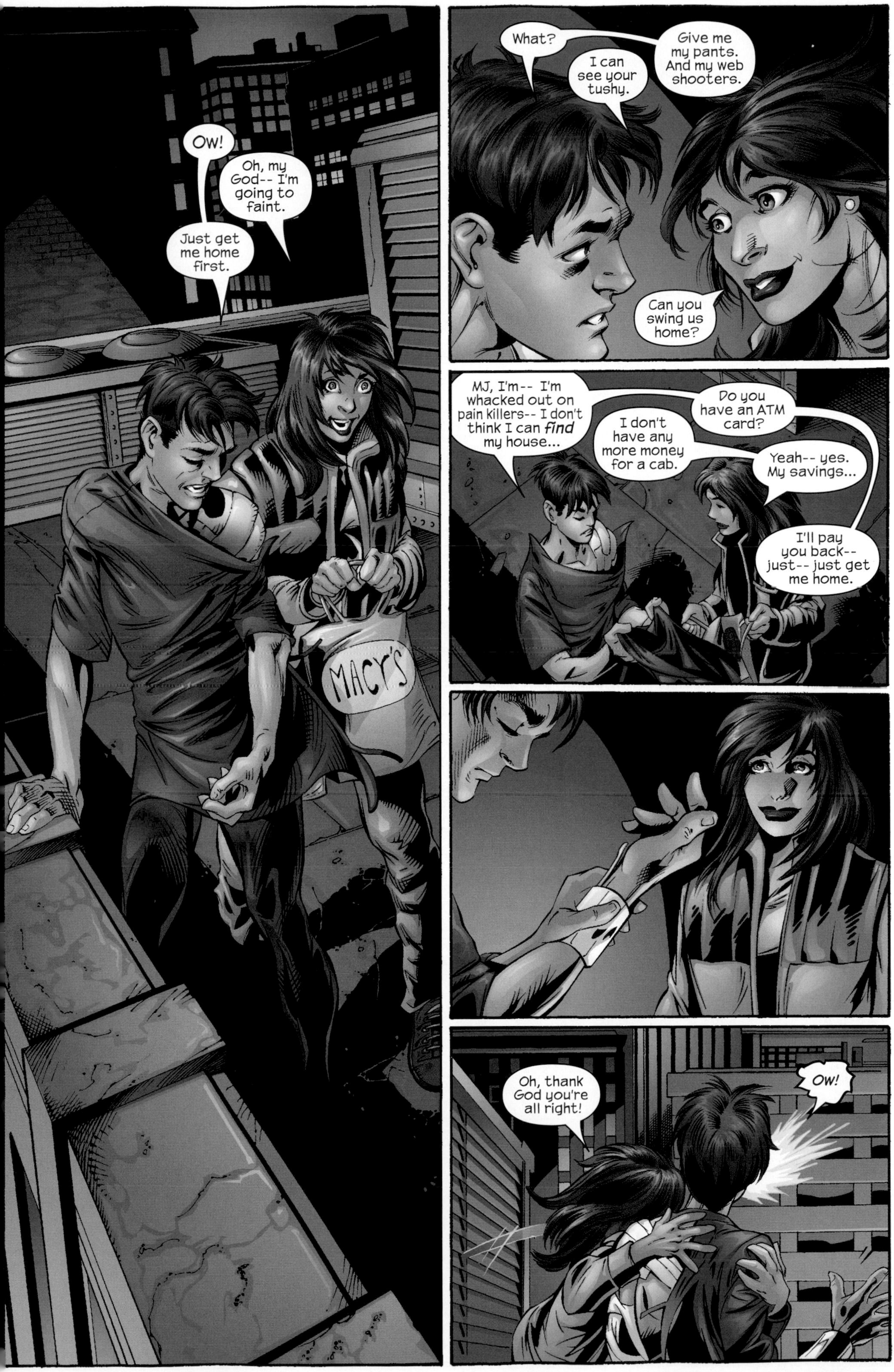
Ow!
Oh, my God-- I'm going to faint.
Just get me home first.
MACY'S
What?
Give me my pants. And my web shooters.
I can see your tushy.
Can you swing us home?
MJ, I'm-- I'm whacked out on pain killers-- I don't think I can *find* my house...
Do you have an ATM card?
I don't have any more money for a cab.
Yeah-- yes. My savings...
I'll pay you back-- just-- just get me home.
Oh, thank God you're all right!
Ow!

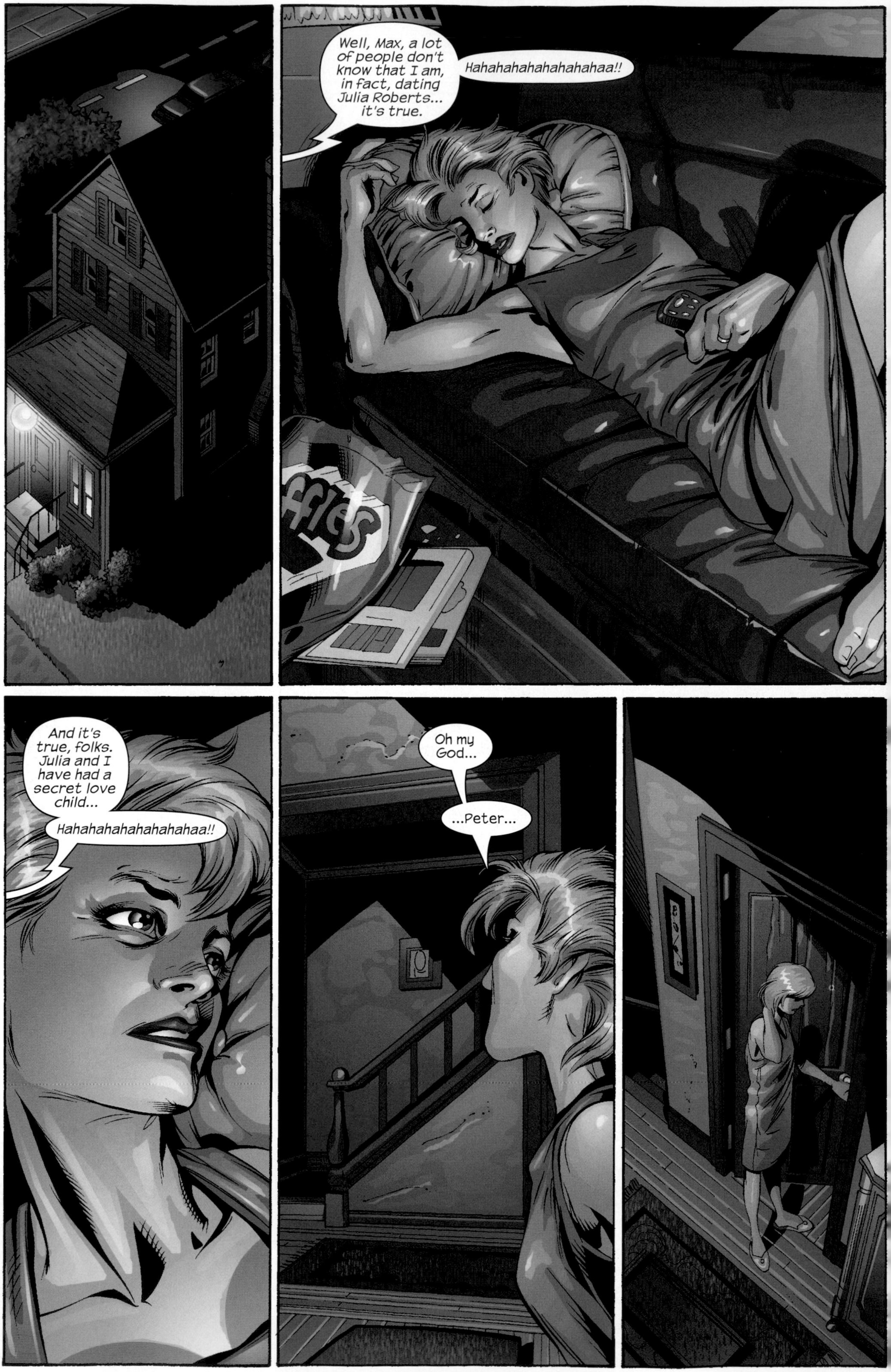

Well, Max, a lot of people don't know that I am, in fact, dating Julia Roberts... it's true.
Hahahahahahahahahaa!!
And it's true, folks. Julia and I have had a secret love child...
Hahahahahahahahahaa!!
Oh my God...
...Peter...

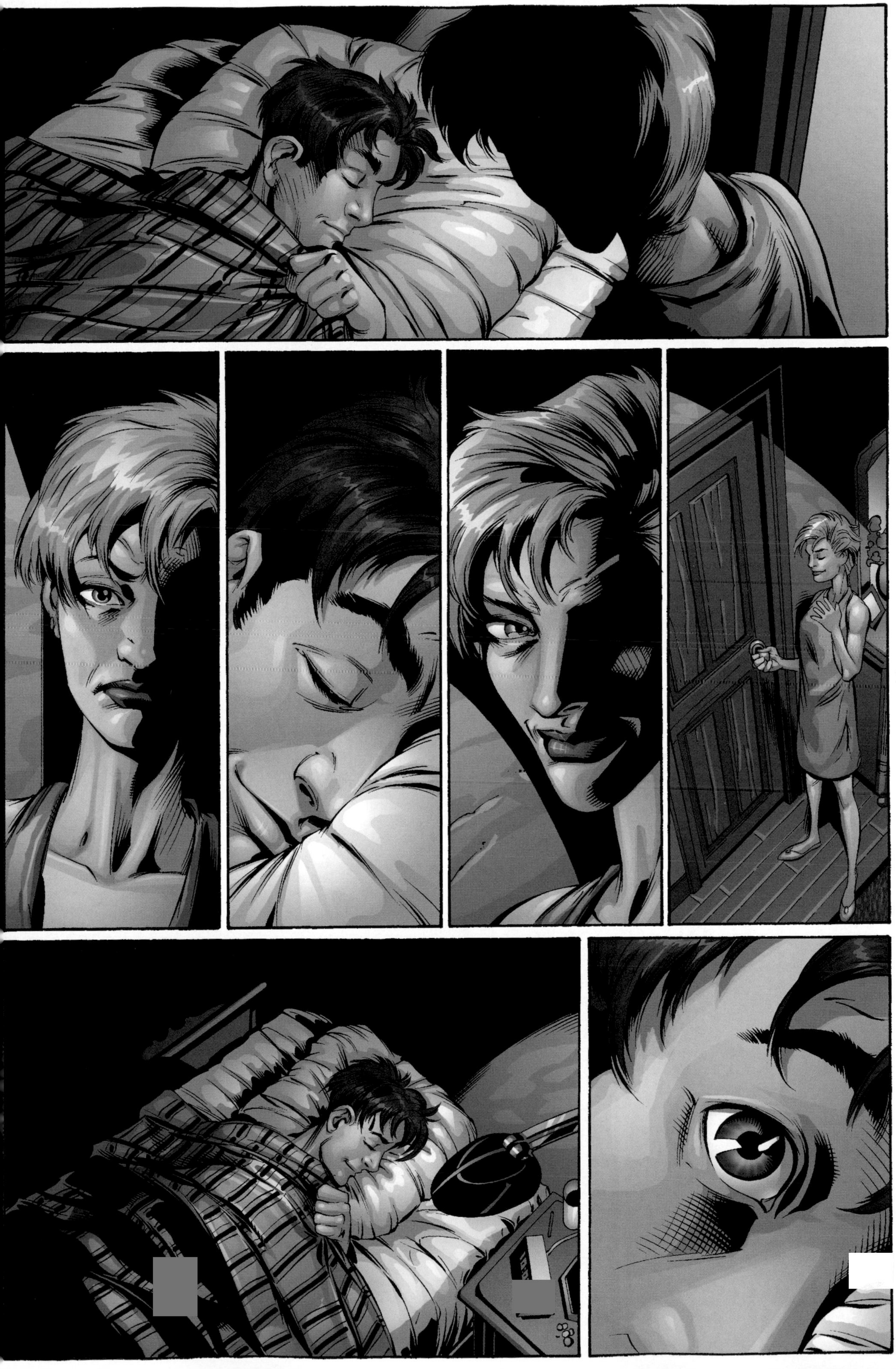

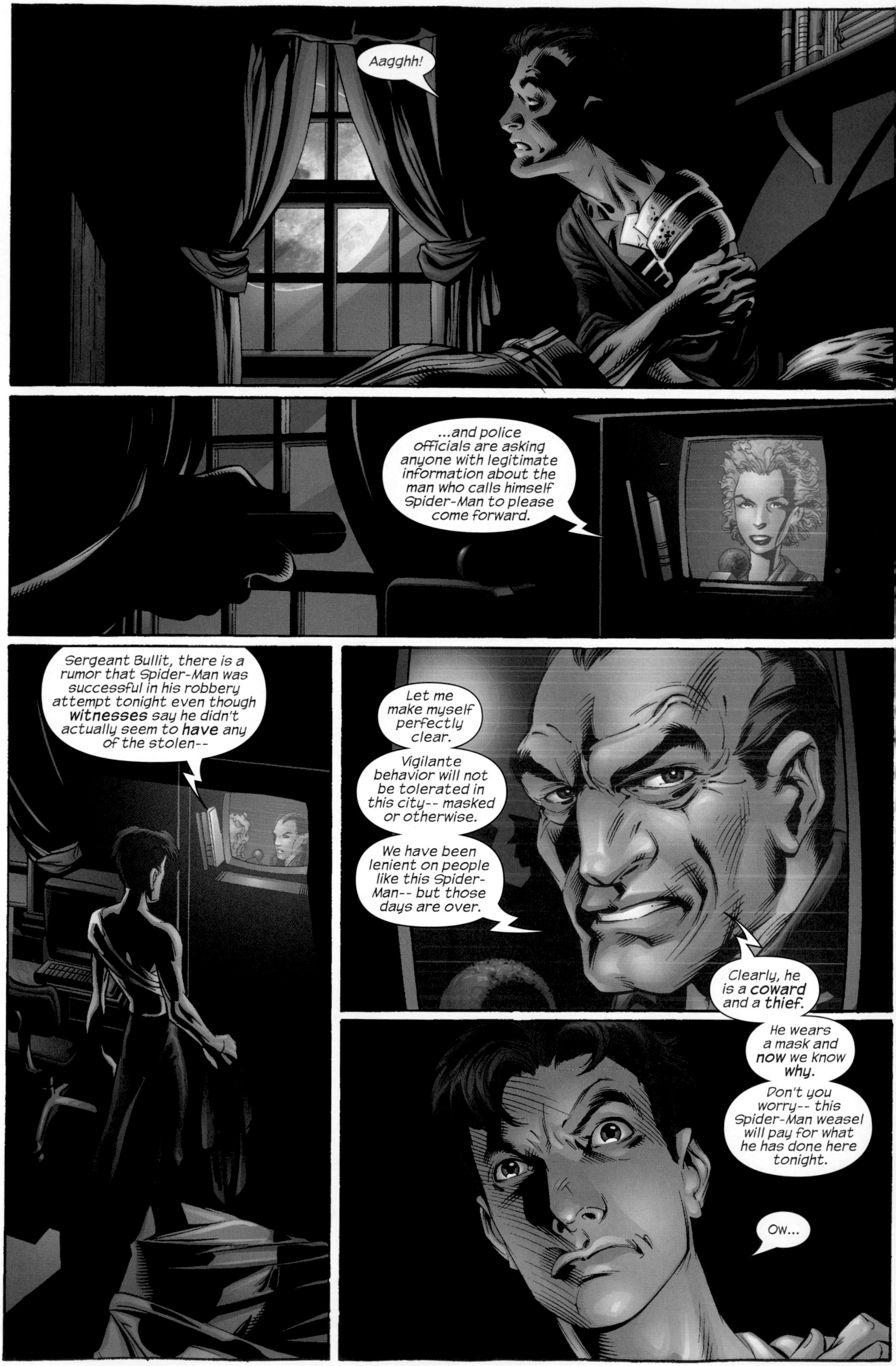
Aagghh!
...and police officials are asking anyone with legitimate information about the man who calls himself Spider-Man to please come forward.
Sergeant Bullit, there is a rumor that Spider-Man was successful in his robbery attempt tonight even though **witnesses** say he didn't actually seem to **have** any of the stolen--
Let me make myself perfectly clear.
Vigilante behavior will not be tolerated in this city-- masked or otherwise.
We have been lenient on people like this Spider-Man-- but those days are over.
Clearly, he is a **coward** and a **thief**.
He wears a mask and **now** we know **why**.
Don't you worry-- this Spider-Man weasel will pay for what he has done here tonight.
Ow...

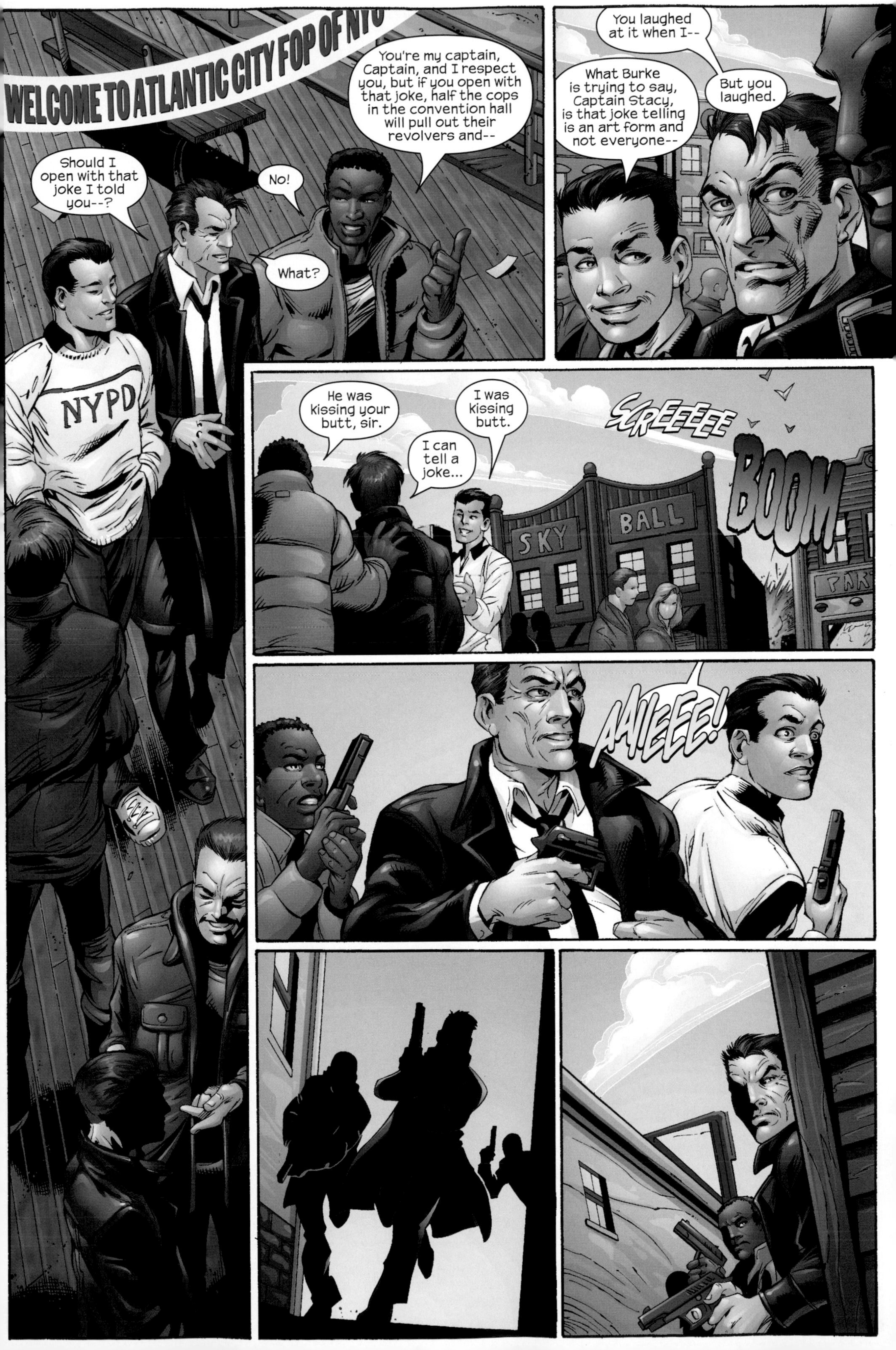
WELCOME TO ATLANTIC CITY FOP OF NYC
Should I open with that joke I told you--?
No!
What?
You're my captain, Captain, and I respect you, but if you open with that joke, half the cops in the convention hall will pull out their revolvers and--
NYPD
You laughed at it when I--
What Burke is trying to say, Captain Stacy, is that joke telling is an art form and not everyone--
But you laughed.
He was kissing your butt, sir.
I can tell a joke...
I was kissing butt.
SCREEEEEE
BOOM
SKY BALL
AAIEEEE!

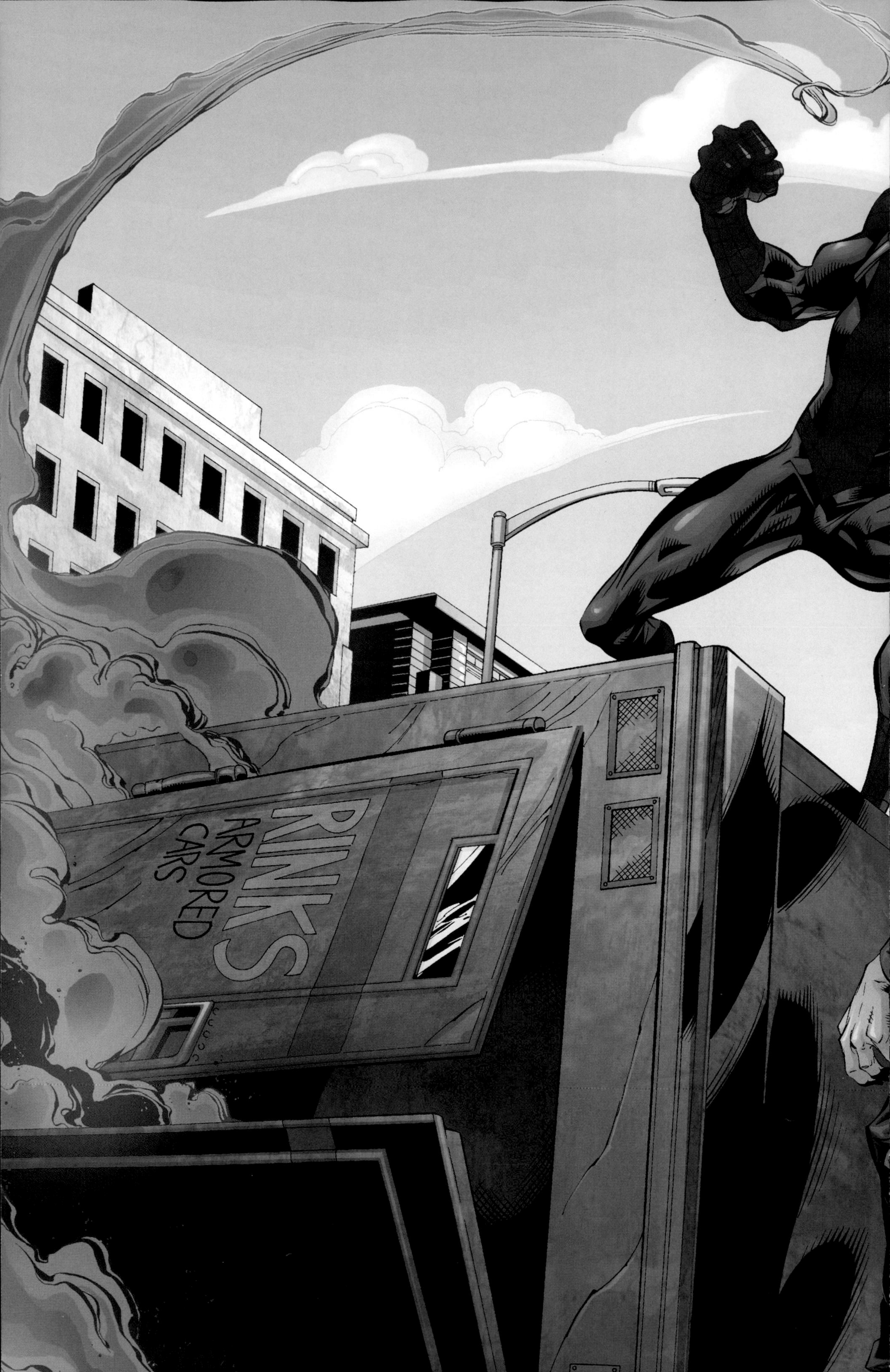
RINKS
ARMORED
CARS

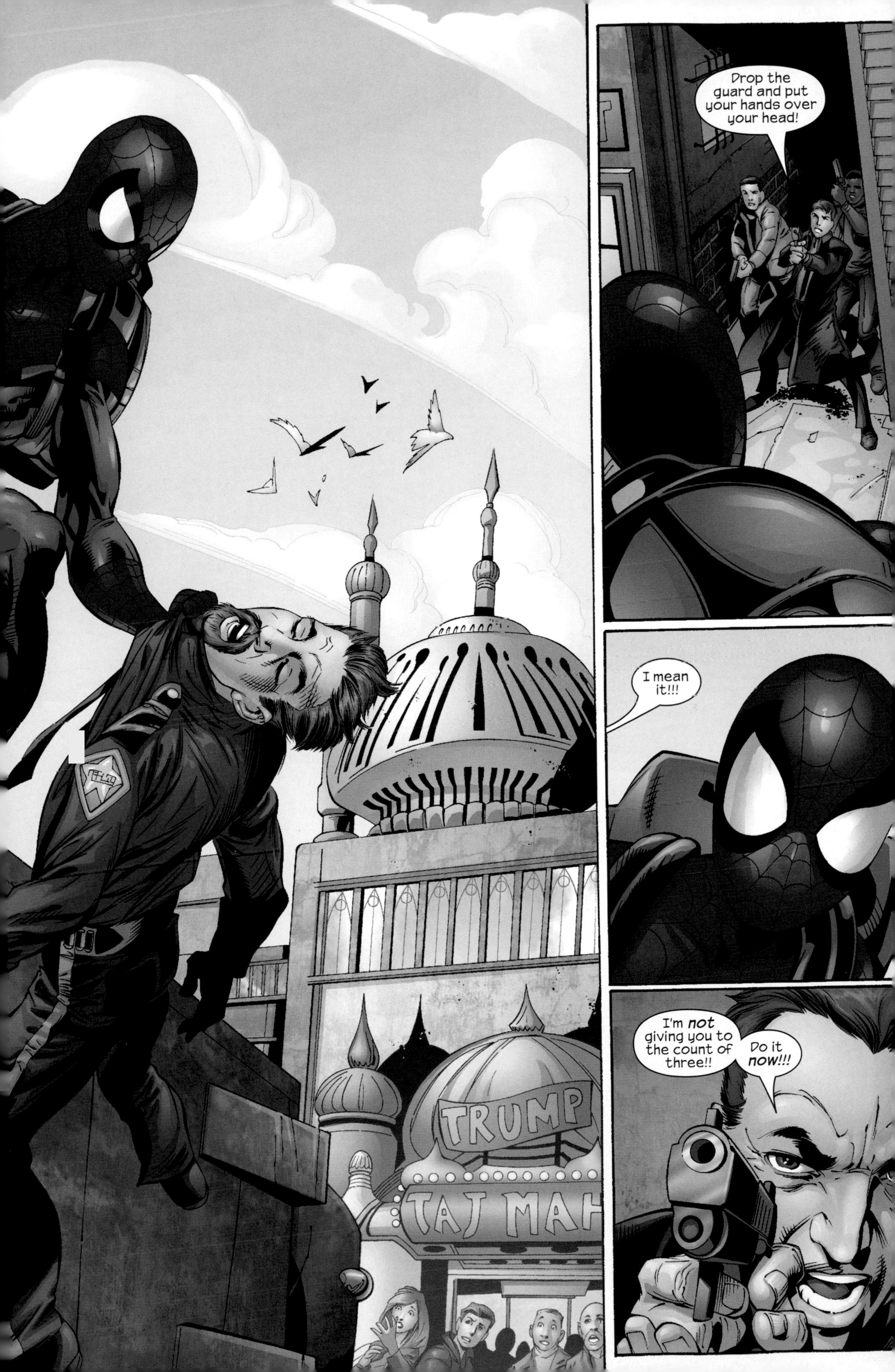
Drop the guard and put your hands over your head!
I mean it!!!
I'm *not* giving you to the count of three!!
Do it *now*!!!
TRUMP
TAJ MAH

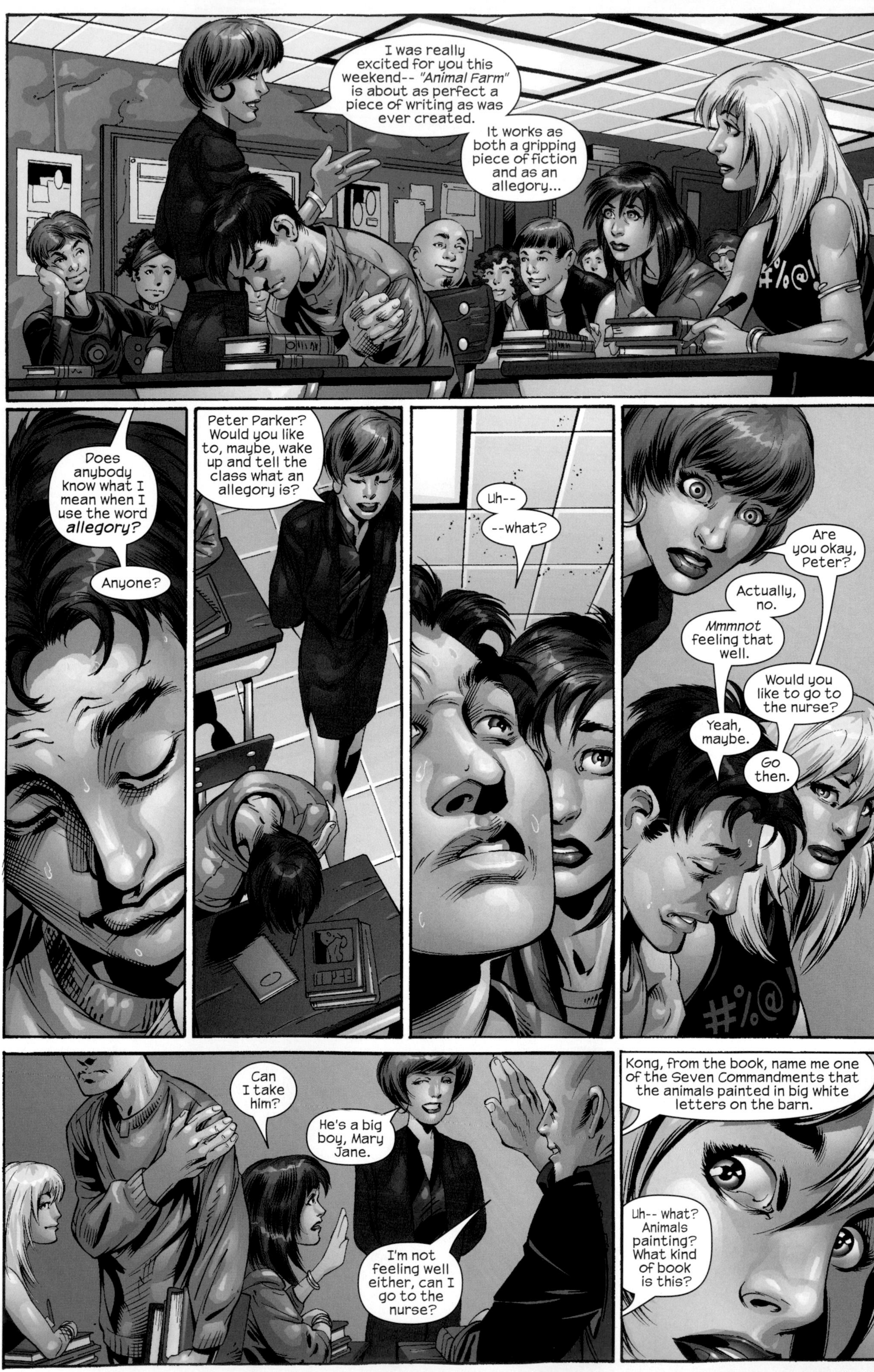
I was really excited for you this weekend-- "Animal Farm" is about as perfect a piece of writing as was ever created.
It works as both a gripping piece of fiction and as an allegory...
Does anybody know what I mean when I use the word allegory?
Anyone?
Peter Parker? Would you like to, maybe, wake up and tell the class what an allegory is?
Uh--
--what?
Are you okay, Peter?
Actually, no.
Mmmnot feeling that well.
Would you like to go to the nurse?
Yeah, maybe.
Go then.
Can I take him?
He's a big boy, Mary Jane.
I'm not feeling well either, can I go to the nurse?
Kong, from the book, name me one of the Seven Commandments that the animals painted in big white letters on the barn.
Uh-- what? Animals painting? What kind of book is this?
#%@!
#%@!

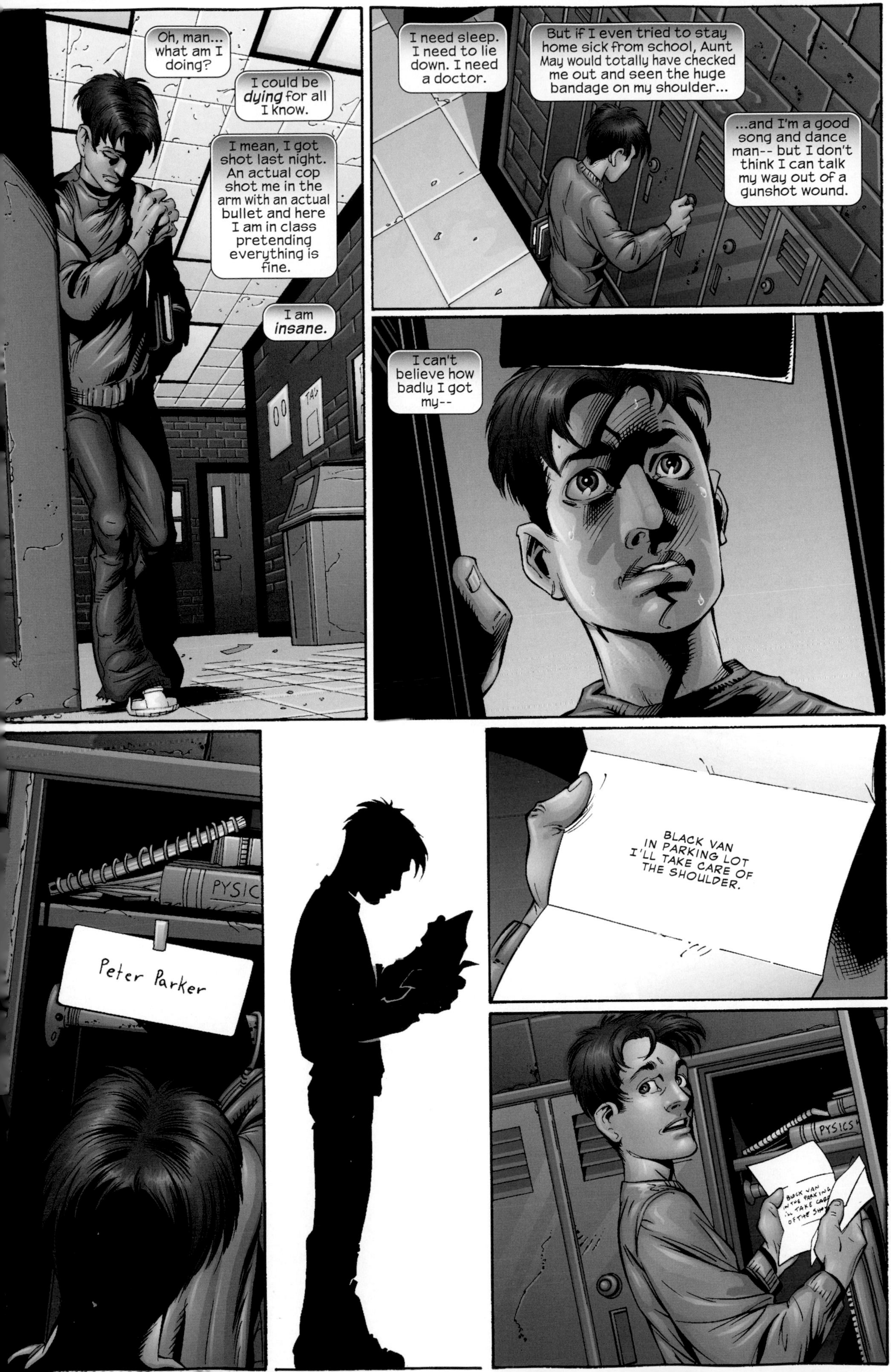
Oh, man... what am I doing?
I could be dying for all I know.
I mean, I got shot last night. An actual cop shot me in the arm with an actual bullet and here I am in class pretending everything is fine.
I am insane.
I need sleep. I need to lie down. I need a doctor.
But if I even tried to stay home sick from school, Aunt May would totally have checked me out and seen the huge bandage on my shoulder...
...and I'm a good song and dance man-- but I don't think I can talk my way out of a gunshot wound.
I can't believe how badly I got my--
PYSIC
Peter Parker
BLACK VAN
IN PARKING LOT
I'LL TAKE CARE OF
THE SHOULDER.
PYSICS

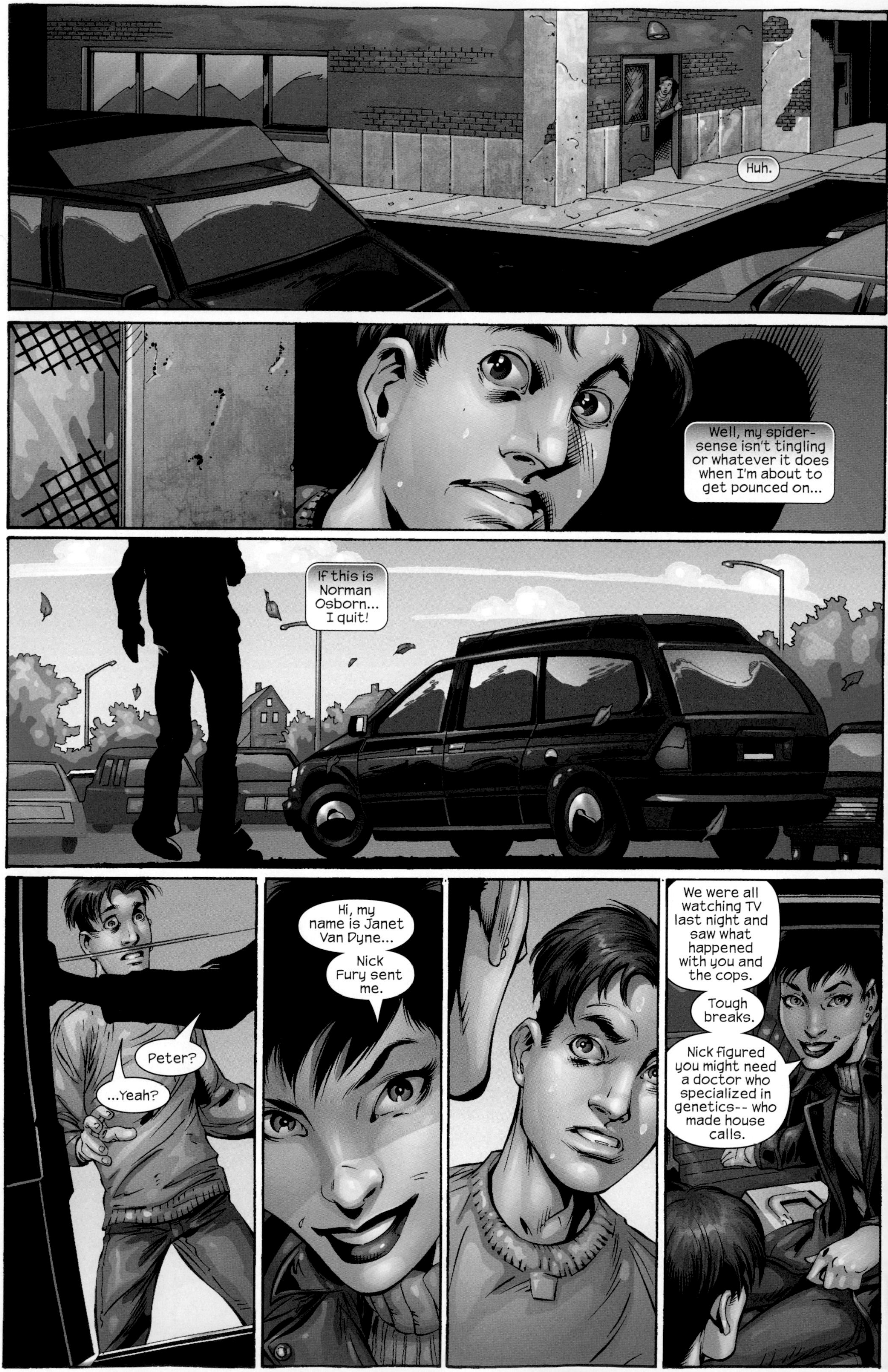
Huh.
Well, my spider-sense isn't tingling or whatever it does when I'm about to get pounced on...
If this is Norman Osborn... I quit!
Peter?
...Yeah?
Hi, my name is Janet Van Dyne...
Nick Fury sent me.
We were all watching TV last night and saw what happened with you and the cops.
Tough breaks.
Nick figured you might need a doctor who specialized in genetics-- who made house calls.

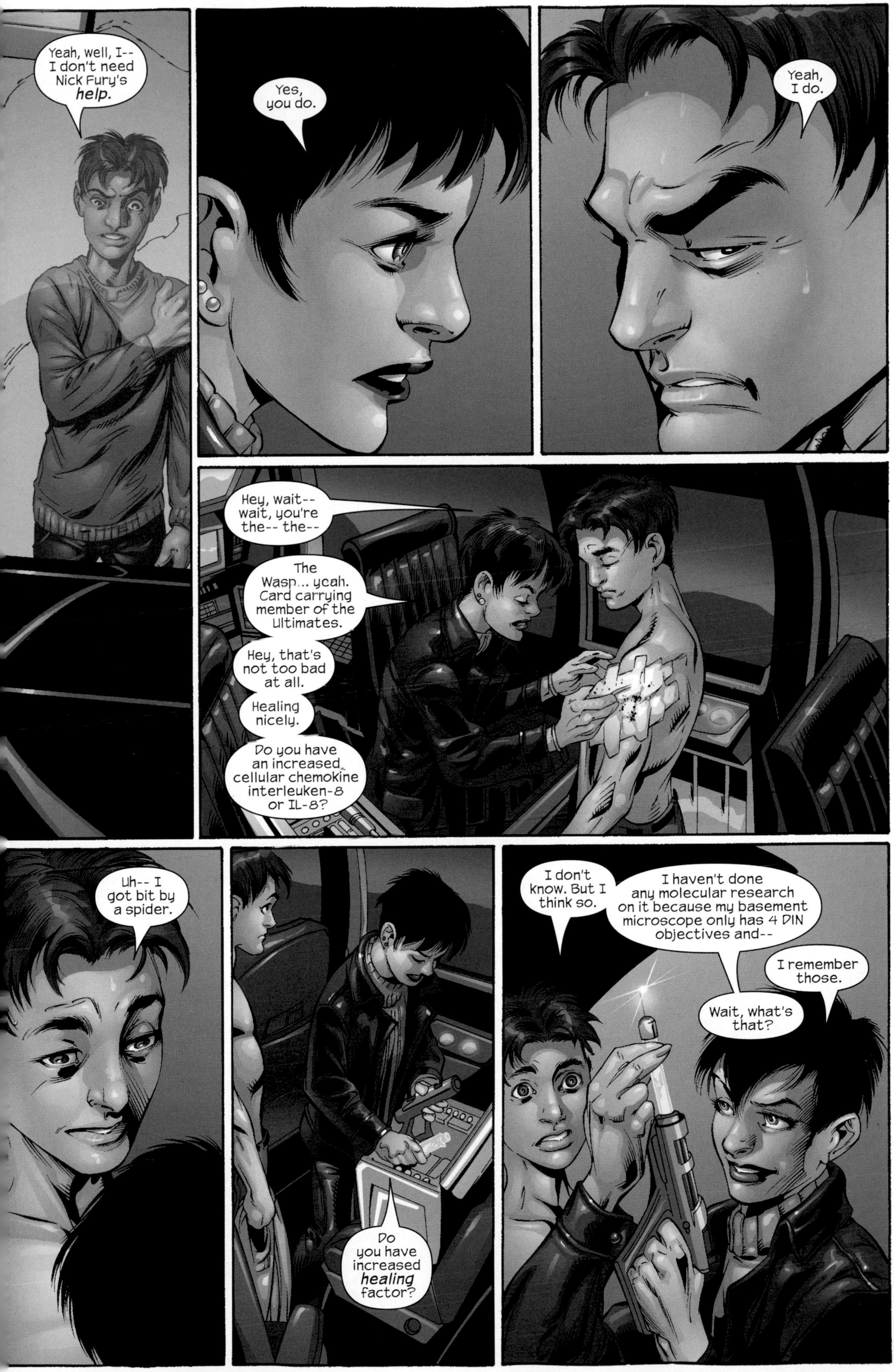

Yeah, well, I-- I don't need Nick Fury's *help.*
Yes, you do.
Yeah, I do.
Hey, wait-- wait, you're the-- the--
The Wasp... yeah. Card carrying member of the Ultimates.
Hey, that's not too bad at all.
Healing nicely.
Do you have an increased cellular chemokine interleuken-8 or IL-8?
Uh-- I got bit by a spider.
Do you have increased *healing* factor?
I don't know. But I think so.
I haven't done any molecular research on it because my basement microscope only has 4 DIN objectives and--
I remember those.
Wait, what's that?

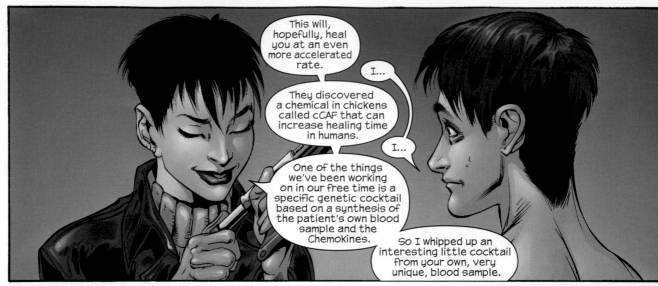

This will, hopefully, heal you at an even more accelerated rate.

I...

They discovered a chemical in chickens called cCAF that can increase healing time in humans.

I...

One of the things we've been working on in our free time is a specific genetic cocktail based on a synthesis of the patient's own blood sample and the Chemokines.

So I whipped up an interesting little cocktail from your own, very unique, blood sample.

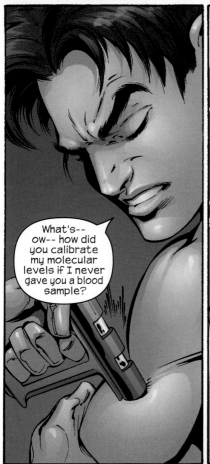

What's-- ow-- how did you calibrate my molecular levels if I never gave you a blood sample?

Look at you, you *are* smart-- that's cute.

I don't know-- Nick Fury had a blood sample from you.

Consider yourself lucky this happened on TV and that we were watching.

Listen, you may or may not get some flu-like symptoms-- but they'll pass.

Just try to take it easy for a couple of days.

Did Fury happen to mention anything to you about a guy named Harry?

Harry? No.

Fury didn't happen to mention if he knows who that guy is that is running around impersonating me and robbing banks?

No, he didn't say.

And no offense, kiddo, but that kind of thing is small potatoes for us.

But, I tell you, if someone was running around in *my* costume doing that... I would find him and beat the holy snot out of him.

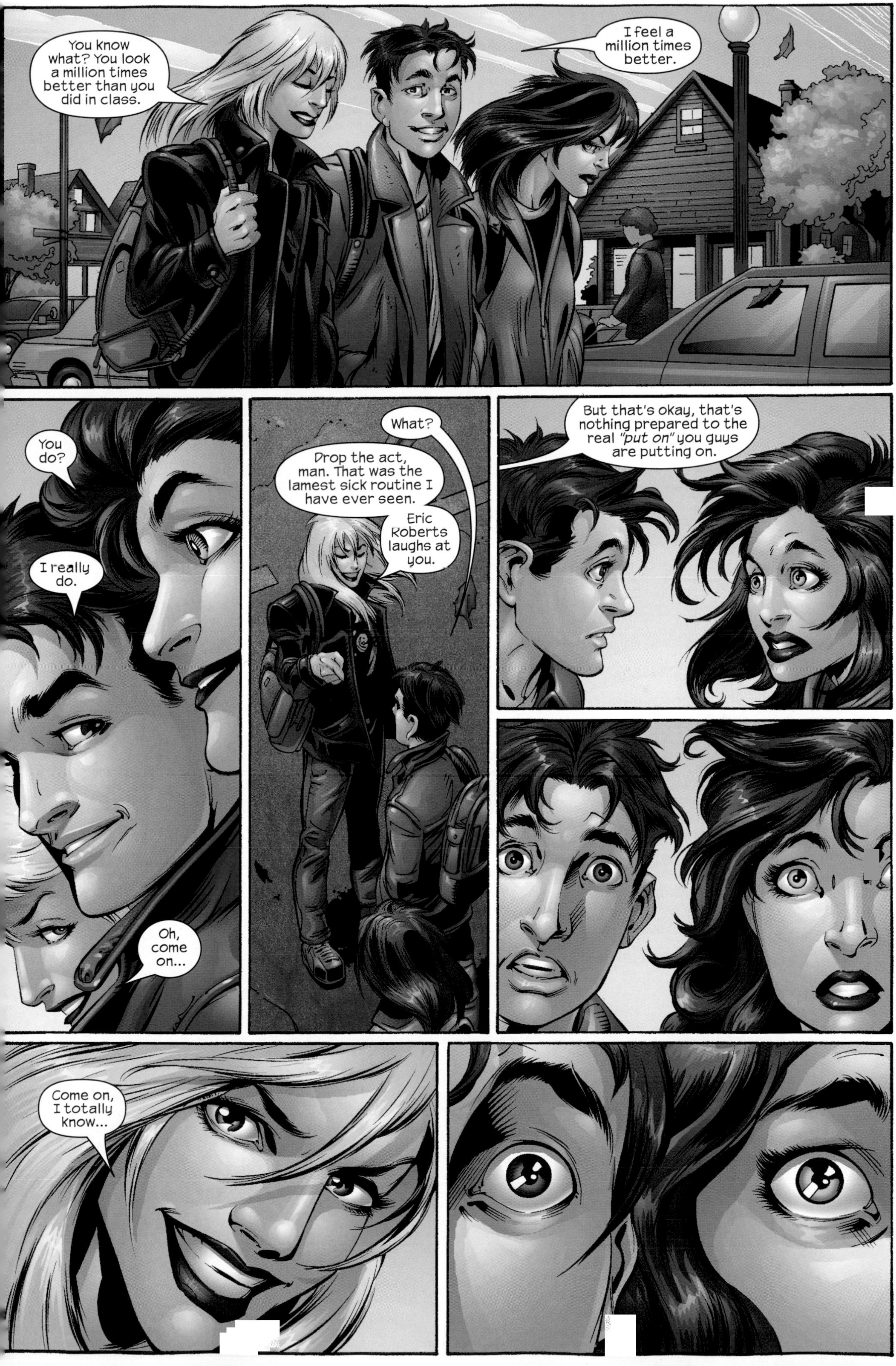
You know what? You look a million times better than you did in class.
I feel a million times better.
You do?
I really do.
Oh, come on...
What?
Drop the act, man. That was the lamest sick routine I have ever seen.
Eric Roberts laughs at you.
But that's okay, that's nothing prepared to the real "put on" you guys are putting on.
Come on, I totally know...

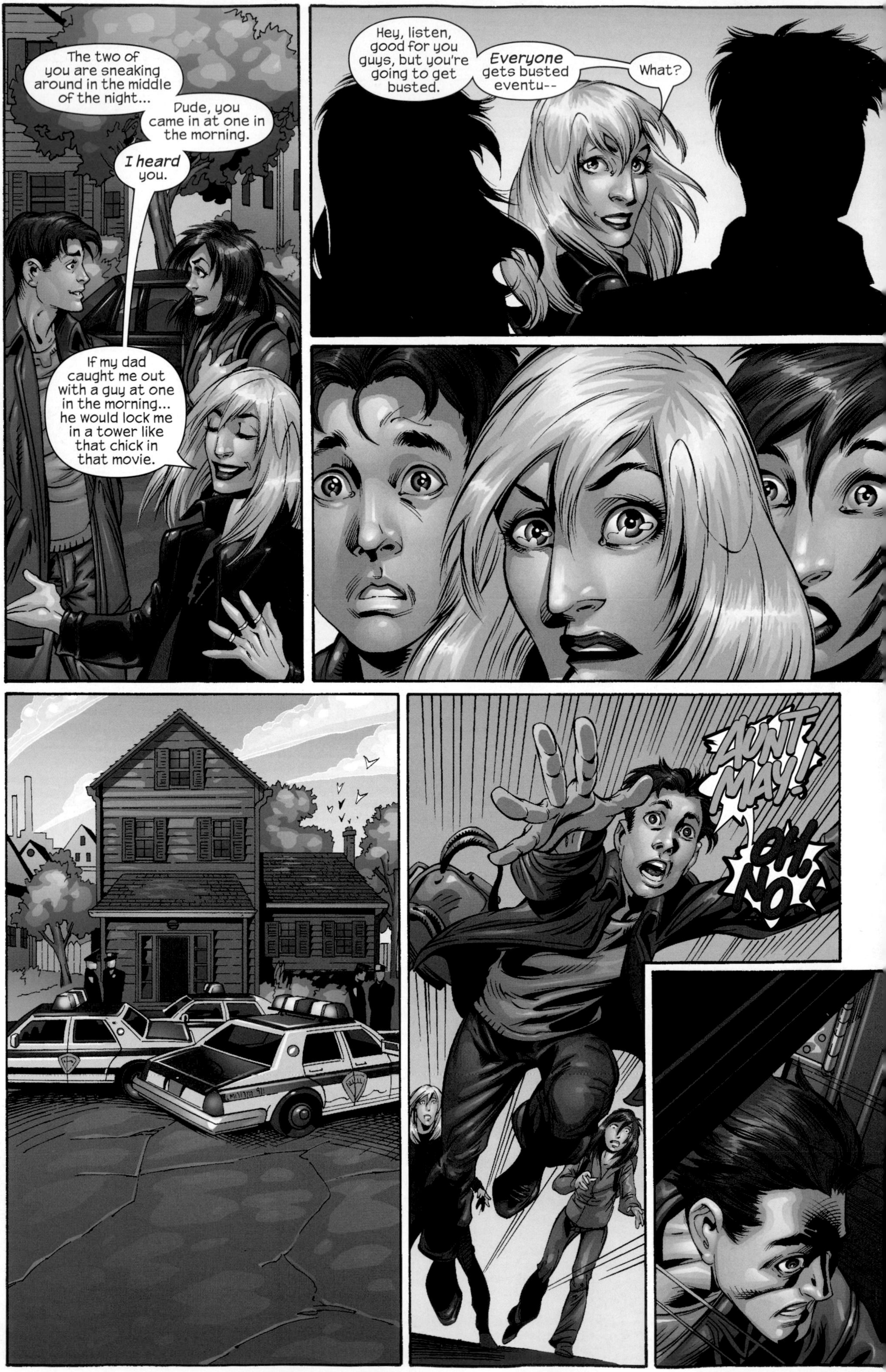
The two of you are sneaking around in the middle of the night...
Dude, you came in at one in the morning.
I heard you.
If my dad caught me out with a guy at one in the morning... he would lock me in a tower like that chick in that movie.
Hey, listen, good for you guys, but you're going to get busted.
Everyone gets busted eventu--
What?
AUNT MAY!
OH, NO!

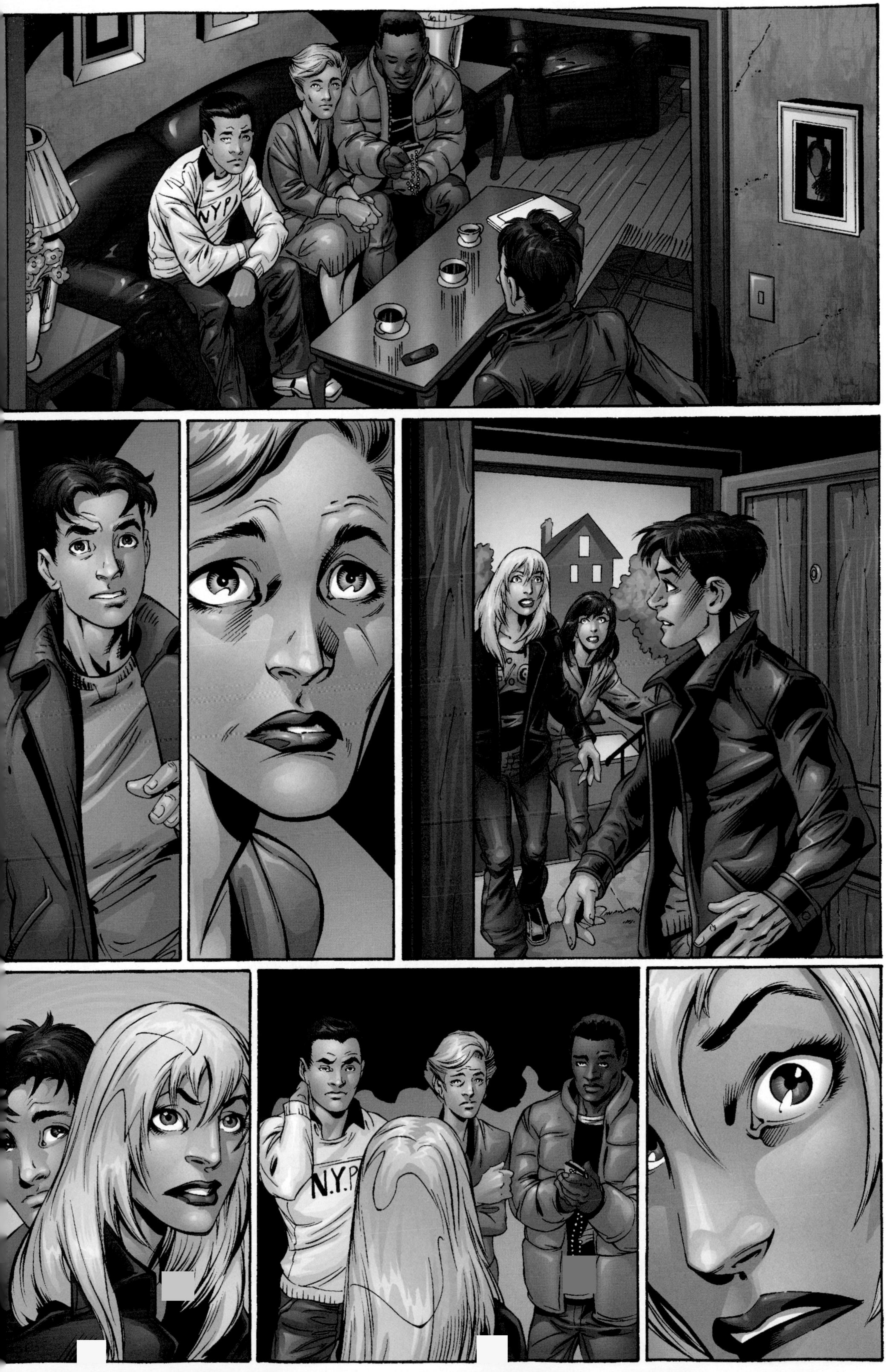
NYP
N.Y.P

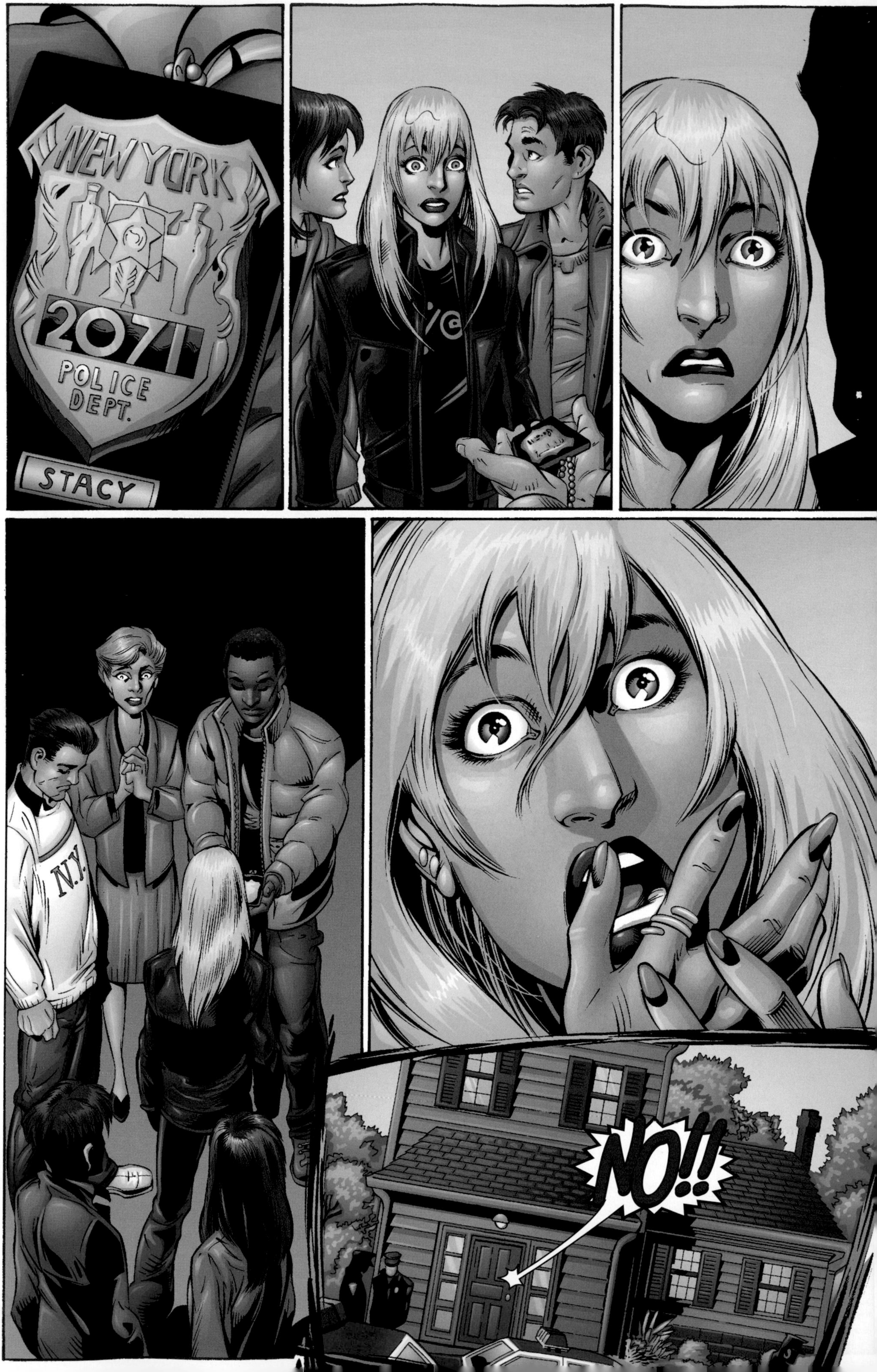
NEW YORK
2071
POLICE DEPT.
STACY
N.Y.
NO!!

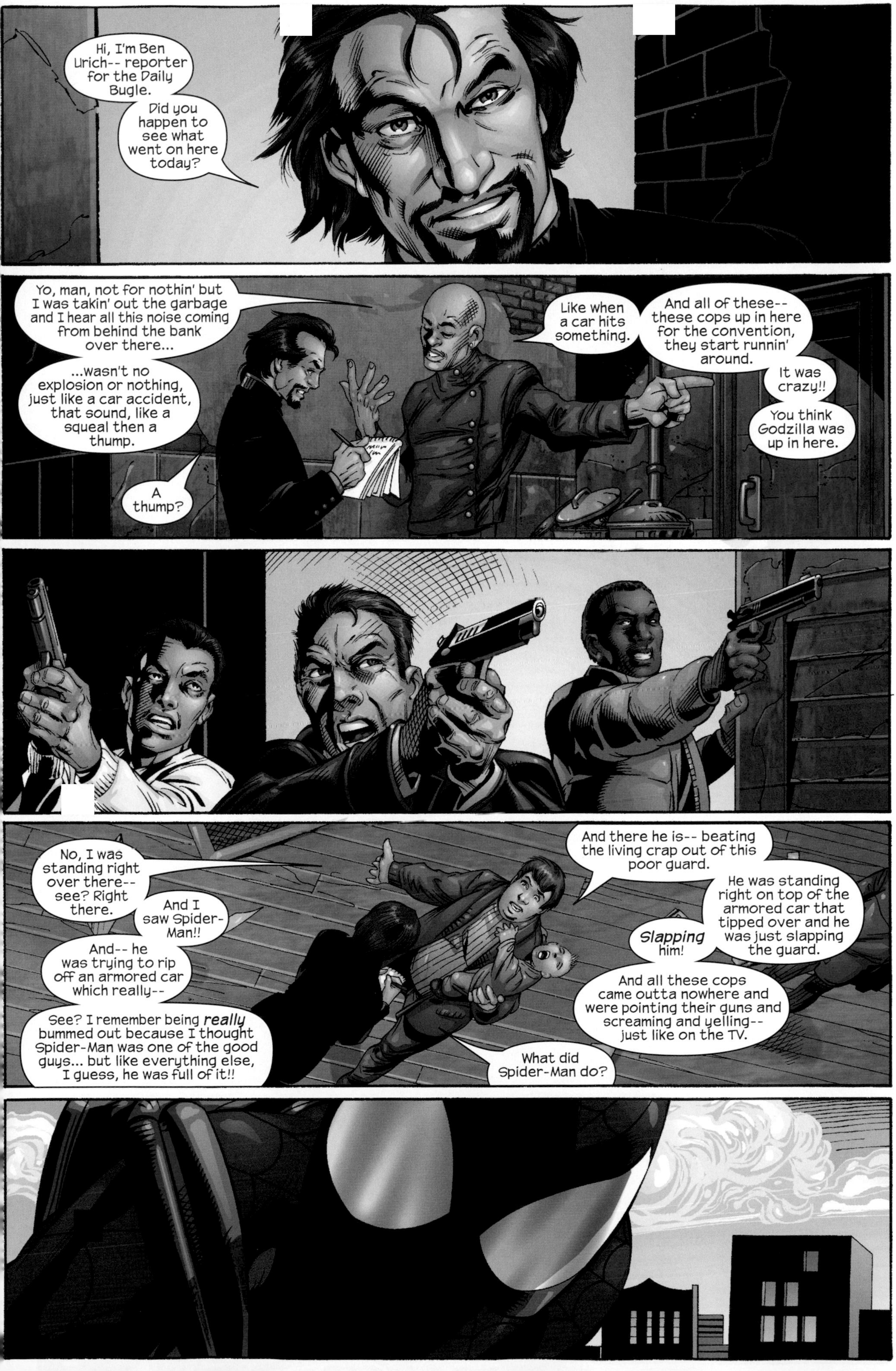

Hi, I'm Ben Urich-- reporter for the Daily Bugle.
Did you happen to see what went on here today?
Yo, man, not for nothin' but I was takin' out the garbage and I hear all this noise coming from behind the bank over there...
...wasn't no explosion or nothing, just like a car accident, that sound, like a squeal then a thump.
A thump?
Like when a car hits something.
And all of these-- these cops up in here for the convention, they start runnin' around.
It was crazy!!
You think Godzilla was up in here.
No, I was standing right over there-- see? Right there.
And I saw Spider-Man!!
And-- he was trying to rip off an armored car which really--
See? I remember being *really* bummed out because I thought Spider-Man was one of the good guys... but like everything else, I guess, he was full of it!!
What did Spider-Man do?
And there he is-- beating the living crap out of this poor guard.
He was standing right on top of the armored car that tipped over and he was just slapping the guard.
Slapping him!
And all these cops came outta nowhere and were pointing their guns and screaming and yelling-- just like on the TV.

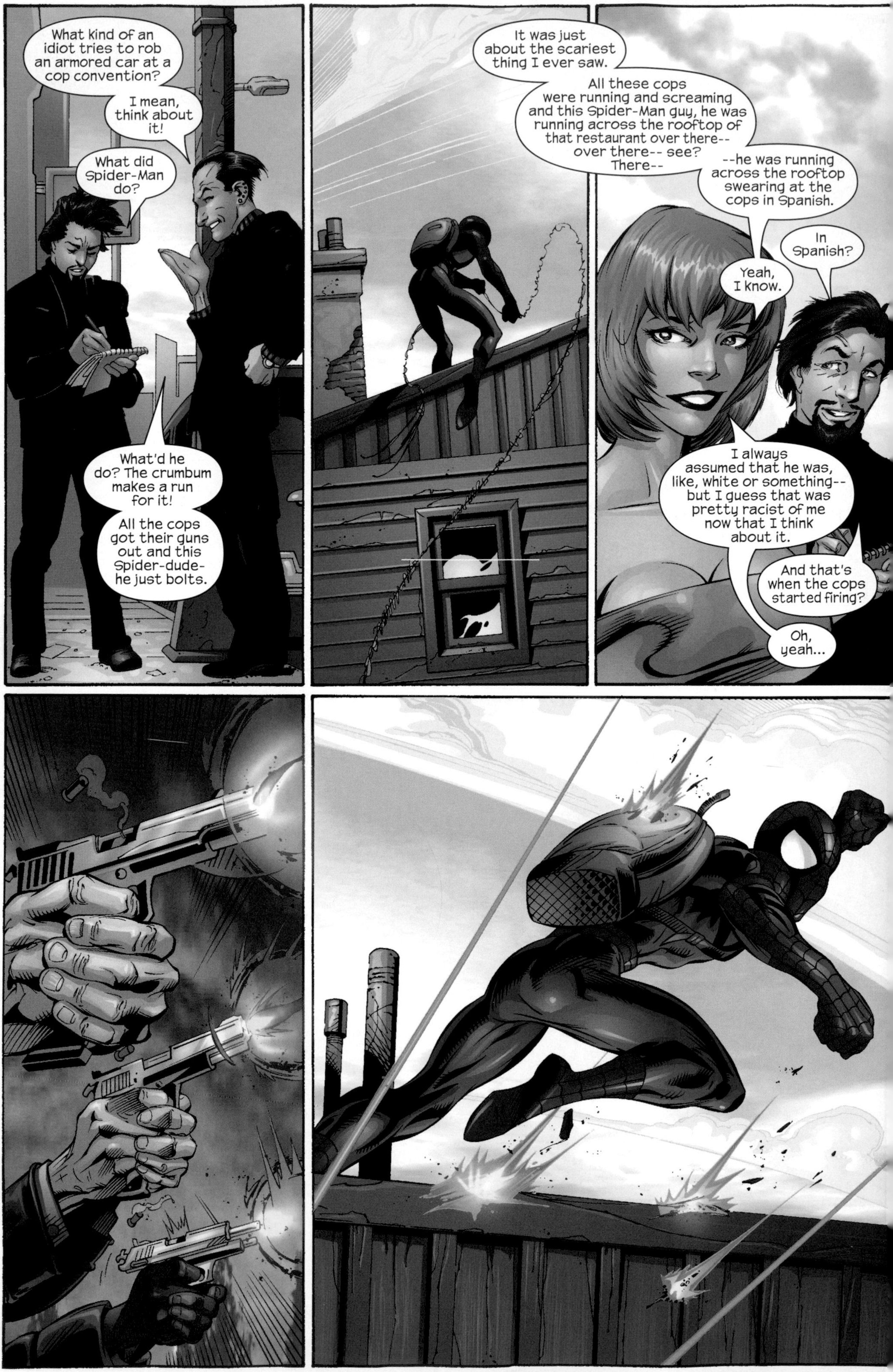
What kind of an idiot tries to rob an armored car at a cop convention?
I mean, think about it!
What did Spider-Man do?
What'd he do? The crumbum makes a run for it!
All the cops got their guns out and this Spider-dude-he just bolts.
It was just about the scariest thing I ever saw.
All these cops were running and screaming and this Spider-Man guy, he was running across the rooftop of that restaurant over there-- over there-- see? There--
--he was running across the rooftop swearing at the cops in Spanish.
In Spanish?
Yeah, I know.
I always assumed that he was, like, white or something-- but I guess that was pretty racist of me now that I think about it.
And that's when the cops started firing?
Oh, yeah...

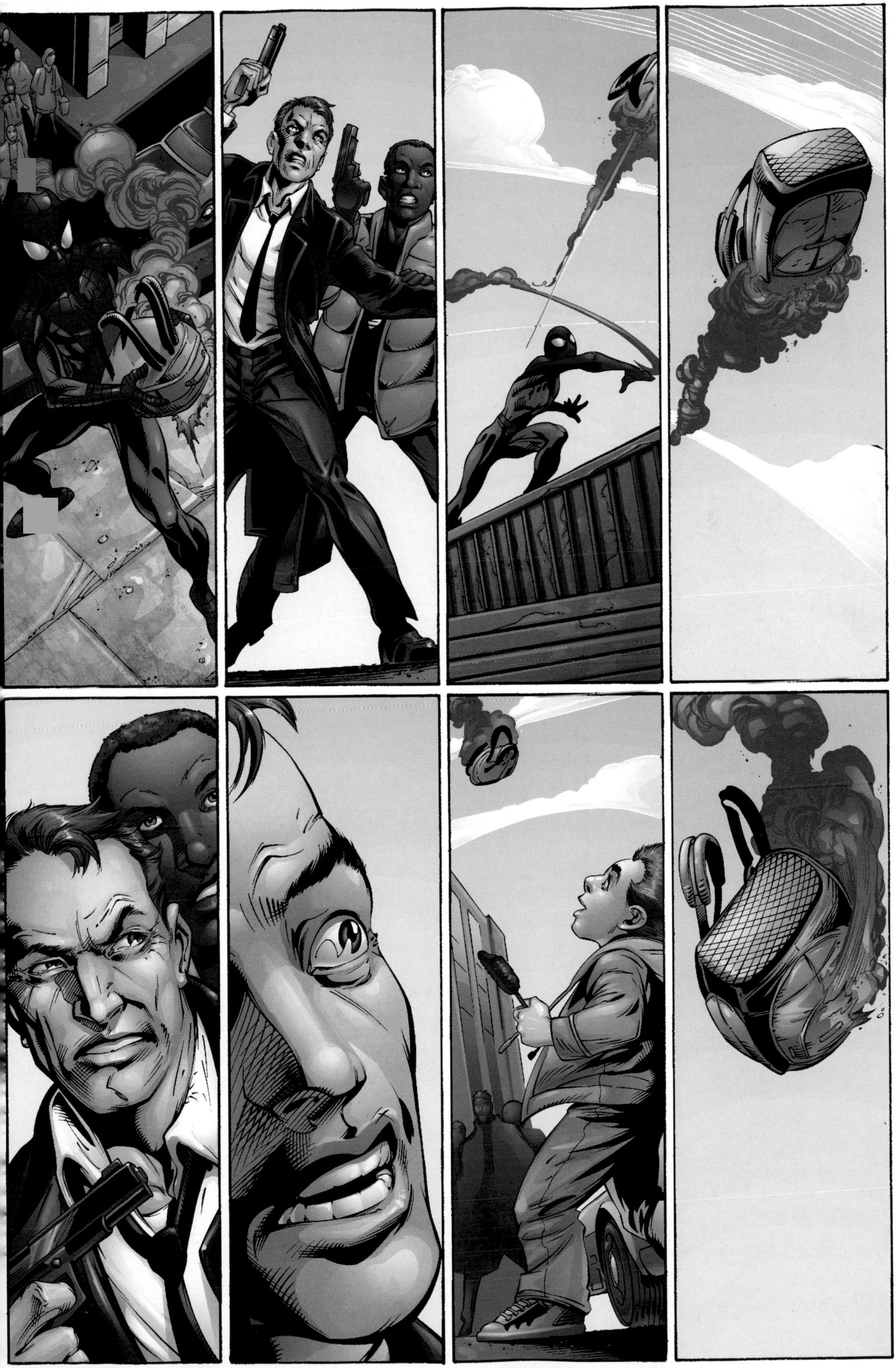

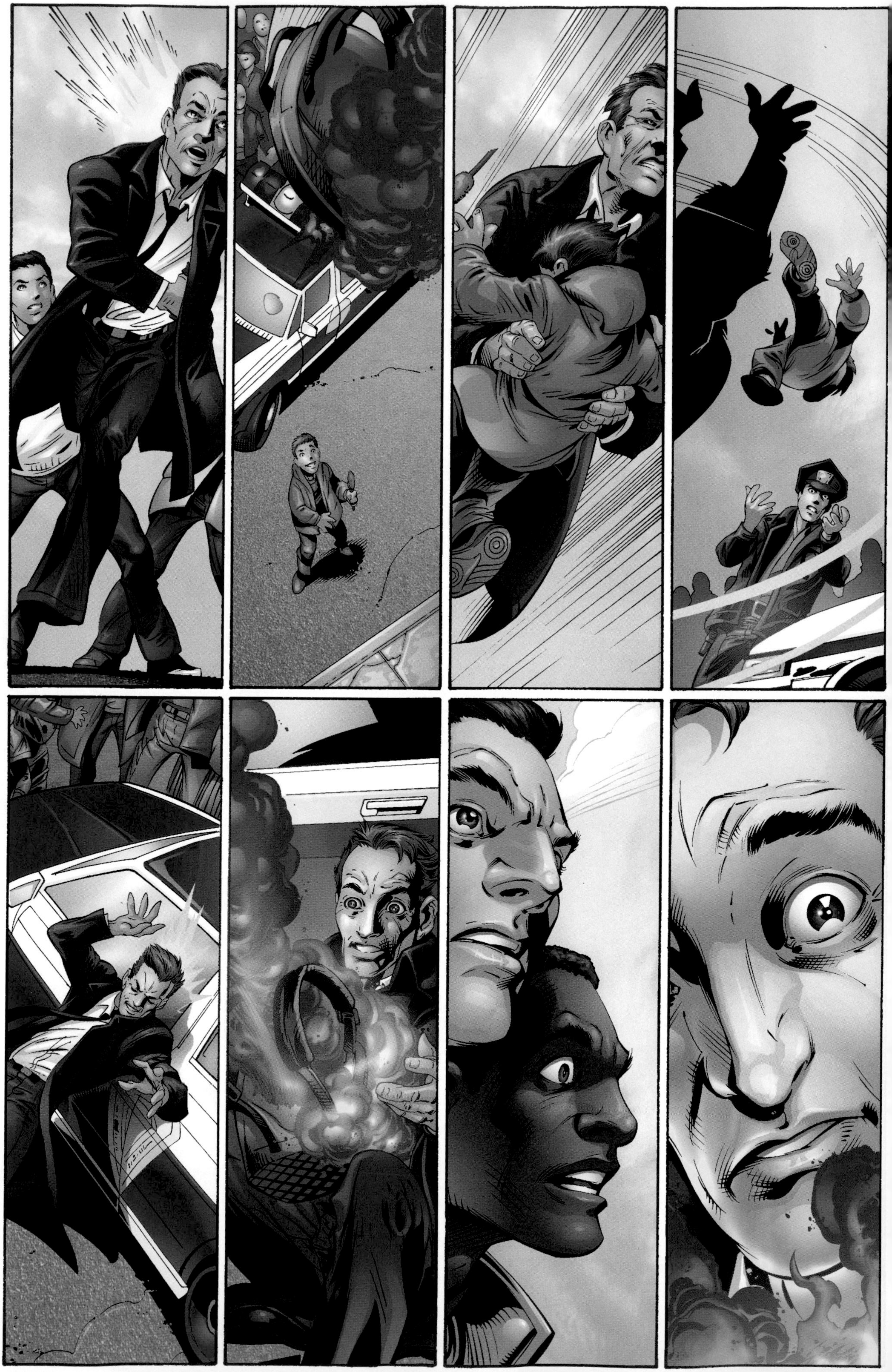

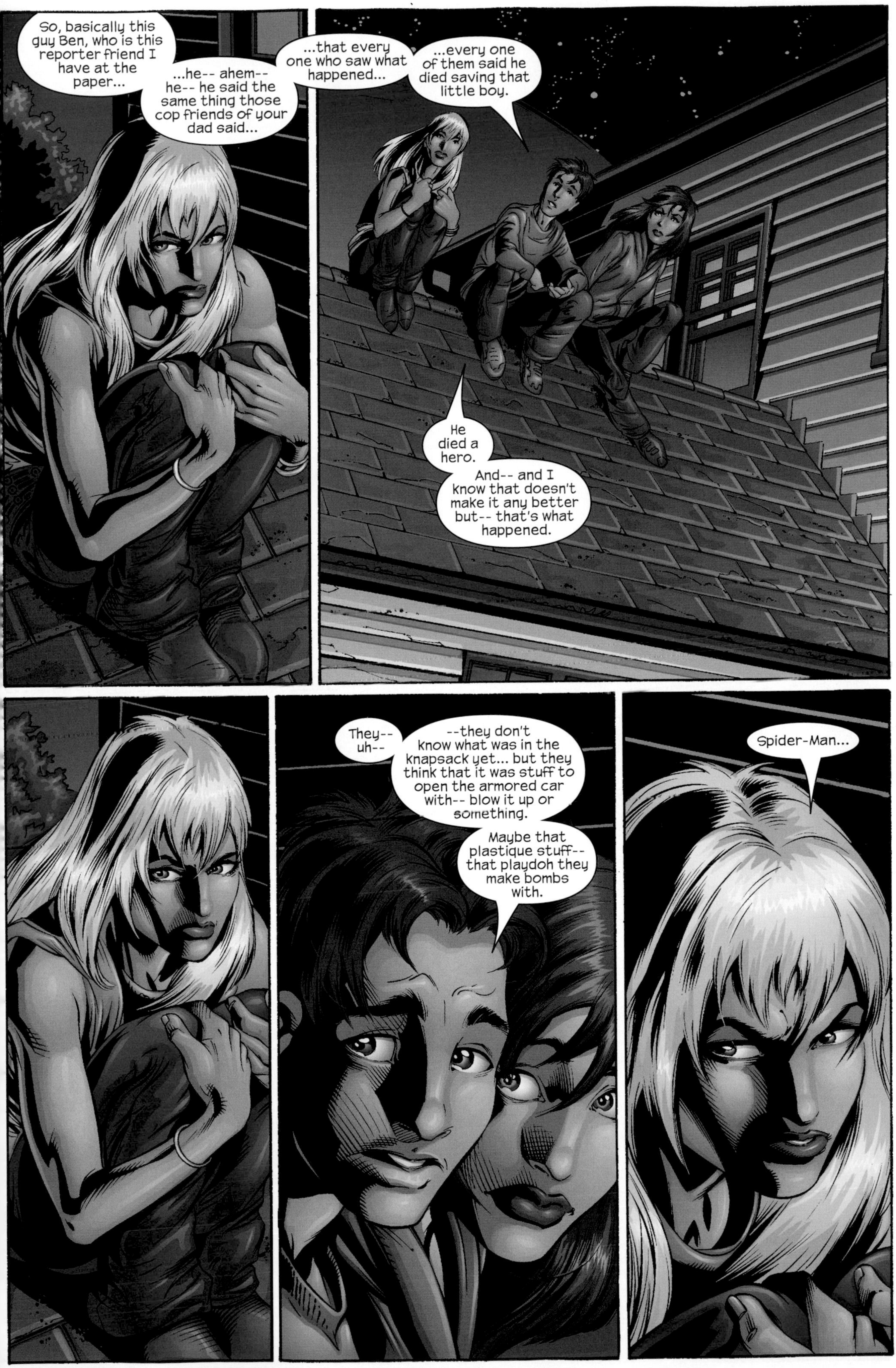
So, basically this guy Ben, who is this reporter friend I have at the paper...
...he-- ahem-- he-- he said the same thing those cop friends of your dad said...
...that every one who saw what happened...
...every one of them said he died saving that little boy.
He died a hero.
And-- and I know that doesn't make it any better but-- that's what happened.
They-- uh--
--they don't know what was in the knapsack yet... but they think that it was stuff to open the armored car with-- blow it up or something.
Maybe that plastique stuff-- that playdoh they make bombs with.
Spider-Man...

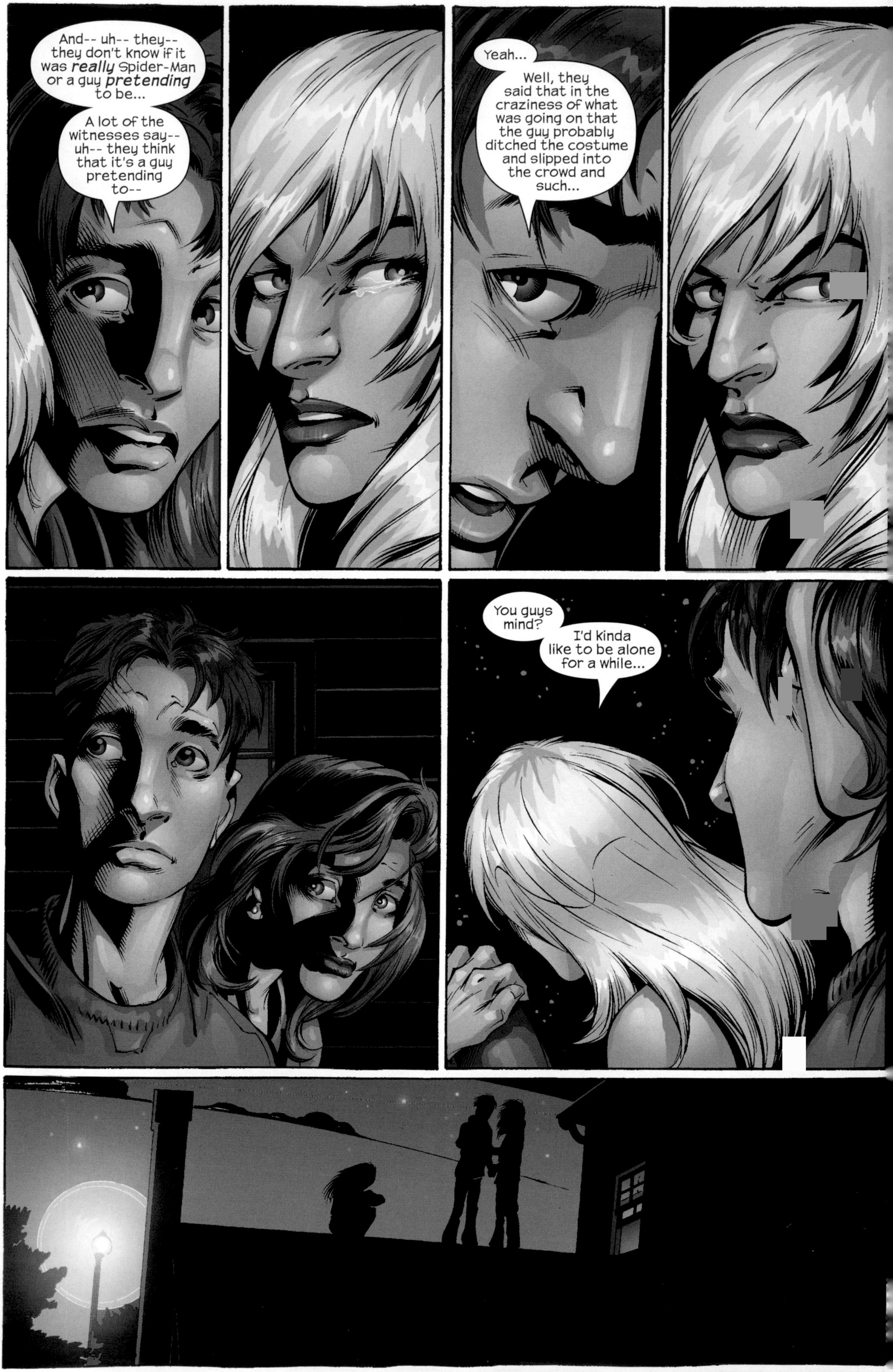
And-- uh-- they-- they don't know if it was *really* Spider-Man or a guy *pretending* to be...
A lot of the witnesses say-- uh-- they think that it's a guy pretending to--
Yeah...
Well, they said that in the craziness of what was going on that the guy probably ditched the costume and slipped into the crowd and such...
You guys mind?
I'd kinda like to be alone for a while...

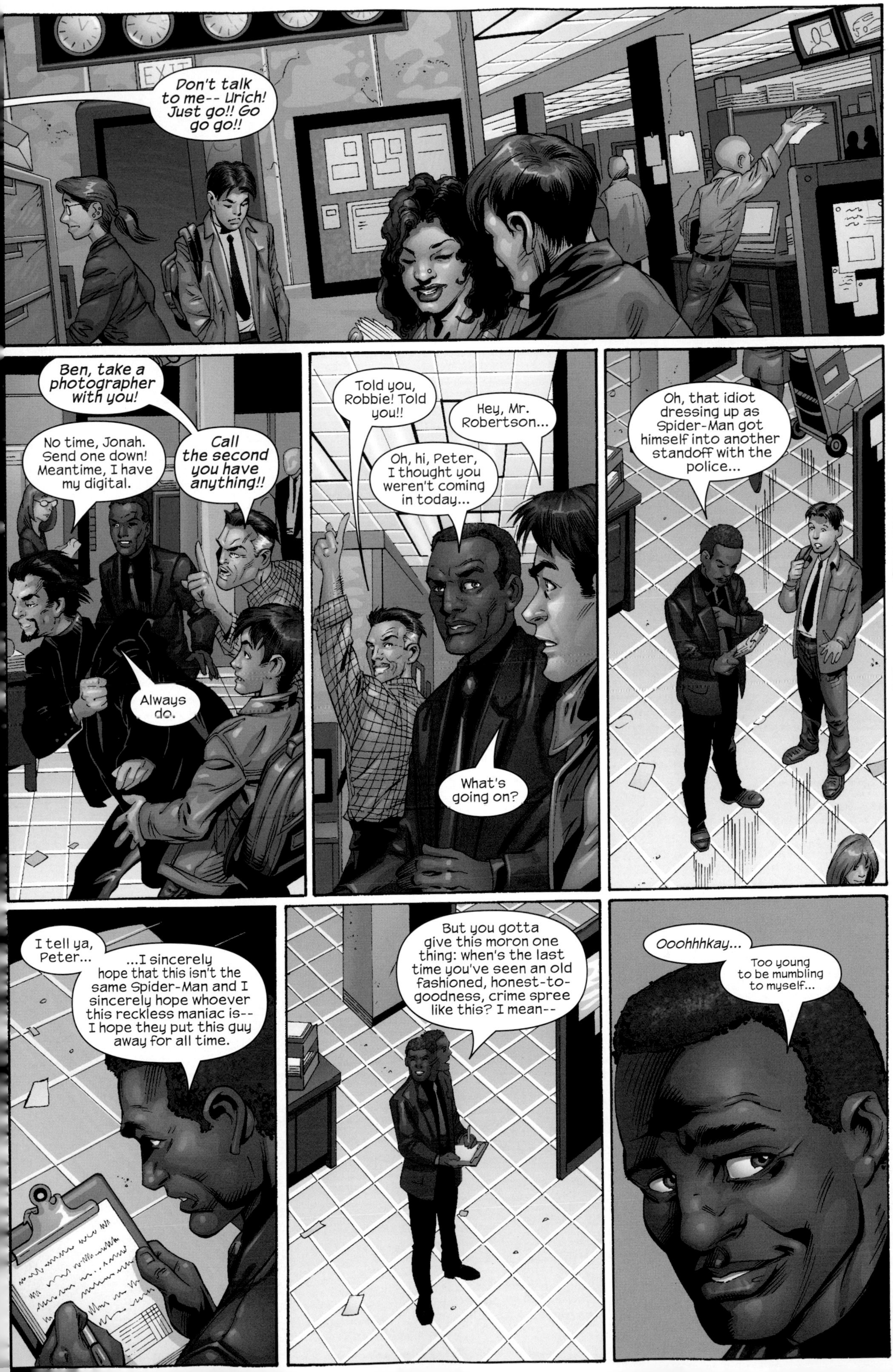
Don't talk to me-- Urich! Just go!! Go go go!!
Ben, take a photographer with you!
No time, Jonah. Send one down! Meantime, I have my digital.
Call the second you have anything!!
Always do.
Told you, Robbie! Told you!!
Hey, Mr. Robertson...
Oh, hi, Peter, I thought you weren't coming in today...
What's going on?
Oh, that idiot dressing up as Spider-Man got himself into another standoff with the police...
I tell ya, Peter...
...I sincerely hope that this isn't the same Spider-Man and I sincerely hope whoever this reckless maniac is-- I hope they put this guy away for all time.
But you gotta give this moron one thing: when's the last time you've seen an old fashioned, honest-to-goodness, crime spree like this? I mean--
Ooohhhkay...
Too young to be mumbling to myself...

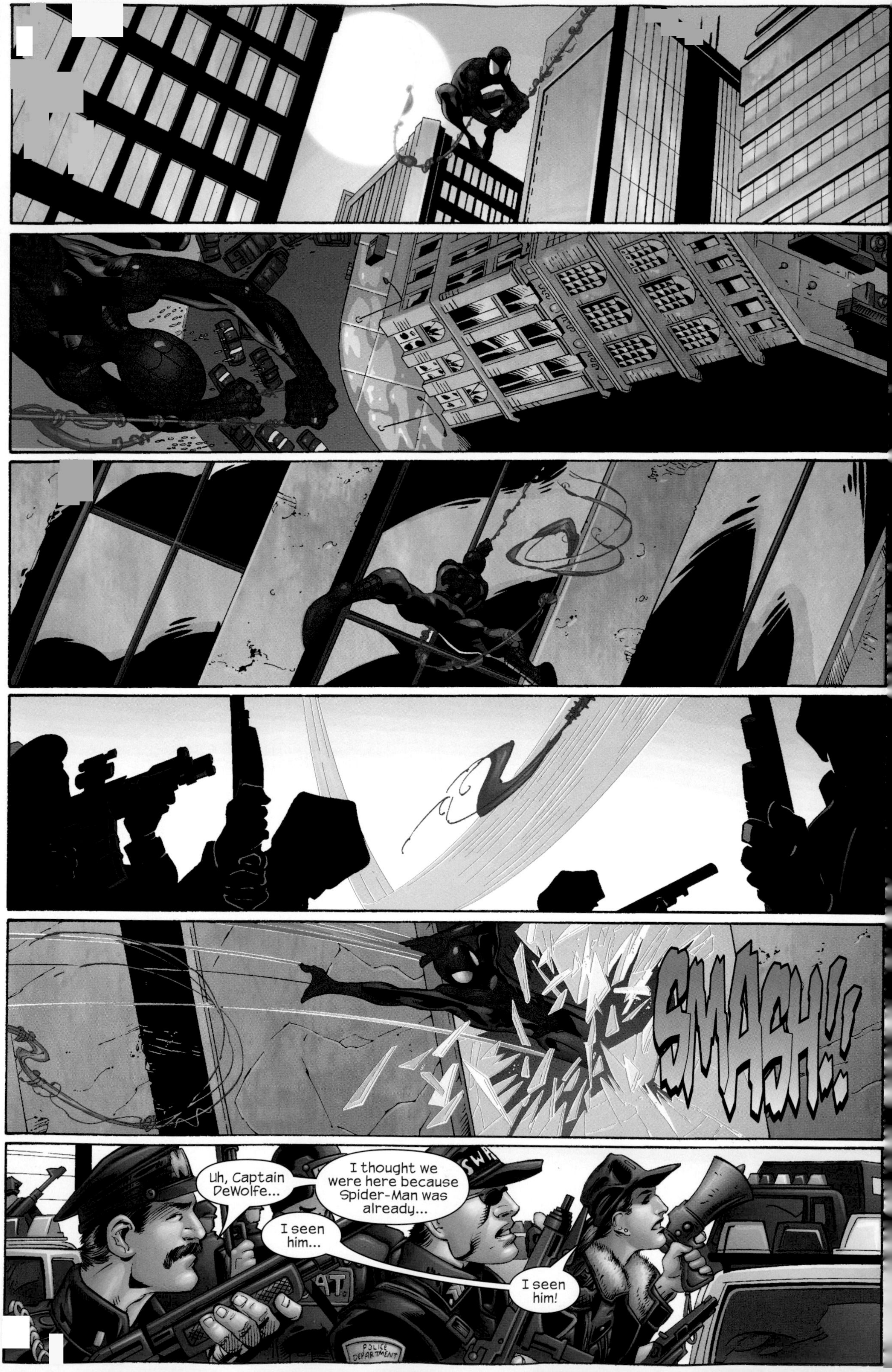
SMASH!!
Uh, Captain DeWolfe...
I thought we were here because Spider-Man was already...
I seen him...
I seen him!

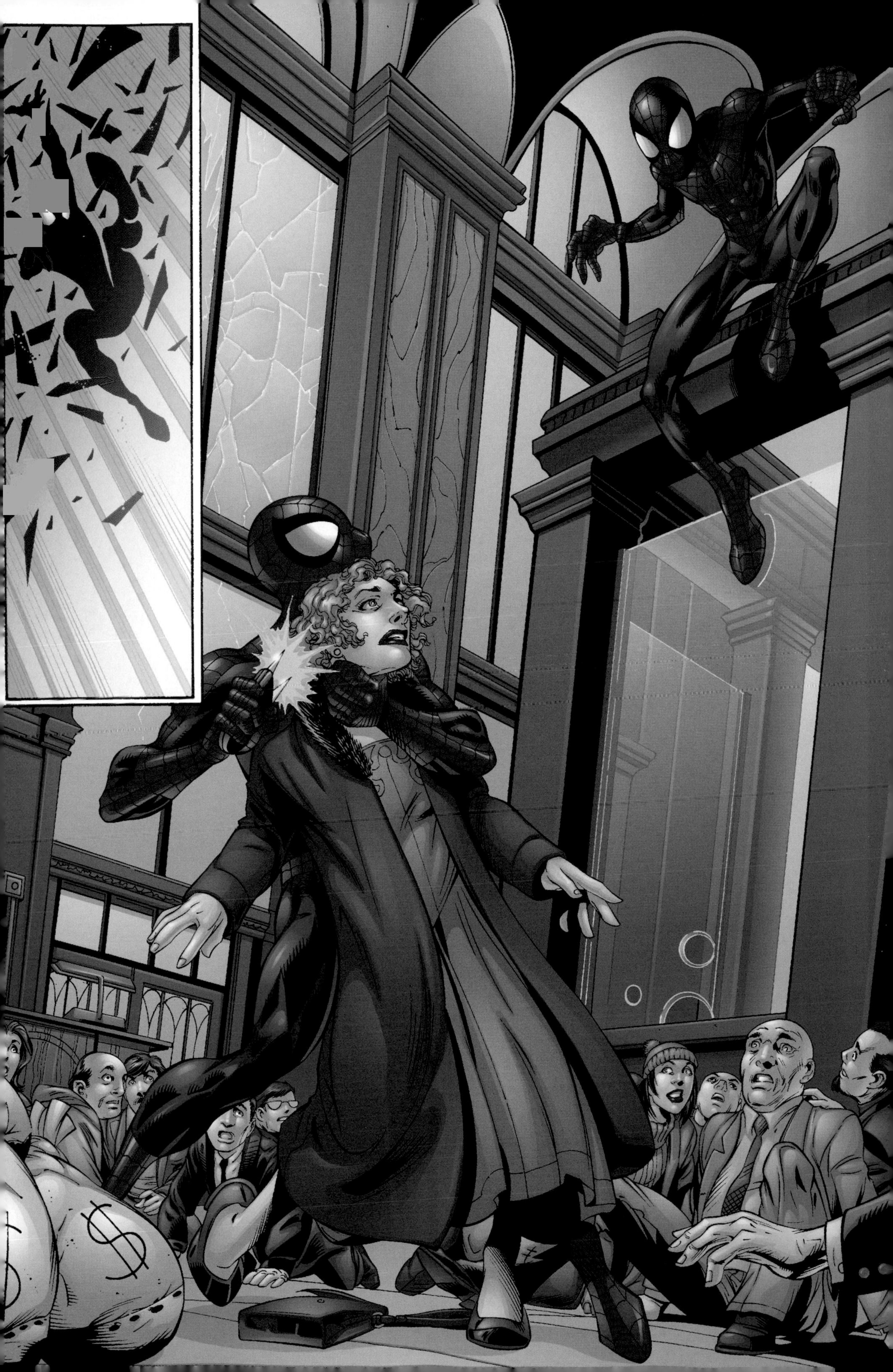

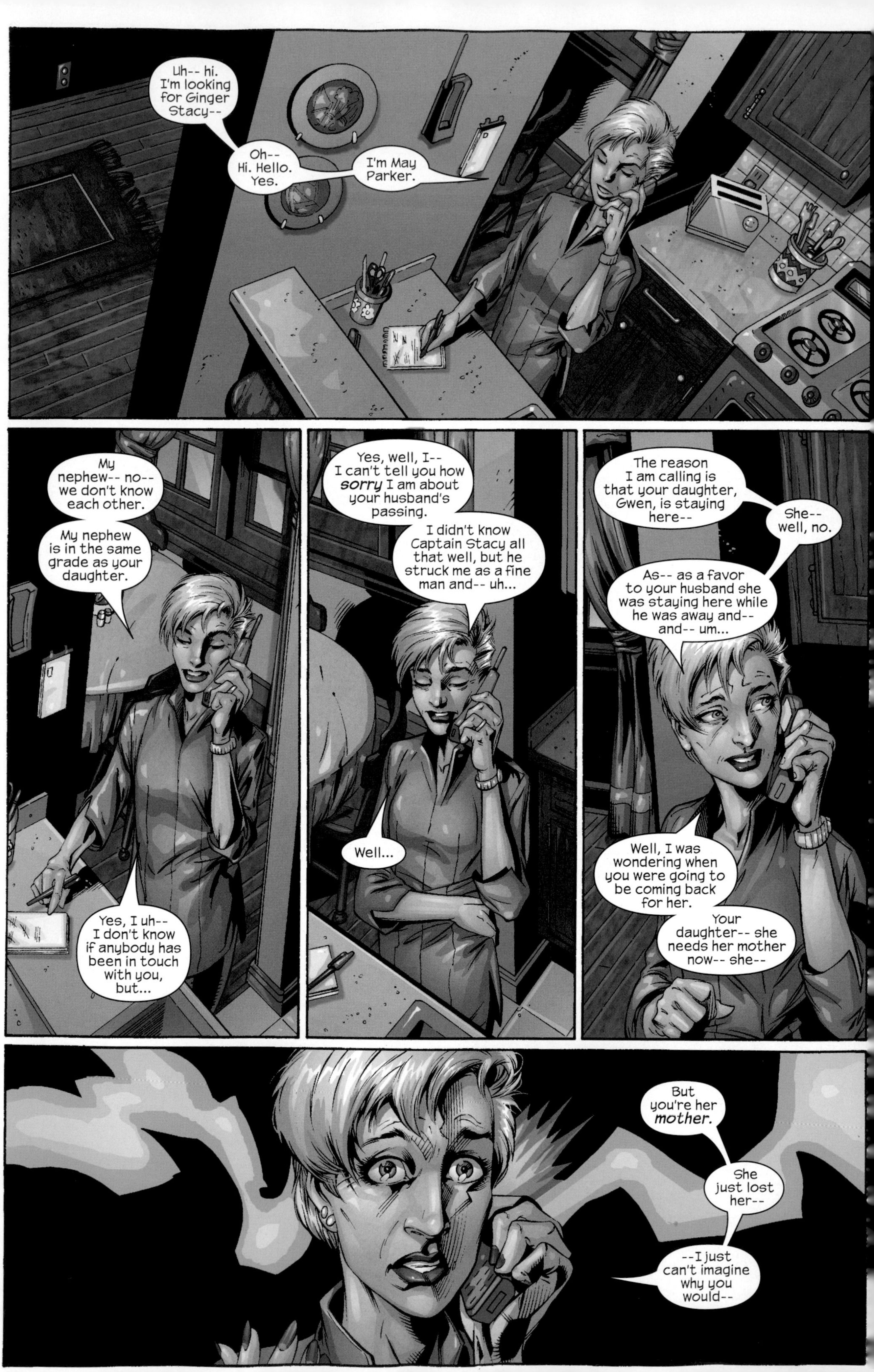
Uh-- hi. I'm looking for Ginger Stacy--
Oh-- Hi. Hello. Yes.
I'm May Parker.
My nephew-- no-- we don't know each other.
My nephew is in the same grade as your daughter.
Yes, I uh-- I don't know if anybody has been in touch with you, but...
Yes, well, I-- I can't tell you how *sorry* I am about your husband's passing.
I didn't know Captain Stacy all that well, but he struck me as a fine man and-- uh...
Well...
The reason I am calling is that your daughter, Gwen, is staying here--
She-- well, no.
As-- as a favor to your husband she was staying here while he was away and-- and-- um...
Well, I was wondering when you were going to be coming back for her.
Your daughter-- she needs her mother now-- she--
But you're her *mother*.
She just lost her--
--I just can't imagine why you would--

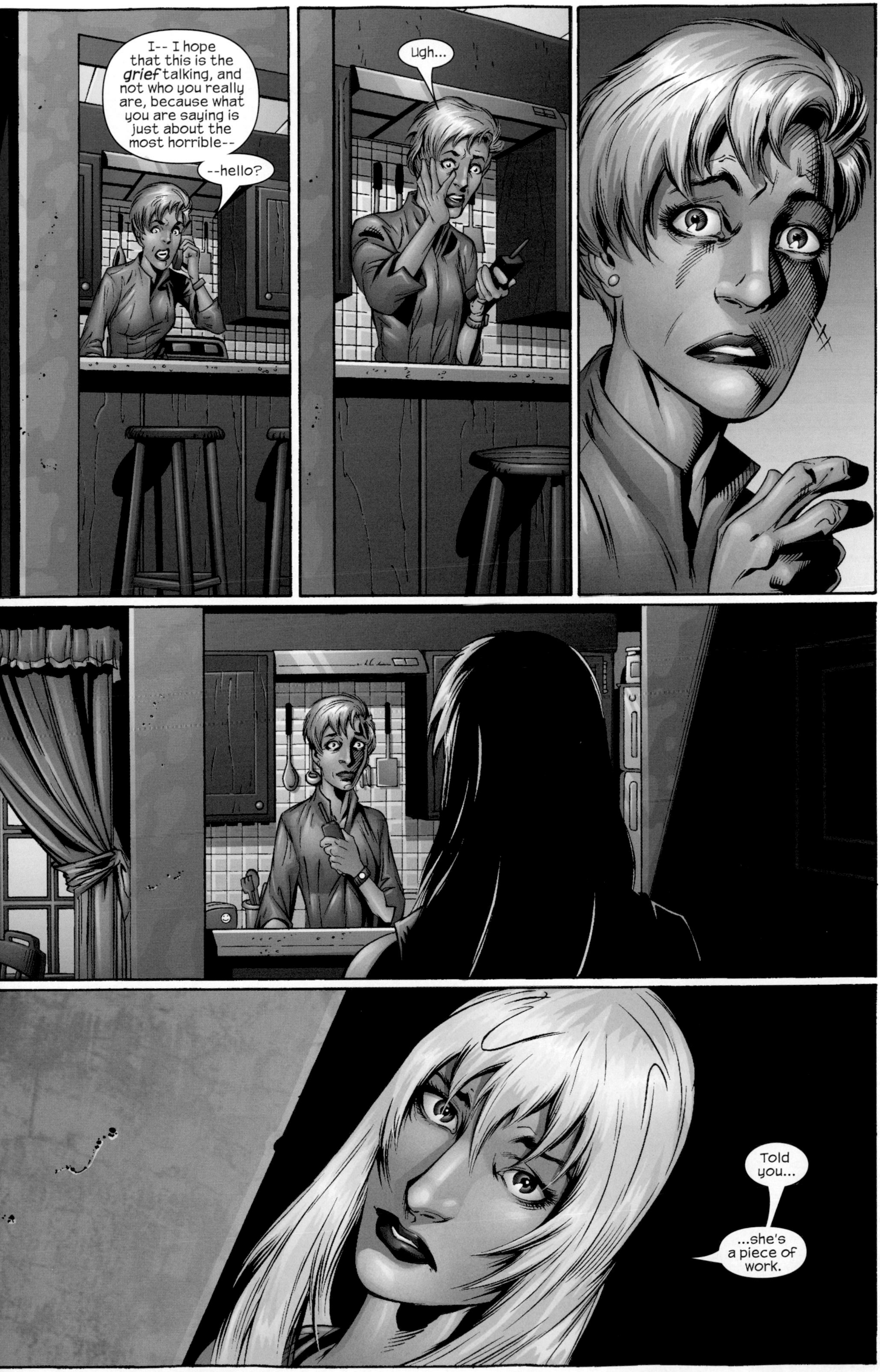

I-- I hope that this is the grief talking, and not who you really are, because what you are saying is just about the most horrible--
--hello?
Ugh...
Told you...
...she's a piece of work.

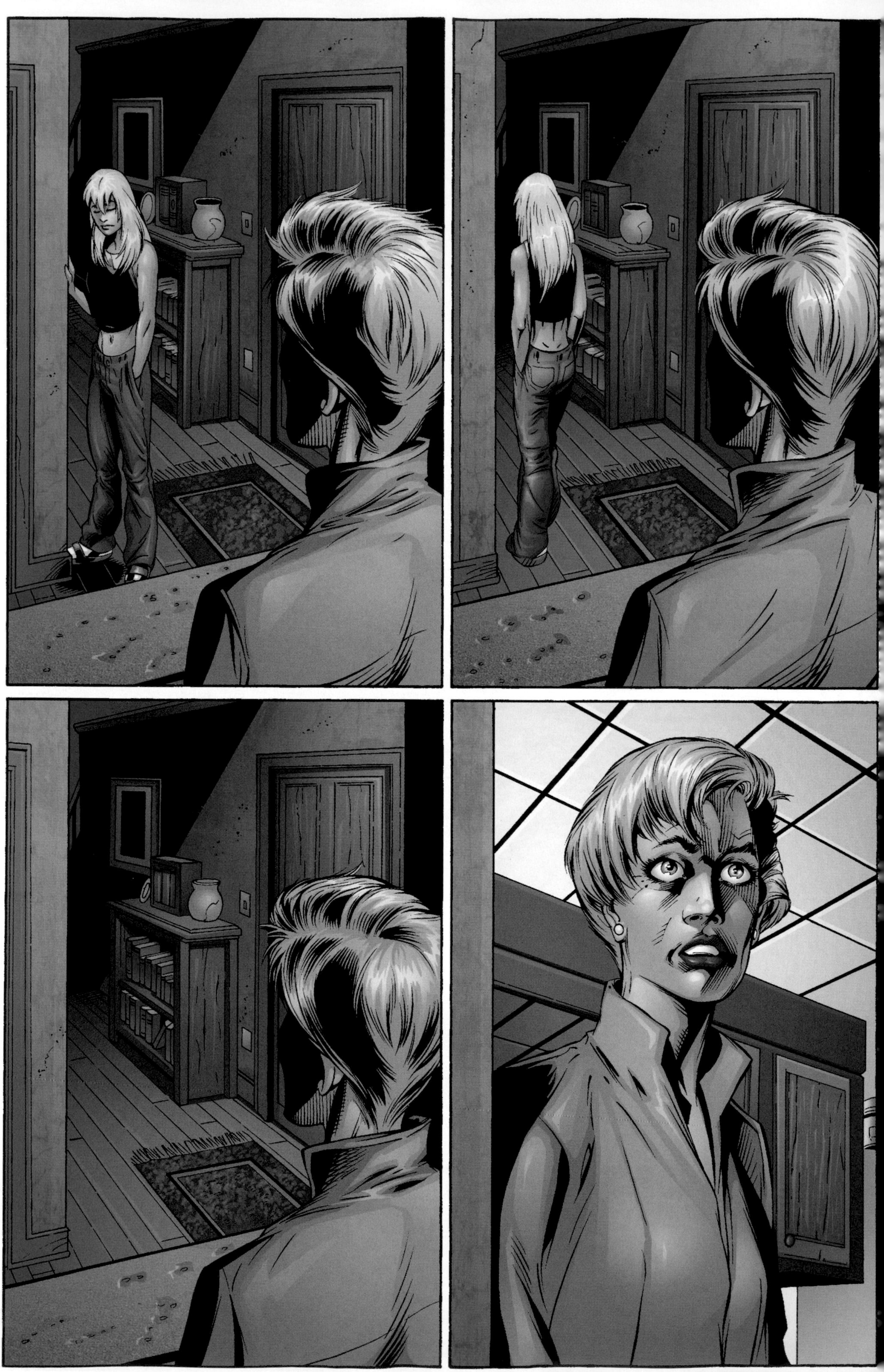

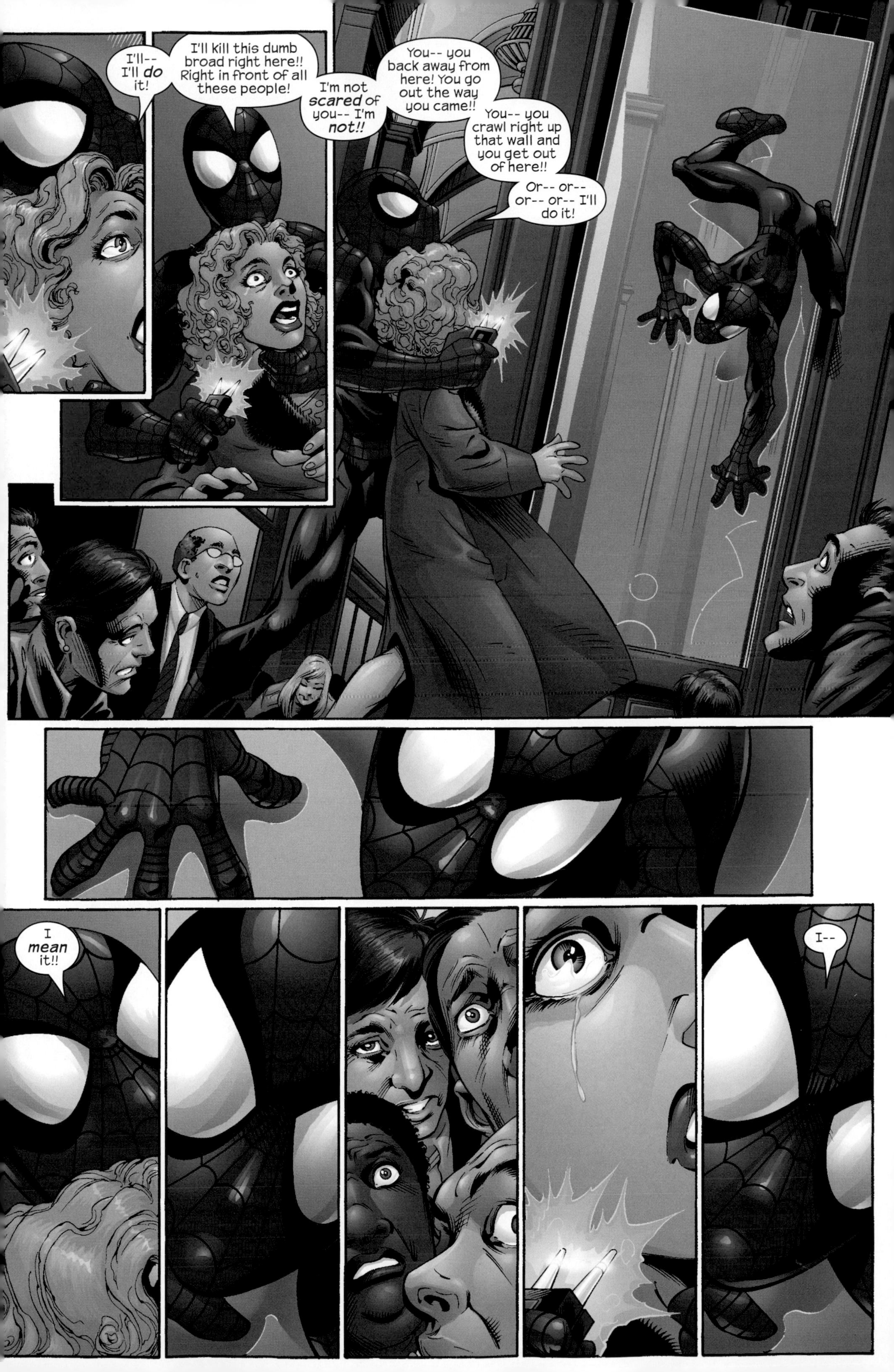
I'll--
I'll *do* it!
I'll kill this dumb broad right here!! Right in front of all these people!
I'm not *scared* of you-- I'm *not!!*
You-- you back away from here! You go out the way you came!!
You-- you crawl right up that wall and you get out of here!!
Or-- or-- or-- or-- I'll do it!
I *mean* it!!
I--

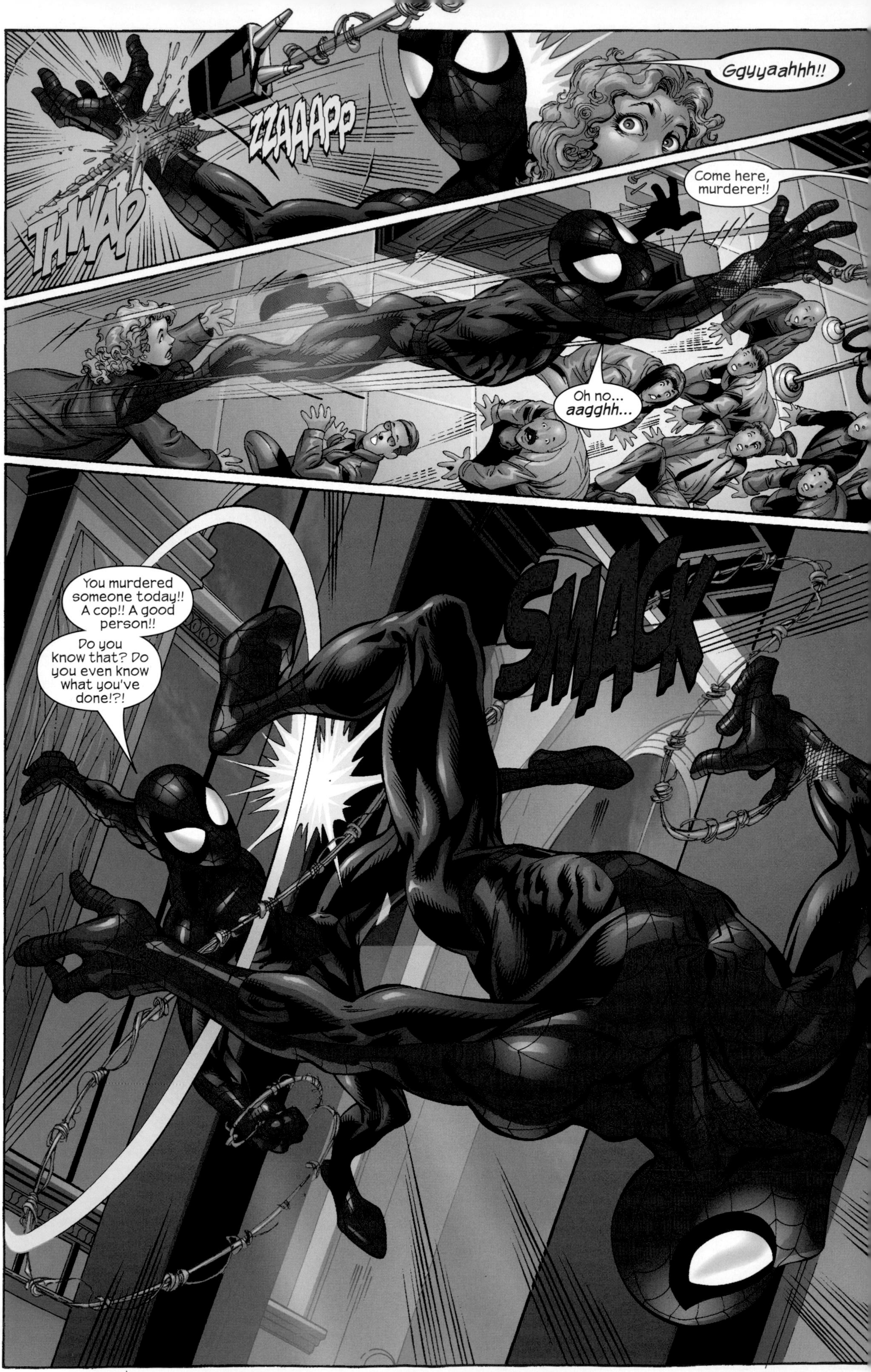
Ggyyaahhh!!
ZZAAAPP
THWAP
Come here, murderer!!
Oh no... aagghh...
SMACK
You murdered someone today!! A cop!! A good person!!
Do you know that? Do you even know what you've done!?!

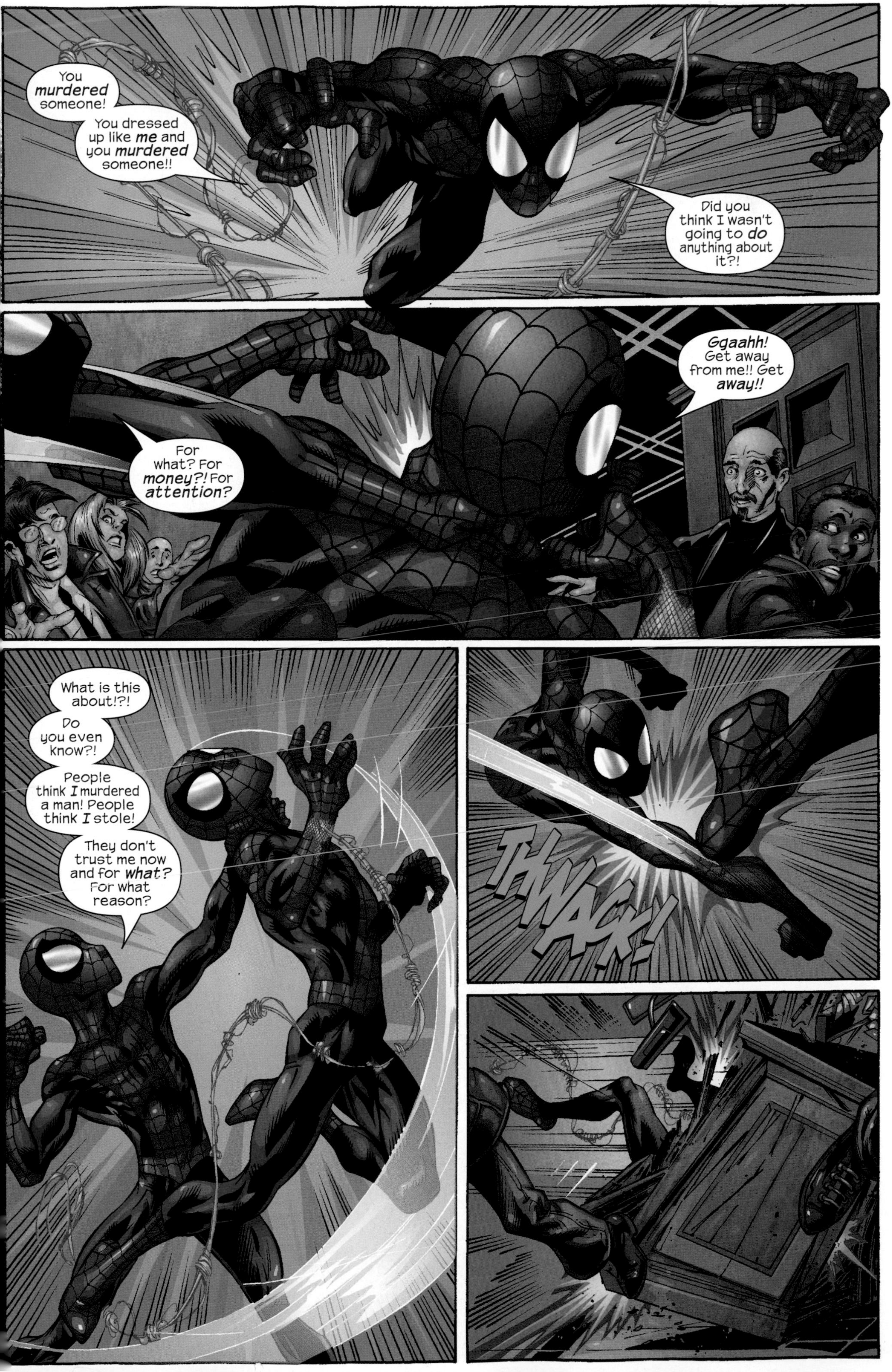
You *murdered* someone!
You dressed up like *me* and you *murdered* someone!!
Did you think I wasn't going to *do* anything about it?!
Ggaahh! Get away from me!! Get *away!!*
For what? For *money?!* For *attention?*
What is this about!?!
Do you even know?!
People think *I* murdered a man! People think *I* stole!
They don't trust me now and for *what?* For what reason?
THWACK!

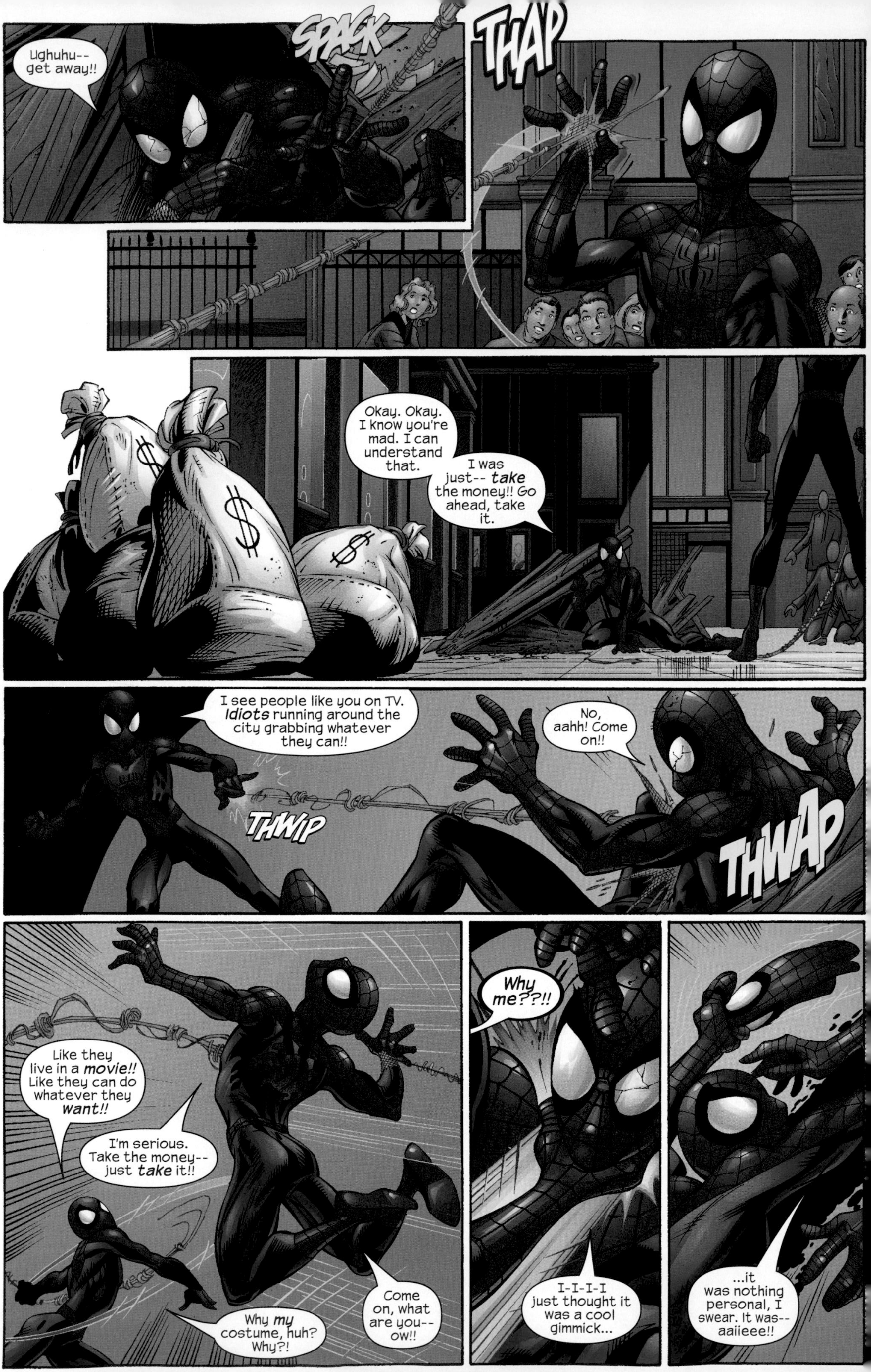
SPACK
THAP
Ughuhu-- get away!!
Okay. Okay. I know you're mad. I can understand that.
I was just-- *take* the money!! Go ahead, take it.
I see people like you on TV. *Idiots* running around the city grabbing whatever they can!!
No, aahh! Come on!!
THWIP
THWAP
Like they live in a *movie!!* Like they can do whatever they *want!!*
I'm serious. Take the money-- just *take* it!!
Why *my* costume, huh? Why?!
Come on, what are you-- ow!!
Why me??!!
I-I-I-I just thought it was a cool gimmick...
...it was nothing personal, I swear. It was-- aaiieee!!

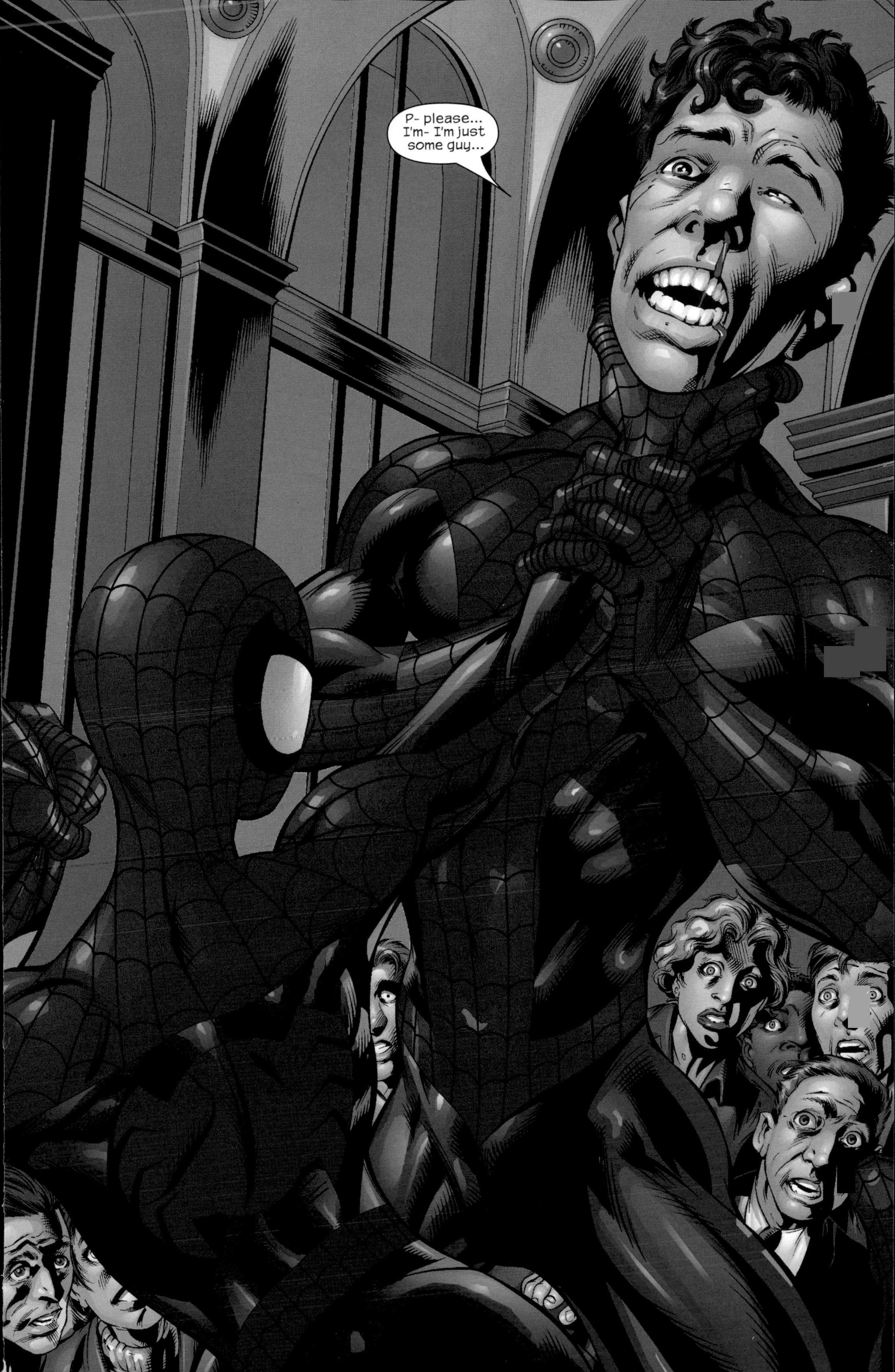
P- please... I'm- I'm just some guy...

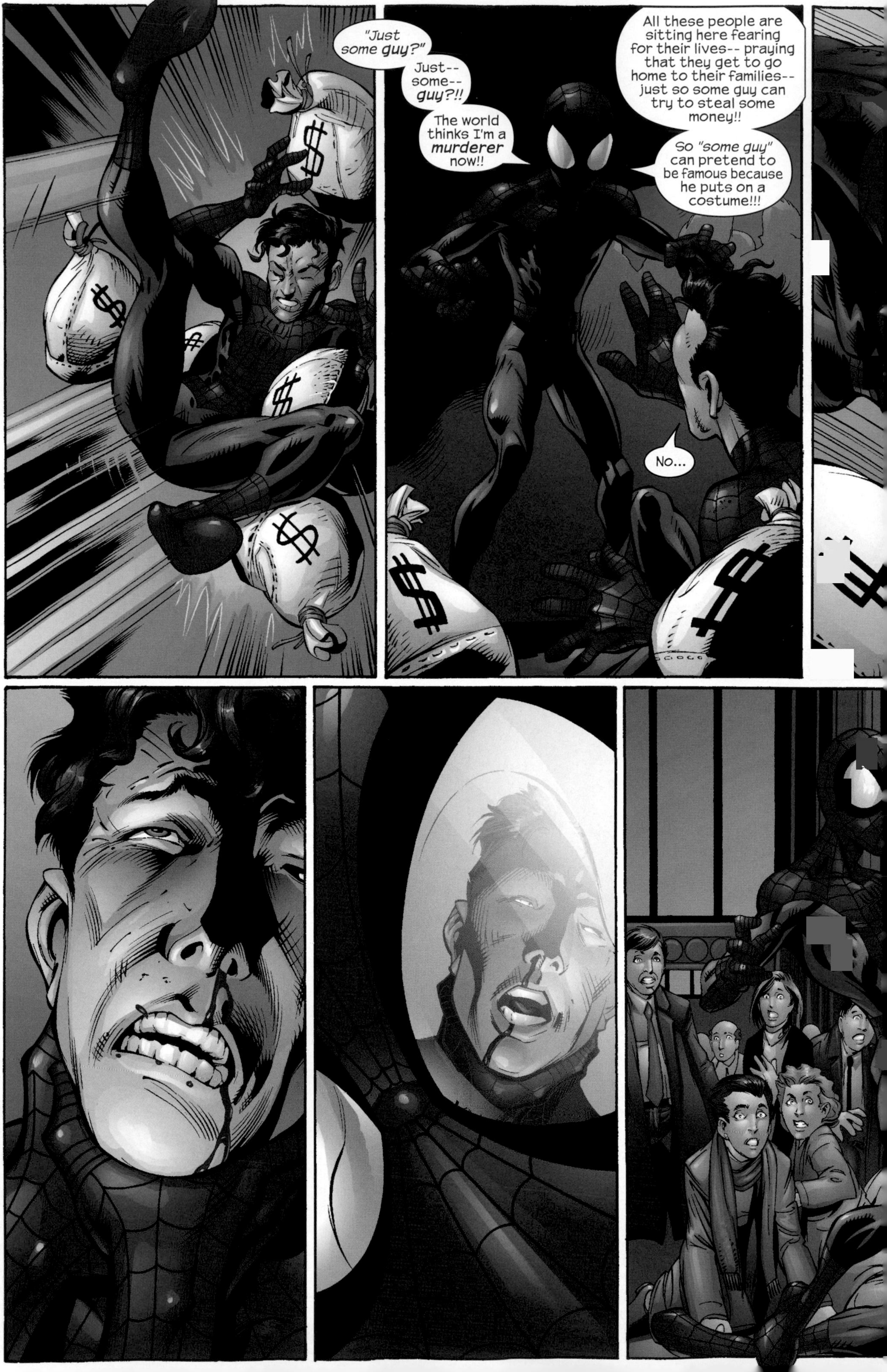
"Just some guy?"
Just-- some-- guy?!!
The world thinks I'm a murderer now!!
All these people are sitting here fearing for their lives-- praying that they get to go home to their families-- just so some guy can try to steal some money!!
So "some guy" can pretend to be famous because he puts on a costume!!!
No...

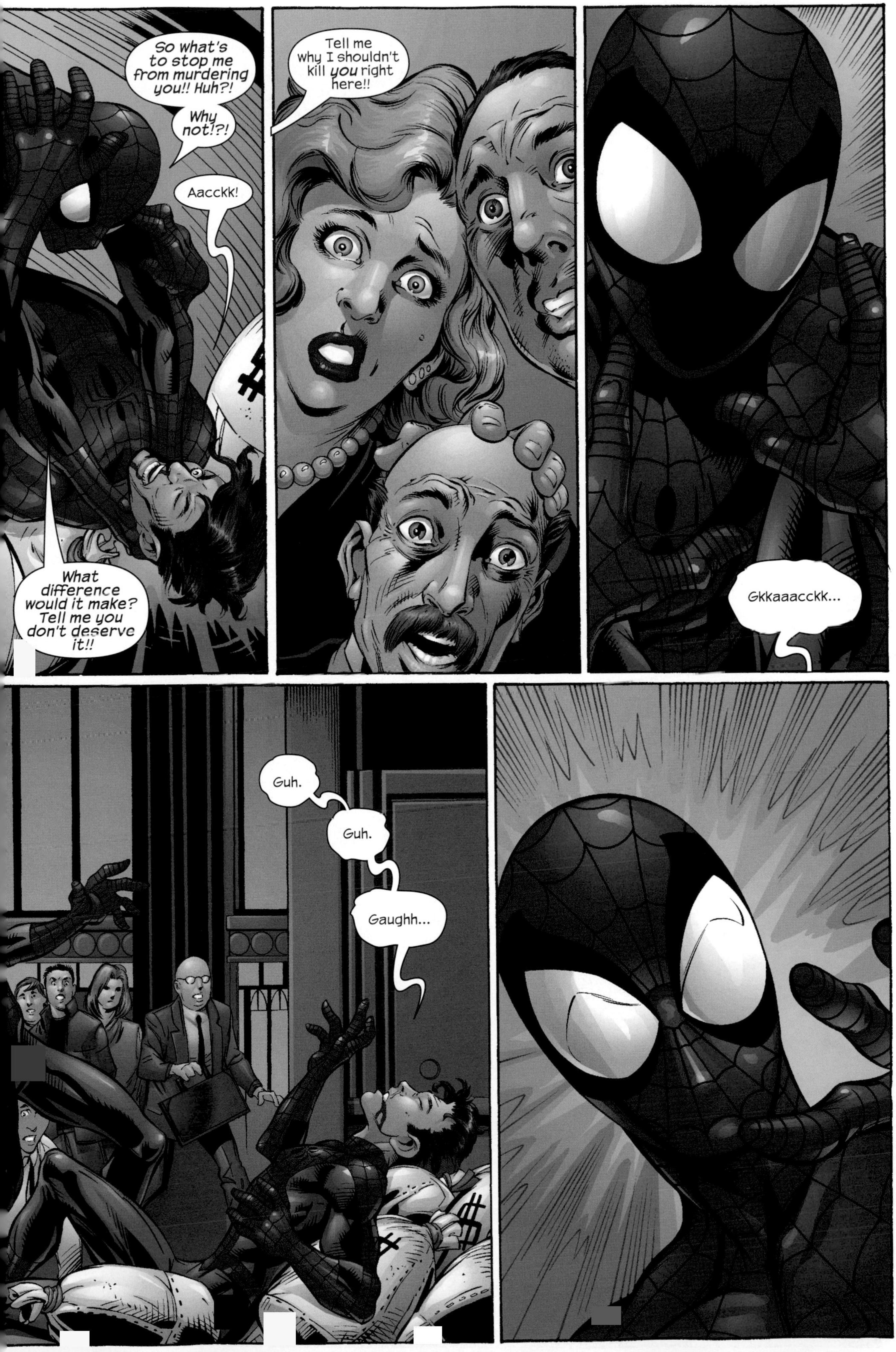
So what's to stop me from murdering you!! Huh?!
Why not!?!
Aacckk!
What difference would it make? Tell me you don't deserve it!!
Tell me why I shouldn't kill you right here!!
Gkkaaacckk...
Guh.
Guh.
Gaughh...

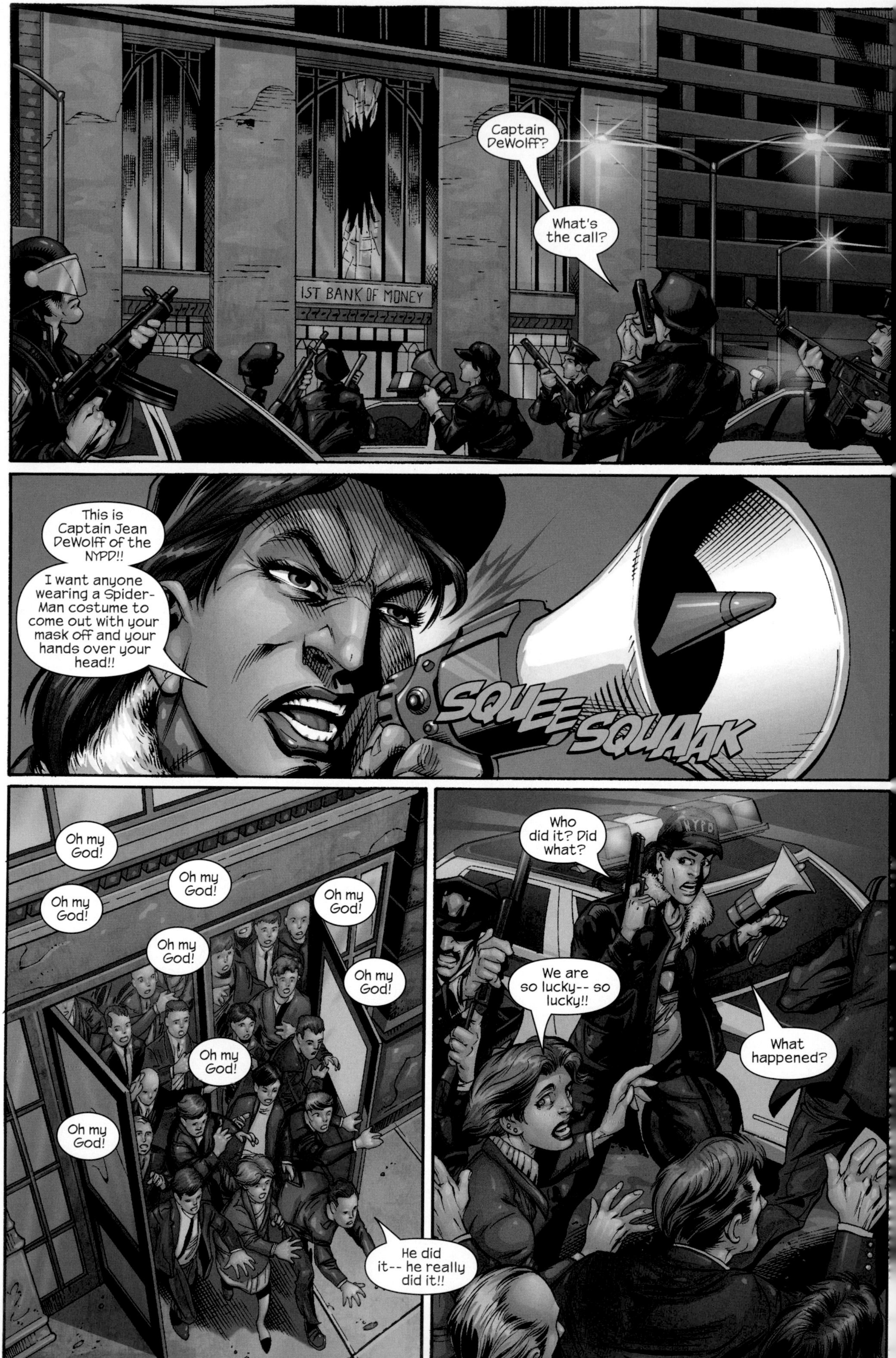
1ST BANK OF MONEY
Captain DeWolff?
What's the call?
This is Captain Jean DeWolff of the NYPD!!
I want anyone wearing a Spider-Man costume to come out with your mask off and your hands over your head!!
SQUEE SQUAAAK
Oh my God!
Oh my God!
Oh my God!
Oh my God!
Oh my God!
Oh my God!
Oh my God!
Oh my God!
He did it-- he really did it!!
Who did it? Did what?
We are so lucky-- so lucky!!
What happened?

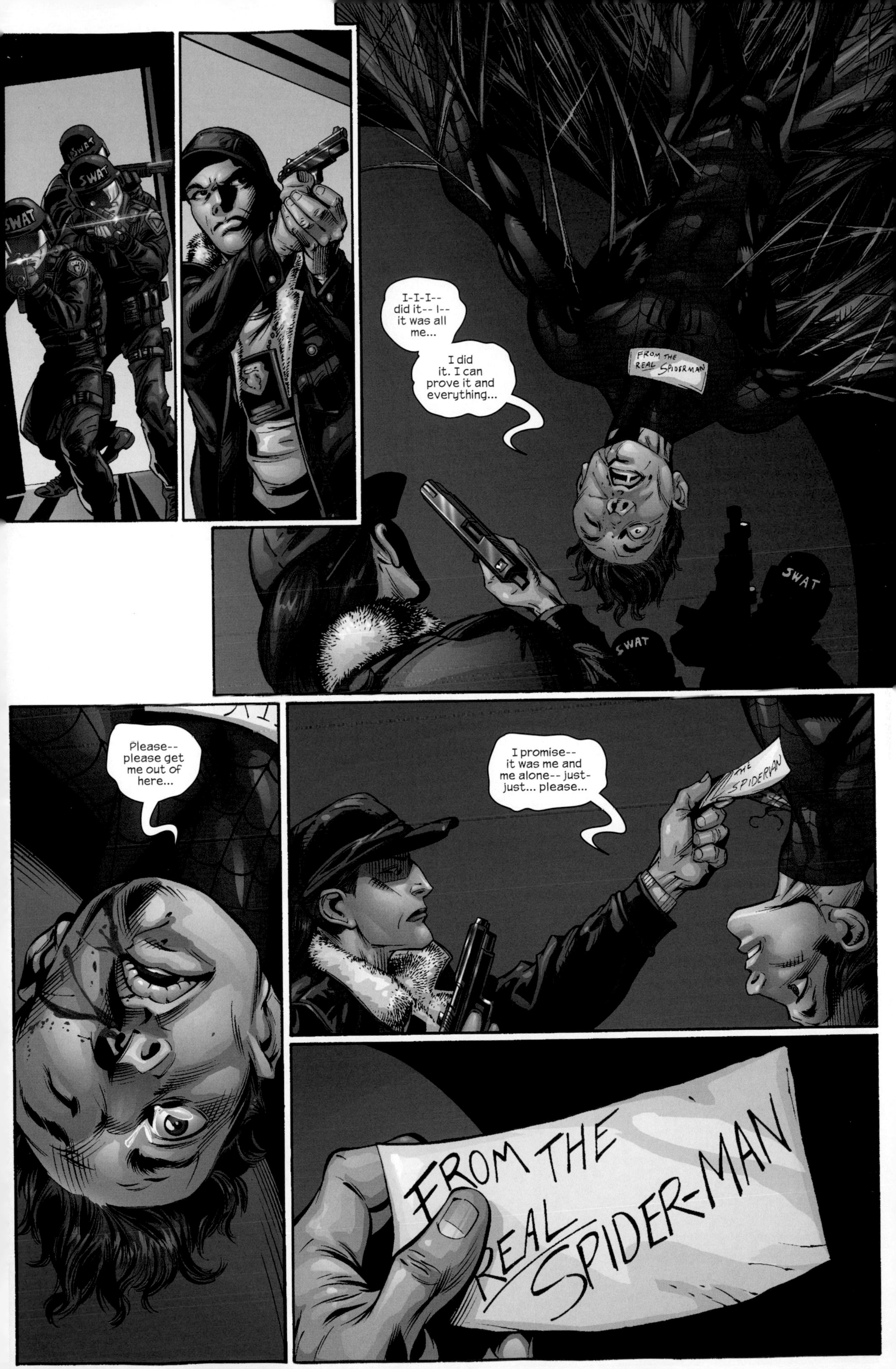
I-I-I-- did it-- I-- it was all me...
I did it. I can prove it and everything...
FROM THE REAL SPIDERMAN
Please-- please get me out of here...
I promise-- it was me and me alone-- just-- just... please...
FROM THE REAL SPIDER-MAN

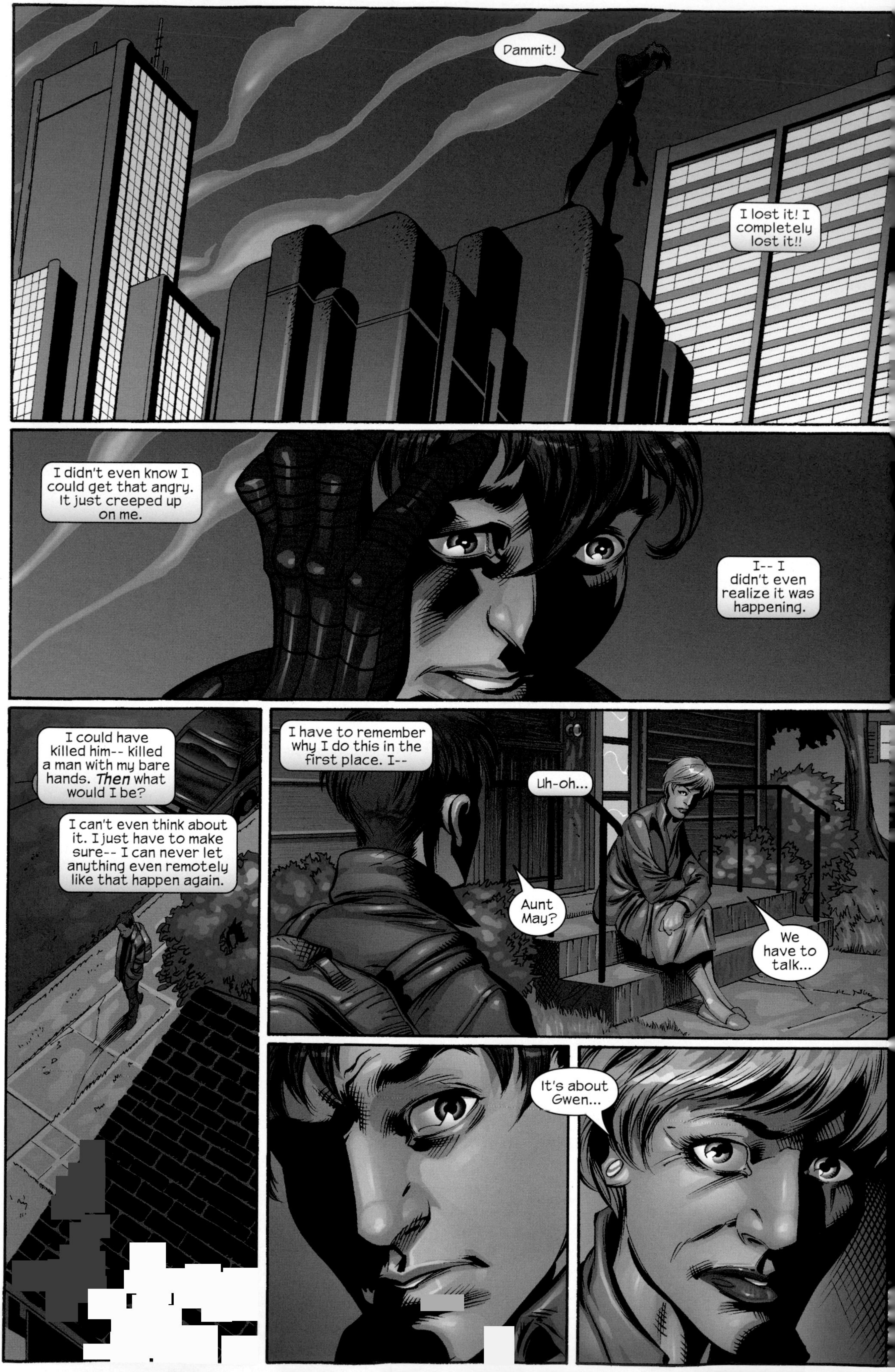
Dammit!
I lost it! I completely lost it!!
I didn't even know I could get that angry. It just creeped up on me.
I-- I didn't even realize it was happening.
I could have killed him-- killed a man with my bare hands. *Then* what would I be?
I can't even think about it. I just have to make sure-- I can never let anything even remotely like that happen again.
I have to remember why I do this in the first place. I--
Uh-oh...
Aunt May?
We have to talk...
It's about Gwen...

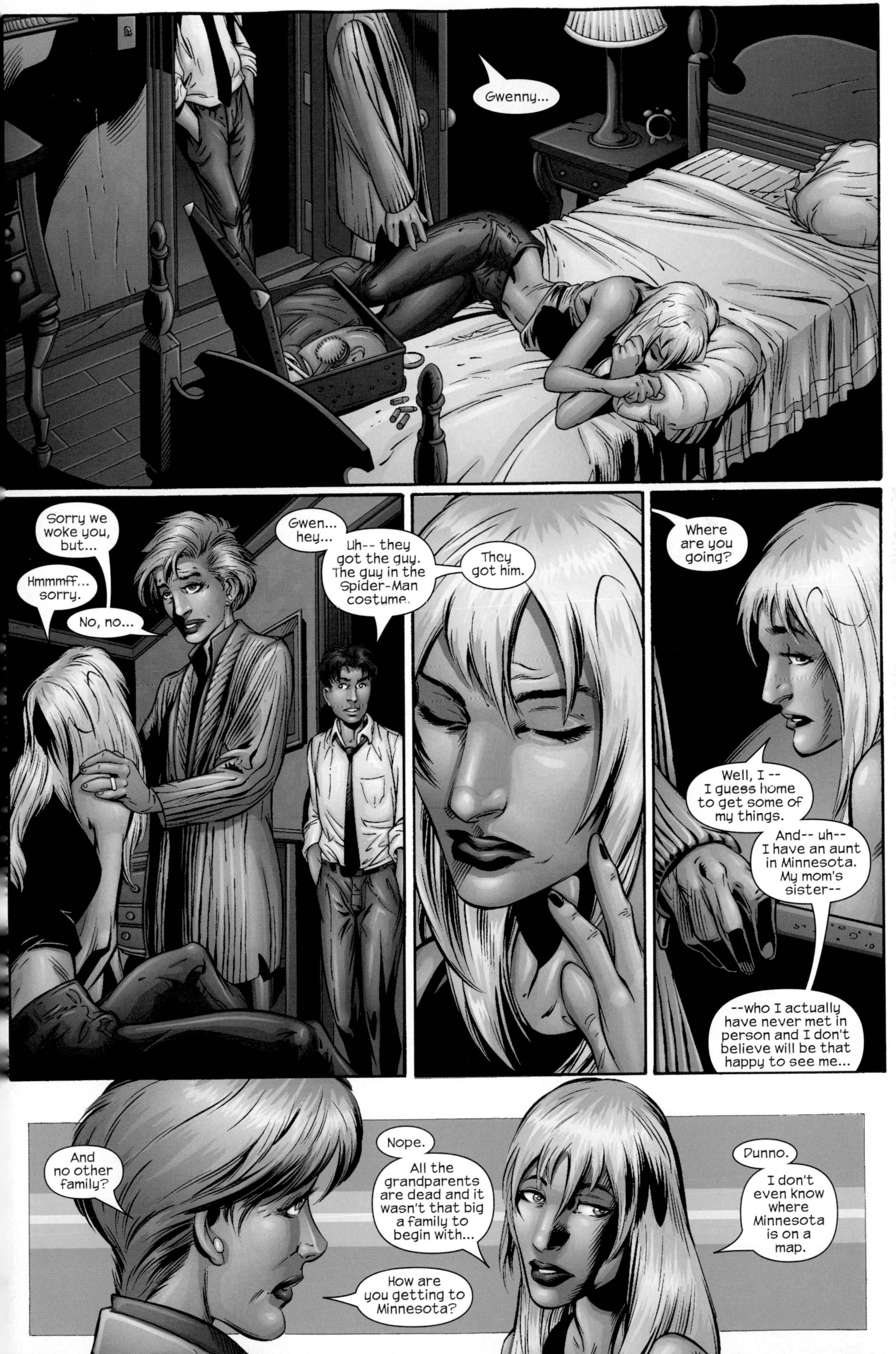
Gwenny...
Sorry we woke you, but...
Hmmmff... sorry.
No, no...
Gwen... hey...
Uh-- they got the guy. The guy in the Spider-Man costume.
They got him.
Where are you going?
Well, I -- I guess home to get some of my things.
And-- uh-- I have an aunt in Minnesota. My mom's sister--
--who I actually have never met in person and I don't believe will be that happy to see me...
And no other family?
Nope.
All the grandparents are dead and it wasn't that big a family to begin with...
How are you getting to Minnesota?
Dunno.
I don't even know where Minnesota is on a map.

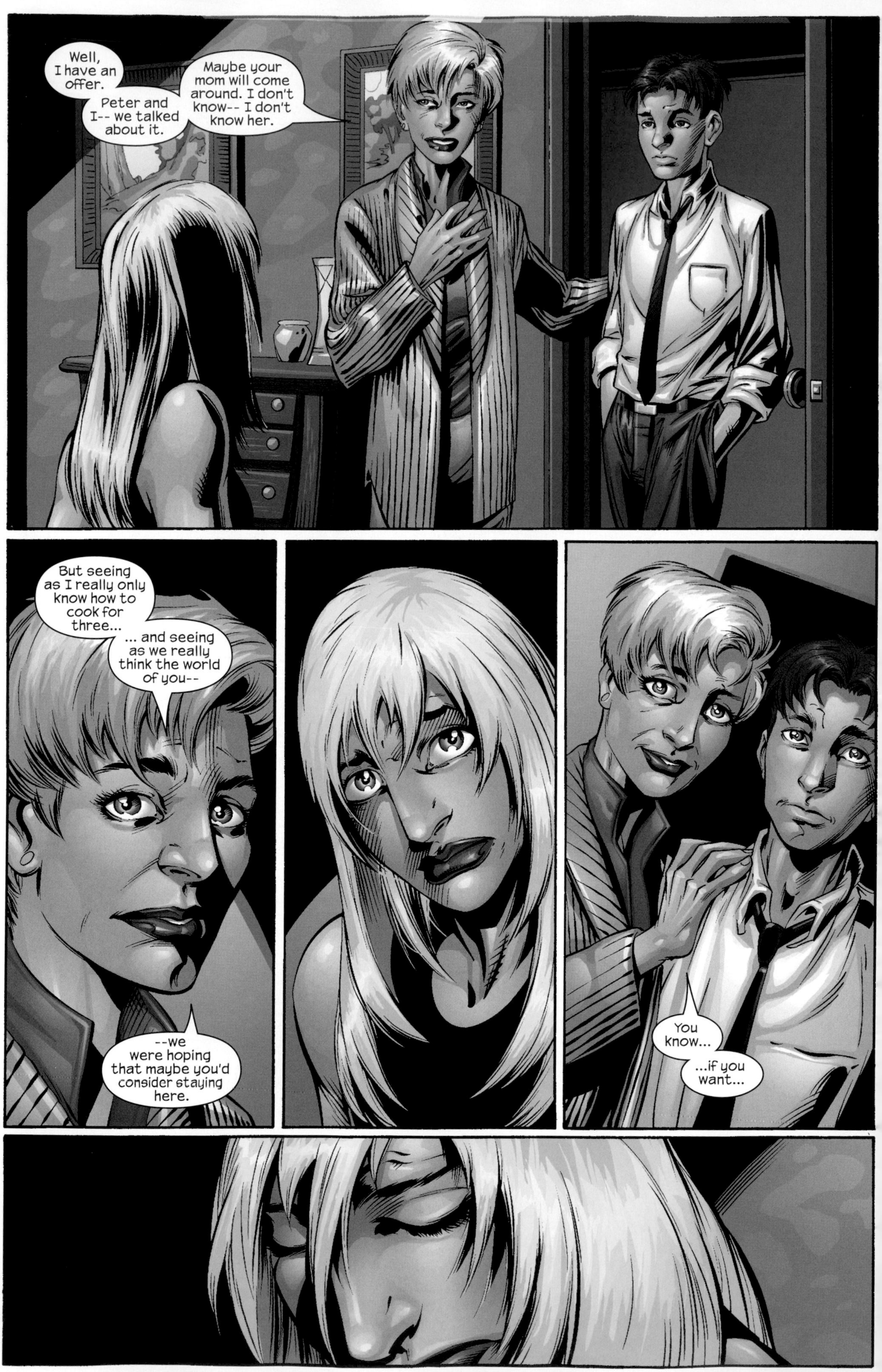
Well, I have an offer.
Peter and I-- we talked about it.
Maybe your mom will come around. I don't know-- I don't know her.
But seeing as I really only know how to cook for three...
... and seeing as we really think the world of you--
--we were hoping that maybe you'd consider staying here.
You know...
...if you want...

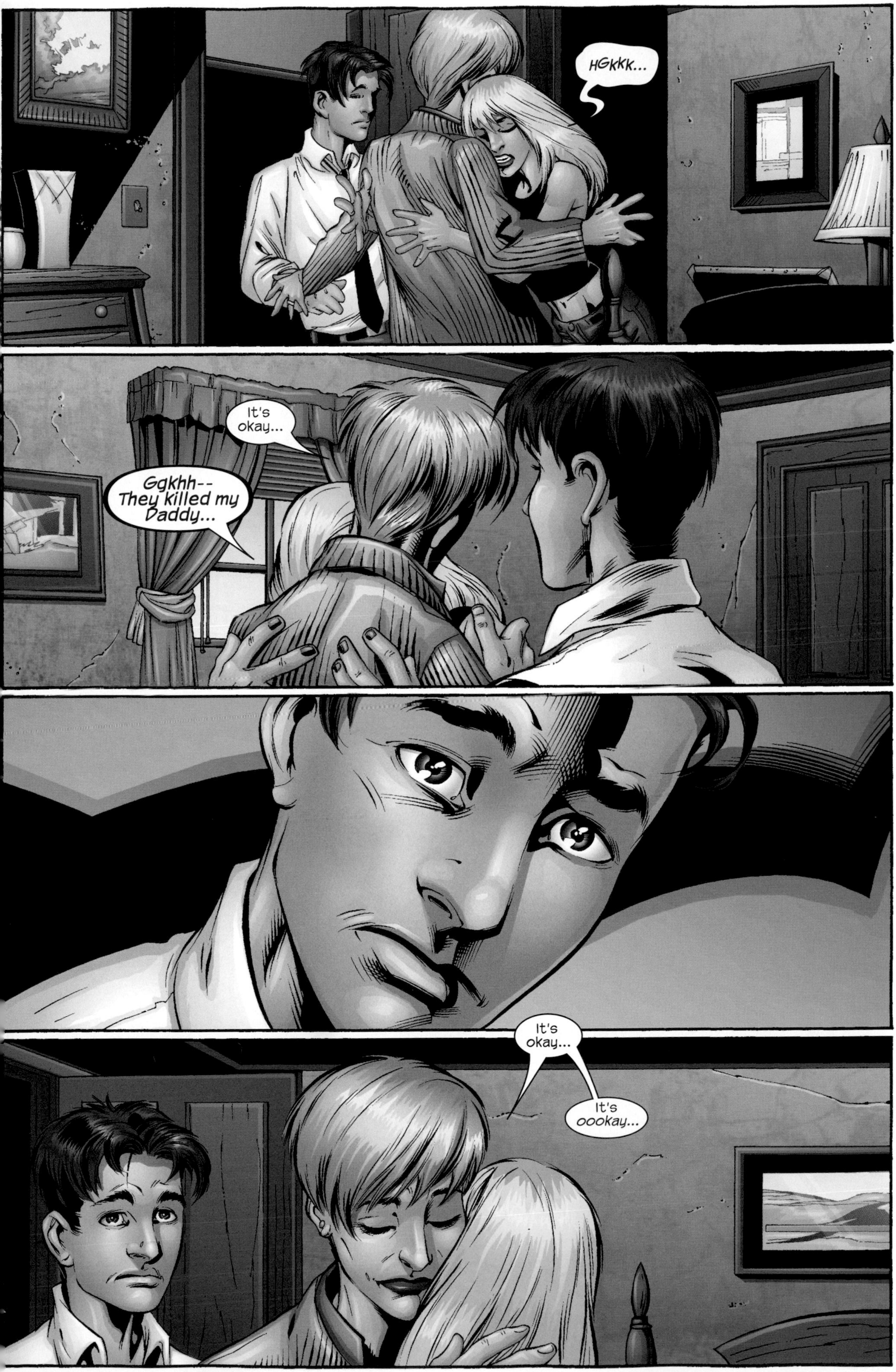
HGKKK...
It's okay...
Ggkhh-- They killed my Daddy...
It's okay...
It's oookay...

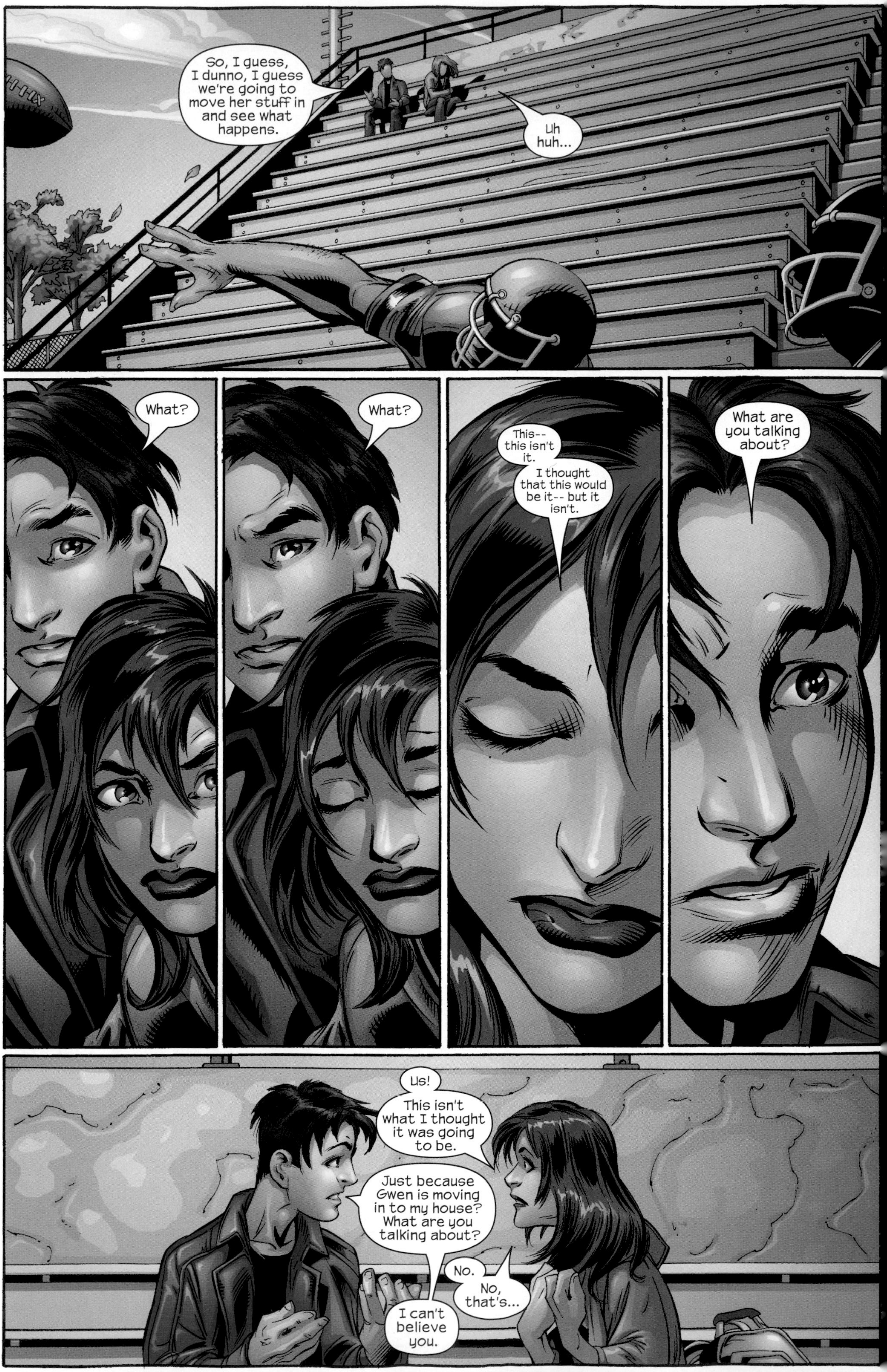
So, I guess, I dunno, I guess we're going to move her stuff in and see what happens.
Uh huh...
What?
What?
This-- this isn't it.
I thought that this would be it-- but it isn't.
What are you talking about?
Us!
This isn't what I thought it was going to be.
Just because Gwen is moving in to my house? What are you talking about?
No.
No, that's...
I can't believe you.

How about because I wake up in the middle of the night-- --every night-- --crying! Did you know that?

I have nightmares, Peter! Horrible nightmares that you *die!*

You die-- or-- or-- or-- or I die.

Every night!

Do you know that I relive the bridge thing?

Sometimes-- sometimes it happens when I'm awake-- right in the middle of class.

I keep reliving the moment-- the exact moment when I was just thrown-- tossed-- off the top of the Queensborough bridge!

I am sitting in class and-- and-- and-- I'll start falling.

At first it-- it was cool.

My boyfriend is a super hero.

Oh, my God-- my boyfriend...

But, Peter-- you're going to die doing this.

You're going to die in that stupid costume!

And I know that there is nothing I can say to stop you from doing it.

But I never in a million years imagined that I would be tossed off a bridge by a maniac or-- or-- or wiping your *gunshot blood* off my clothes so my mom doesn't see it

Someone is going to *kill* you.

I-I-I-I can't do this.

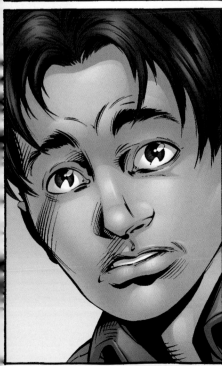

‡Sniff‡

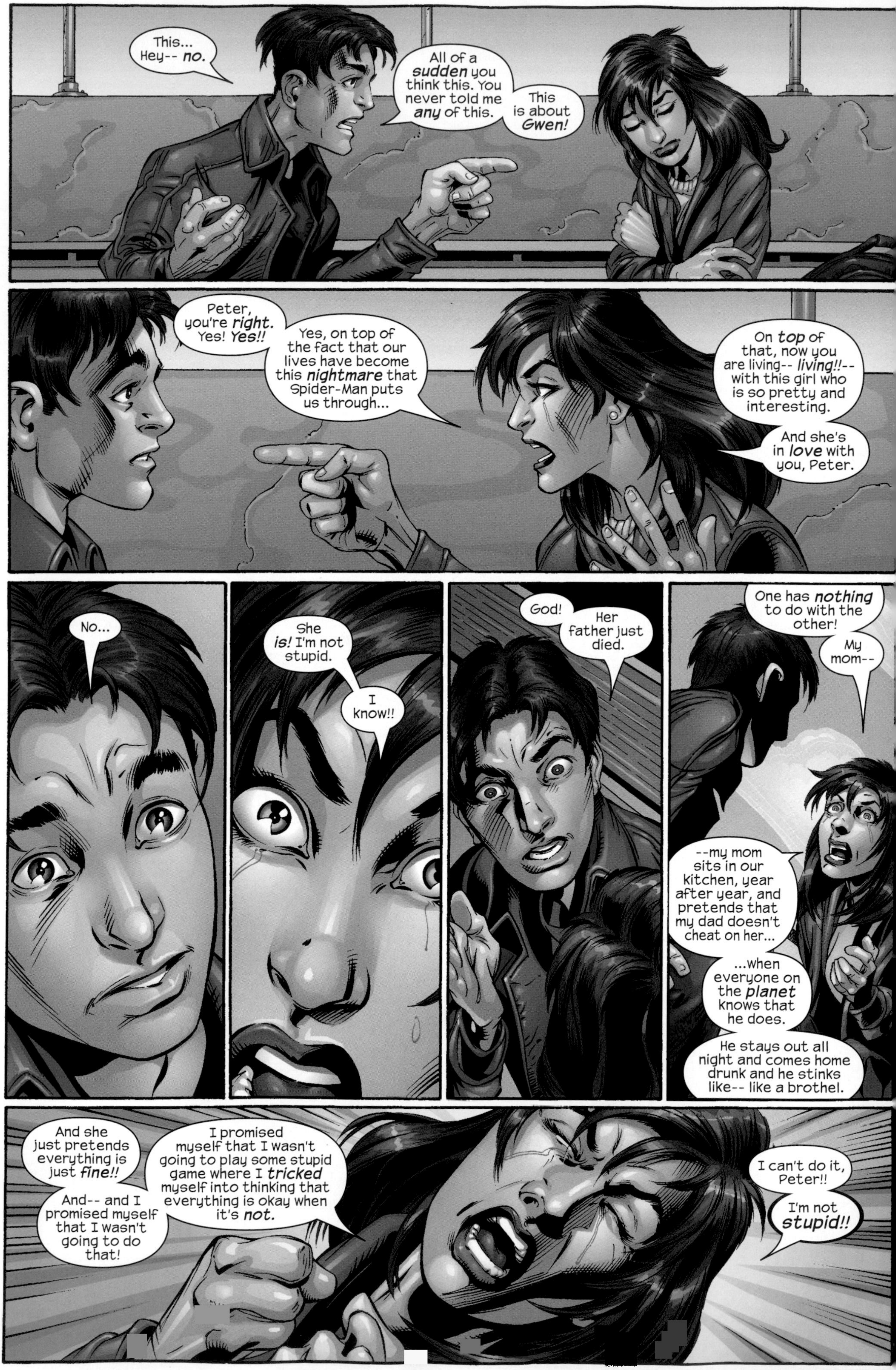
This... Hey-- *no.*
All of a *sudden* you think this. You never told me *any* of this.
This is about *Gwen!*
Peter, you're *right.* Yes! *Yes!!*
Yes, on top of the fact that our lives have become this *nightmare* that Spider-Man puts us through...
On *top* of that, now you are living-- *living!!*-- with this girl who is so pretty and interesting.
And she's in *love* with you, Peter.
No...
She *is!* I'm not stupid.
I know!!
God!
Her father just died.
One has *nothing* to do with the other!
My mom--
--my mom sits in our kitchen, year after year, and pretends that my dad doesn't cheat on her...
...when everyone on the *planet* knows that he does.
He stays out all night and comes home drunk and he stinks like-- like a brothel.
And she just pretends everything is just *fine!!*
And-- and I promised myself that I wasn't going to do that!
I promised myself that I wasn't going to play some stupid game where I *tricked* myself into thinking that everything is okay when it's *not.*
I can't do it, Peter!!
I'm not *stupid!!*

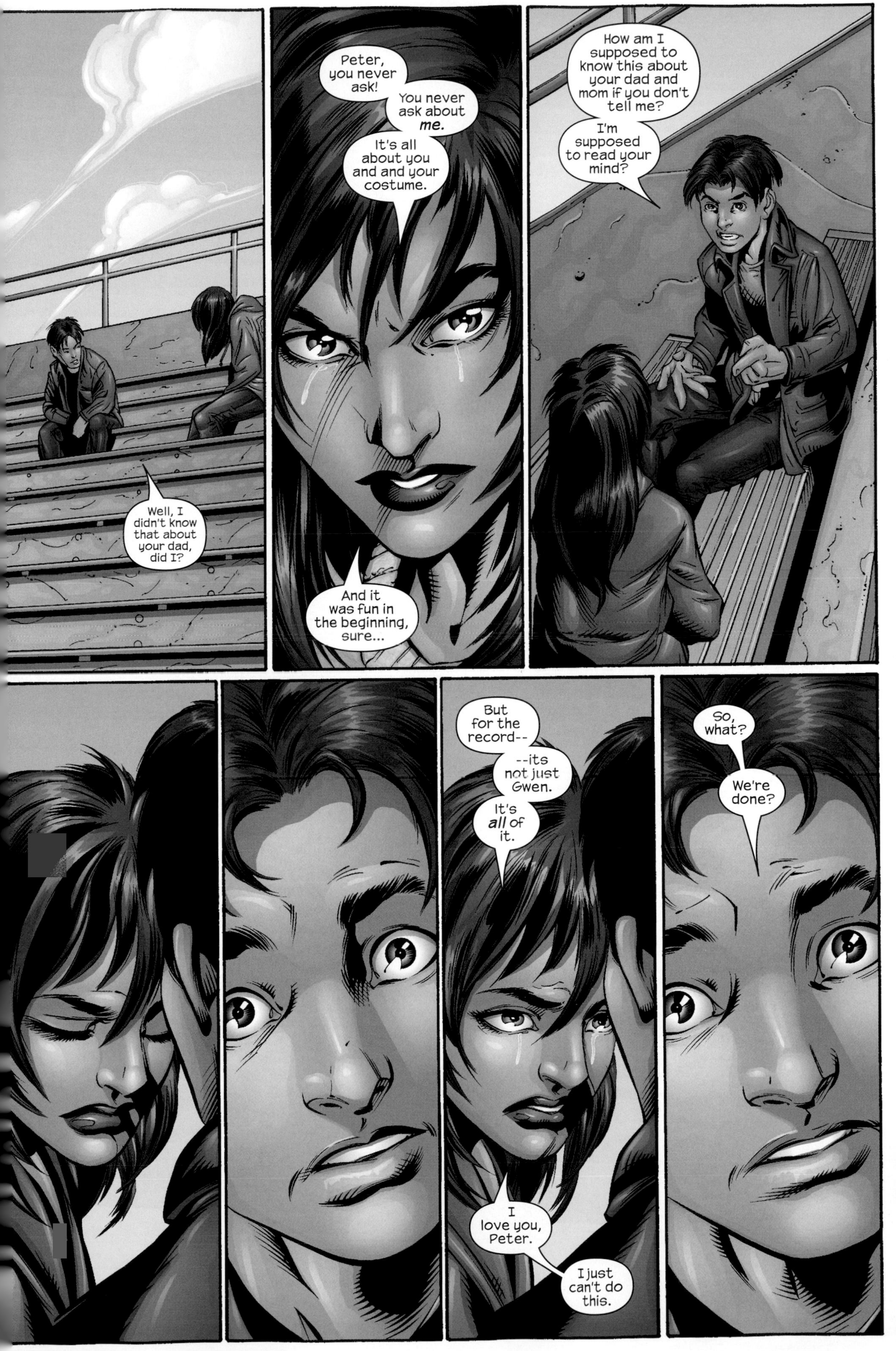
Well, I didn't know that about your dad, did I?
Peter, you never ask!
You never ask about *me.*
It's all about you and and your costume.
And it was fun in the beginning, sure...
How am I supposed to know this about your dad and mom if you don't tell me?
I'm supposed to read your mind?
But for the record--
--its not just Gwen.
It's *all* of it.
I love you, Peter.
I just can't do this.
So, what?
We're done?

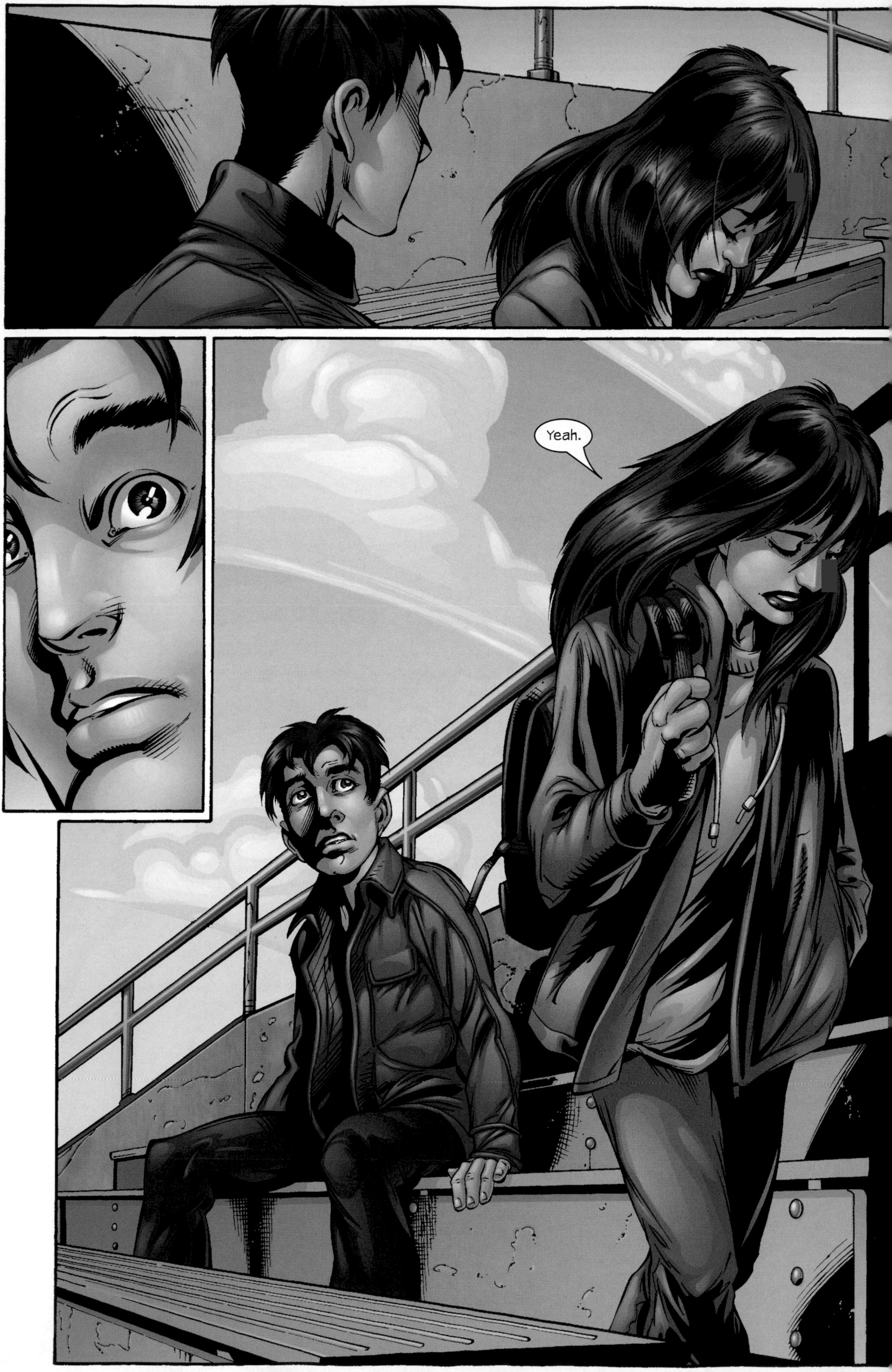
Yeah.

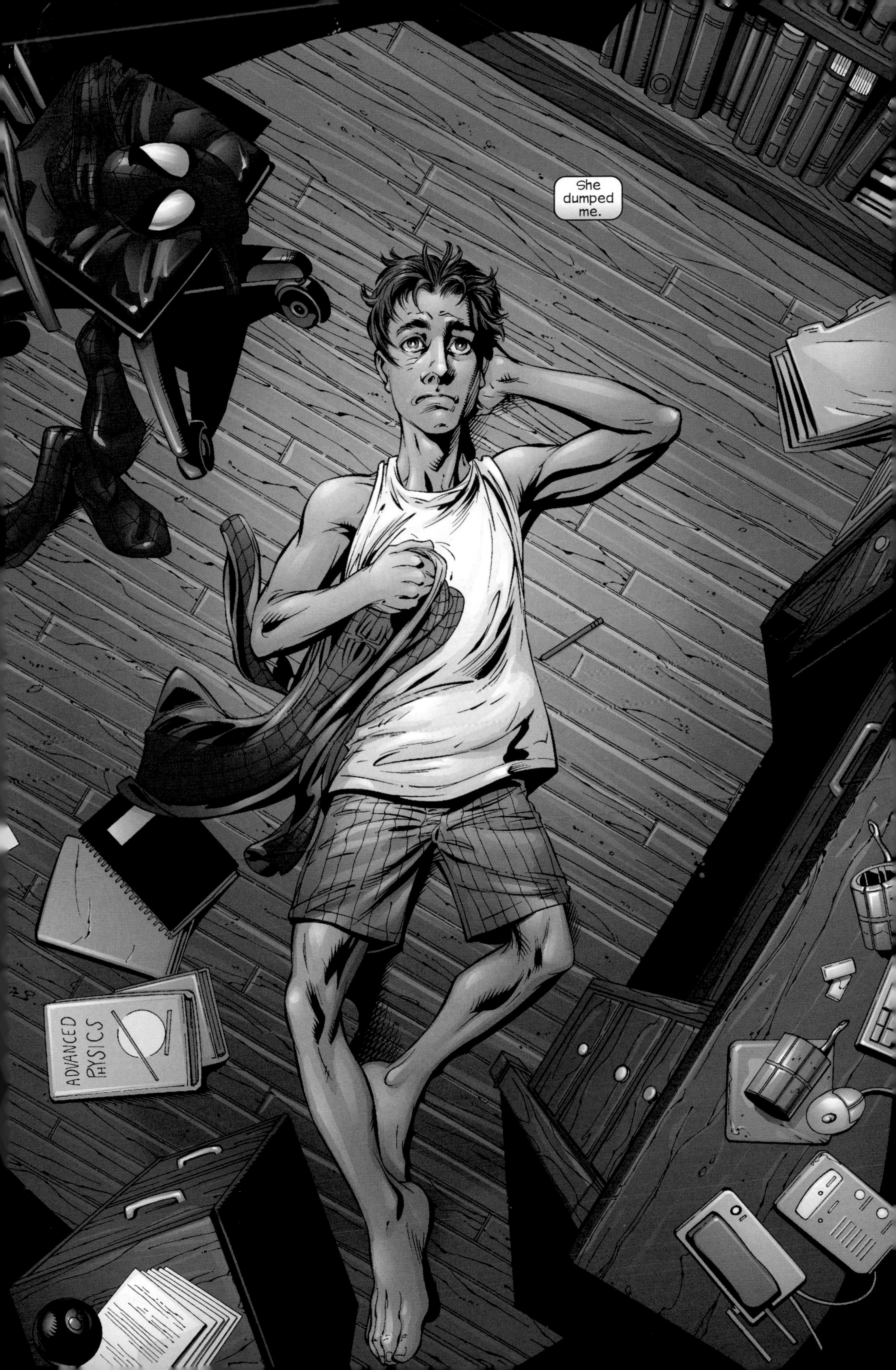
She dumped me.
ADVANCED PHYSICS

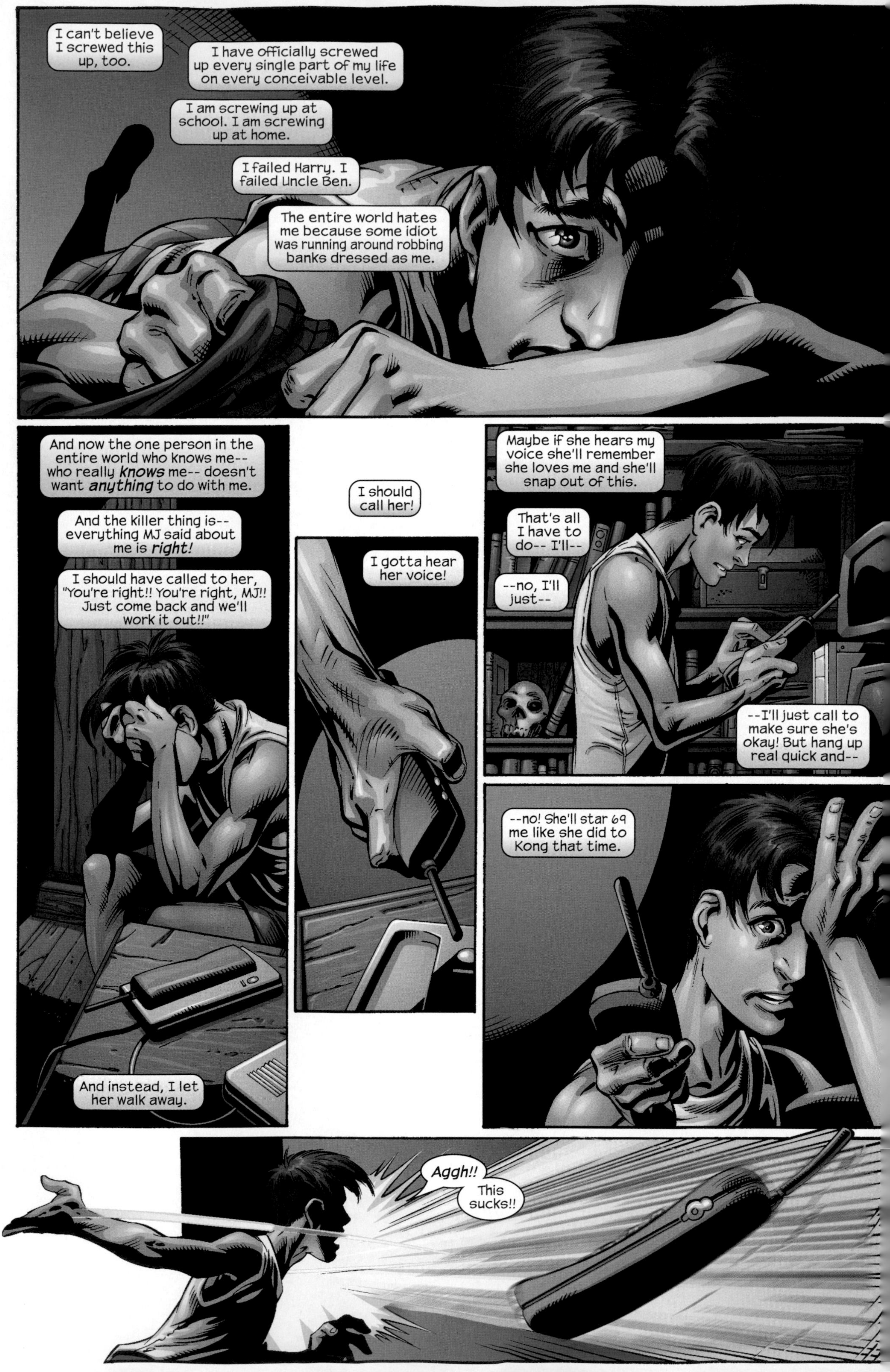
I can't believe I screwed this up, too.
I have officially screwed up every single part of my life on every conceivable level.
I am screwing up at school. I am screwing up at home.
I failed Harry. I failed Uncle Ben.
The entire world hates me because some idiot was running around robbing banks dressed as me.
And now the one person in the entire world who knows me-- who really *knows* me-- doesn't want *anything* to do with me.
And the killer thing is-- everything MJ said about me is *right!*
I should have called to her, "You're right!! You're right, MJ!! Just come back and we'll work it out!!"
And instead, I let her walk away.
I should call her!
I gotta hear her voice!
Maybe if she hears my voice she'll remember she loves me and she'll snap out of this.
That's all I have to do-- I'll--
--no, I'll just--
--I'll just call to make sure she's okay! But hang up real quick and--
--no! She'll star 69 me like she did to Kong that time.
Aggh!!
This sucks!!

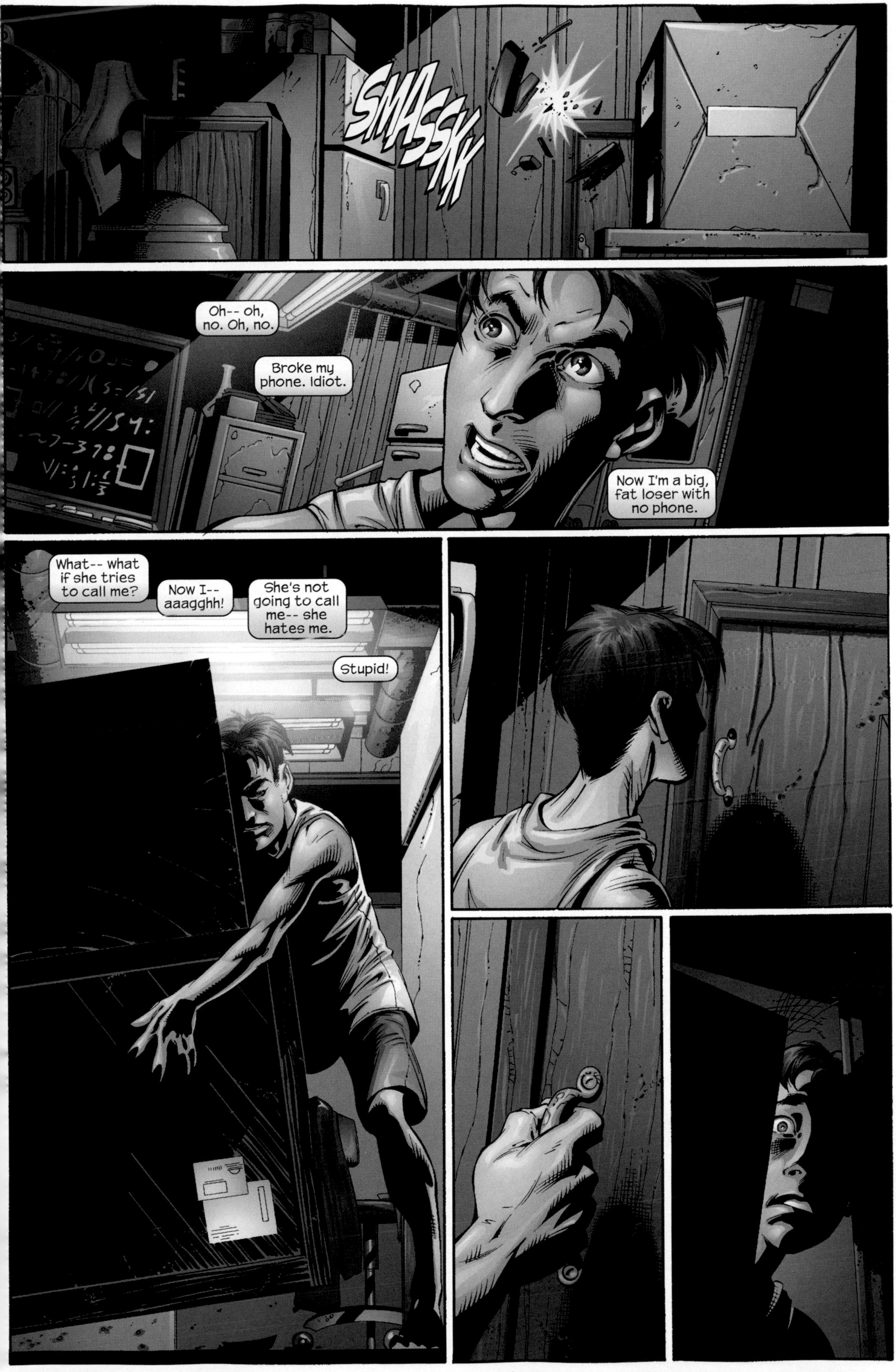
SMASSKK
Oh-- oh, no. Oh, no.
Broke my phone. Idiot.
Now I'm a big, fat loser with no phone.
What-- what if she tries to call me?
Now I-- aaagghh!
She's not going to call me-- she hates me.
Stupid!

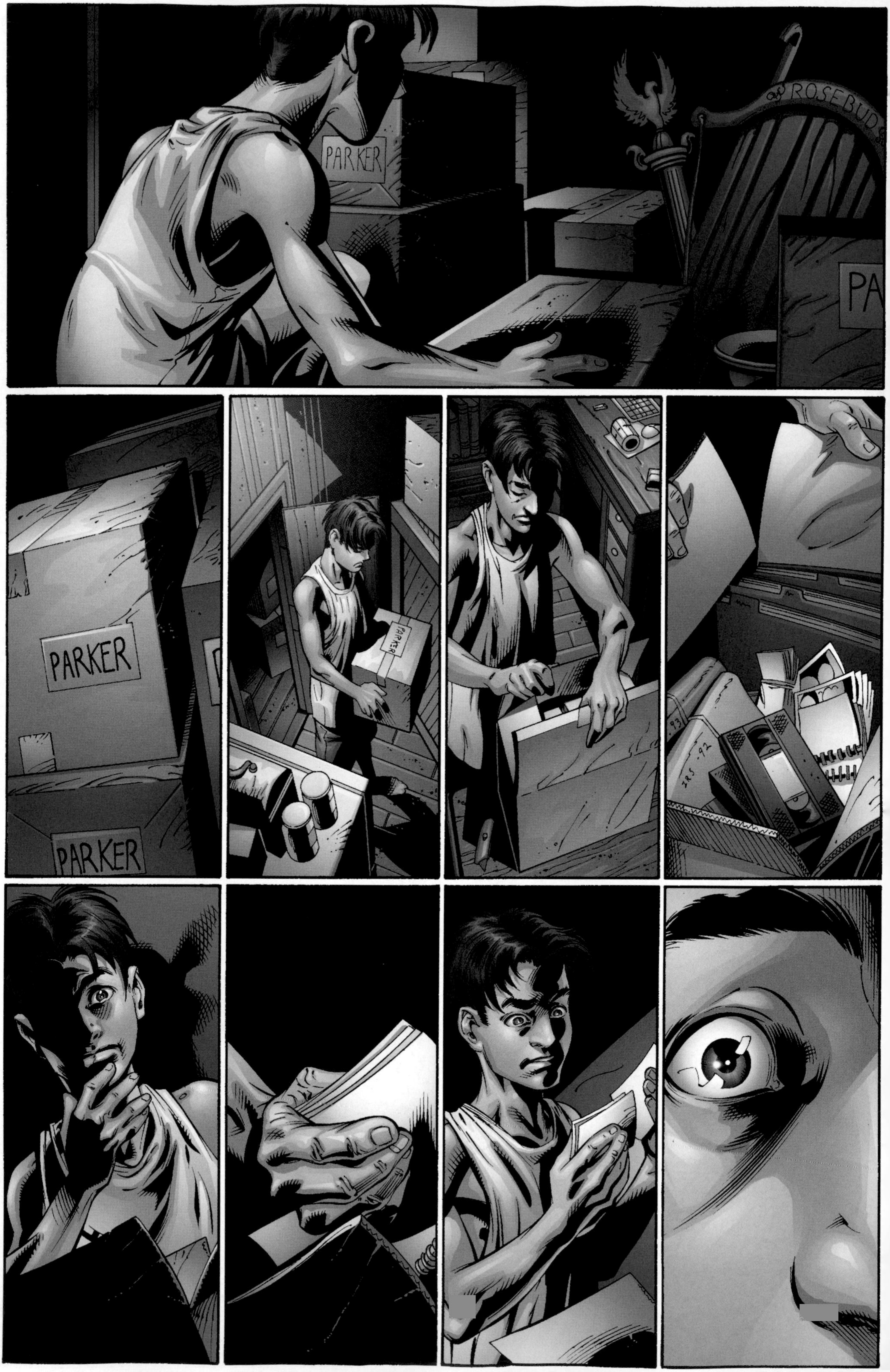
ROSEBUD
PARKER
PARKER
PARKER
PARKER
PARKER

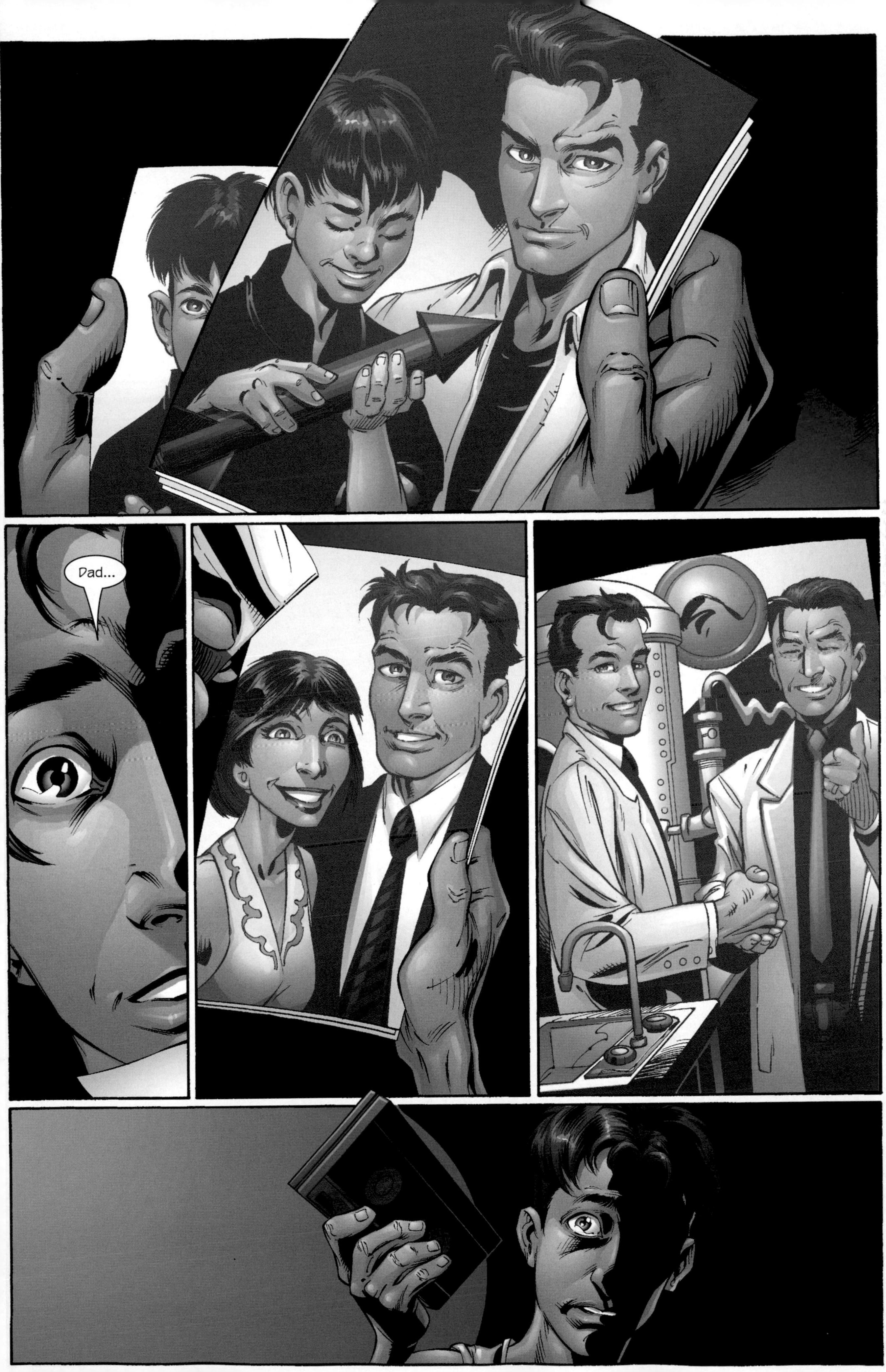
Dad...

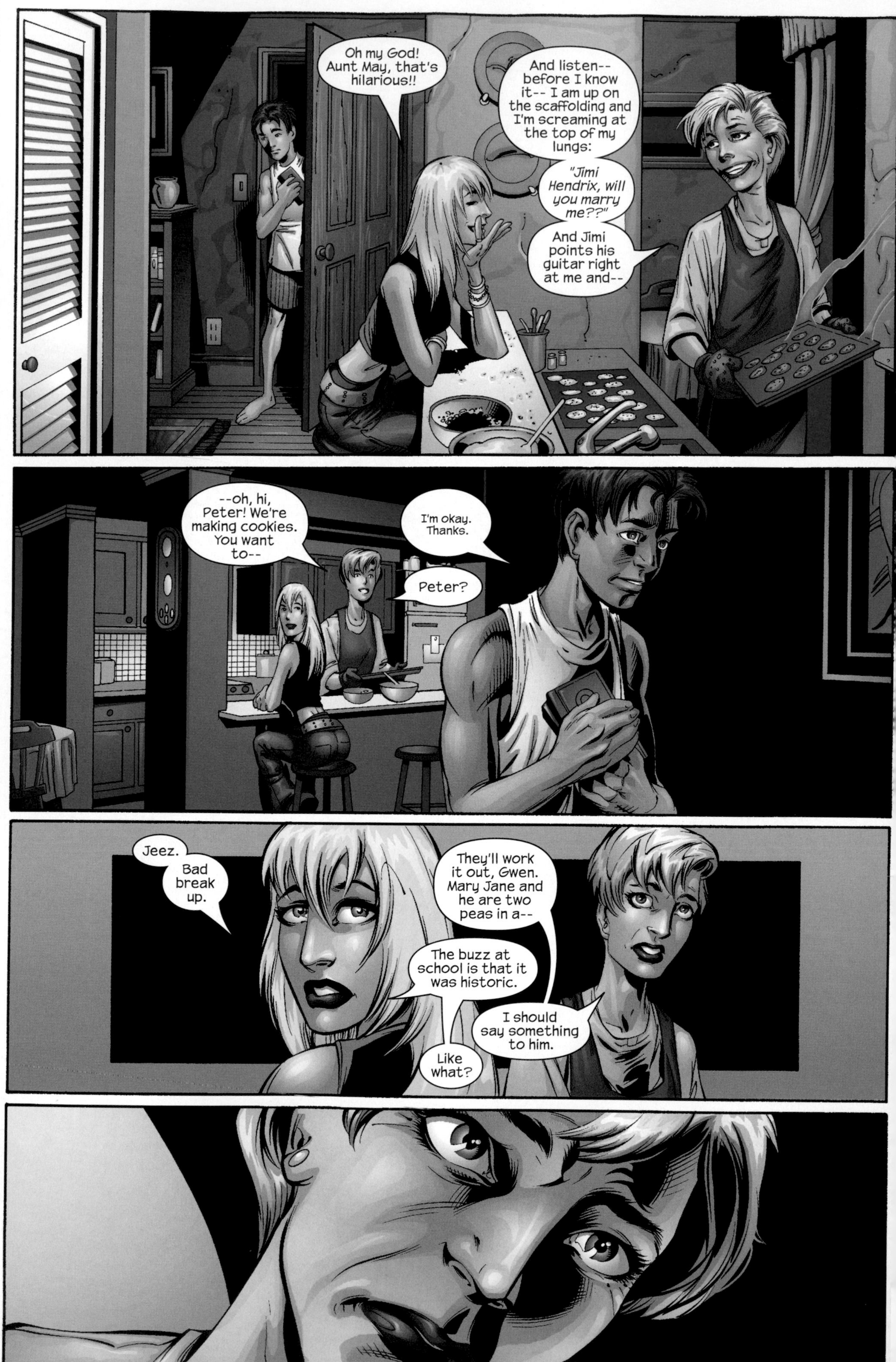
Oh my God! Aunt May, that's hilarious!!
And listen-- before I know it-- I am up on the scaffolding and I'm screaming at the top of my lungs:
"Jimi Hendrix, will you marry me??"
And Jimi points his guitar right at me and--
--oh, hi, Peter! We're making cookies. You want to--
I'm okay. Thanks.
Peter?
Jeez. Bad break up.
They'll work it out, Gwen. Mary Jane and he are two peas in a--
The buzz at school is that it was historic.
I should say something to him.
Like what?

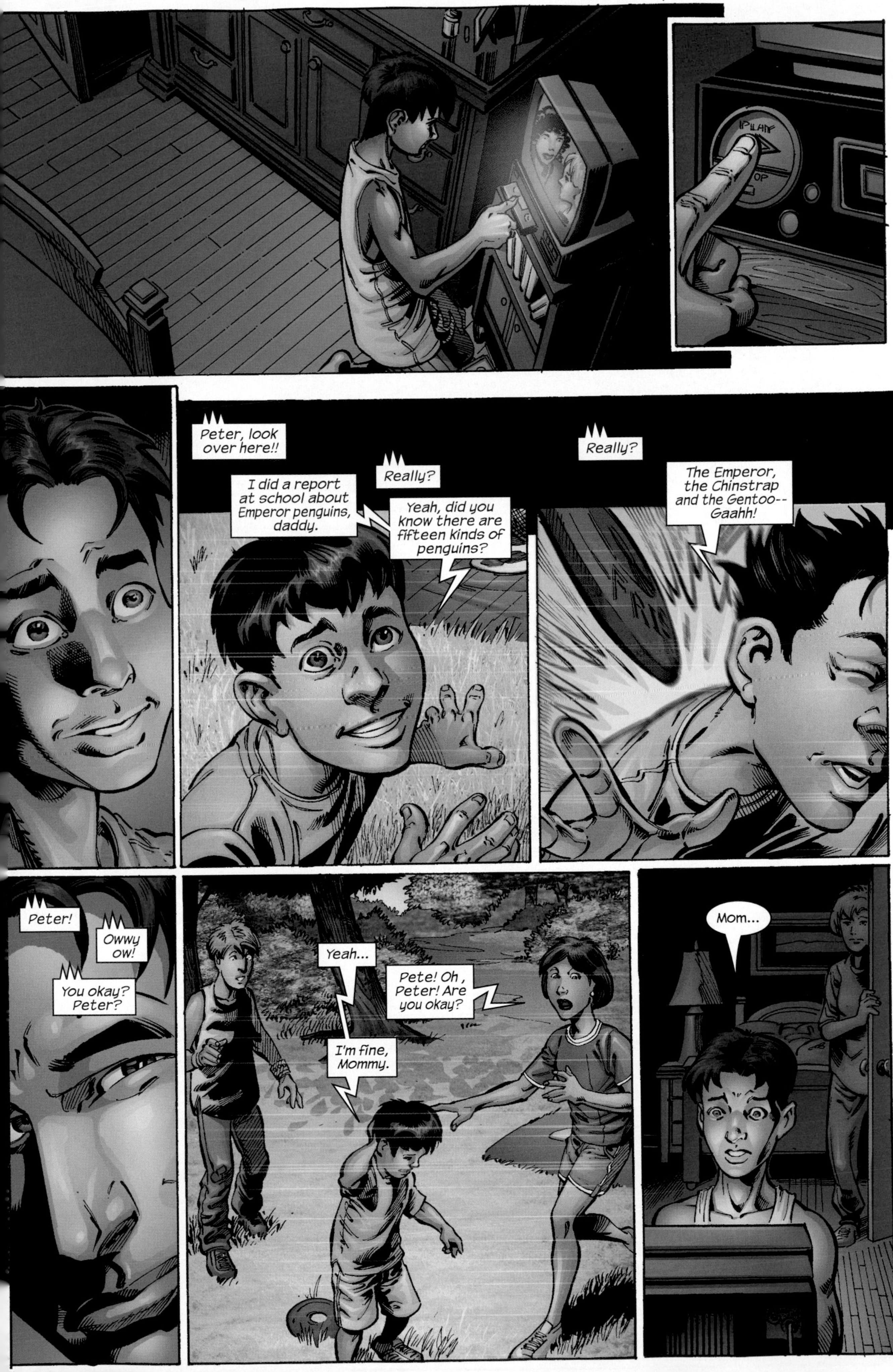

PLAY
Peter, look over here!!
I did a report at school about Emperor penguins, daddy.
Really?
Yeah, did you know there are fifteen kinds of penguins?
Really?
The Emperor, the Chinstrap and the Gentoo-- Gaahh!
Peter!
Owwy ow!
You okay? Peter?
Yeah...
Pete! Oh, Peter! Are you okay?
I'm fine, Mommy.
Mom...

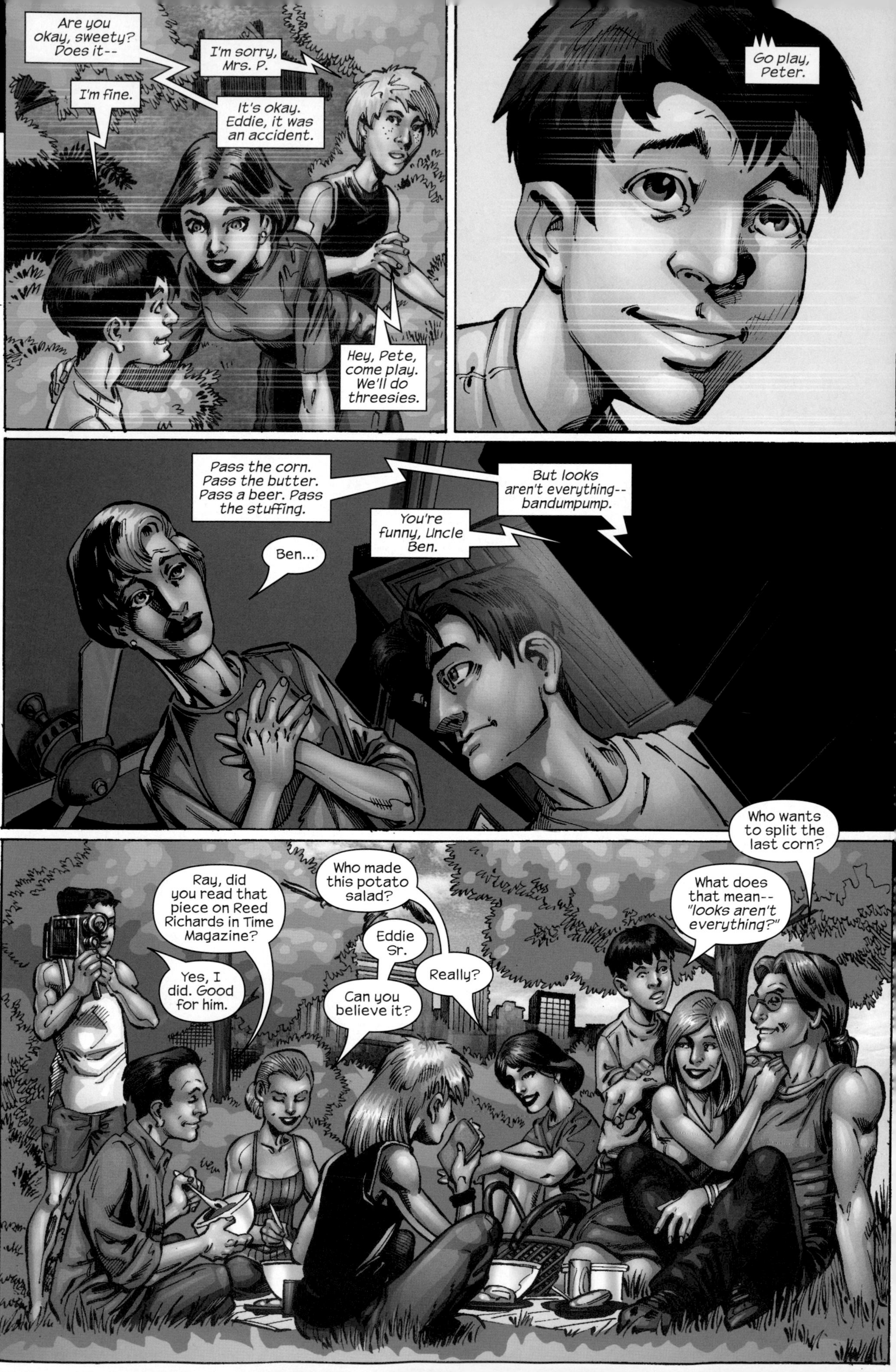
Are you okay, sweety? Does it--
I'm sorry, Mrs. P.
I'm fine.
It's okay. Eddie, it was an accident.
Hey, Pete, come play. We'll do threesies.
Go play, Peter.
Pass the corn. Pass the butter. Pass a beer. Pass the stuffing.
But looks aren't everything-- bandumpump.
You're funny, Uncle Ben.
Ben...
Ray, did you read that piece on Reed Richards in Time Magazine?
Yes, I did. Good for him.
Who made this potato salad?
Eddie Sr.
Really?
Can you believe it?
Who wants to split the last corn?
What does that mean-- "looks aren't everything?"

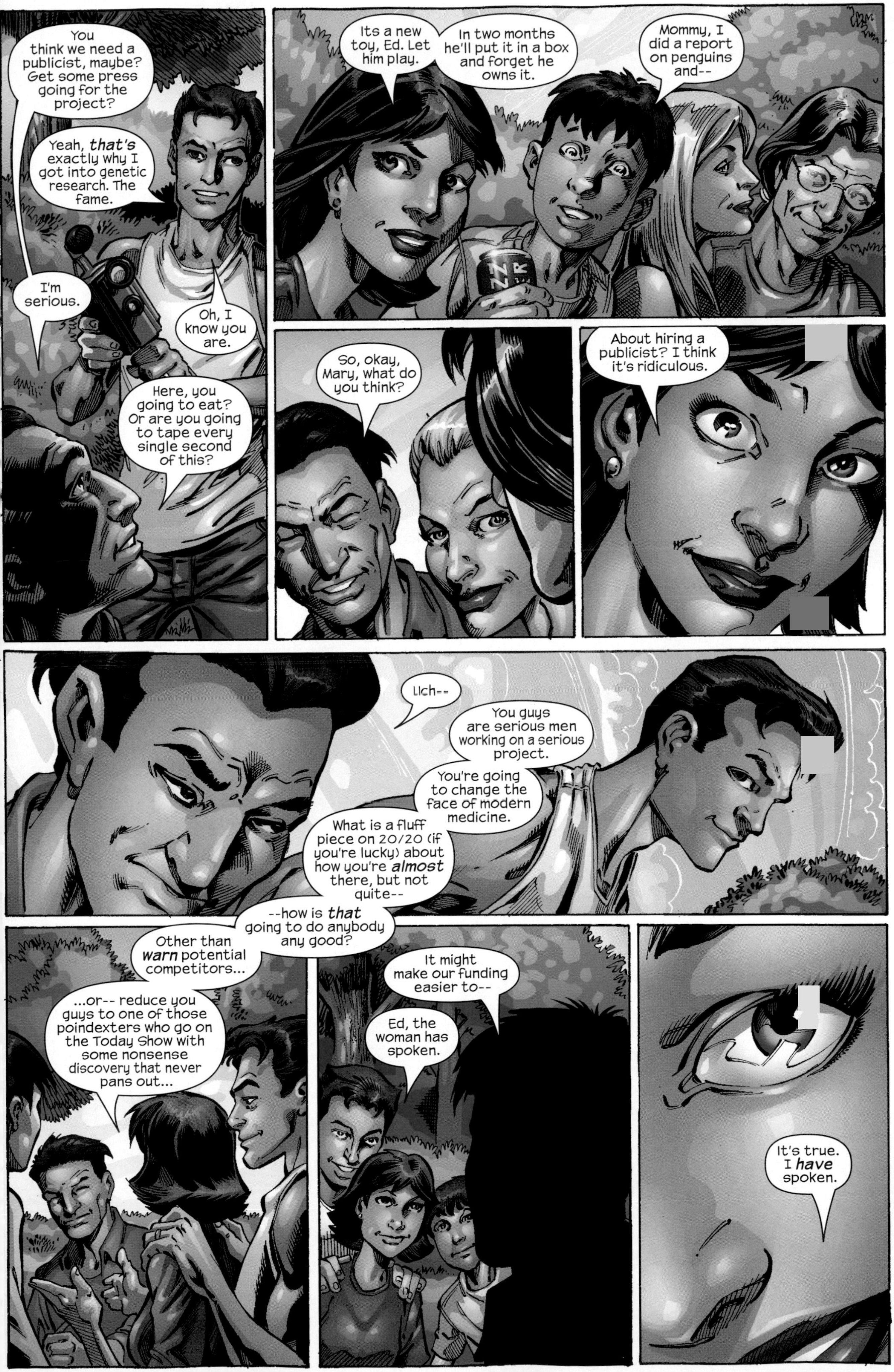
You think we need a publicist, maybe? Get some press going for the project?
Yeah, ***that's*** exactly why I got into genetic research. The fame.
I'm serious.
Oh, I know you are.
Here, you going to eat? Or are you going to tape every single second of this?
Its a new toy, Ed. Let him play.
In two months he'll put it in a box and forget he owns it.
Mommy, I did a report on penguins and--
So, okay, Mary, what do you think?
About hiring a publicist? I think it's ridiculous.
Uch--
You guys are serious men working on a serious project.
You're going to change the face of modern medicine.
What is a fluff piece on 20/20 (if you're lucky) about how you're ***almost*** there, but not quite--
--how is ***that*** going to do anybody any good?
Other than ***warn*** potential competitors...
...or-- reduce you guys to one of those poindexters who go on the Today Show with some nonsense discovery that never pans out...
It might make our funding easier to--
Ed, the woman has spoken.
It's true. I ***have*** spoken.

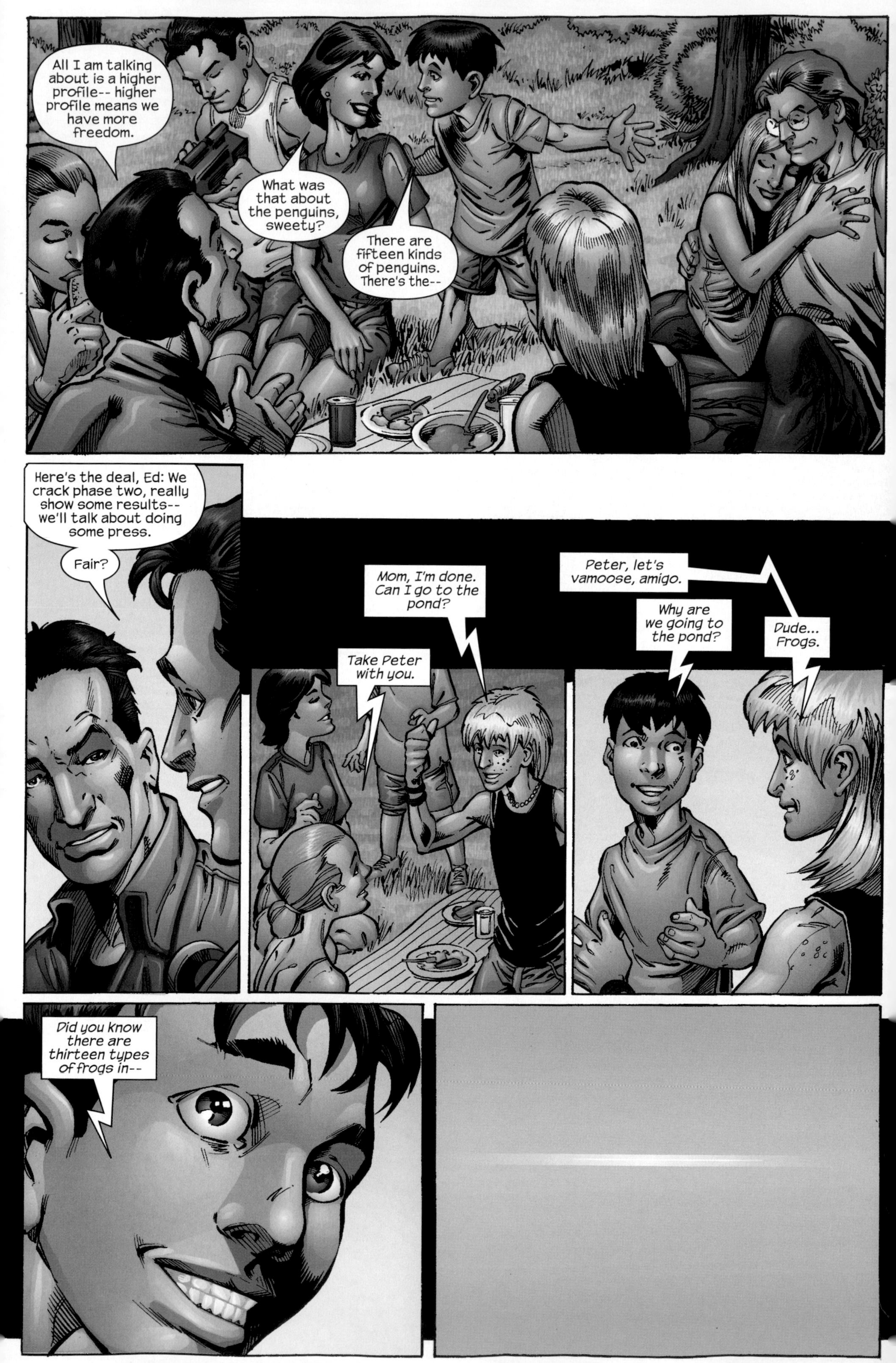

All I am talking about is a higher profile-- higher profile means we have more freedom.
What was that about the penguins, sweety?
There are fifteen kinds of penguins. There's the--
Here's the deal, Ed: We crack phase two, really show some results-- we'll talk about doing some press.
Fair?
Mom, I'm done. Can I go to the pond?
Take Peter with you.
Peter, let's vamoose, amigo.
Why are we going to the pond?
Dude... Frogs.
Did you know there are thirteen types of frogs in--

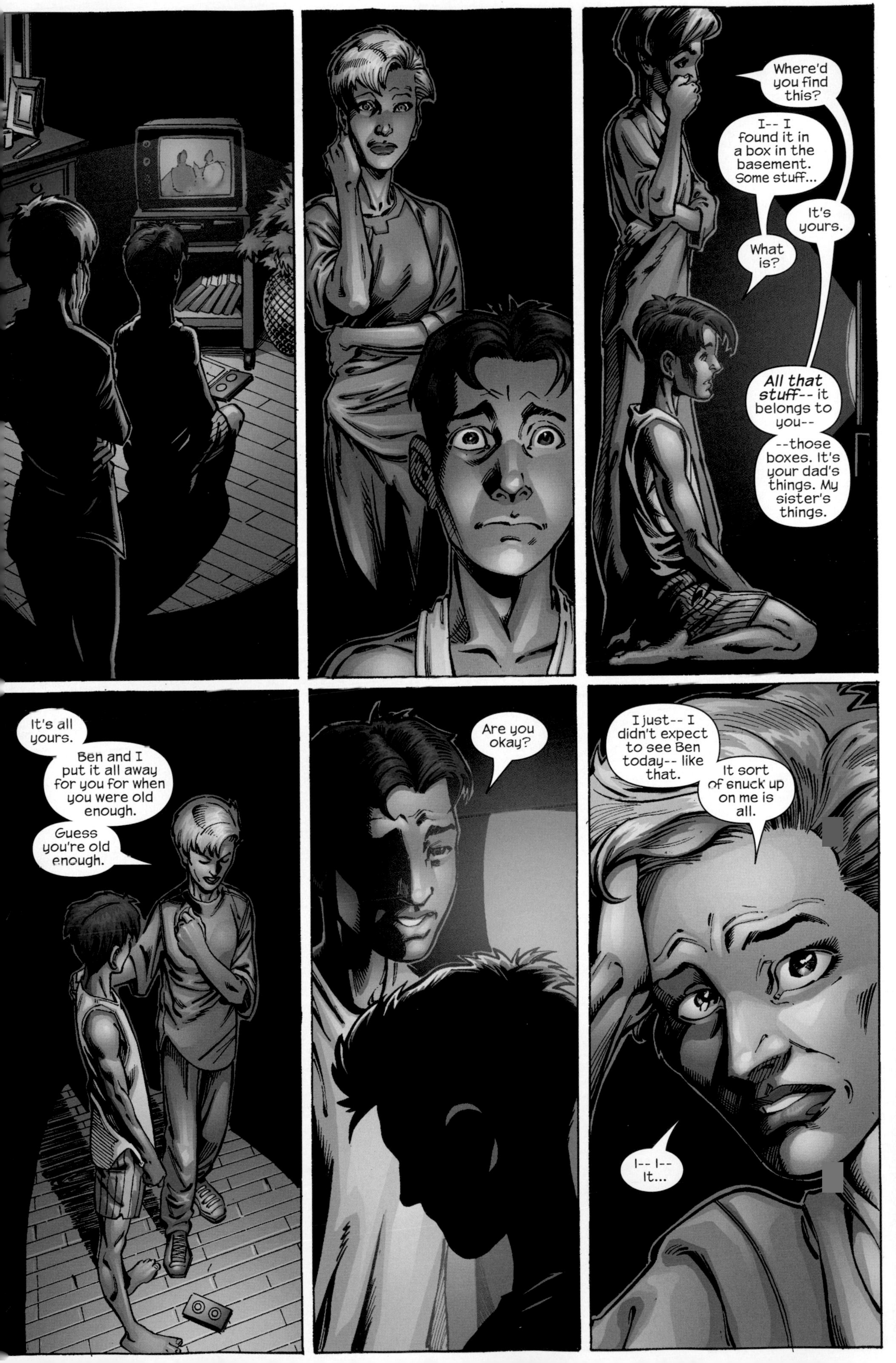
Where'd you find this?
I-- I found it in a box in the basement. Some stuff...
It's yours.
What is?
All that stuff-- it belongs to you--
--those boxes. It's your dad's things. My sister's things.
It's all yours.
Ben and I put it all away for you for when you were old enough.
Guess you're old enough.
Are you okay?
I just-- I didn't expect to see Ben today-- like that.
It sort of snuck up on me is all.
I-- I-- It...

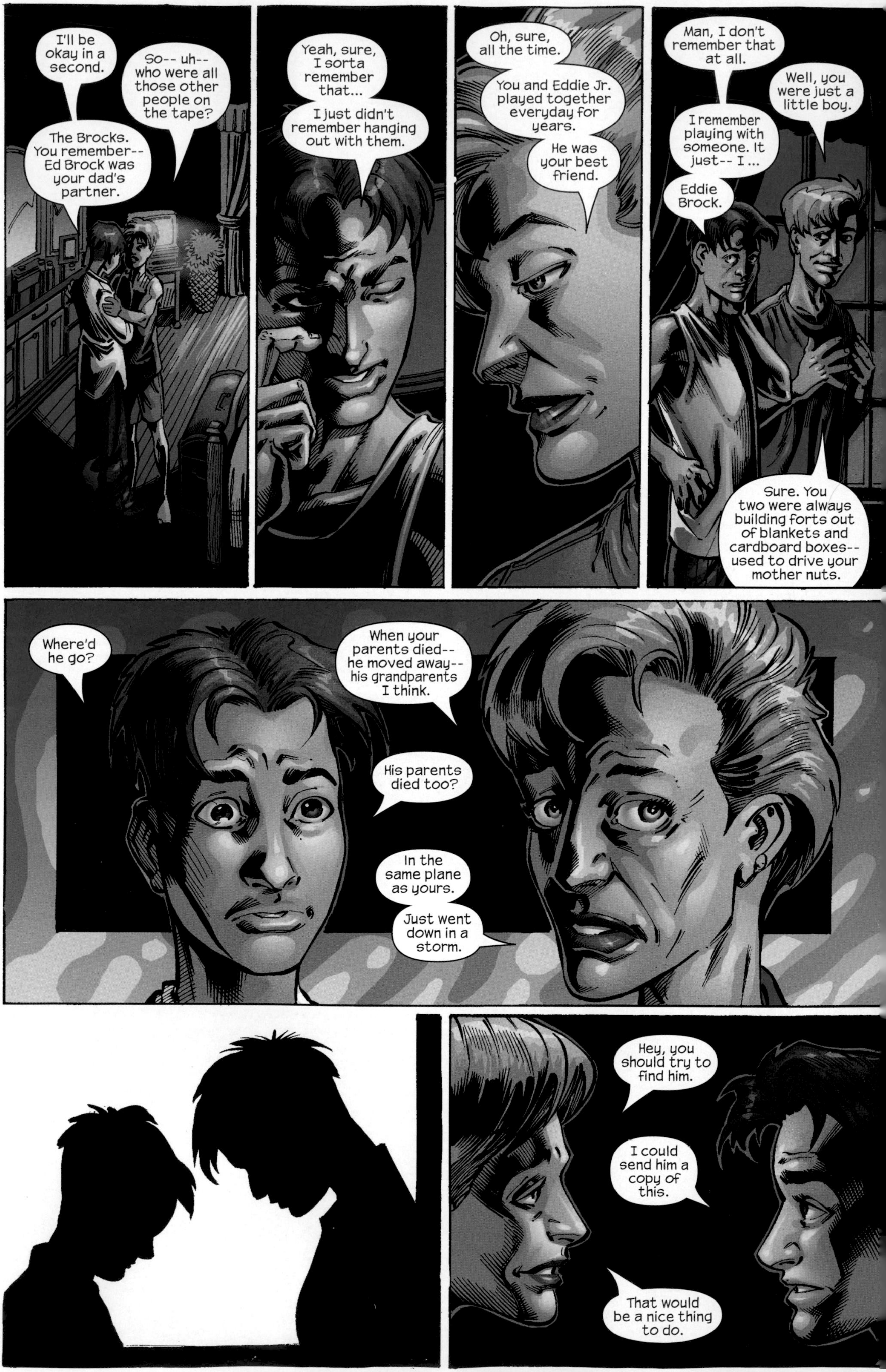

I'll be okay in a second.
So-- uh-- who were all those other people on the tape?
The Brocks. You remember-- Ed Brock was your dad's partner.
Yeah, sure, I sorta remember that...
I just didn't remember hanging out with them.
Oh, sure, all the time.
You and Eddie Jr. played together everyday for years.
He was your best friend.
Man, I don't remember that at all.
Well, you were just a little boy.
I remember playing with someone. It just-- I ...
Eddie Brock.
Sure. You two were always building forts out of blankets and cardboard boxes-- used to drive your mother nuts.
Where'd he go?
When your parents died-- he moved away-- his grandparents I think.
His parents died too?
In the same plane as yours.
Just went down in a storm.
Hey, you should try to find him.
I could send him a copy of this.
That would be a nice thing to do.

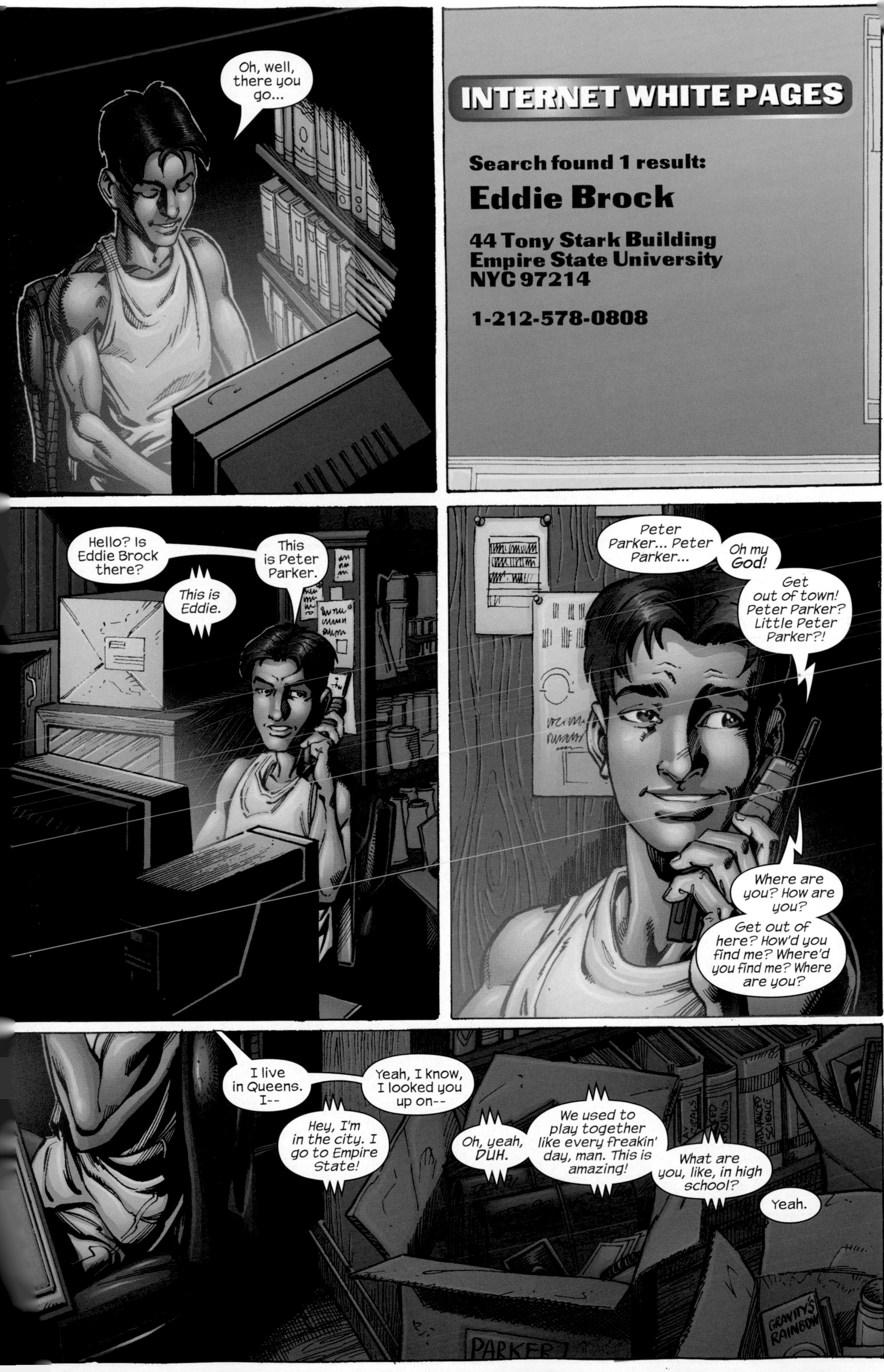
Oh, well, there you go...
INTERNET WHITE PAGES
Search found 1 result:
Eddie Brock
44 Tony Stark Building
Empire State University
NYC 97214
1-212-578-0808
Hello? Is Eddie Brock there?
This is Peter Parker.
This is Eddie.
Peter Parker... Peter Parker...
Oh my God!
Get out of town! Peter Parker? Little Peter Parker?!
Where are you? How are you?
Get out of here? How'd you find me? Where'd you find me? Where are you?
I live in Queens. I--
Yeah, I know, I looked you up on--
Hey, I'm in the city. I go to Empire State!
Oh, yeah, DUH.
We used to play together like every freakin' day, man. This is amazing!
What are you, like, in high school?
Yeah.
ADVANCED SCIENCE
GRAVITY'S RAINBOW
PARKER

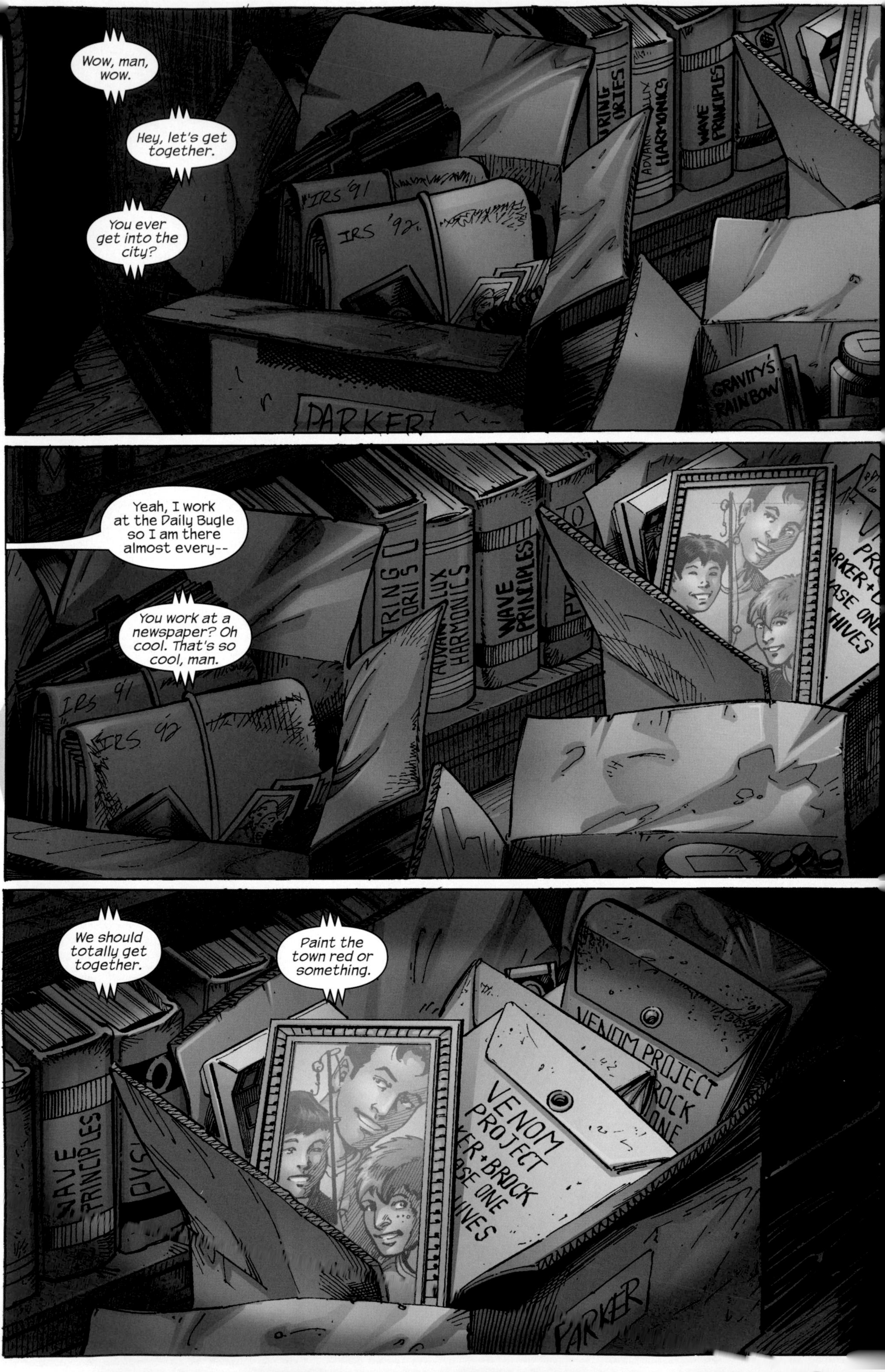
Wow, man, wow.
Hey, let's get together.
You ever get into the city?
IRS '91
IRS '92
WAVE PRINCIPLES
HARMONICS
GRAVITY'S RAINBOW
PARKER
Yeah, I work at the Daily Bugle so I am there almost every--
You work at a newspaper? Oh cool. That's so cool, man.
We should totally get together.
Paint the town red or something.
VENOM PROJECT
PARKER

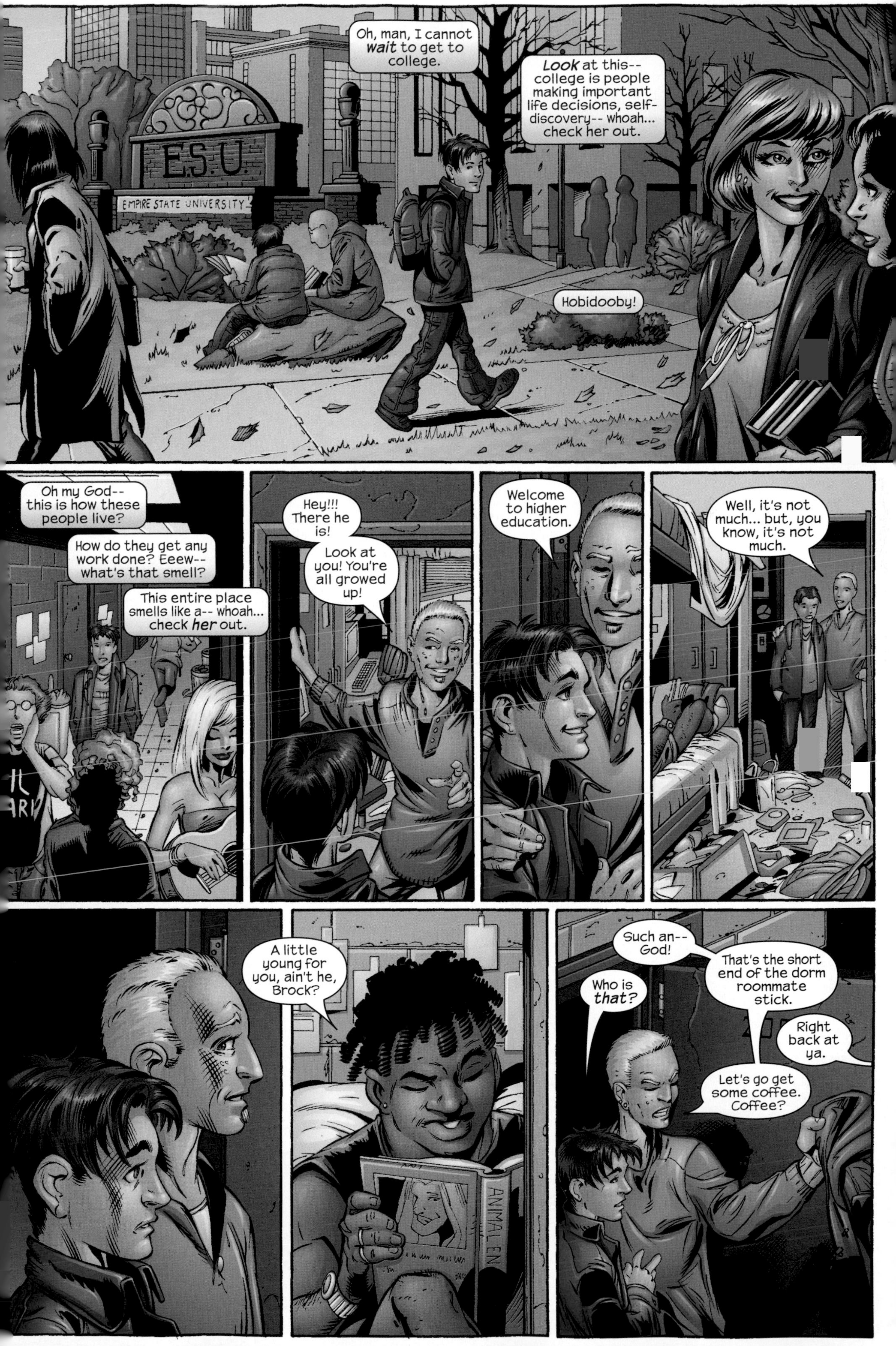
E.S.U.
EMPIRE STATE UNIVERSITY
Oh, man, I cannot *wait* to get to college.
Look at this-- college is people making important life decisions, self-discovery-- whoah... check her out.
Hobidooby!
Oh my God-- this is how these people live?
How do they get any work done? Eeew-- what's that smell?
This entire place smells like a-- whoah... check *her* out.
Hey!!! There he is!
Look at you! You're all growed up!
Welcome to higher education.
Well, it's not much... but, you know, it's not much.
A little young for you, ain't he, Brock?
ANIMAL EN
Such an-- God!
Who is *that?*
That's the short end of the dorm roommate stick.
Right back at ya.
Let's go get some coffee. Coffee?

...astrophysics. So now I'm in the bioengineering program.

Really, that's-- wow. That's going to be my major, too.

Wow, aren't we two pieces of work.

What do you mean?

Two little ghost chasers-- me and you.

Trying to impress our daddies.

Well, I--

I read some of my dad's papers and I-- I really believe in his work.

No, I do, too.

I mean at first I'm sure I was trying to-- I don't know-- relive my dad's... something. Right?

But I really do believe in what they were doing because, let me tell you...

If I didn't... bio is a crapload of reading to be into it for the wrong reason.

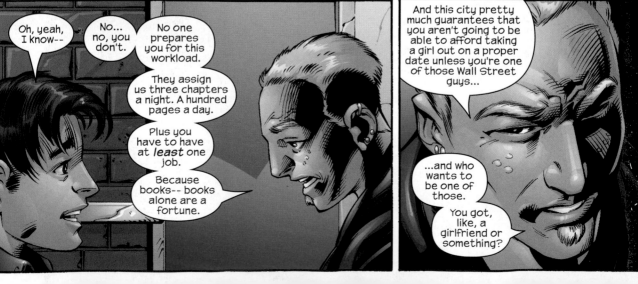

Oh, yeah, I know--

No... no, you don't.

No one prepares you for this workload.

They assign us three chapters a night. A hundred pages a day.

Plus you have to have at least one job.

Because books-- books alone are a fortune.

And this city pretty much guarantees that you aren't going to be able to afford taking a girl out on a proper date unless you're one of those Wall Street guys...

...and who wants to be one of those.

You got, like, a girlfriend or something?

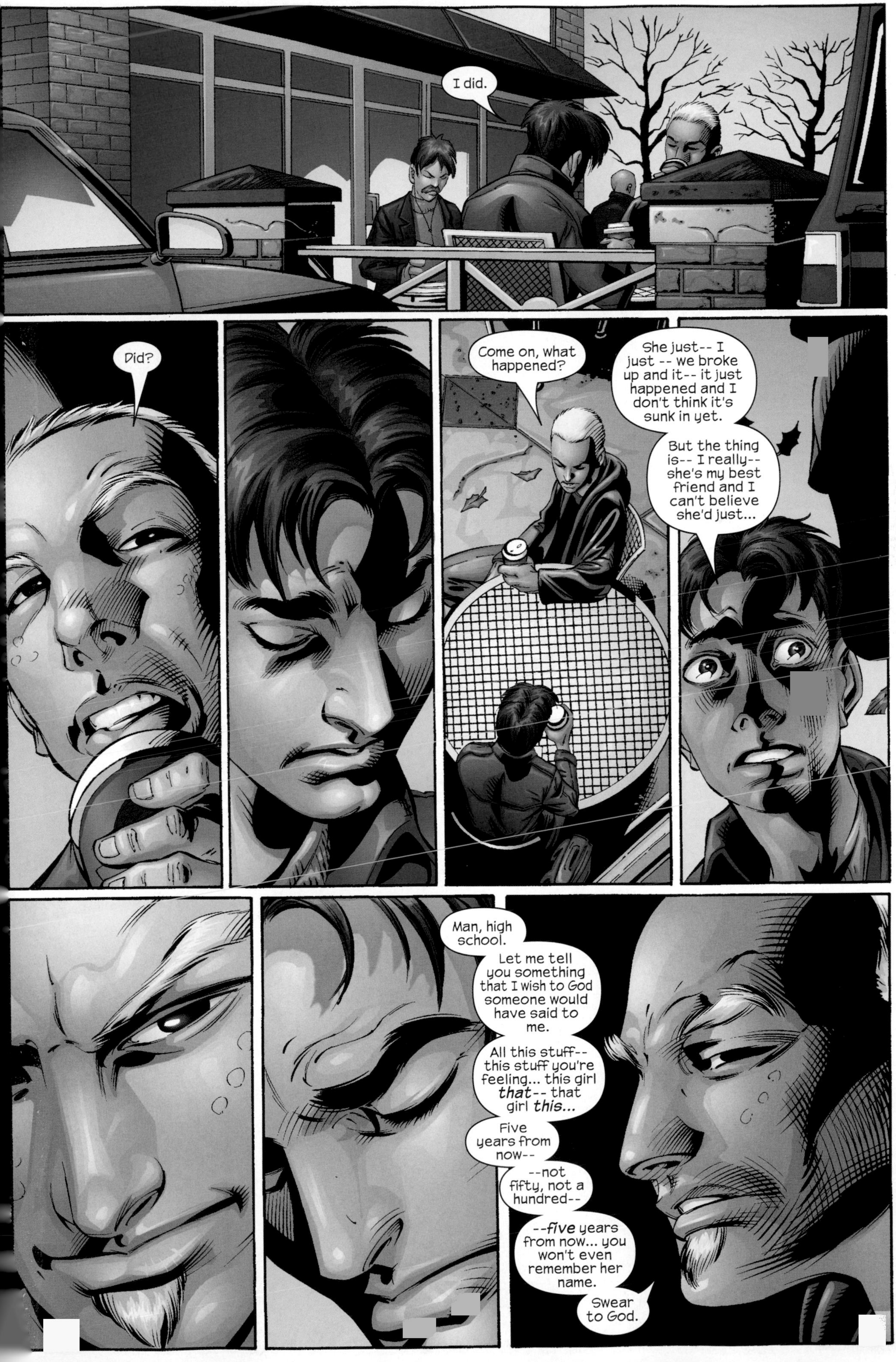
I did.
Did?
Come on, what happened?
She just-- I just -- we broke up and it-- it just happened and I don't think it's sunk in yet.
But the thing is-- I really-- she's my best friend and I can't believe she'd just...
Man, high school.
Let me tell you something that I wish to God someone would have said to me.
All this stuff-- this stuff you're feeling... this girl *that*-- that girl *this*...
Five years from now--
--not fifty, not a hundred--
--*five* years from now... you won't even remember her name.
Swear to God.

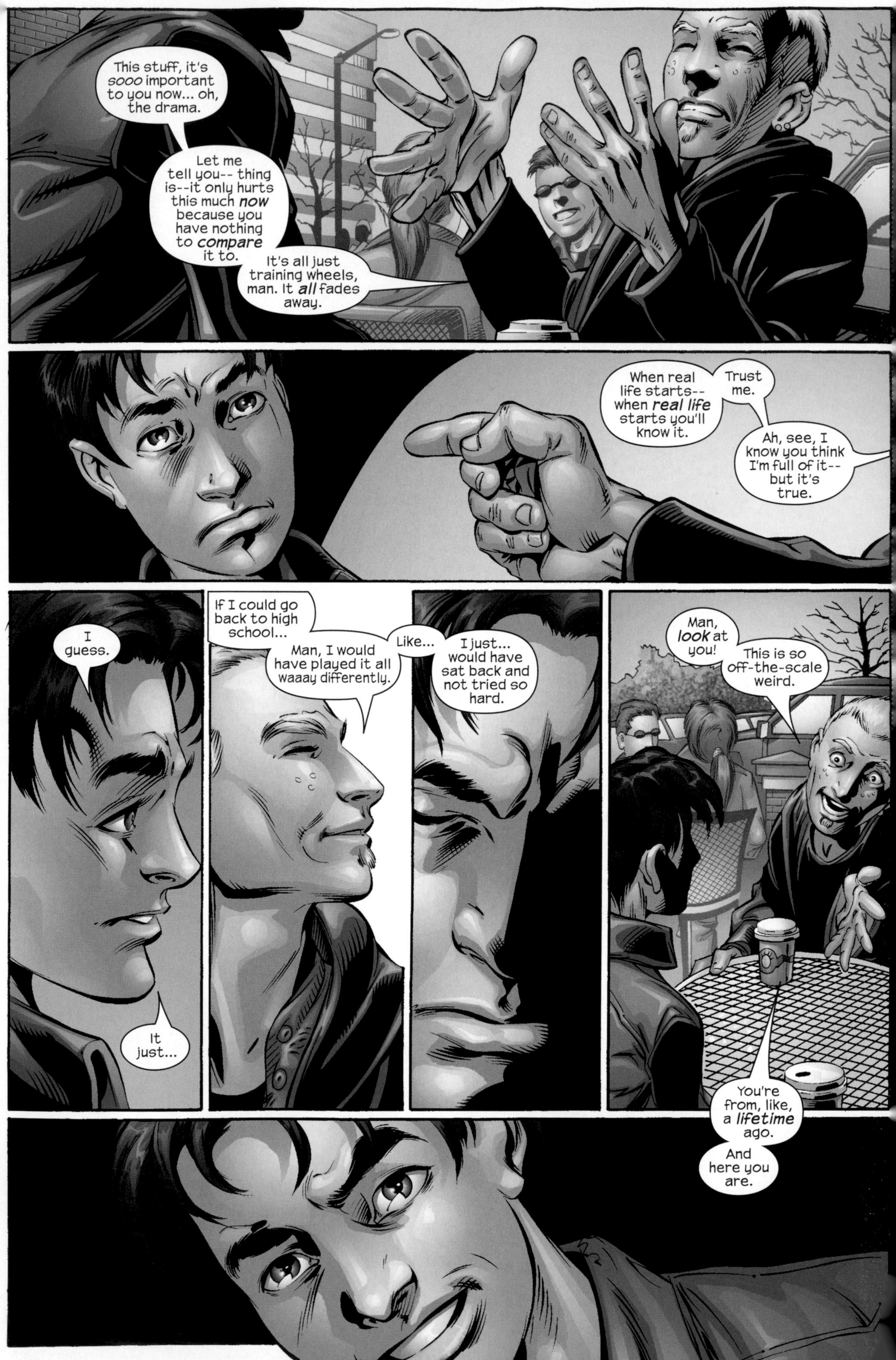
This stuff, it's sooo important to you now... oh, the drama.
Let me tell you-- thing is--it only hurts this much now because you have nothing to compare it to.
It's all just training wheels, man. It all fades away.
When real life starts-- when real life starts you'll know it.
Trust me.
Ah, see, I know you think I'm full of it-- but it's true.
I guess.
It just...
If I could go back to high school...
Man, I would have played it all waaay differently.
Like...
I just... would have sat back and not tried so hard.
Man, look at you!
This is so off-the-scale weird.
You're from, like, a lifetime ago.
And here you are.

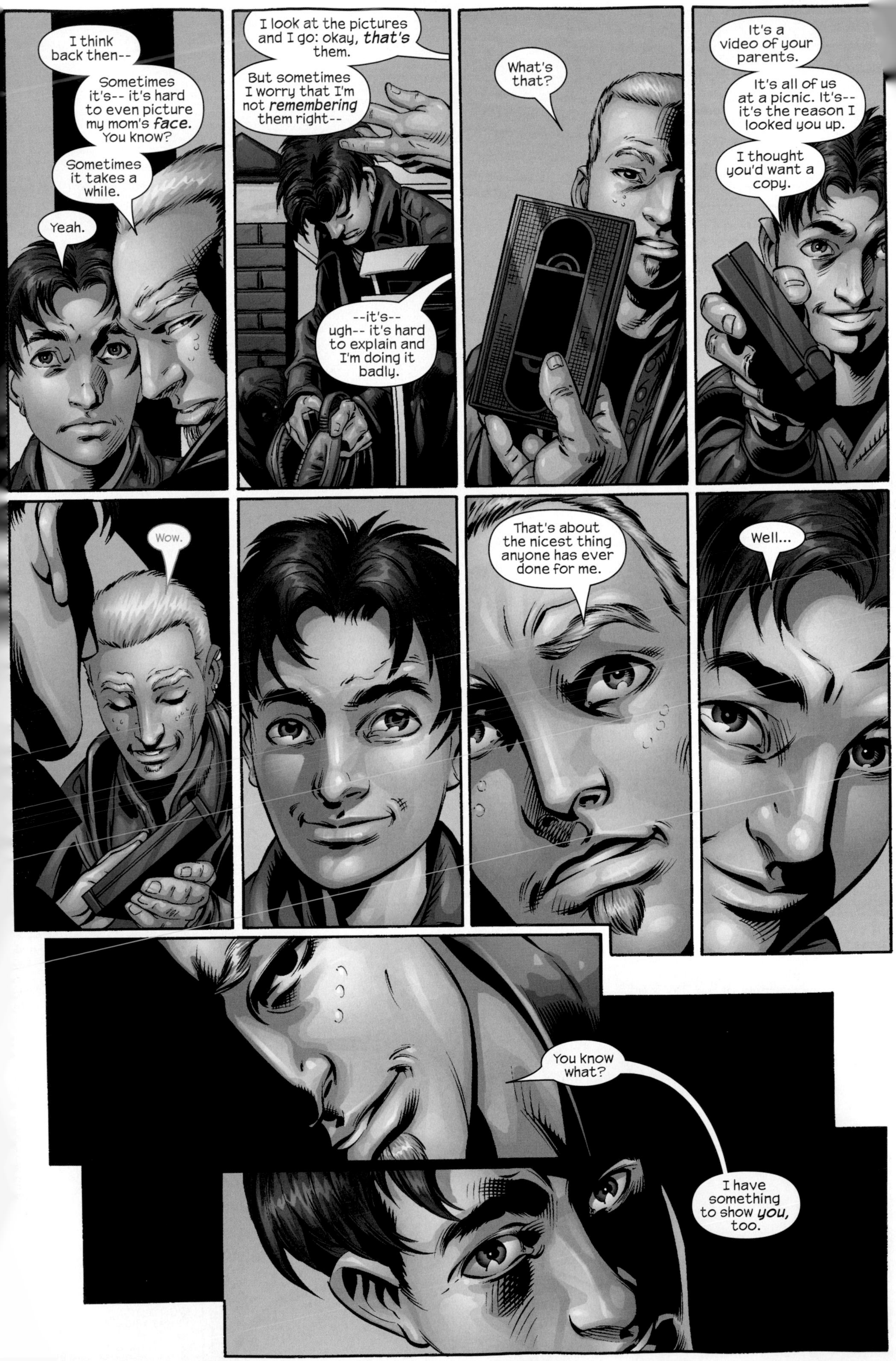
I think back then--
Sometimes it's-- it's hard to even picture my mom's *face.* You know?
Sometimes it takes a while.
Yeah.
I look at the pictures and I go: okay, *that's* them.
But sometimes I worry that I'm not *remembering* them right--
--it's-- ugh-- it's hard to explain and I'm doing it badly.
What's that?
It's a video of your parents.
It's all of us at a picnic. It's-- it's the reason I looked you up.
I thought you'd want a copy.
Wow.
That's about the nicest thing anyone has ever done for me.
Well...
You know what?
I have something to show *you,* too.

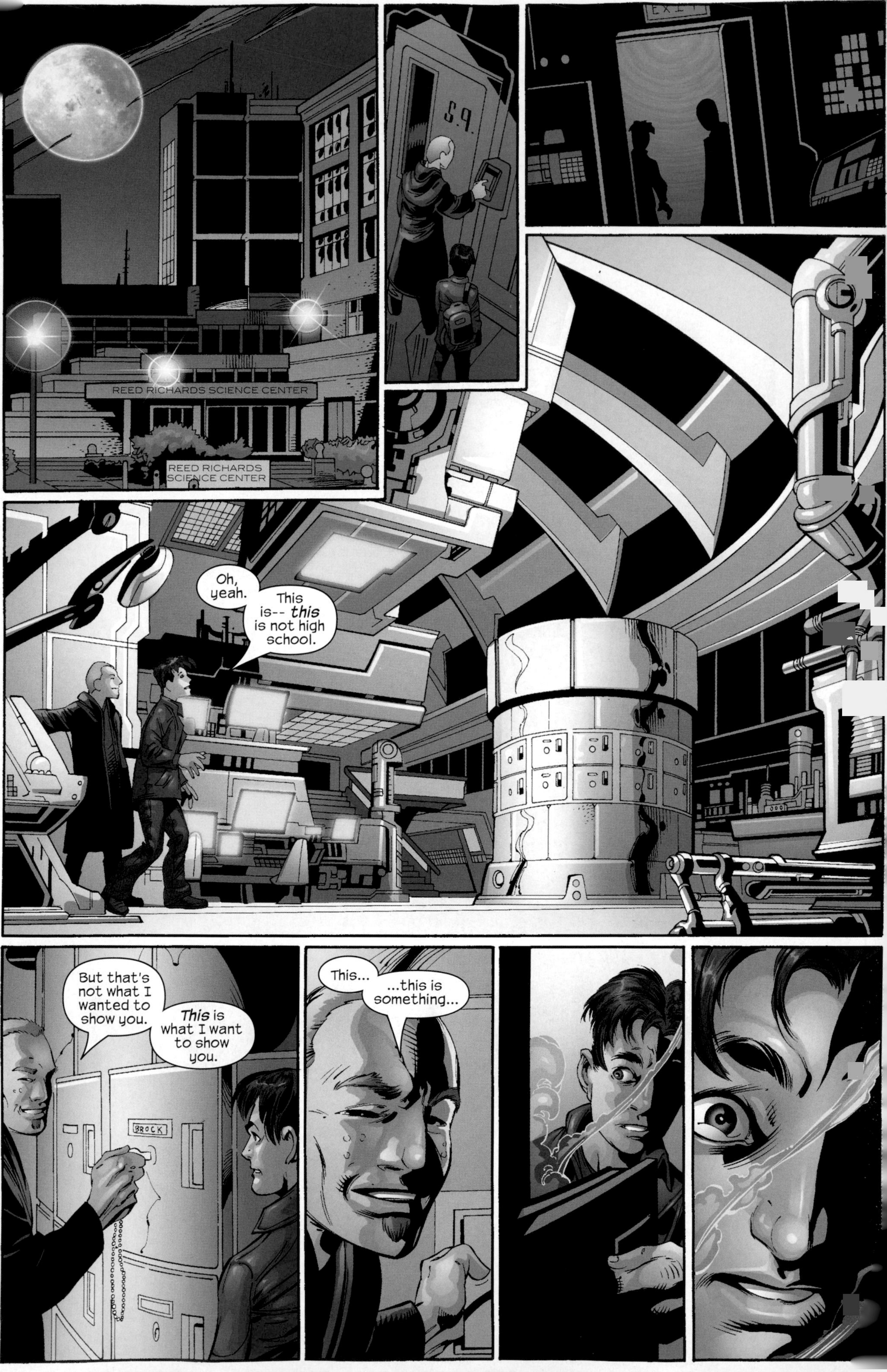
S.Q.
EXIT
REED RICHARDS SCIENCE CENTER
REED RICHARDS SCIENCE CENTER
Oh, yeah.
This is-- *this* is not high school.
But that's not what I wanted to show you.
This is what I want to show you.
BROCK
This...
...this is something...

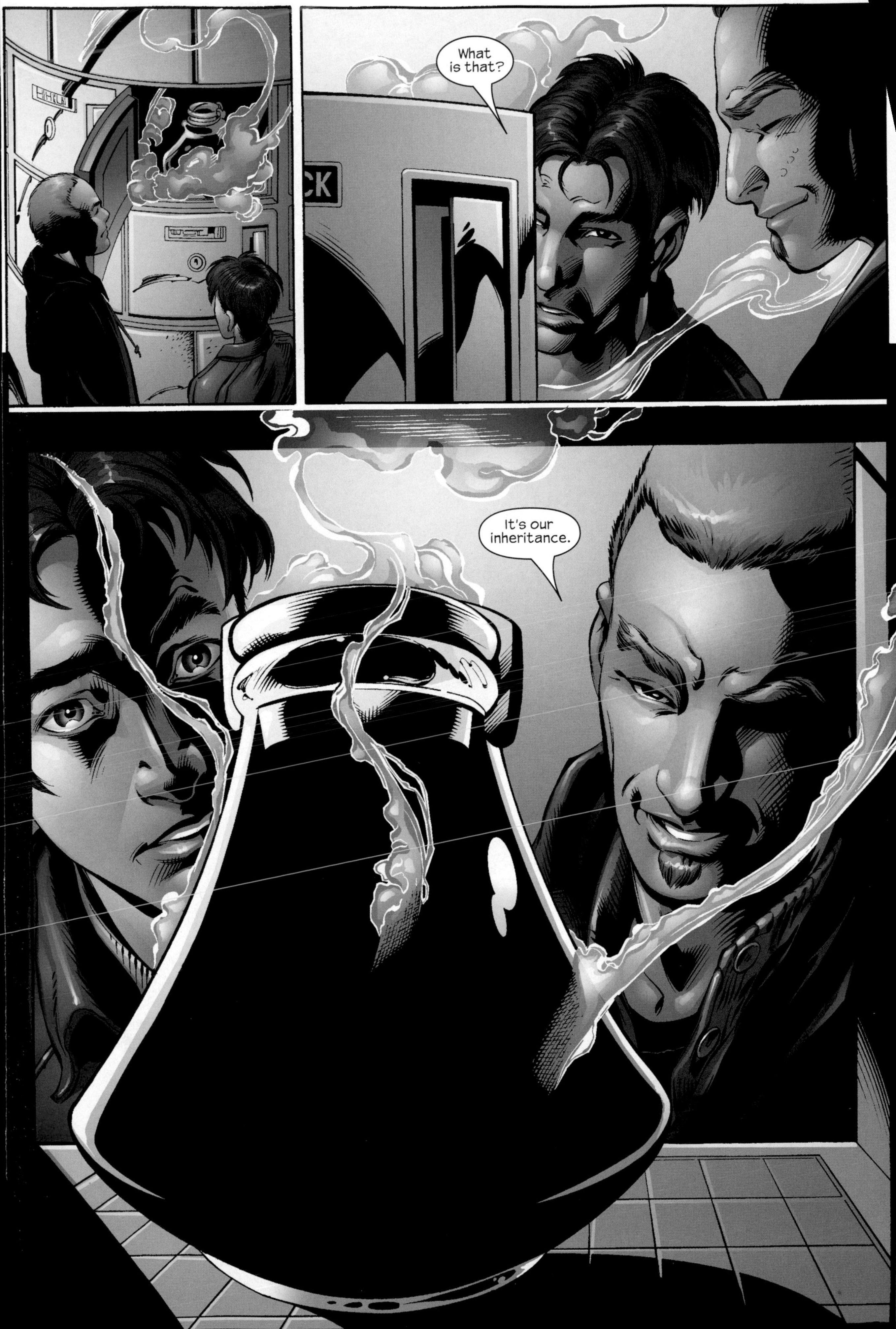
What is that?
It's our inheritance.

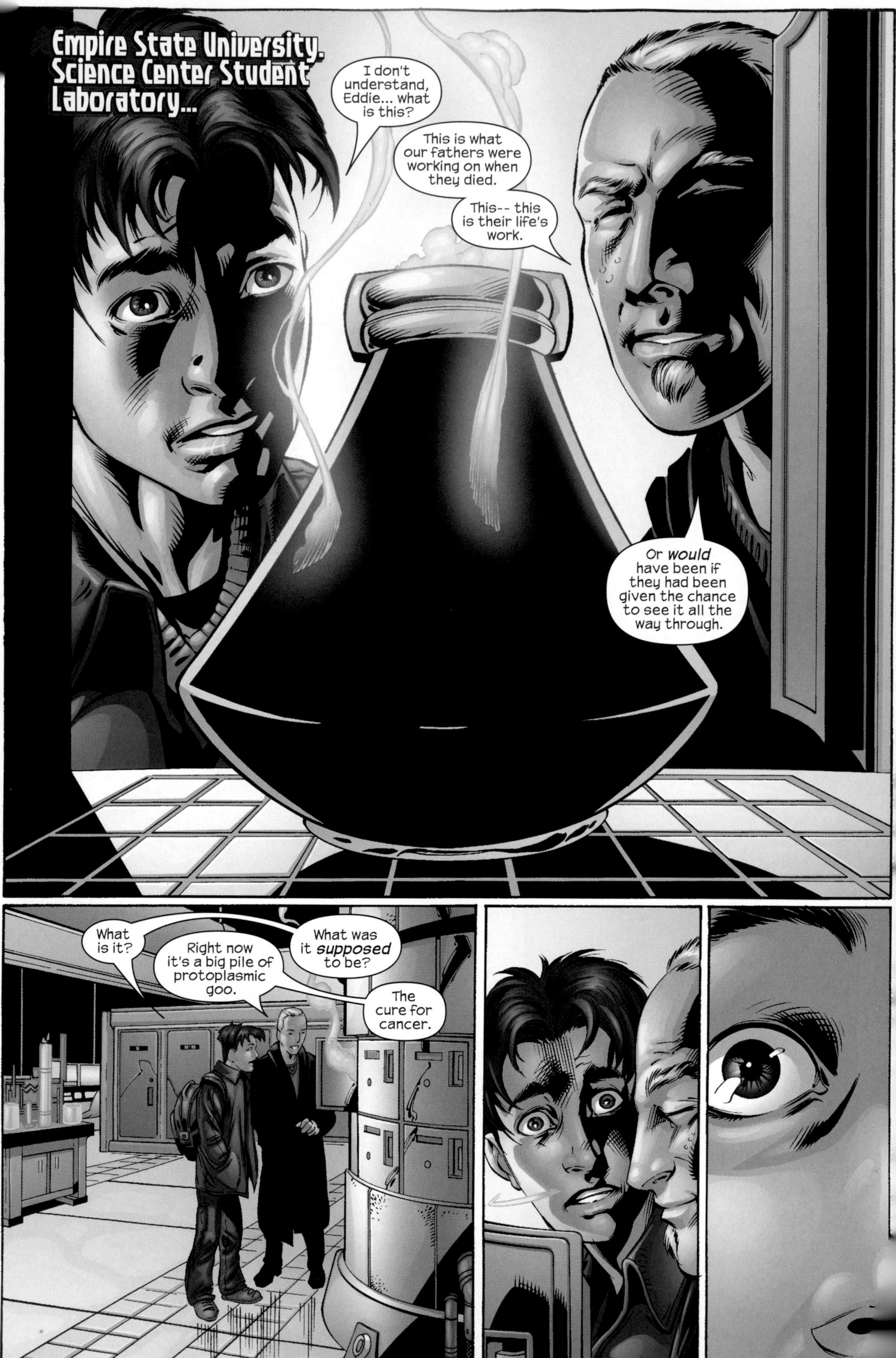
Empire State University. Science Center Student Laboratory...
I don't understand, Eddie... what is this?
This is what our fathers were working on when they died.
This-- this is their life's work.
Or *would* have been if they had been given the chance to see it all the way through.
What is it?
Right now it's a big pile of protoplasmic goo.
What was it *supposed* to be?
The cure for cancer.

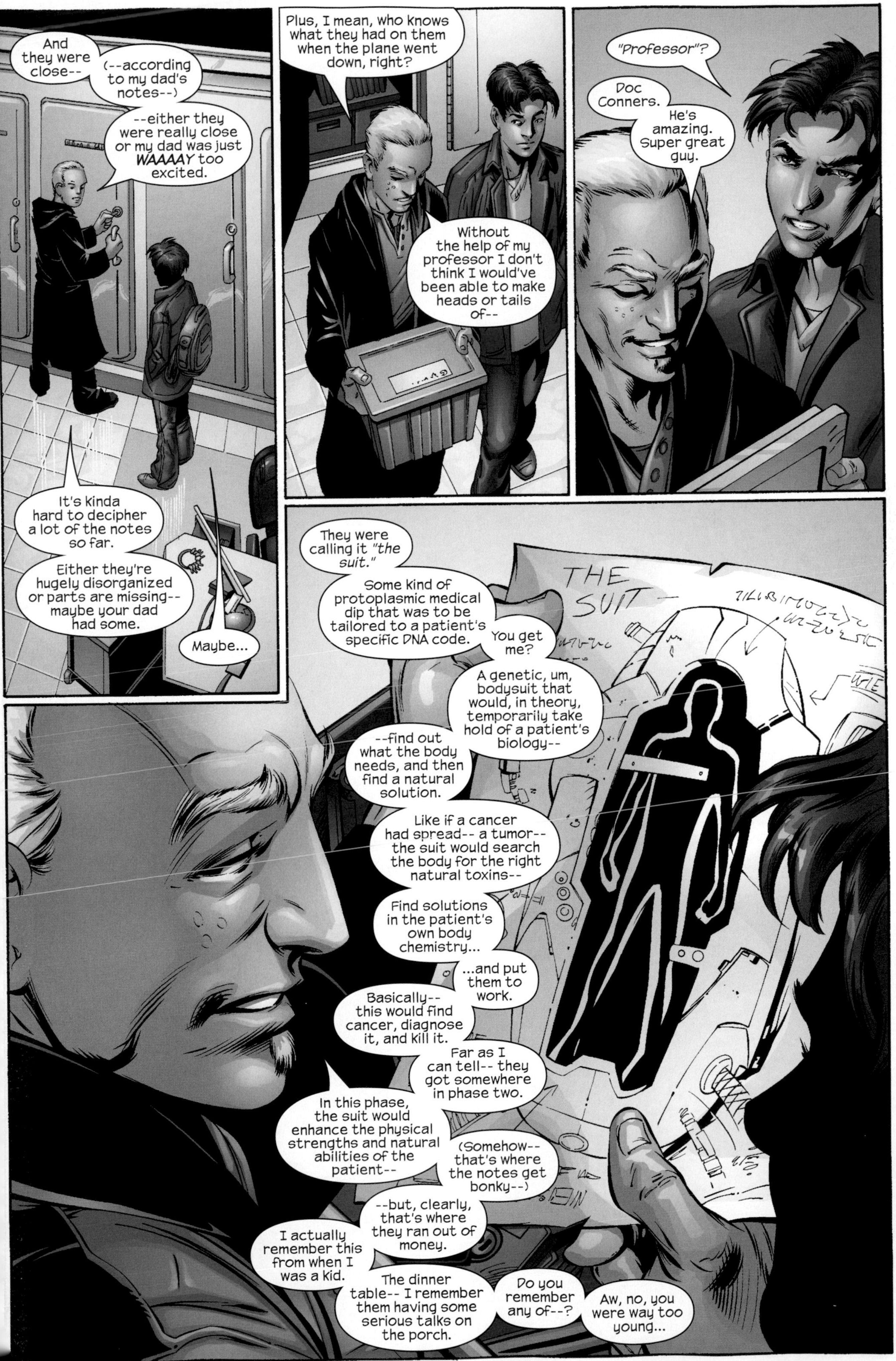
And they were close--
(--according to my dad's notes--)
--either they were really close or my dad was just WAAAAY too excited.
Plus, I mean, who knows what they had on them when the plane went down, right?
Without the help of my professor I don't think I would've been able to make heads or tails of--
"Professor"?
Doc Conners.
He's amazing. Super great guy.
It's kinda hard to decipher a lot of the notes so far.
Either they're hugely disorganized or parts are missing-- maybe your dad had some.
Maybe...
They were calling it "the suit."
Some kind of protoplasmic medical dip that was to be tailored to a patient's specific DNA code.
You get me?
A genetic, um, bodysuit that would, in theory, temporarily take hold of a patient's biology--
--find out what the body needs, and then find a natural solution.
Like if a cancer had spread-- a tumor-- the suit would search the body for the right natural toxins--
Find solutions in the patient's own body chemistry...
...and put them to work.
Basically-- this would find cancer, diagnose it, and kill it.
Far as I can tell-- they got somewhere in phase two.
In this phase, the suit would enhance the physical strengths and natural abilities of the patient--
(Somehow-- that's where the notes get bonky--)
--but, clearly, that's where they ran out of money.
I actually remember this from when I was a kid.
The dinner table-- I remember them having some serious talks on the porch.
Do you remember any of--?
Aw, no, you were way too young...
THE SUIT

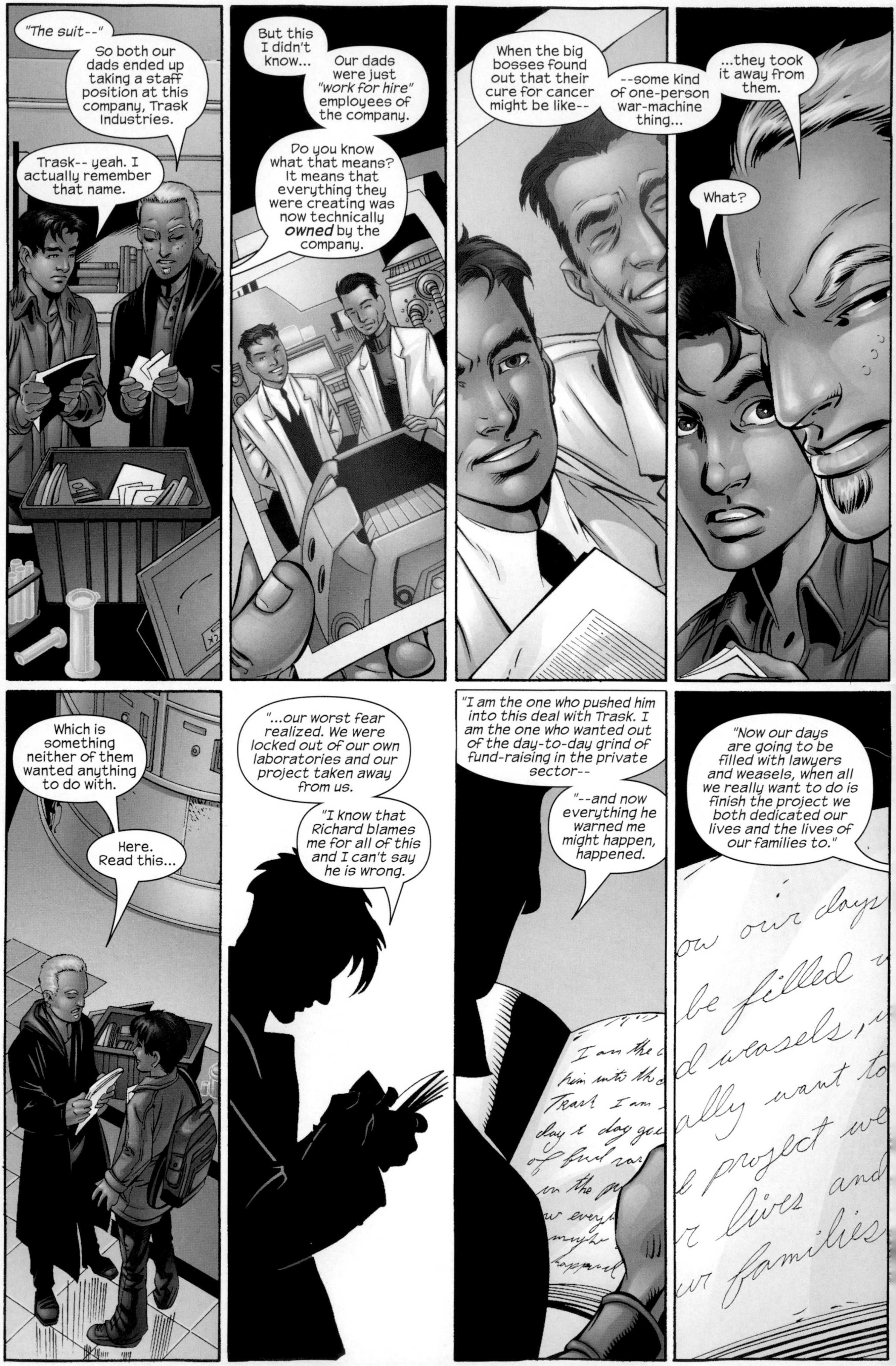
"The suit--"
So both our dads ended up taking a staff position at this company, Trask Industries.
Trask-- yeah. I actually remember that name.
But this I didn't know...
Our dads were just *"work for hire"* employees of the company.
Do you know what that means? It means that everything they were creating was now technically ***owned*** by the company.
When the big bosses found out that their cure for cancer might be like--
--some kind of one-person war-machine thing...
...they took it away from them.
What?
Which is something neither of them wanted anything to do with.
Here. Read this...
"...our worst fear realized. We were locked out of our own laboratories and our project taken away from us.
"I know that Richard blames me for all of this and I can't say he is wrong.
"I am the one who pushed him into this deal with Trask. I am the one who wanted out of the day-to-day grind of fund-raising in the private sector--
"--and now everything he warned me might happen, happened.
"Now our days are going to be filled with lawyers and weasels, when all we really want to do is finish the project we both dedicated our lives and the lives of our families to."

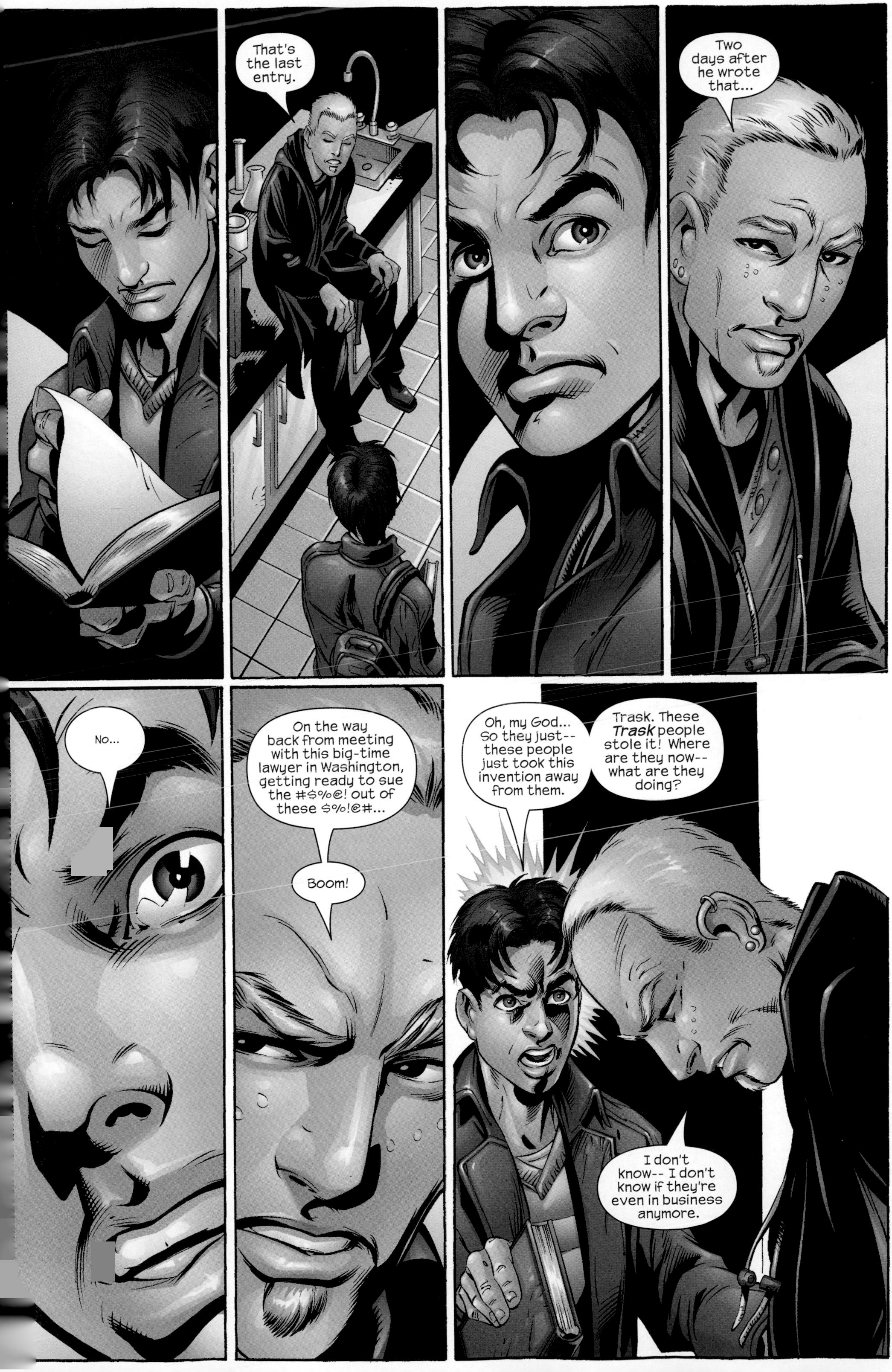
That's the last entry.
Two days after he wrote that...
No...
On the way back from meeting with this big-time lawyer in Washington, getting ready to sue the #$%@! out of these $%!@#...
Boom!
Oh, my God... So they just-- these people just took this invention away from them.
Trask. These *Trask* people stole it! Where are they now-- what are they doing?
I don't know-- I don't know if they're even in business anymore.

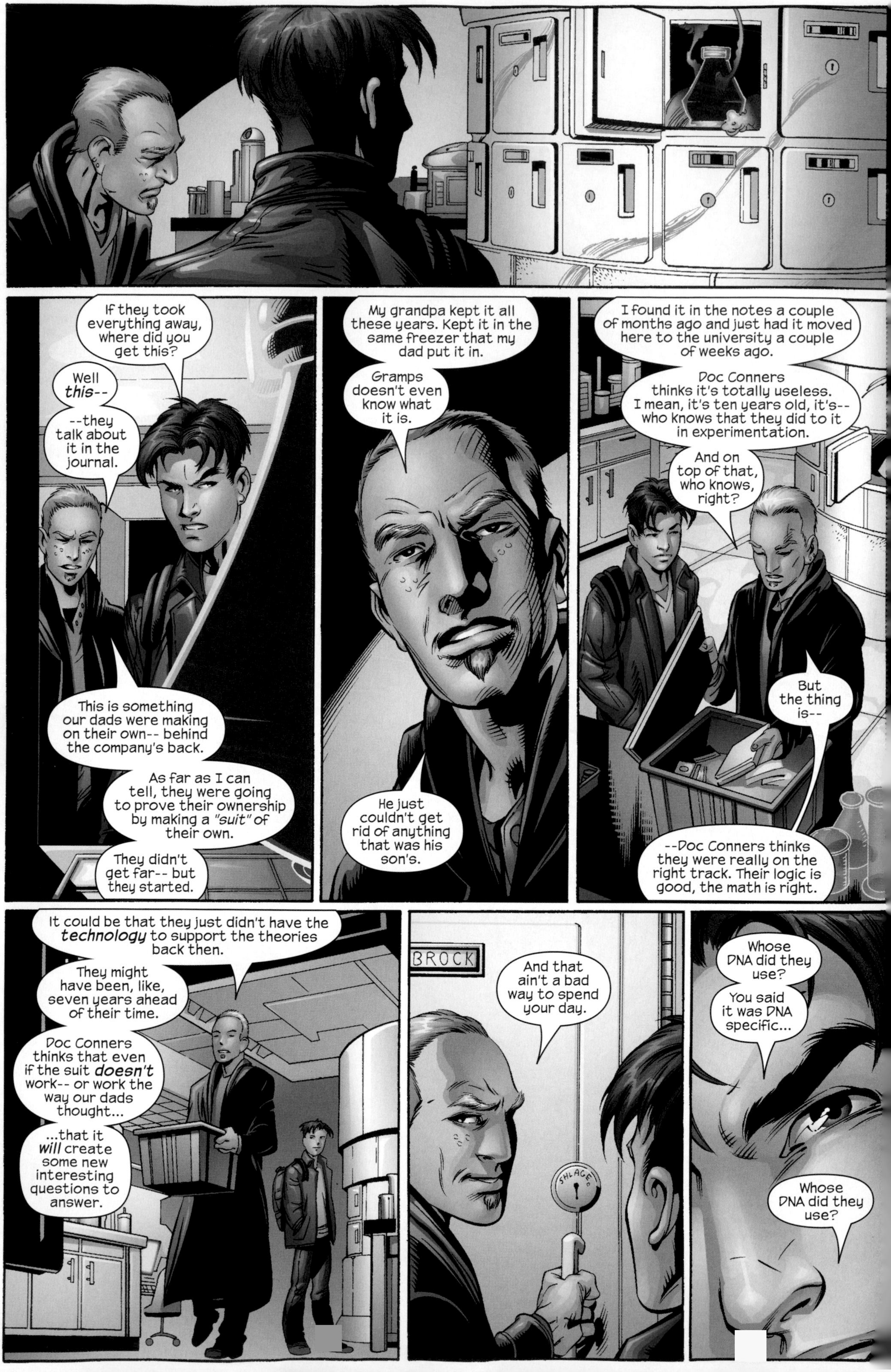

If they took everything away, where did you get this?
Well *this*--
--they talk about it in the journal.
This is something our dads were making on their own-- behind the company's back.
As far as I can tell, they were going to prove their ownership by making a *"suit"* of their own.
They didn't get far-- but they started.
My grandpa kept it all these years. Kept it in the same freezer that my dad put it in.
Gramps doesn't even know what it is.
He just couldn't get rid of anything that was his son's.
I found it in the notes a couple of months ago and just had it moved here to the university a couple of weeks ago.
Doc Conners thinks it's totally useless. I mean, it's ten years old, it's-- who knows that they did to it in experimentation.
And on top of that, who knows, right?
But the thing is--
--Doc Conners thinks they were really on the right track. Their logic is good, the math is right.
It could be that they just didn't have the *technology* to support the theories back then.
They might have been, like, seven years ahead of their time.
Doc Conners thinks that even if the suit *doesn't* work-- or work the way our dads thought...
...that it *will* create some new interesting questions to answer.
BROCK
And that ain't a bad way to spend your day.
SHLAGE
Whose DNA did they use?
You said it was DNA specific...
Whose DNA did they use?

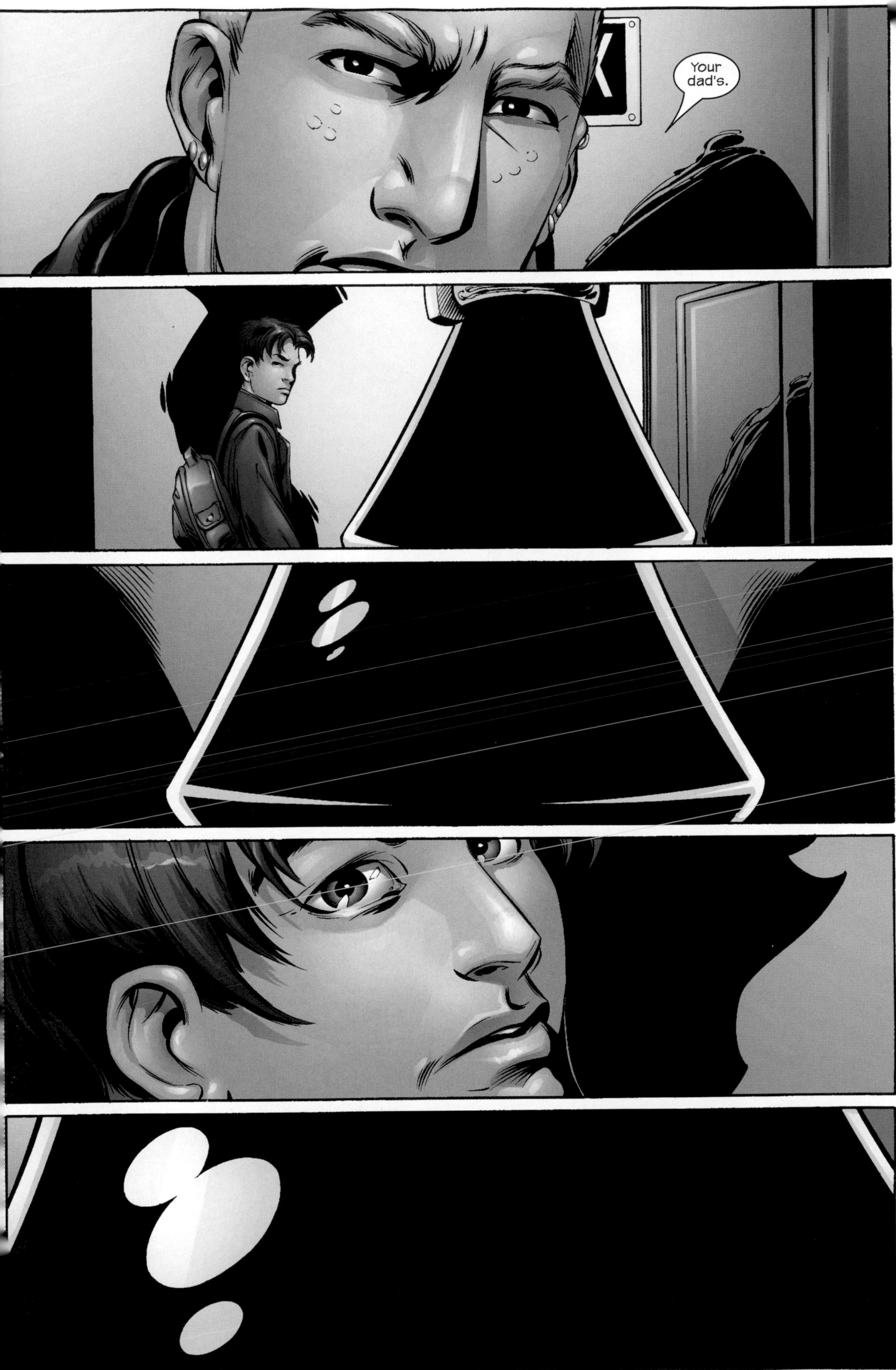
Your dad's.

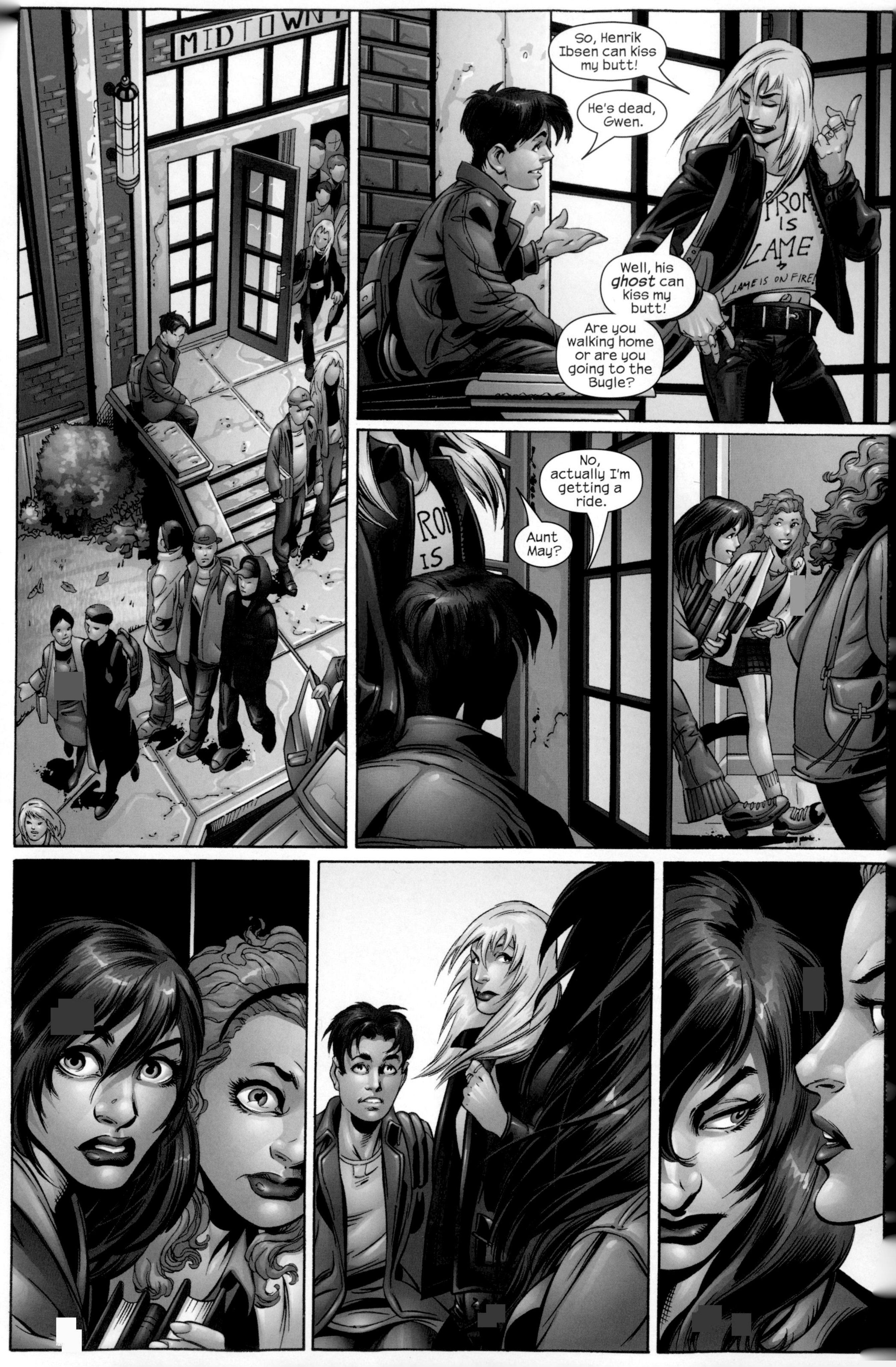
MIDTOWN
So, Henrik Ibsen can kiss my butt!
He's dead, Gwen.
PROM IS LAME
LAME IS ON FIRE!
Well, his *ghost* can kiss my butt!
Are you walking home or are you going to the Bugle?
Aunt May?
No, actually I'm getting a ride.

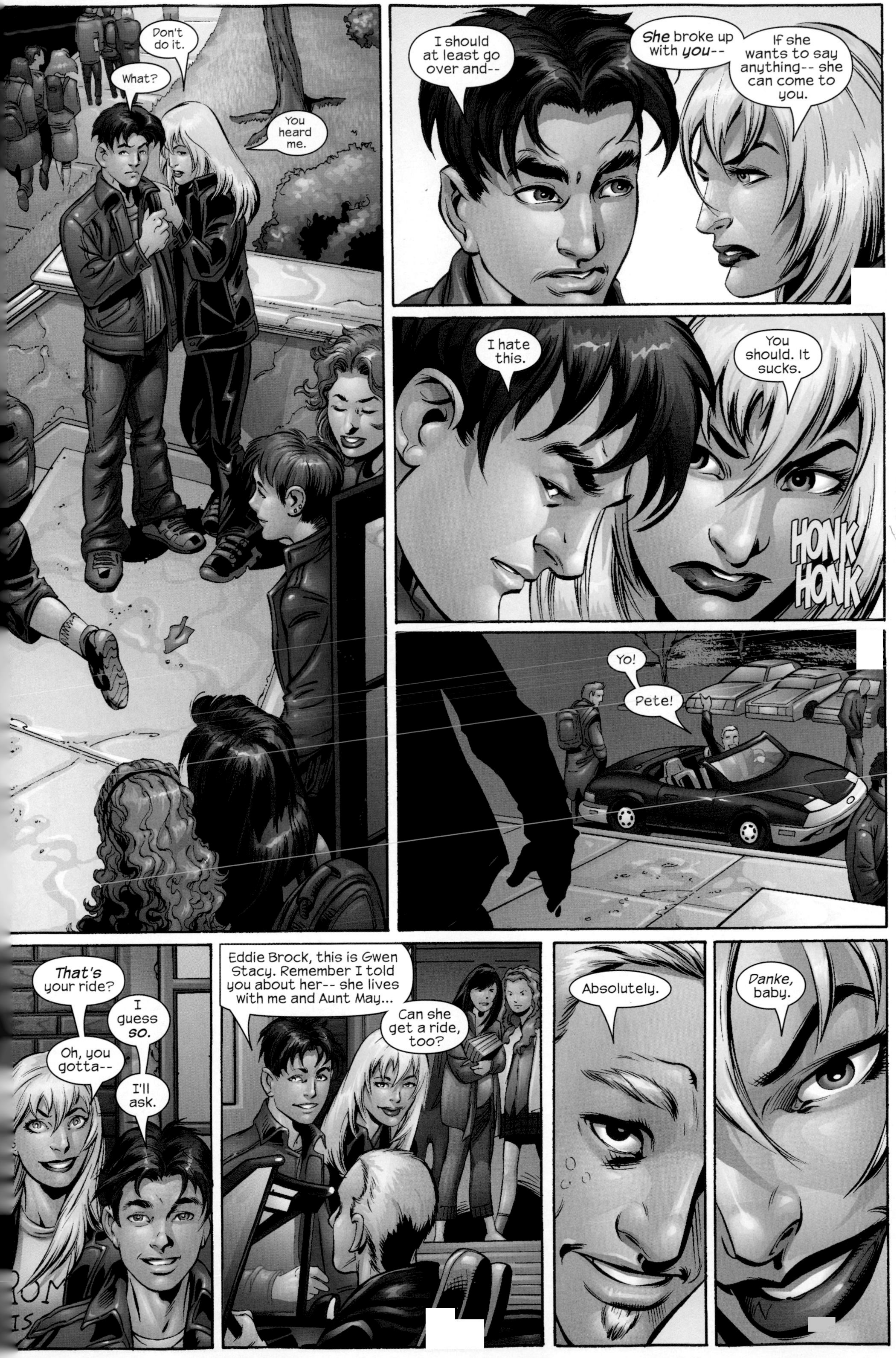
Don't do it.
What?
You heard me.
I should at least go over and--
She broke up with you--
If she wants to say anything-- she can come to you.
I hate this.
You should. It sucks.
HONK HONK
Yo!
Pete!
That's your ride?
I guess so.
Oh, you gotta--
I'll ask.
Eddie Brock, this is Gwen Stacy. Remember I told you about her-- she lives with me and Aunt May...
Can she get a ride, too?
Absolutely.
Danke, baby.

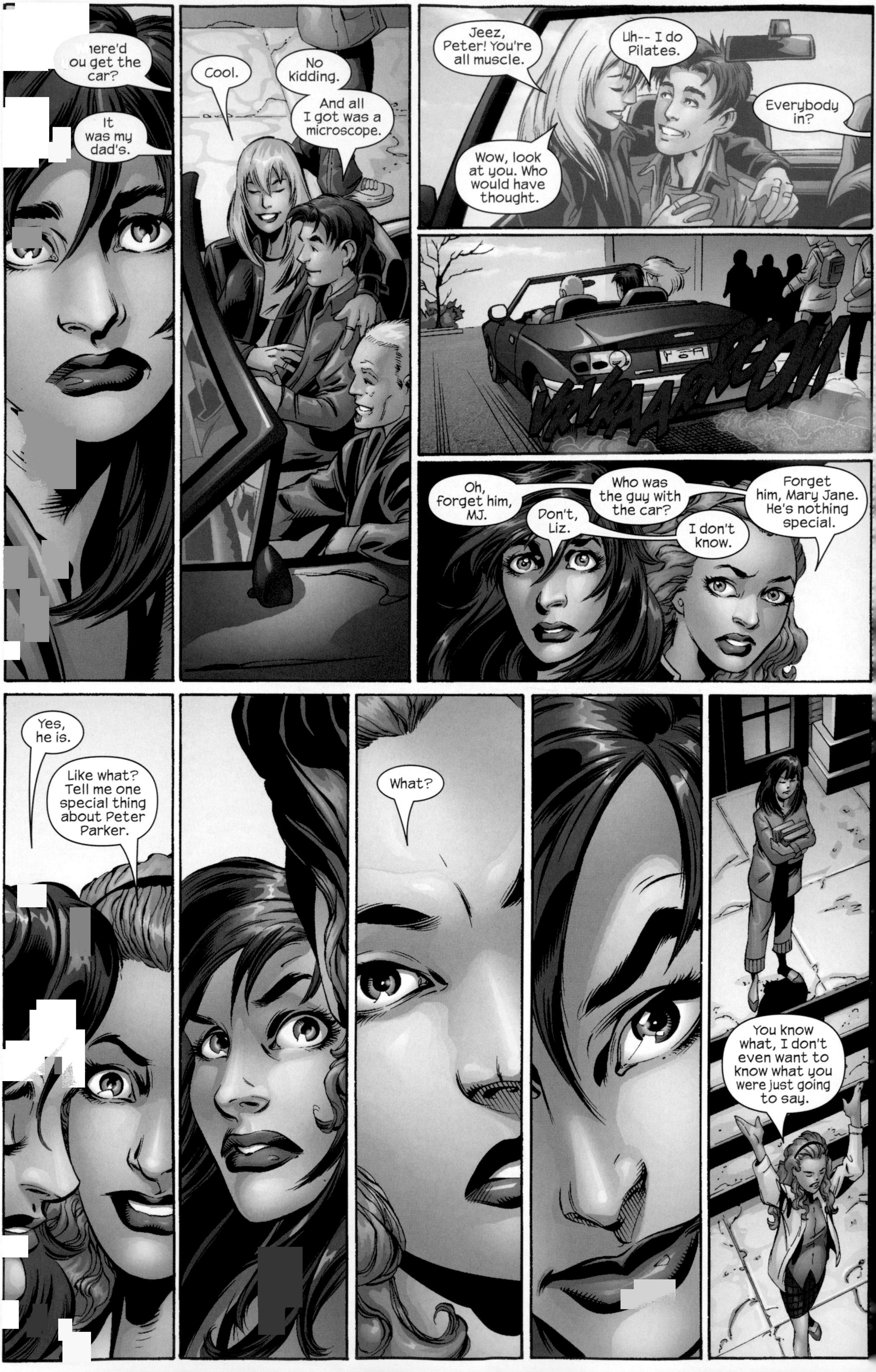

here'd
ou get the car?
It was my dad's.
Cool.
No kidding.
And all I got was a microscope.
Jeez, Peter! You're all muscle.
Uh-- I do Pilates.
Everybody in?
Wow, look at you. Who would have thought.
Oh, forget him, MJ.
Who was the guy with the car?
Forget him, Mary Jane. He's nothing special.
Don't, Liz.
I don't know.
Yes, he is.
Like what? Tell me one special thing about Peter Parker.
What?
You know what, I don't even want to know what you were just going to say.

--no way, I would never join a frat.

Are you kidding me? No way.

They are the *worst*.

What do they do there?

Let me ask-- who's the biggest lame-o in your school?

Flash Thompson.

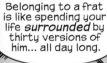

Belonging to a frat is like spending your life *surrounded* by thirty versions of him... all day long.

Eeeww.

Exactly.

Oop-- hold on.

Hello?

Oh, Hey, Doc--

--yes. Uh-huh. What?

Yes.

No, it was *me*.

BEEDOO BEEDOO BEE-

Well I signed in on the sign-in sheet.

I wanted to show it to my friend.

No, no, not some girl! No, this was my father's partner's son.

Peter Parker. Yeah.

No. No, I know. When have I ever done that before? I know.

Okay, yeah.

Okay.

That was my professor-- the one I was telling you about.

Great guy but he can be a spaz.

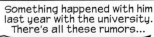

Something happened with him last year with the university. There's all these rumors...

...he *really* wants our work on this to go smoothly... and he spazzes sometimes.

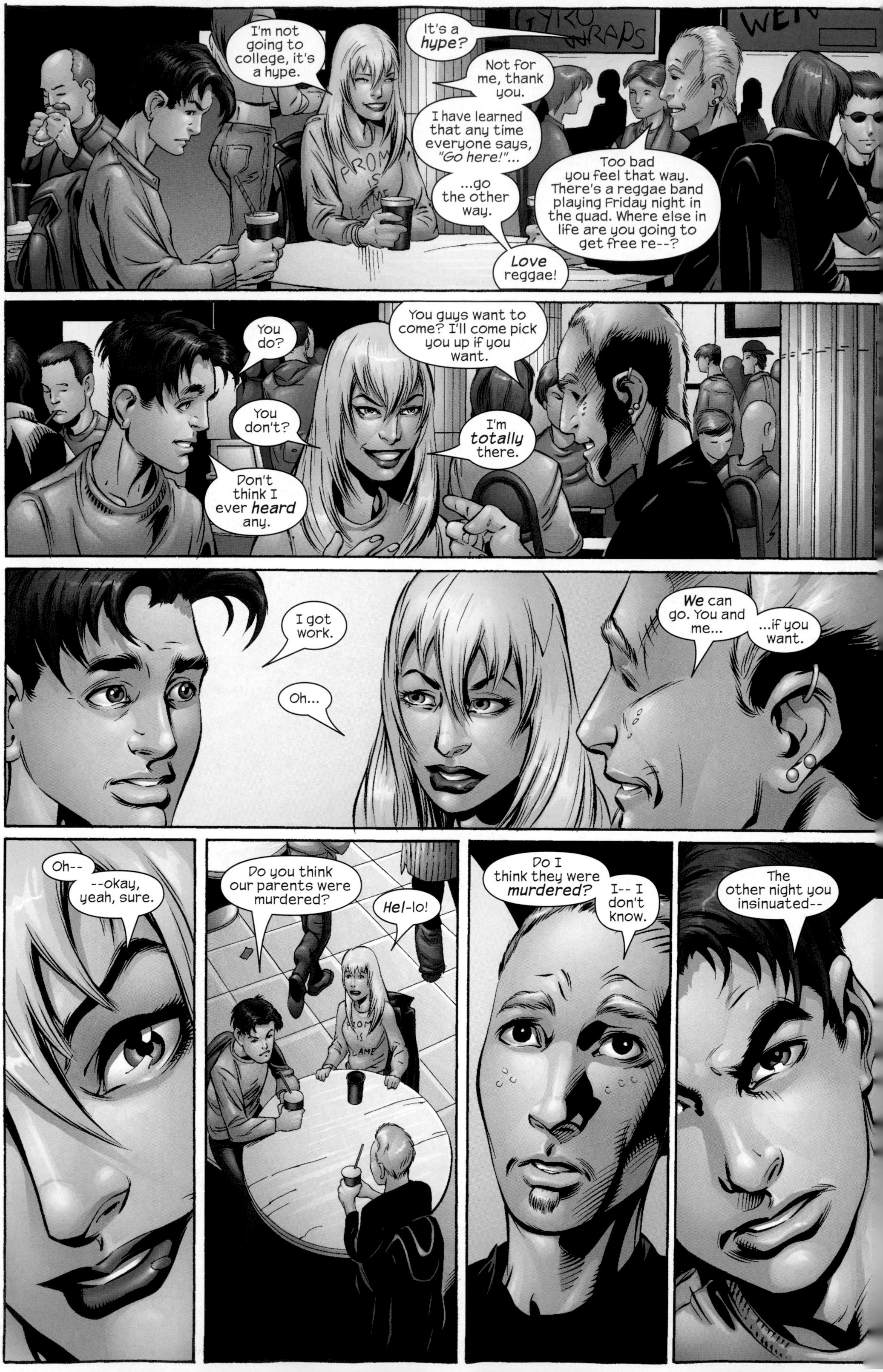
GYRO WRAPS
WEN
I'm not going to college, it's a hype.
It's a *hype*?
Not for me, thank you.
I have learned that any time everyone says, *"Go here!"*...
...go the other way.
Too bad you feel that way. There's a reggae band playing Friday night in the quad. Where else in life are you going to get free re--?
Love reggae!
PROM IS LAME
You do?
You guys want to come? I'll come pick you up if you want.
You don't?
I'm *totally* there.
Don't think I ever *heard* any.
I got work.
Oh...
We can go. You and me...
...if you want.
Oh--
--okay, yeah, sure.
Do you think our parents were murdered?
Hel-lo!
Do I think they were *murdered?*
I-- I don't know.
The other night you insinuated--

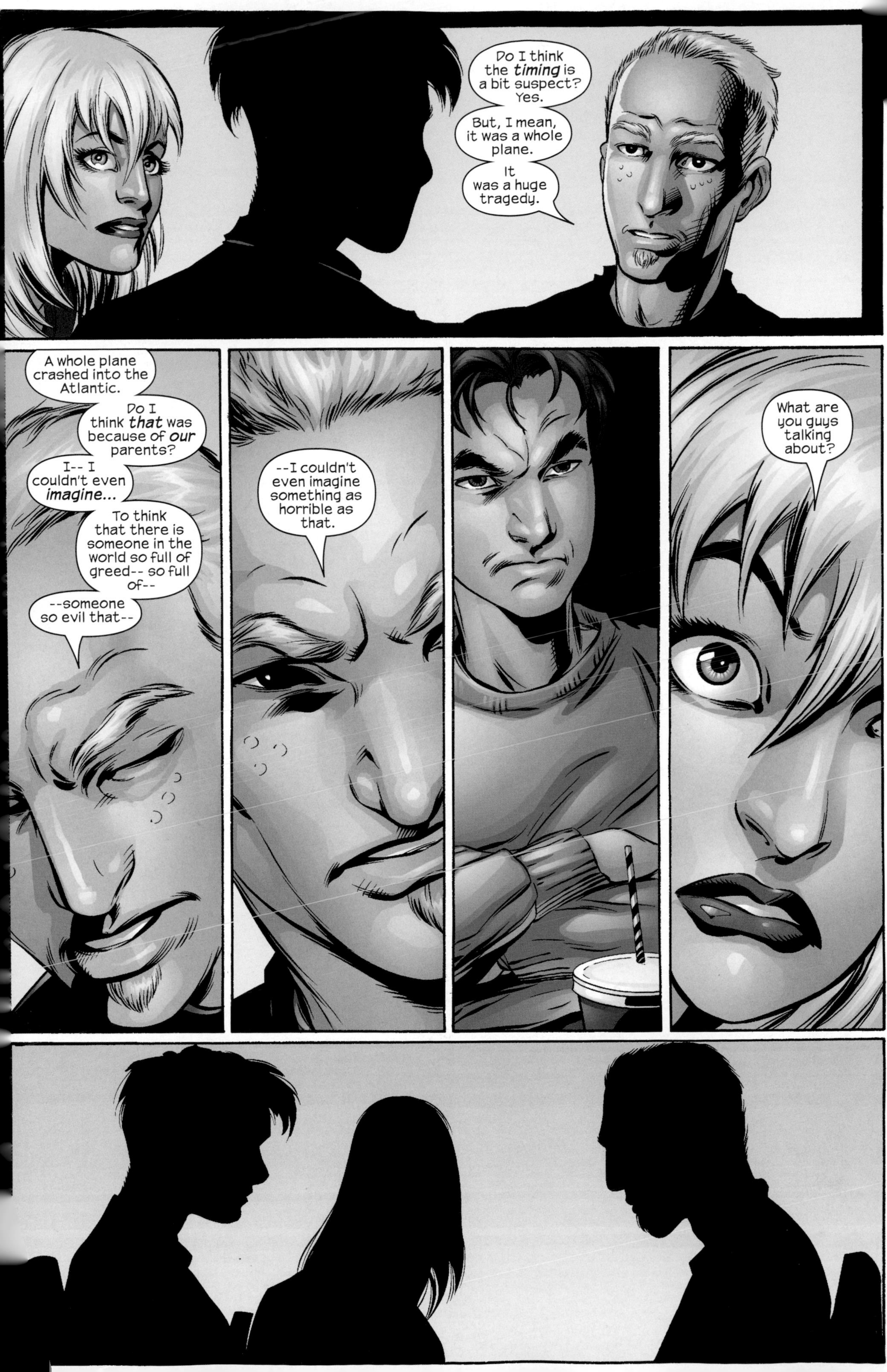
Do I think the *timing* is a bit suspect? Yes.
But, I mean, it was a whole plane.
It was a huge tragedy.
A whole plane crashed into the Atlantic.
Do I think *that* was because of *our* parents?
I-- I couldn't even *imagine...*
To think that there is someone in the world so full of greed-- so full of--
--someone so evil that--
--I couldn't even imagine something as horrible as that.
What are you guys talking about?

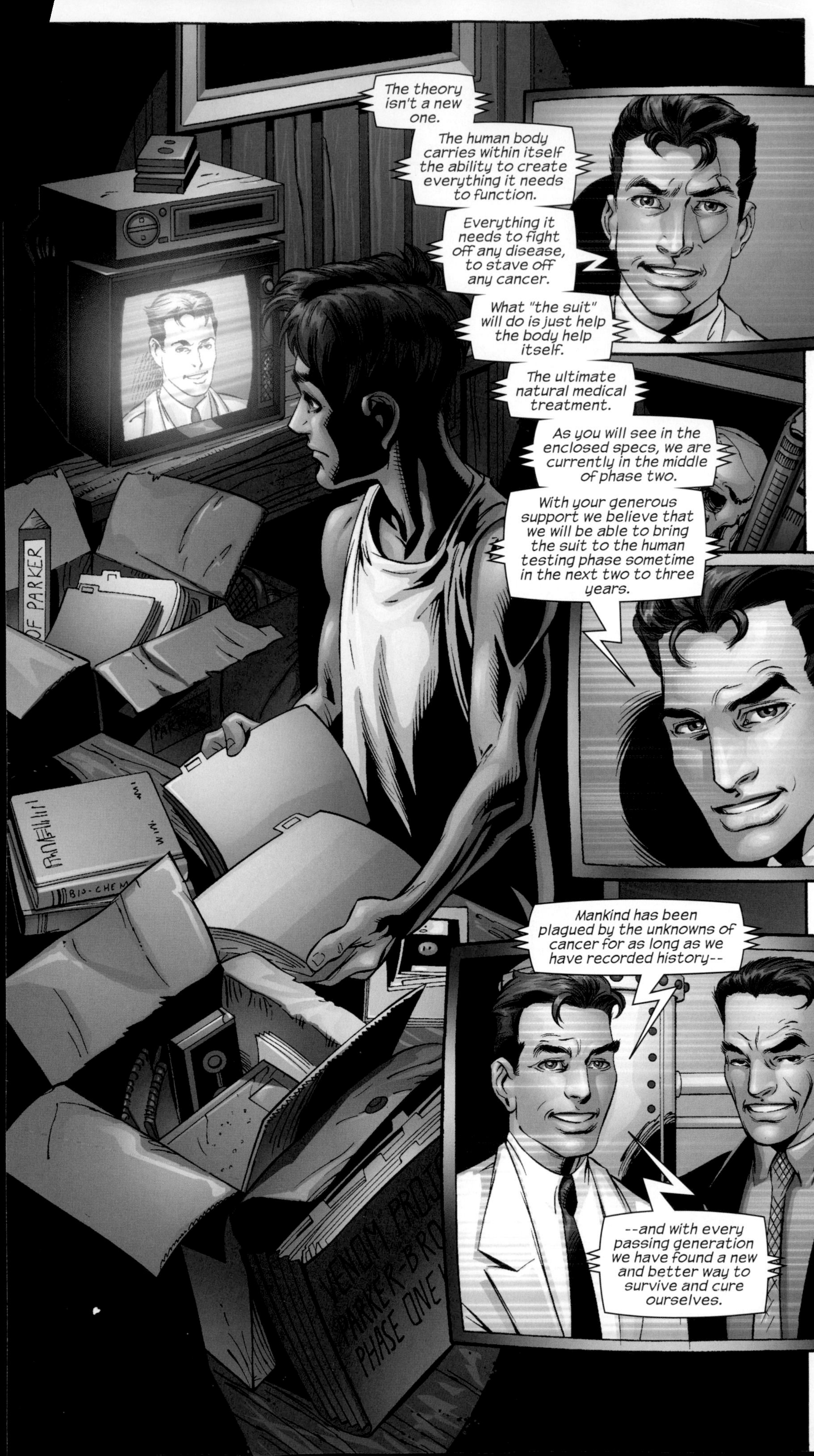
The theory isn't a new one.
The human body carries within itself the ability to create everything it needs to function.
Everything it needs to fight off any disease, to stave off any cancer.
What "the suit" will do is just help the body help itself.
The ultimate natural medical treatment.
As you will see in the enclosed specs, we are currently in the middle of phase two.
With your generous support we believe that we will be able to bring the suit to the human testing phase sometime in the next two to three years.
BIO-CHEM
Mankind has been plagued by the unknowns of cancer for as long as we have recorded history--
--and with every passing generation we have found a new and better way to survive and cure ourselves.

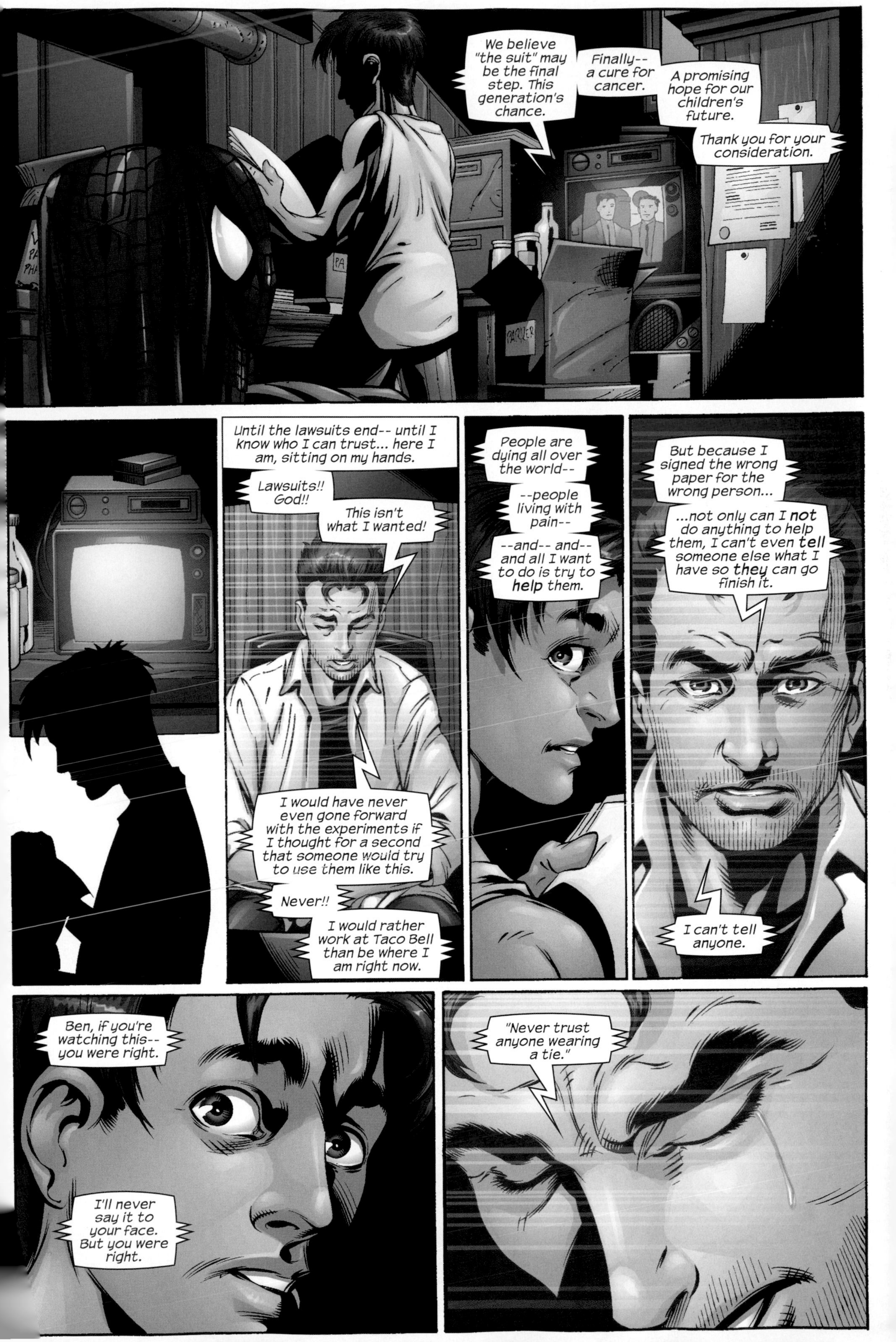

We believe "the suit" may be the final step. This generation's chance.
Finally-- a cure for cancer.
A promising hope for our children's future.
Thank you for your consideration.
Until the lawsuits end-- until I know who I can trust... here I am, sitting on my hands.
Lawsuits!! God!!
This isn't what I wanted!
I would have never even gone forward with the experiments if I thought for a second that someone would try to use them like this.
Never!!
I would rather work at Taco Bell than be where I am right now.
People are dying all over the world--
--people living with pain--
--and-- and-- and all I want to do is try to help them.
But because I signed the wrong paper for the wrong person...
...not only can I not do anything to help them, I can't even tell someone else what I have so they can go finish it.
I can't tell anyone.
Ben, if you're watching this-- you were right.
I'll never say it to your face. But you were right.
"Never trust anyone wearing a tie."

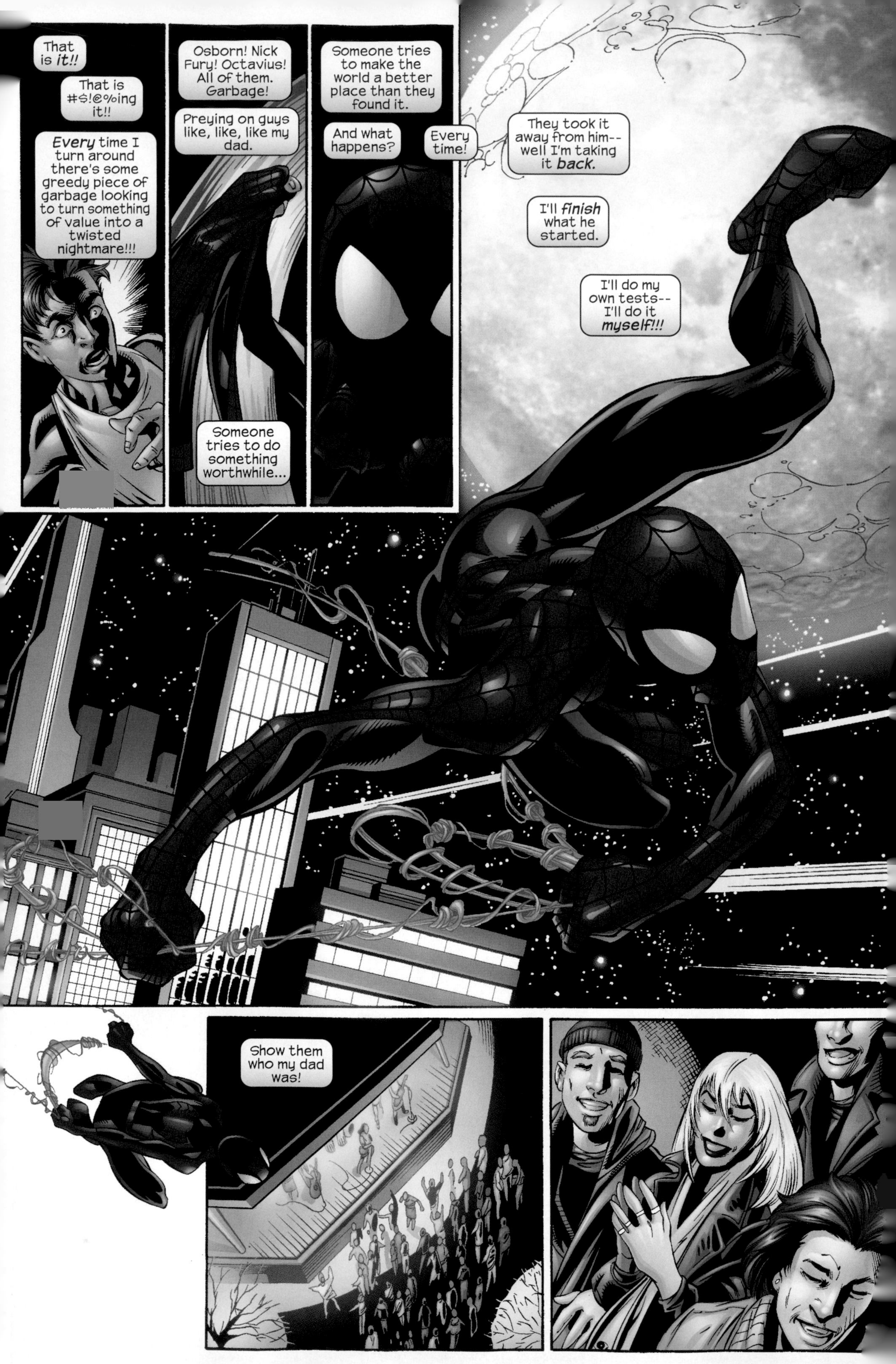

That is *it*!!
That is #$!@%ing it!!
Every time I turn around there's some greedy piece of garbage looking to turn something of value into a twisted nightmare!!!
Osborn! Nick Fury! Octavius! All of them. Garbage!
Preying on guys like, like, like my dad.
Someone tries to do something worthwhile...
Someone tries to make the world a better place than they found it.
And what happens?
Every time!
They took it away from him--well I'm taking it *back*.
I'll *finish* what he started.
I'll do my own tests--I'll do it *myself*!!!
Show them who my dad was!

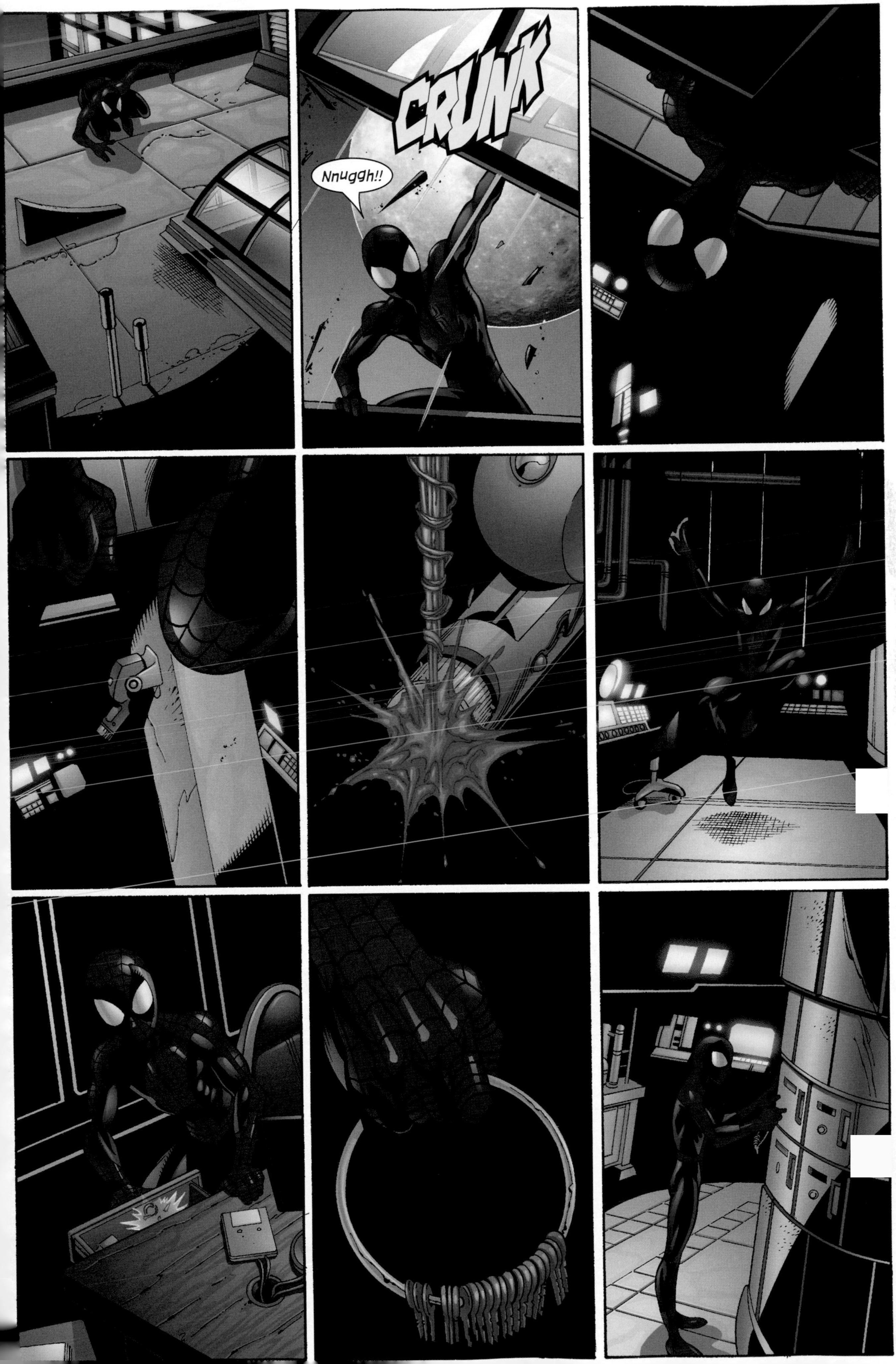
CRUNK
Nnuggh!!

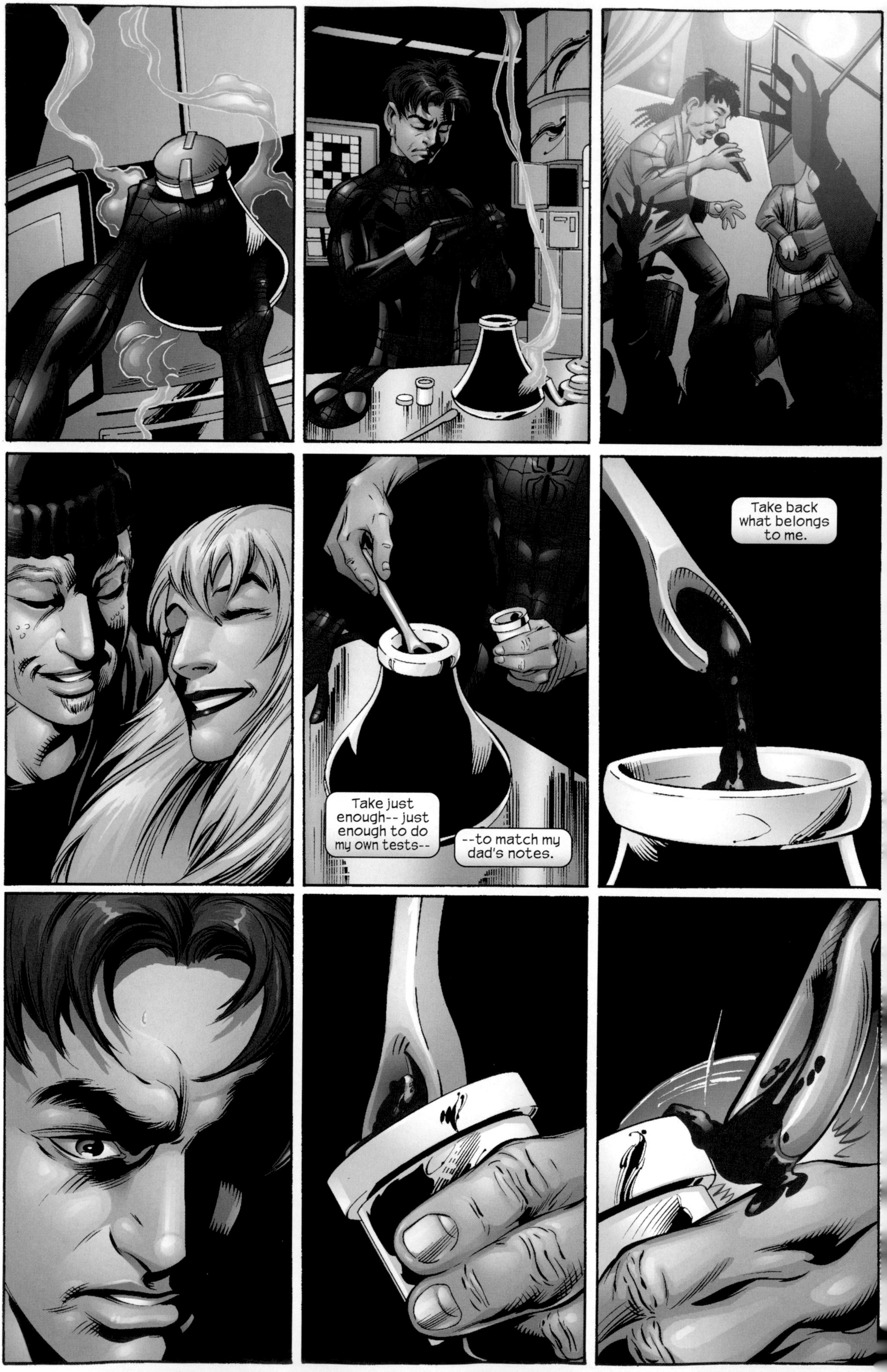
Take just enough-- just enough to do my own tests--
--to match my dad's notes.
Take back what belongs to me.

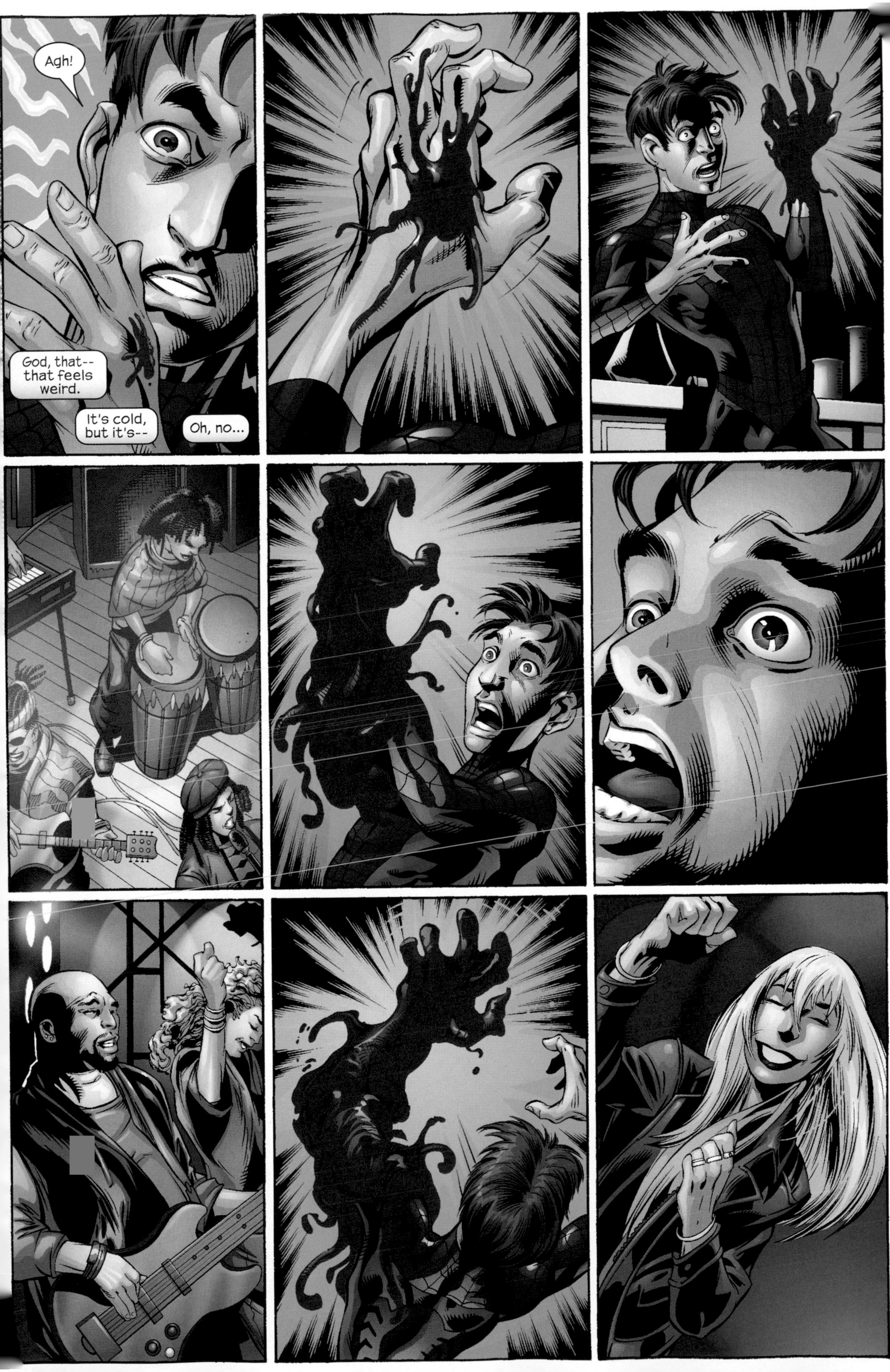
Agh!
God, that-- that feels weird.
It's cold, but it's--
Oh, no...

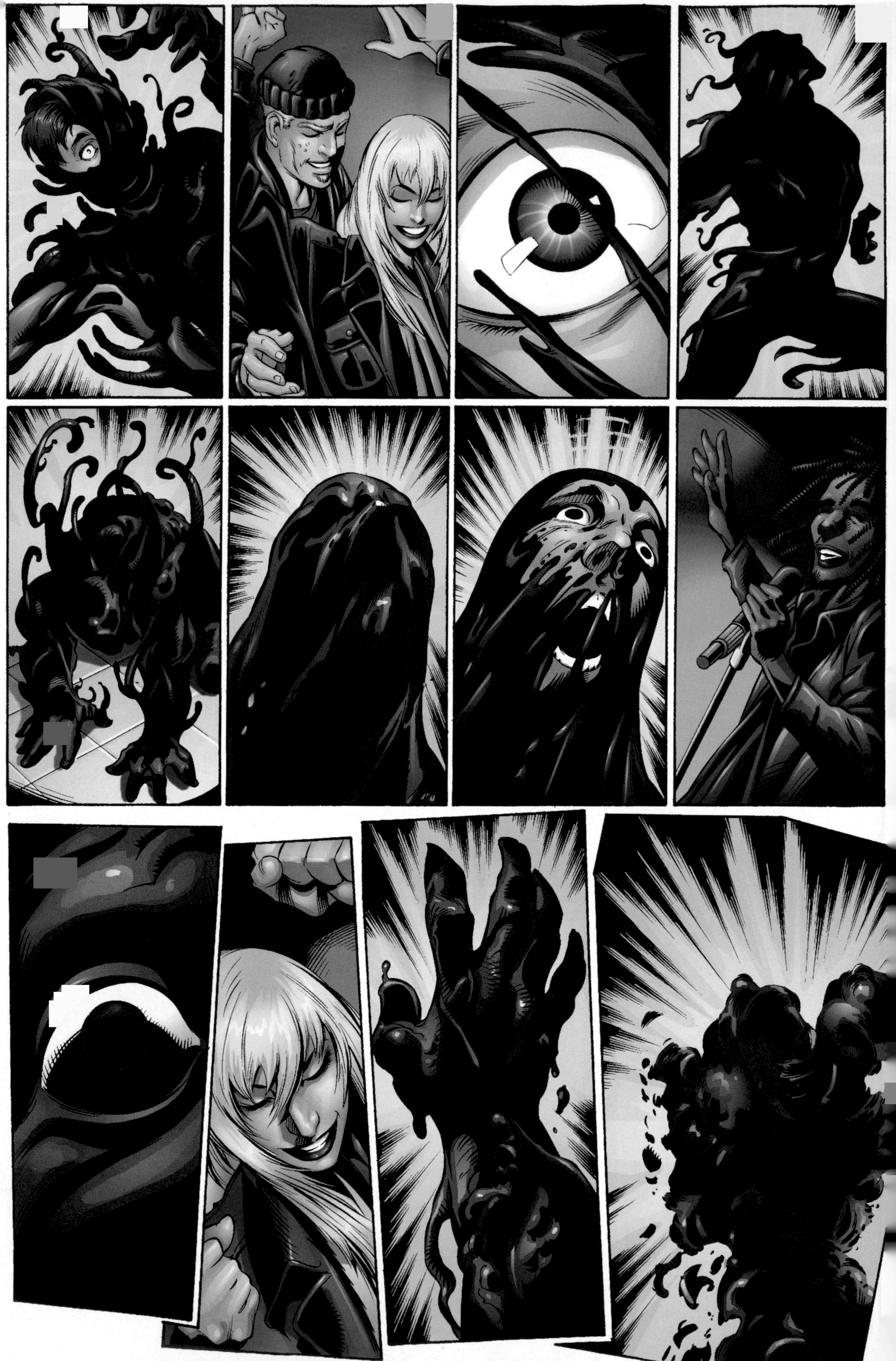

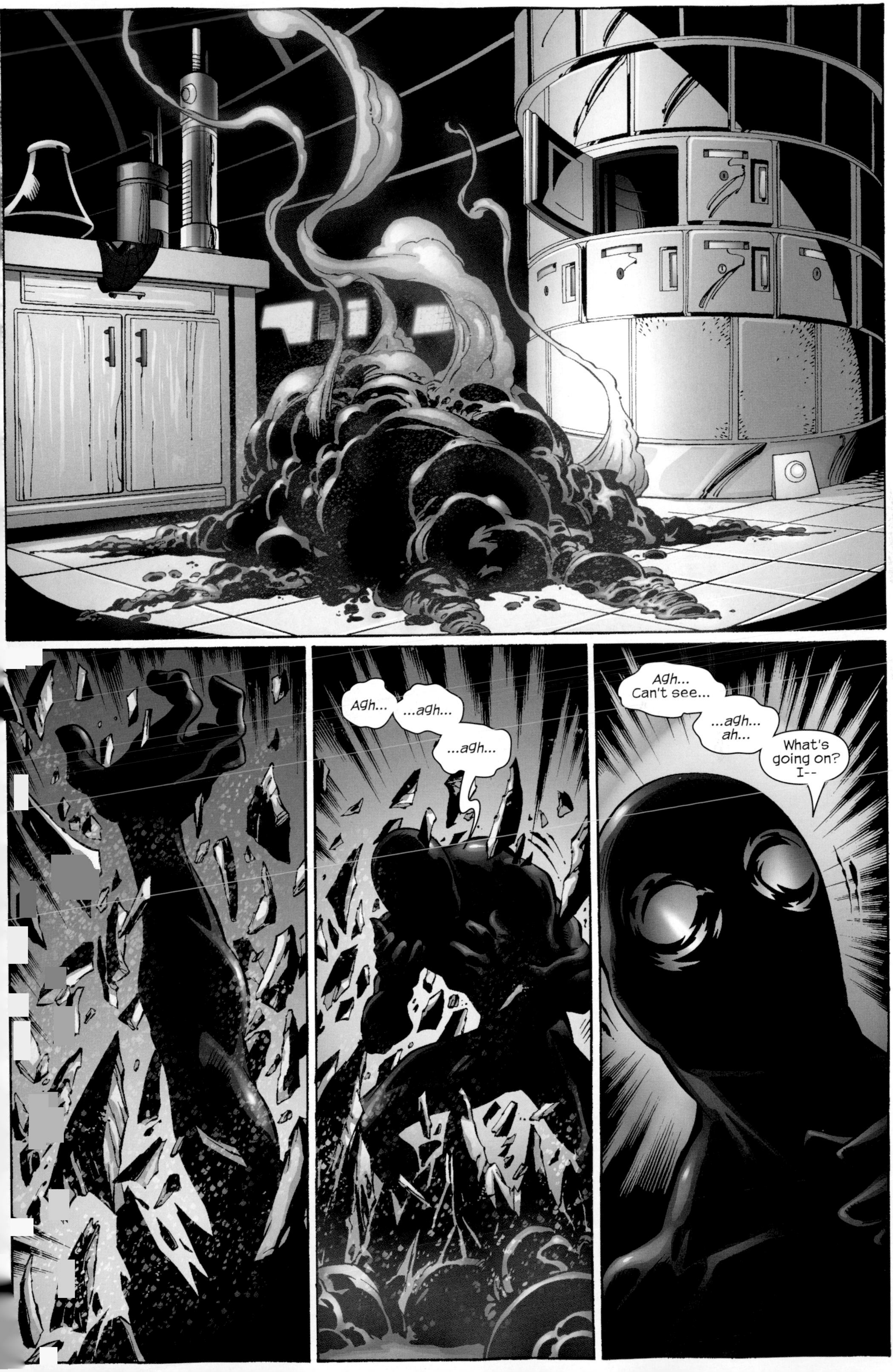
Agh...
...agh...
...agh...
Agh... Can't see...
...agh... ah...
What's going on? I--

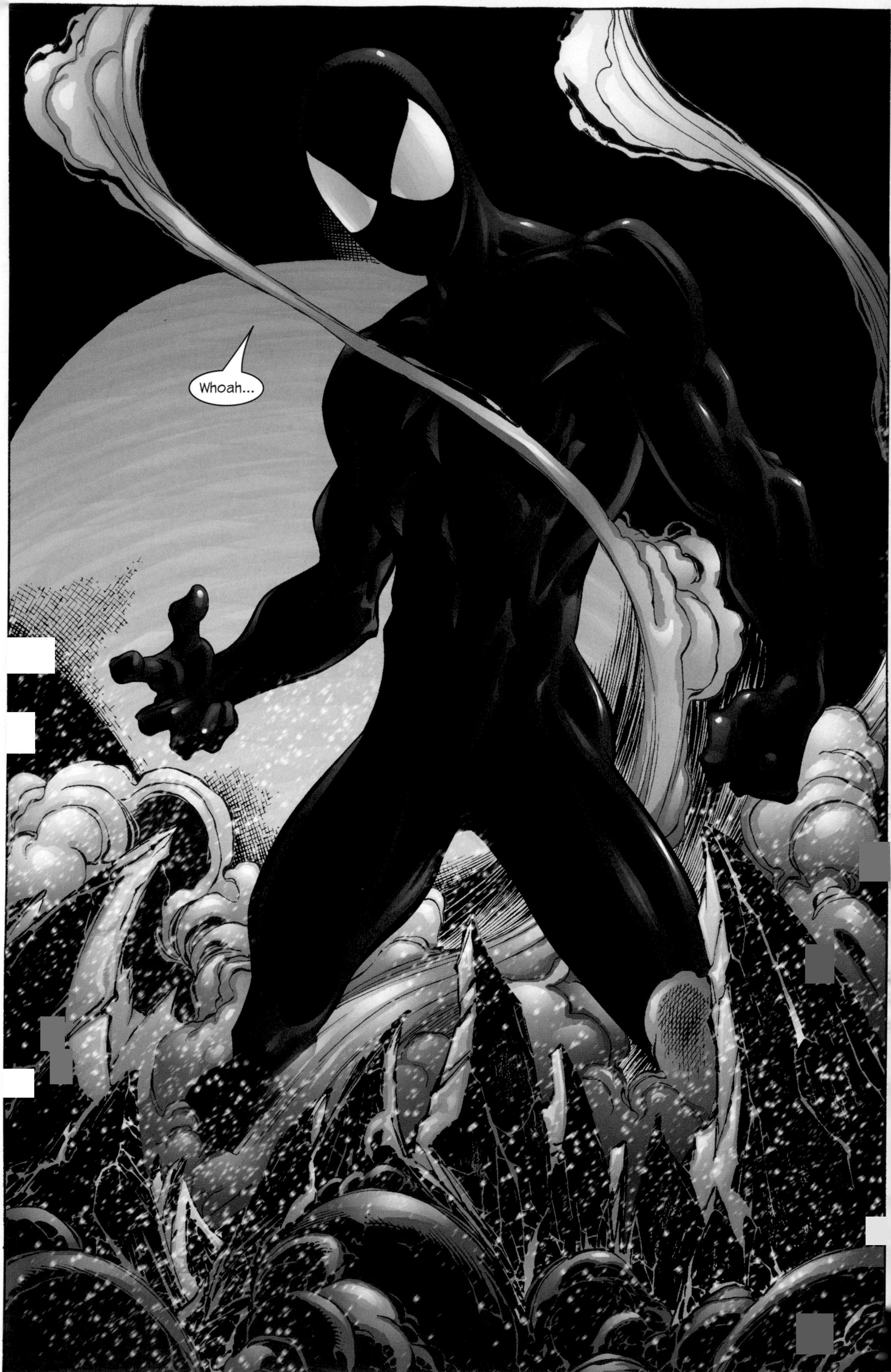
Whoah...

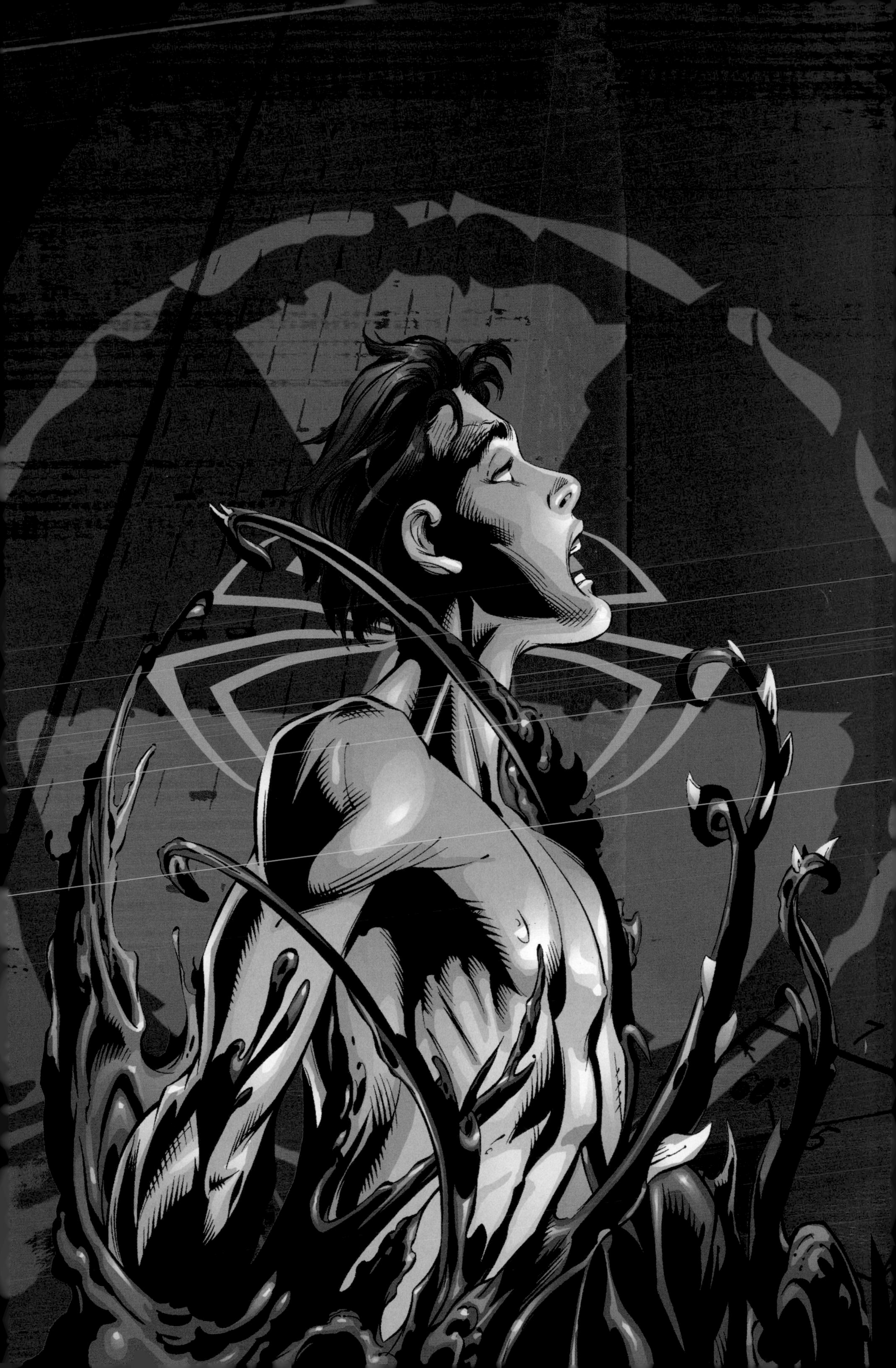

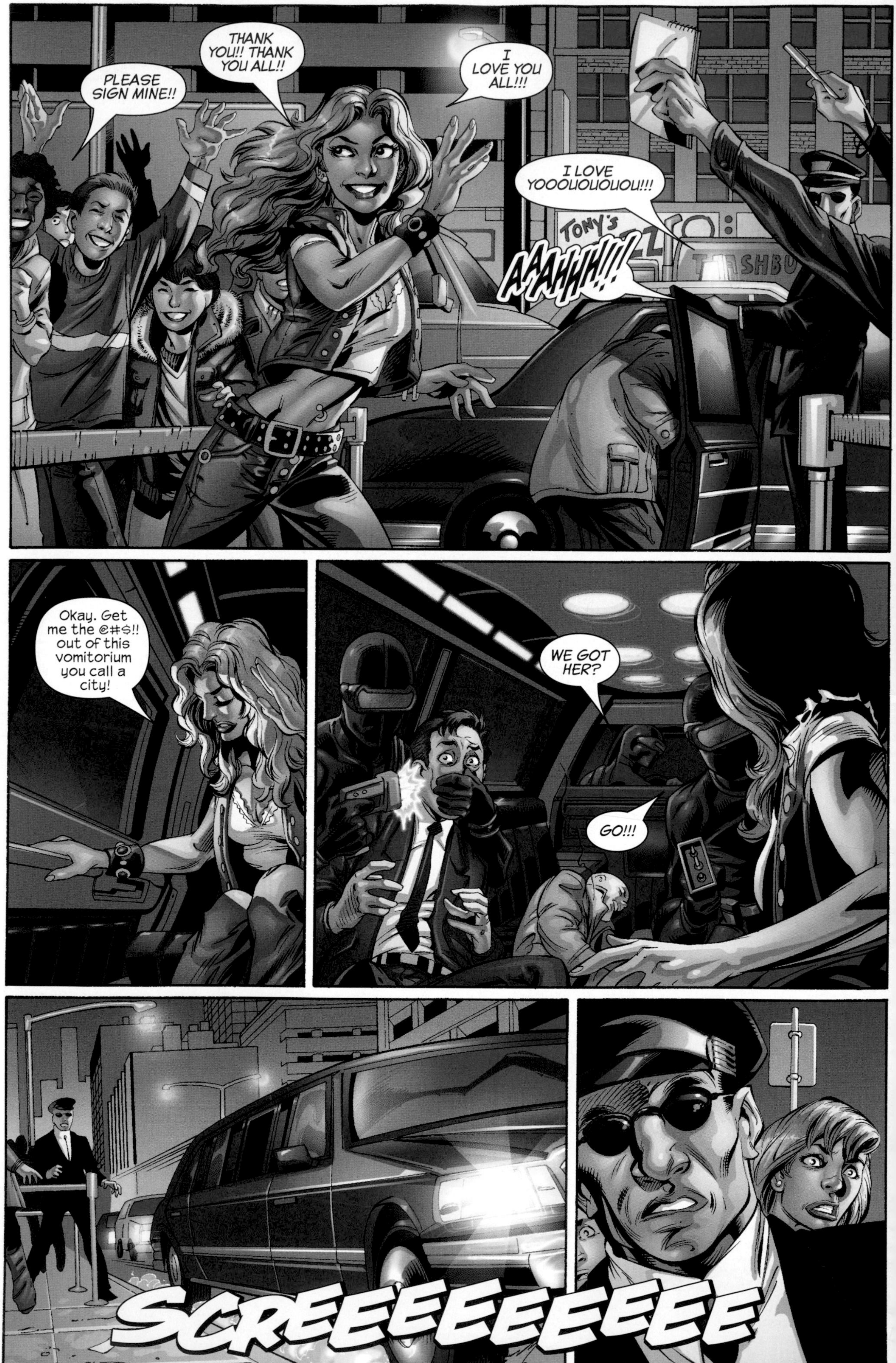
PLEASE SIGN MINE!!
THANK YOU!! THANK YOU ALL!!
I LOVE YOU ALL!!!
I LOVE YOOOUOUOUOU!!!
TONY'S
AAAHHH!!!
Okay. Get me the @#$!! out of this vomitorium you call a city!
WE GOT HER?
GO!!!
SCREEEEEEEEEE

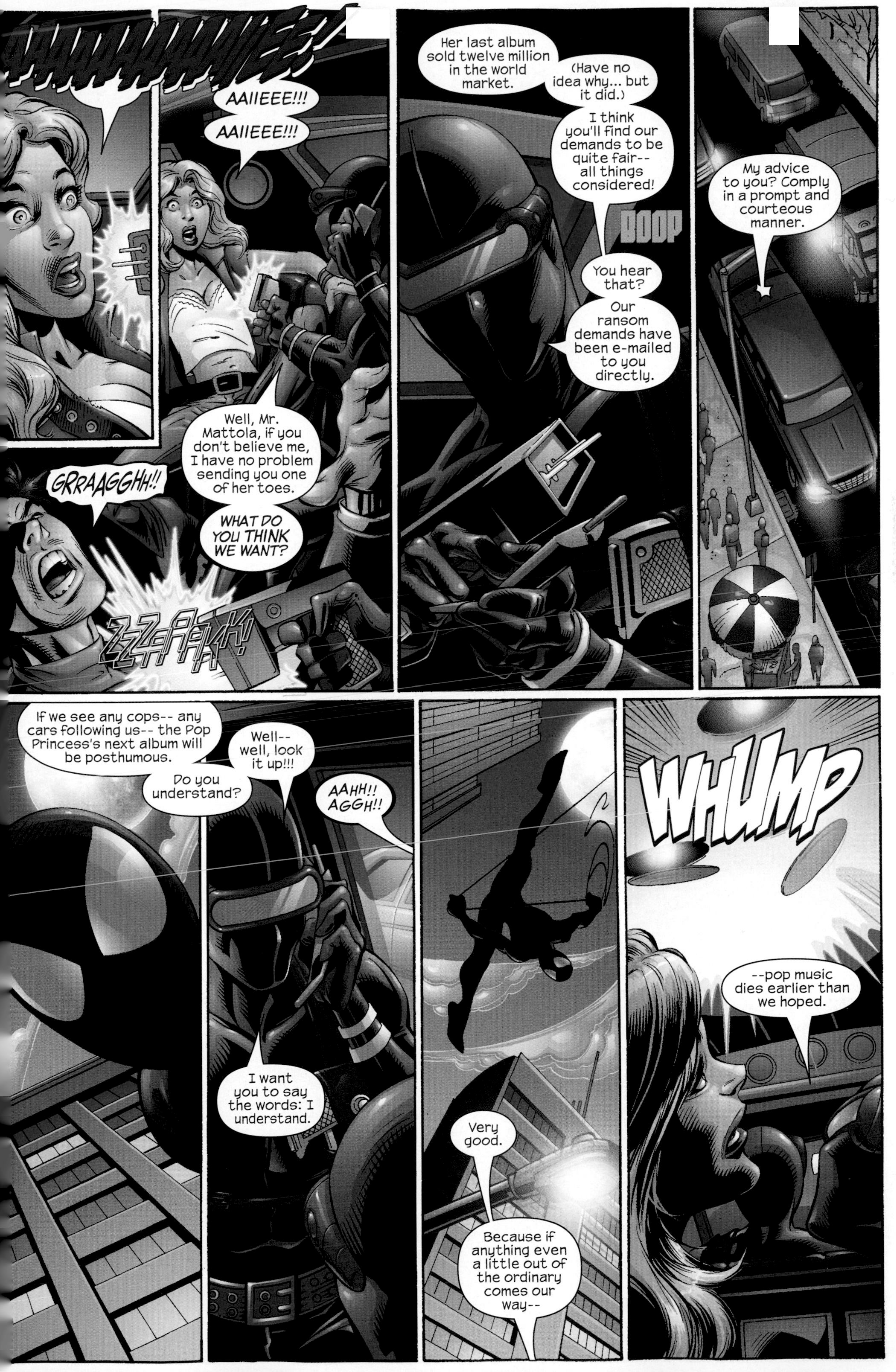
AAAAAAAAAIIEEE!
AAIIEEE!!!
AAIIEEE!!!
Well, Mr. Mattola, if you don't believe me, I have no problem sending you one of her toes.
GRRAAGGHH!!
WHAT DO YOU THINK WE WANT?
ZZZAAKK!
Her last album sold twelve million in the world market.
(Have no idea why... but it did.)
I think you'll find our demands to be quite fair-- all things considered!
BOOP
You hear that?
Our ransom demands have been e-mailed to you directly.
My advice to you? Comply in a prompt and courteous manner.
If we see any cops-- any cars following us-- the Pop Princess's next album will be posthumous.
Do you understand?
Well-- well, look it up!!!
AAHH!! AGGH!!
I want you to say the words: I understand.
Very good.
Because if anything even a little out of the ordinary comes our way--
WHUMP
--pop music dies earlier than we hoped.

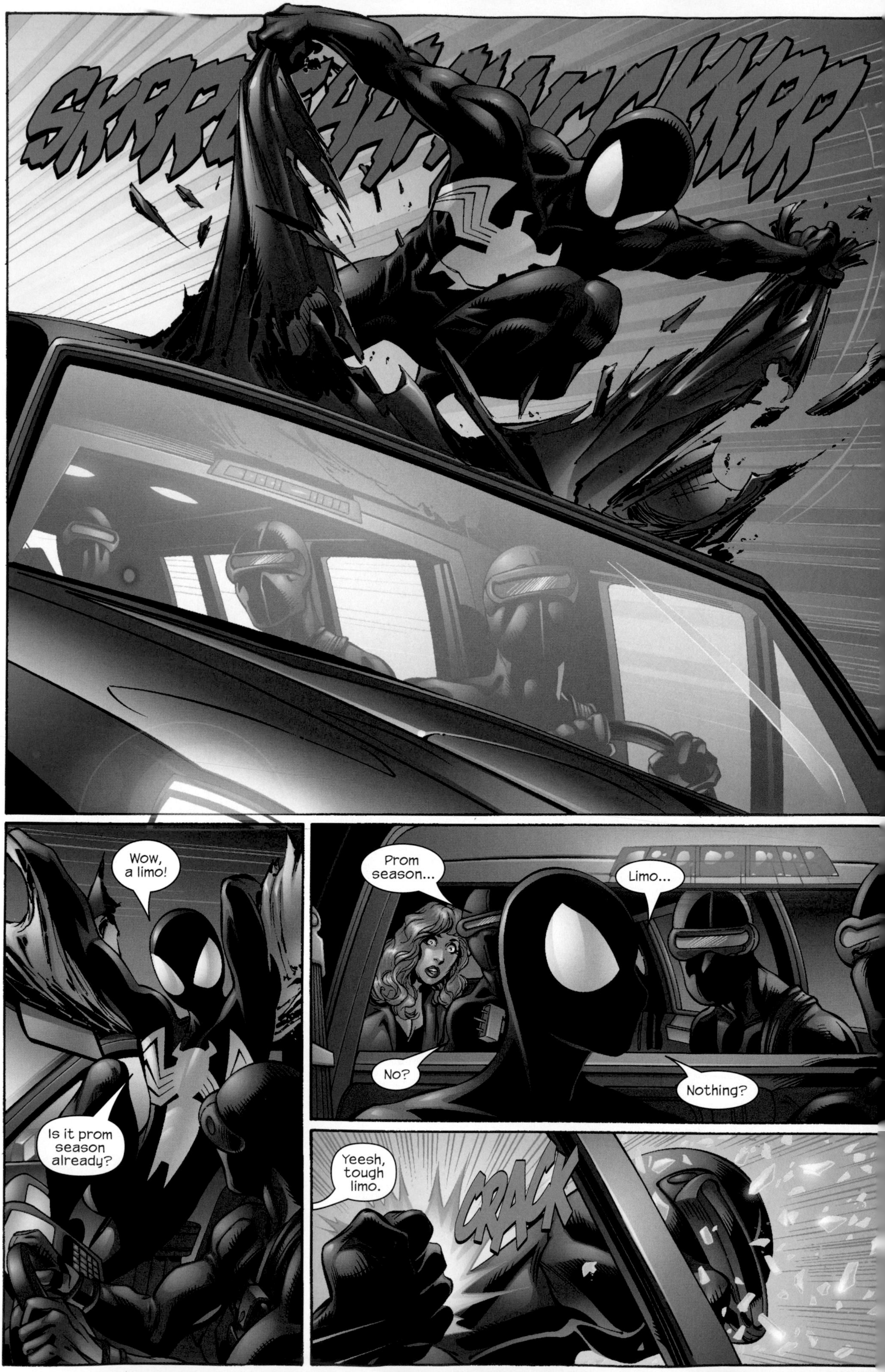
Wow, a limo!
Is it prom season already?
Prom season...
Limo...
No?
Nothing?
Yeesh, tough limo.
CRACK

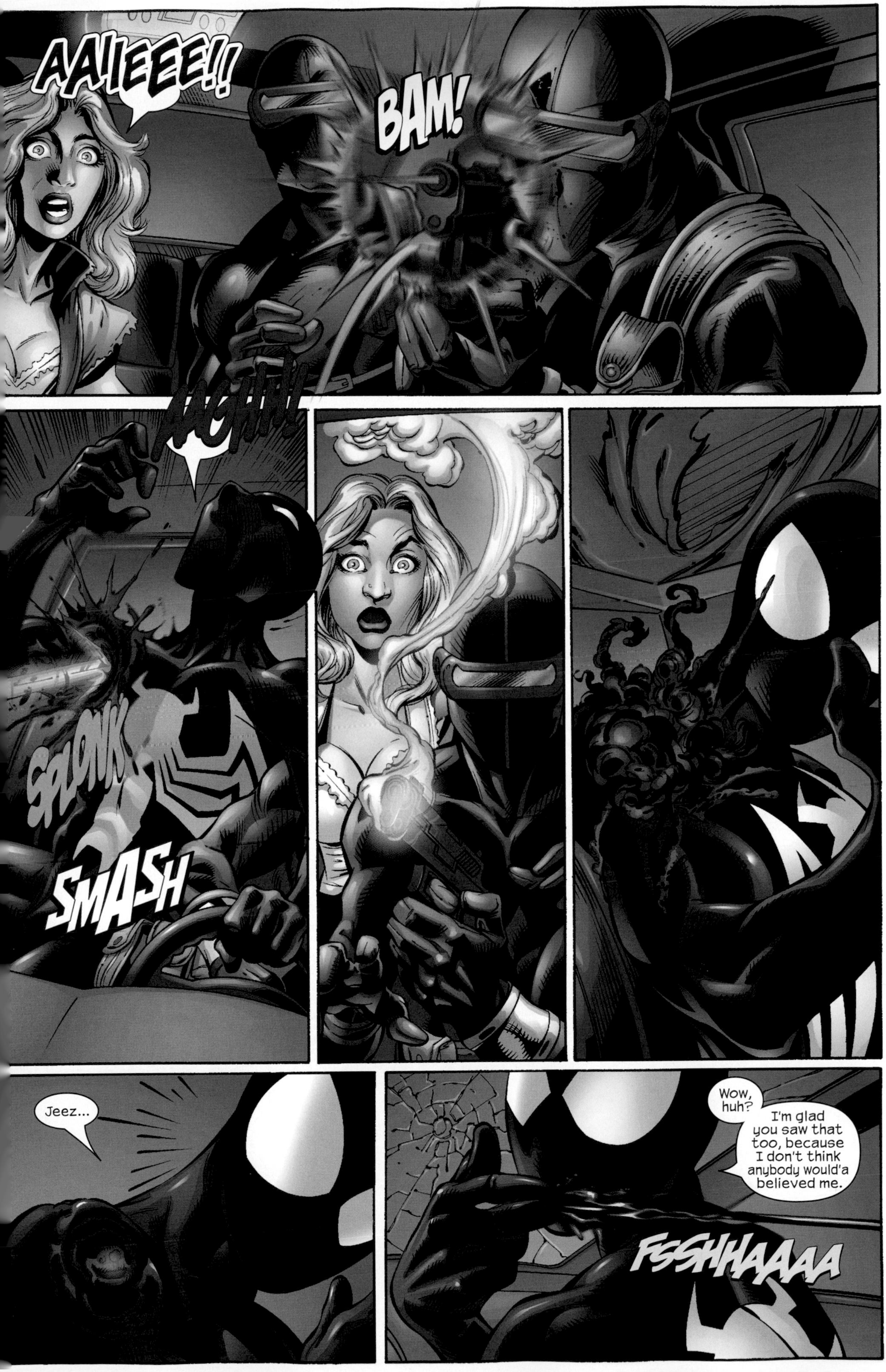
AAIIEEE!!
BAM!
AAGHH!
SPLONK
SMASH
Jeez...
Wow, huh?
I'm glad you saw that too, because I don't think anybody would'a believed me.
FSSHHAAAA

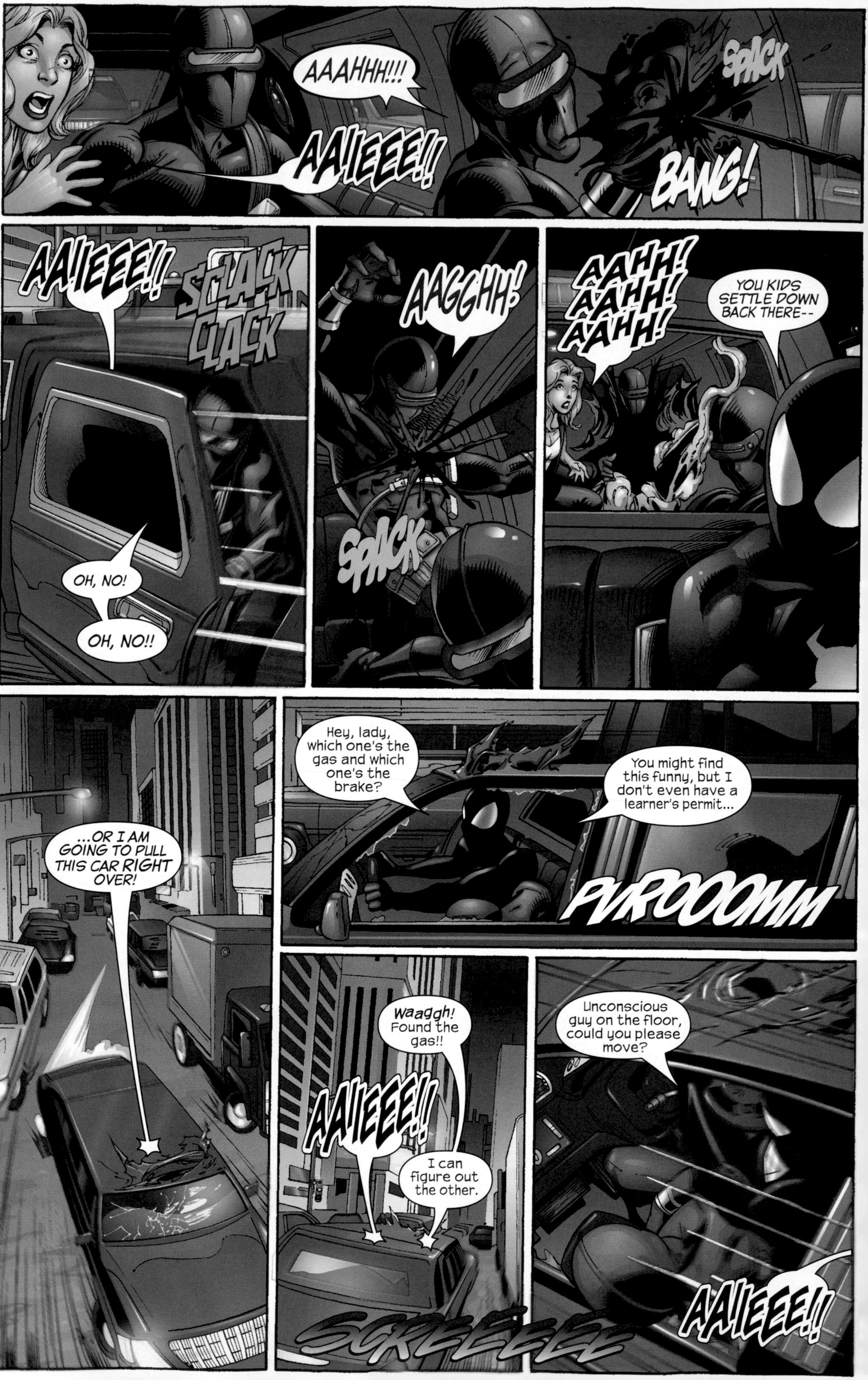
AAAHHH!!!
AA!IEEE!!
SPACK
BANG!
AA!IEEE!!
SCLACK CLACK
OH, NO!
OH, NO!!
AAGGHH!
SPACK
AAHH! AAHH! AAHH!
YOU KIDS SETTLE DOWN BACK THERE--
...OR I AM GOING TO PULL THIS CAR RIGHT OVER!
Hey, lady, which one's the gas and which one's the brake?
You might find this funny, but I don't even have a learner's permit...
PVROOOOMM
Waaggh! Found the gas!!
AA!IEEE!!
I can figure out the other.
SCREEEEE
Unconscious guy on the floor, could you please move?
AA!IEEE!!

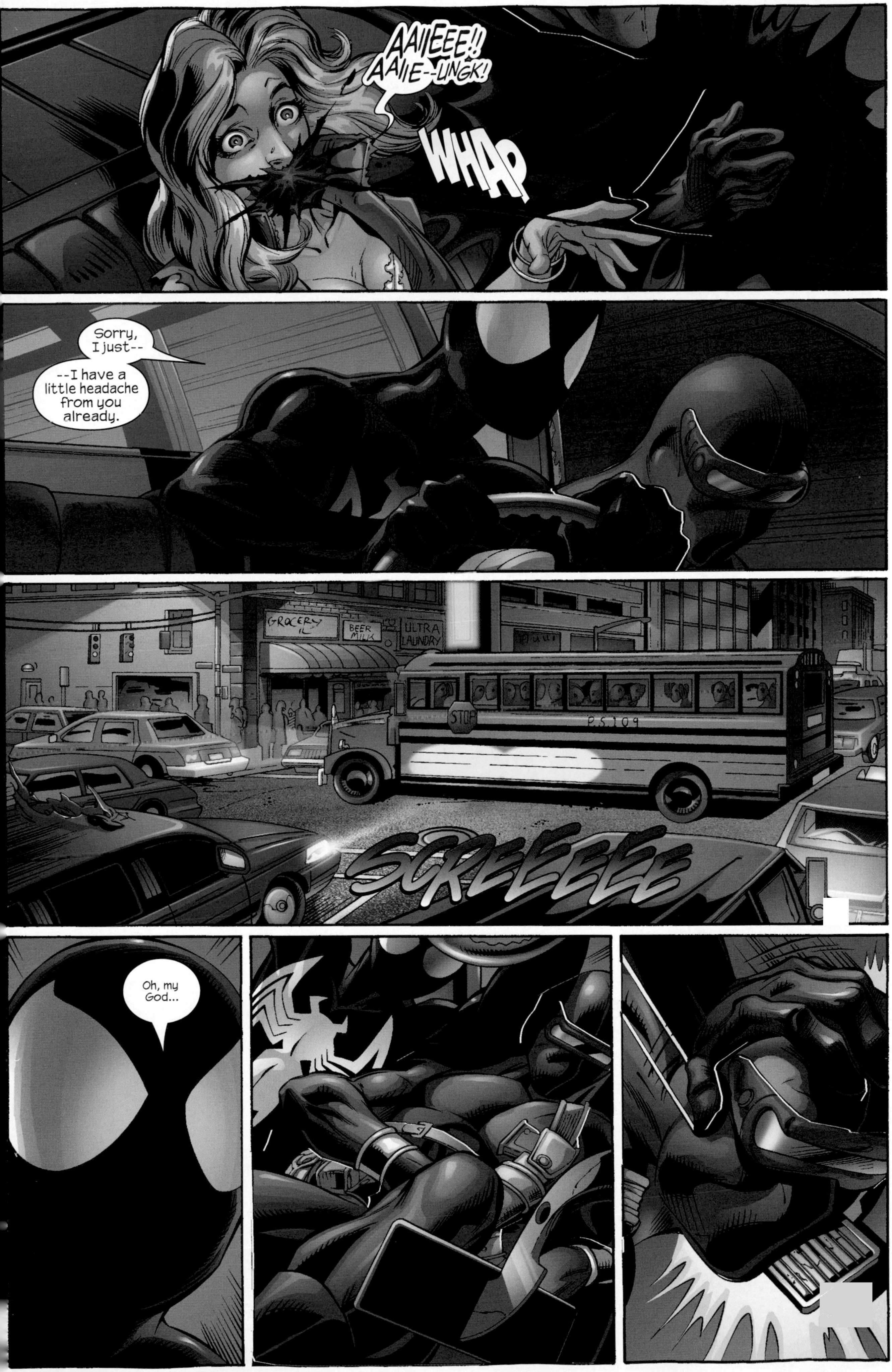
AAIIEEE!! AAIIE--UNGK!
WHAP
Sorry, I just--
--I have a little headache from you already.
GROCERY
BEER MILK
ULTRA LAUNDRY
STOP
P.S. 109
SCREEEEEE
Oh, my God...

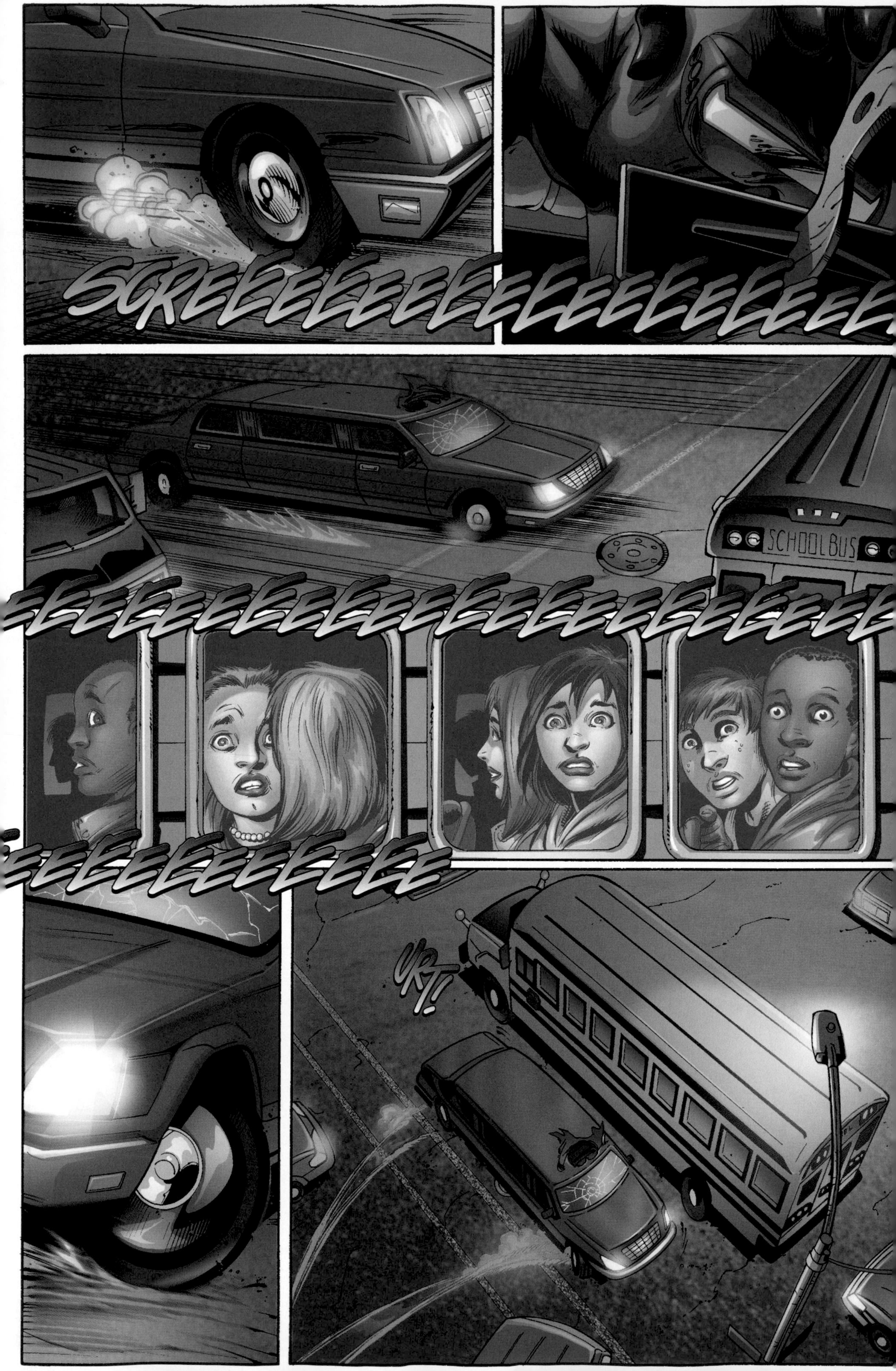
SCREEEEEEEEEEEEEEEEEEE
SCHOOLBUS
EEEEEEEEEEEEEEEEEEEEEEEEE
EEEEEEEEEEEEE
URT!!

Ma'am...

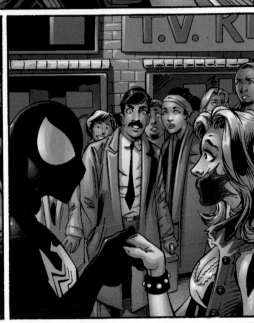

Just for the record, everyone...

...we're just friends.

WEEEEEDOOOWEEEEDOOO

Hands in the air, freak!!

Oh, come on, man. I so rocked it this time.

I mean it! Put out your #$@#in' hands in the air, right @$@#@in' now!

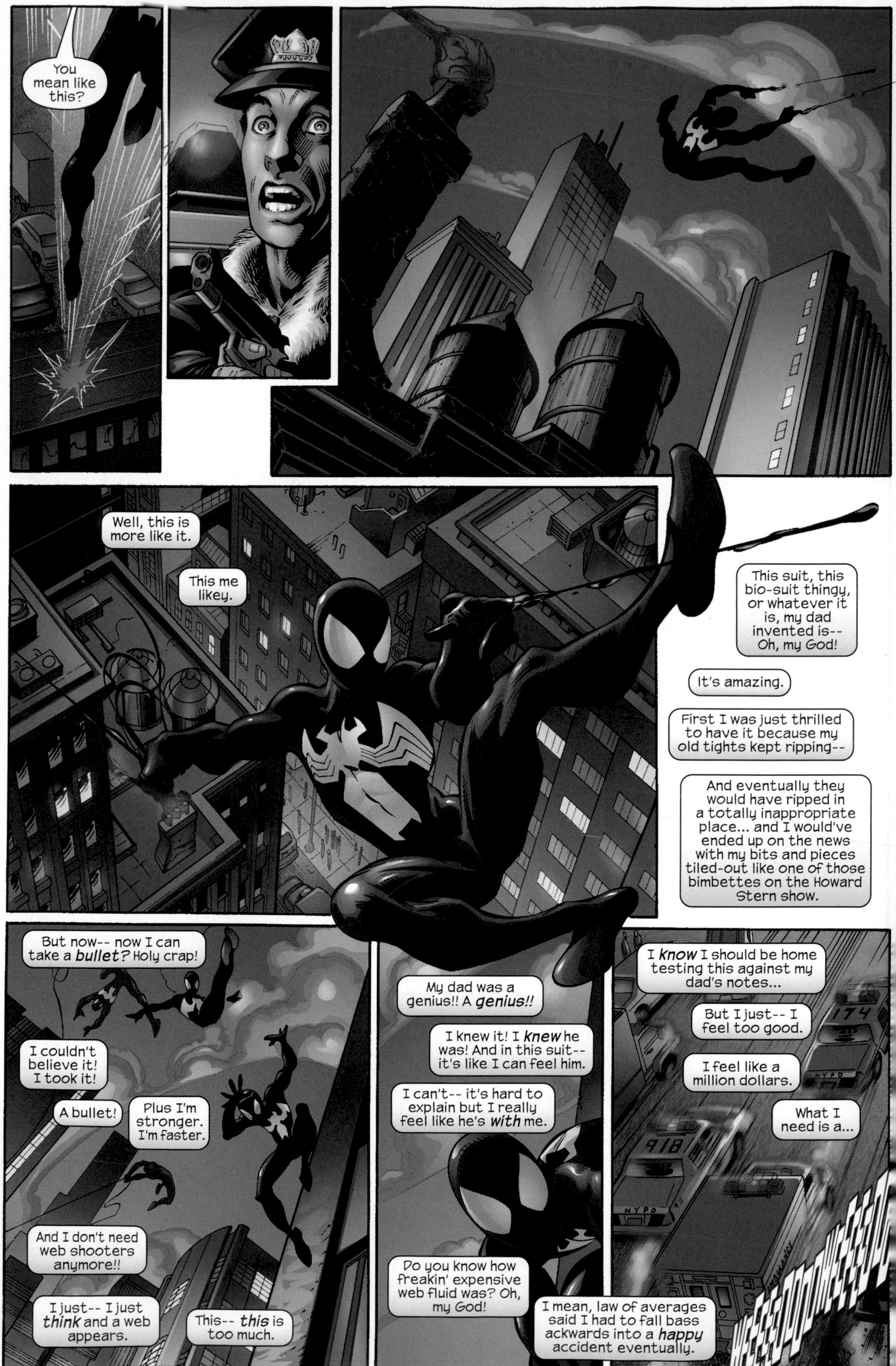

You mean like this?
Well, this is more like it.
This me likey.
This suit, this bio-suit thingy, or whatever it is, my dad invented is-- Oh, my God!
It's amazing.
First I was just thrilled to have it because my old tights kept ripping--
And eventually they would have ripped in a totally inappropriate place... and I would've ended up on the news with my bits and pieces tiled-out like one of those bimbettes on the Howard Stern show.
But now-- now I can take a bullet? Holy crap!
I couldn't believe it! I took it!
A bullet!
Plus I'm stronger. I'm faster.
And I don't need web shooters anymore!!
I just-- I just think and a web appears.
This-- this is too much.
My dad was a genius!! A genius!!
I knew it! I knew he was! And in this suit-- it's like I can feel him.
I can't-- it's hard to explain but I really feel like he's with me.
Do you know how freakin' expensive web fluid was? Oh, my God!
I mean, law of averages said I had to fall bass ackwards into a happy accident eventually.
I know I should be home testing this against my dad's notes...
But I just-- I feel too good.
I feel like a million dollars.
What I need is a...
WHEEEEOOOOWHEEEEOO

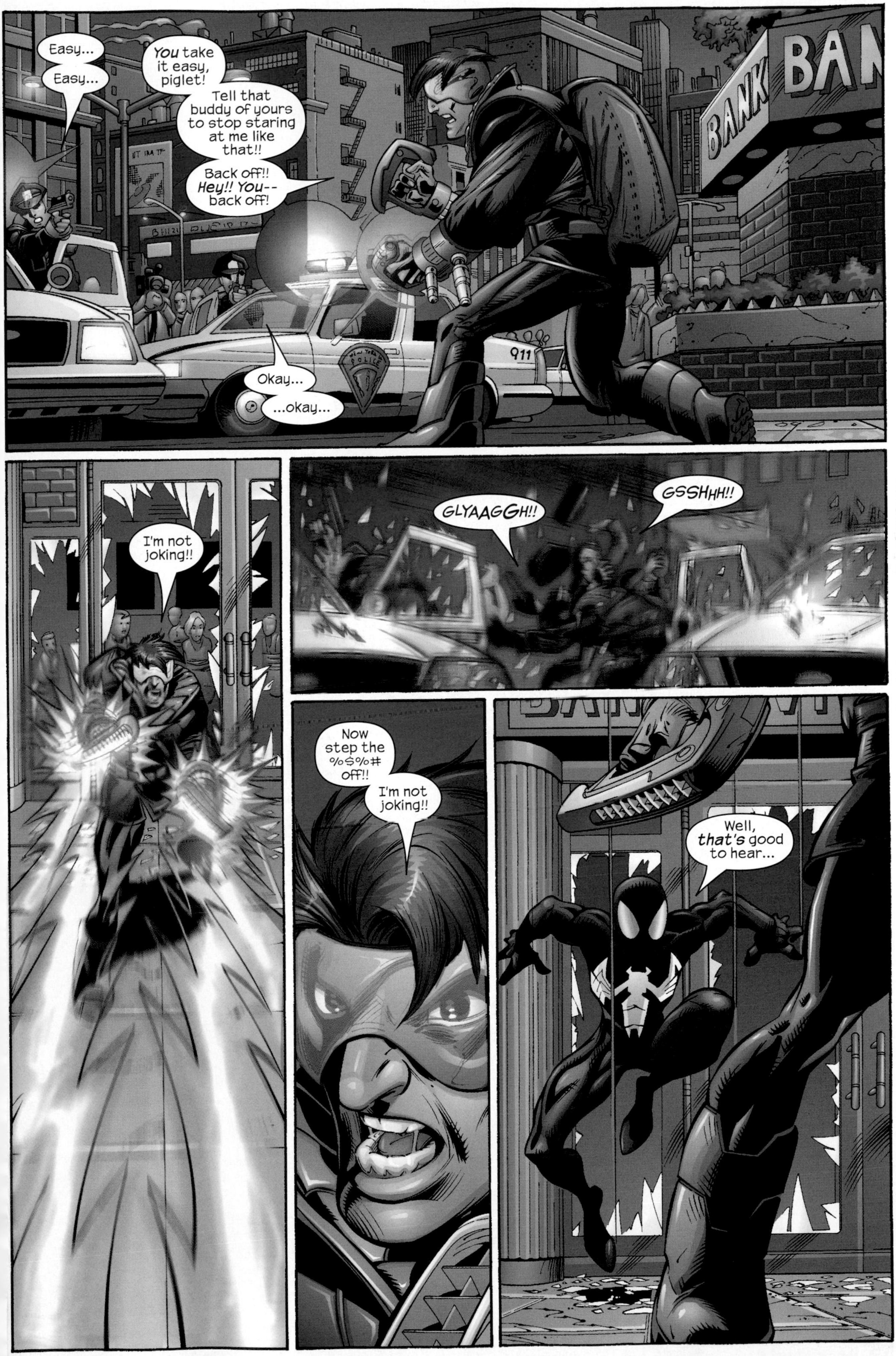

Easy...
Easy...
You take it easy, piglet!
Tell that buddy of yours to stop staring at me like that!!
Back off!! Hey!! You-- back off!
Okay...
...okay...
BANK
I'm not joking!!
GLYAAGGH!!
GSSHHH!!
Now step the %$%# off!!
I'm not joking!!
Well, that's good to hear...

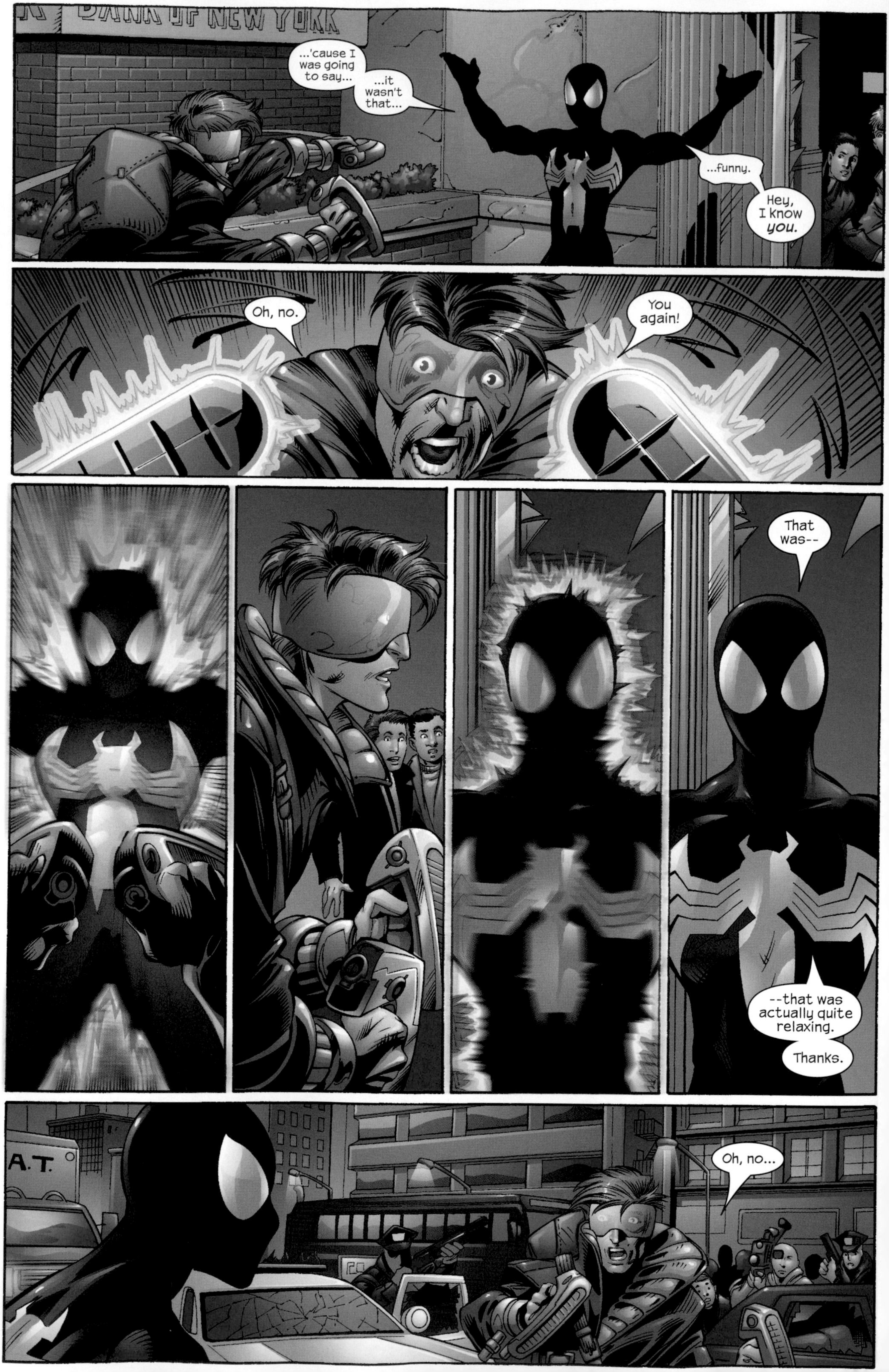
BANK OF NEW YORK
...'cause I was going to say...
...it wasn't that...
...funny.
Hey, I know *you.*
Oh, no.
You again!
That was--
--that was actually quite relaxing.
Thanks.
A.T.
Oh, no...

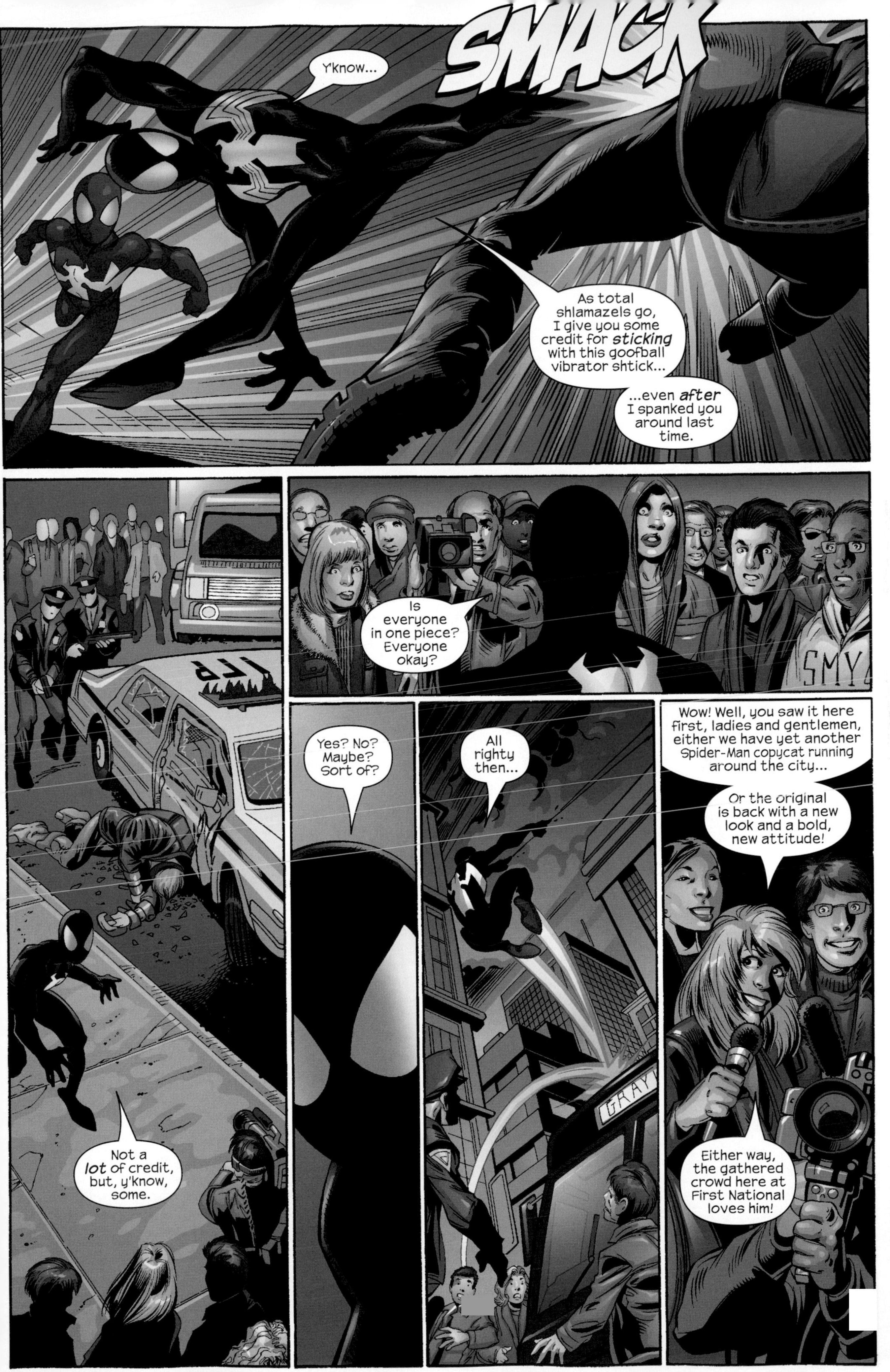
SMACK
Y'know...
As total shlamazels go, I give you some credit for sticking with this goofball vibrator shtick...
...even after I spanked you around last time.
Not a lot of credit, but, y'know, some.
Is everyone in one piece? Everyone okay?
Yes? No? Maybe? Sort of?
All righty then...
Wow! Well, you saw it here first, ladies and gentlemen, either we have yet another Spider-Man copycat running around the city...
Or the original is back with a new look and a bold, new attitude!
Either way, the gathered crowd here at First National loves him!

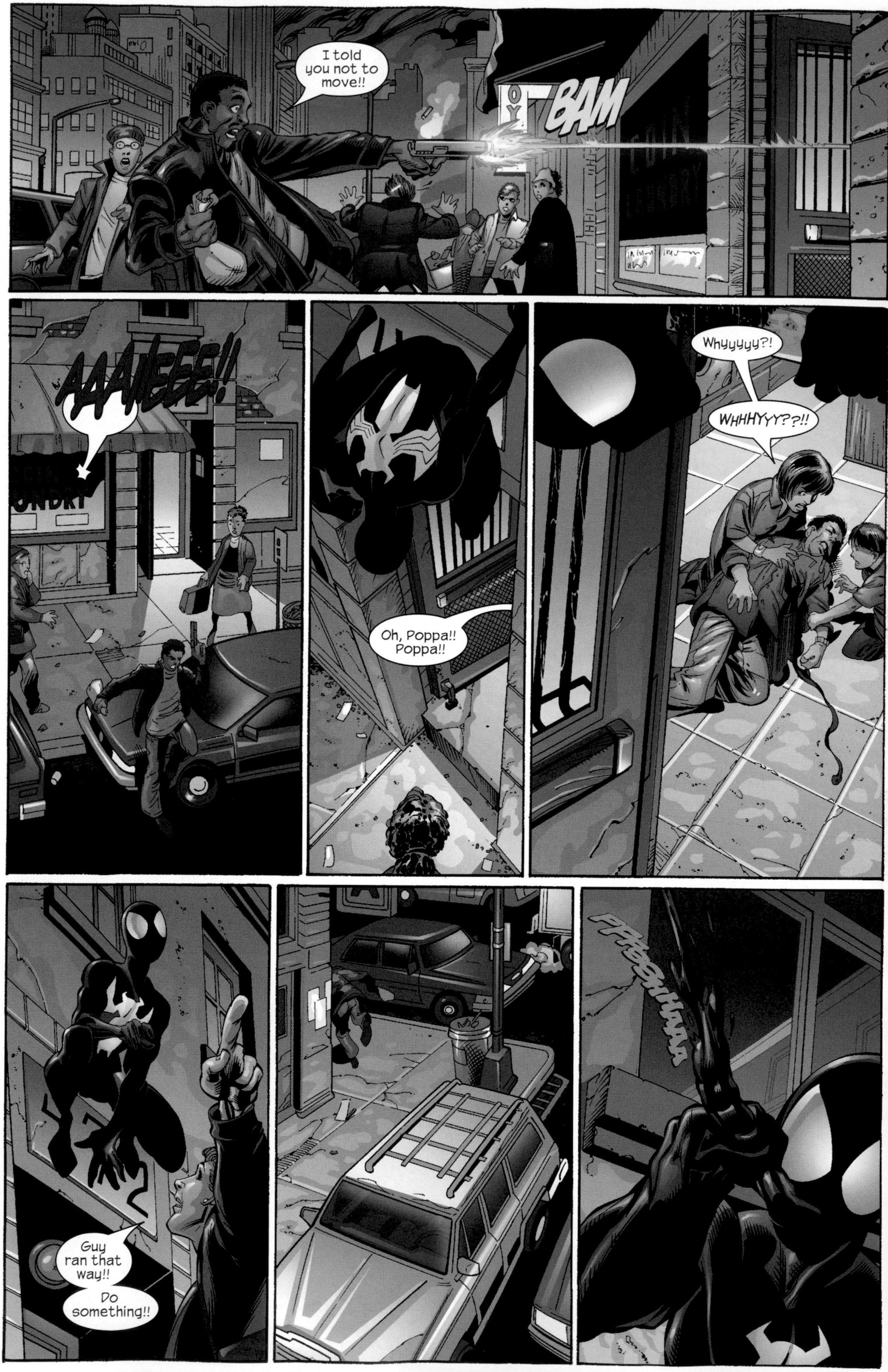
I told you not to move!!
BAM
AAAIEEE!!
Oh, Poppa!! Poppa!!
Whyyyyy?!
WHHHYYY??!!
Guy ran that way!!
Do something!!

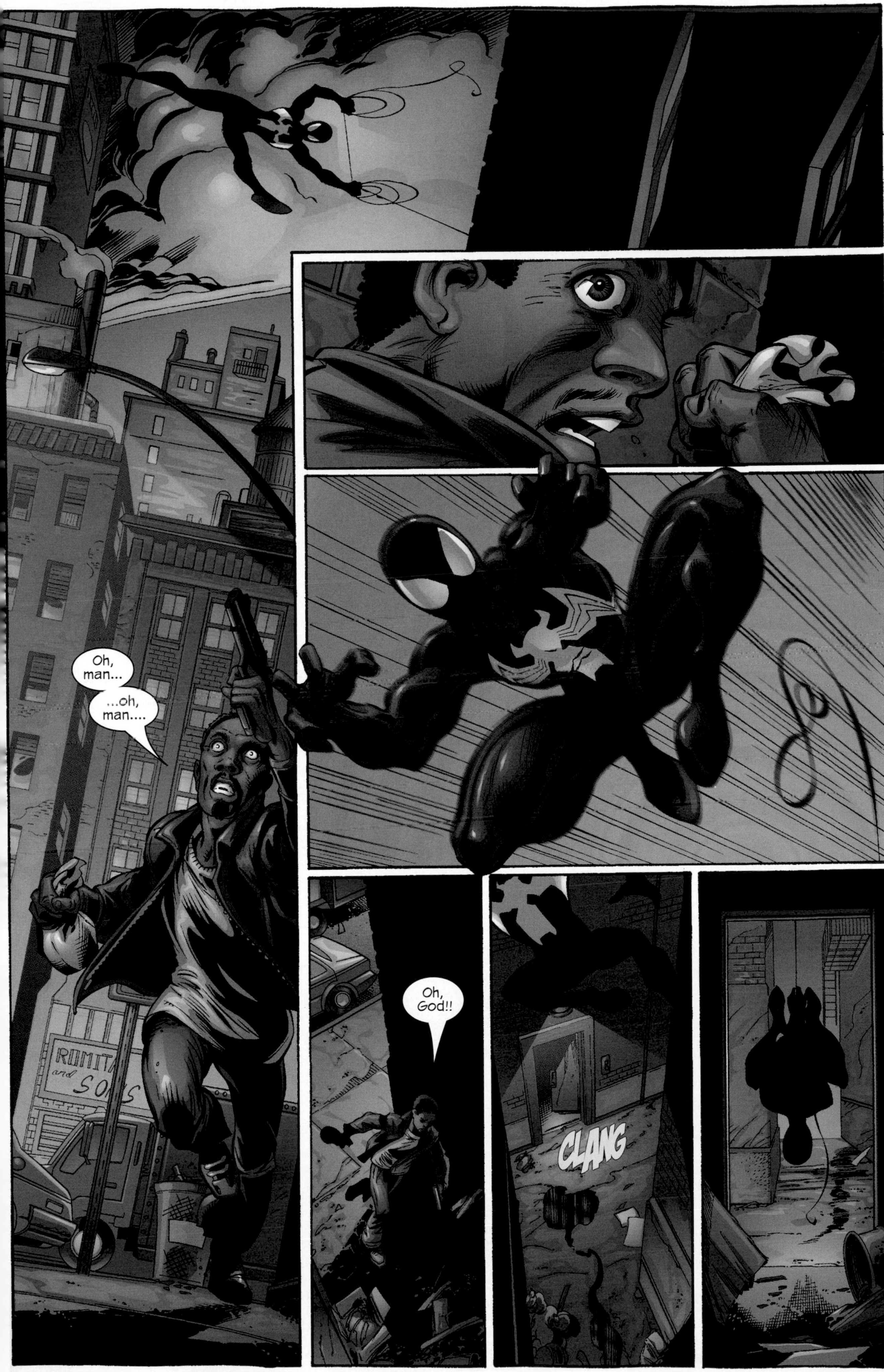
Oh, man...
...oh, man....
Oh, God!!
CLANG
ROMITA and SONS

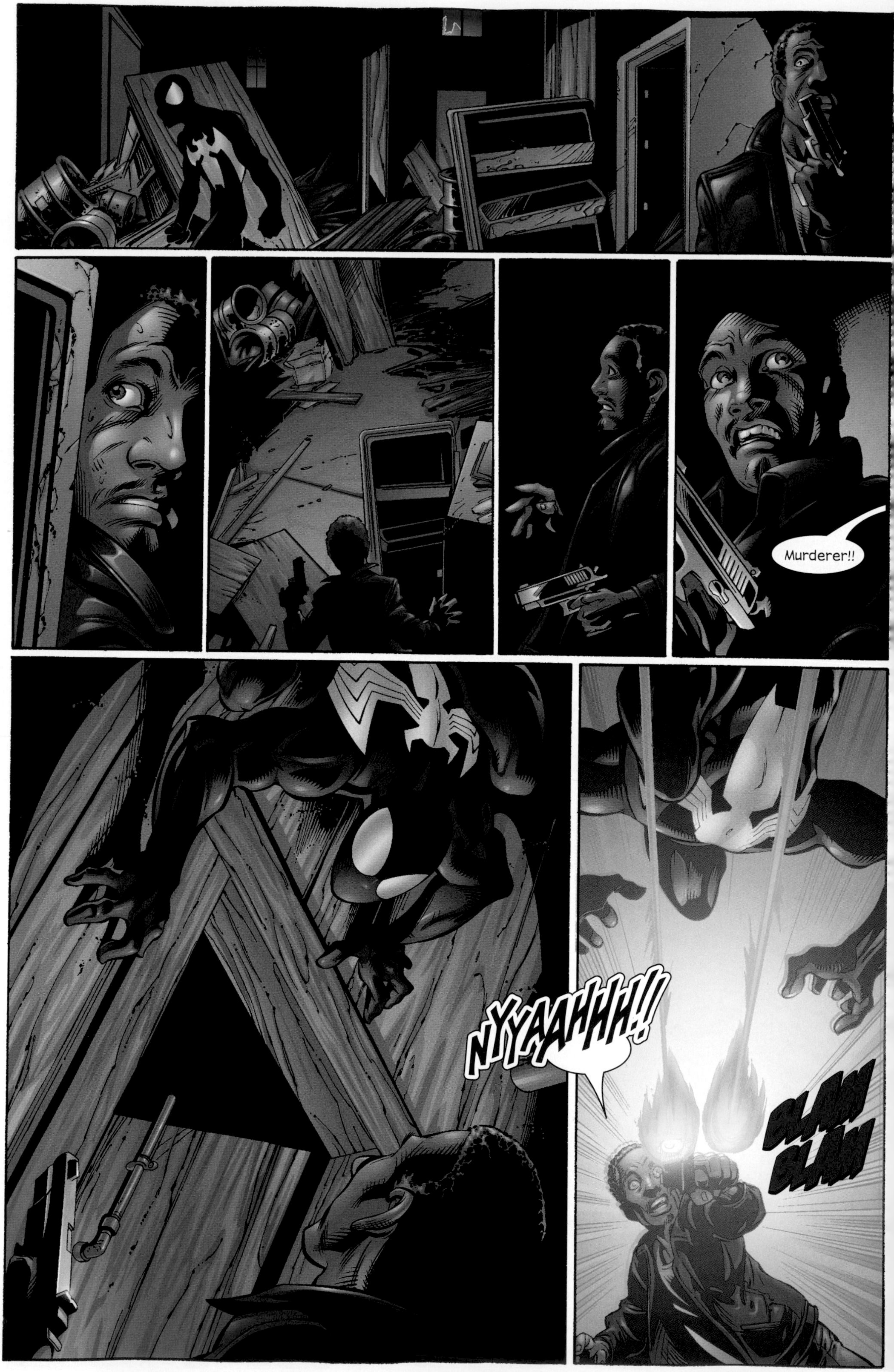
Murderer!!
NYYAAHHHH!!
BLAM
BLAM

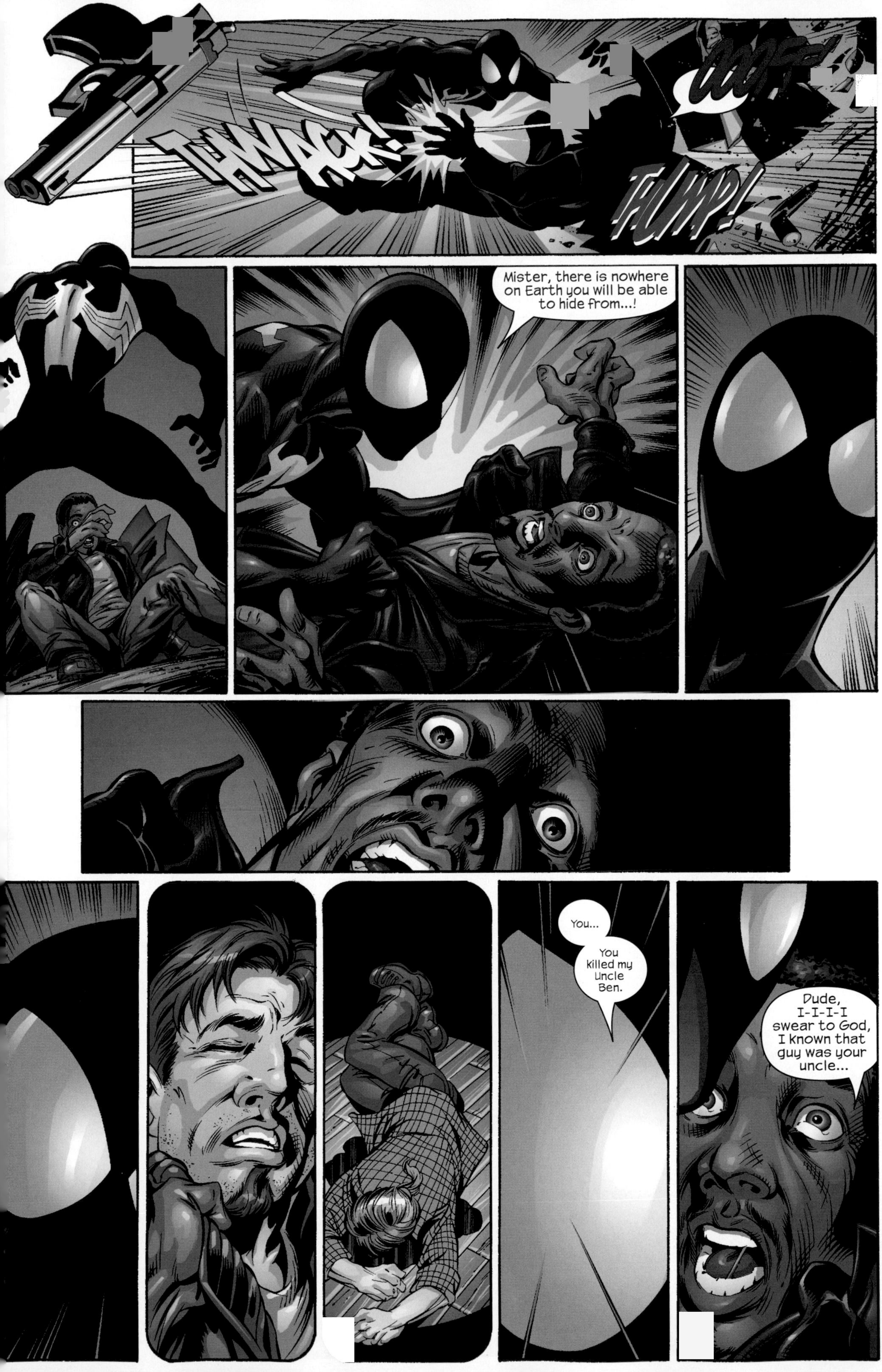
THWACK!
OOOF!
THUMP!
Mister, there is nowhere on Earth you will be able to hide from...!
You...
You killed my Uncle Ben.
Dude, I-I-I-I swear to God, I known that guy was your uncle...

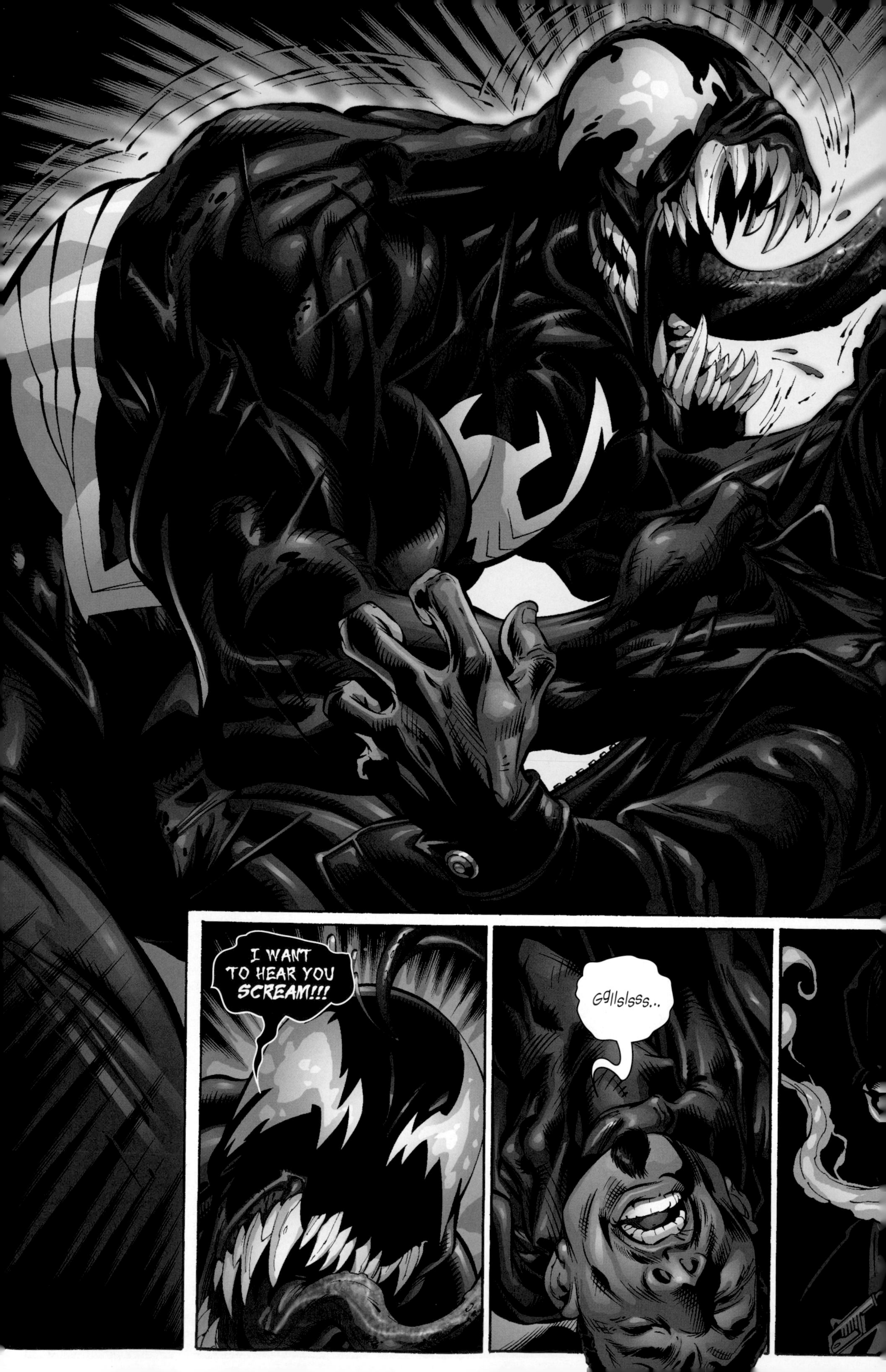
I WANT TO HEAR YOU SCREAM!!!
Ggllslsss...

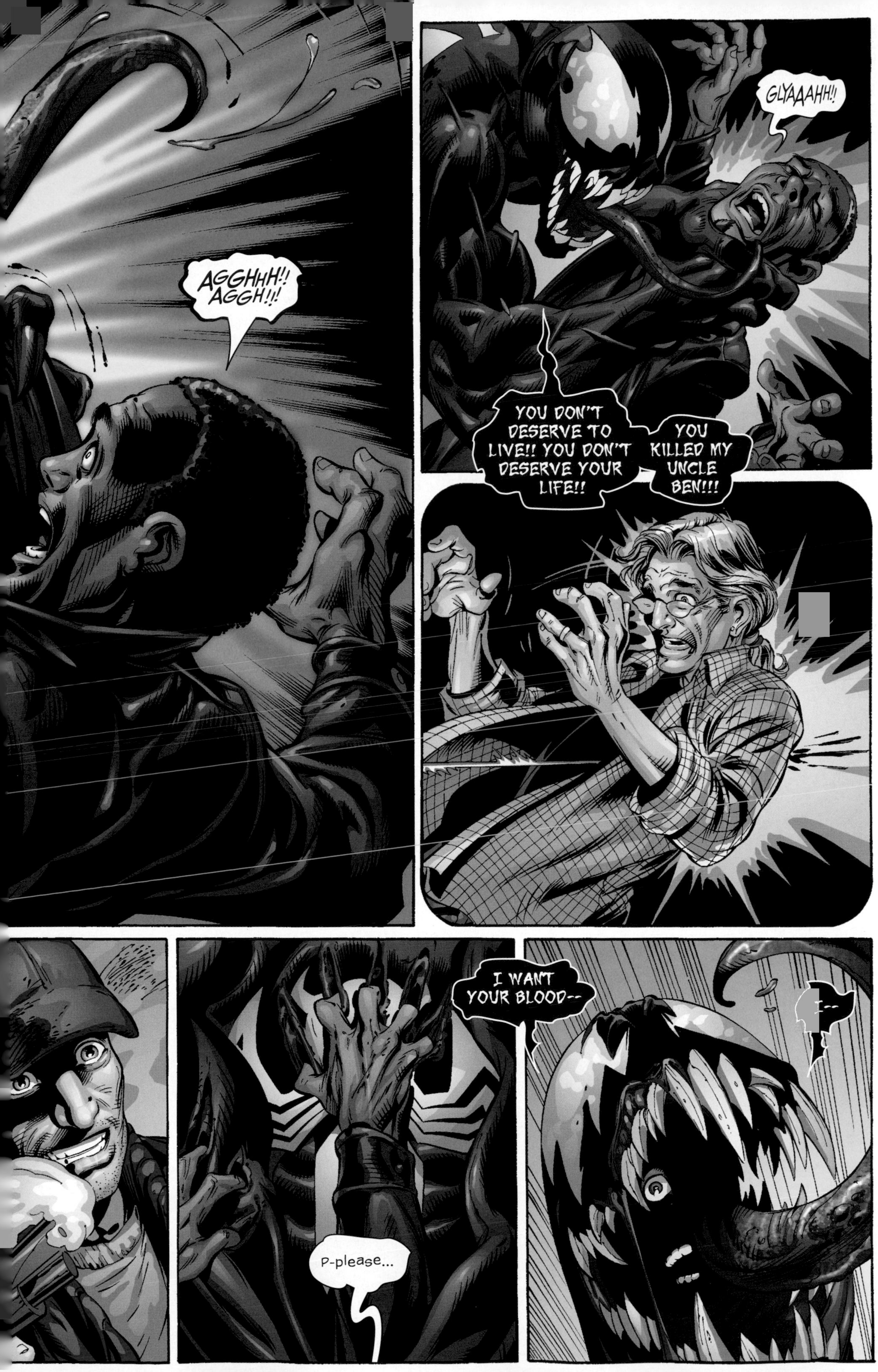
AGGHHH!! AGGH!!!
GLYAAAHH!!
YOU DON'T DESERVE TO LIVE!! YOU DON'T DESERVE YOUR LIFE!!
YOU KILLED MY UNCLE BEN!!!
P-please...
I WANT YOUR BLOOD--
I--

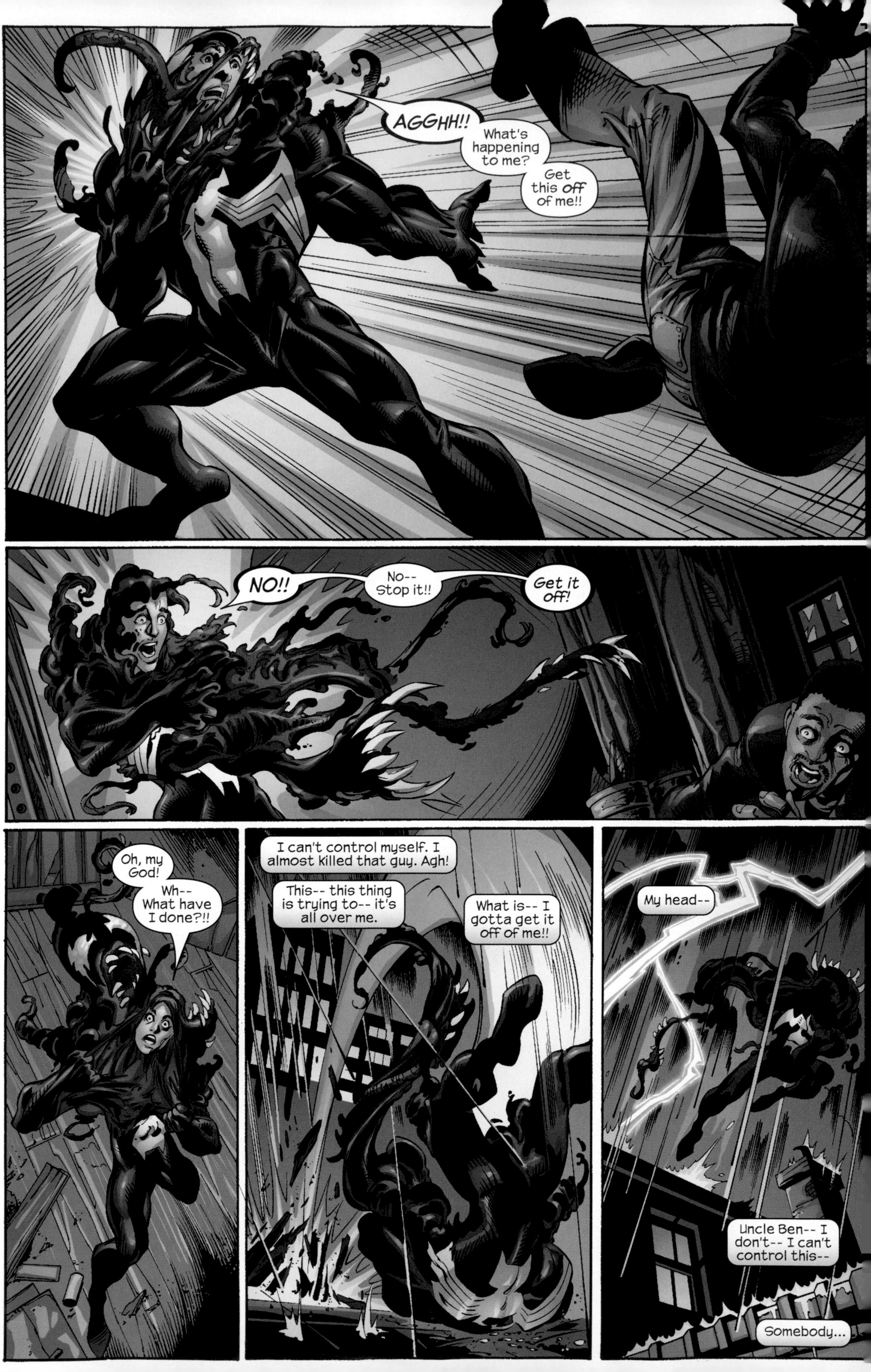
AGGHH!!
What's happening to me?
Get this off of me!!
NO!!
No-- Stop it!!
Get it off!
Oh, my God!
Wh-- What have I done?!!
I can't control myself. I almost killed that guy. Agh!
This-- this thing is trying to-- it's all over me.
What is-- I gotta get it off of me!!
My head--
Uncle Ben-- I don't-- I can't control this--
Somebody...

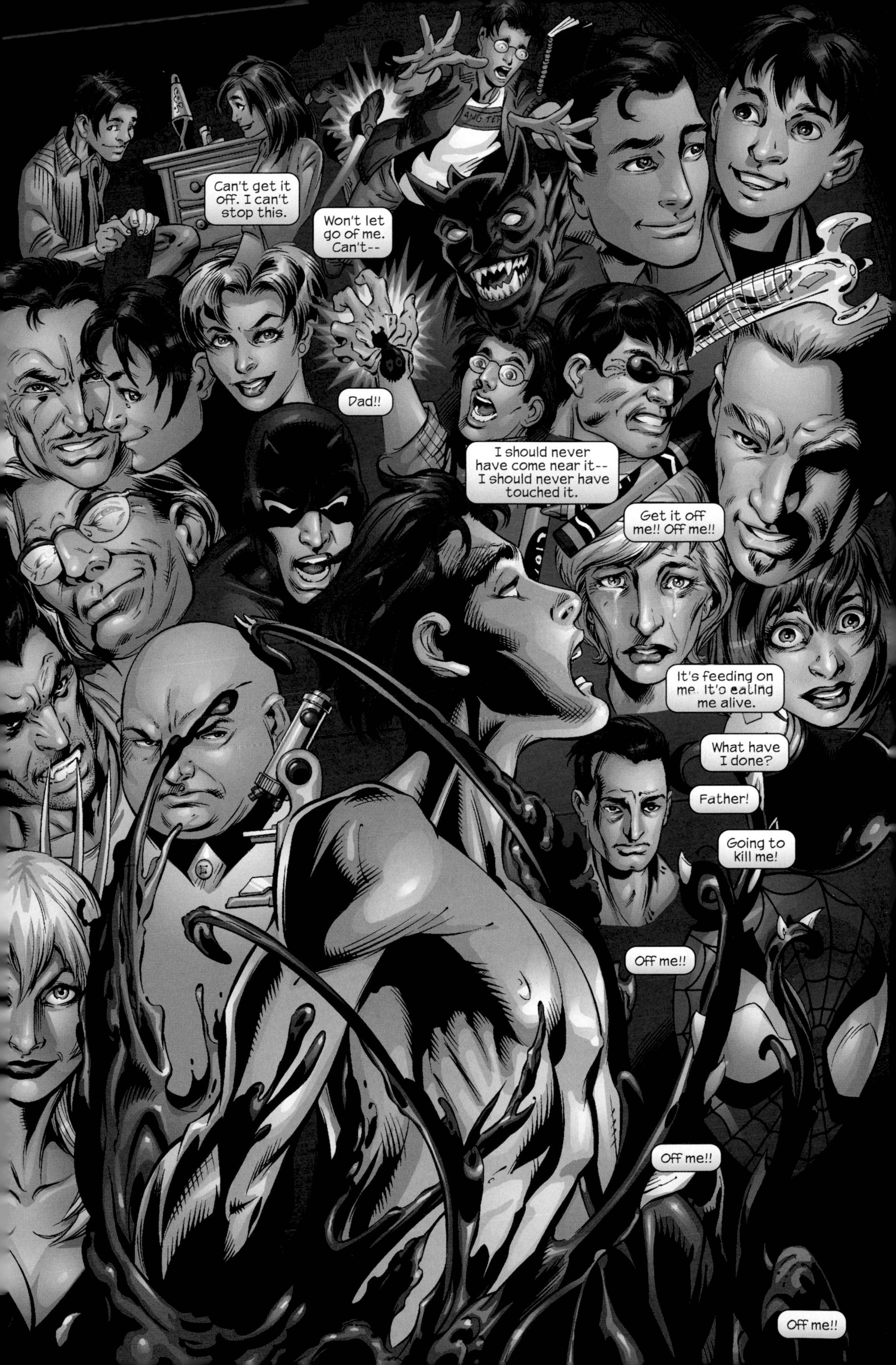

Can't get it off. I can't stop this.
Won't let go of me. Can't--
Dad!!
I should never have come near it-- I should never have touched it.
Get it off me!! Off me!!
It's feeding on me. It's eating me alive.
What have I done?
Father!
Going to kill me!
Off me!!
Off me!!
Off me!!

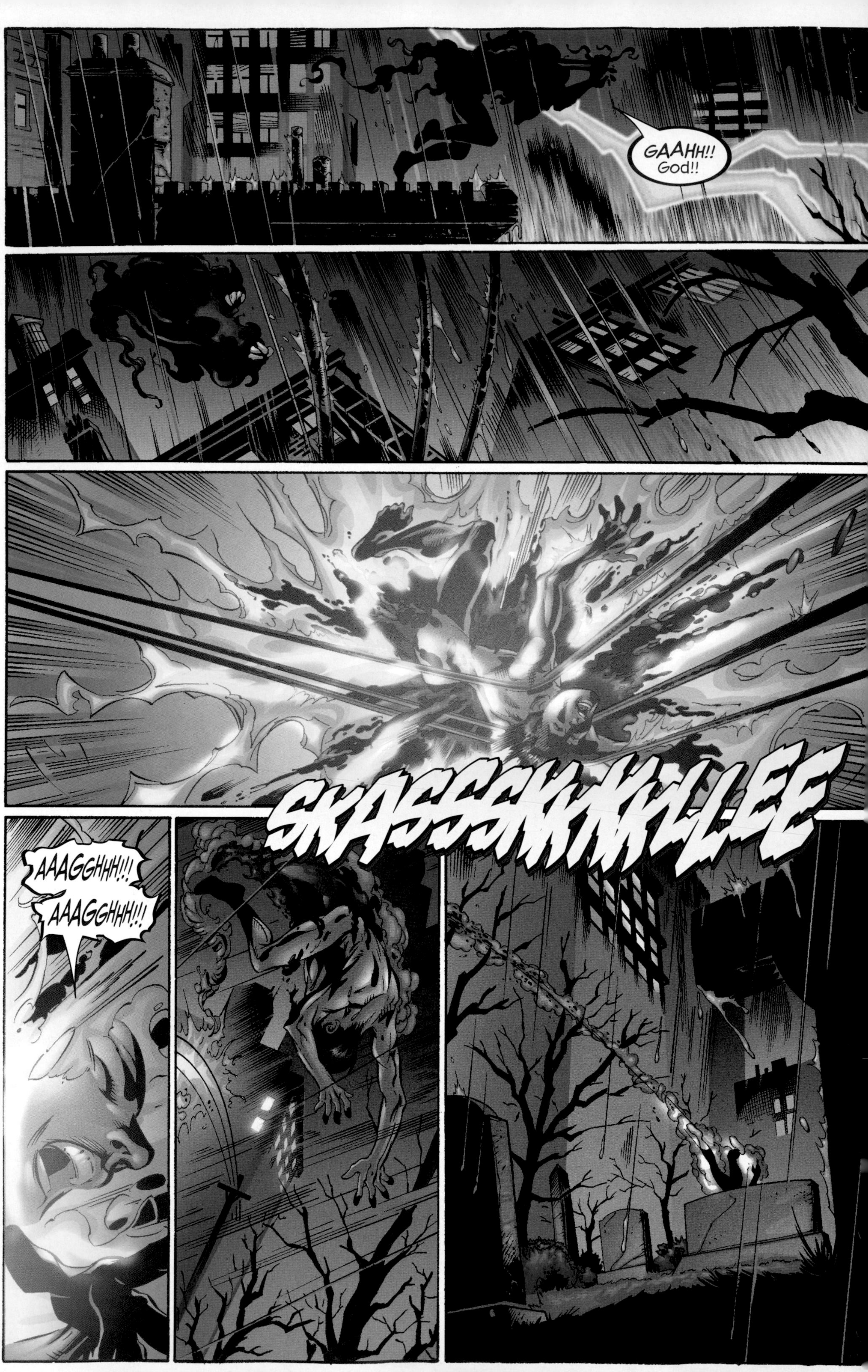
GAAHH!! God!!
SKASSSKKKKLLEE
AAAGGHHH!!!
AAAGGHHH!!!

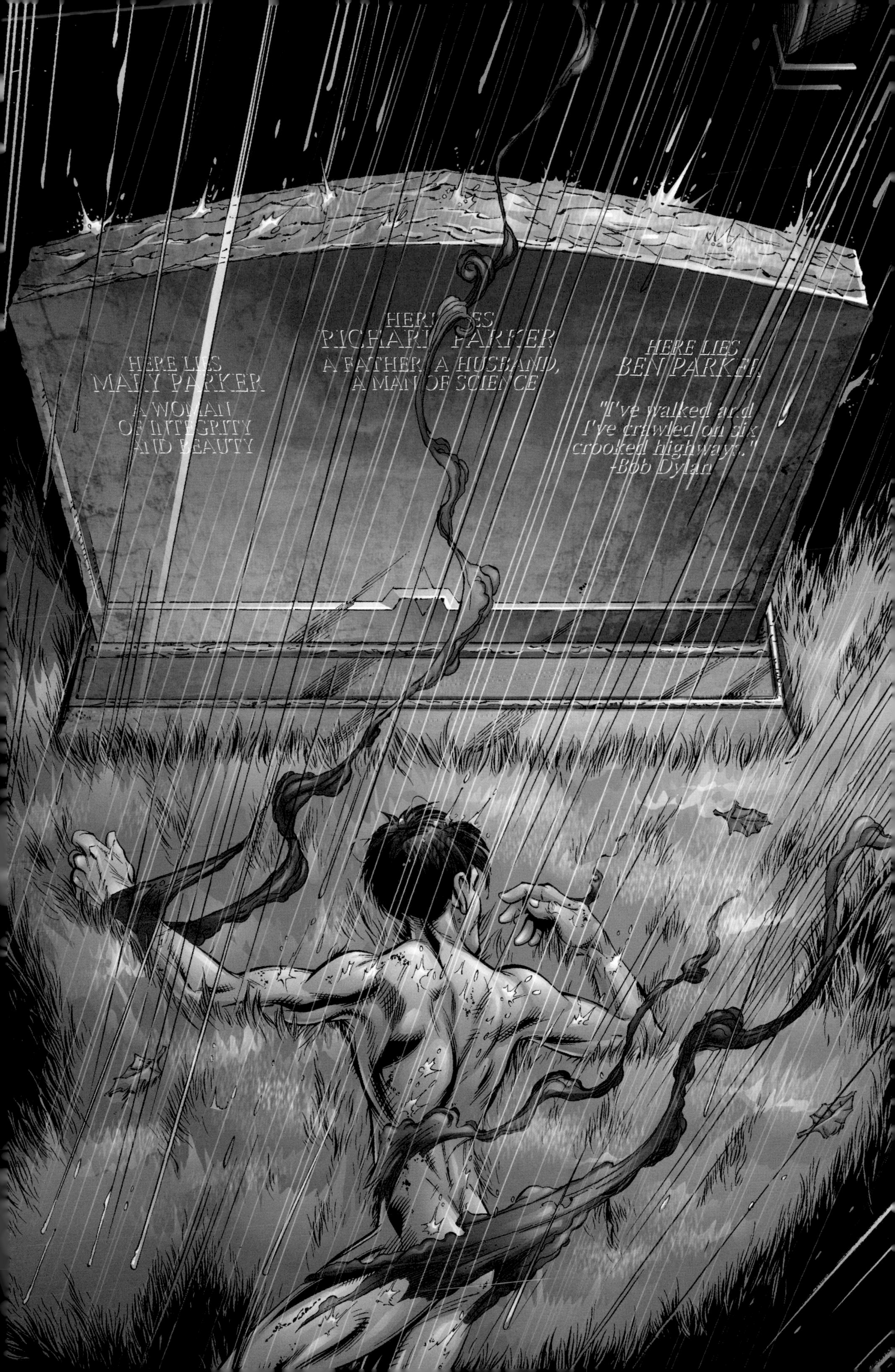
HERE LIES
MARY PARKER
A WOMAN
OF INTEGRITY
AND BEAUTY
HERE LIES
RICHARD PARKER
A FATHER, A HUSBAND,
A MAN OF SCIENCE
HERE LIES
BEN PARKER
"I've walked and
I've crawled on six
crooked highways."
-Bob Dylan

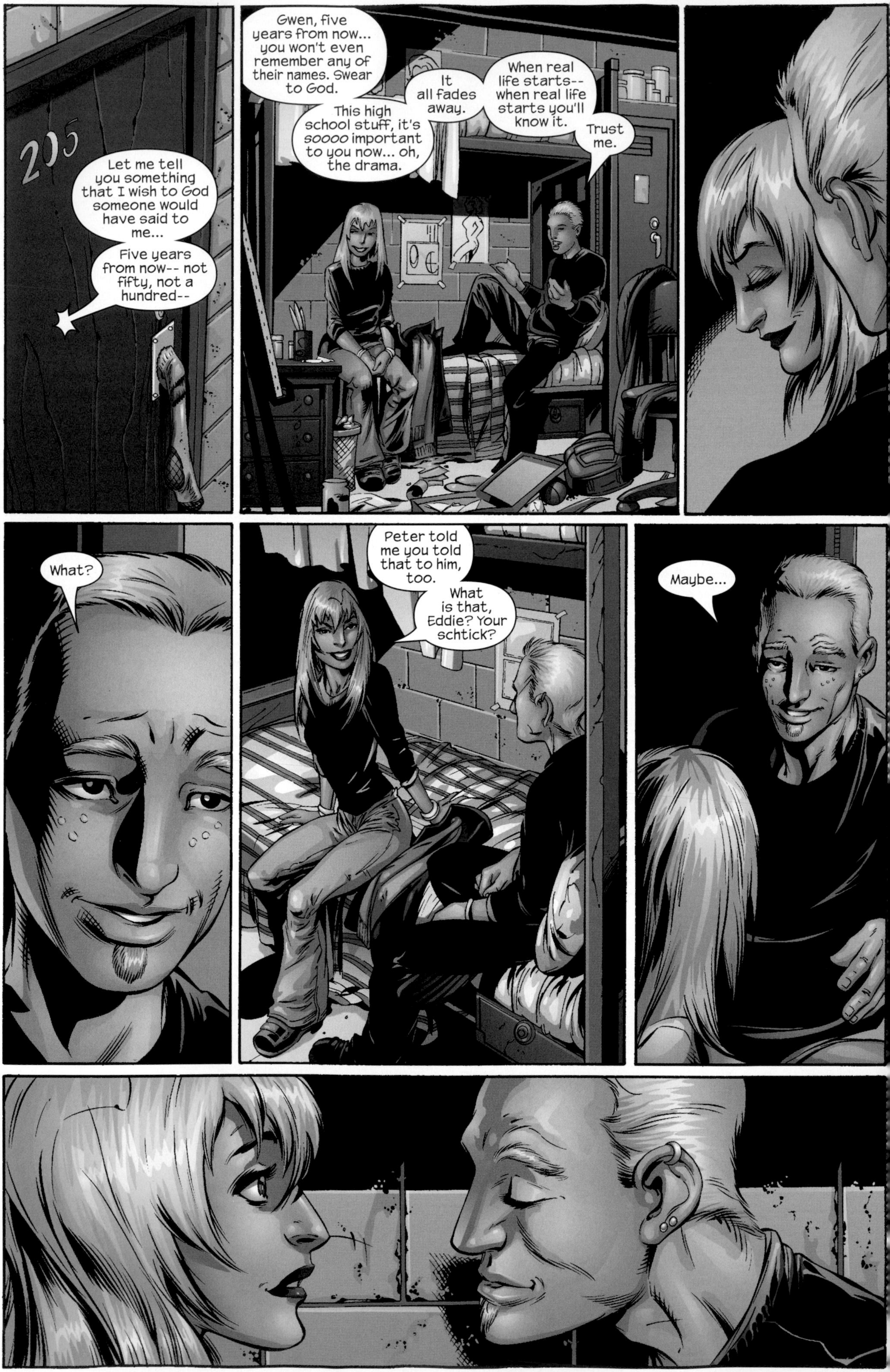
205
Let me tell you something that I wish to God someone would have said to me...
Five years from now-- not fifty, not a hundred--
Gwen, five years from now... you won't even remember any of their names. Swear to God.
This high school stuff, it's soooo important to you now... oh, the drama.
It all fades away.
When real life starts-- when real life starts you'll know it.
Trust me.
What?
Peter told me you told that to him, too.
What is that, Eddie? Your schtick?
Maybe...

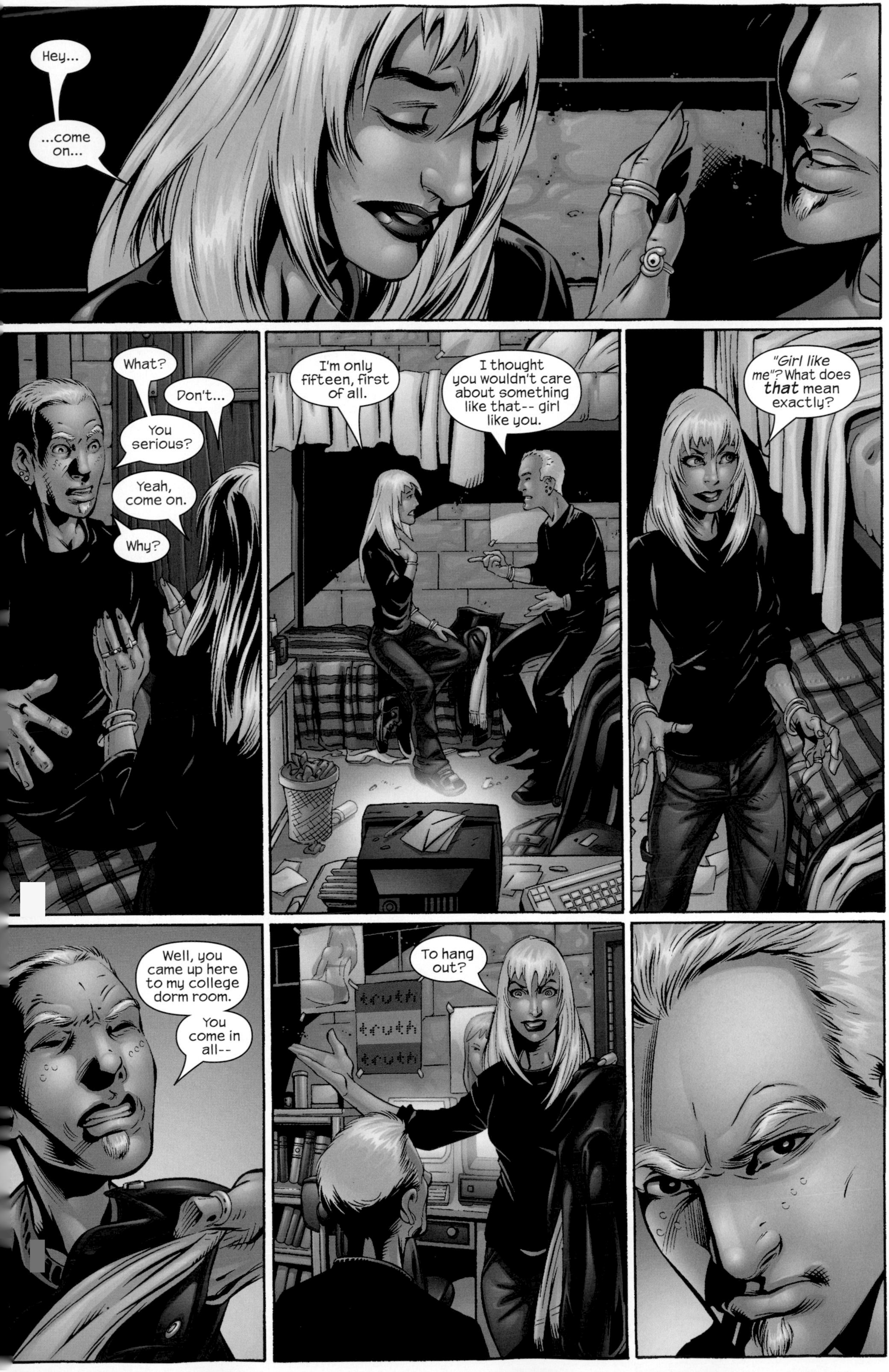
Hey...
...come on...
What?
Don't...
You serious?
Yeah, come on.
Why?
I'm only fifteen, first of all.
I thought you wouldn't care about something like that-- girl like you.
"Girl like me"? What does *that* mean exactly?
Well, you came up here to my college dorm room.
You come in all--
To hang out?
truth
truth
truth

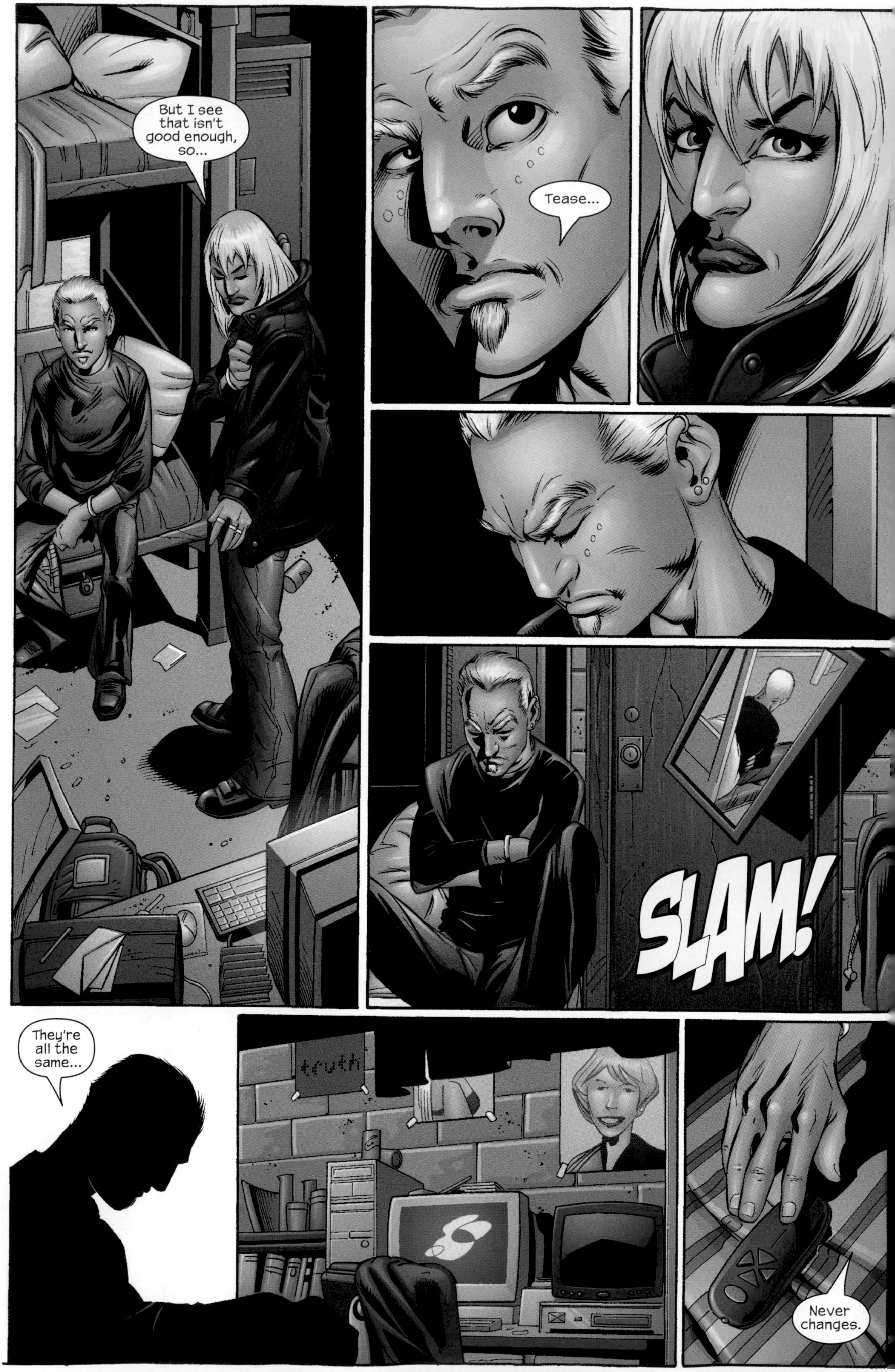
But I see that isn't good enough, so...
Tease...
SLAM!
They're all the same...
truth
Never changes.

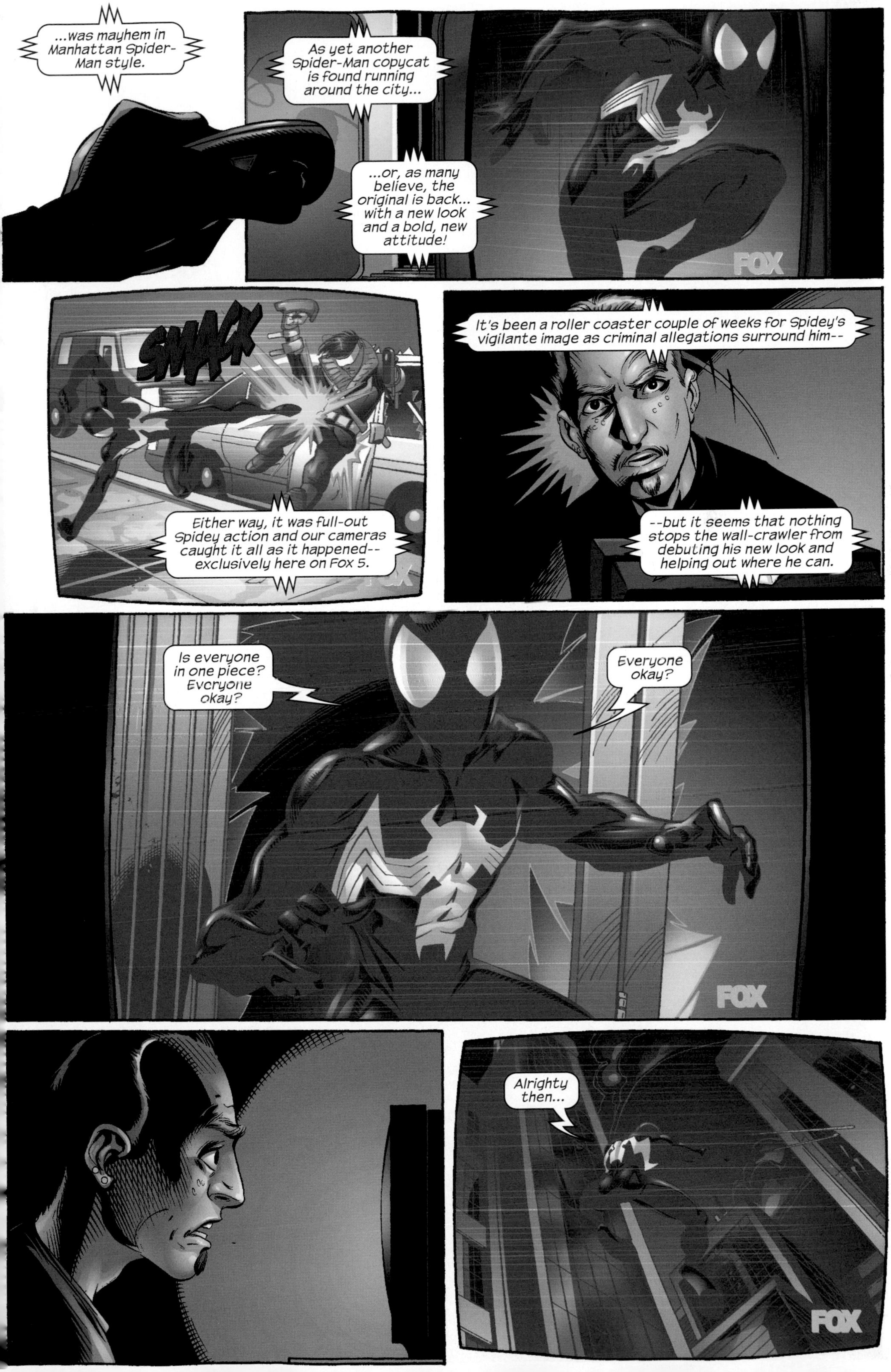
...was mayhem in Manhattan Spider-Man style.
As yet another Spider-Man copycat is found running around the city...
...or, as many believe, the original is back... with a new look and a bold, new attitude!
FOX
SMACK
Either way, it was full-out Spidey action and our cameras caught it all as it happened--exclusively here on Fox 5.
It's been a roller coaster couple of weeks for Spidey's vigilante image as criminal allegations surround him--
--but it seems that nothing stops the wall-crawler from debuting his new look and helping out where he can.
Is everyone in one piece? Everyone okay?
Everyone okay?
FOX
Alrighty then...
FOX

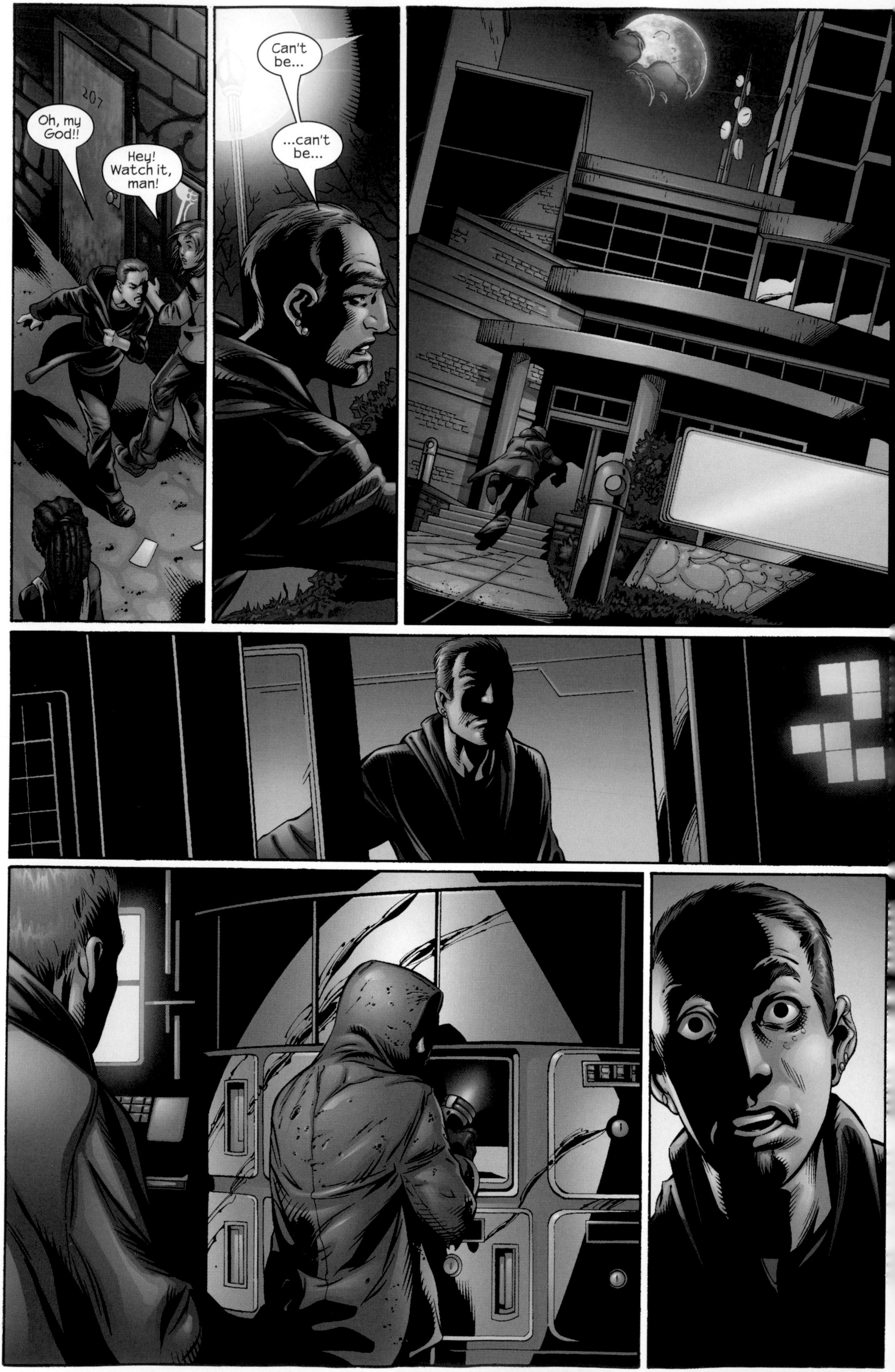

Oh, my God!!
Hey! Watch it, man!
Can't be...
...can't be...

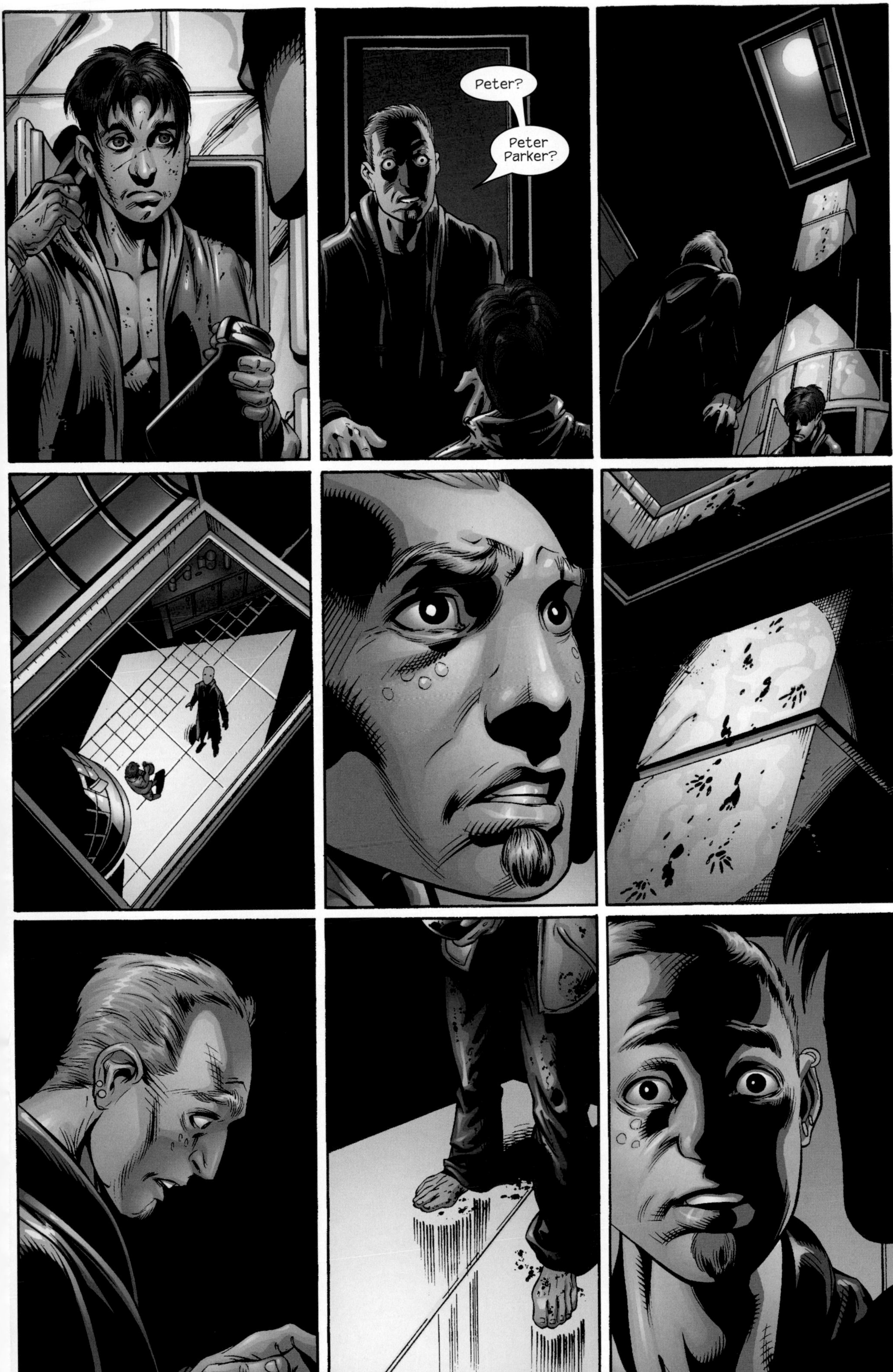
Peter?
Peter Parker?

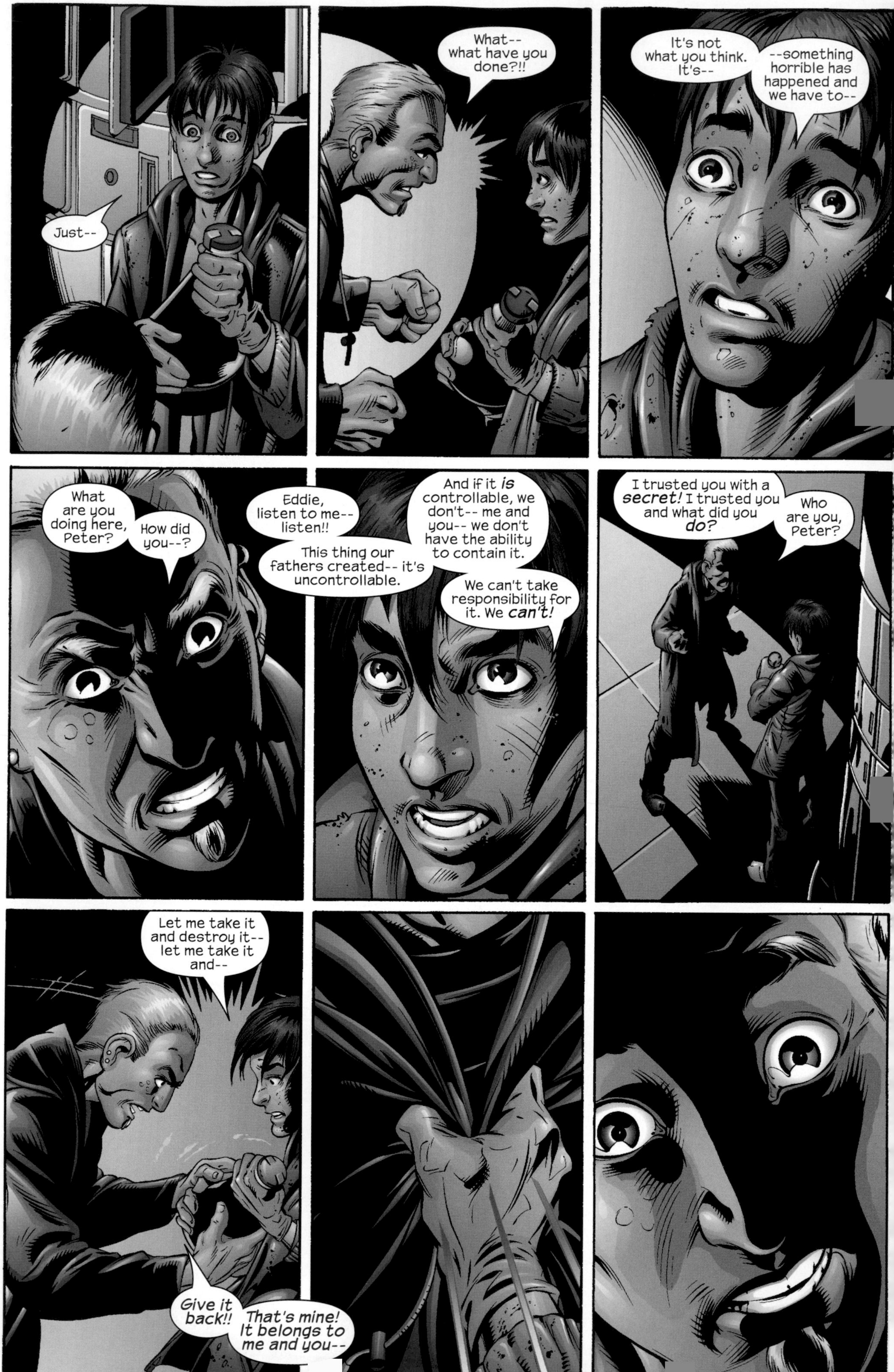
Just--
What-- what have you done?!!
It's not what you think. It's--
--something horrible has happened and we have to--
What are you doing here, Peter?
How did you--?
Eddie, listen to me-- listen!!
This thing our fathers created-- it's uncontrollable.
And if it *is* controllable, we don't-- me and you-- we don't have the ability to contain it.
We can't take responsibility for it. We *can't!*
I trusted you with a *secret!* I trusted you and what did you *do?*
Who are you, Peter?
Let me take it and destroy it-- let me take it and--
Give it back!!
That's mine! It belongs to me and you--

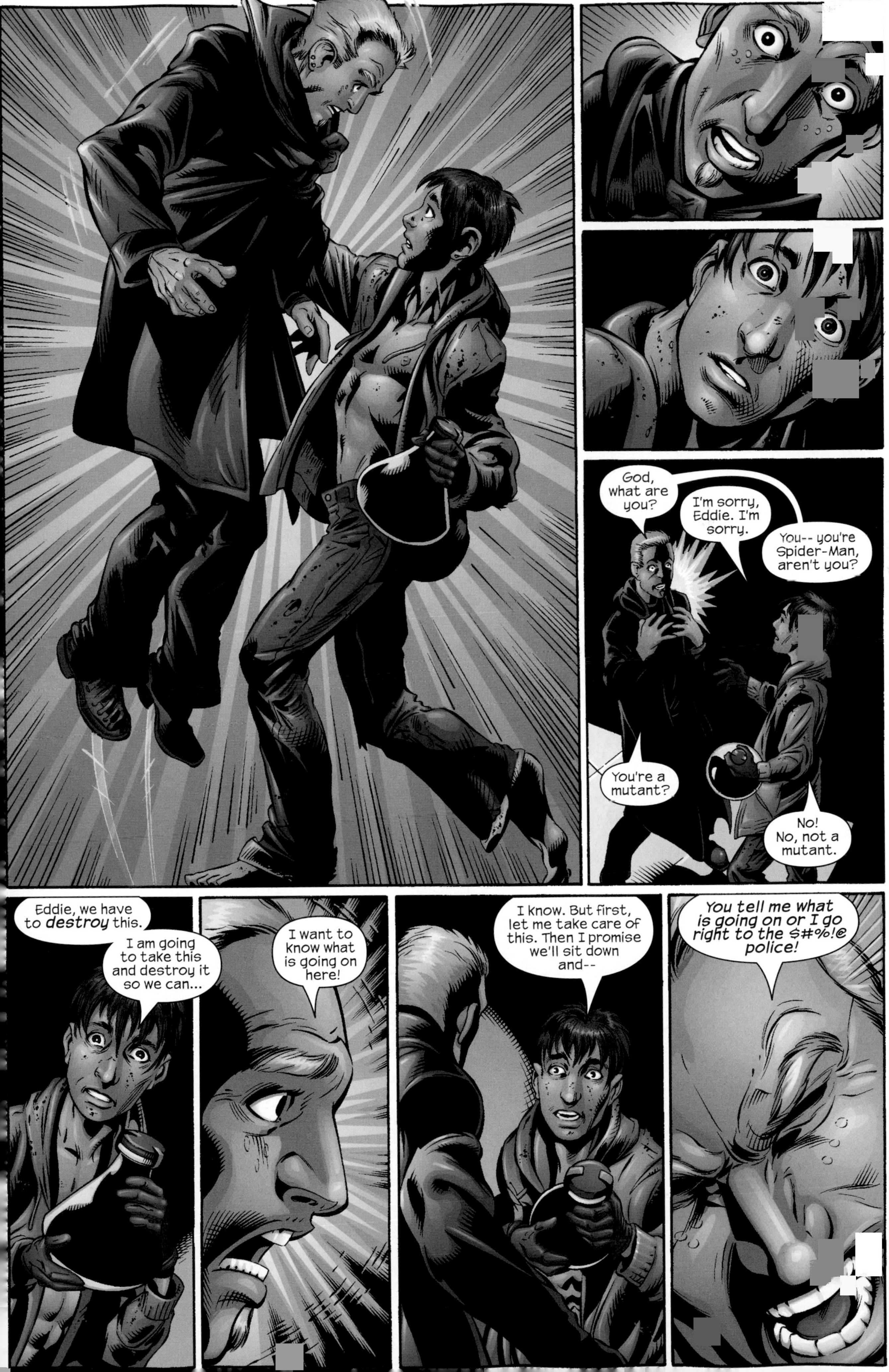
God, what are you?
I'm sorry, Eddie. I'm sorry.
You-- you're Spider-Man, aren't you?
You're a mutant?
No! No, not a mutant.
Eddie, we have to *destroy* this.
I am going to take this and destroy it so we can...
I want to know what is going on here!
I know. But first, let me take care of this. Then I promise we'll sit down and--
You tell me what is going on or I go right to the $#%!@ police!

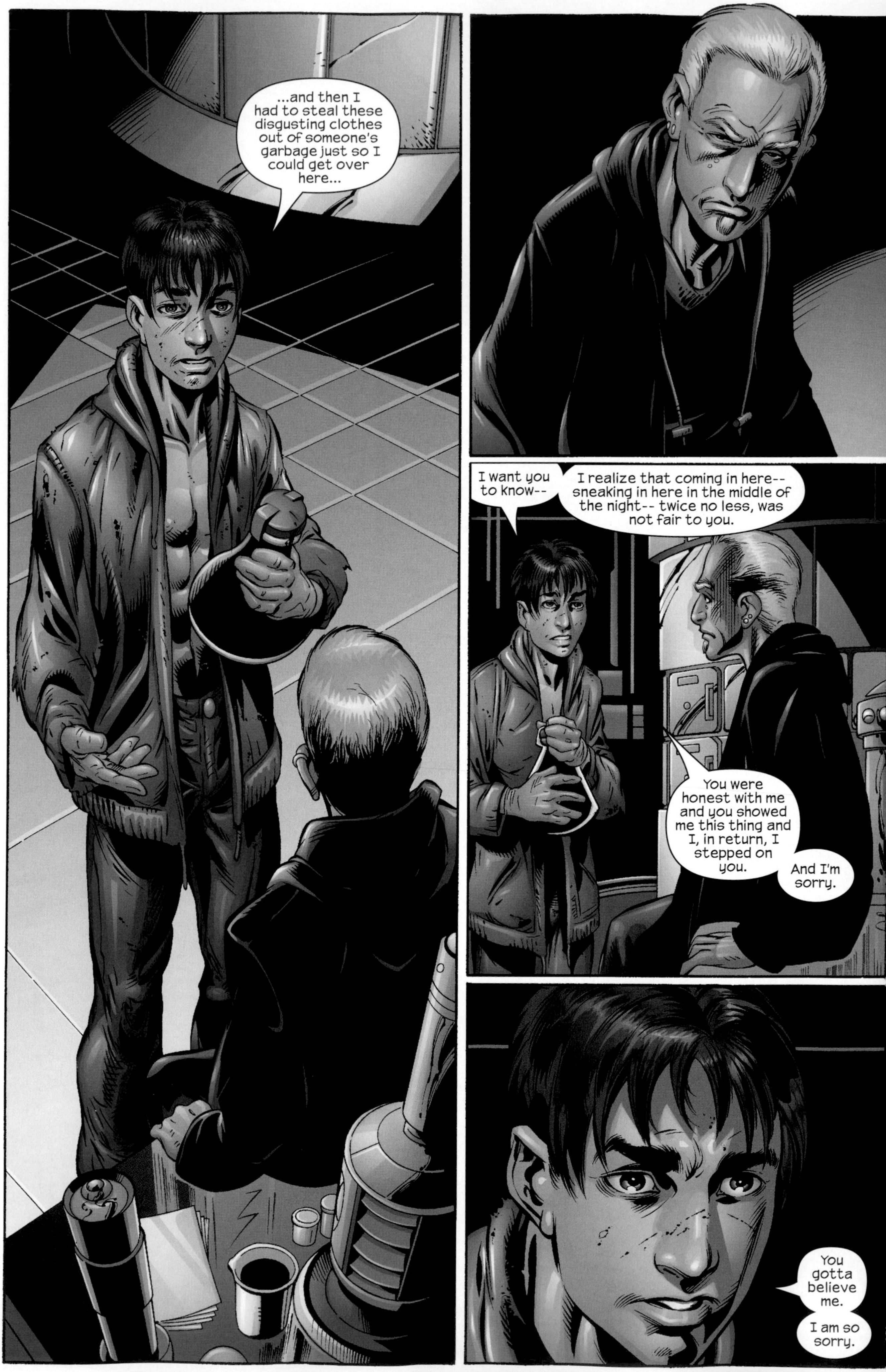
...and then I had to steal these disgusting clothes out of someone's garbage just so I could get over here...
I want you to know--
I realize that coming in here-- sneaking in here in the middle of the night-- twice no less, was not fair to you.
You were honest with me and you showed me this thing and I, in return, I stepped on you.
And I'm sorry.
You gotta believe me.
I am so sorry.

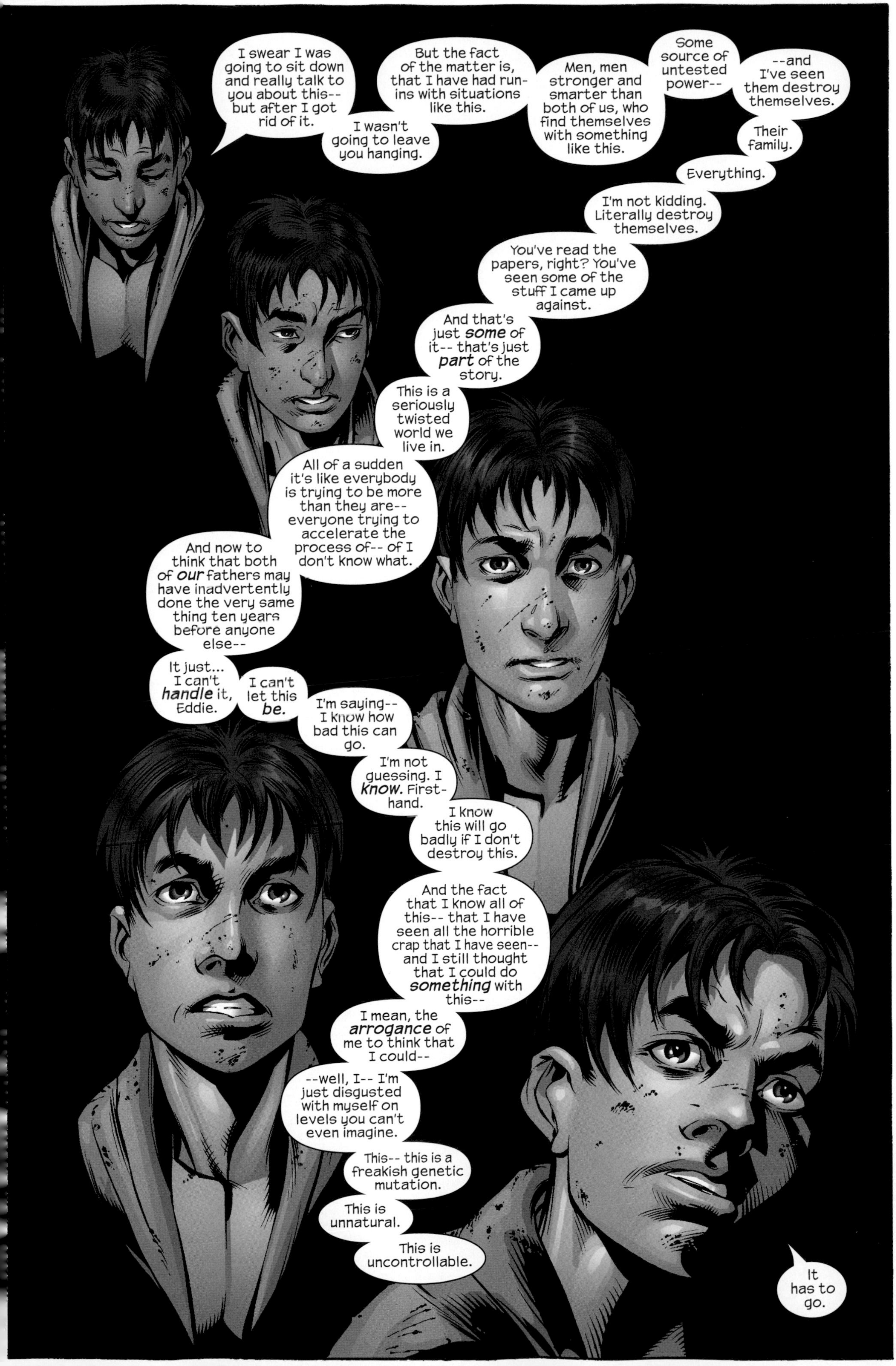
I swear I was going to sit down and really talk to you about this-- but after I got rid of it.
But the fact of the matter is, that I have had run-ins with situations like this.
I wasn't going to leave you hanging.
Men, men stronger and smarter than both of us, who find themselves with something like this.
Some source of untested power--
--and I've seen them destroy themselves.
Their family.
Everything.
I'm not kidding. Literally destroy themselves.
You've read the papers, right? You've seen some of the stuff I came up against.
And that's just some of it-- that's just part of the story.
This is a seriously twisted world we live in.
All of a sudden it's like everybody is trying to be more than they are-- everyone trying to accelerate the process of-- of I don't know what.
And now to think that both of our fathers may have inadvertently done the very same thing ten years before anyone else--
It just... I can't handle it, Eddie.
I can't let this be.
I'm saying-- I know how bad this can go.
I'm not guessing. I know. First-hand.
I know this will go badly if I don't destroy this.
And the fact that I know all of this-- that I have seen all the horrible crap that I have seen-- and I still thought that I could do something with this--
I mean, the arrogance of me to think that I could--
--well, I-- I'm just disgusted with myself on levels you can't even imagine.
This-- this is a freakish genetic mutation.
This is unnatural.
This is uncontrollable.
It has to go.

Peter--

This is *all* I have left of my father.

It's all I have left.

I know.

I know exactly how you feel.

Look at me-- I had the thing for an hour and look what happened.

I almost *killed* a man with my bare hands.

It's a cancer. It's a virus.

Just a little drop accidently fell on my skin and my whole body-- my mind--

--it was horrible.

If I didn't have my *powers* I don't know if I would have been able to *survive* it.

Our fathers died for this and we can't-- we aren't smart enough to contain this.

And we can't trust anybody else with it.

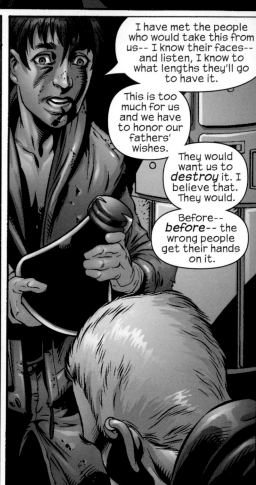

I have met the people who would take this from us-- I know their faces-- and listen, I know to what lengths they'll go to have it.

This is too much for us and we have to honor our fathers' wishes.

They would want us to *destroy* it. I believe that. They would.

Before-- *before*-- the wrong people get their hands on it.

Okay? I'm going to take this and I'm going to destroy it.

It's not like I can stop you.

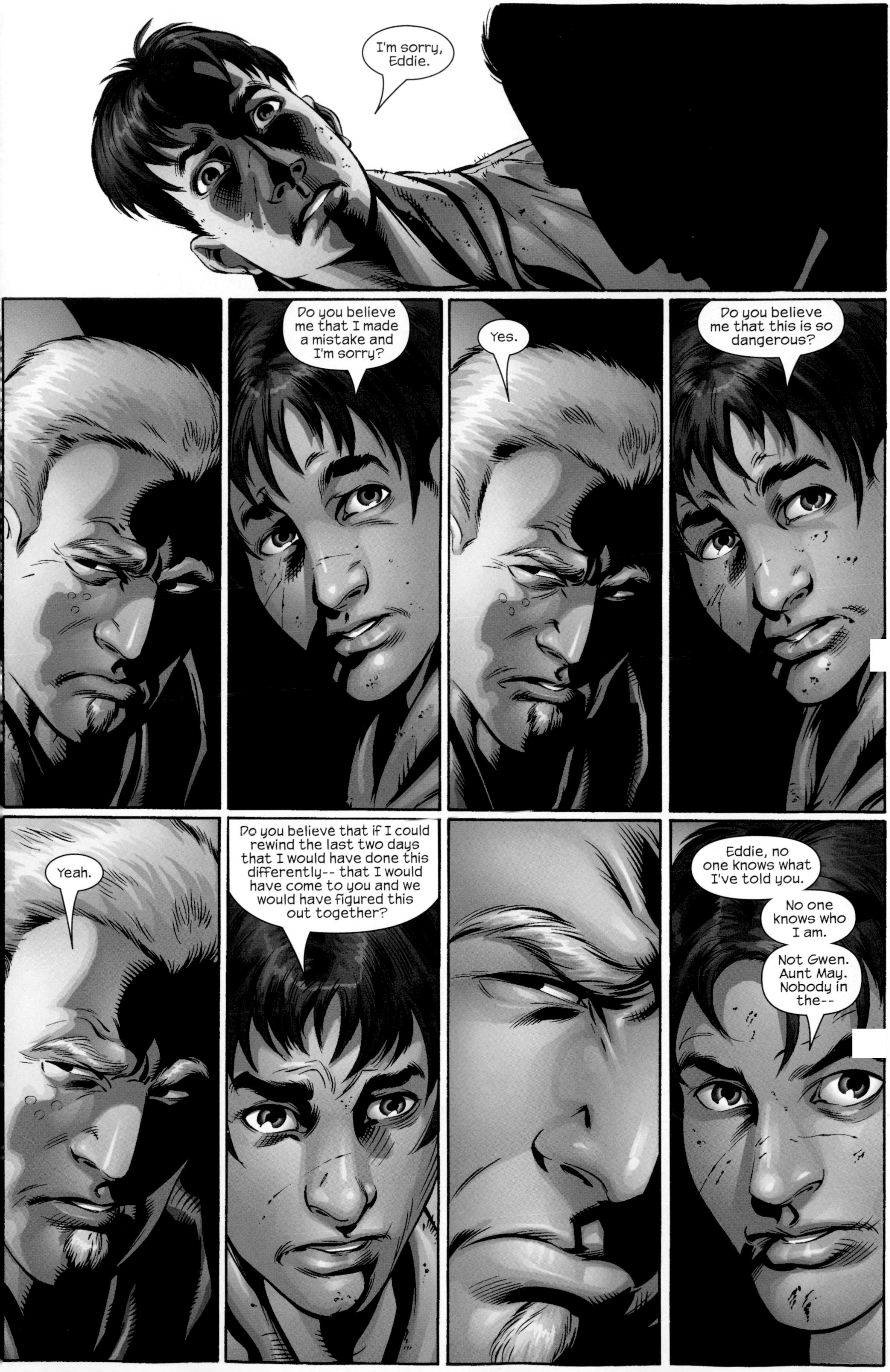
I'm sorry, Eddie.
Do you believe me that I made a mistake and I'm sorry?
Yes.
Do you believe me that this is so dangerous?
Yeah.
Do you believe that if I could rewind the last two days that I would have done this differently-- that I would have come to you and we would have figured this out together?
Eddie, no one knows what I've told you.
No one knows who I am.
Not Gwen. Aunt May. Nobody in the--

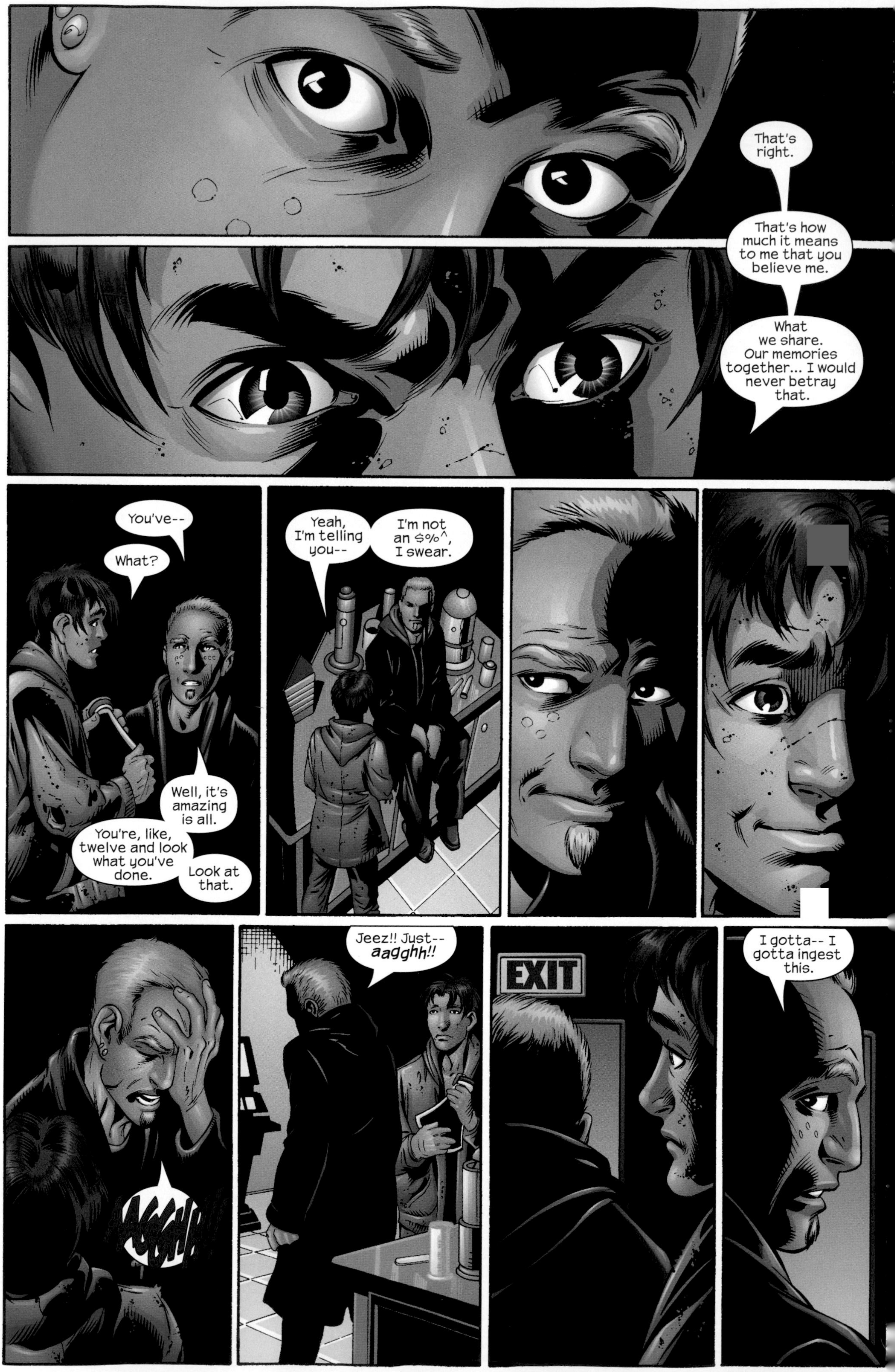
That's right.
That's how much it means to me that you believe me.
What we share. Our memories together... I would never betray that.
You've--
What?
Well, it's amazing is all.
You're, like, twelve and look what you've done.
Look at that.
Yeah, I'm telling you--
I'm not an $%^, I swear.
Jeez!! Just-- aagghh!!
EXIT
I gotta-- I gotta ingest this.

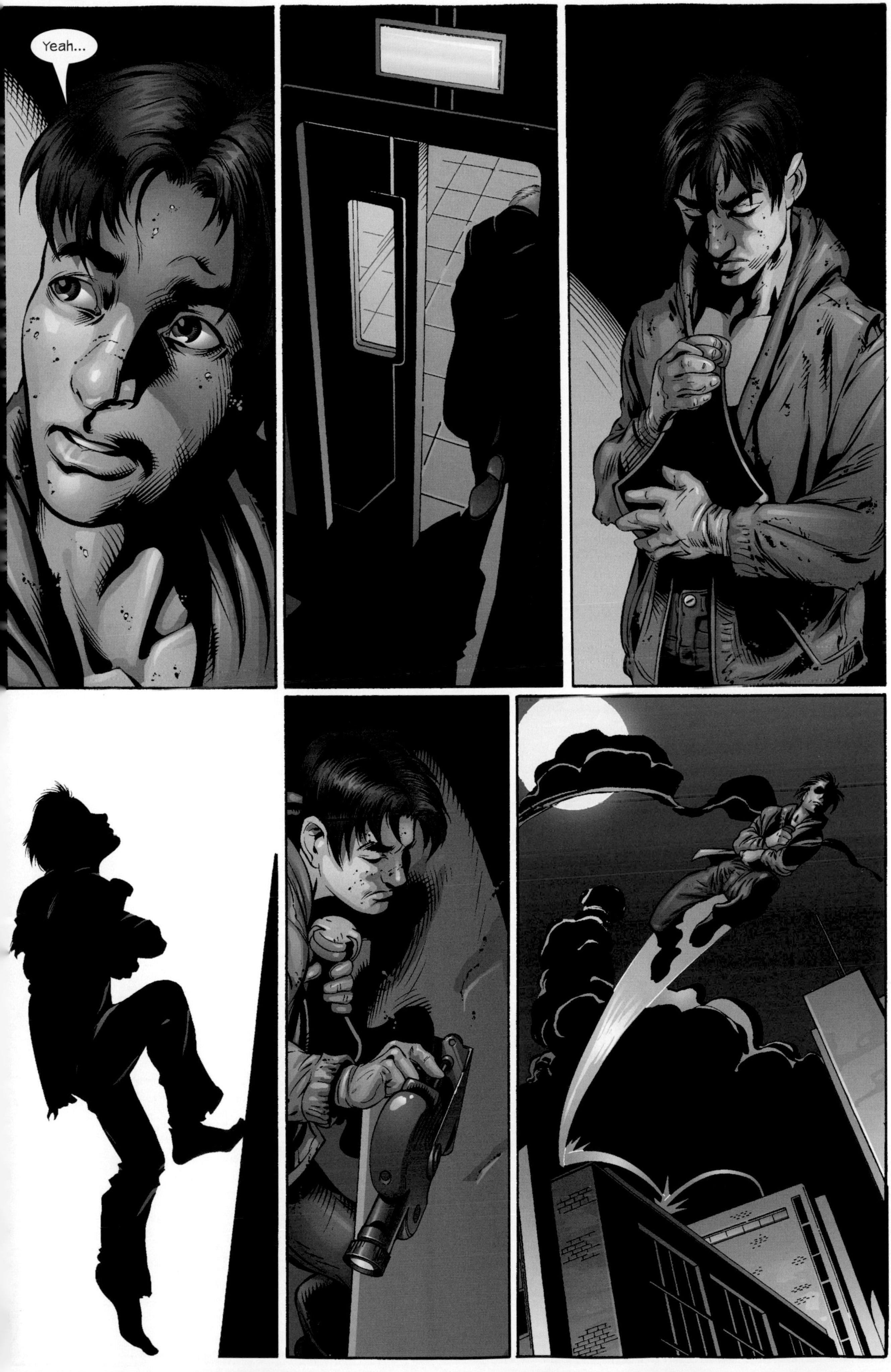
Yeah...

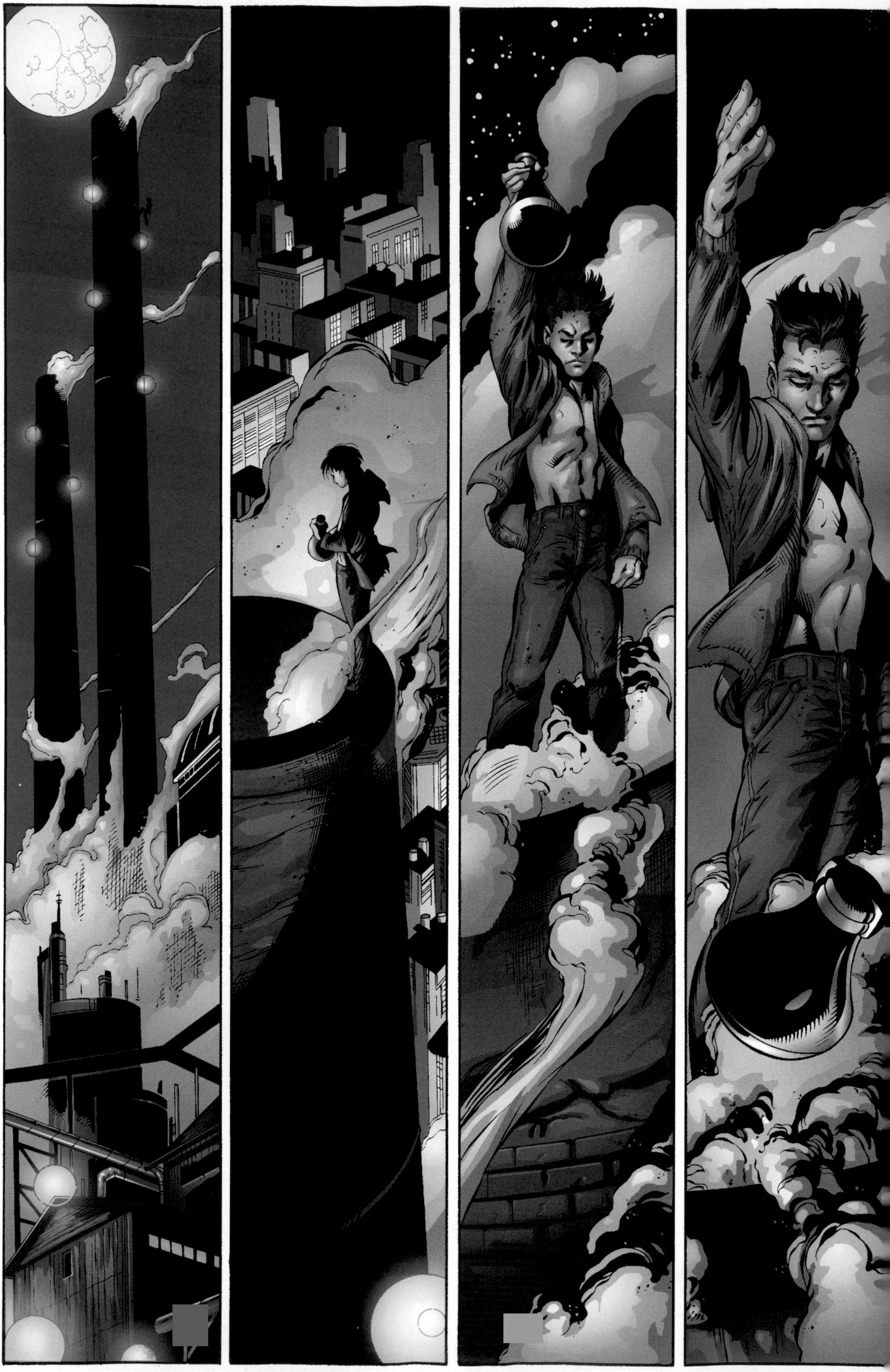

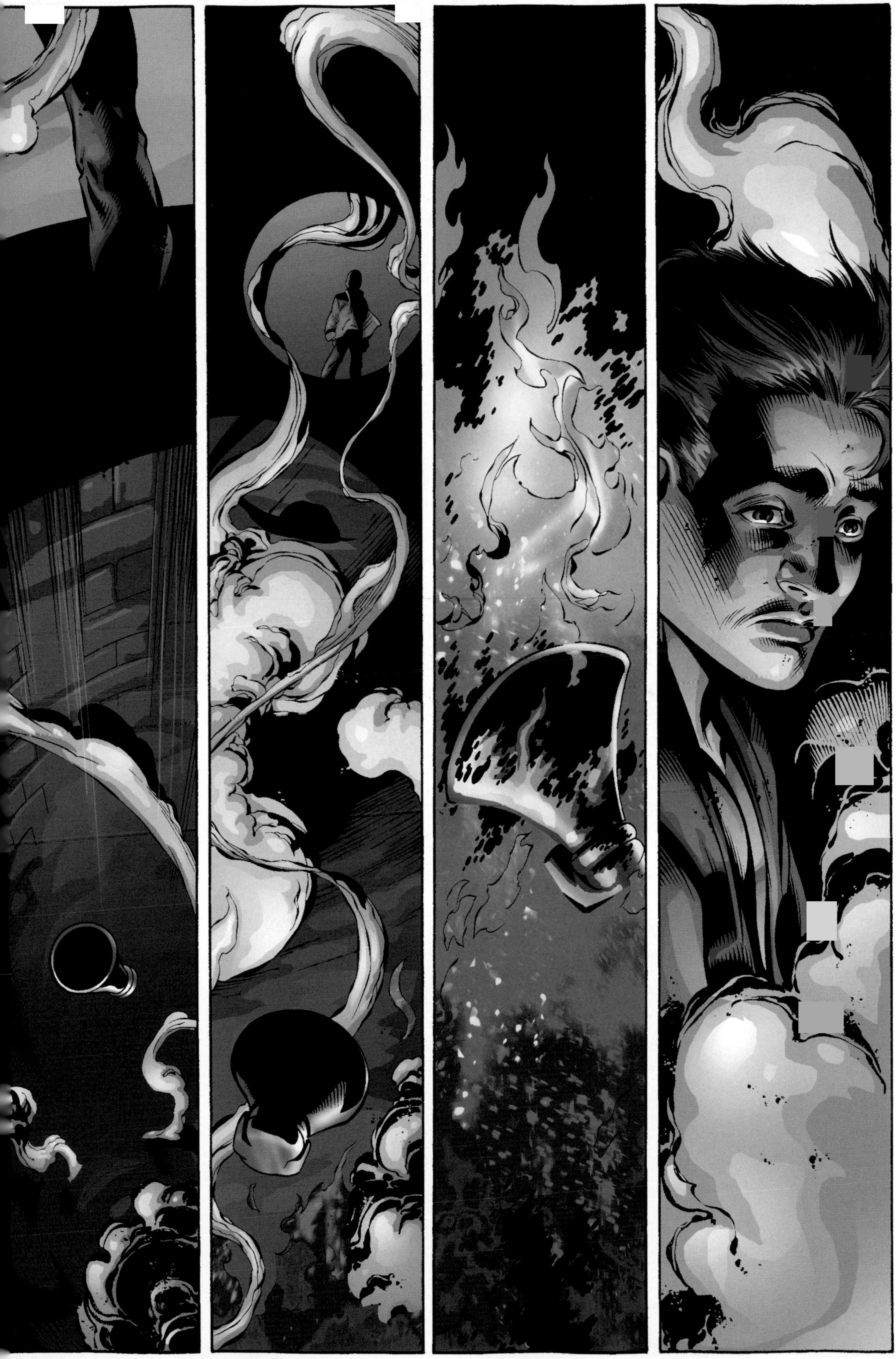

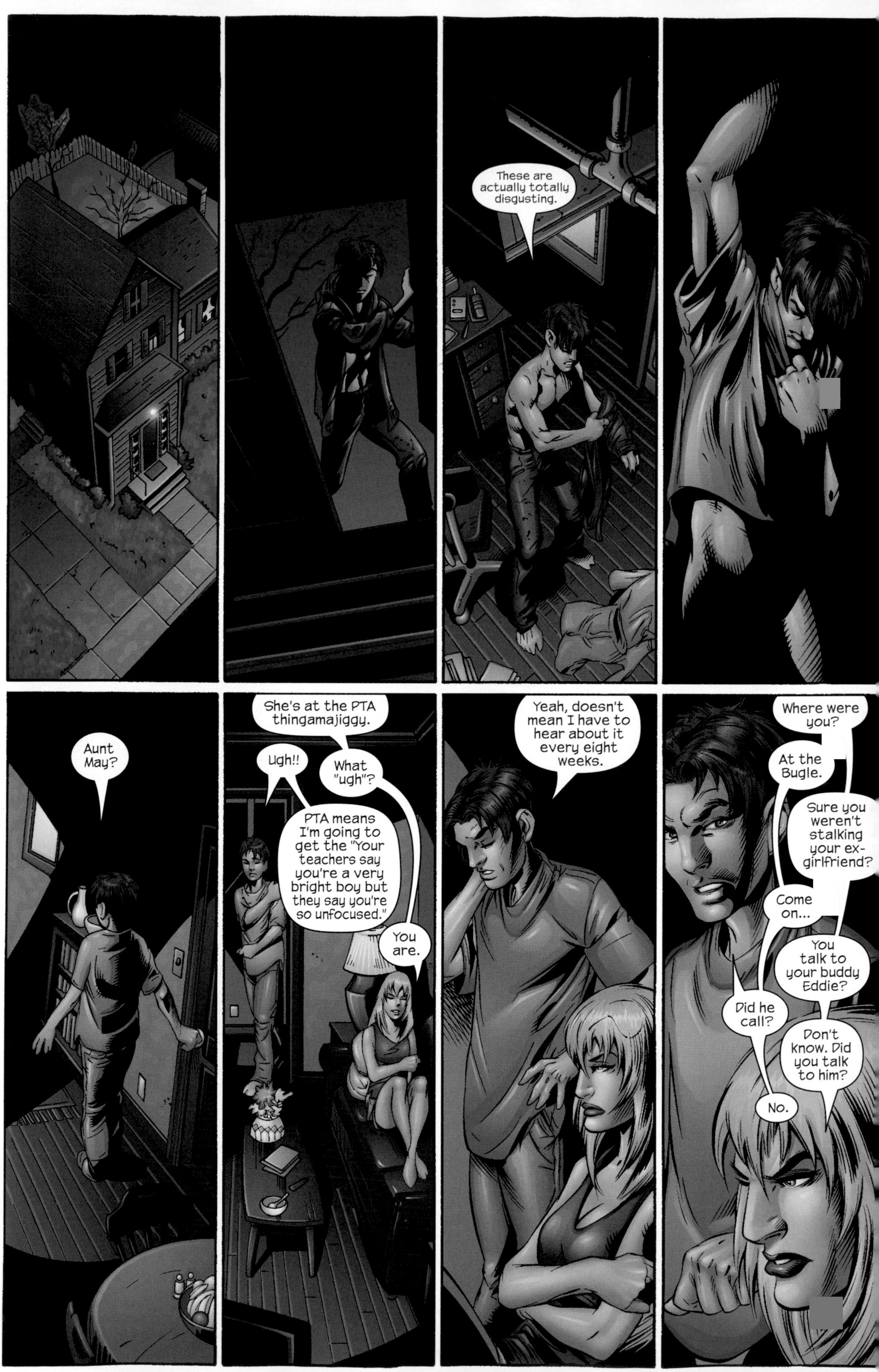
These are actually totally disgusting.
Aunt May?
She's at the PTA thingamajiggy.
Ugh!!
What "ugh"?
PTA means I'm going to get the "Your teachers say you're a very bright boy but they say you're so unfocused."
You are.
Yeah, doesn't mean I have to hear about it every eight weeks.
Where were you?
At the Bugle.
Sure you weren't stalking your ex-girlfriend?
Come on...
You talk to your buddy Eddie?
Did he call?
Don't know. Did you talk to him?
No.

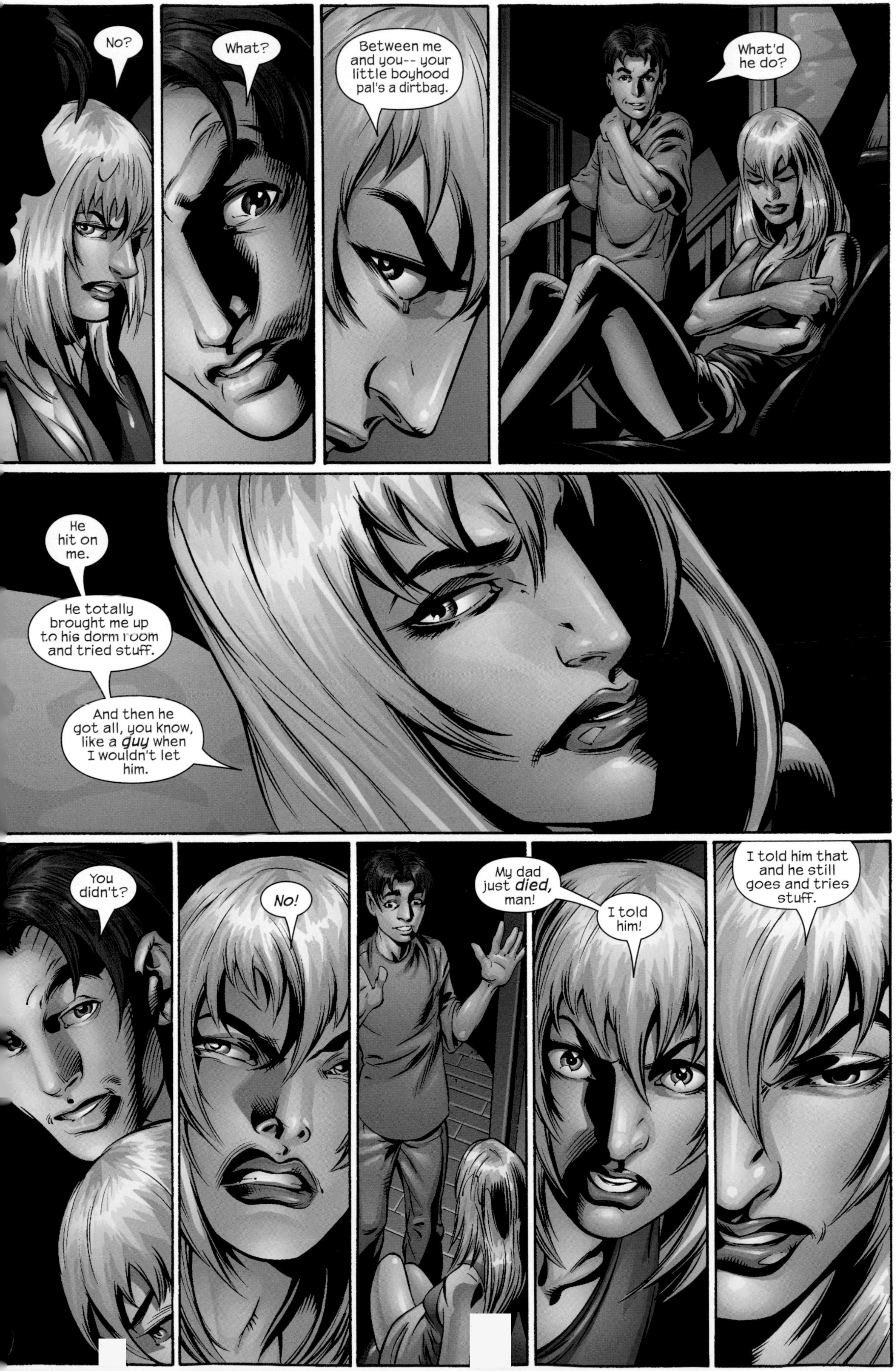
No?
What?
Between me and you-- your little boyhood pal's a dirtbag.
What'd he do?
He hit on me.
He totally brought me up to his dorm room and tried stuff.
And then he got all, you know, like a *guy* when I wouldn't let him.
You didn't?
No!
My dad just *died,* man!
I told him!
I told him that and he still goes and tries stuff.

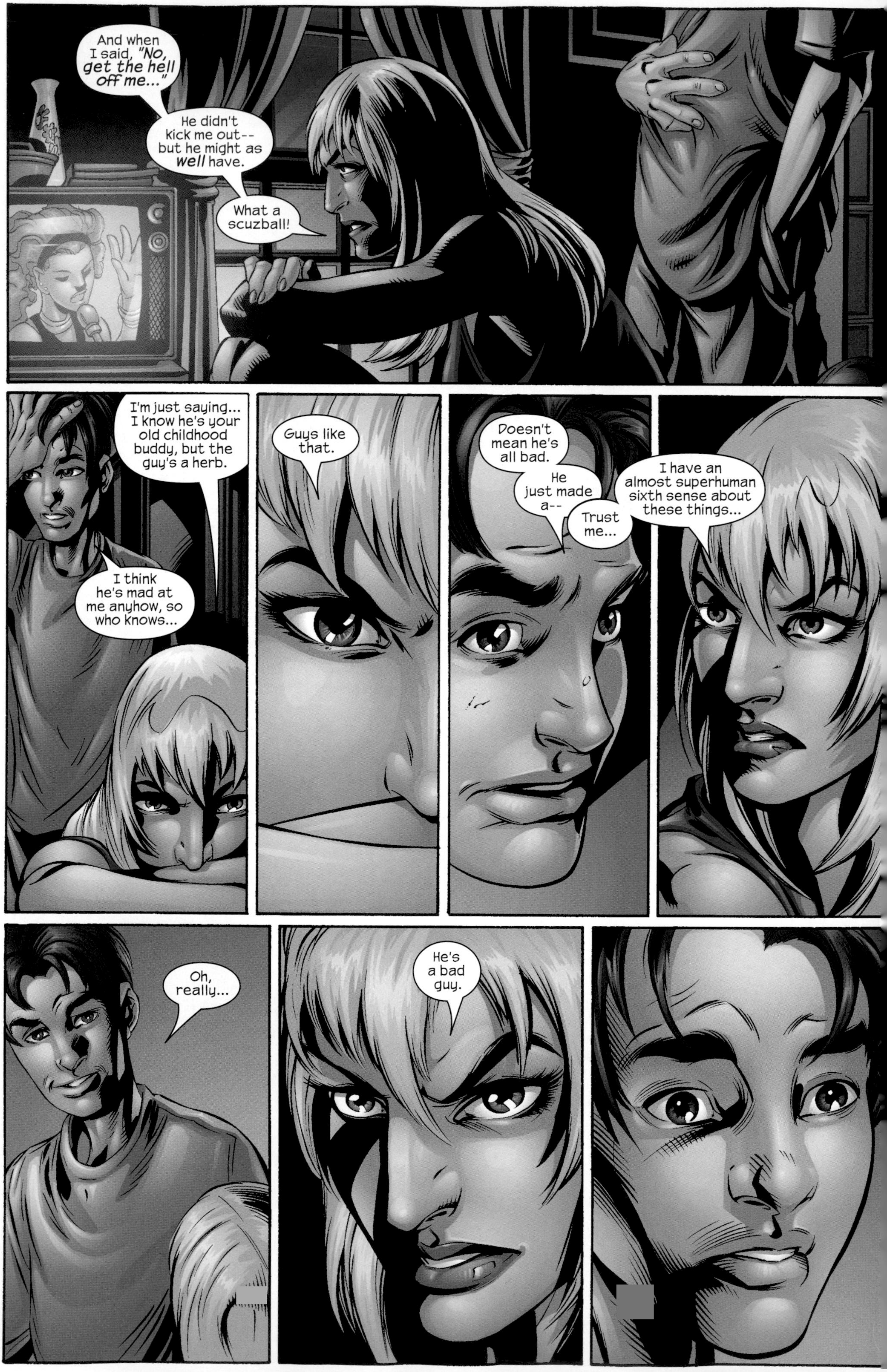
And when I said, "No, get the hell off me..."
He didn't kick me out-- but he might as well have.
What a scuzball!
I'm just saying... I know he's your old childhood buddy, but the guy's a herb.
I think he's mad at me anyhow, so who knows...
Guys like that.
Doesn't mean he's all bad.
He just made a--
Trust me...
I have an almost superhuman sixth sense about these things...
Oh, really...
He's a bad guy.

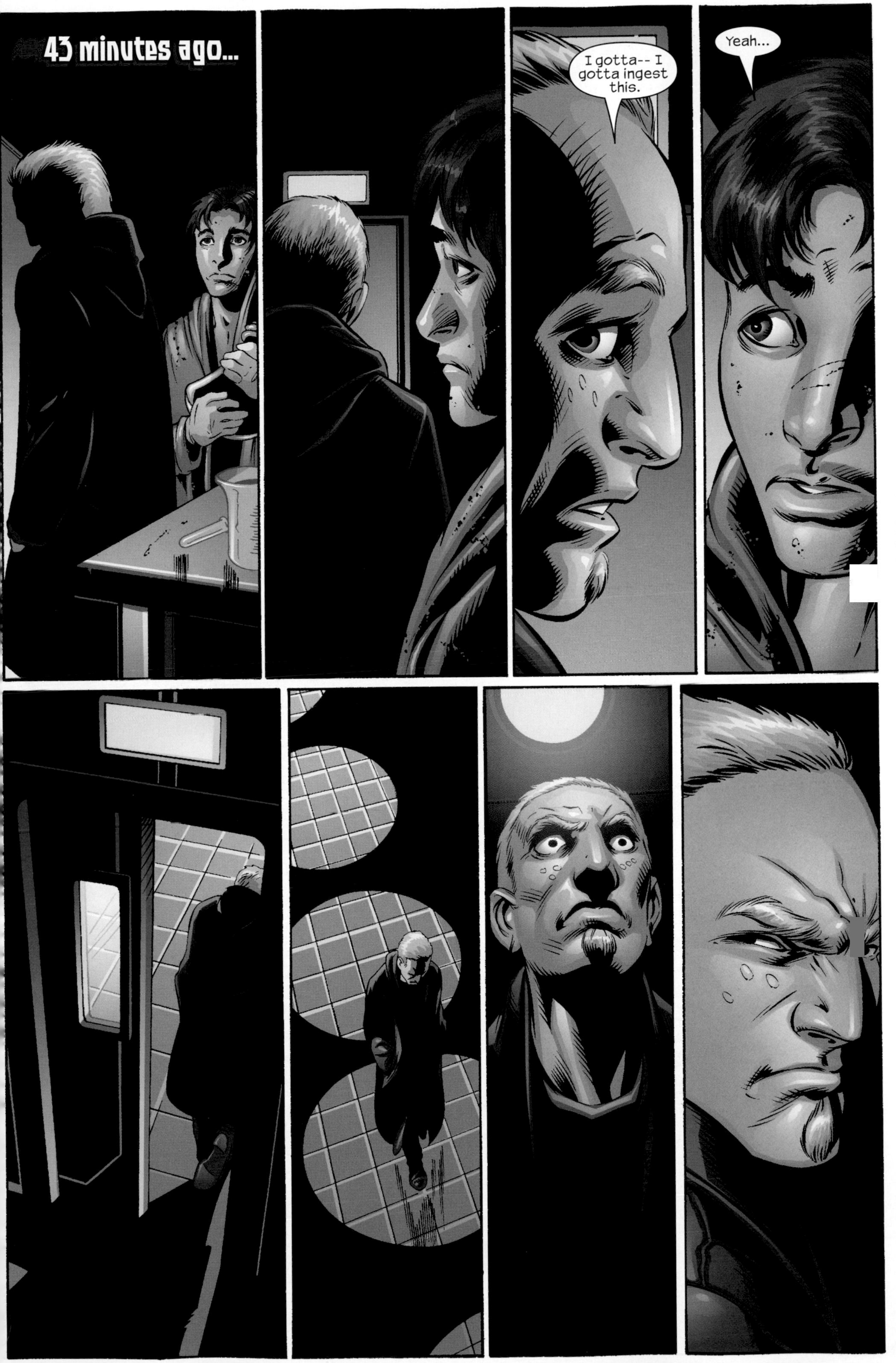
43 minutes ago...
I gotta-- I gotta ingest this.
Yeah...

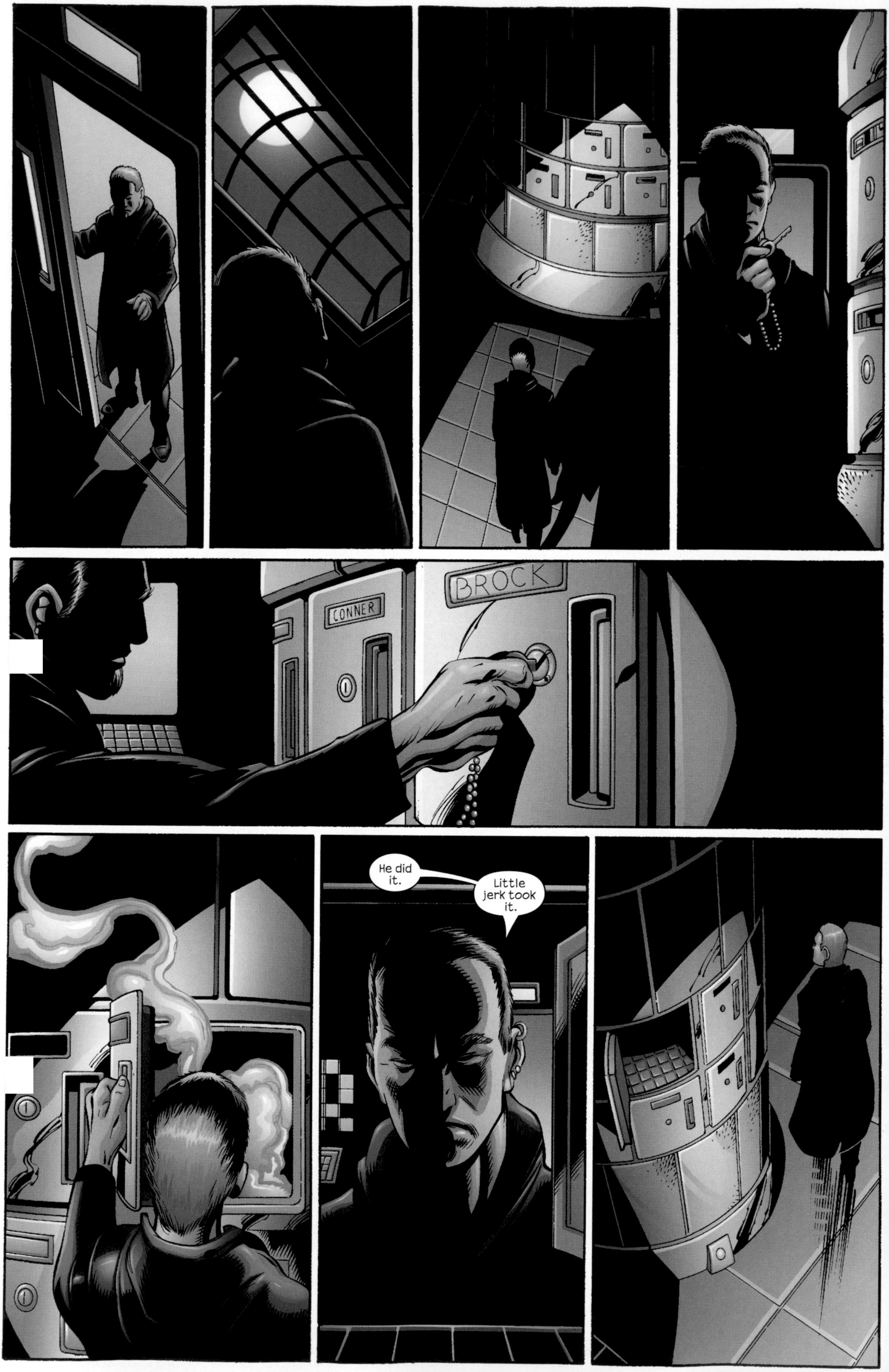
CONNER
BROCK
He did it.
Little jerk took it.

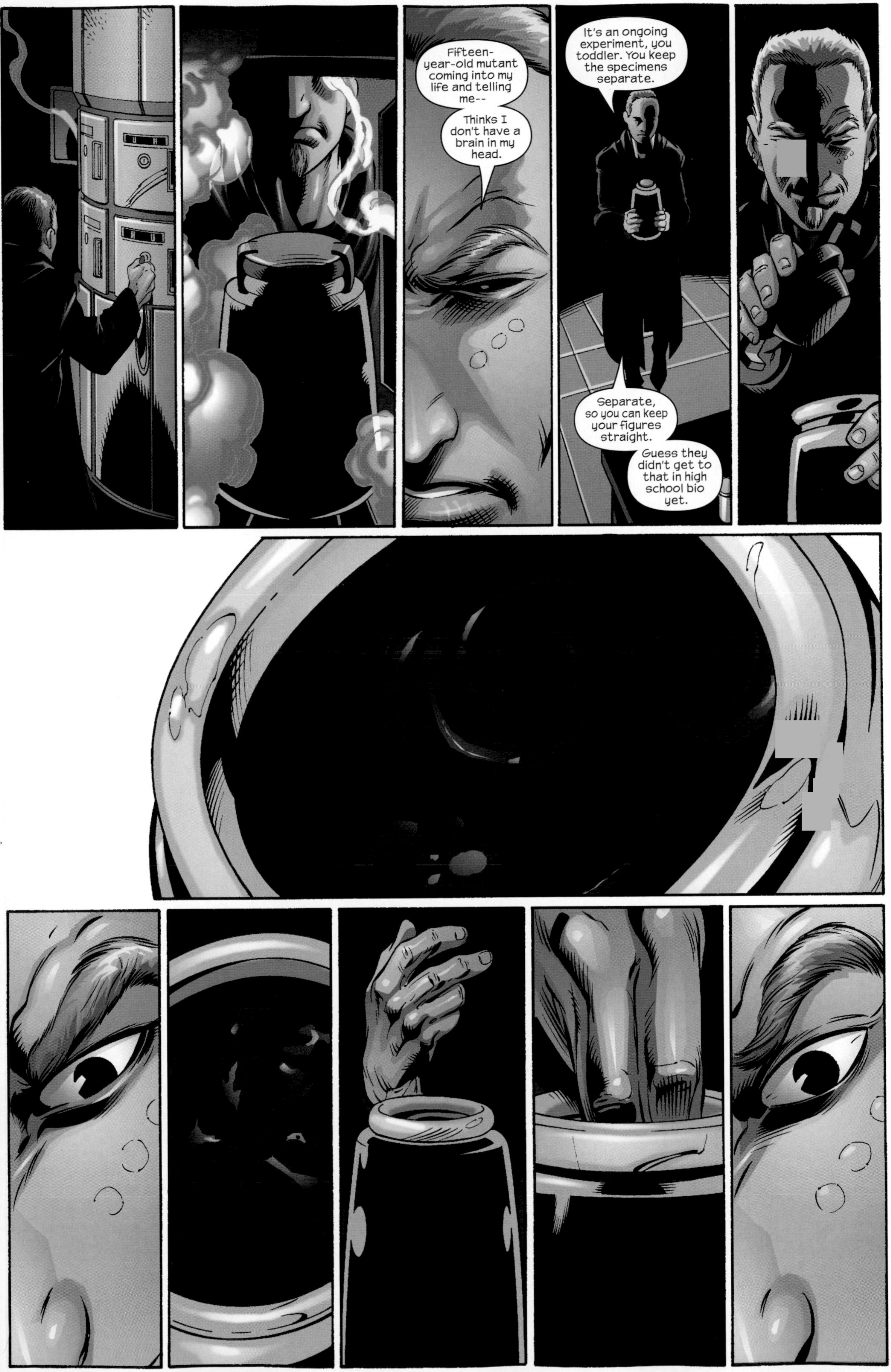
Fifteen-year-old mutant coming into my life and telling me--
Thinks I don't have a brain in my head.
It's an ongoing experiment, you toddler. You keep the specimens separate.
Separate, so you can keep your figures straight.
Guess they didn't get to that in high school bio yet.

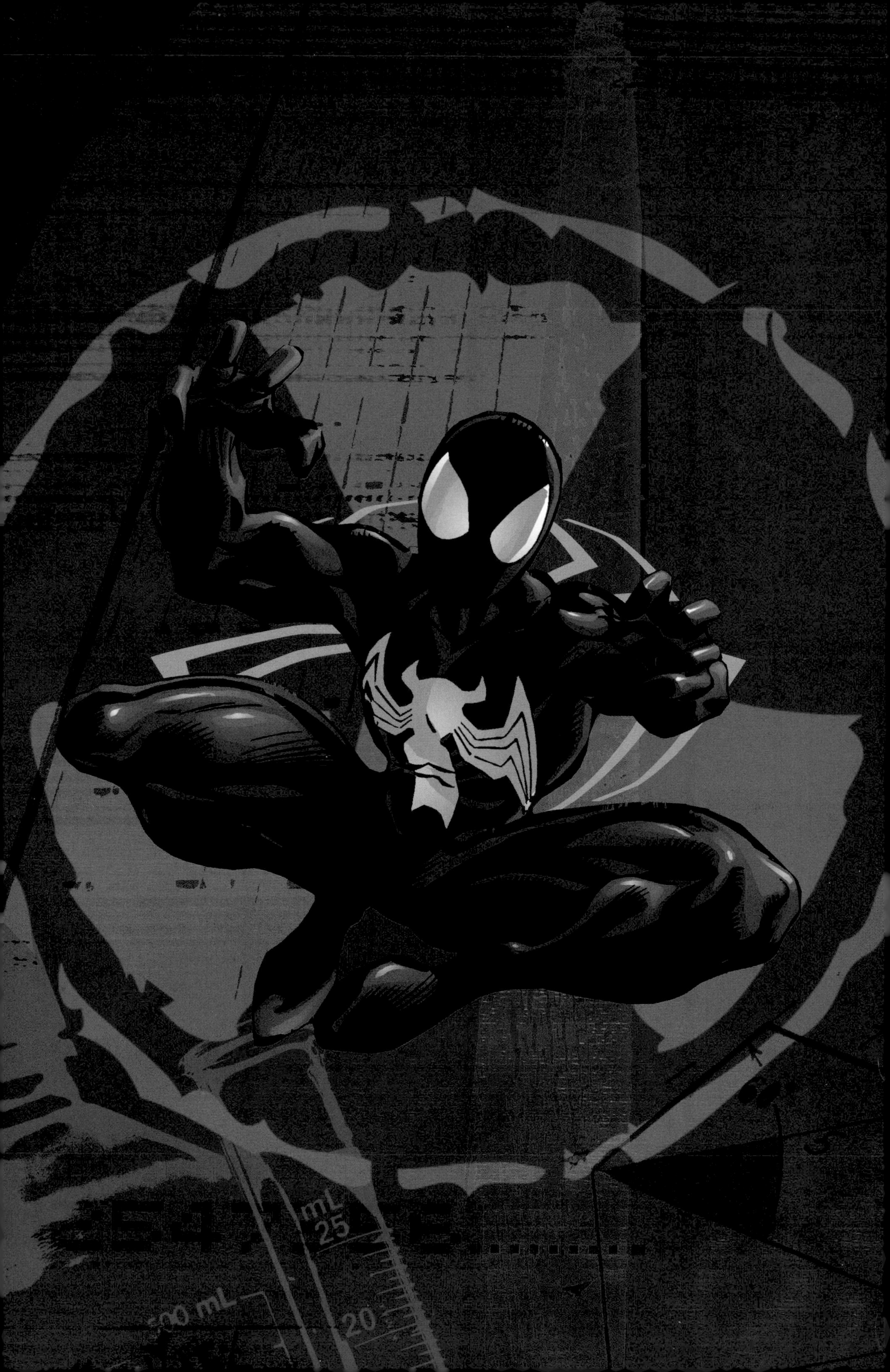
mL
25
20

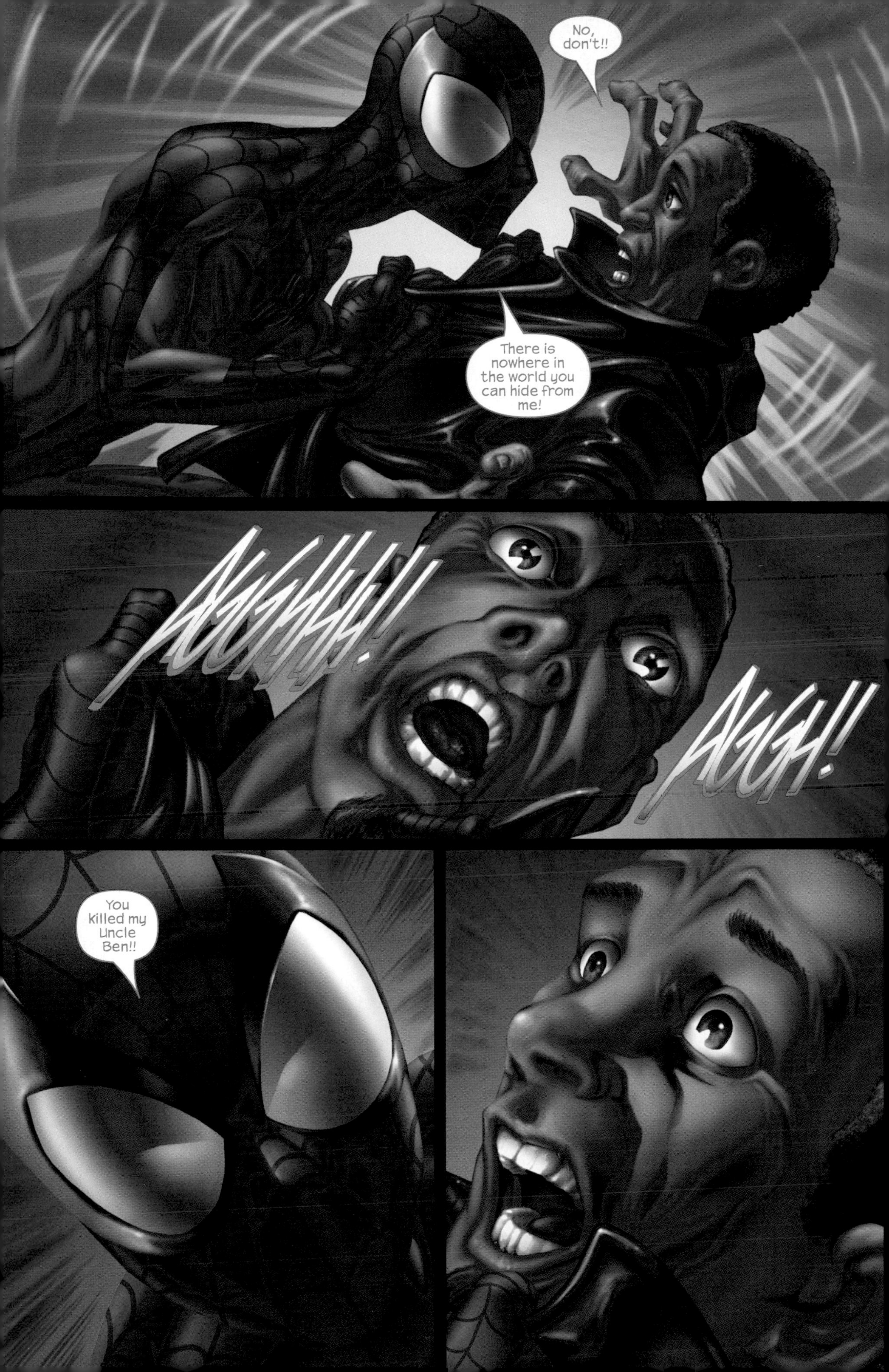
No, don't!!
There is nowhere in the world you can hide from me!
AAAGHHH!!
AUGH!
You killed my Uncle Ben!!

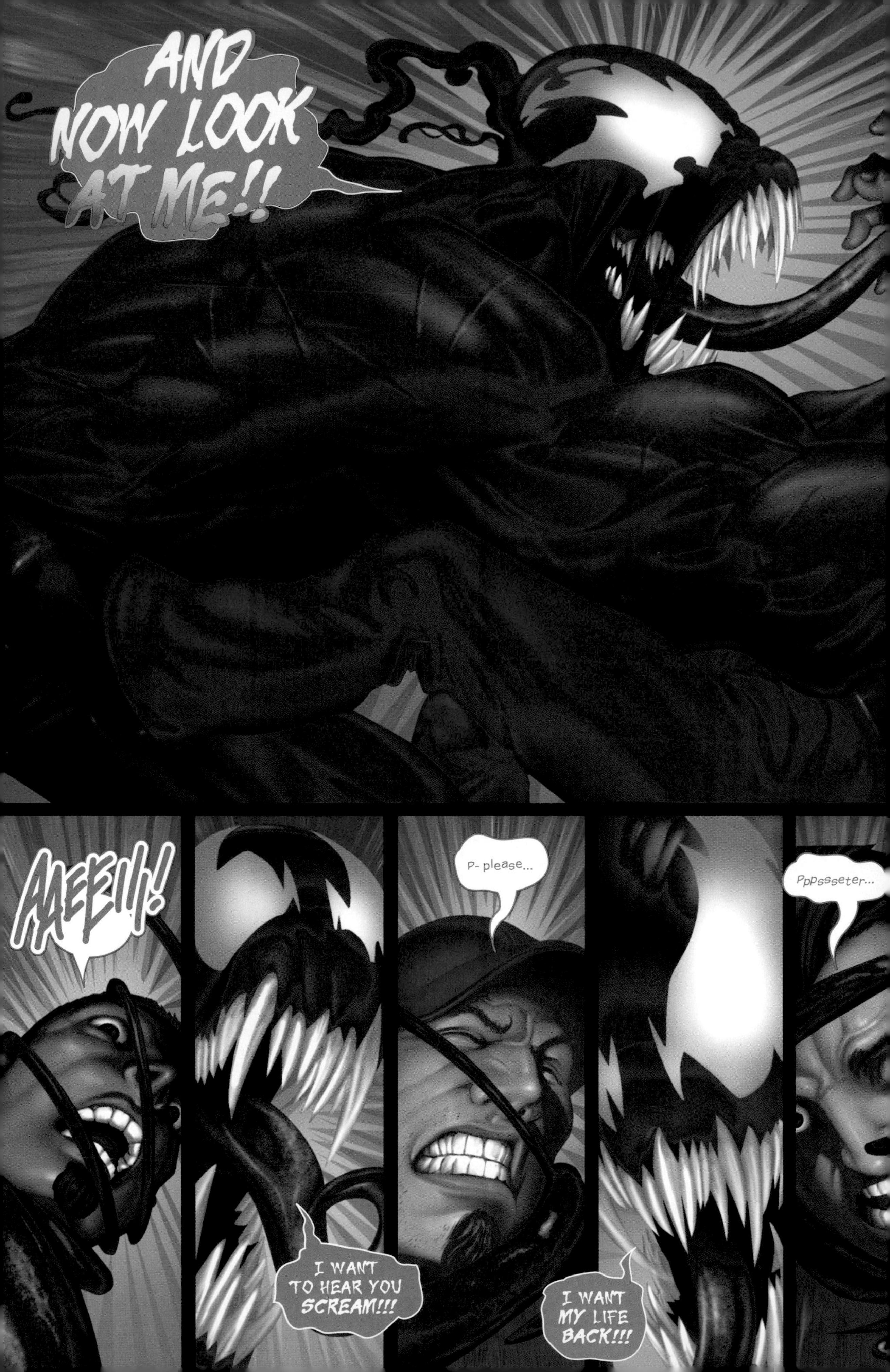
AND NOW LOOK AT ME!!
AAEEIIII!
I WANT TO HEAR YOU SCREAM!!!
P- please...
I WANT MY LIFE BACK!!!
Pppsssseter...

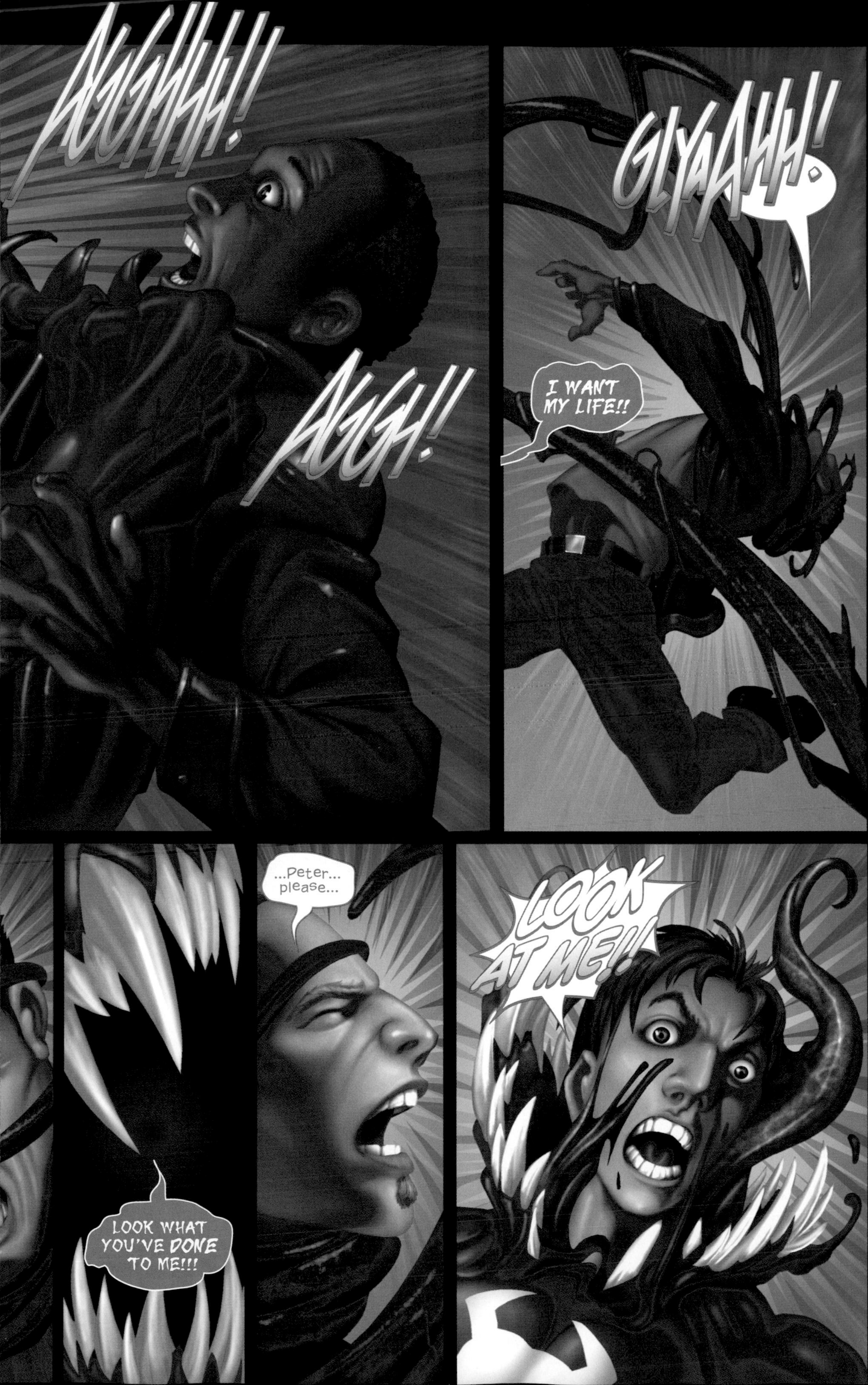
AUGHHH!
AUGH!
GLYAAHH!
I WANT MY LIFE!!
LOOK WHAT YOU'VE DONE TO ME!!!
...Peter... please...
LOOK AT ME!!

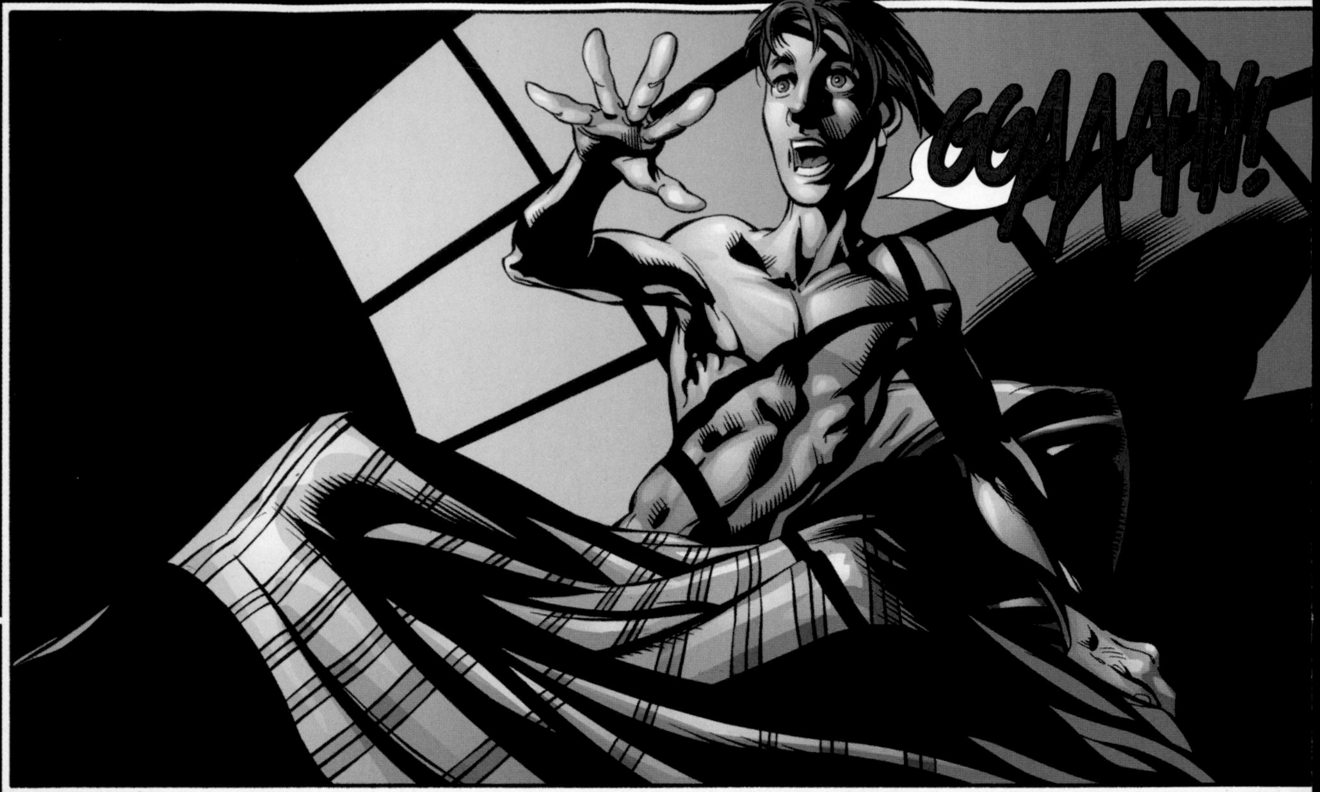
GGAAAHH!
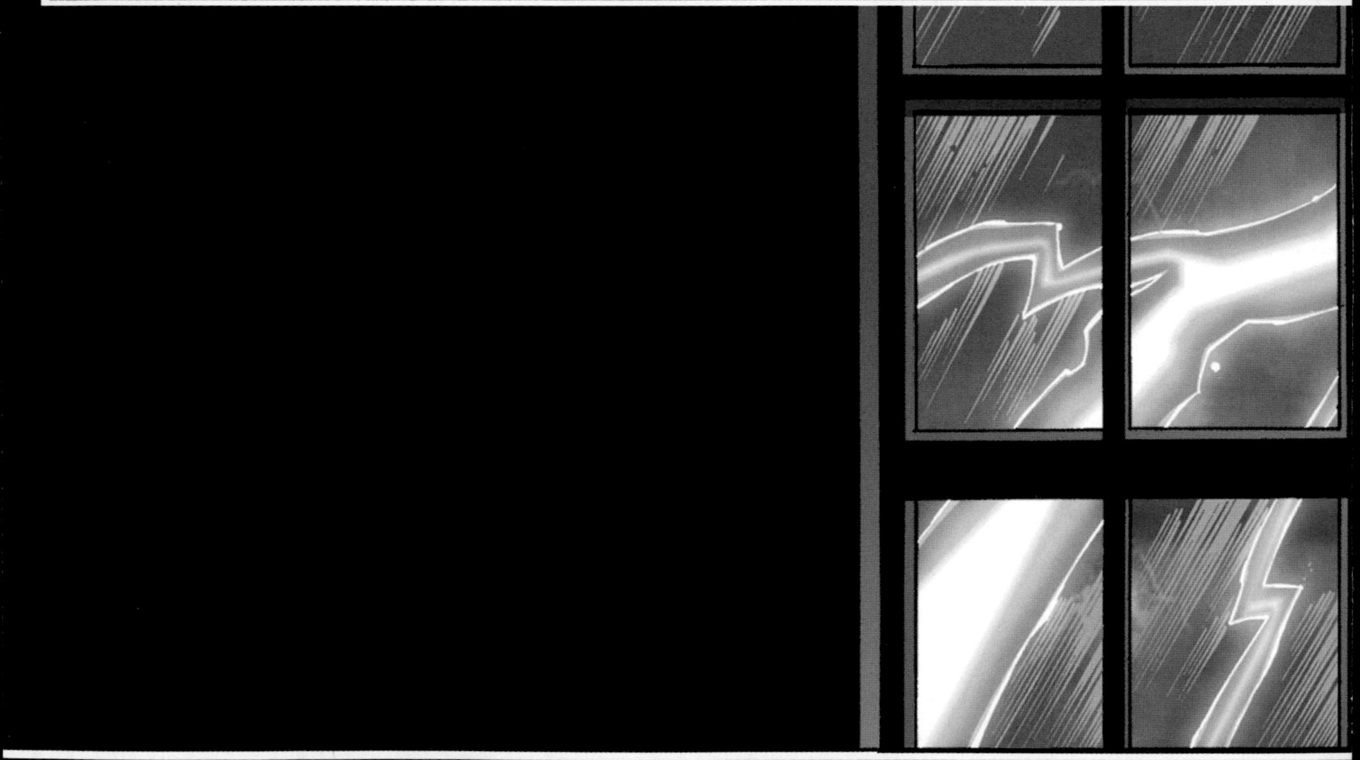

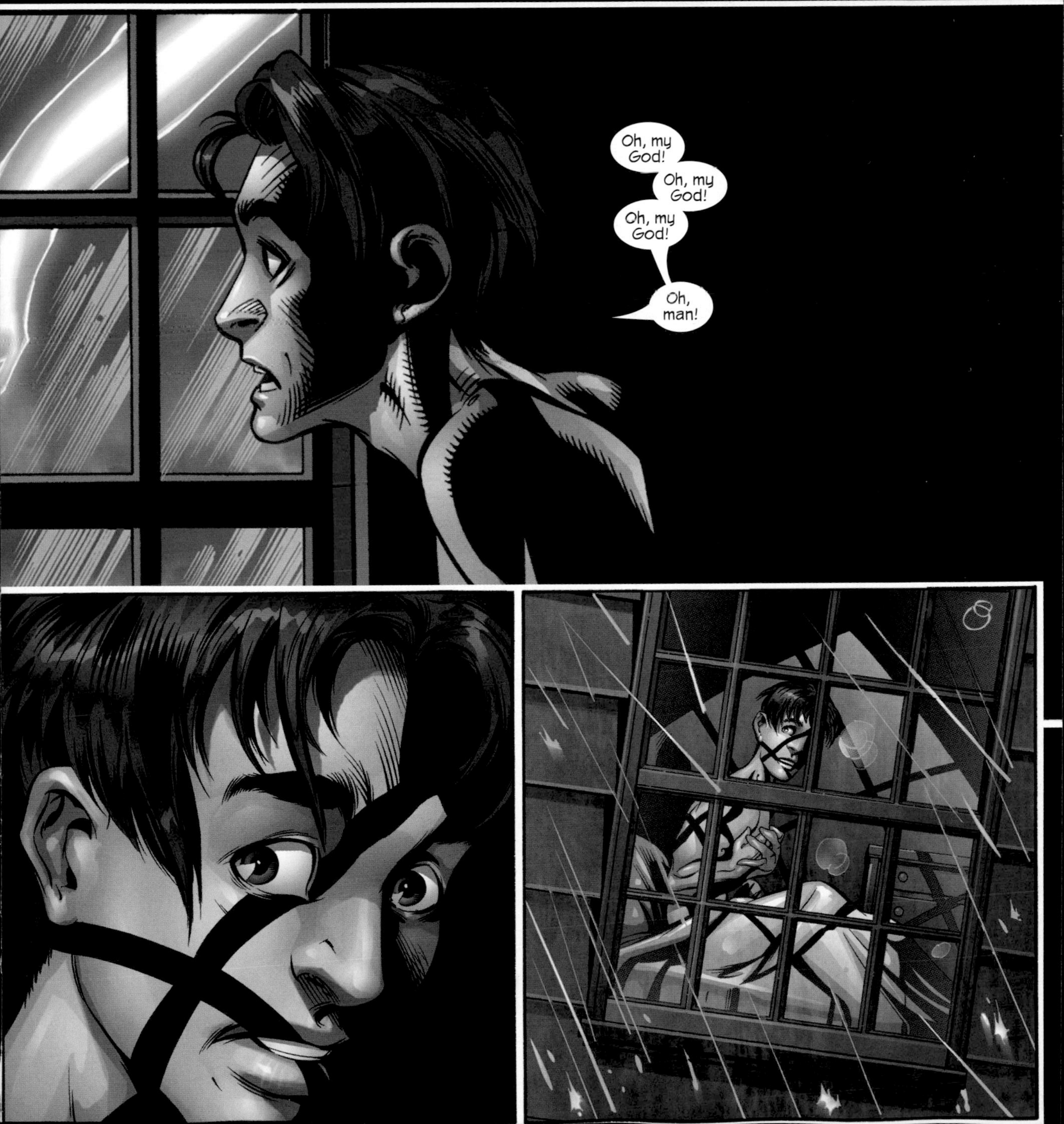
Oh, my God!
Oh, my God!
Oh, my God!
Oh, man!

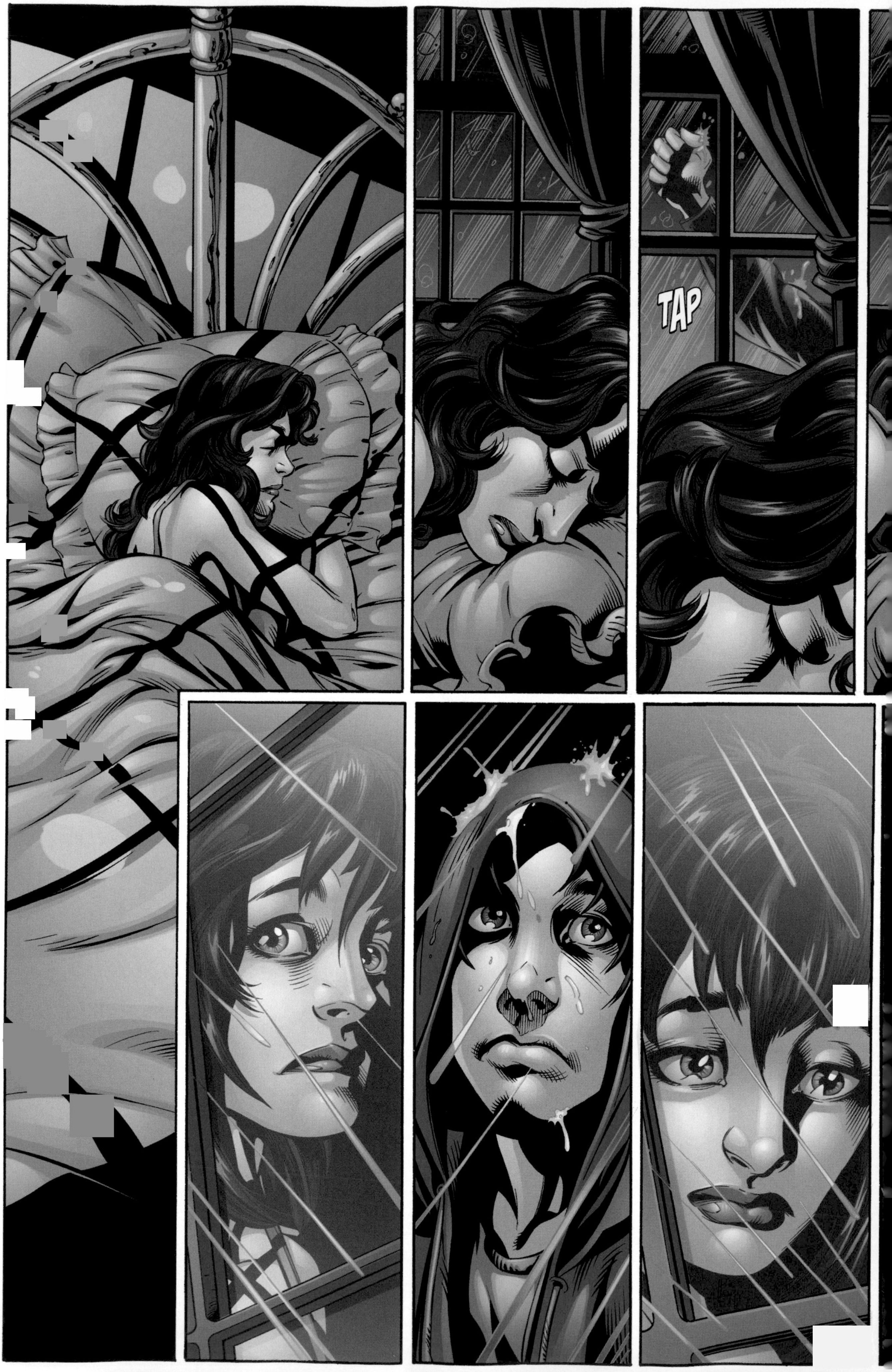
TAP

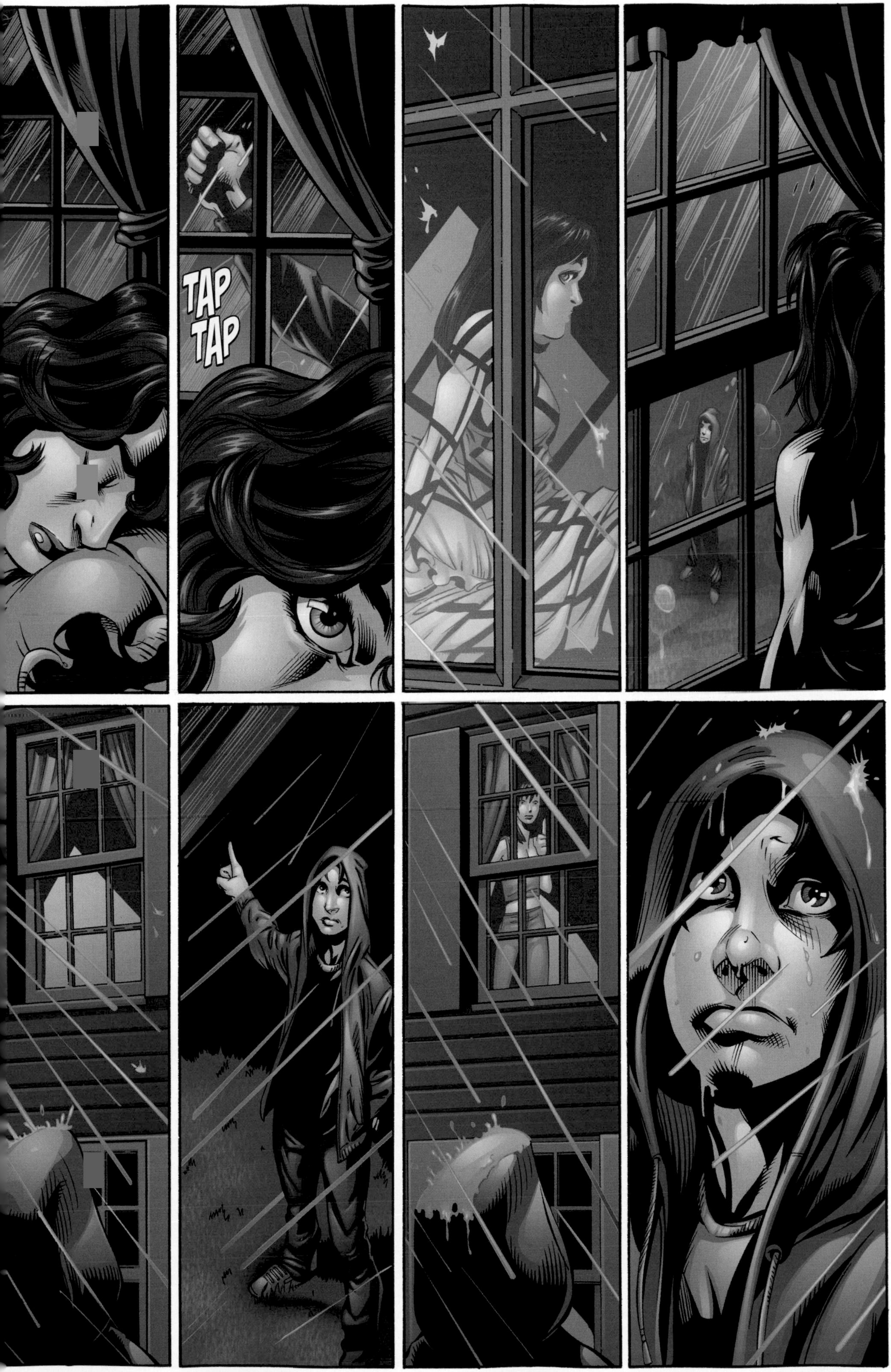
TAP
TAP

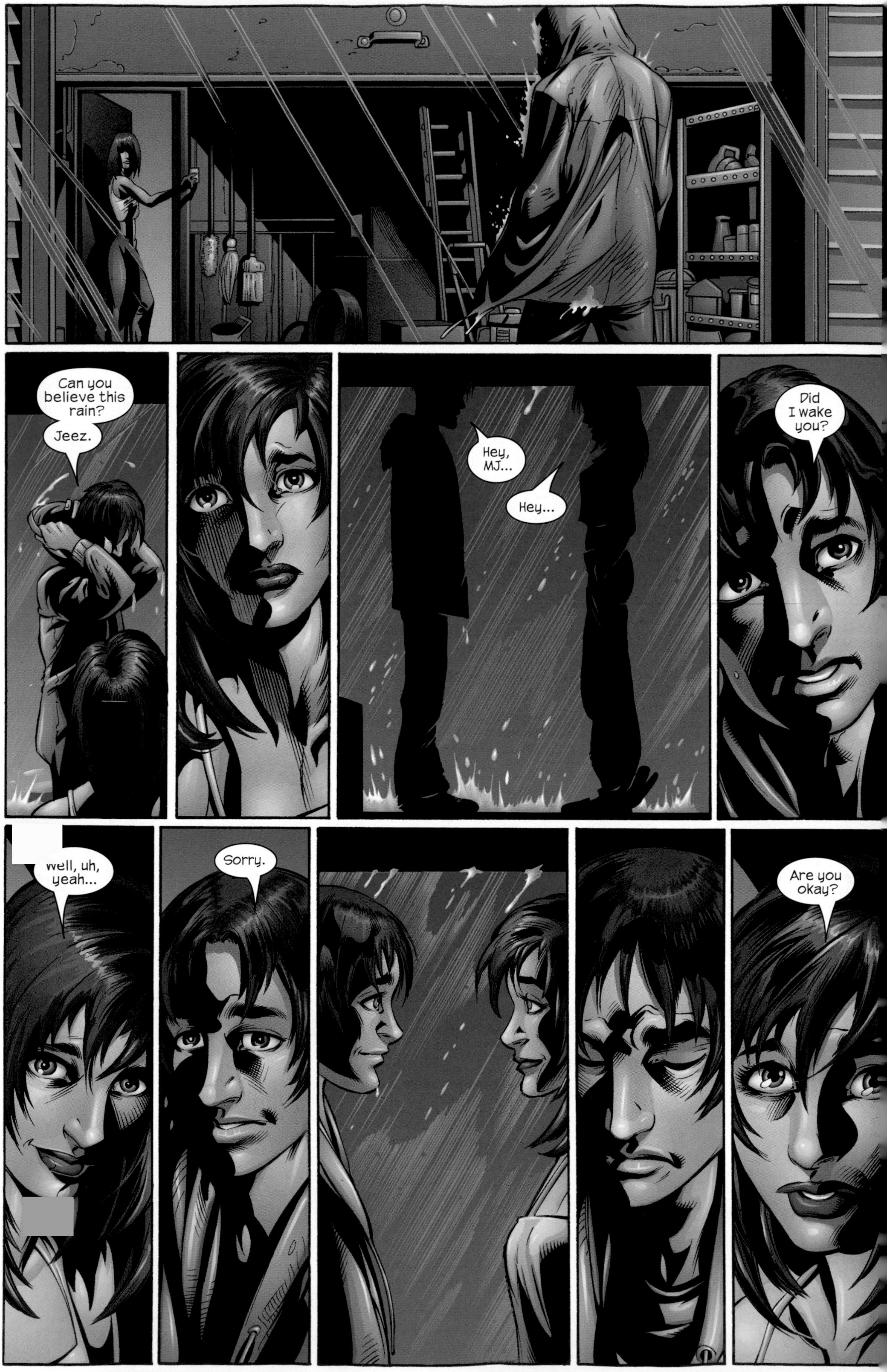
Can you believe this rain?
Jeez.
Hey, MJ...
Hey...
Did I wake you?
Well, uh, yeah...
Sorry.
Are you okay?

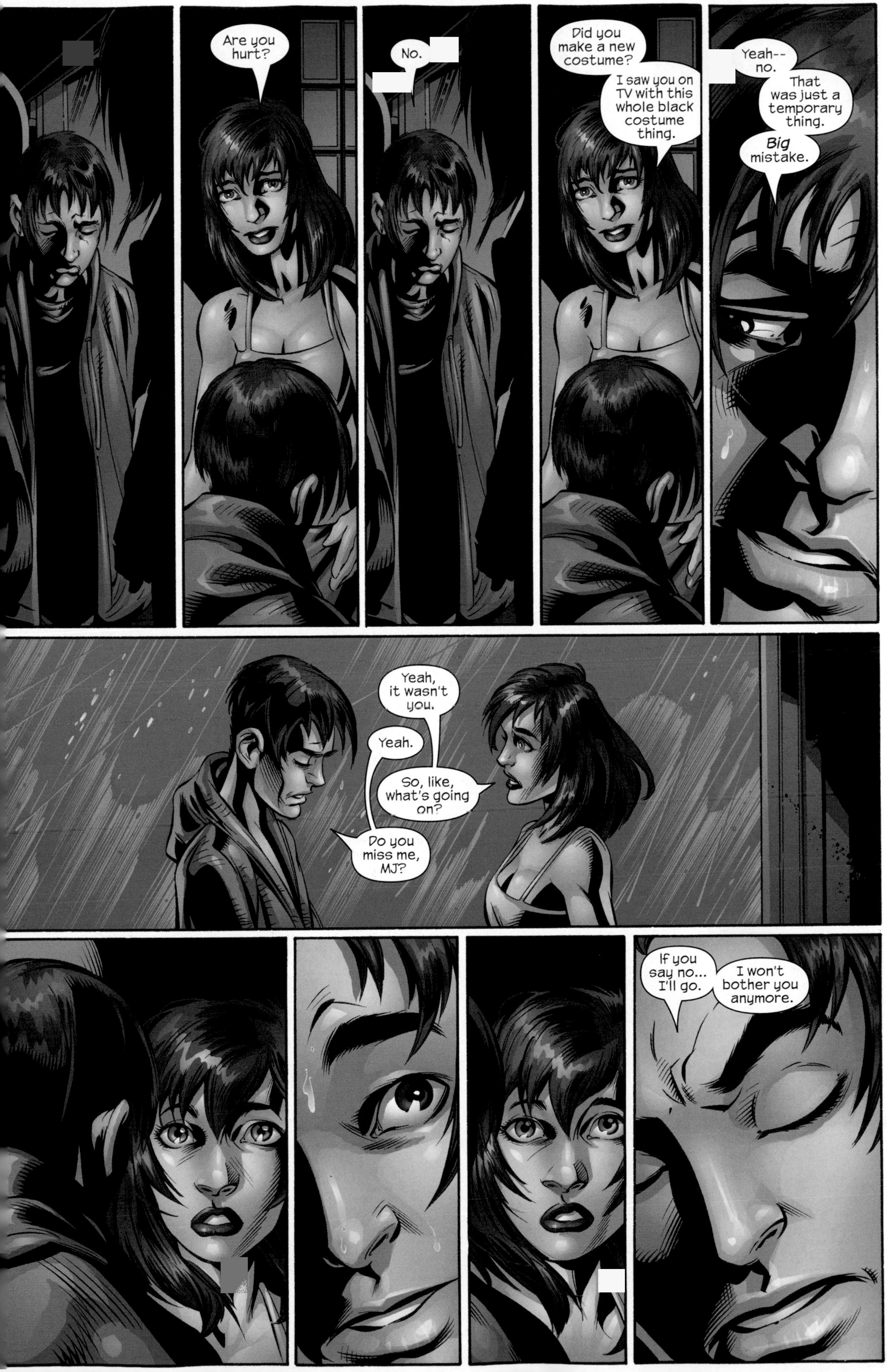
Are you hurt?
No.
Did you make a new costume?
I saw you on TV with this whole black costume thing.
Yeah-- no.
That was just a temporary thing.
Big mistake.
Yeah.
Yeah, it wasn't you.
So, like, what's going on?
Do you miss me, MJ?
If you say no... I'll go.
I won't bother you anymore.

Of course I do.

I see you at school--

--it-- uh-- it doesn't *look* like you do at all.

Me? What about *you?* You're all hoppin' rides with college guys and Gwen.

Gwen?

You two are always--

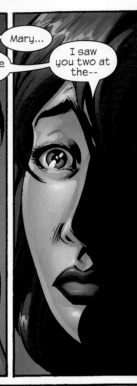

Mary...

I saw you two at the--

Nothing is going on with me and Gwen.

Nothing.

No-thing.

Are you-- are you seeing anyone?

Yeah, Liz Allen.

Really?

You wish.

No, Peter. I'm not seeing anyone.

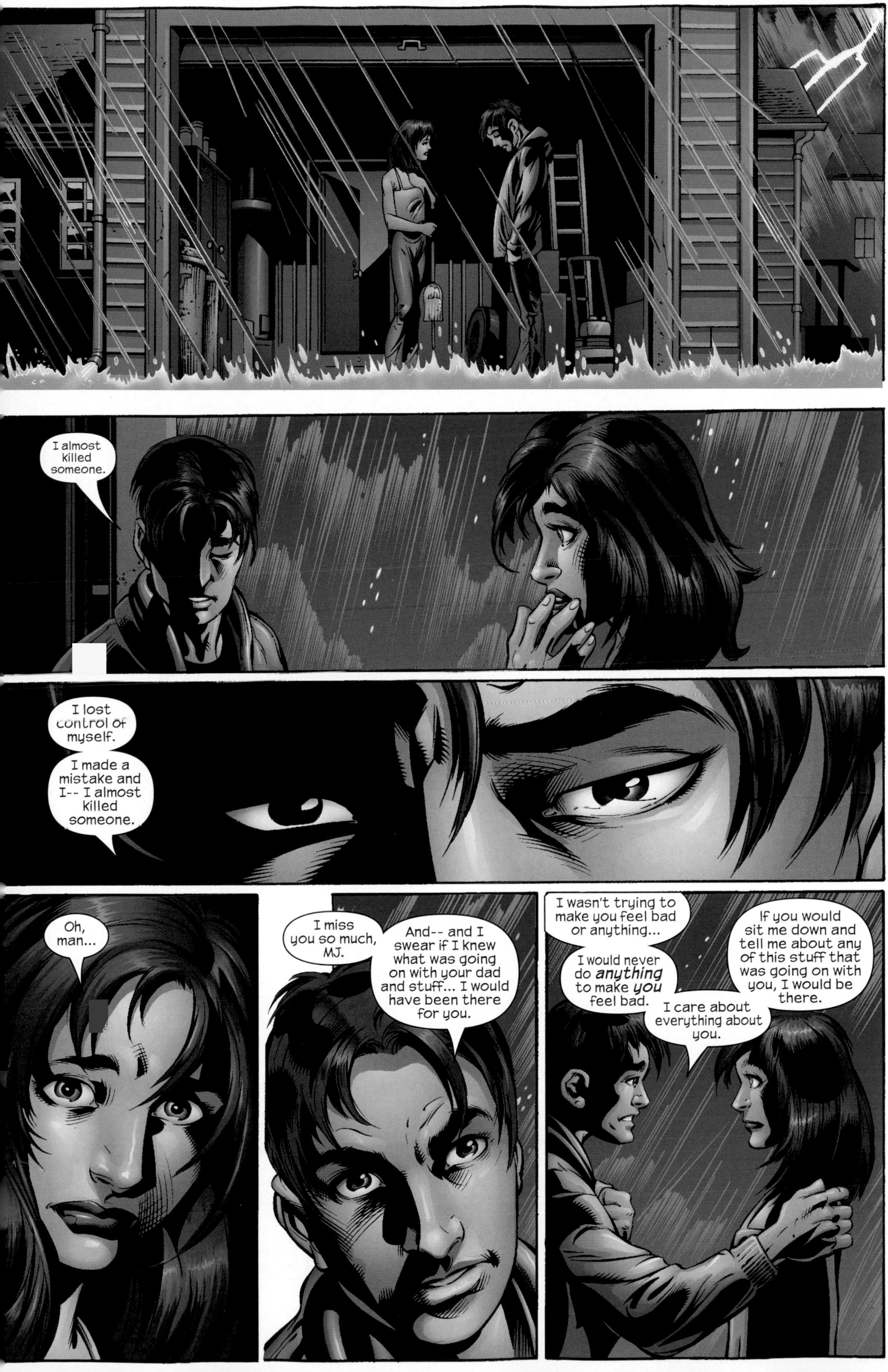

I almost killed someone.
I lost control of myself.
I made a mistake and I-- I almost killed someone.
Oh, man...
I miss you so much, MJ.
And-- and I swear if I knew what was going on with your dad and stuff... I would have been there for you.
I wasn't trying to make you feel bad or anything...
I would never do *anything* to make *you* feel bad.
If you would sit me down and tell me about any of this stuff that was going on with you, I would be there.
I care about everything about you.

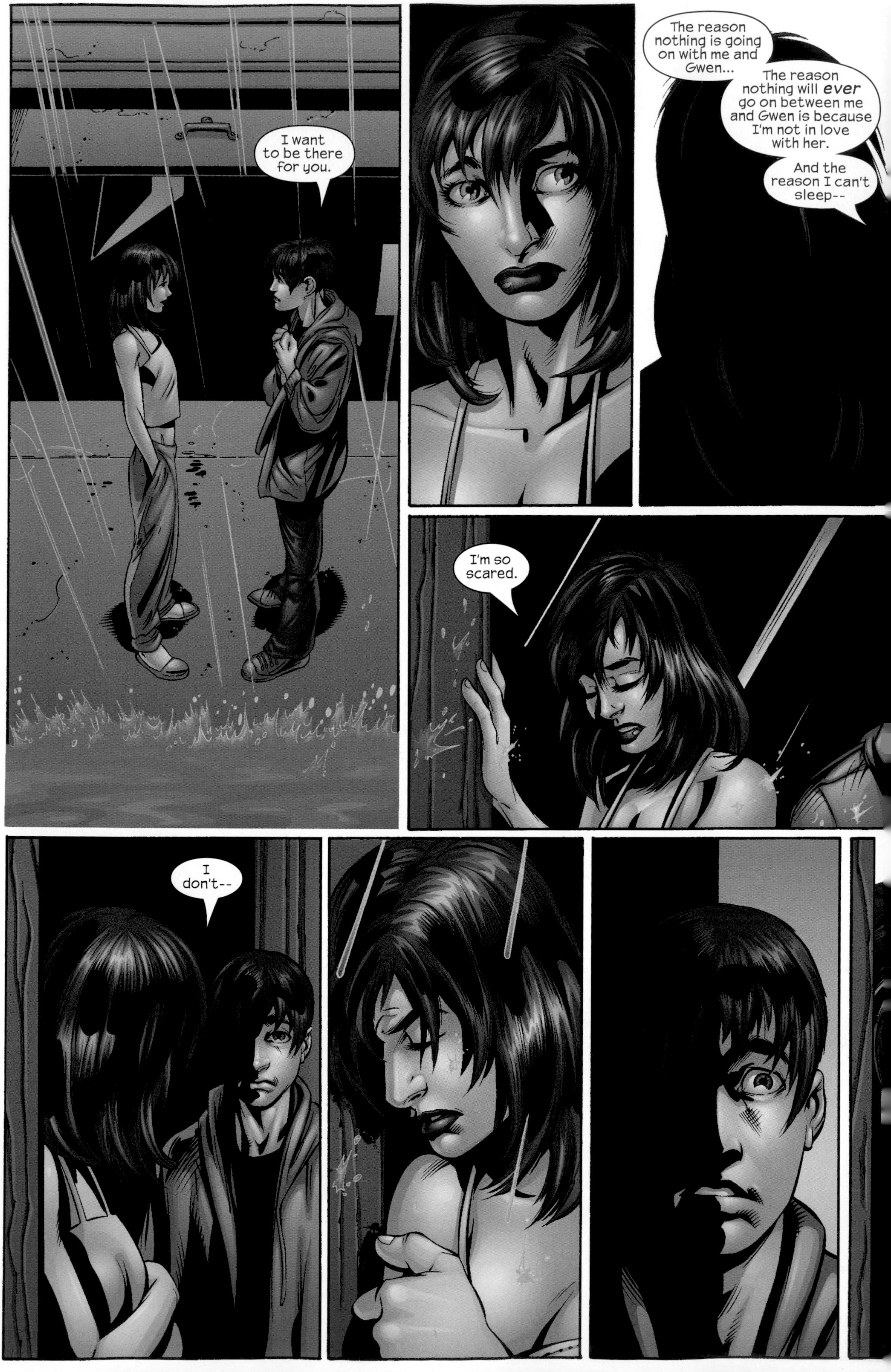
I want to be there for you.
The reason nothing is going on with me and Gwen...
The reason nothing will *ever* go on between me and Gwen is because I'm not in love with her.
And the reason I can't sleep--
I'm so scared.
I don't--

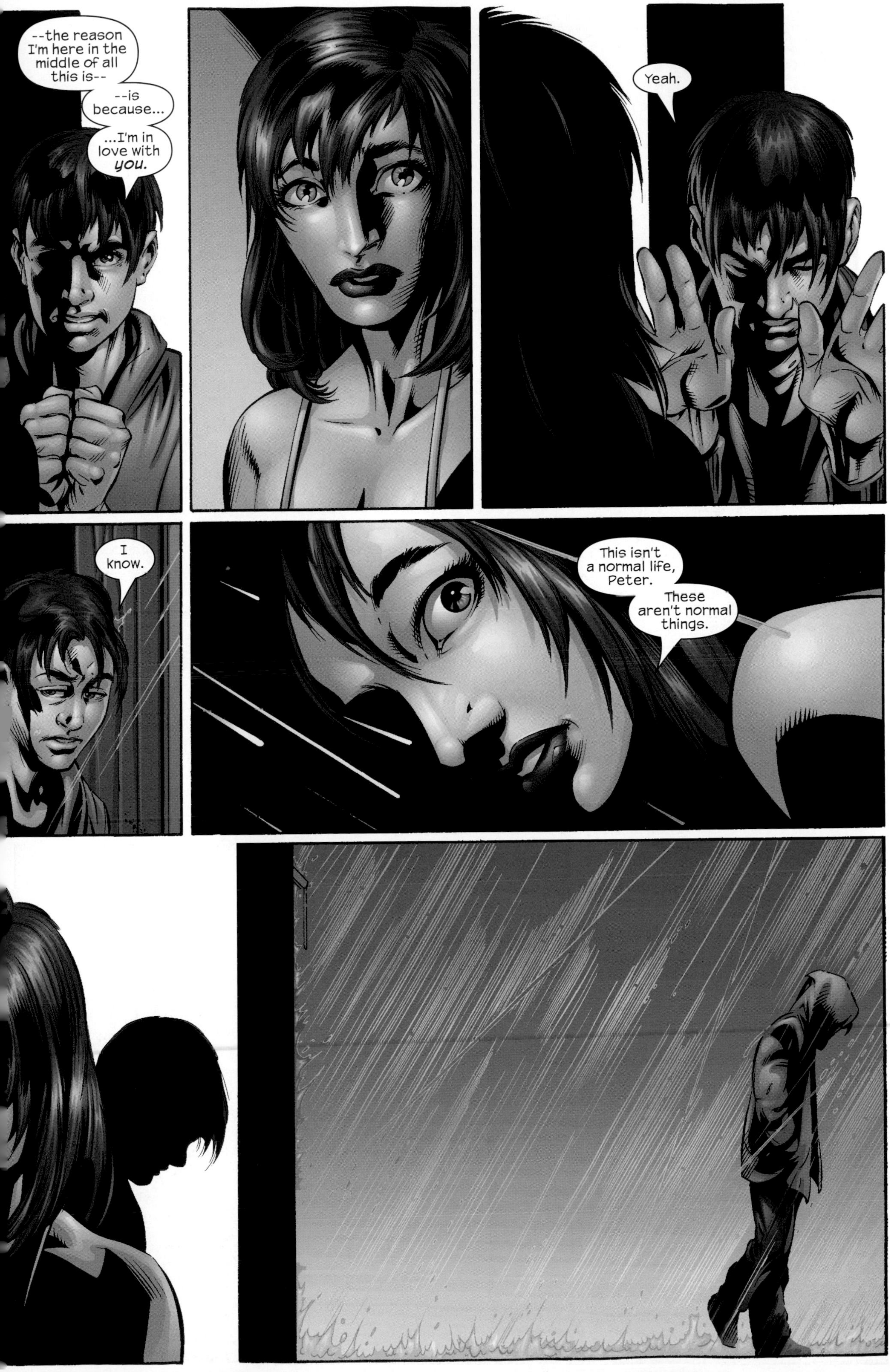
--the reason I'm here in the middle of all this is--
--is because...
...I'm in love with *you.*
Yeah.
I know.
This isn't a normal life, Peter.
These aren't normal things.

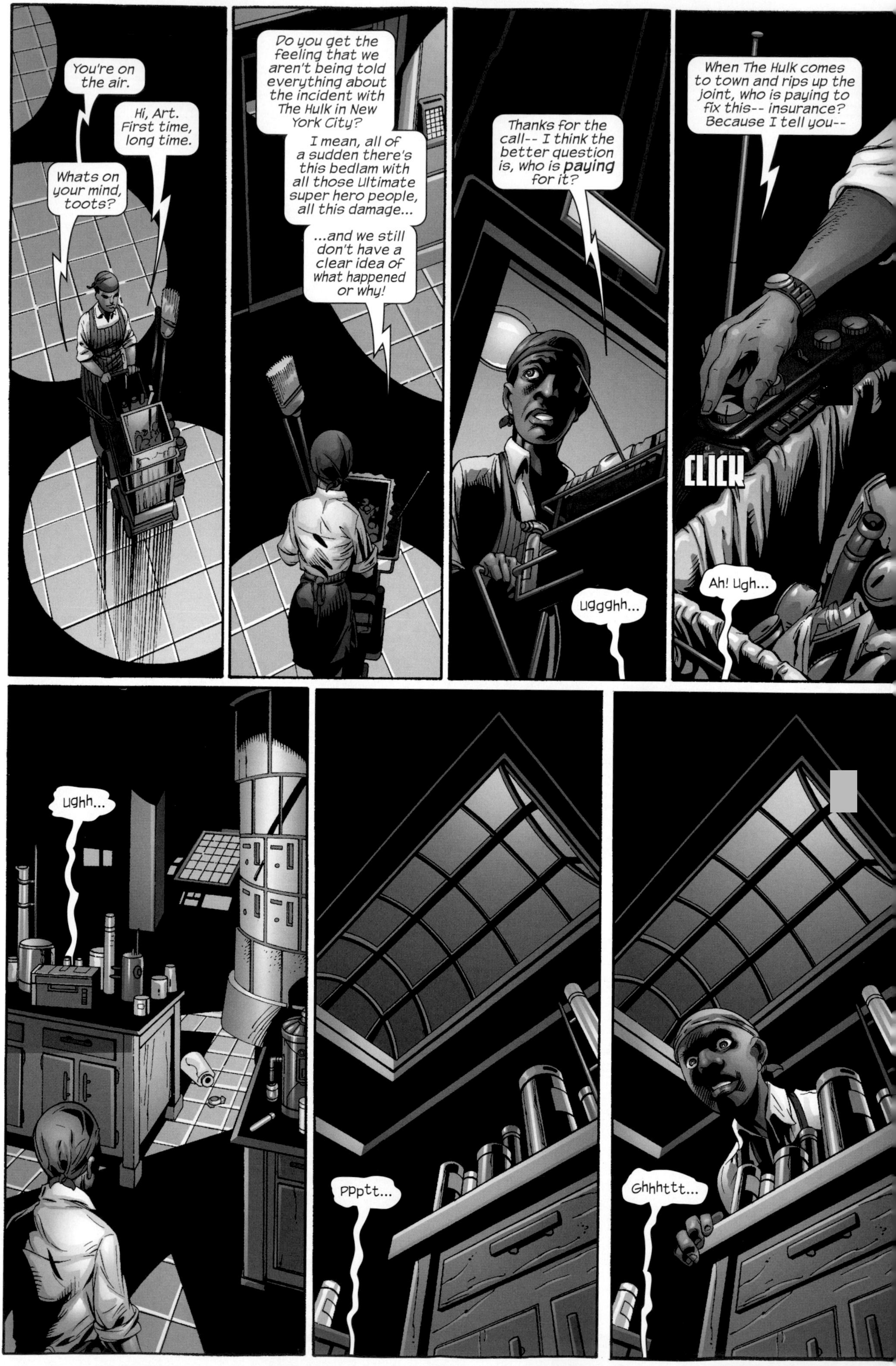
You're on the air.
Hi, Art. First time, long time.
Whats on your mind, toots?
Do you get the feeling that we aren't being told everything about the incident with The Hulk in New York City?
I mean, all of a sudden there's this bedlam with all those Ultimate super hero people, all this damage...
...and we still don't have a clear idea of what happened or why!
Thanks for the call-- I think the better question is, who is paying for it?
Uggghh...
When The Hulk comes to town and rips up the joint, who is paying to fix this-- insurance? Because I tell you--
CLICK
Ah! Ugh...
Ughh...
Ppptt...
Ghhhttt...

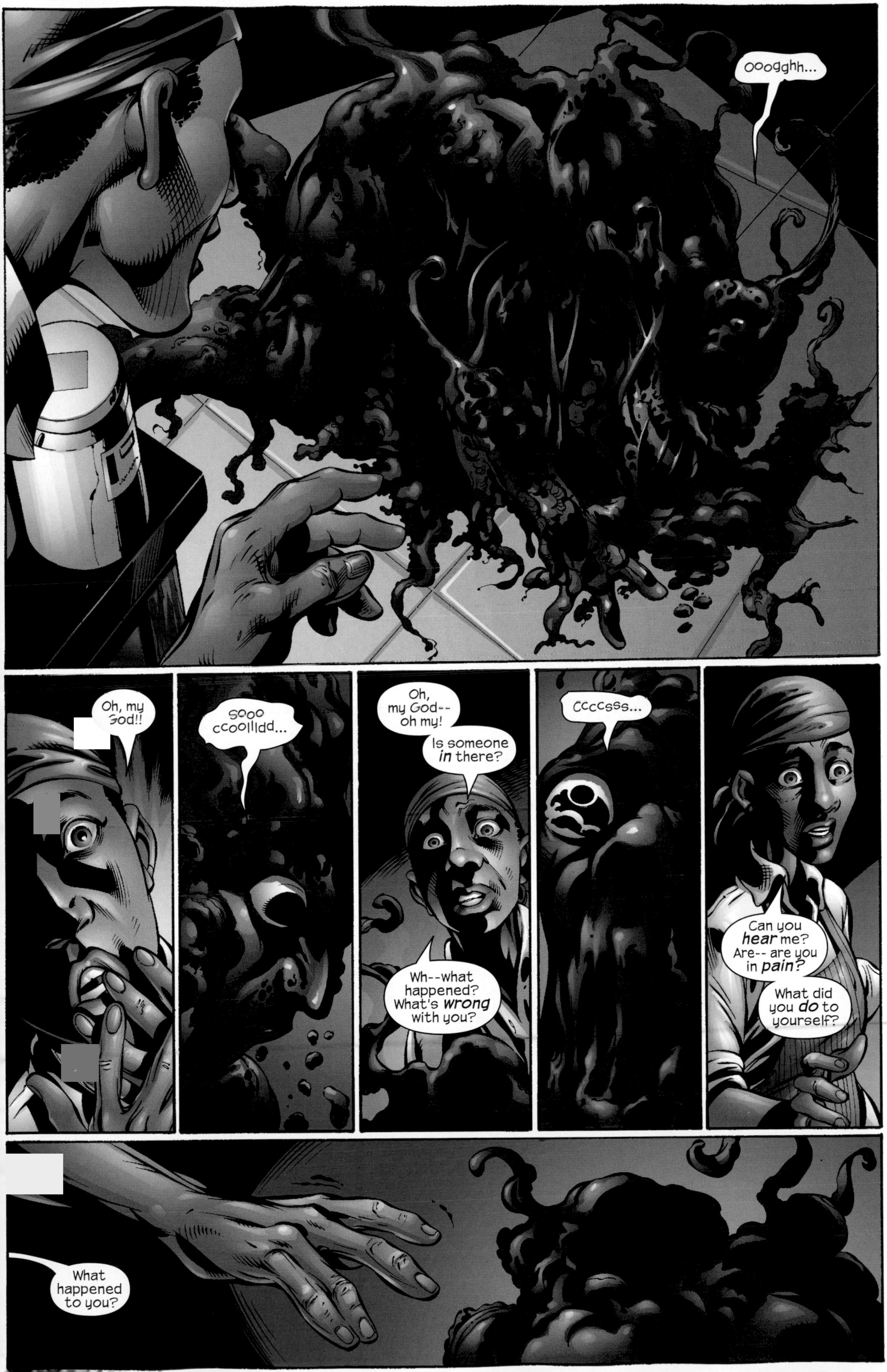
Ooogghh...
Oh, my God!!
Sooo ccoollldd...
Oh, my God-- oh my!
Is someone in there?
Wh--what happened? What's wrong with you?
Ccccsss...
Can you hear me? Are-- are you in pain?
What did you do to yourself?
What happened to you?

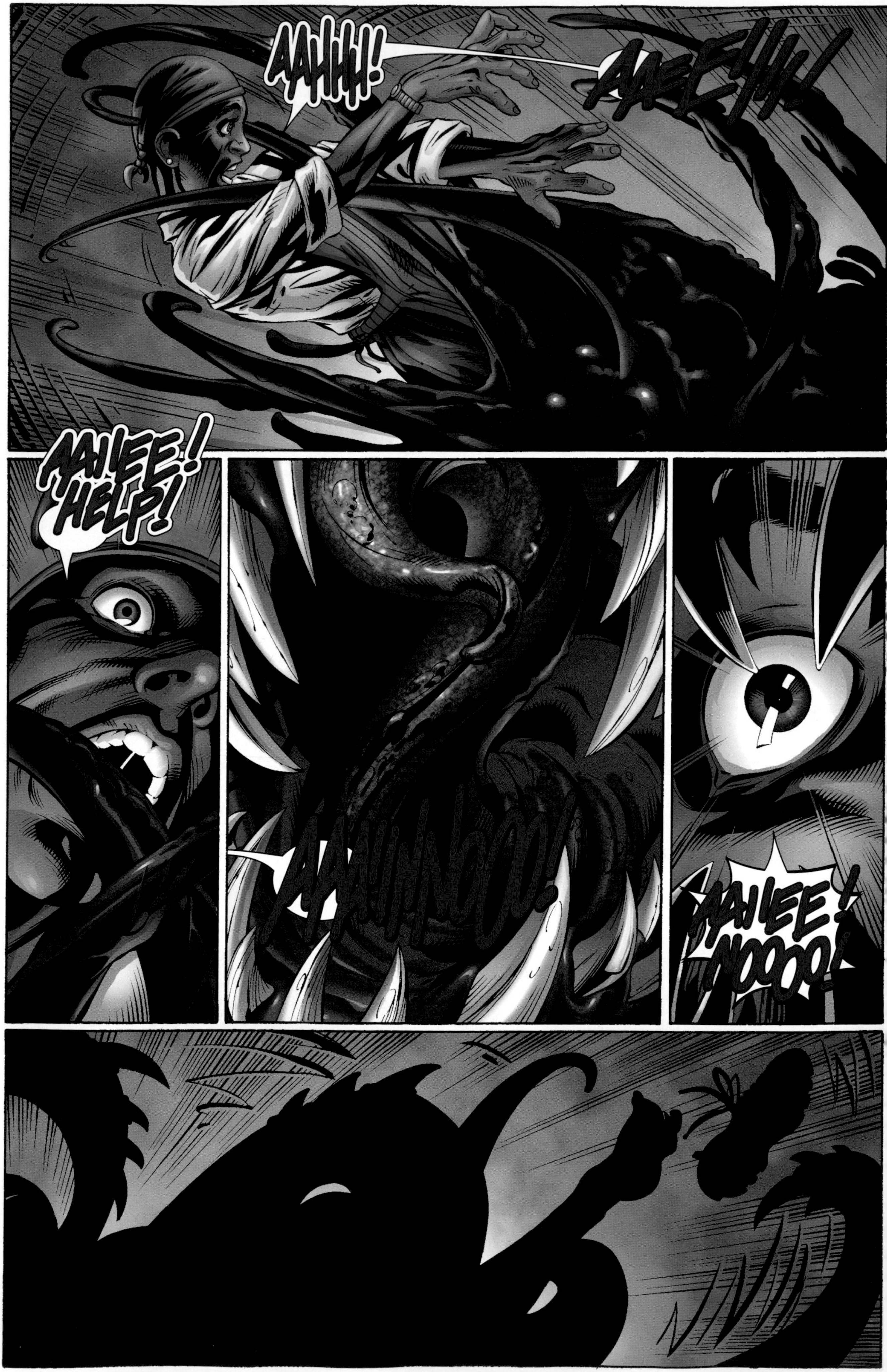
AAHHH!
AAEEHHH!!
AAIEE! HELP!
AAHHNOOO!
AAIEE! NOOOO!

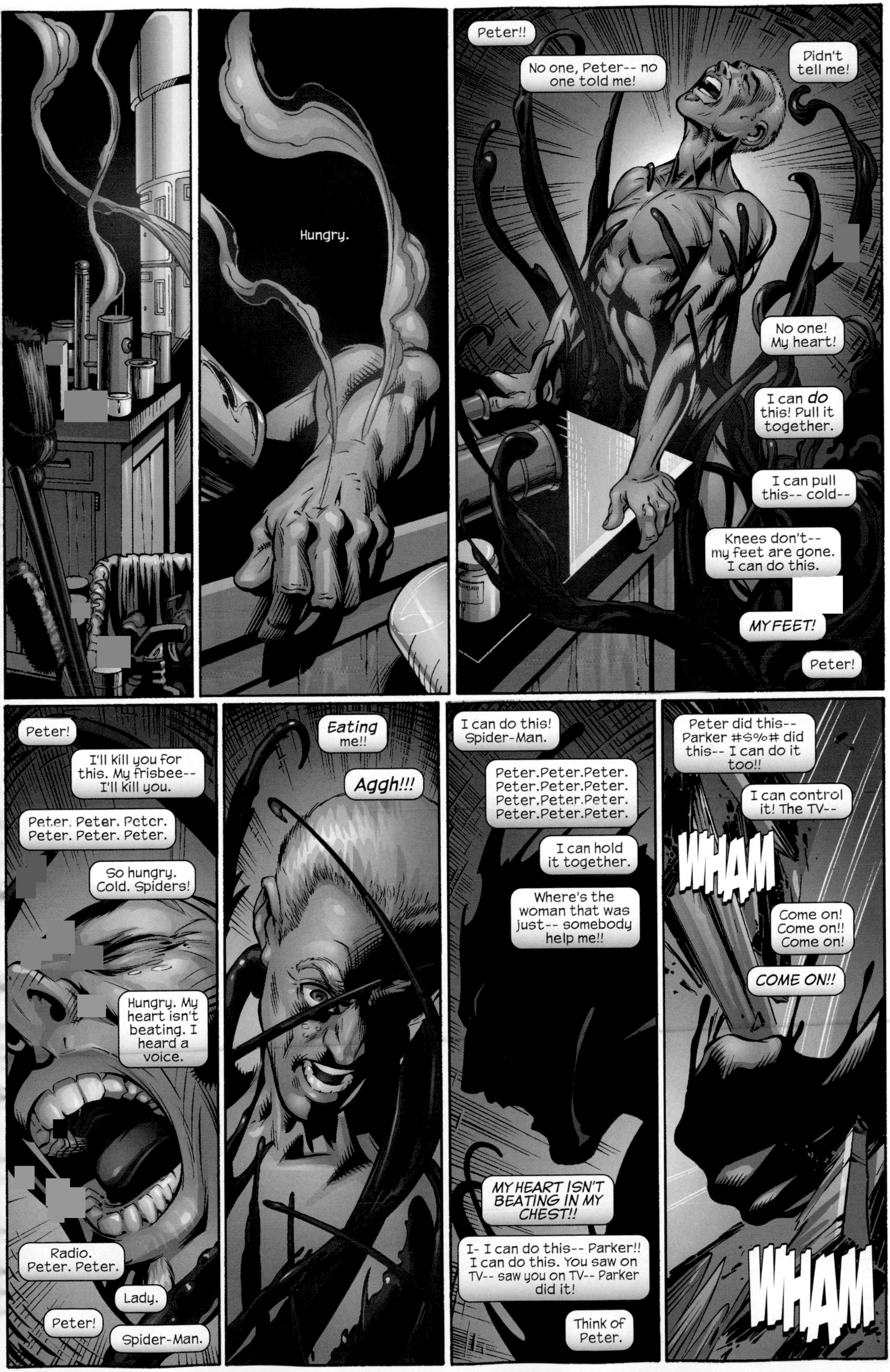

Hungry.
Peter!!
No one, Peter-- no one told me!
Didn't tell me!
No one! My heart!
I can *do* this! Pull it together.
I can pull this-- cold--
Knees don't-- my feet are gone. I can do this.
MY FEET!
Peter!
Peter!
I'll kill you for this. My frisbee-- I'll kill you.
Peter. Peter. Peter. Peter. Peter. Peter.
So hungry. Cold. Spiders!
Hungry. My heart isn't beating. I heard a voice.
Radio. Peter. Peter.
Lady.
Peter!
Spider-Man.
Eating me!!
Aggh!!!
I can do this! Spider-Man.
Peter.Peter.Peter. Peter.Peter.Peter. Peter.Peter.Peter. Peter.Peter.Peter.
I can hold it together.
Where's the woman that was just-- somebody help me!!
MY HEART ISN'T BEATING IN MY CHEST!!
I- I can do this-- Parker!! I can do this. You saw on TV-- saw you on TV-- Parker did it!
Think of Peter.
Peter did this-- Parker #$%# did this-- I can do it too!!
I can control it! The TV--
WHAM
Come on! Come on!! Come on!
COME ON!!
WHAM

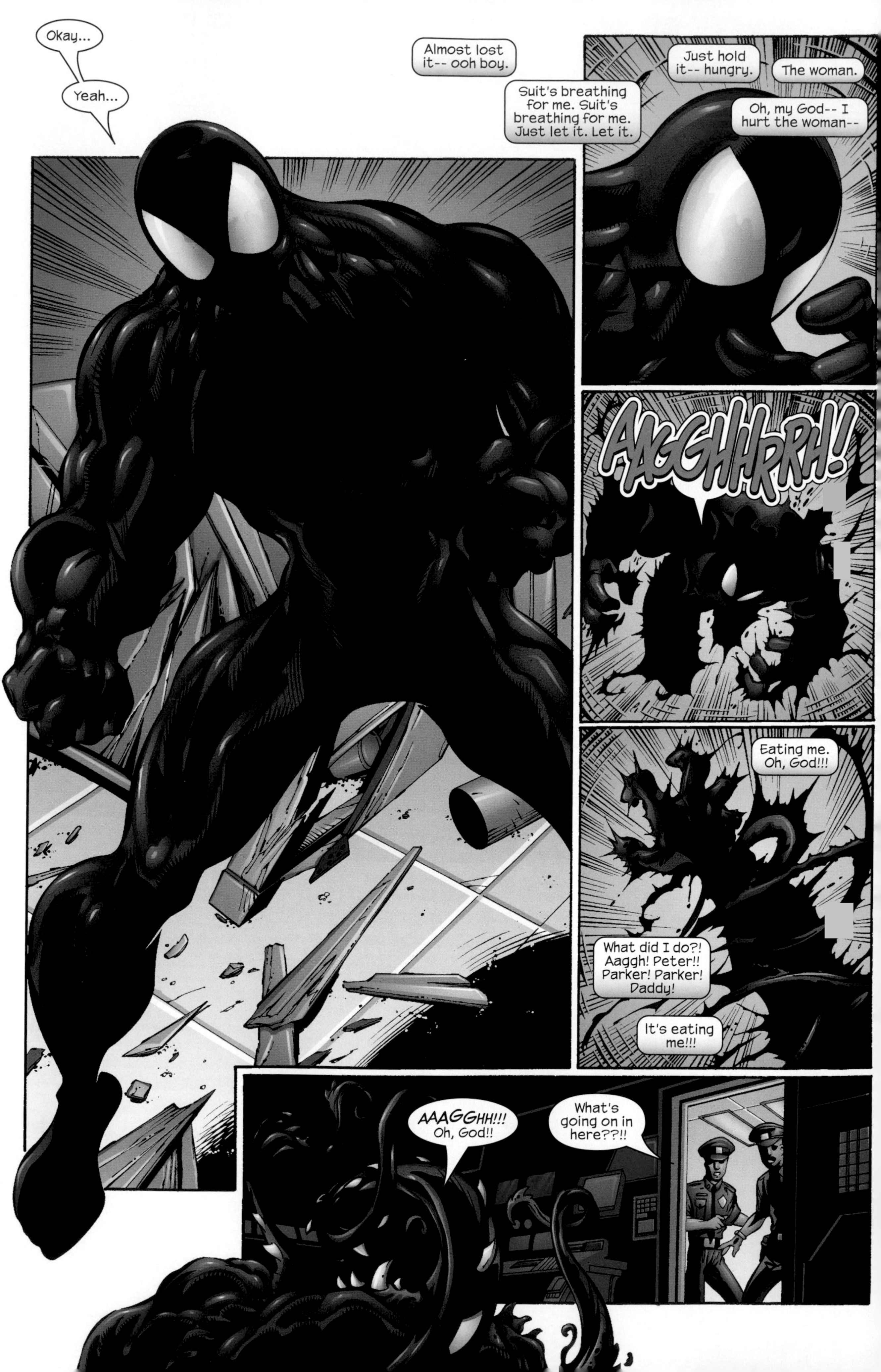
Okay...
Yeah...
Almost lost it-- ooh boy.
Suit's breathing for me. Suit's breathing for me. Just let it. Let it.
Just hold it-- hungry.
The woman.
Oh, my God-- I hurt the woman--
AAGGHHRRH!
Eating me. Oh, God!!!
What did I do?! Aaggh! Peter!! Parker! Parker! Daddy!
It's eating me!!!
AAAGGHH!!! Oh, God!!
What's going on in here??!!

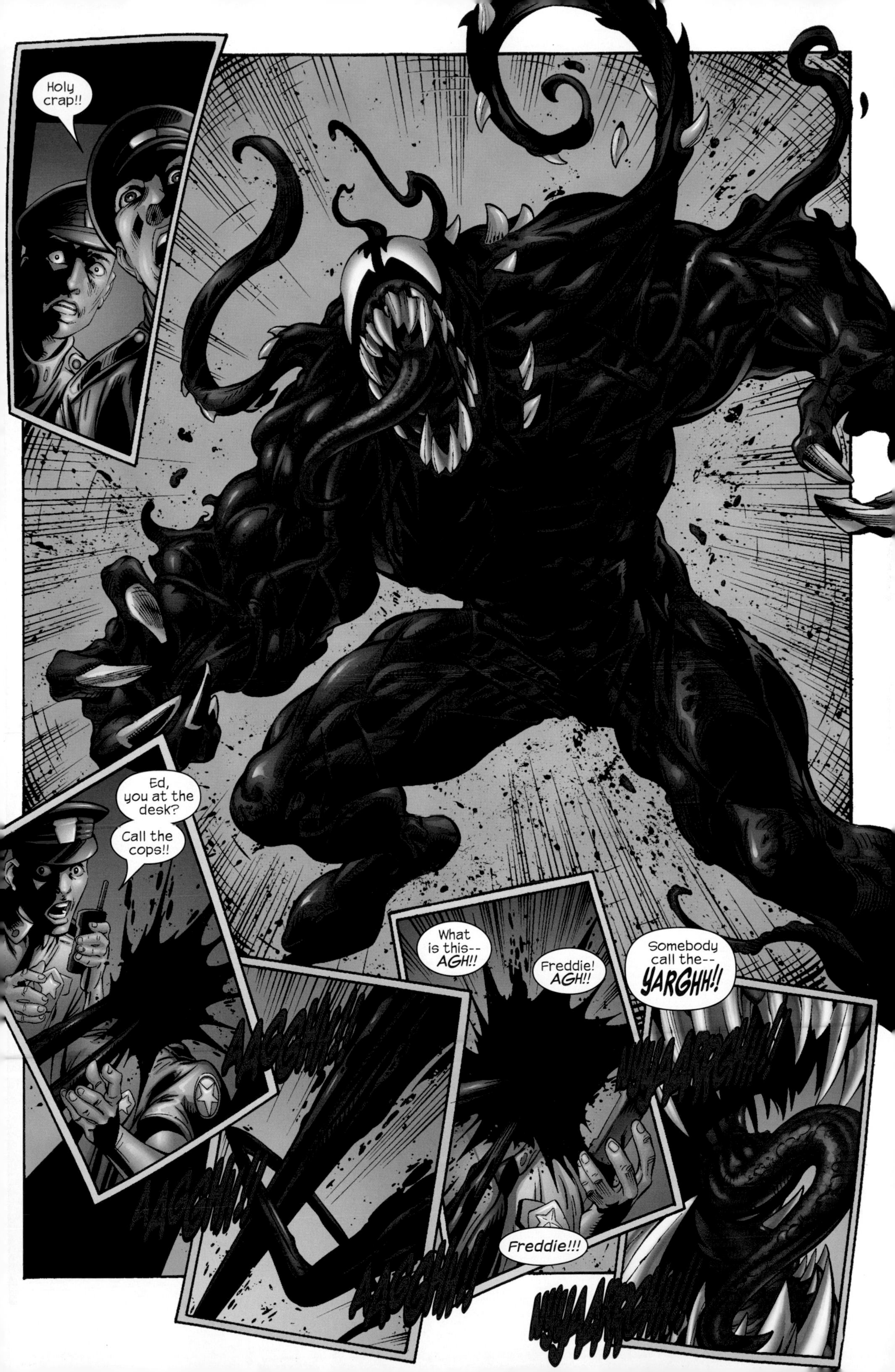
Holy crap!!
Ed, you at the desk?
Call the cops!!
What is this-- AGH!!
Freddie! AGH!!
Somebody call the-- YARGHH!!
Freddie!!!

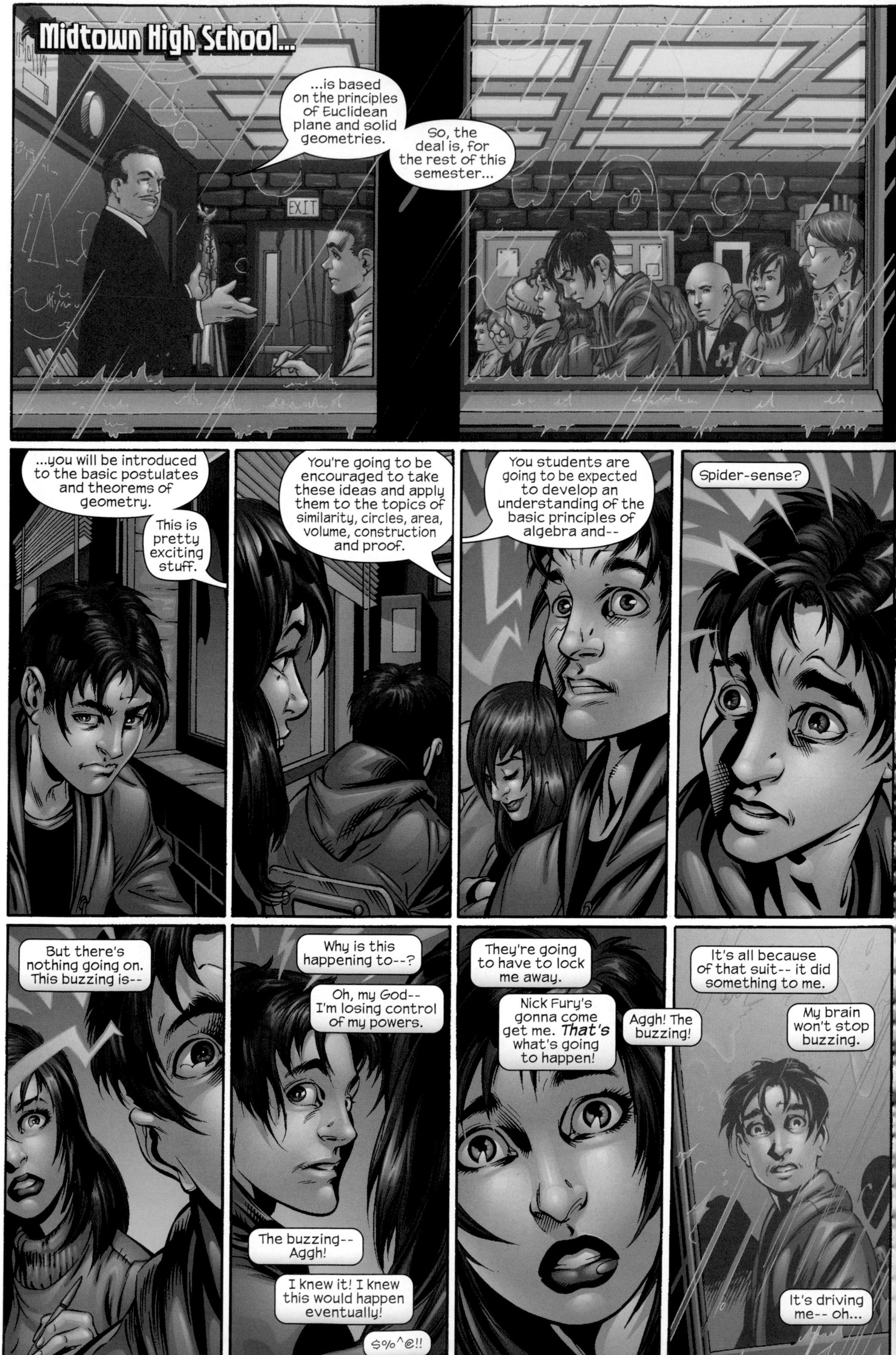
Midtown High School...
...is based on the principles of Euclidean plane and solid geometries.
So, the deal is, for the rest of this semester...
...you will be introduced to the basic postulates and theorems of geometry.
This is pretty exciting stuff.
You're going to be encouraged to take these ideas and apply them to the topics of similarity, circles, area, volume, construction and proof.
You students are going to be expected to develop an understanding of the basic principles of algebra and--
Spider-sense?
But there's nothing going on. This buzzing is--
Why is this happening to--?
Oh, my God-- I'm losing control of my powers.
The buzzing-- Aggh!
I knew it! I knew this would happen eventually!
$%^@!!
They're going to have to lock me away.
Nick Fury's gonna come get me. That's what's going to happen!
Aggh! The buzzing!
It's all because of that suit-- it did something to me.
My brain won't stop buzzing.
It's driving me-- oh...

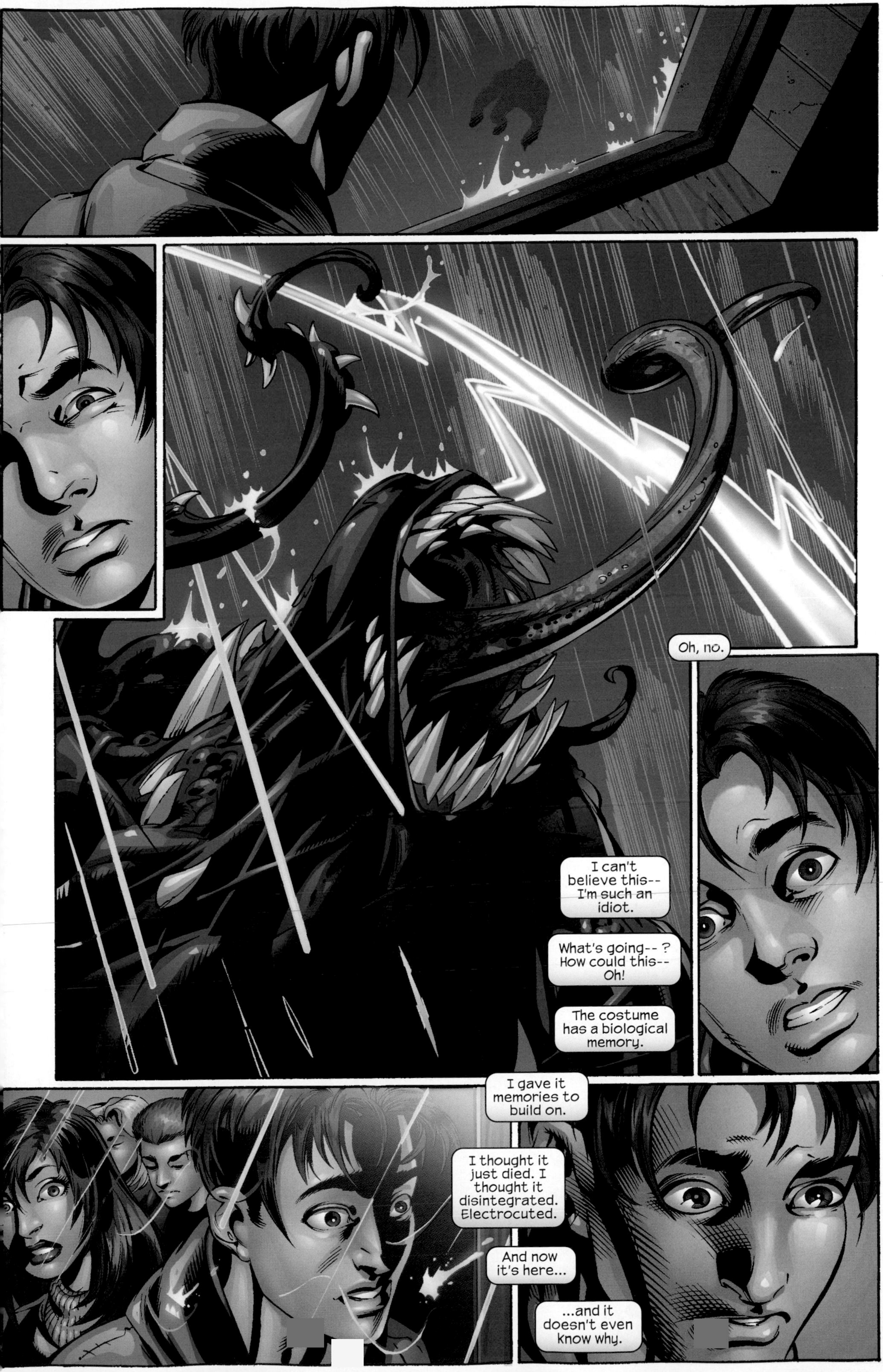
Oh, no.
I can't believe this-- I'm such an idiot.
What's going-- ? How could this-- Oh!
The costume has a biological memory.
I gave it memories to build on.
I thought it just died. I thought it disintegrated. Electrocuted.
And now it's here...
...and it doesn't even know why.

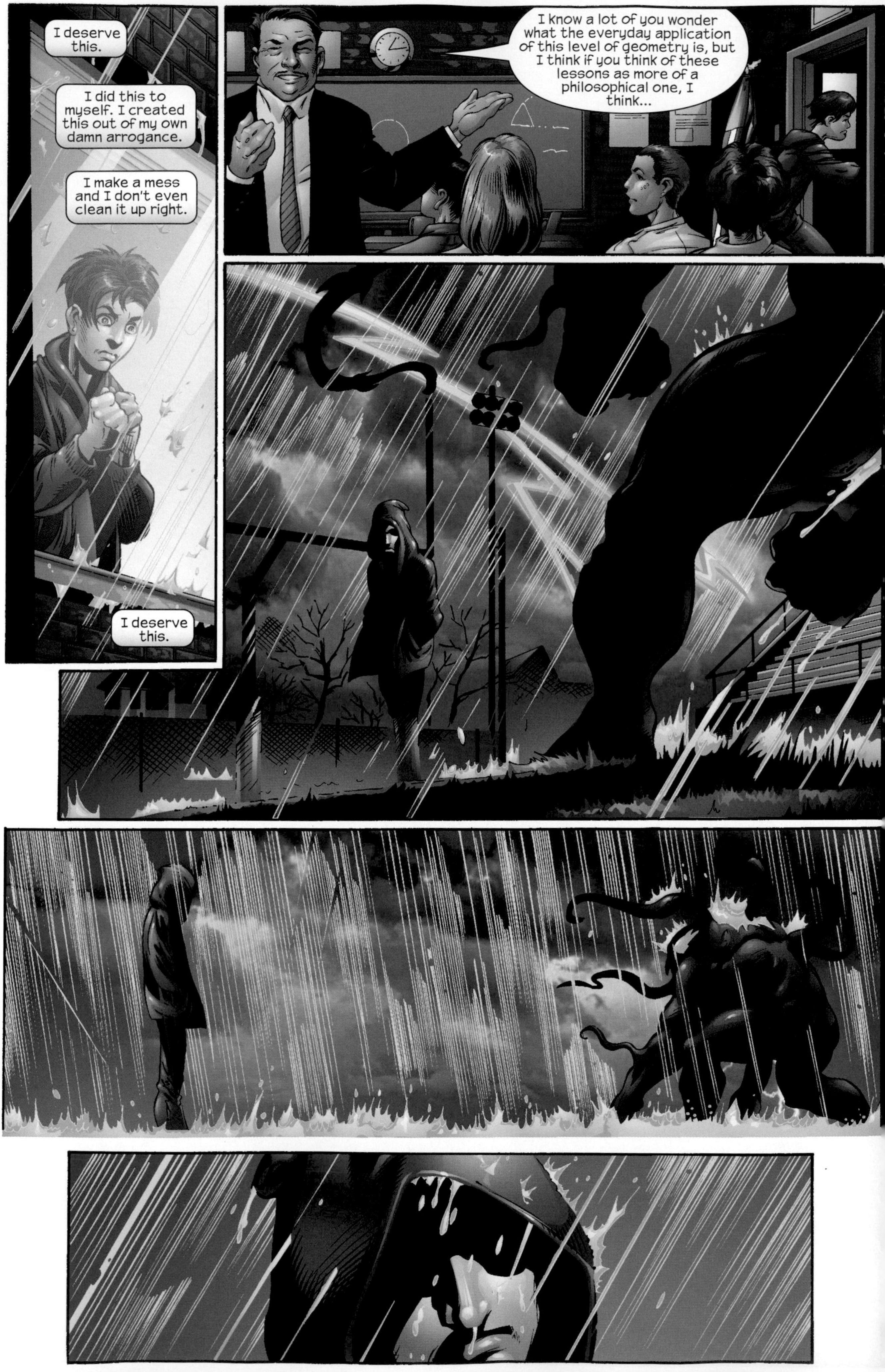
I deserve this.
I did this to myself. I created this out of my own damn arrogance.
I make a mess and I don't even clean it up right.
I deserve this.
I know a lot of you wonder what the everyday application of this level of geometry is, but I think if you think of these lessons as more of a philosophical one, I think...

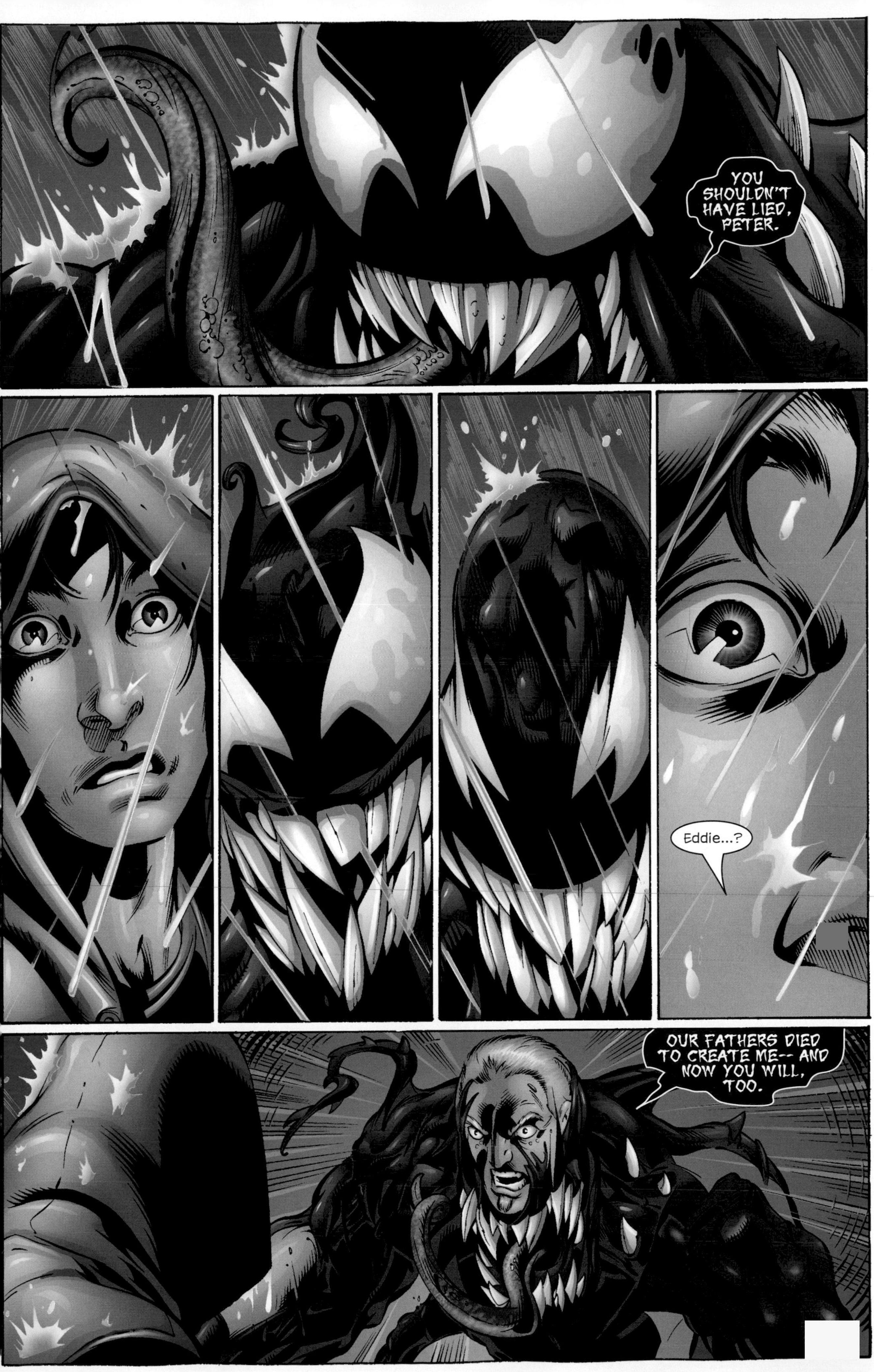
YOU SHOULDN'T HAVE LIED, PETER.
Eddie...?
OUR FATHERS DIED TO CREATE ME-- AND NOW YOU WILL, TOO.

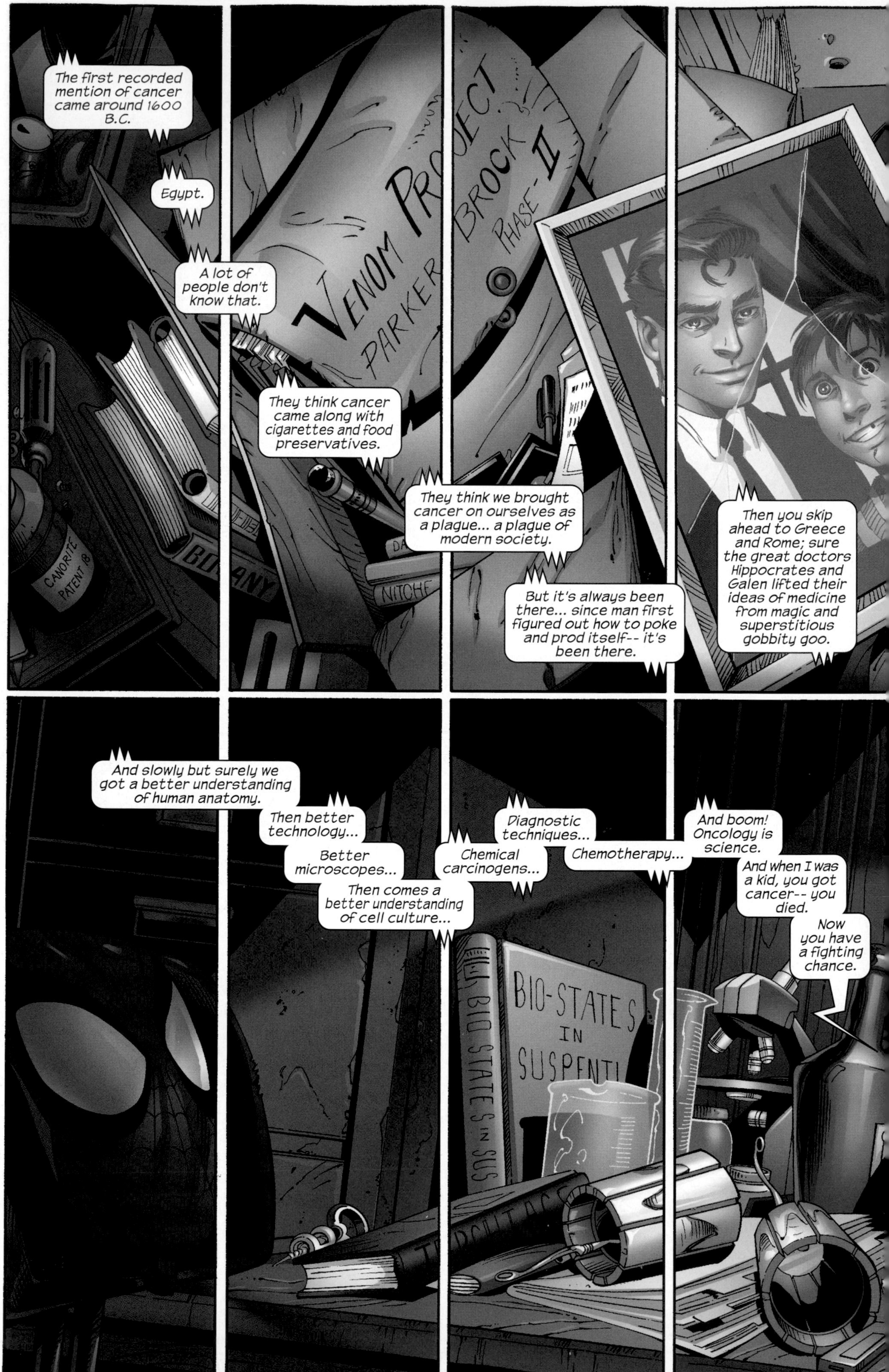
The first recorded mention of cancer came around 1600 B.C.
Egypt.
A lot of people don't know that.
VENOM PROJECT
PARKER
BROCK
PHASE-II
They think cancer came along with cigarettes and food preservatives.
CANORITE PATENT 8
BOTANY
NITCHE
They think we brought cancer on ourselves as a plague... a plague of modern society.
But it's always been there... since man first figured out how to poke and prod itself-- it's been there.
Then you skip ahead to Greece and Rome; sure the great doctors Hippocrates and Galen lifted their ideas of medicine from magic and superstitious gobbity goo.
And slowly but surely we got a better understanding of human anatomy.
Then better technology...
Better microscopes...
Then comes a better understanding of cell culture...
Chemical carcinogens...
Diagnostic techniques...
Chemotherapy...
And boom! Oncology is science.
And when I was a kid, you got cancer-- you died.
Now you have a fighting chance.
BIO-STATES IN SUSPENTI
BIO STATES IN SUS

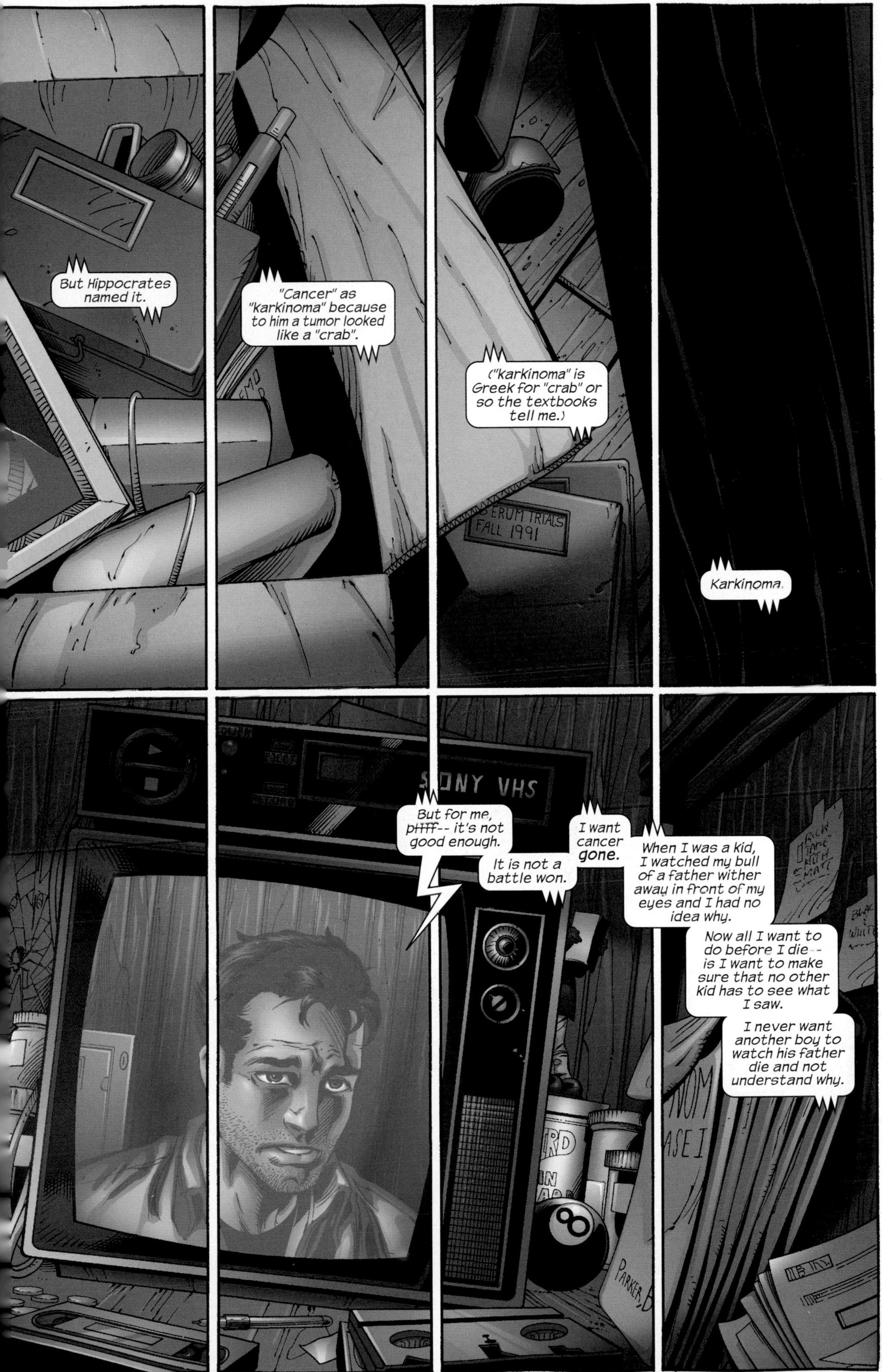

But Hippocrates named it.
"Cancer" as "karkinoma" because to him a tumor looked like a "crab".
("karkinoma" is Greek for "crab" or so the textbooks tell me.)
SERUM TRIALS FALL 1991
Karkinoma.
SONY VHS
But for me, phhf-- it's not good enough.
It is not a battle won.
I want cancer **gone.**
When I was a kid, I watched my bull of a father wither away in front of my eyes and I had no idea why.
Now all I want to do before I die-- is I want to make sure that no other kid has to see what I saw.
I never want another boy to watch his father die and not understand why.
PARKER, B

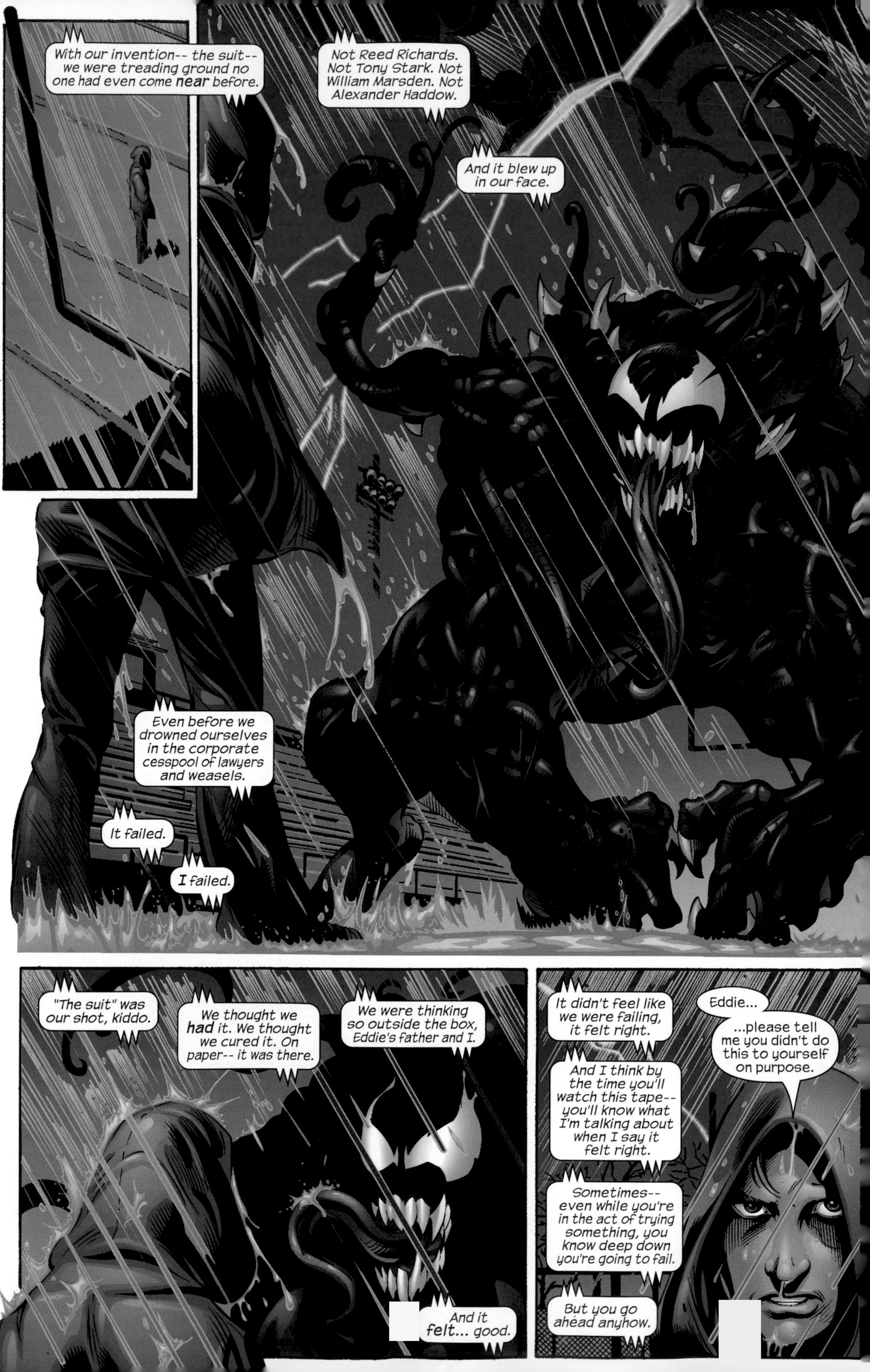
With our invention-- the suit-- we were treading ground no one had even come **near** before.
Not Reed Richards. Not Tony Stark. Not William Marsden. Not Alexander Haddow.
And it blew up in our face.
Even before we drowned ourselves in the corporate cesspool of lawyers and weasels.
It failed.
I failed.
"The suit" was our shot, kiddo.
We thought we **had** it. We thought we cured it. On paper-- it was there.
We were thinking so outside the box, Eddie's father and I.
And it **felt...** good.
It didn't feel like we were failing, it felt right.
And I think by the time you'll watch this tape-- you'll know what I'm talking about when I say it felt right.
Sometimes-- even while you're in the act of trying something, you know deep down you're going to fail.
But you go ahead anyhow.
Eddie...
...please tell me you didn't do this to yourself on purpose.

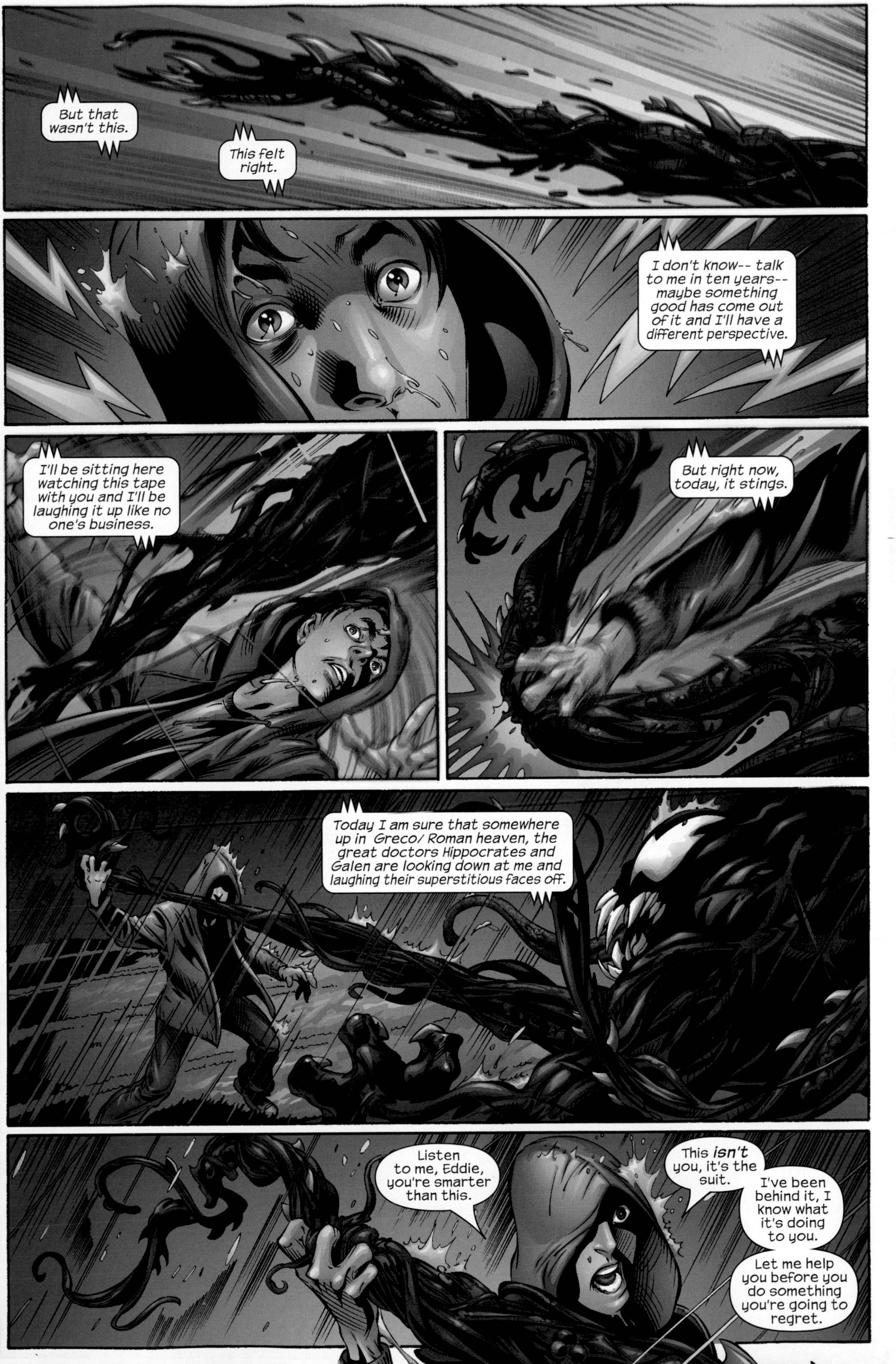
But that wasn't this.
This felt right.
I don't know-- talk to me in ten years-- maybe something good has come out of it and I'll have a different perspective.
I'll be sitting here watching this tape with you and I'll be laughing it up like no one's business.
But right now, today, it stings.
Today I am sure that somewhere up in Greco/ Roman heaven, the great doctors Hippocrates and Galen are looking down at me and laughing their superstitious faces off.
Listen to me, Eddie, you're smarter than this.
This *isn't* you, it's the suit.
I've been behind it, I know what it's doing to you.
Let me help you before you do something you're going to regret.

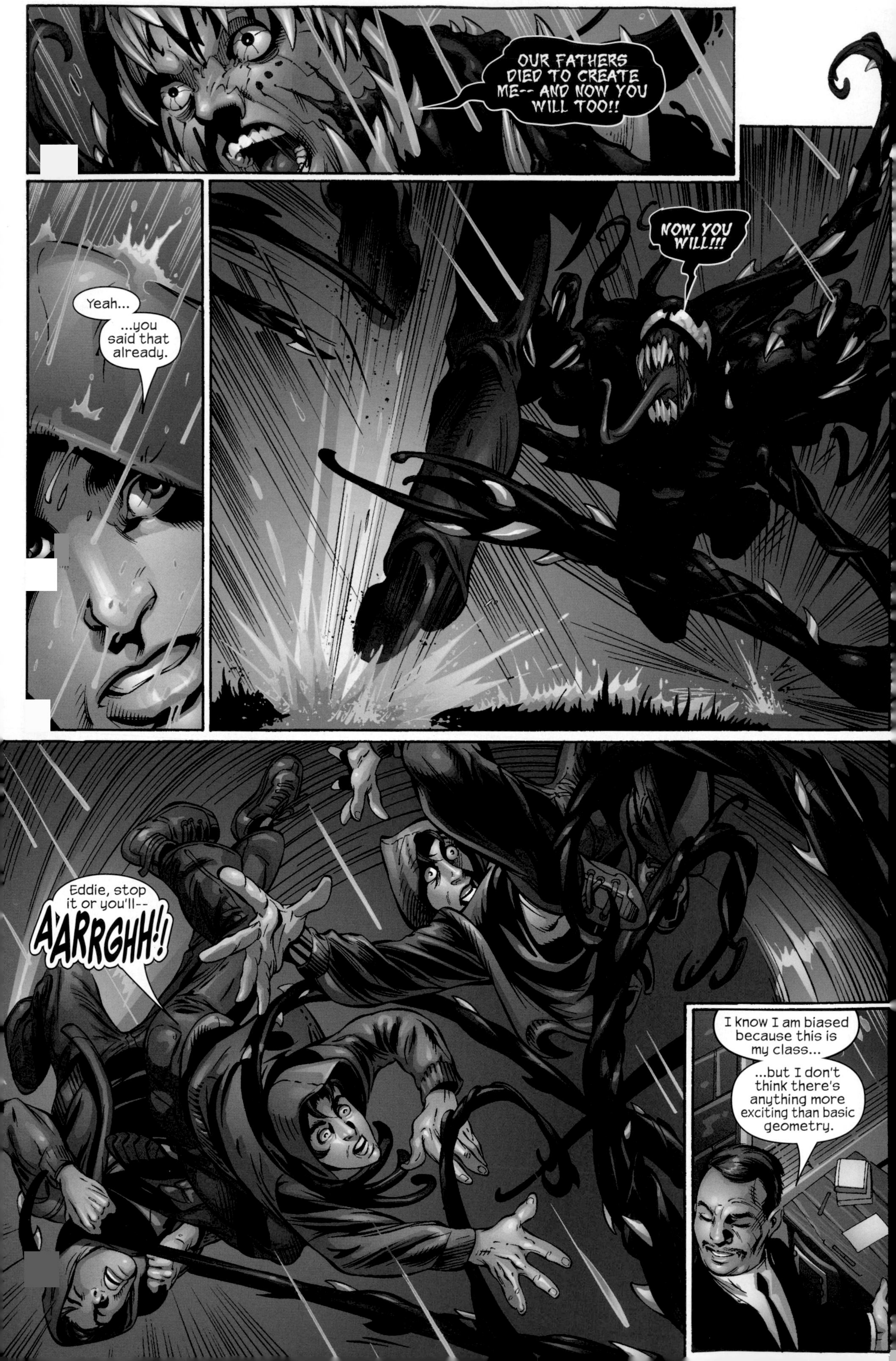
OUR FATHERS DIED TO CREATE ME-- AND NOW YOU WILL TOO!!
Yeah... ...you said that already.
NOW YOU WILL!!!
Eddie, stop it or you'll--
AARRGHH!!
I know I am biased because this is my class...
...but I don't think there's anything more exciting than basic geometry.

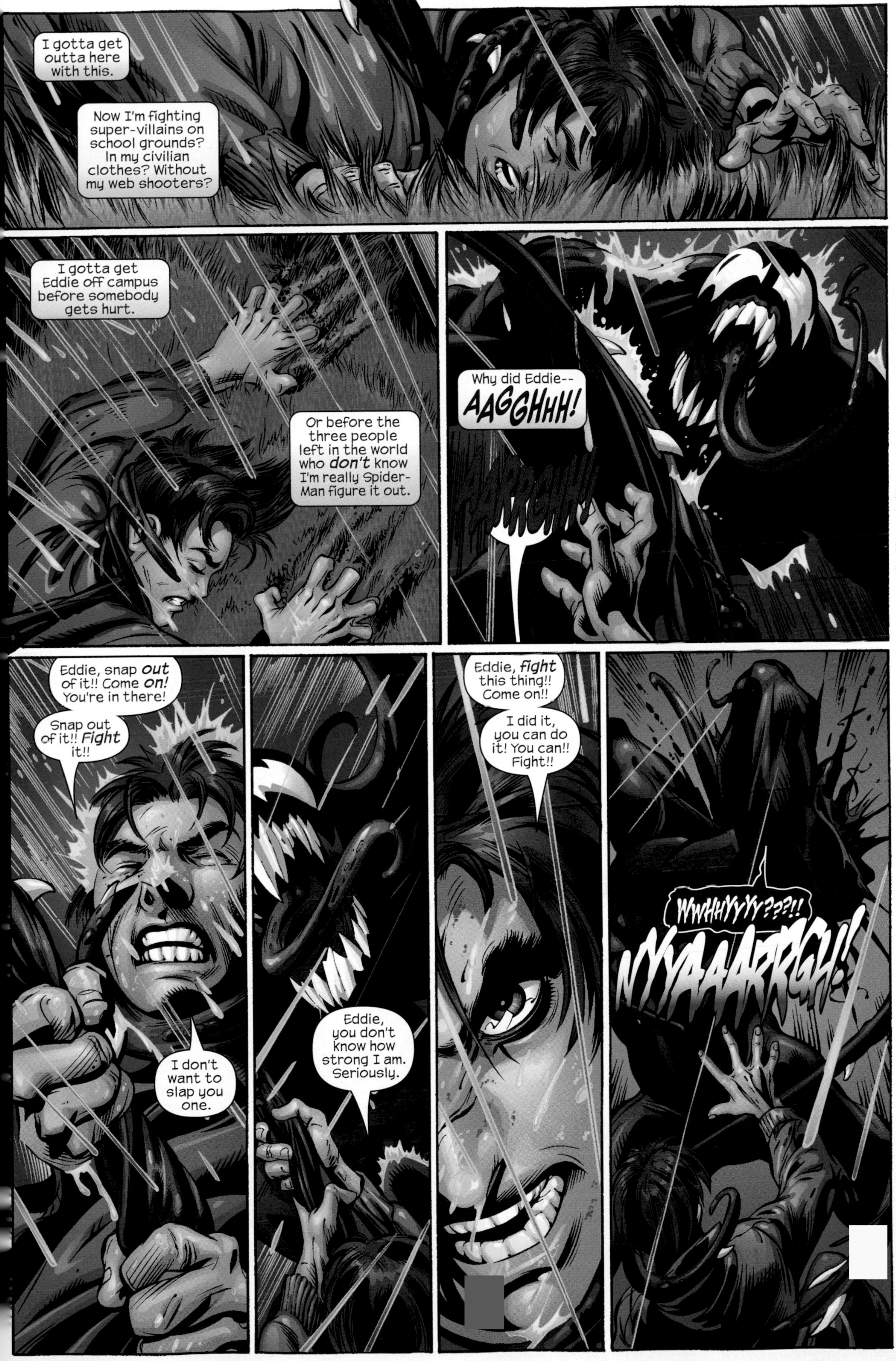

I gotta get outta here with this.
Now I'm fighting super-villains on school grounds? In my civilian clothes? Without my web shooters?
I gotta get Eddie off campus before somebody gets hurt.
Or before the three people left in the world who *don't* know I'm really Spider-Man figure it out.
Why did Eddie-- AAGGHHH!
Eddie, snap *out* of it!! Come *on!* You're in there!
Snap out of it!! *Fight* it!!
I don't want to slap you one.
Eddie, you don't know how strong I am. Seriously.
Eddie, *fight* this thing!! Come on!!
I did it, you can do it! You can!! Fight!!
WWHHYYYY???!!
NYYAAARRGH!!

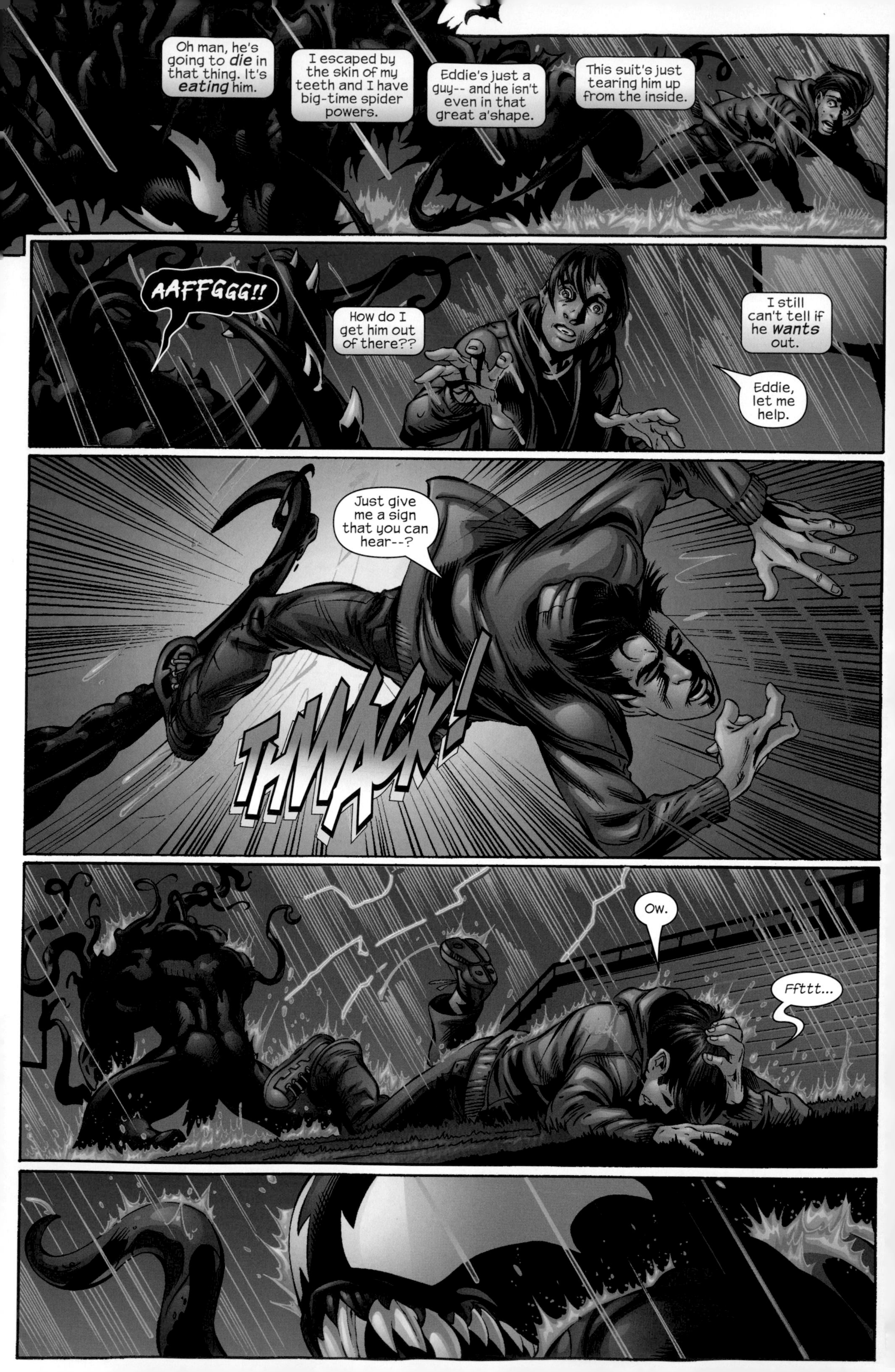

Oh man, he's going to *die* in that thing. It's *eating* him.
I escaped by the skin of my teeth and I have big-time spider powers.
Eddie's just a guy-- and he isn't even in that great a'shape.
This suit's just tearing him up from the inside.
AAFFGGG!!
How do I get him out of there??
I still can't tell if he *wants* out.
Eddie, let me help.
Just give me a sign that you can hear--?
THWACK!
Ow.
Ffttt...

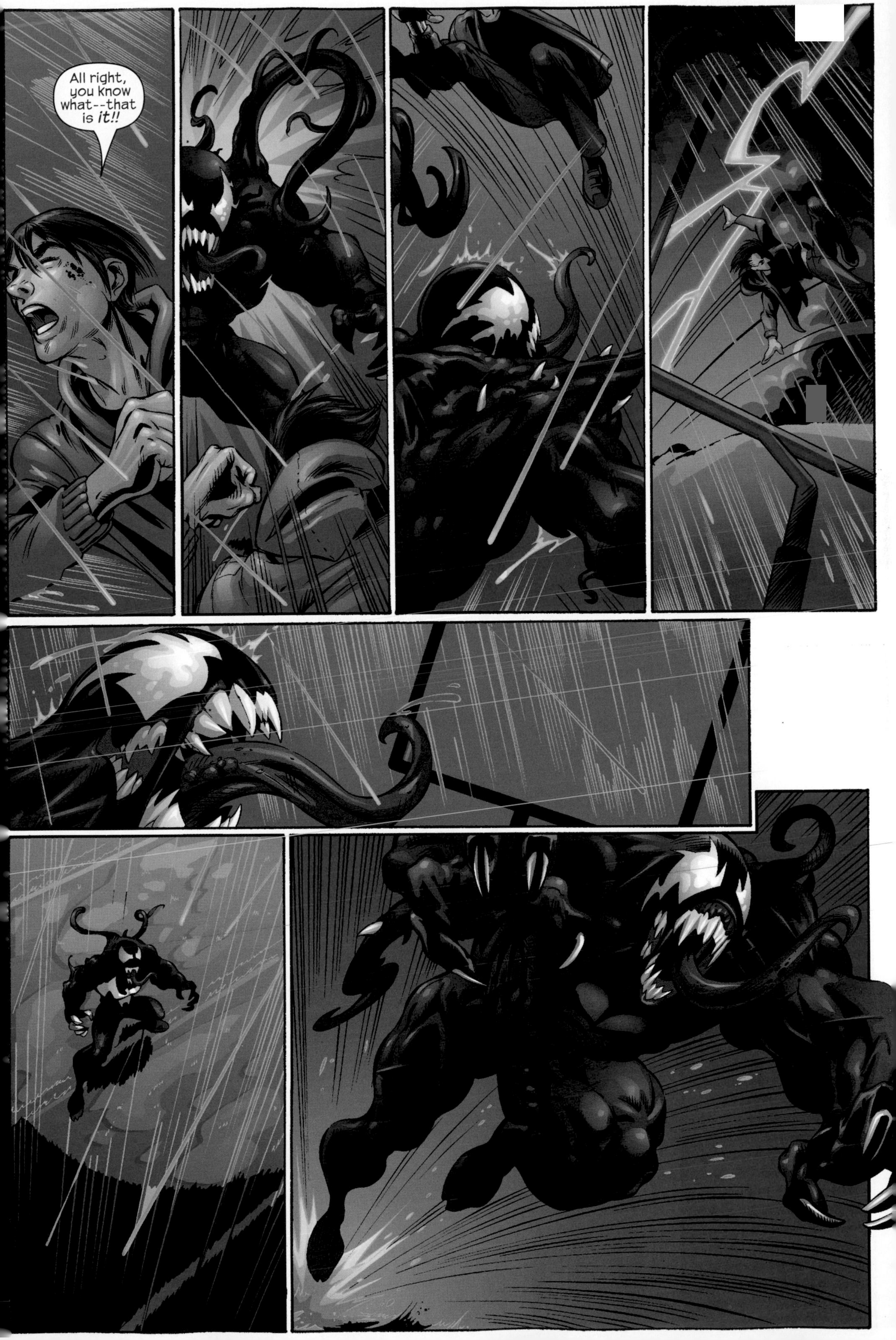
All right, you know what--that is *it!!*

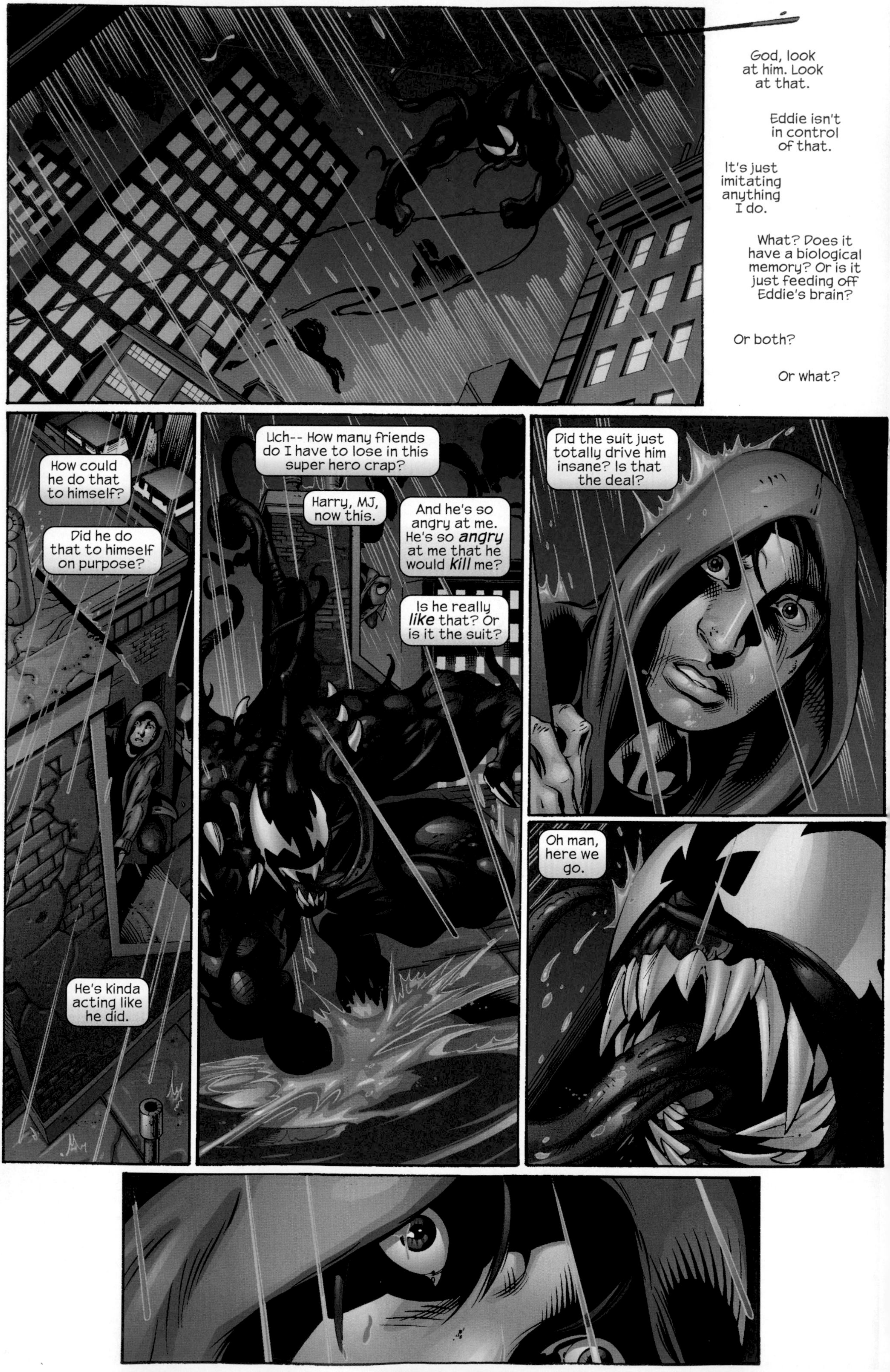
God, look at him. Look at that.
Eddie isn't in control of that.
It's just imitating anything I do.
What? Does it have a biological memory? Or is it just feeding off Eddie's brain?
Or both?
Or what?
How could he do that to himself?
Did he do that to himself on purpose?
He's kinda acting like he did.
Uch-- How many friends do I have to lose in this super hero crap?
Harry, MJ, now this.
And he's so angry at me. He's so angry at me that he would kill me?
Is he really like that? Or is it the suit?
Did the suit just totally drive him insane? Is that the deal?
Oh man, here we go.

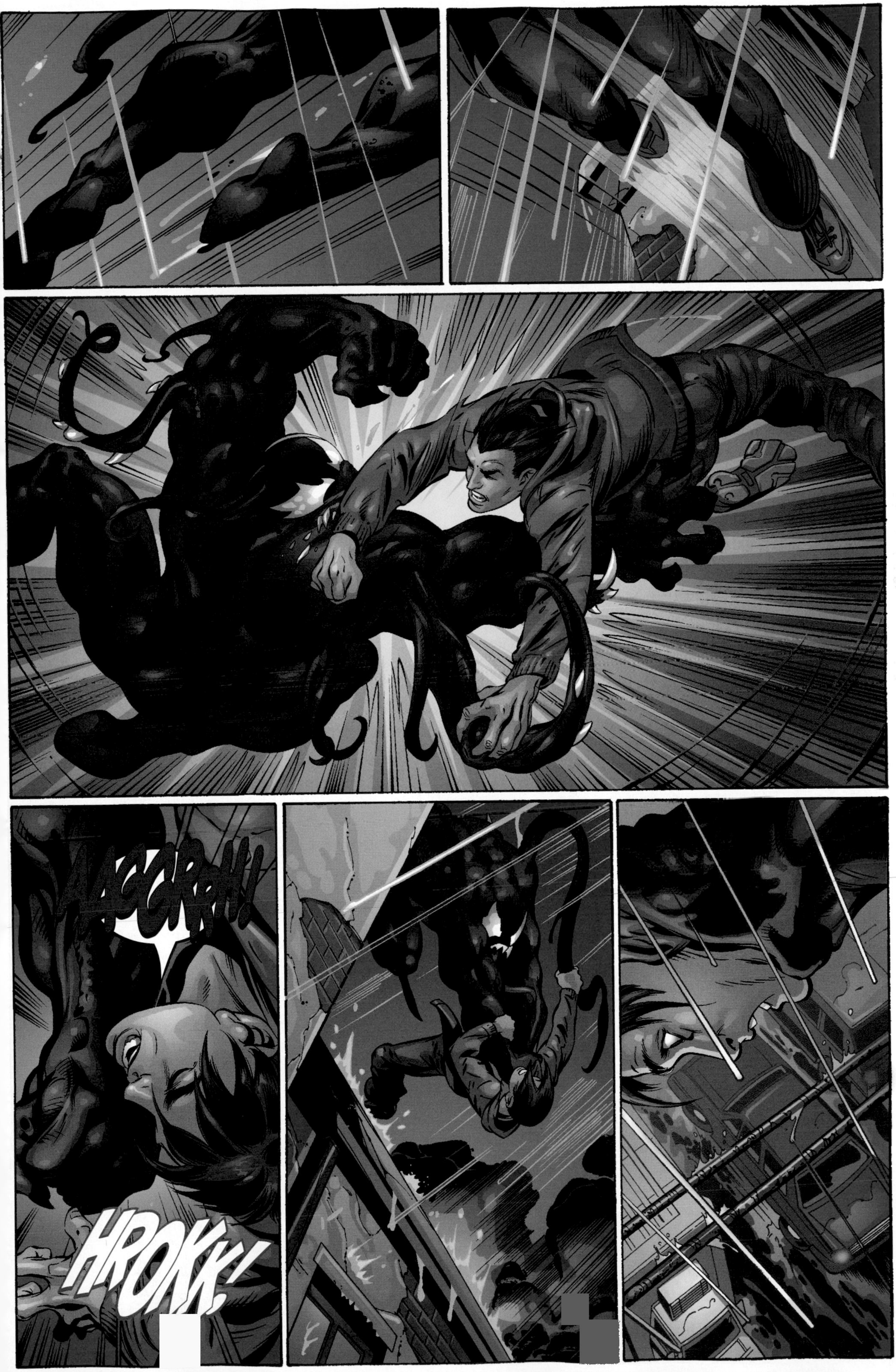
AAGGRAH!
HROKK!

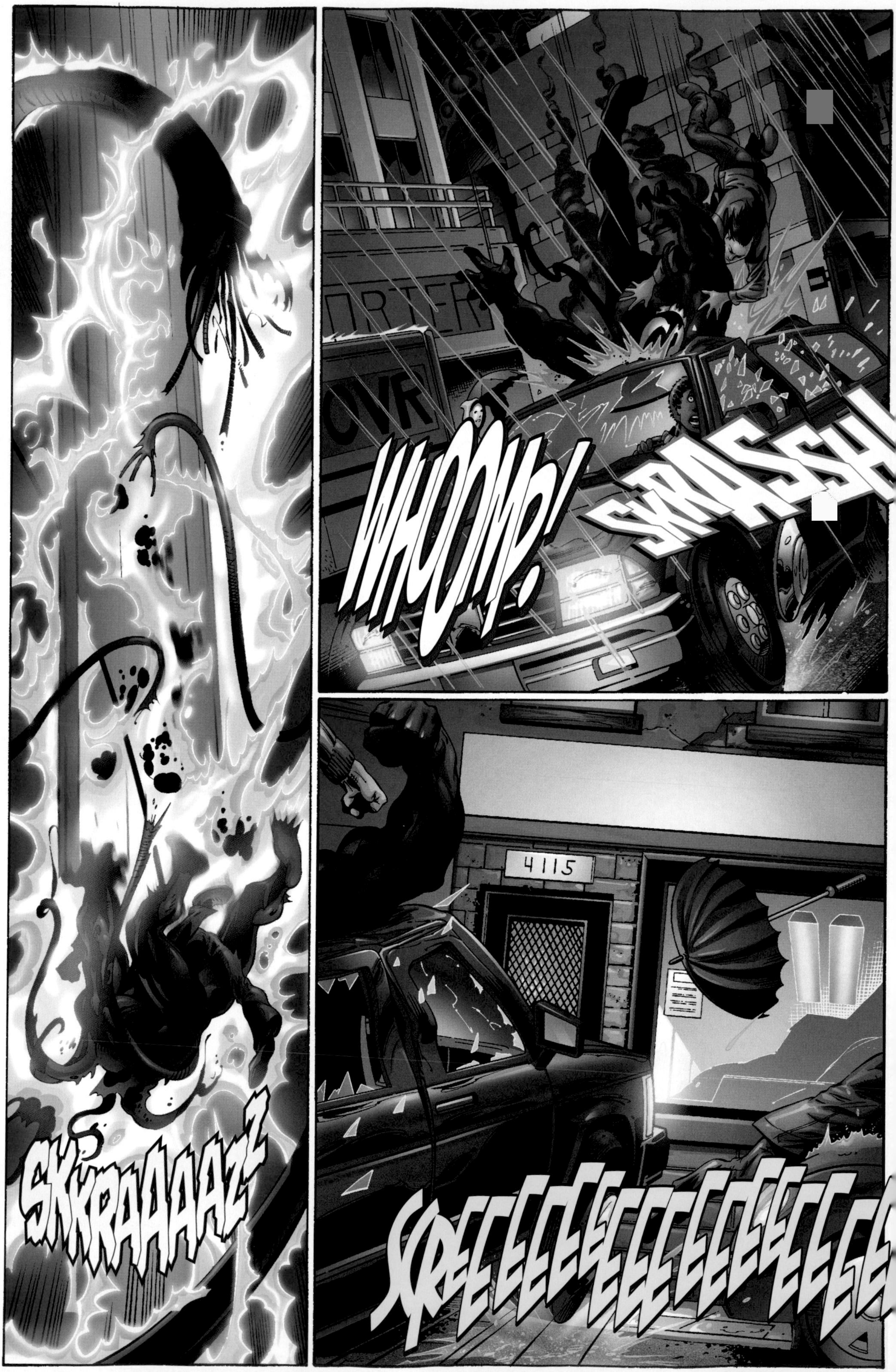
SKRAAAAZ
WHOOMP!
SKRASSH
SKREEEEEEEEEEEEEEEE

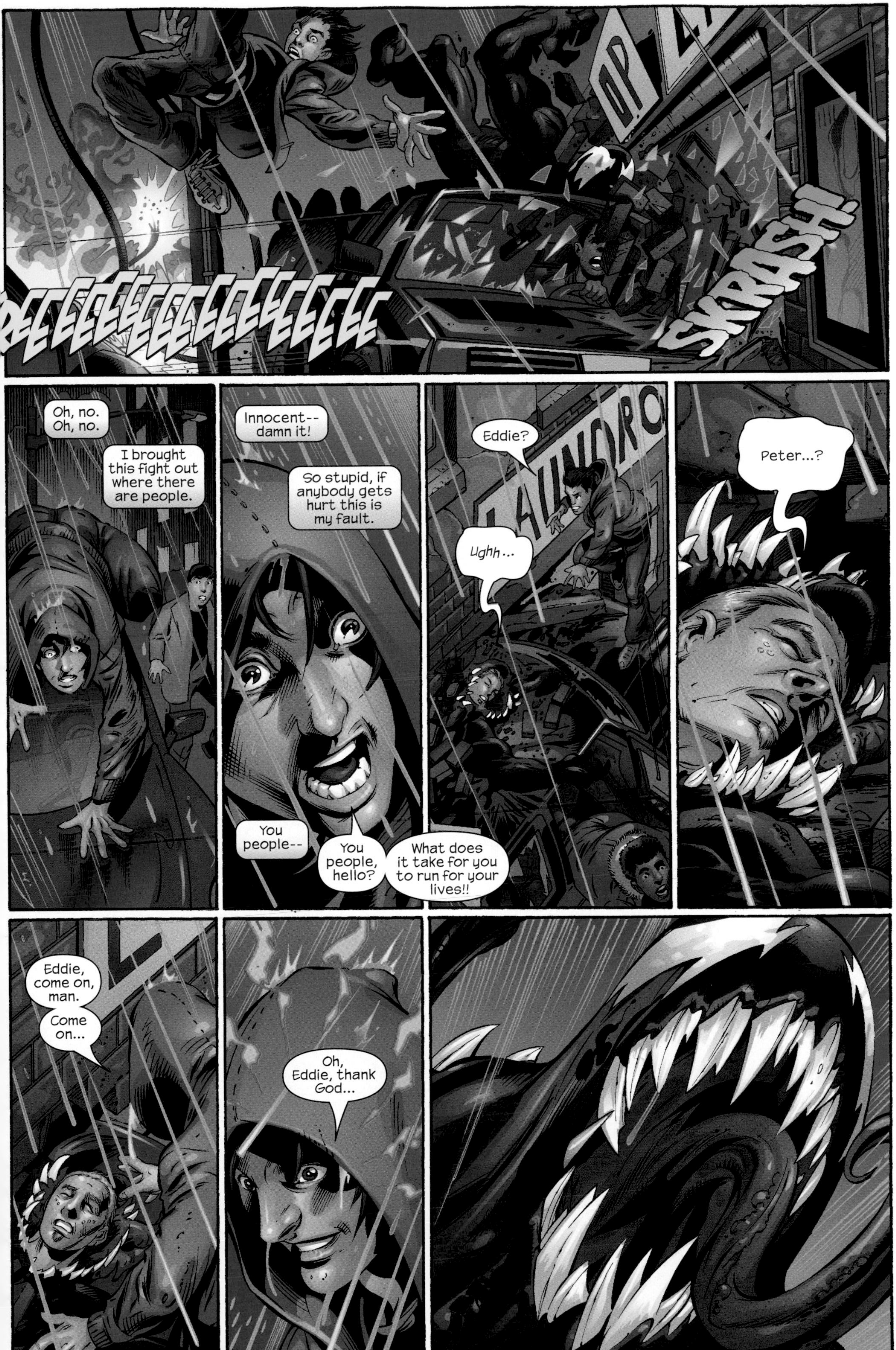

EEEEEEEEEEEEEEEEEEEEEE
SHRASH
Oh, no. Oh, no.
I brought this fight out where there are people.
Innocent--damn it!
So stupid, if anybody gets hurt this is my fault.
You people--
You people, hello?
What does it take for you to run for your lives!!
Eddie?
Ughh...
Peter...?
Eddie, come on, man.
Come on...
Oh, Eddie, thank God...

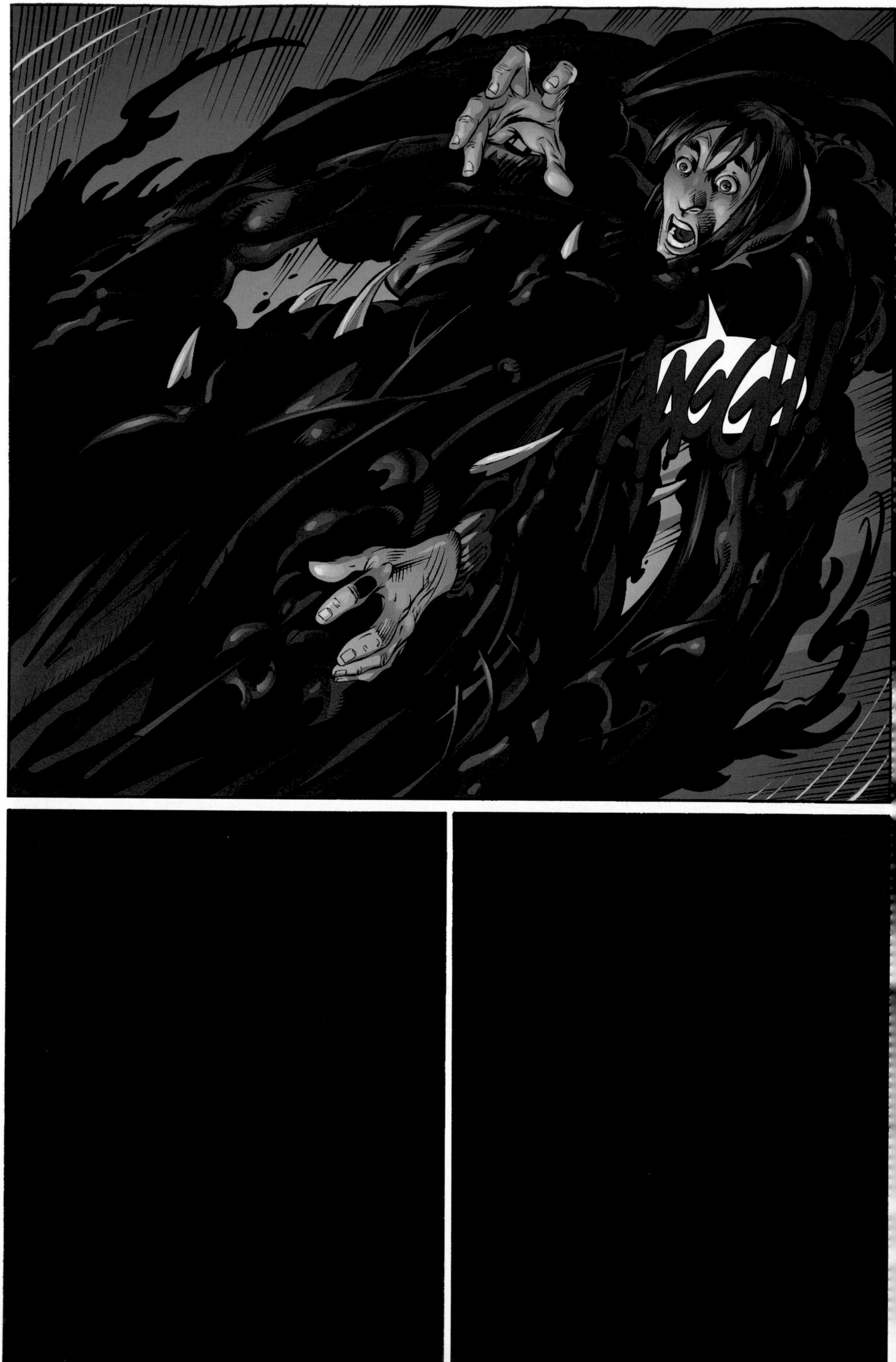
AAGGH!!

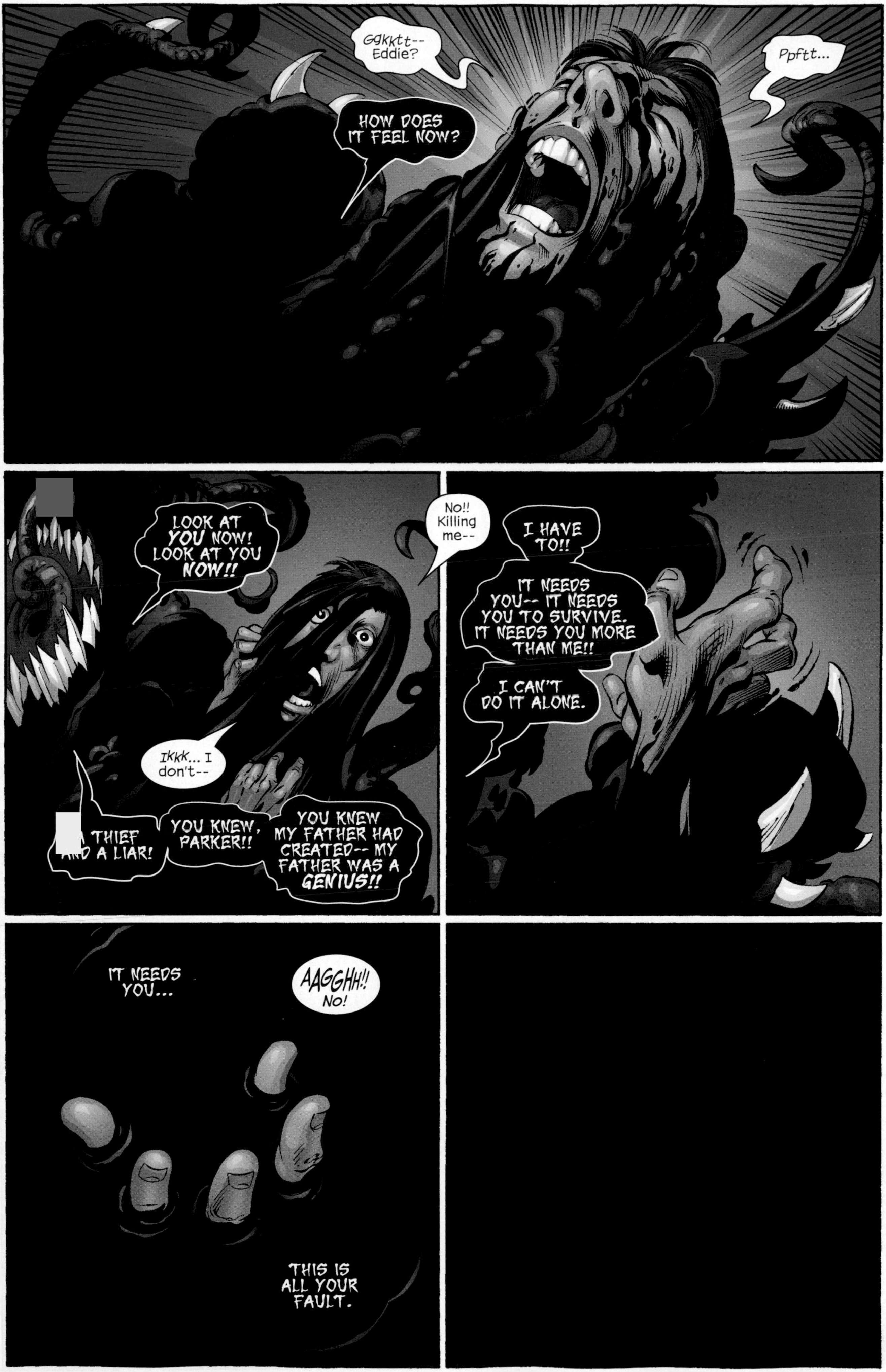
Ggkktt-- Eddie?
HOW DOES IT FEEL NOW?
Ppftt...
LOOK AT YOU NOW! LOOK AT YOU NOW!!
Ikkk... I don't--
THIEF AND A LIAR!
YOU KNEW, PARKER!!
YOU KNEW MY FATHER HAD CREATED-- MY FATHER WAS A GENIUS!!
No!! Killing me--
I HAVE TO!!
IT NEEDS YOU-- IT NEEDS YOU TO SURVIVE. IT NEEDS YOU MORE THAN ME!!
I CAN'T DO IT ALONE.
IT NEEDS YOU...
AAGGHH!! No!
THIS IS ALL YOUR FAULT.

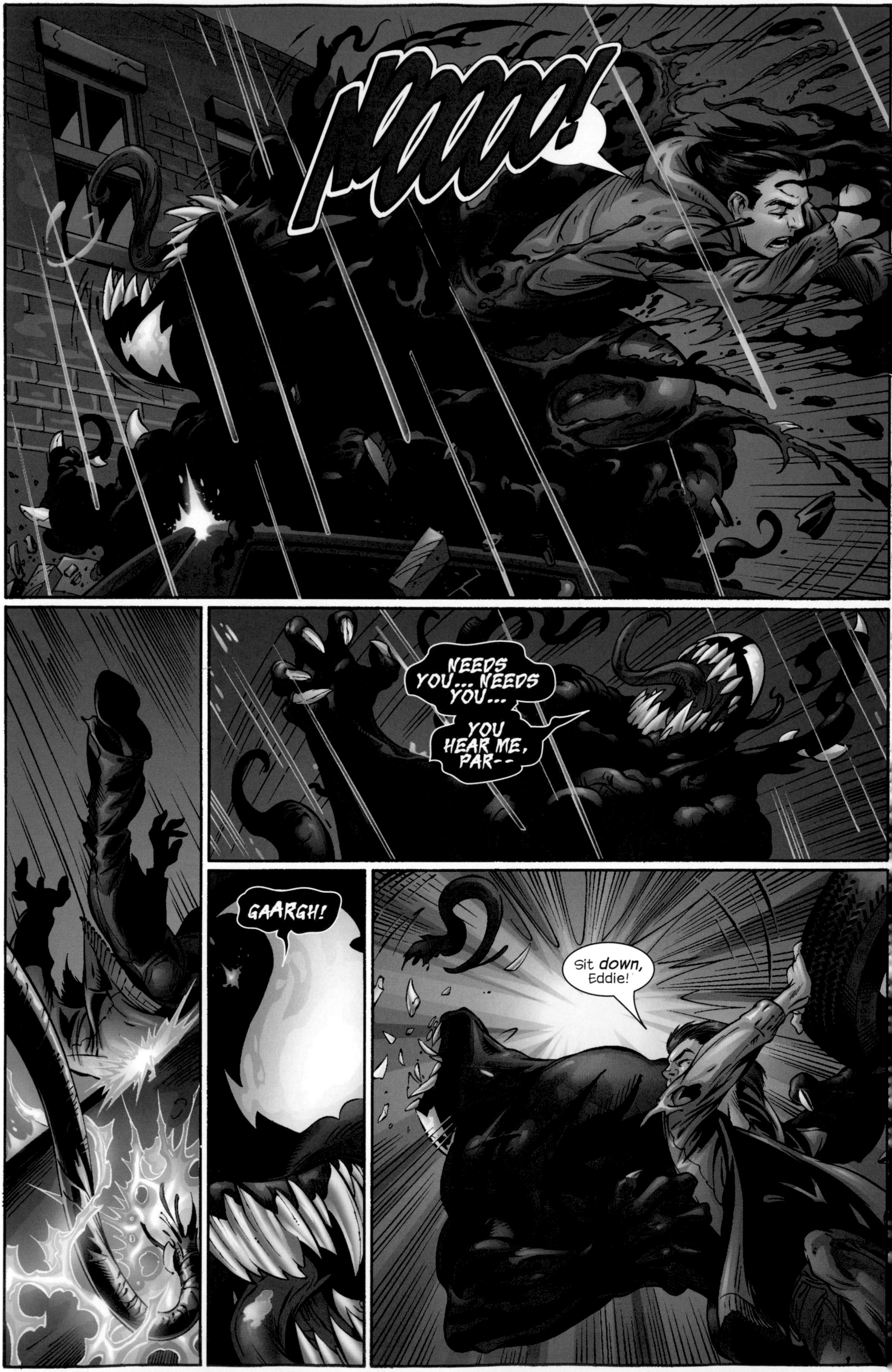
NOOOO!
NEEDS YOU... NEEDS YOU...
YOU HEAR ME, PAR--
GAARGH!
Sit down, Eddie!

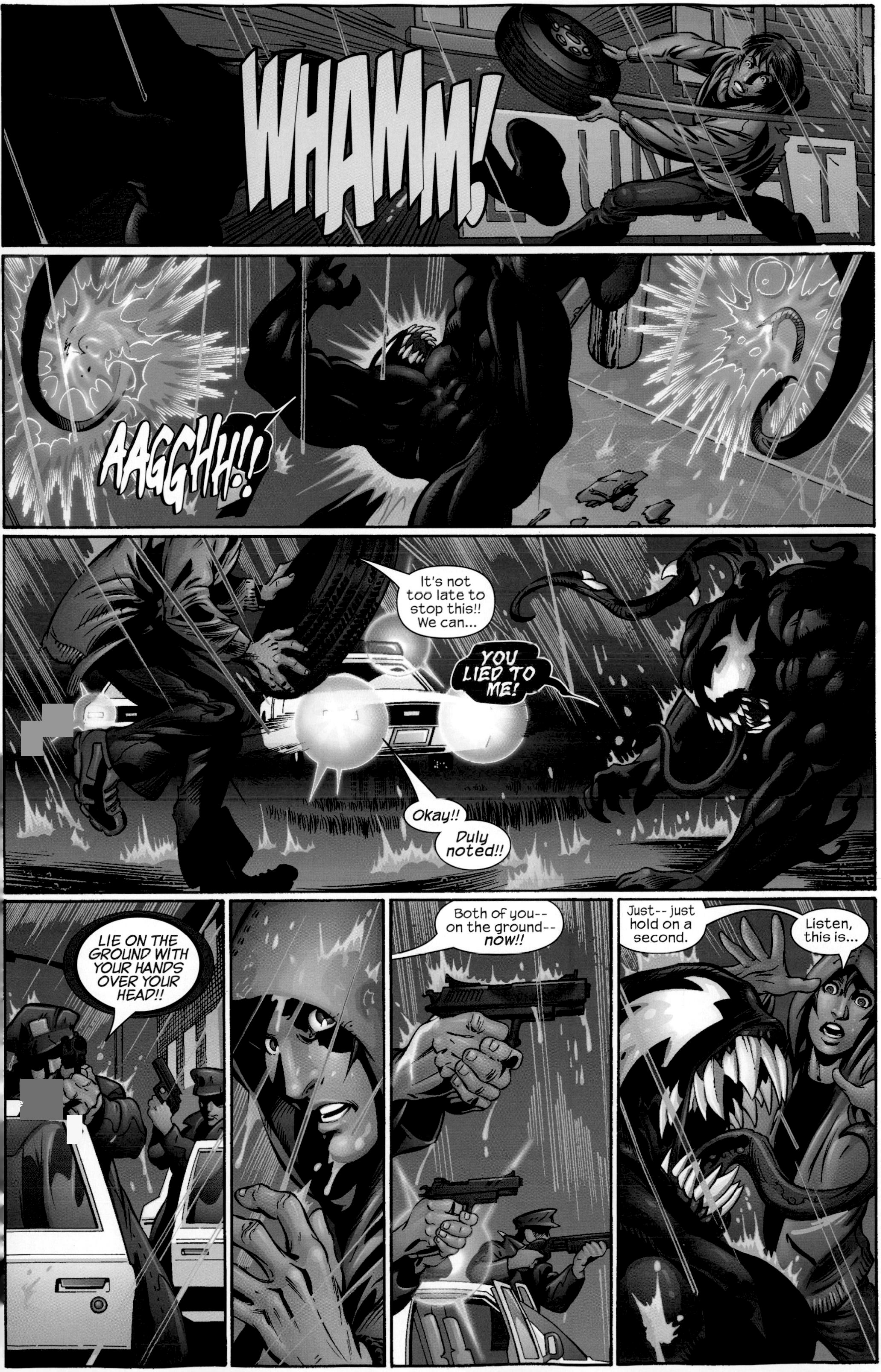
WHAMM!
AAGGHH!!
It's not too late to stop this!! We can...
YOU LIED TO ME!
Okay!!
Duly noted!!
LIE ON THE GROUND WITH YOUR HANDS OVER YOUR HEAD!!
Both of you-- on the ground-- now!!
Just-- just hold on a second.
Listen, this is...

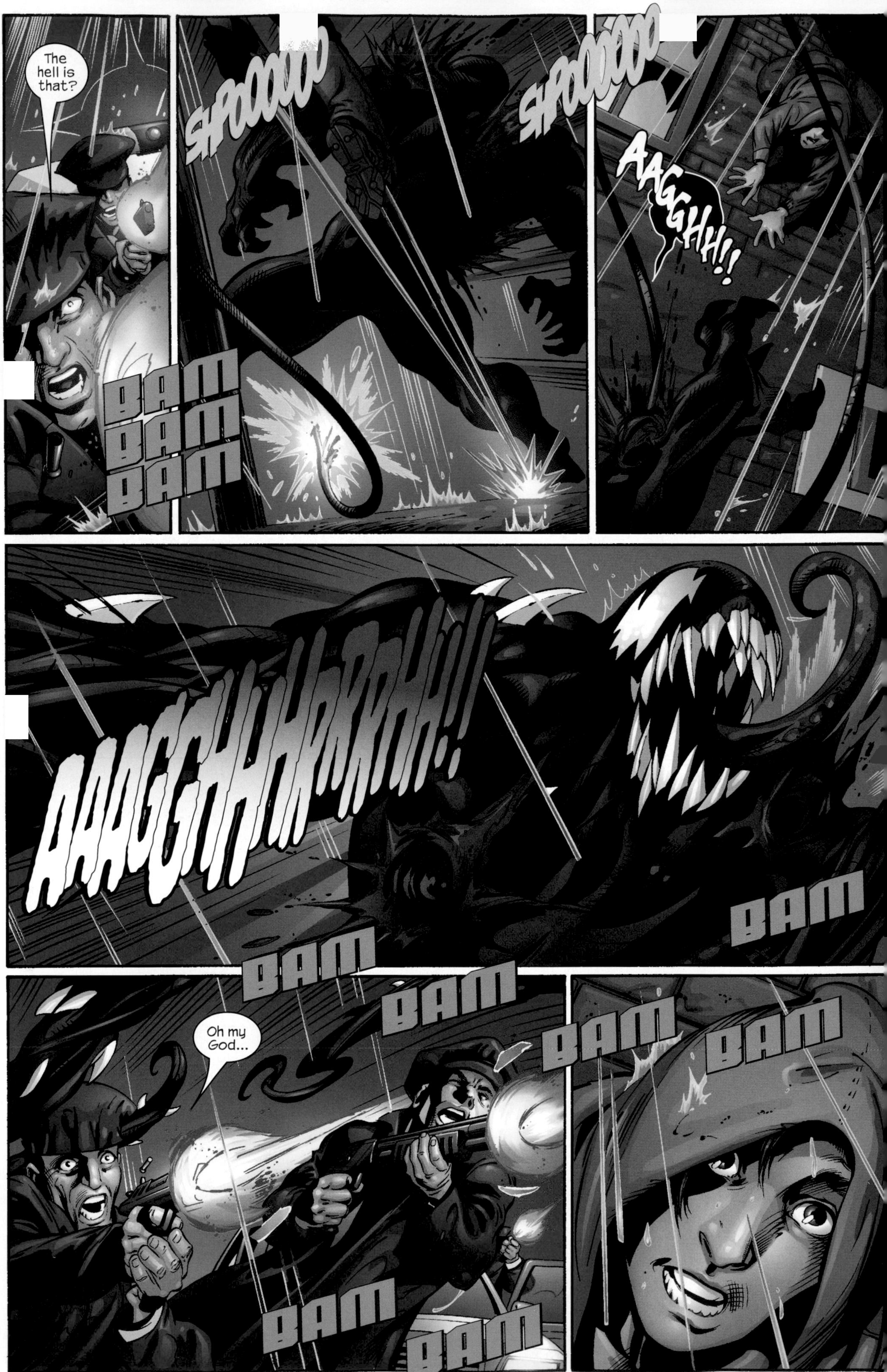

The hell is that?
BAM
BAM
BAM
SHPOOOOOO
SHPOOOOOO
AAGGHH!!
AAAGHHHRRRHH!!
BAM
BAM
BAM
Oh my God...
BAM
BAM
BAM
BAM

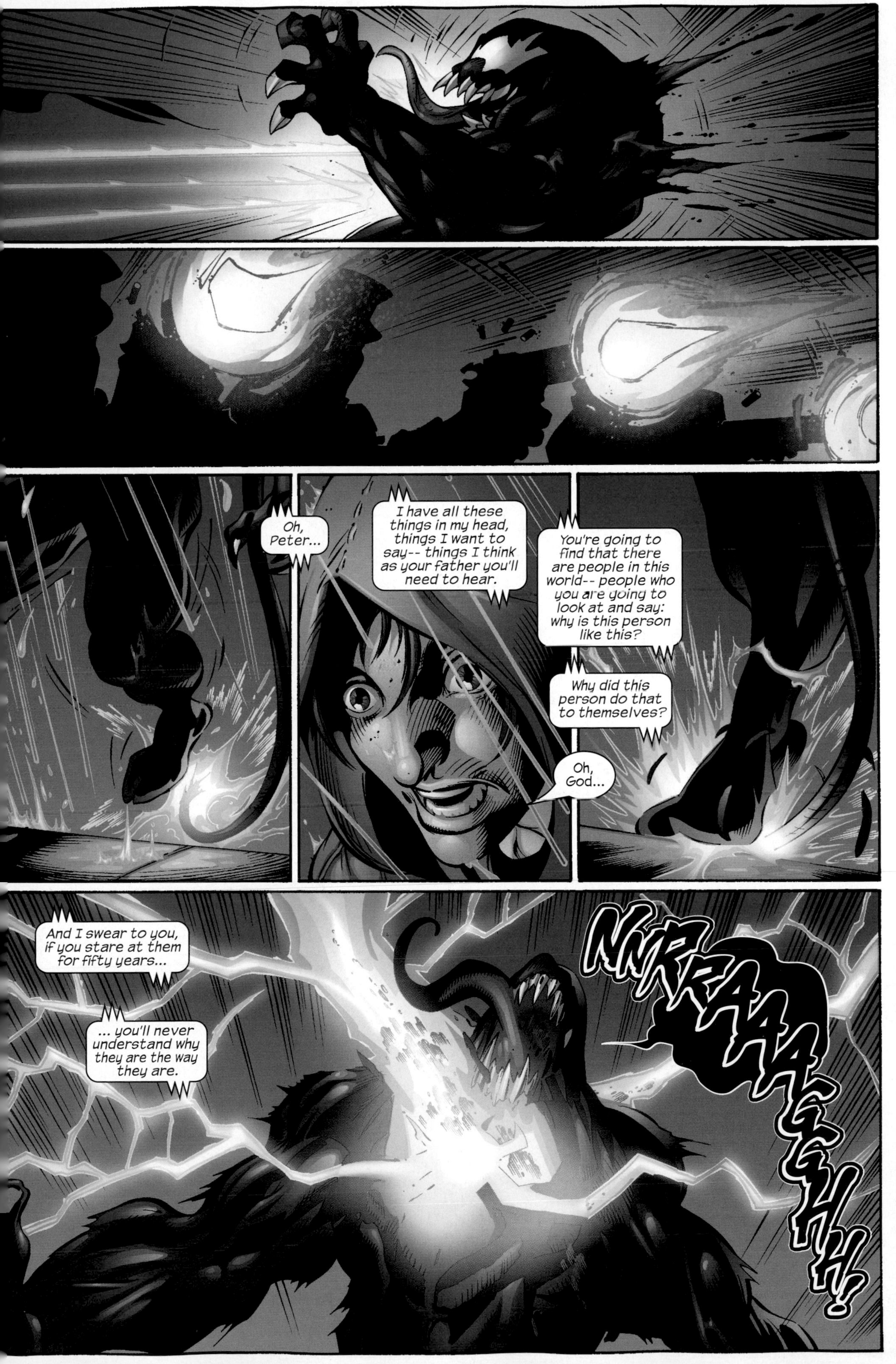
Oh, Peter...
I have all these things in my head, things I want to say-- things I think as your father you'll need to hear.
You're going to find that there are people in this world-- people who you are going to look at and say: why is this person like this?
Why did this person do that to themselves?
Oh, God...
And I swear to you, if you stare at them for fifty years...
... you'll never understand why they are the way they are.
NNRRAAAAGGHHH!

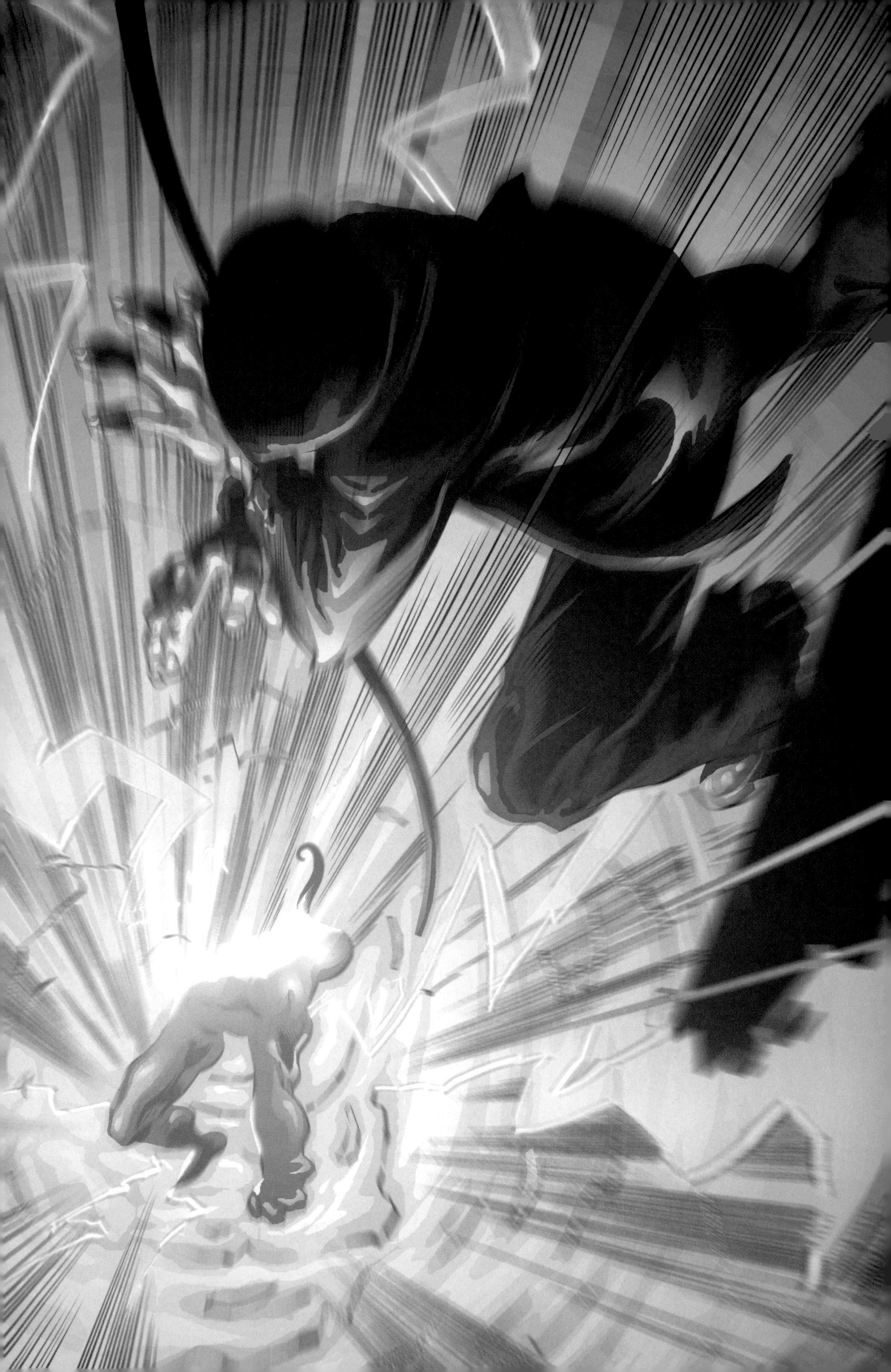

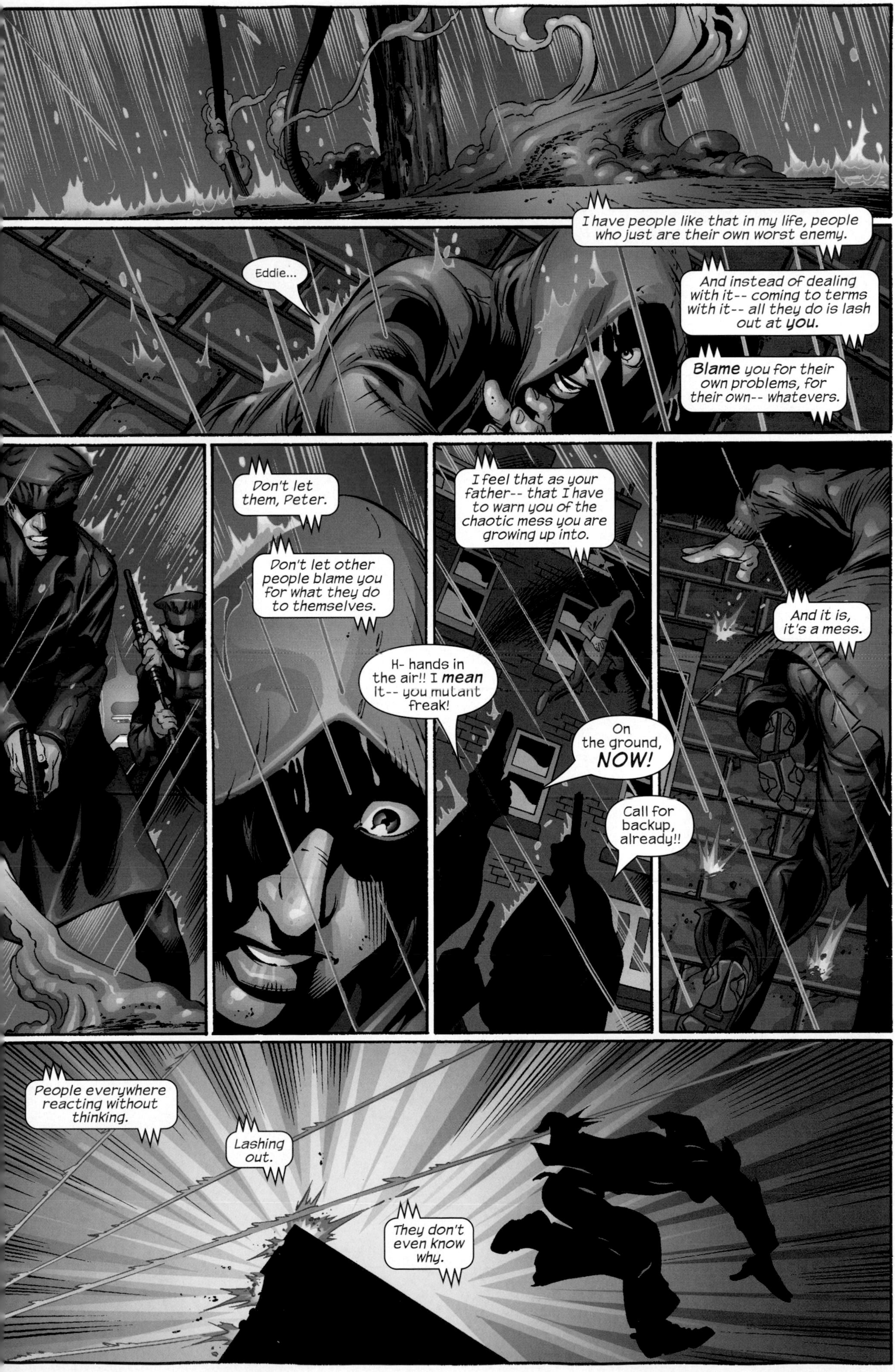

I have people like that in my life, people who just are their own worst enemy.
Eddie...
And instead of dealing with it-- coming to terms with it-- all they do is lash out at **you.**
Blame you for their own problems, for their own-- whatevers.
Don't let them, Peter.
Don't let other people blame you for what they do to themselves.
I feel that as your father-- that I have to warn you of the chaotic mess you are growing up into.
H- hands in the air!! I **mean** it-- you mutant freak!
On the ground, **NOW!**
Call for backup, already!!
And it is, it's a mess.
People everywhere reacting without thinking.
Lashing out.
They don't even know why.

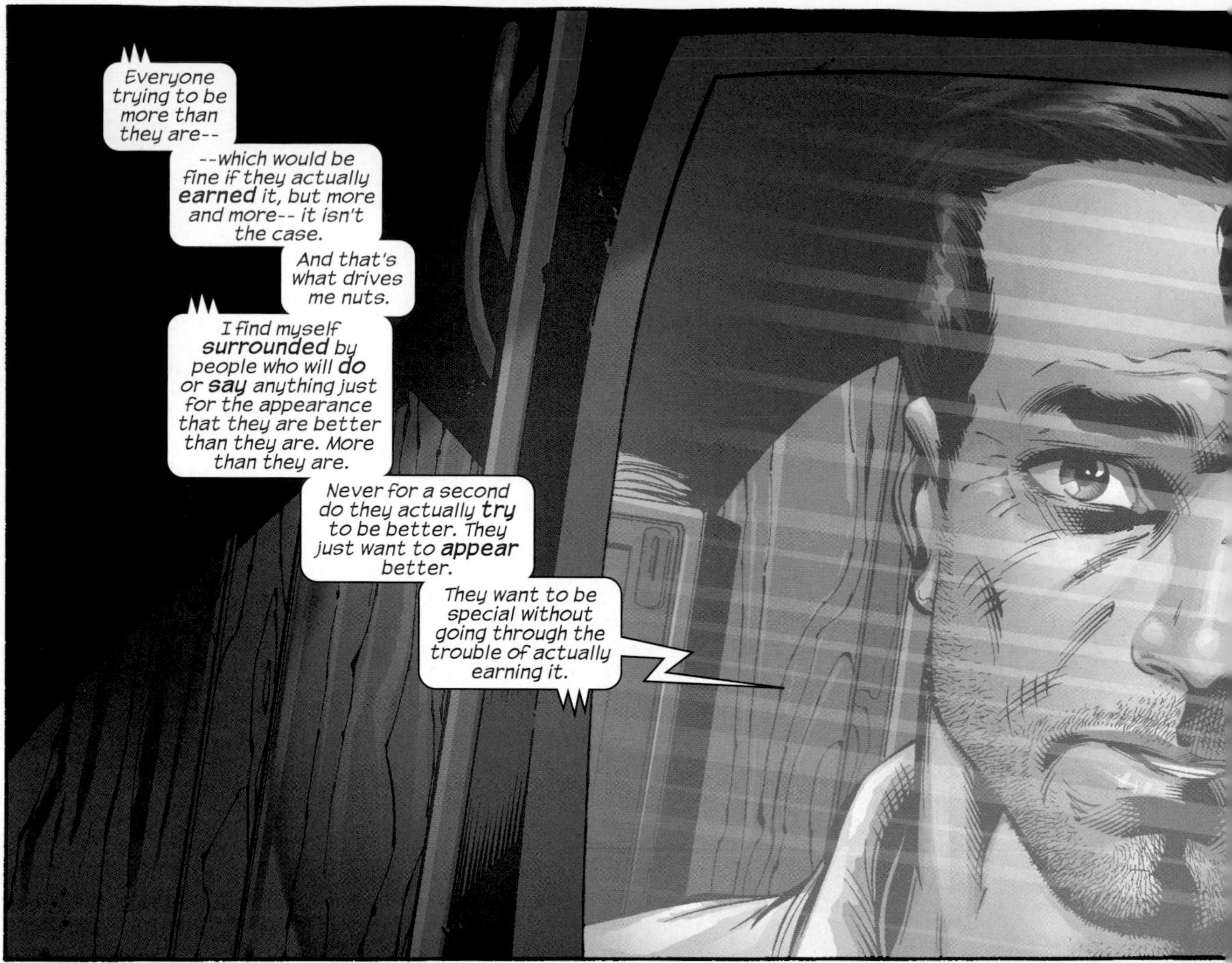
Everyone trying to be more than they are--
--which would be fine if they actually earned it, but more and more-- it isn't the case.
And that's what drives me nuts.
I find myself surrounded by people who will do or say anything just for the appearance that they are better than they are. More than they are.
Never for a second do they actually try to be better. They just want to appear better.
They want to be special without going through the trouble of actually earning it.
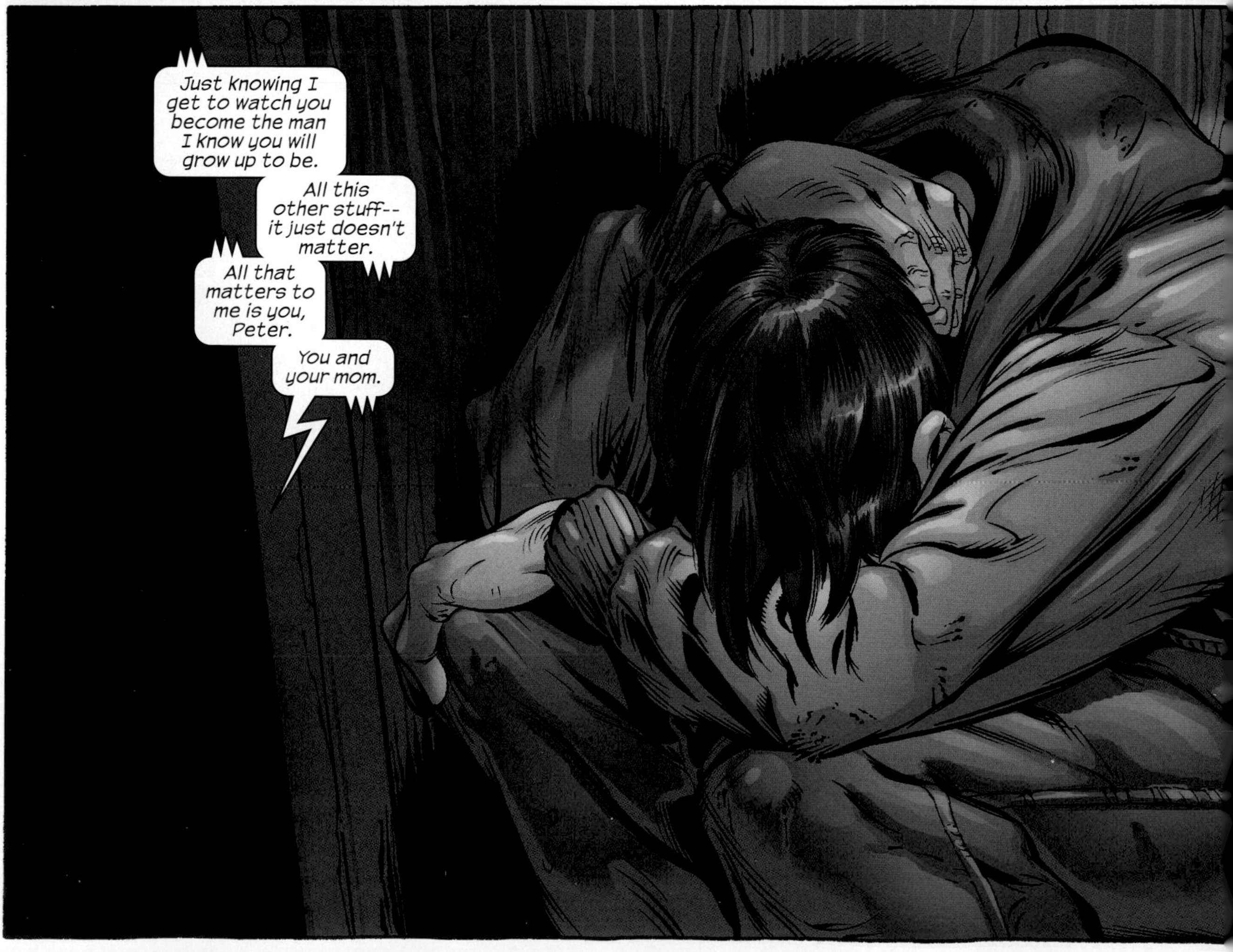
Just knowing I get to watch you become the man I know you will grow up to be.
All this other stuff-- it just doesn't matter.
All that matters to me is you, Peter.
You and your mom.

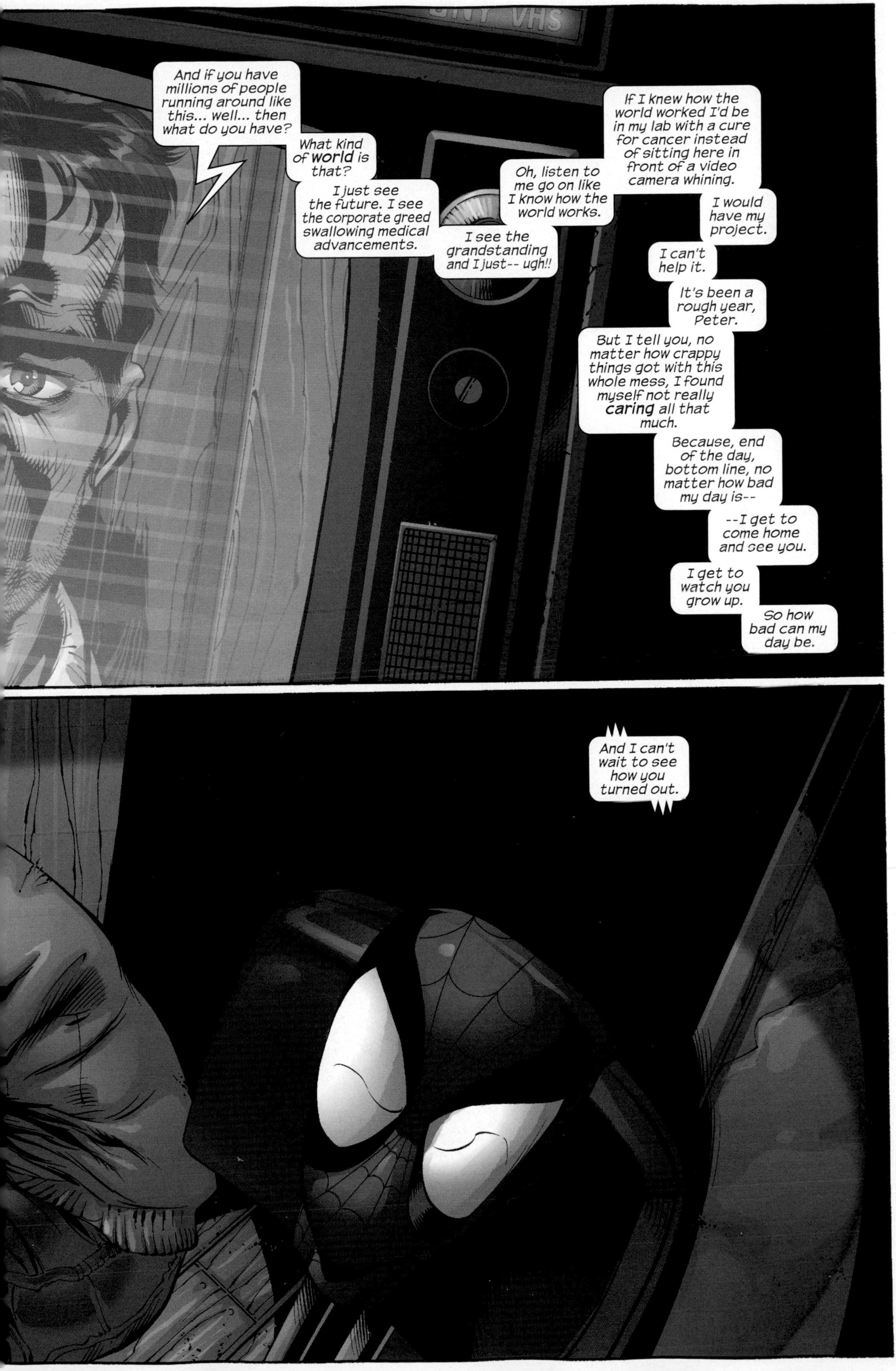

SONY VHS
And if you have millions of people running around like this... well... then what do you have?
What kind of world is that?
I just see the future. I see the corporate greed swallowing medical advancements.
I see the grandstanding and I just-- ugh!!
Oh, listen to me go on like I know how the world works.
If I knew how the world worked I'd be in my lab with a cure for cancer instead of sitting here in front of a video camera whining.
I would have my project.
I can't help it.
It's been a rough year, Peter.
But I tell you, no matter how crappy things got with this whole mess, I found myself not really caring all that much.
Because, end of the day, bottom line, no matter how bad my day is--
--I get to come home and see you.
I get to watch you grow up.
So how bad can my day be.
And I can't wait to see how you turned out.

General Fury, can I get you more wine?

No. This is fine.

Please tell the kitchen that the General Tso's is fantastic.

GLEEK

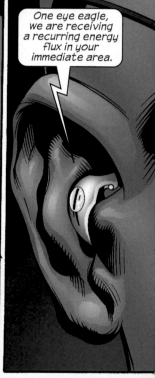

One eye eagle, we are receiving a recurring energy flux in your immediate area.

I have it.

Here comes the matching intelligence.

Thank you.

Huh.

Request command sequence.

No, I got it.

Sir?

I'll take care of it myself.

But sir, procedure.

Soldier?

Yes, sir. Sorry, sir.

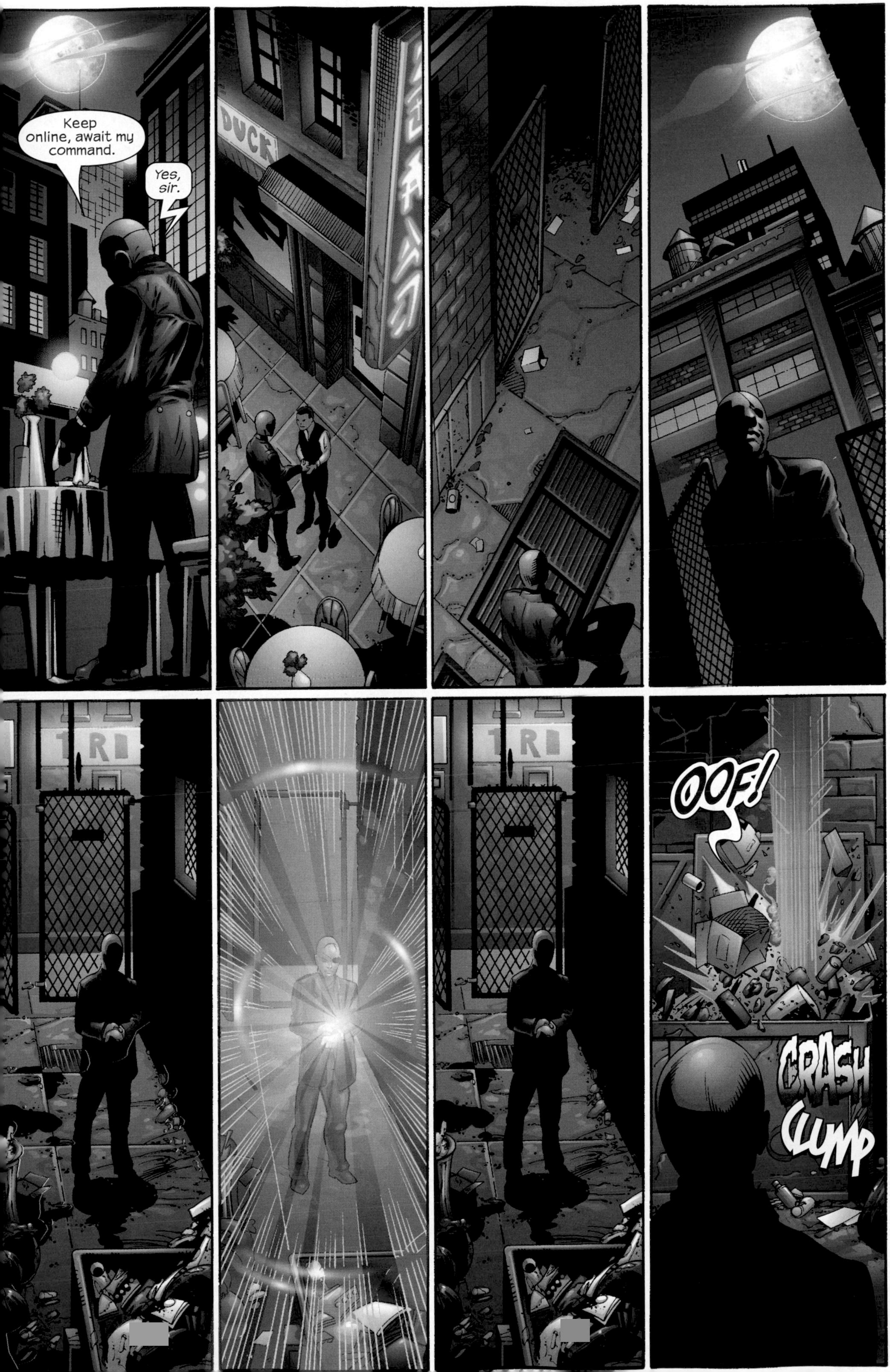
Keep online, await my command.
Yes, sir.
DUCK
OOF!
CRASH
CLUMP

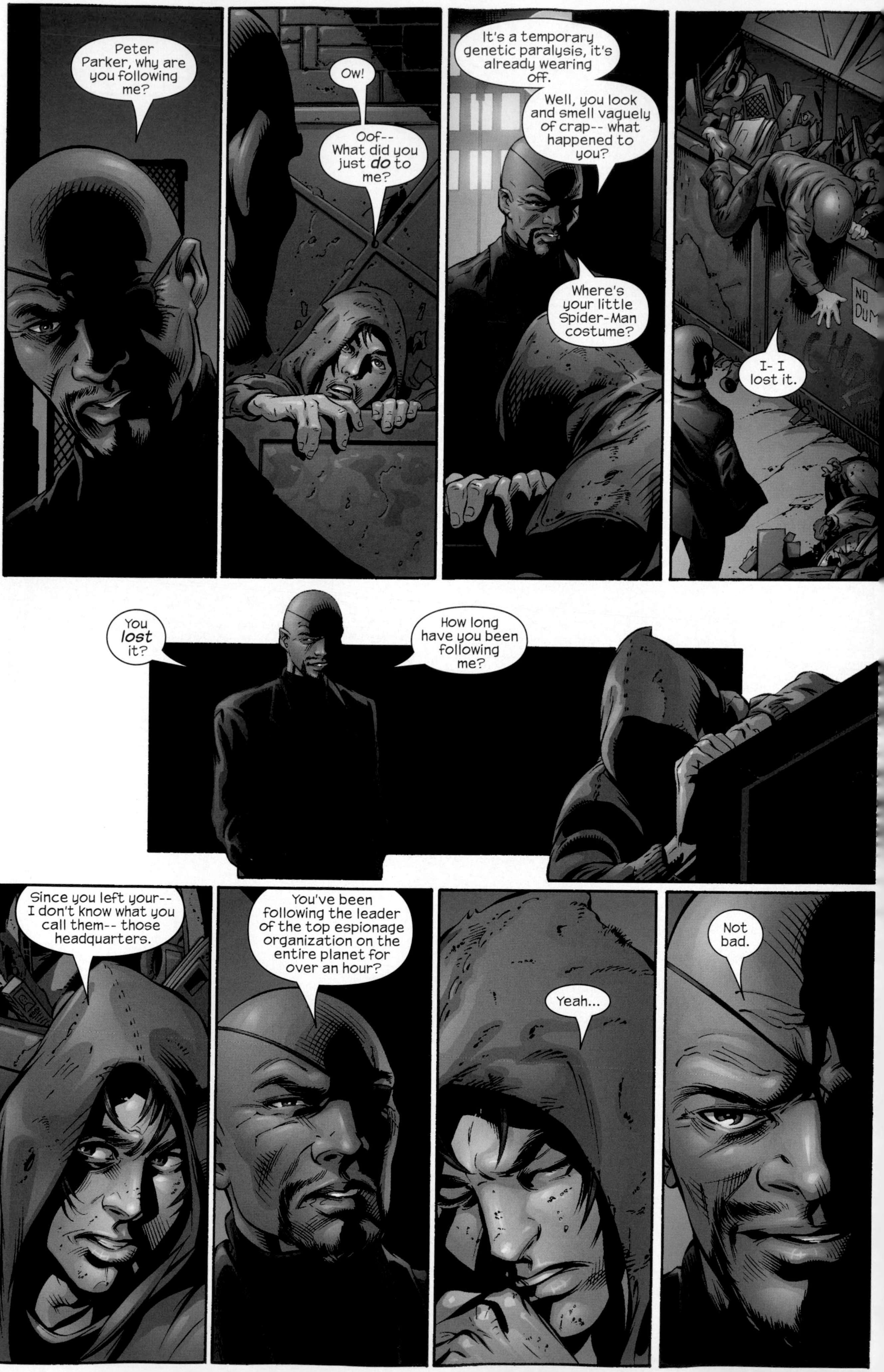
Peter Parker, why are you following me?
Ow!
Oof-- What did you just *do* to me?
It's a temporary genetic paralysis, it's already wearing off.
Well, you look and smell vaguely of crap-- what happened to you?
Where's your little Spider-Man costume?
I- I lost it.
NO DUM
You *lost* it?
How long have you been following me?
Since you left your-- I don't know what you call them-- those headquarters.
You've been following the leader of the top espionage organization on the entire planet for over an hour?
Yeah...
Not bad.

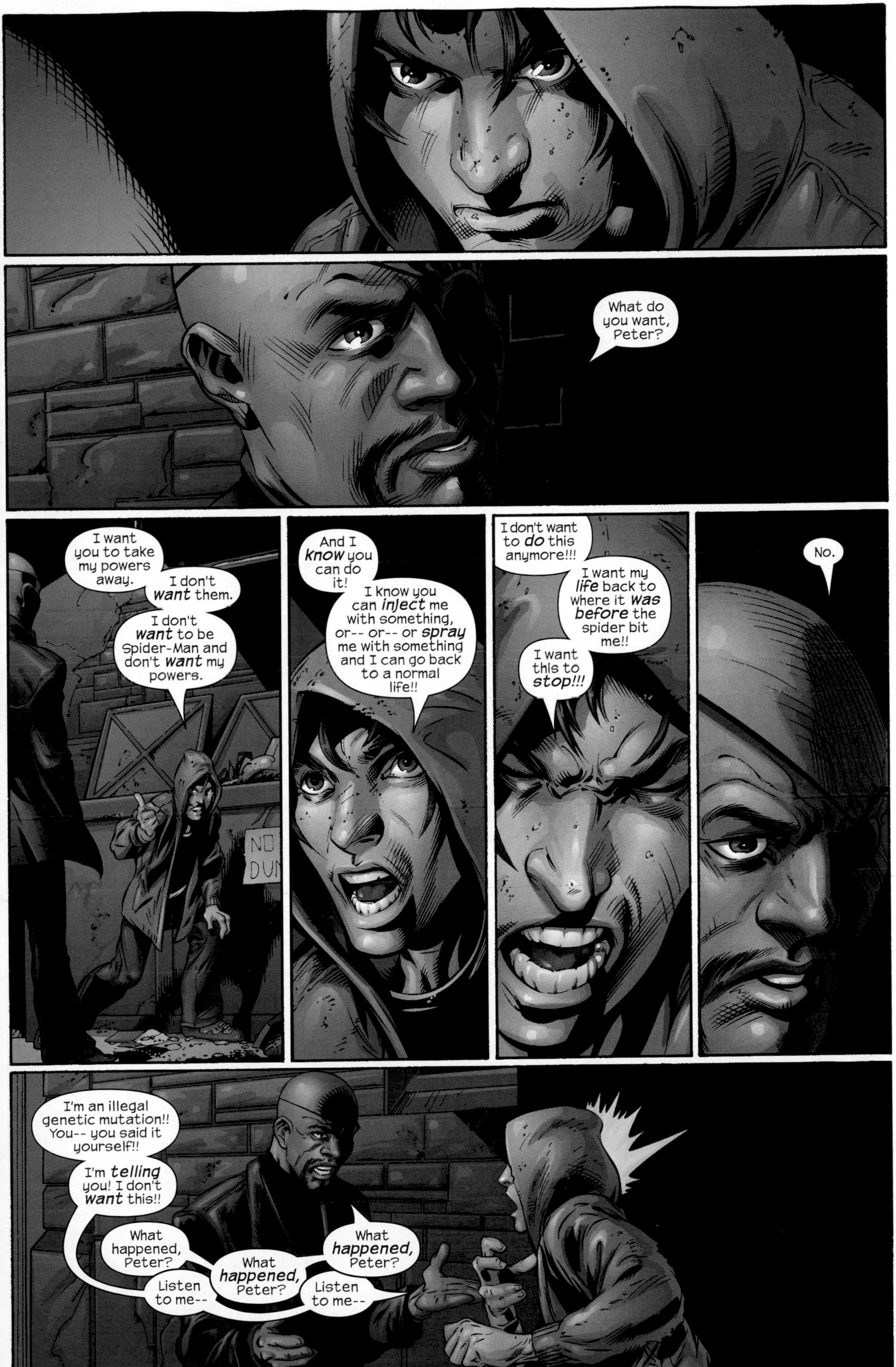
What do you want, Peter?
I want you to take my powers away.
I don't want them.
I don't want to be Spider-Man and don't want my powers.
NO DUM
And I know you can do it!
I know you can inject me with something, or-- or-- or spray me with something and I can go back to a normal life!!
I don't want to do this anymore!!!
I want my life back to where it was before the spider bit me!!
I want this to stop!!!
No.
I'm an illegal genetic mutation!! You-- you said it yourself!!
I'm telling you! I don't want this!!
What happened, Peter?
Listen to me--
What happened, Peter?
Listen to me--
What happened, Peter?

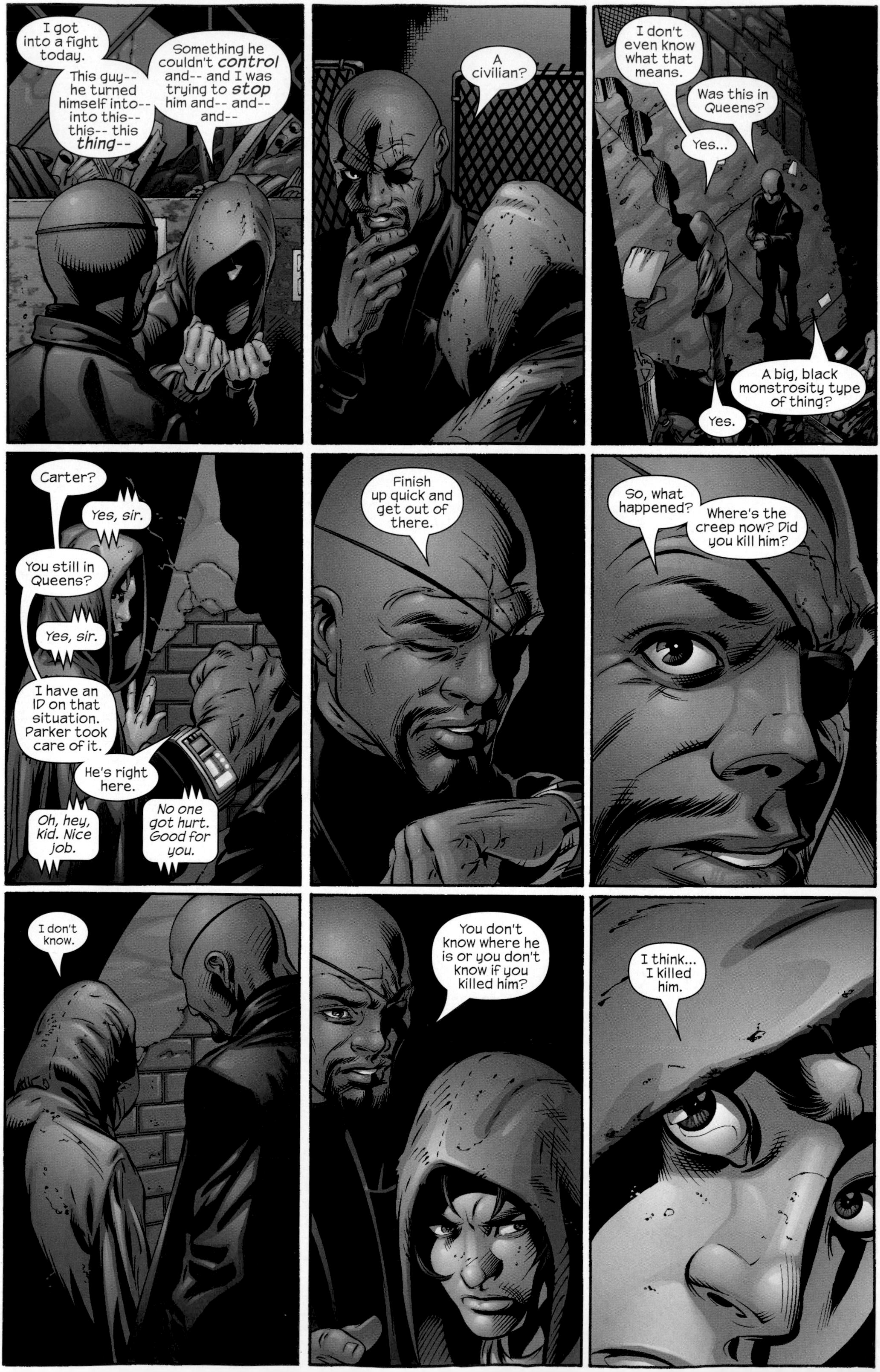
I got into a fight today.
This guy-- he turned himself into-- into this-- this-- this *thing*--
Something he couldn't **control** and-- and I was trying to **stop** him and-- and-- and--
A civilian?
I don't even know what that means.
Was this in Queens?
Yes...
A big, black monstrosity type of thing?
Yes.
Carter?
Yes, sir.
You still in Queens?
Yes, sir.
I have an ID on that situation. Parker took care of it.
He's right here.
Oh, hey, kid. Nice job.
No one got hurt. Good for you.
Finish up quick and get out of there.
So, what happened?
Where's the creep now? Did you kill him?
I don't know.
You don't know where he is or you don't know if you killed him?
I think... I killed him.

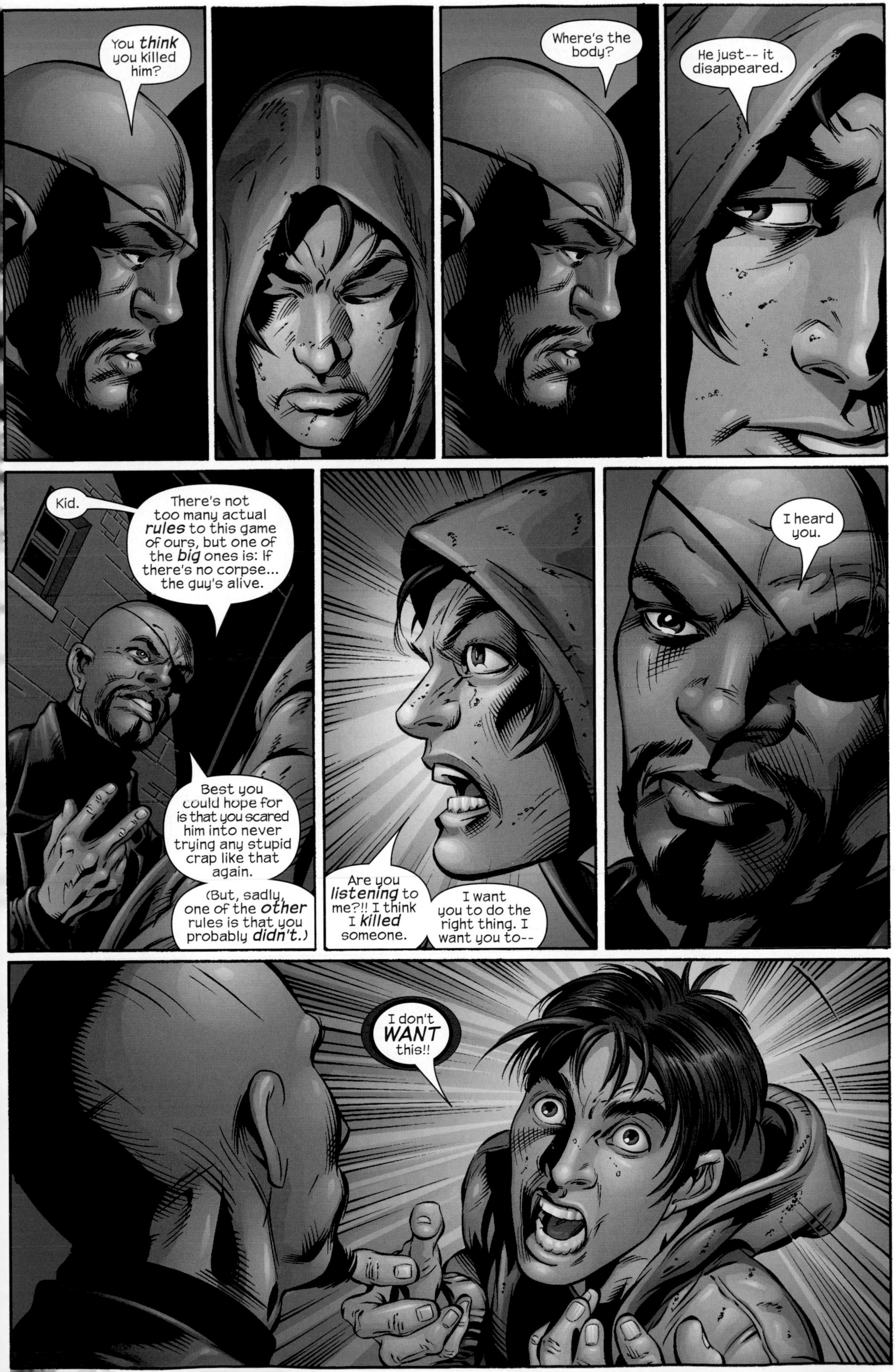
You *think* you killed him?
Where's the body?
He just-- it disappeared.
Kid.
There's not too many actual *rules* to this game of ours, but one of the *big* ones is: If there's no corpse... the guy's alive.
Best you could hope for is that you scared him into never trying any stupid crap like that again.
(But, sadly, one of the *other* rules is that you probably *didn't.*)
Are you *listening* to me?!! I think I *killed* someone.
I want you to do the right thing. I want you to--
I heard you.
I don't *WANT* this!!

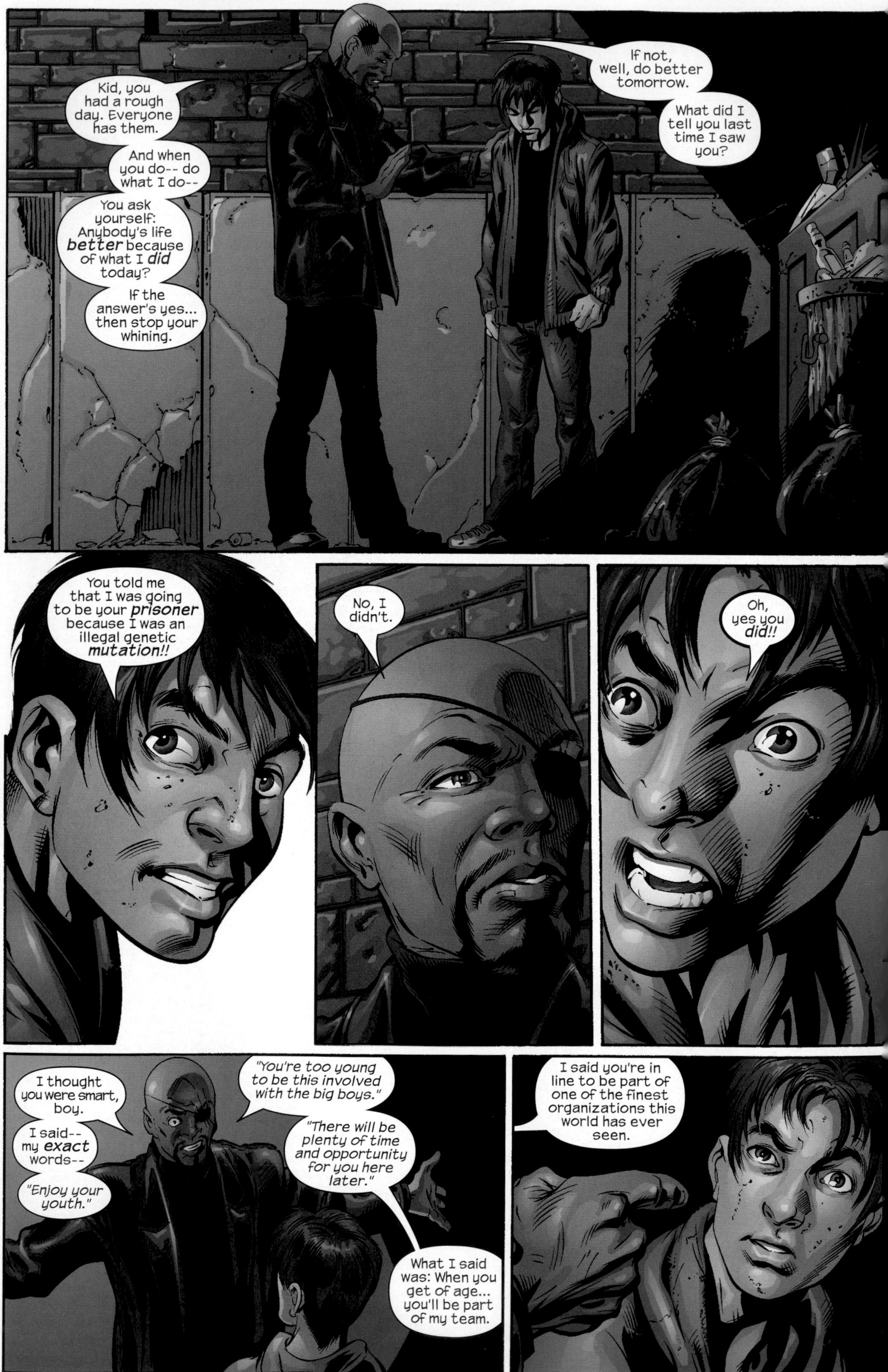
Kid, you had a rough day. Everyone has them.
And when you do-- do what I do--
You ask yourself: Anybody's life *better* because of what I *did* today?
If the answer's yes... then stop your whining.
If not, well, do better tomorrow.
What did I tell you last time I saw you?
You told me that I was going to be your *prisoner* because I was an illegal genetic *mutation!!*
No, I didn't.
Oh, yes you *did!!*
I thought you were smart, boy.
I said-- my *exact* words--
"Enjoy your youth."
"You're too young to be this involved with the big boys."
"There will be plenty of time and opportunity for you here later."
What I said was: When you get of age... you'll be part of my team.
I said you're in line to be part of one of the finest organizations this world has ever seen.

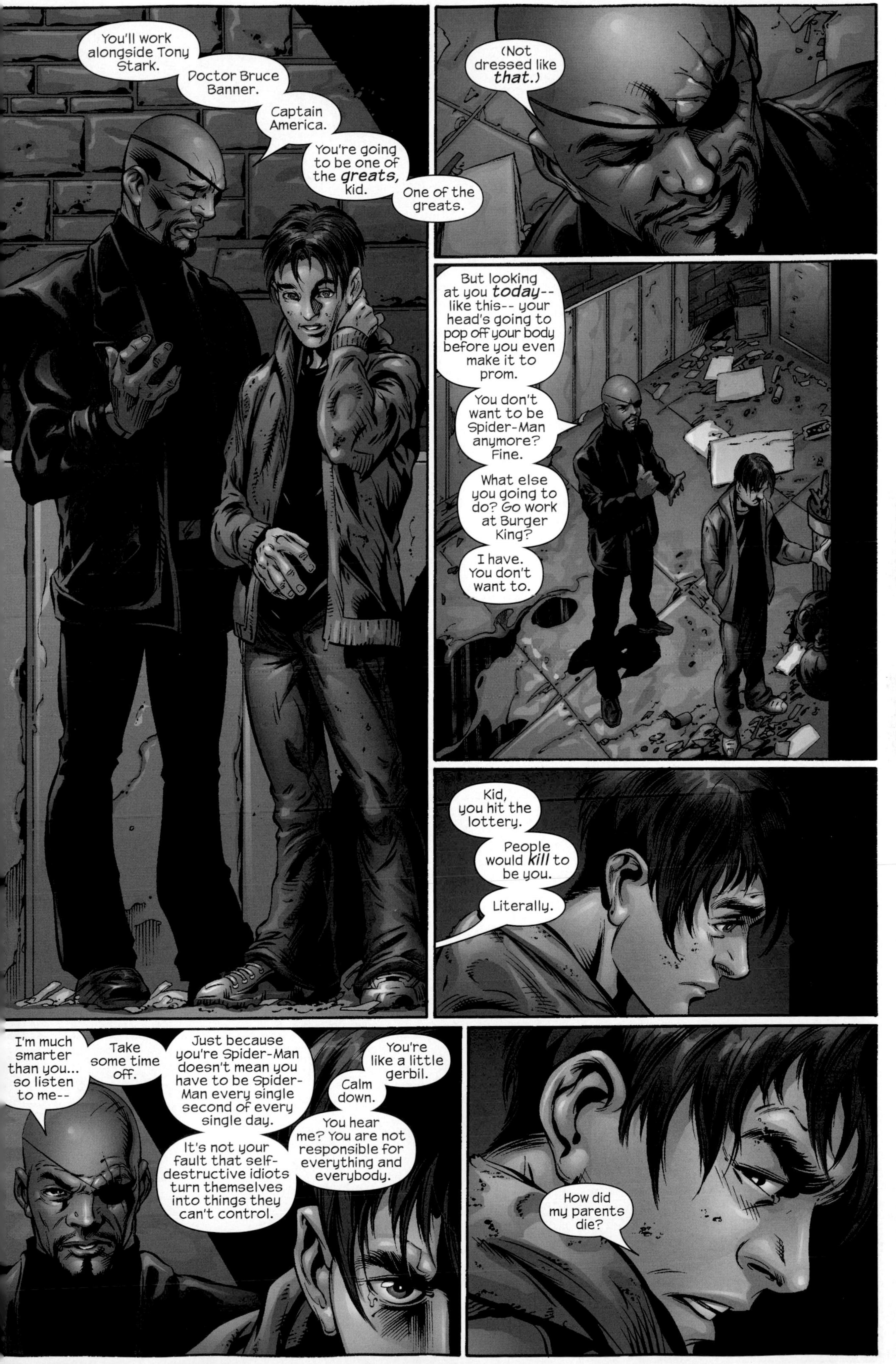

You'll work alongside Tony Stark.
Doctor Bruce Banner.
Captain America.
You're going to be one of the *greats,* kid.
One of the greats.
(Not dressed like *that.*)
But looking at you *today*-- like this-- your head's going to pop off your body before you even make it to prom.
You don't want to be Spider-Man anymore? Fine.
What else you going to do? Go work at Burger King?
I have. You don't want to.
Kid, you hit the lottery.
People would *kill* to be you.
Literally.
I'm much smarter than you... so listen to me--
Take some time off.
Just because you're Spider-Man doesn't mean you have to be Spider-Man every single second of every single day.
It's not your fault that self-destructive idiots turn themselves into things they can't control.
You're like a little gerbil.
Calm down.
You hear me? You are not responsible for everything and everybody.
How did my parents die?

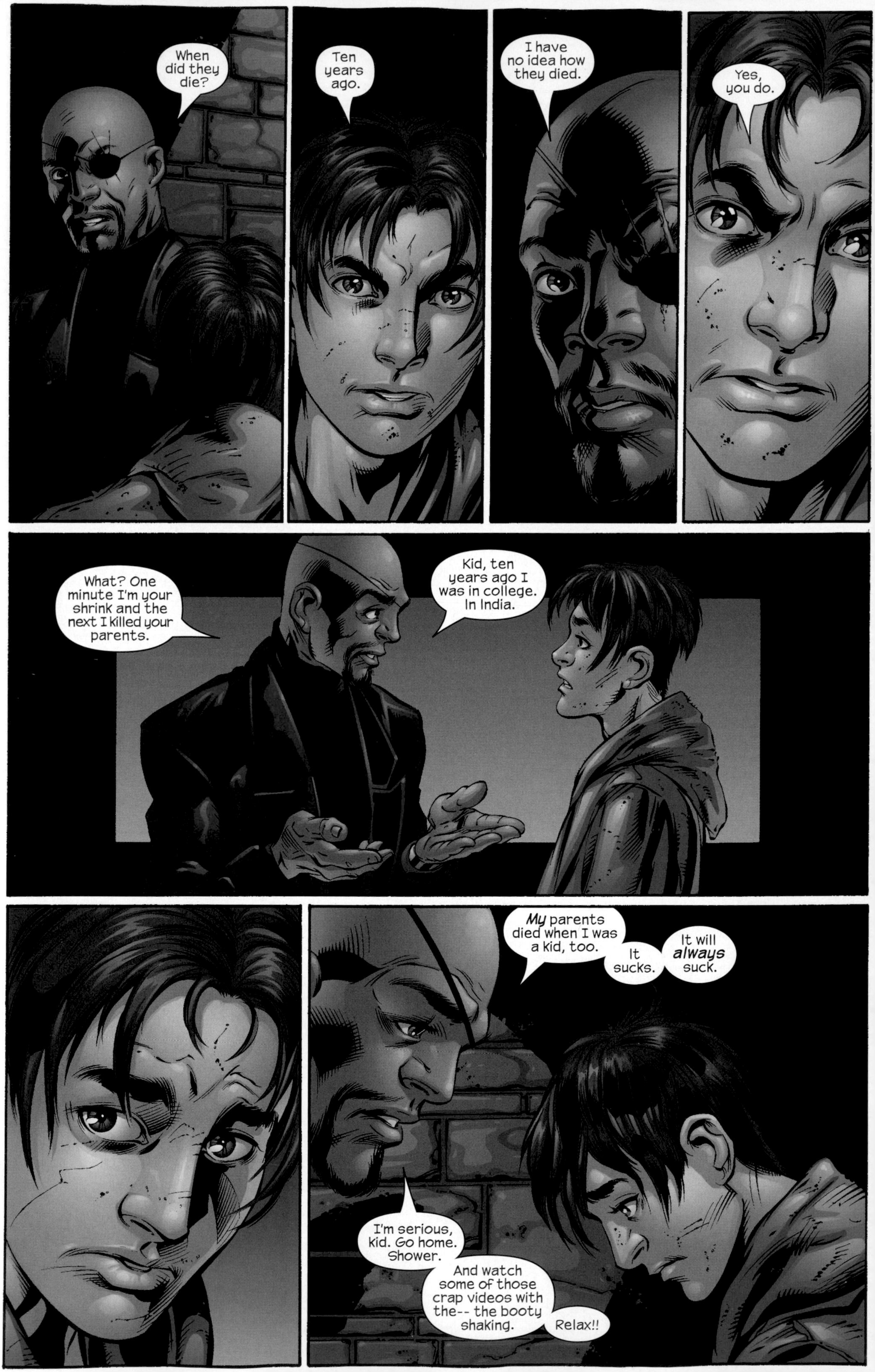
When did they die?
Ten years ago.
I have no idea how they died.
Yes, you do.
What? One minute I'm your shrink and the next I killed your parents.
Kid, ten years ago I was in college. In India.
My parents died when I was a kid, too.
It sucks.
It will *always* suck.
I'm serious, kid. Go home. Shower.
And watch some of those crap videos with the-- the booty shaking.
Relax!!

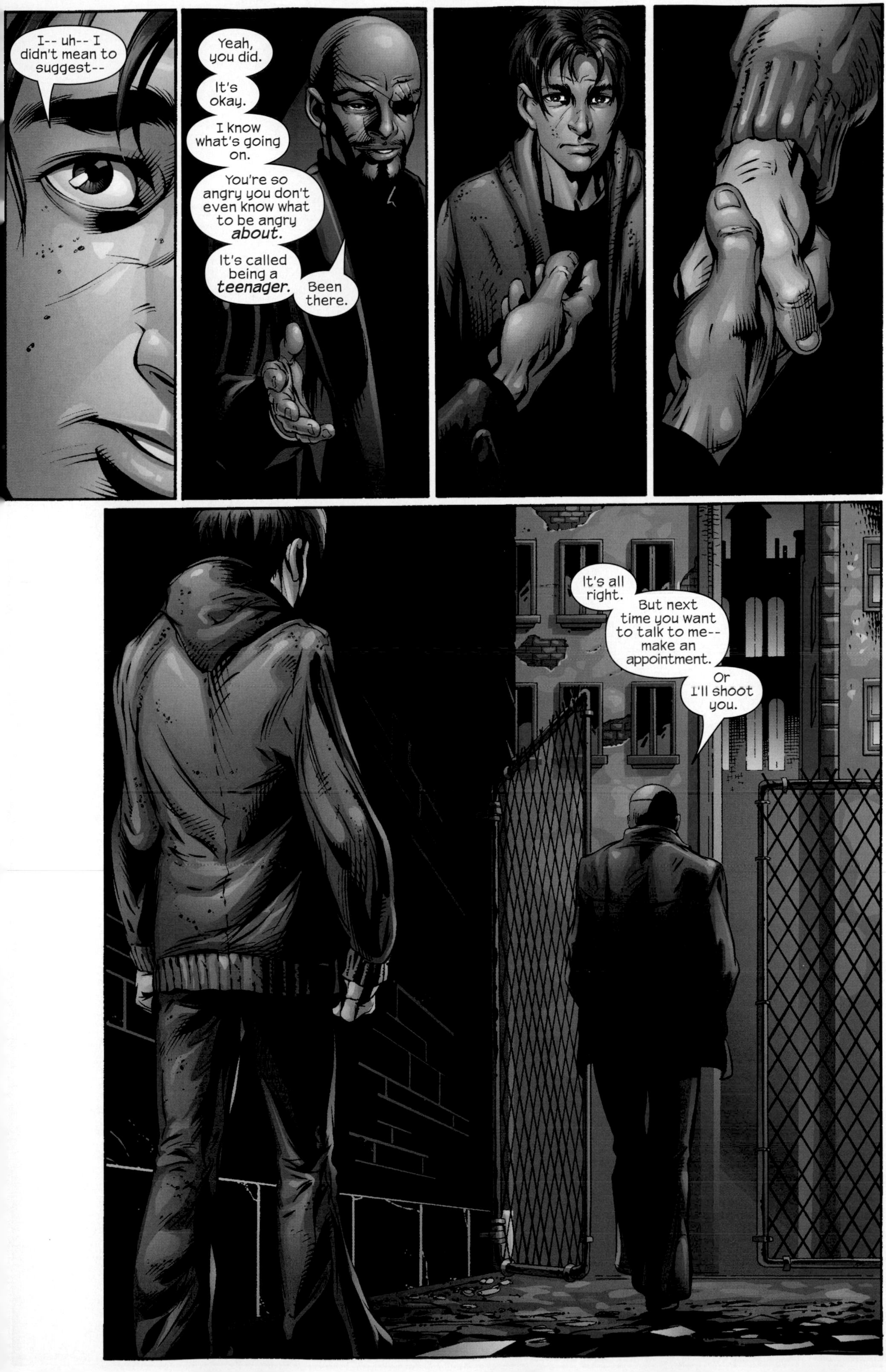
I-- uh-- I didn't mean to suggest--
Yeah, you did.
It's okay.
I know what's going on.
You're so angry you don't even know what to be angry *about.*
It's called being a *teenager.*
Been there.
It's all right.
But next time you want to talk to me-- make an appointment.
Or I'll shoot you.

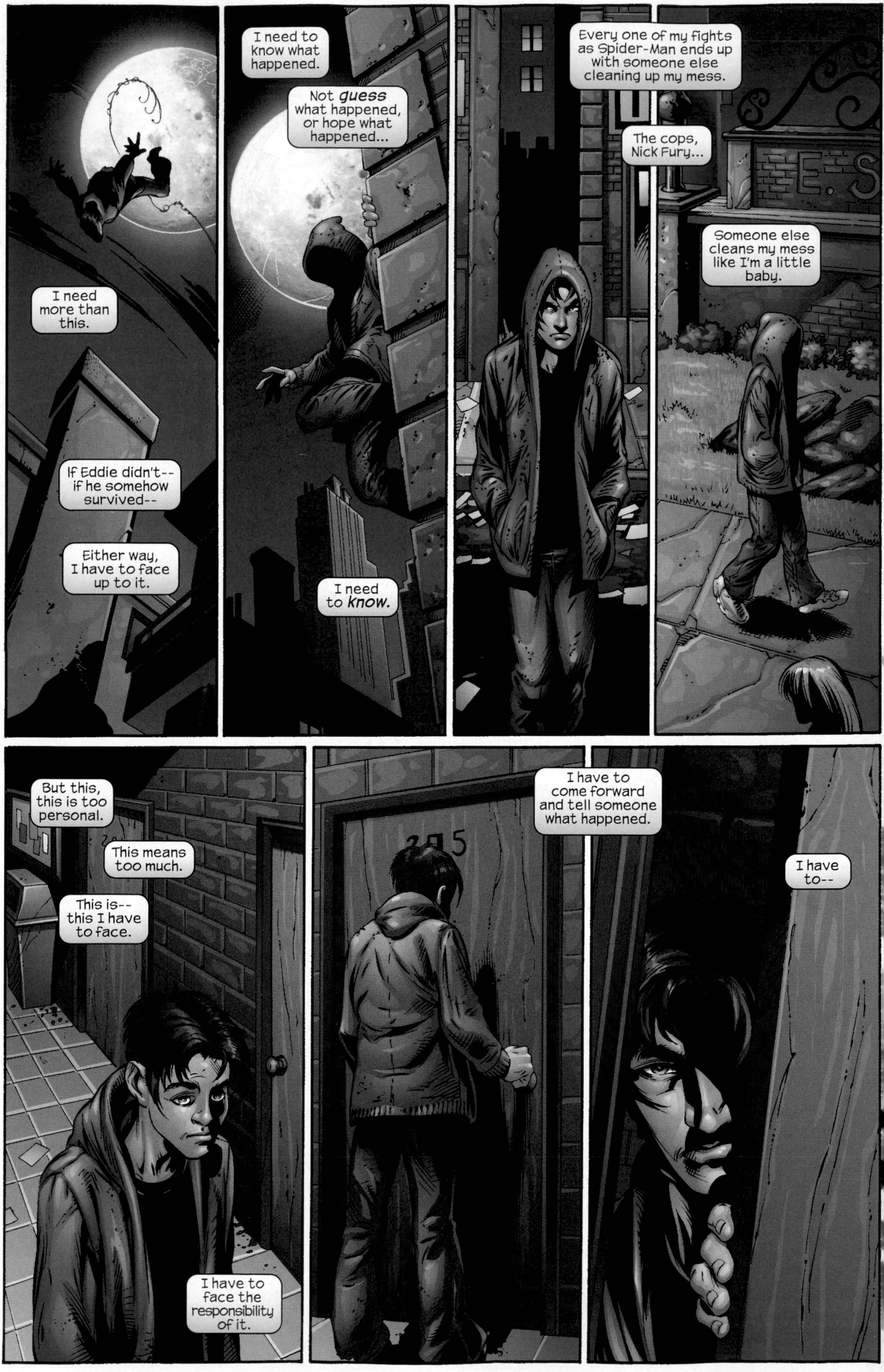
I need more than this.
If Eddie didn't-- if he somehow survived--
Either way, I have to face up to it.
I need to know what happened.
Not *guess* what happened, or hope what happened...
I need to *know.*
Every one of my fights as Spider-Man ends up with someone else cleaning up my mess.
The cops, Nick Fury...
Someone else cleans my mess like I'm a little baby.
But this, this is too personal.
This means too much.
This is-- this I have to face.
I have to face the responsibility of it.
I have to come forward and tell someone what happened.
I have to--

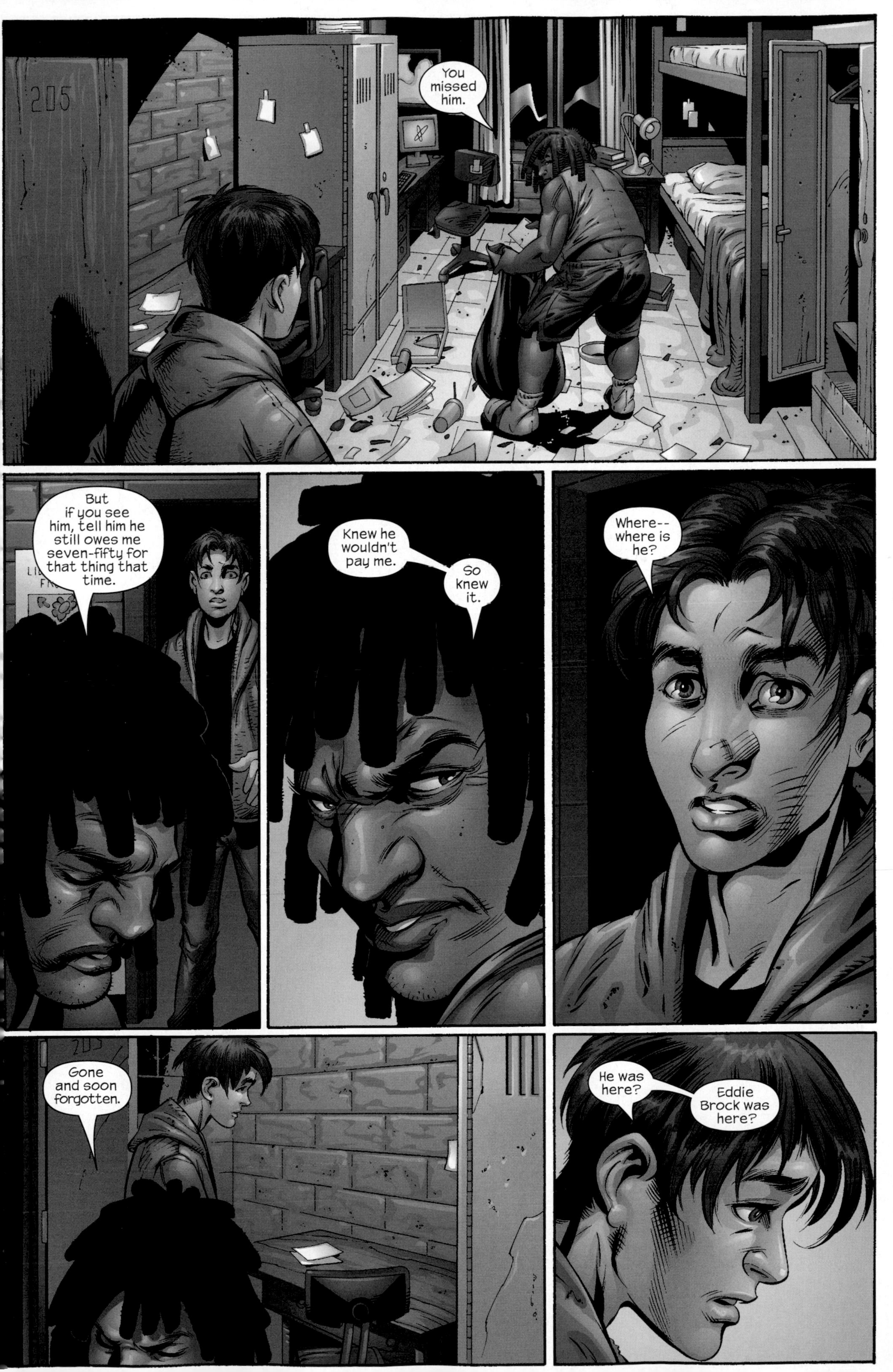
You missed him.
But if you see him, tell him he still owes me seven-fifty for that thing that time.
Knew he wouldn't pay me.
So knew it.
Where-- where is he?
Gone and soon forgotten.
He was here?
Eddie Brock was here?

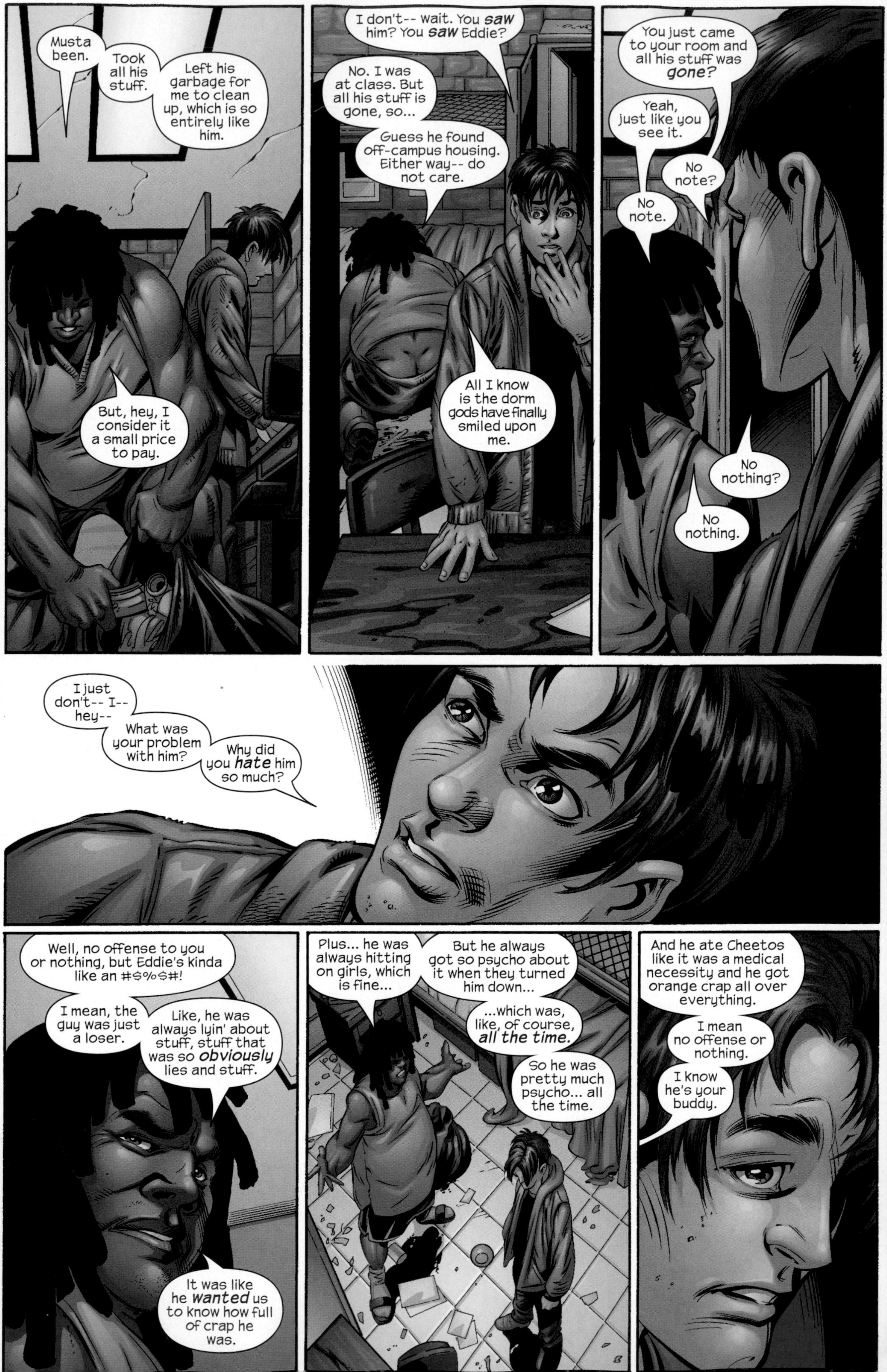

Musta been.
Took all his stuff.
Left his garbage for me to clean up, which is so entirely like him.
But, hey, I consider it a small price to pay.
I don't-- wait. You saw him? You saw Eddie?
No. I was at class. But all his stuff is gone, so...
Guess he found off-campus housing. Either way-- do not care.
All I know is the dorm gods have finally smiled upon me.
You just came to your room and all his stuff was gone?
Yeah, just like you see it.
No note?
No note.
No nothing?
No nothing.
I just don't-- I-- hey--
What was your problem with him?
Why did you hate him so much?
Well, no offense to you or nothing, but Eddie's kinda like an #$%$#!
I mean, the guy was just a loser.
Like, he was always lyin' about stuff, stuff that was so obviously lies and stuff.
It was like he wanted us to know how full of crap he was.
Plus... he was always hitting on girls, which is fine...
But he always got so psycho about it when they turned him down...
...which was, like, of course, all the time.
So he was pretty much psycho... all the time.
And he ate Cheetos like it was a medical necessity and he got orange crap all over everything.
I mean no offense or nothing.
I know he's your buddy.

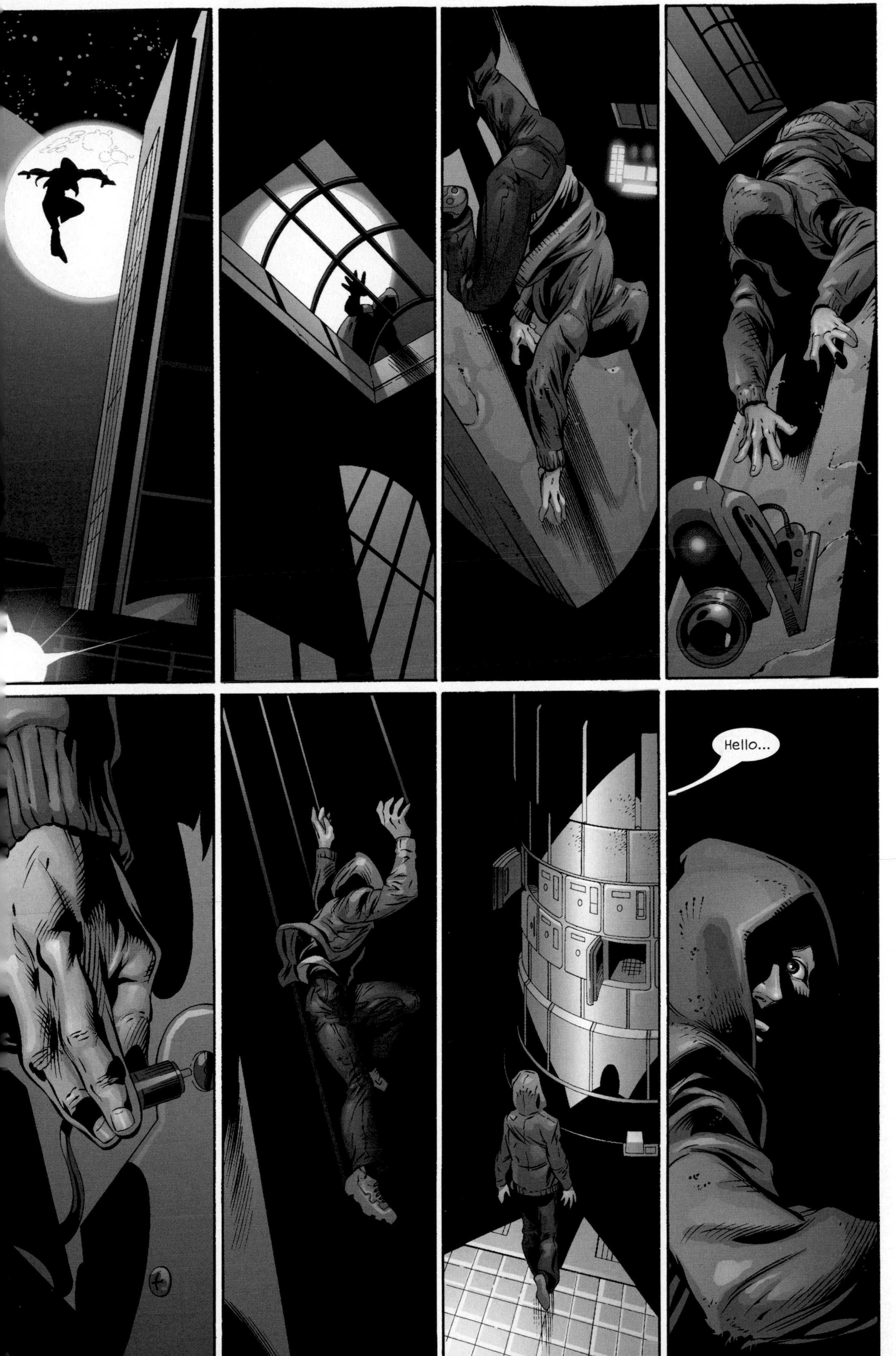
Hello...

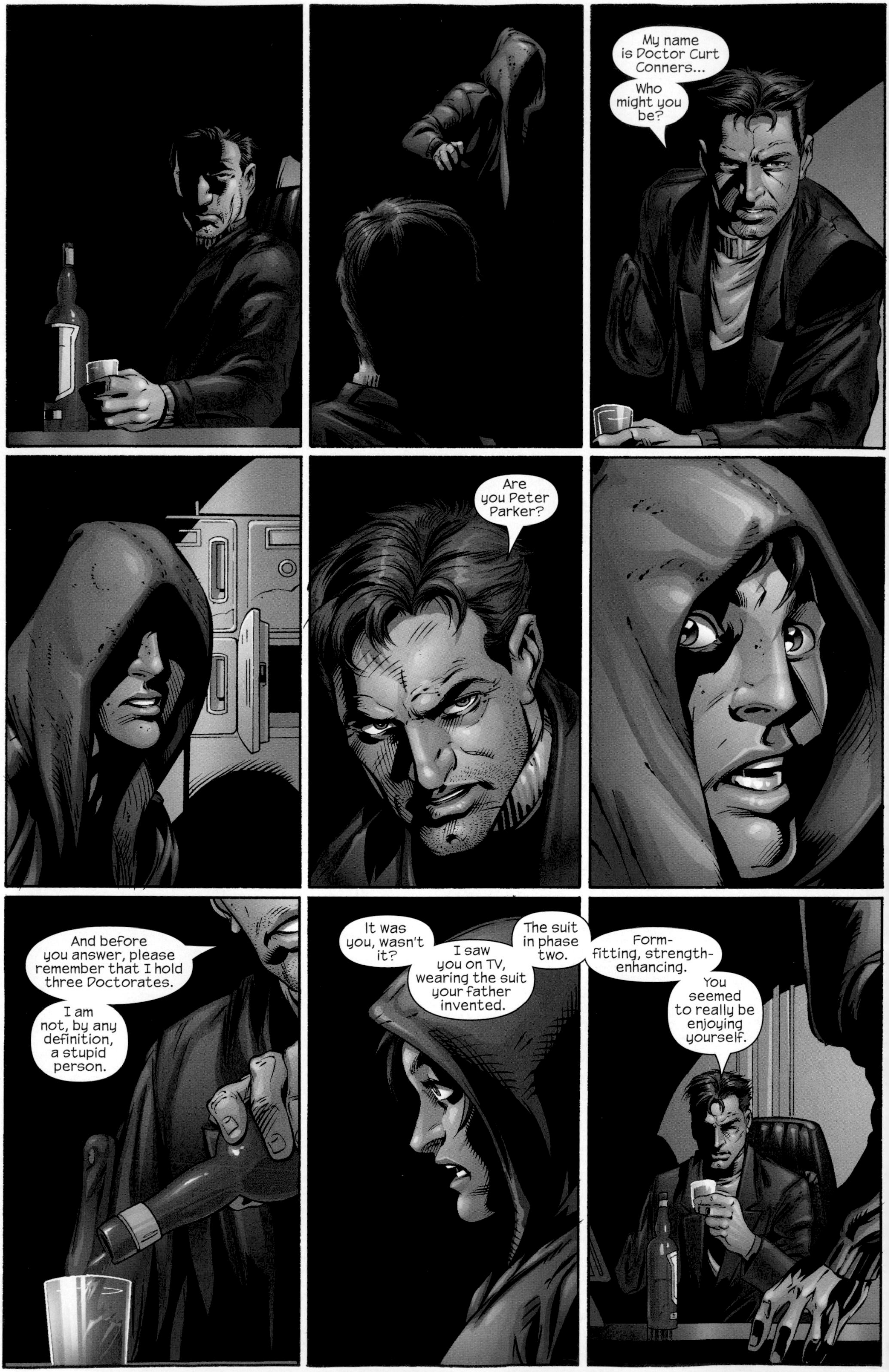

My name is Doctor Curt Conners...
Who might you be?
Are you Peter Parker?
And before you answer, please remember that I hold three Doctorates.
I am not, by any definition, a stupid person.
It was you, wasn't it?
I saw you on TV, wearing the suit your father invented.
The suit in phase two.
Form-fitting, strength-enhancing.
You seemed to really be enjoying yourself.

And I stood there staring at my TV, asking myself: How on earth did this Spider-Man guy get his hands on "the suit"?

I never put together that Spider-Man could actually be Ray Parker's son.

My student, your pal, Eddie Brock told me you were just a kid. As you are.

I would never have put the two together if I didn't see you here just now, like this.

Peter Parker.

Spider-Man.

Good for you.

We've met before, you and I, right?

You saved my life.

Yes.

You saved my family.

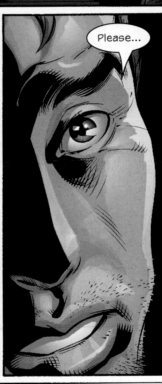

Please...

Yes.

Did you ever tell anyone what happened that night?

When you found me-- when you saw what I had done to myself?

Did you tell anyone?

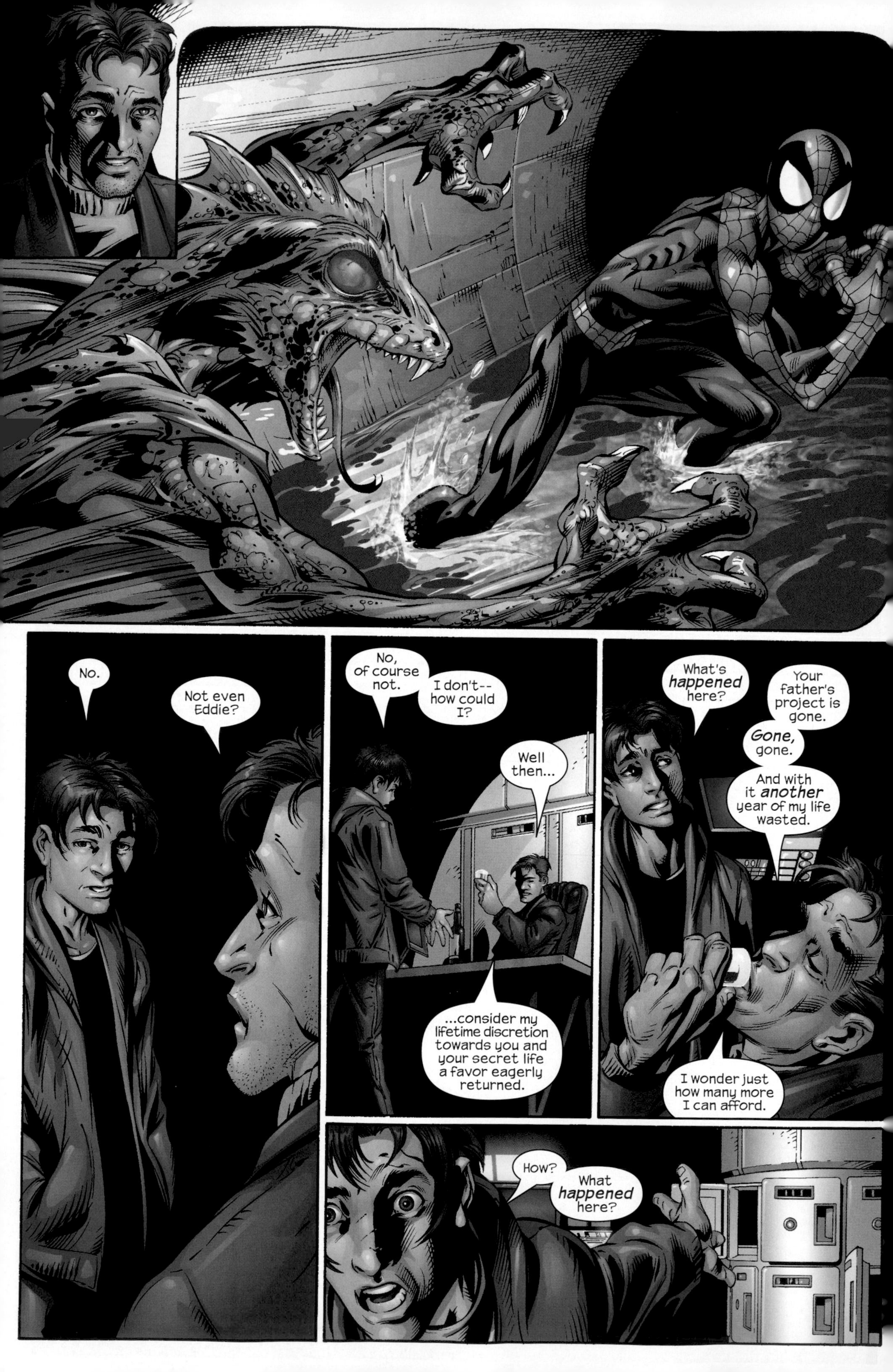

No.
Not even Eddie?
No, of course not.
I don't-- how could I?
Well then...
...consider my lifetime discretion towards you and your secret life a favor eagerly returned.
What's *happened* here?
Your father's project is gone.
Gone, gone.
And with it *another* year of my life wasted.
I wonder just how many more I can afford.
How?
What *happened* here?

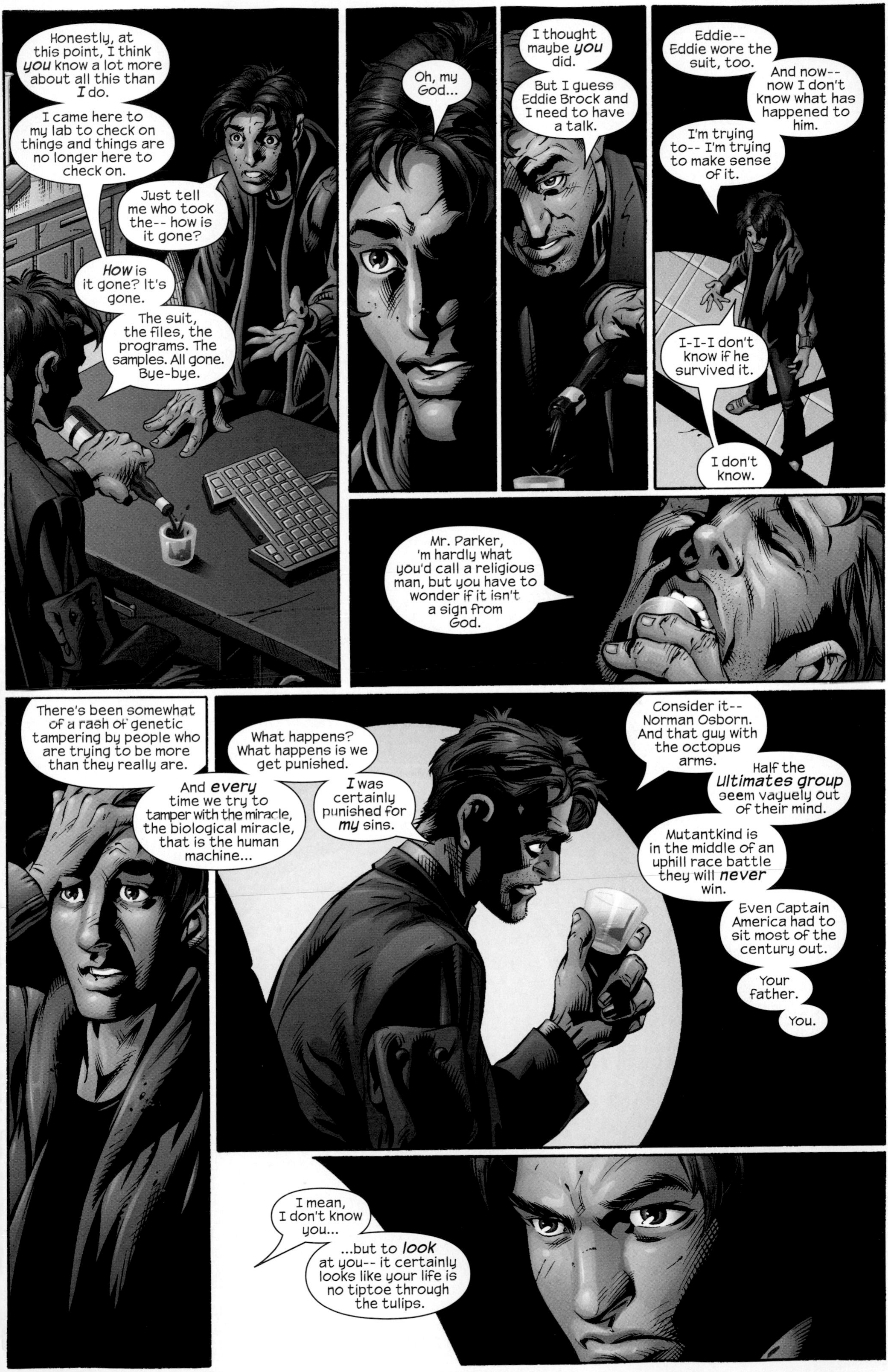
Honestly, at this point, I think *you* know a lot more about all this than *I* do.
I came here to my lab to check on things and things are no longer here to check on.
Just tell me who took the-- how is it gone?
How is it gone? It's gone.
The suit, the files, the programs. The samples. All gone. Bye-bye.
Oh, my God...
I thought maybe *you* did.
But I guess Eddie Brock and I need to have a talk.
Eddie-- Eddie wore the suit, too.
And now-- now I don't know what has happened to him.
I'm trying to-- I'm trying to make sense of it.
I-I-I don't know if he survived it.
I don't know.
Mr. Parker, 'm hardly what you'd call a religious man, but you have to wonder if it isn't a sign from God.
There's been somewhat of a rash of genetic tampering by people who are trying to be more than they really are.
And *every* time we try to tamper with the miracle, the biological miracle, that is the human machine...
What happens? What happens is we get punished.
I was certainly punished for *my* sins.
Consider it-- Norman Osborn. And that guy with the octopus arms.
Half the *Ultimates group* seem vaguely out of their mind.
Mutantkind is in the middle of an uphill race battle they will *never* win.
Even Captain America had to sit most of the century out.
Your father.
You.
I mean, I don't know you...
...but to *look* at you-- it certainly looks like your life is no tiptoe through the tulips.

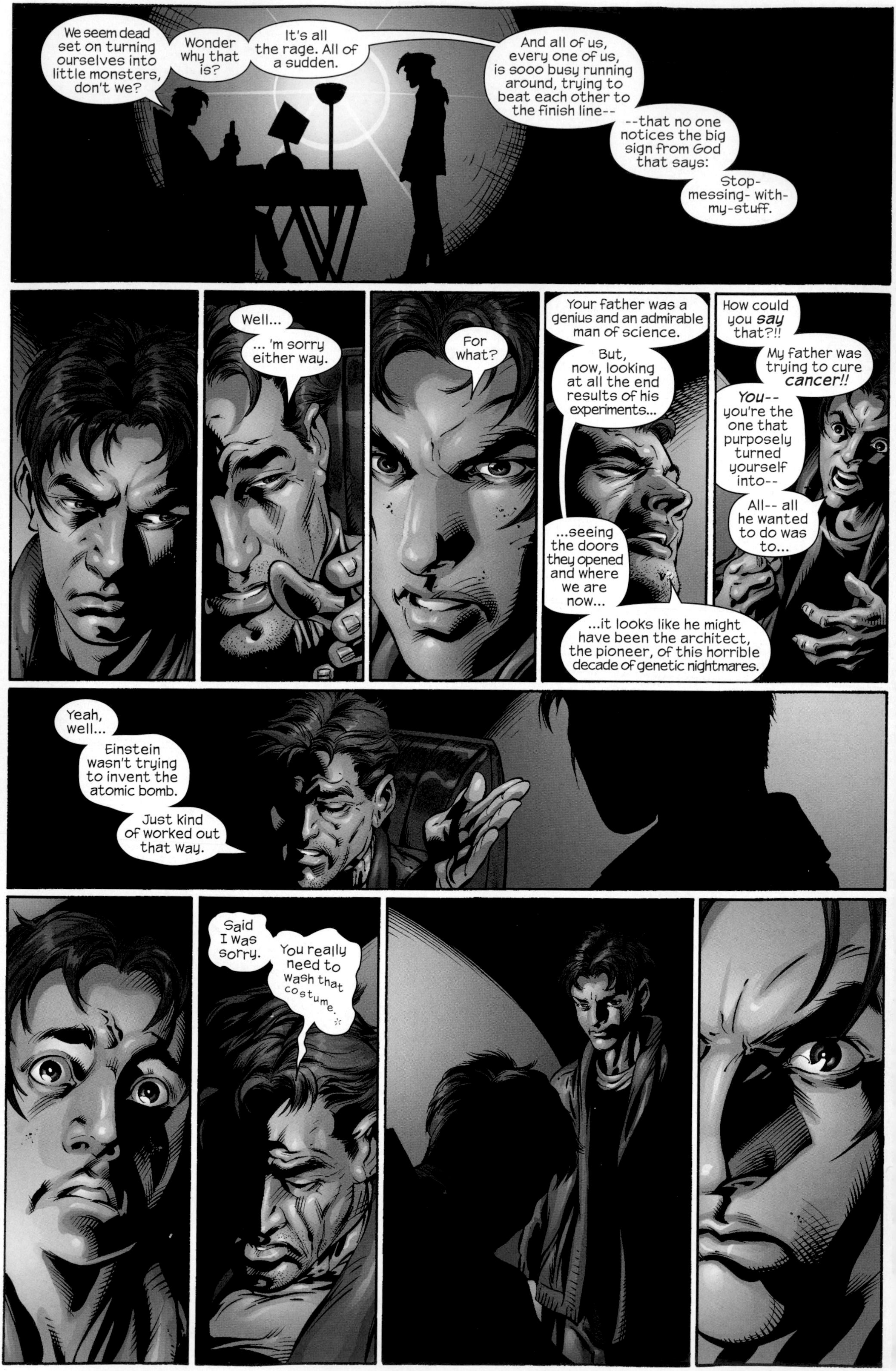
We seem dead set on turning ourselves into little monsters, don't we?
Wonder why that is?
It's all the rage. All of a sudden.
And all of us, every one of us, is sooo busy running around, trying to beat each other to the finish line--
--that no one notices the big sign from God that says:
Stop- messing- with- my-stuff.
Well...
... 'm sorry either way.
For what?
Your father was a genius and an admirable man of science.
But, now, looking at all the end results of his experiments...
...seeing the doors they opened and where we are now...
...it looks like he might have been the architect, the pioneer, of this horrible decade of genetic nightmares.
How could you *say* that?!!
My father was trying to cure *cancer!!*
You-- you're the one that purposely turned yourself into--
All-- all he wanted to do was to...
Yeah, well...
Einstein wasn't trying to invent the atomic bomb.
Just kind of worked out that way.
Said I was sorry.
You really need to wash that costume.

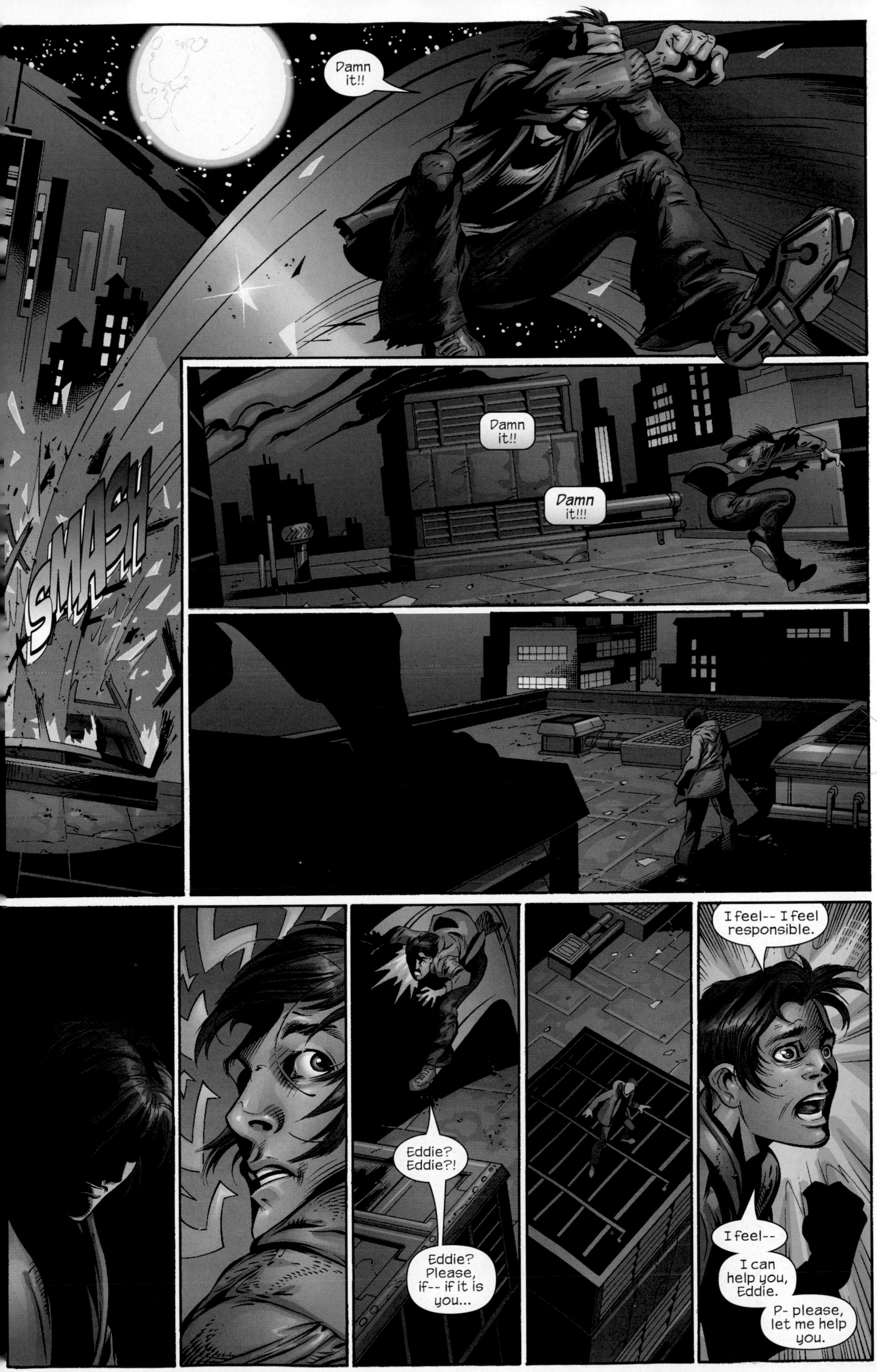
Damn it!!
SMASH
Damn it!!
Damn it!!!
Eddie? Eddie?!
Eddie? Please, if-- if it is you...
I feel-- I feel responsible.
I feel--
I can help you, Eddie.
P- please, let me help you.

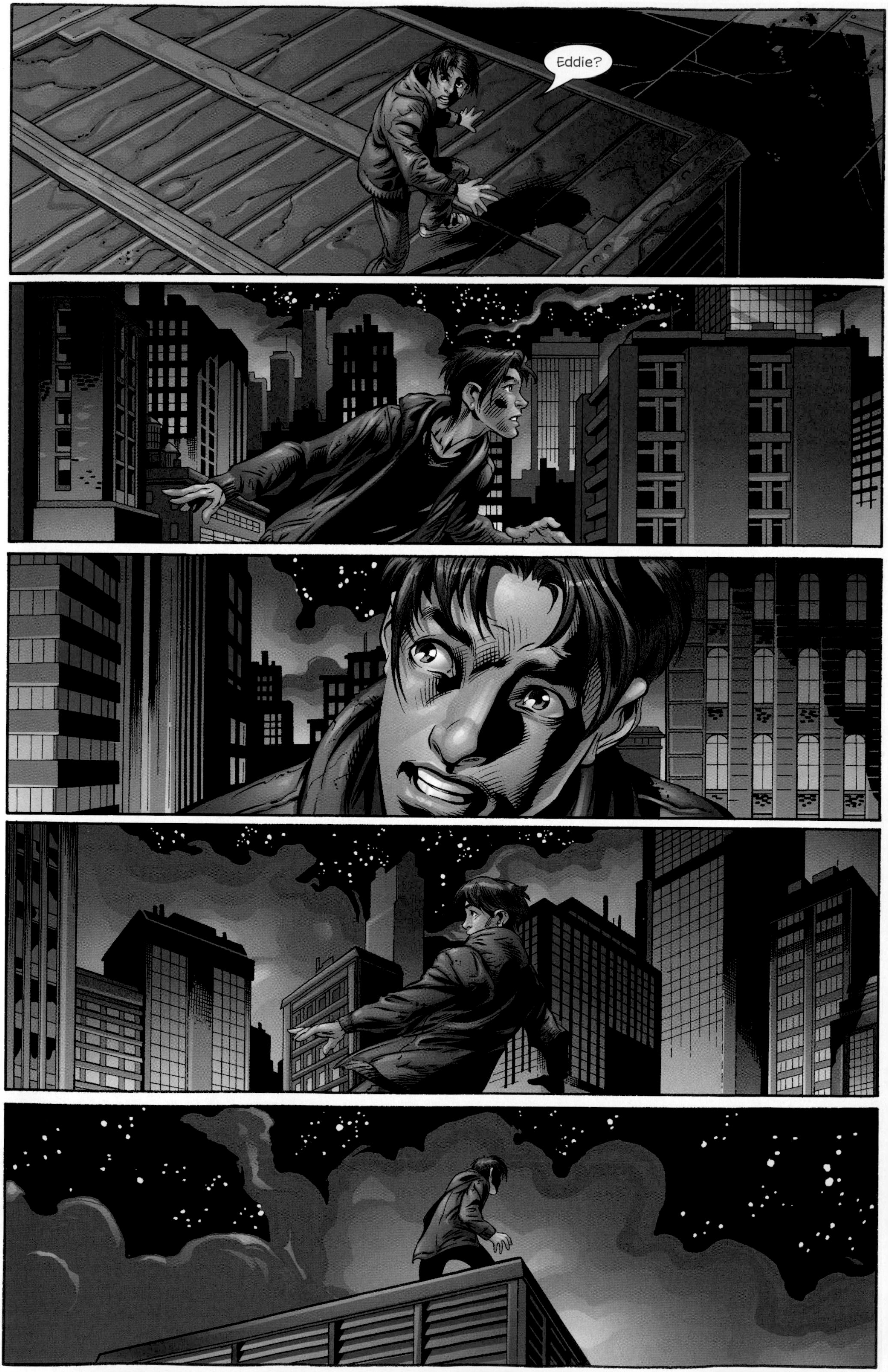
Eddie?

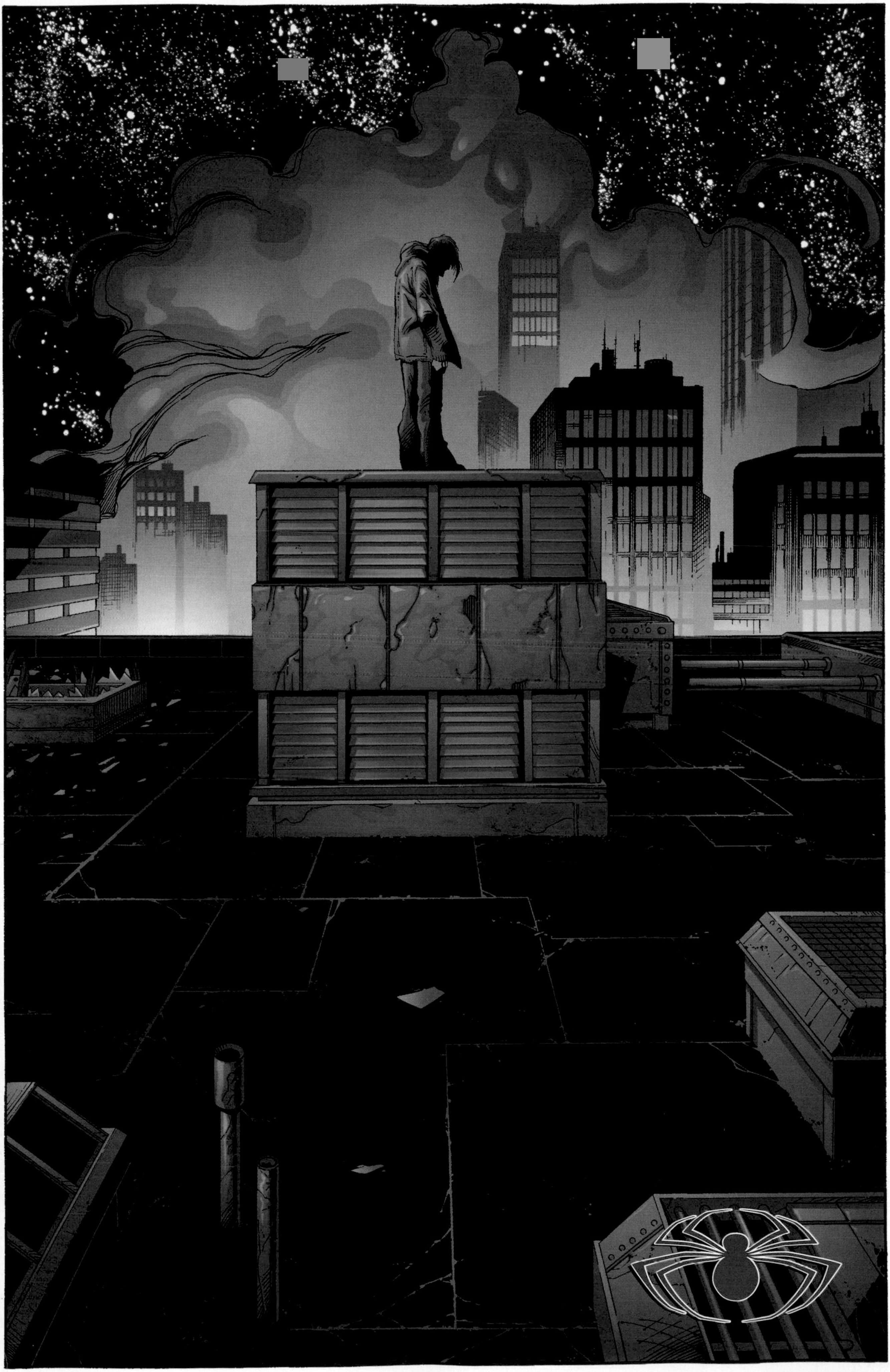

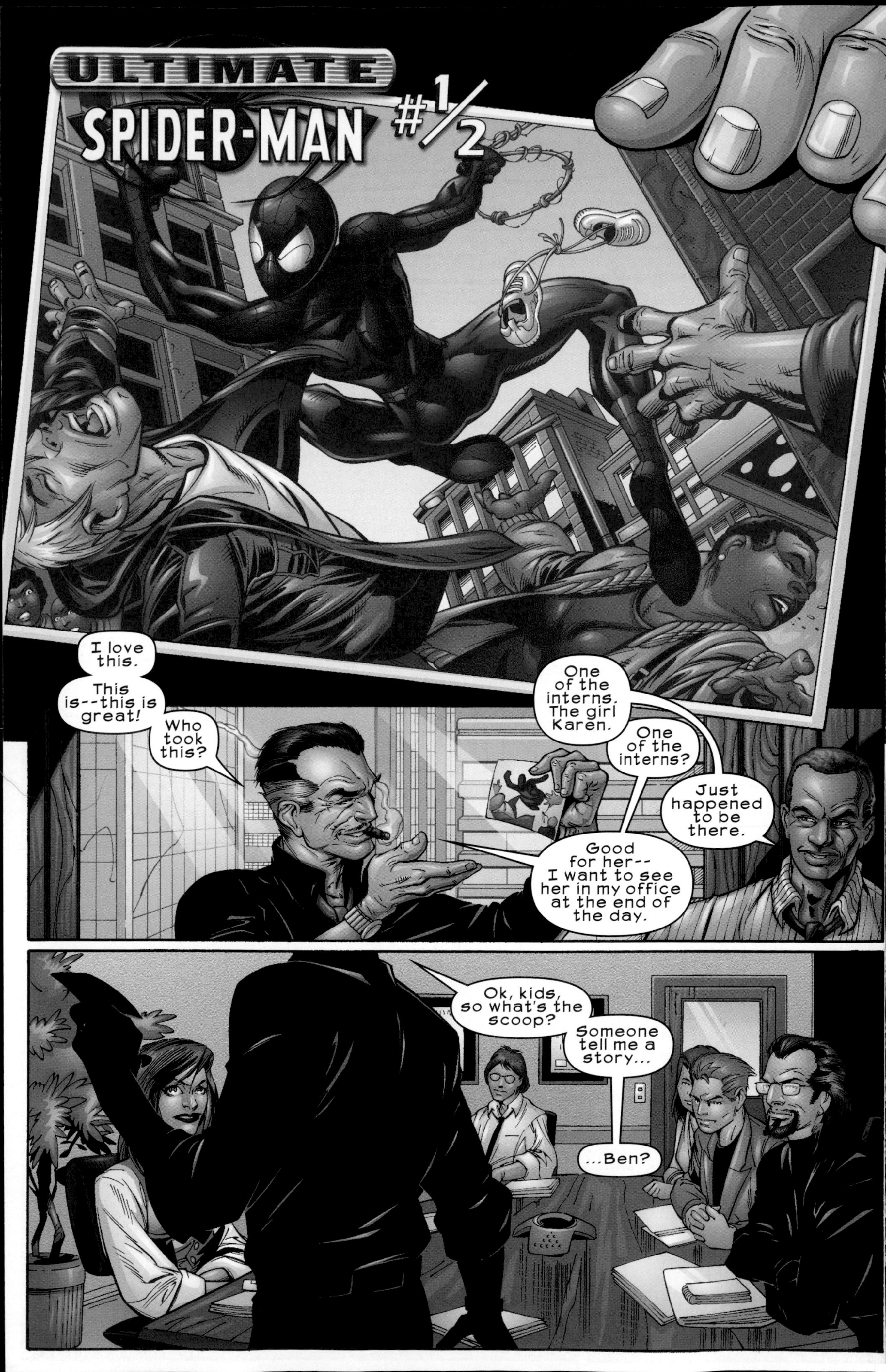

ULTIMATE SPIDER-MAN #1/2
I love this.
This is--this is great!
Who took this?
One of the interns. The girl Karen.
One of the interns?
Just happened to be there.
Good for her-- I want to see her in my office at the end of the day.
Ok, kids, so what's the scoop?
Someone tell me a story...
...Ben?

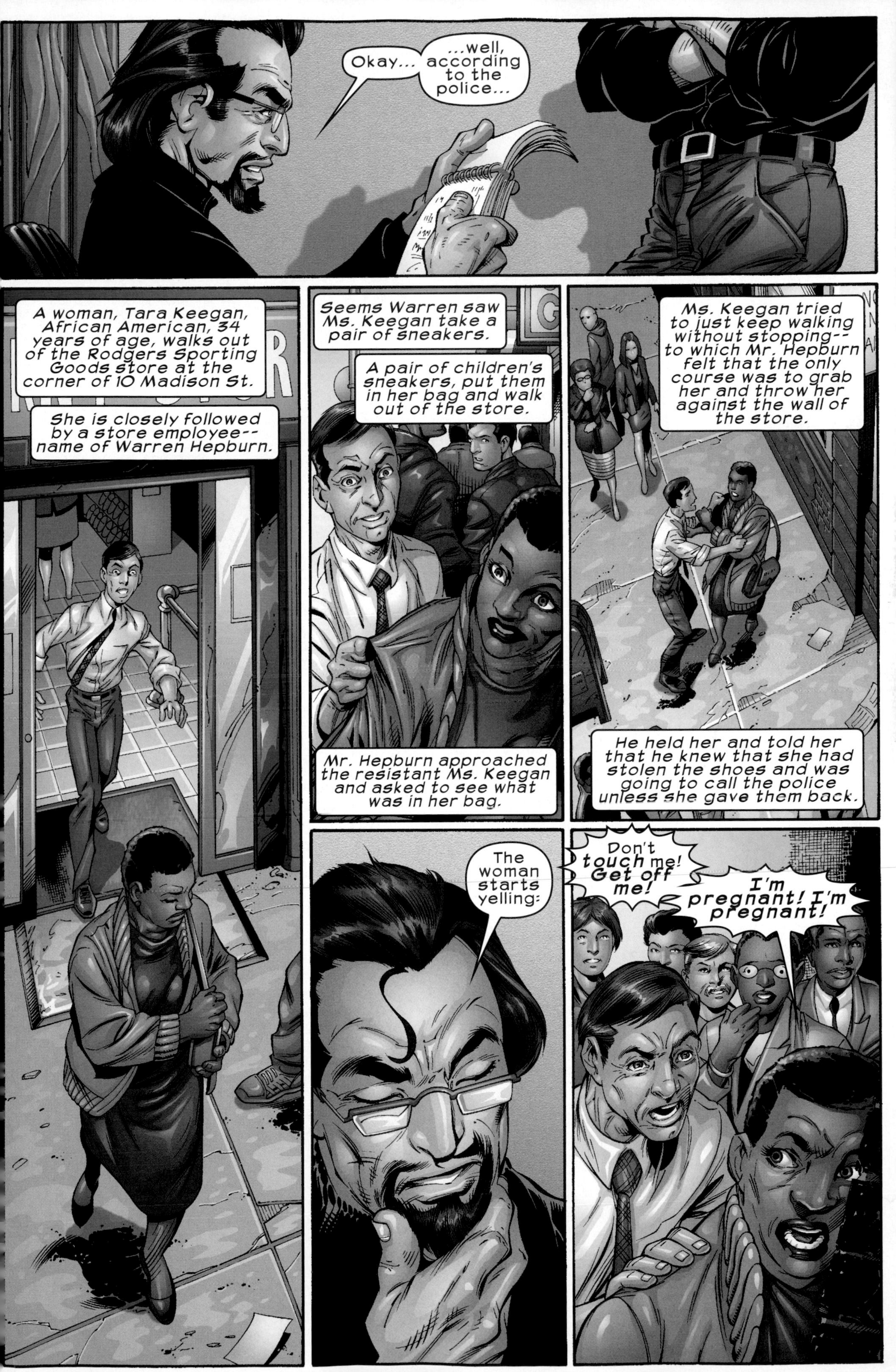
Okay...
...well, according to the police...
A woman, Tara Keegan, African American, 34 years of age, walks out of the Rodgers Sporting Goods store at the corner of 10 Madison St.
She is closely followed by a store employee-- name of Warren Hepburn.
Seems Warren saw Ms. Keegan take a pair of sneakers.
A pair of children's sneakers, put them in her bag and walk out of the store.
Mr. Hepburn approached the resistant Ms. Keegan and asked to see what was in her bag.
Ms. Keegan tried to just keep walking without stopping-- to which Mr. Hepburn felt that the only course was to grab her and throw her against the wall of the store.
He held her and told her that he knew that she had stolen the shoes and was going to call the police unless she gave them back.
The woman starts yelling:
Don't touch me! Get off me!
I'm pregnant! I'm pregnant!

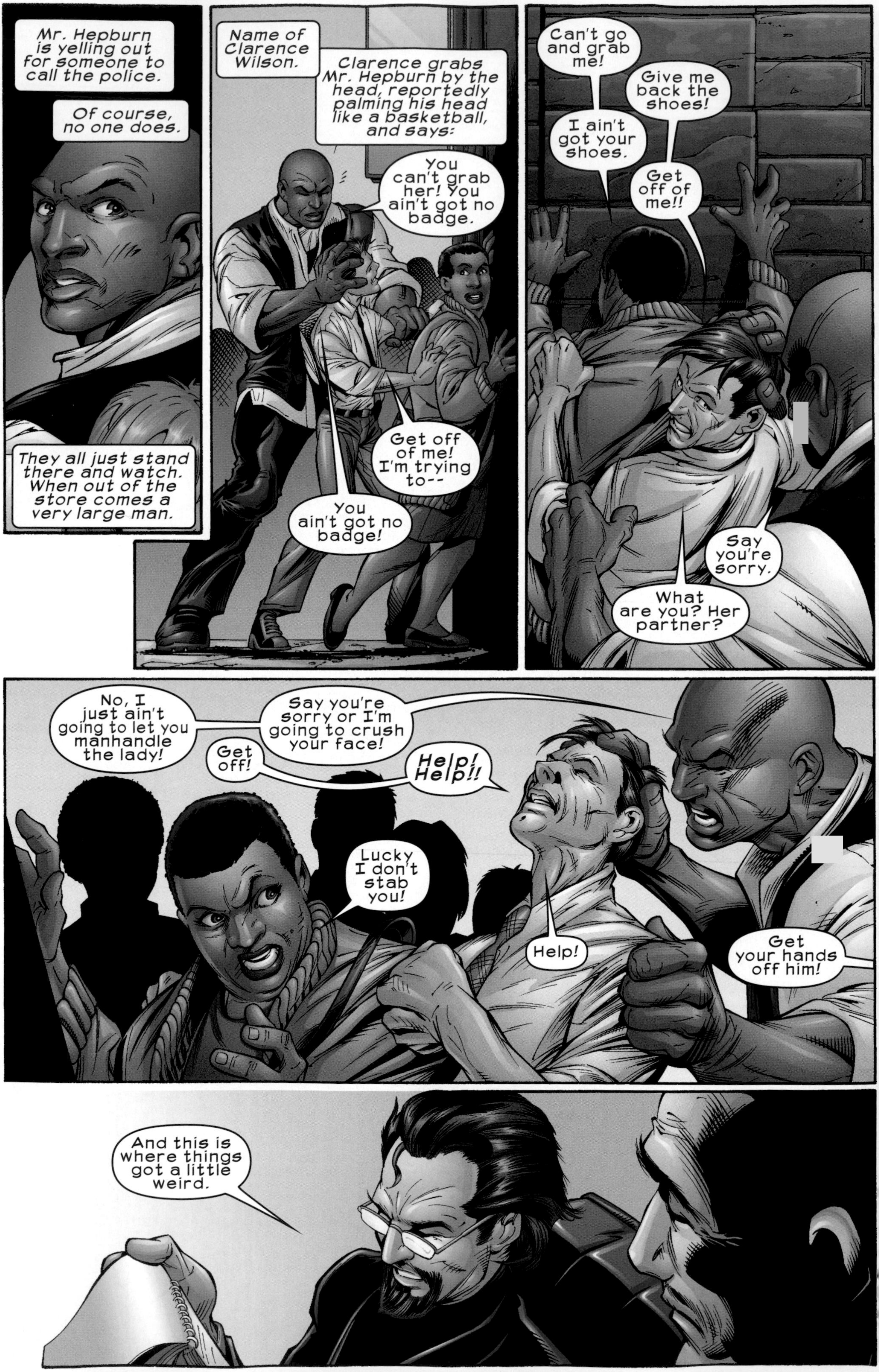
Mr. Hepburn is yelling out for someone to call the police.
Of course, no one does.
They all just stand there and watch. When out of the store comes a very large man.
Name of Clarence Wilson.
Clarence grabs Mr. Hepburn by the head, reportedly palming his head like a basketball, and says:
You can't grab her! You ain't got no badge.
Get off of me! I'm trying to--
You ain't got no badge!
Can't go and grab me!
I ain't got your shoes.
Give me back the shoes!
Get off of me!!
Say you're sorry.
What are you? Her partner?
No, I just ain't going to let you manhandle the lady!
Say you're sorry or I'm going to crush your face!
Get off!
Help! Help!!
Lucky I don't stab you!
Help!
Get your hands off him!
And this is where things got a little weird.

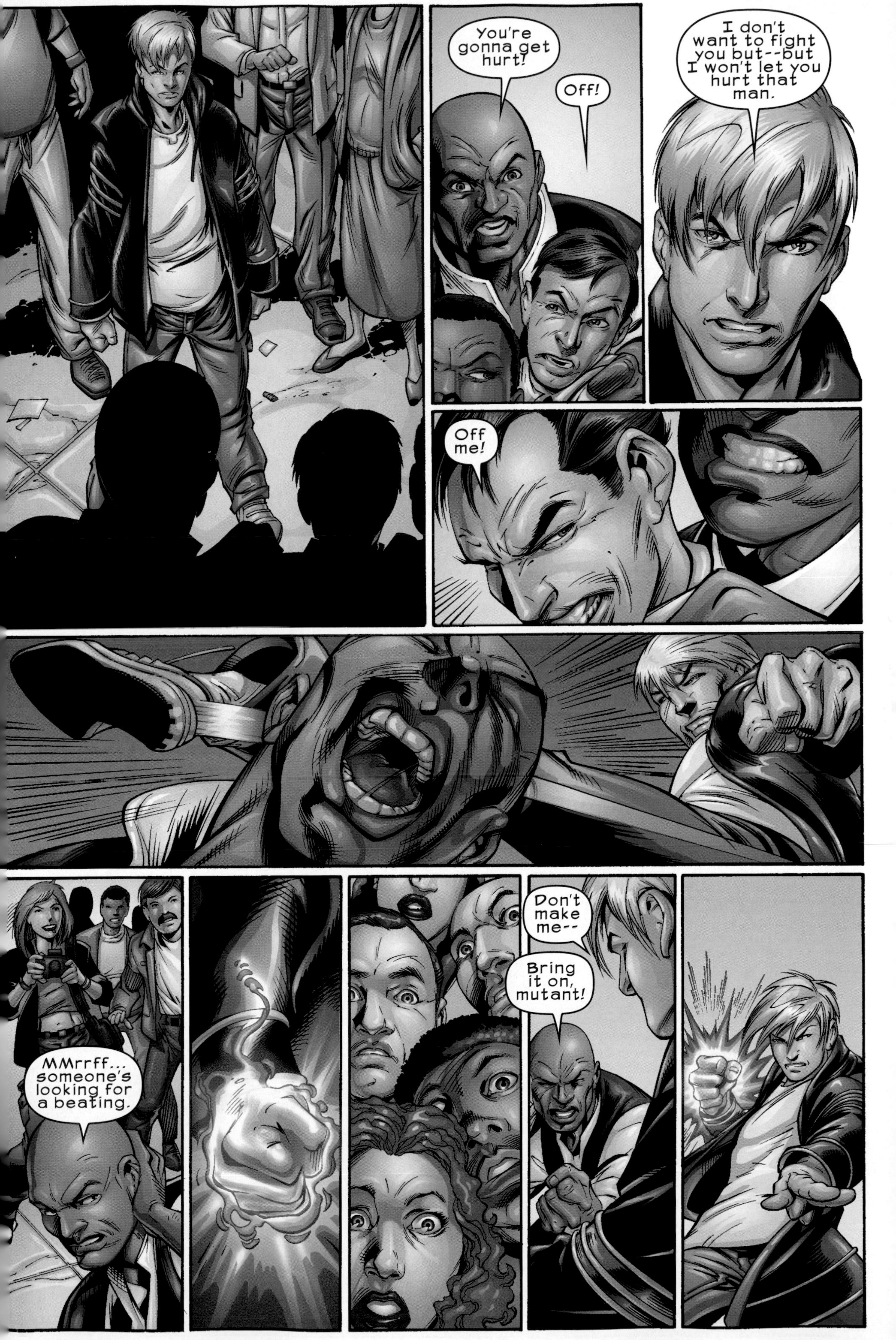

You're gonna get hurt!
Off!
I don't want to fight you but--but I won't let you hurt that man.
Off me!
MMrrff... someone's looking for a beating.
Don't make me--
Bring it on, mutant!

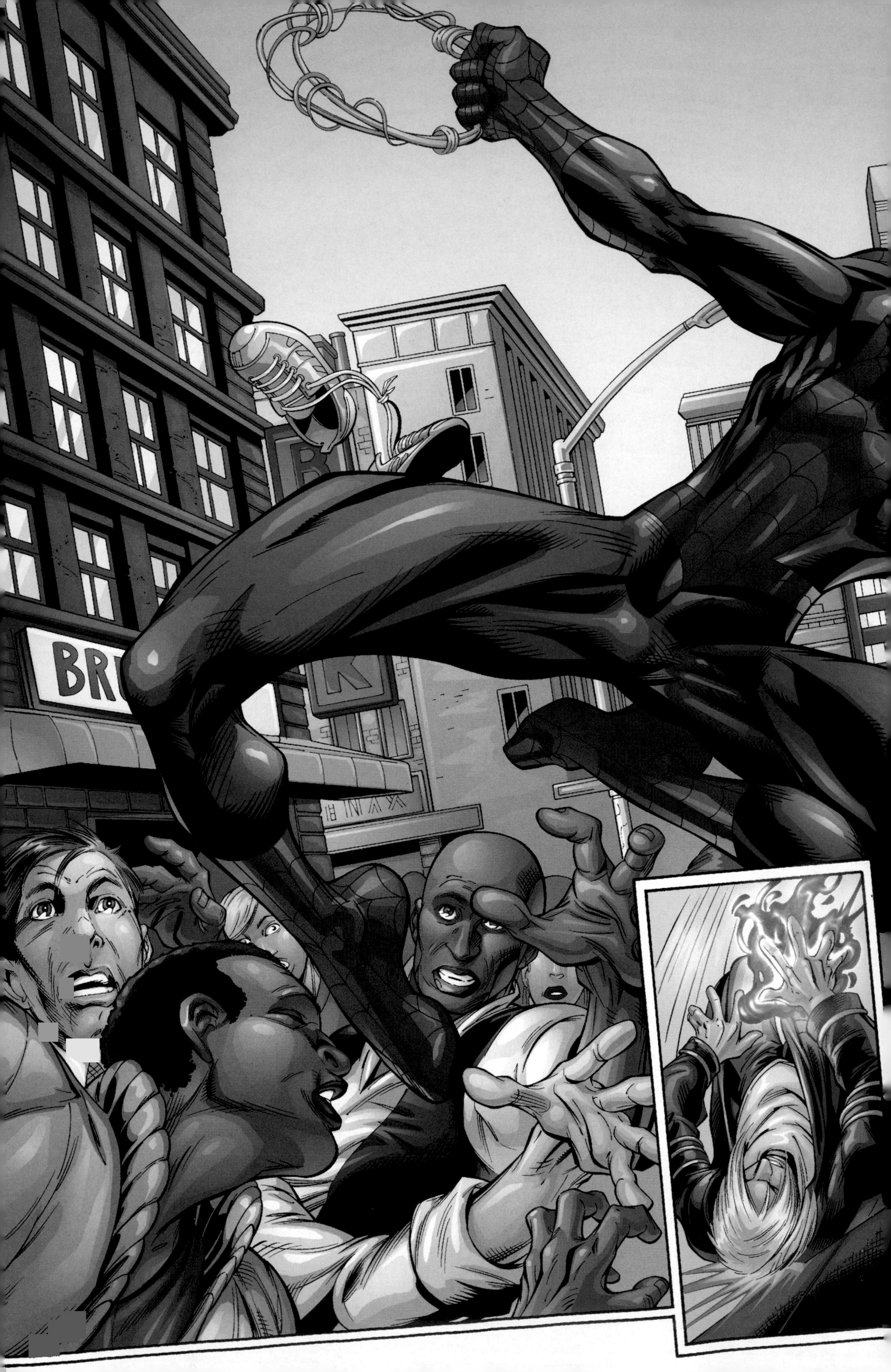
BR

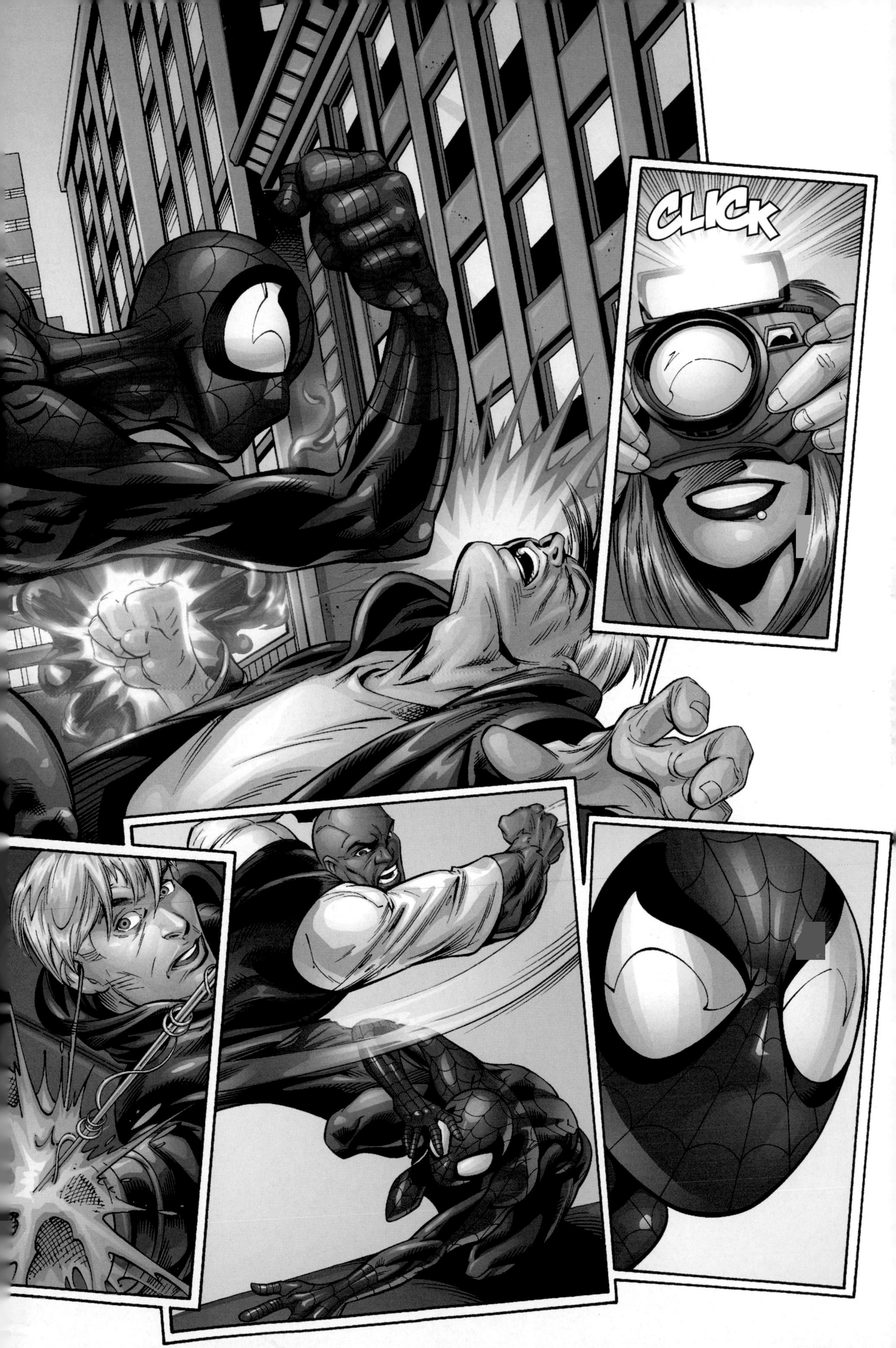
CLICK

Ha! Anyone talk to the guy with this glowing hand?

Well, he wouldn't return calls but a friend of mine at the precinct gave me a look-see at his statement. (Under the table. Of course.) Guy is named Danny Rand.

In his statement he said that he wasn't a mutant, but he did have 'abilities'.

"According to his statement, he has mastered the ability to focus his spiritual energy into an impervious fist of iron."

A martial artist?

I guess.

Says he focuses his chi? Chi. Anyone knows what that means?

No? Okay.

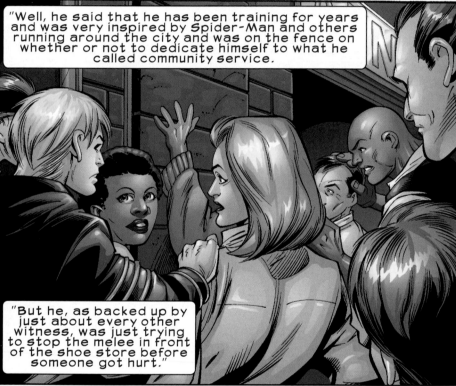

"Well, he said that he has been training for years and was very inspired by Spider-Man and others running around the city and was on the fence on whether or not to dedicate himself to what he called community service.

"But he, as backed up by just about every other witness, was just trying to stop the melee in front of the shoe store before someone got hurt."

Don't make me--

Bring it on, mutant!

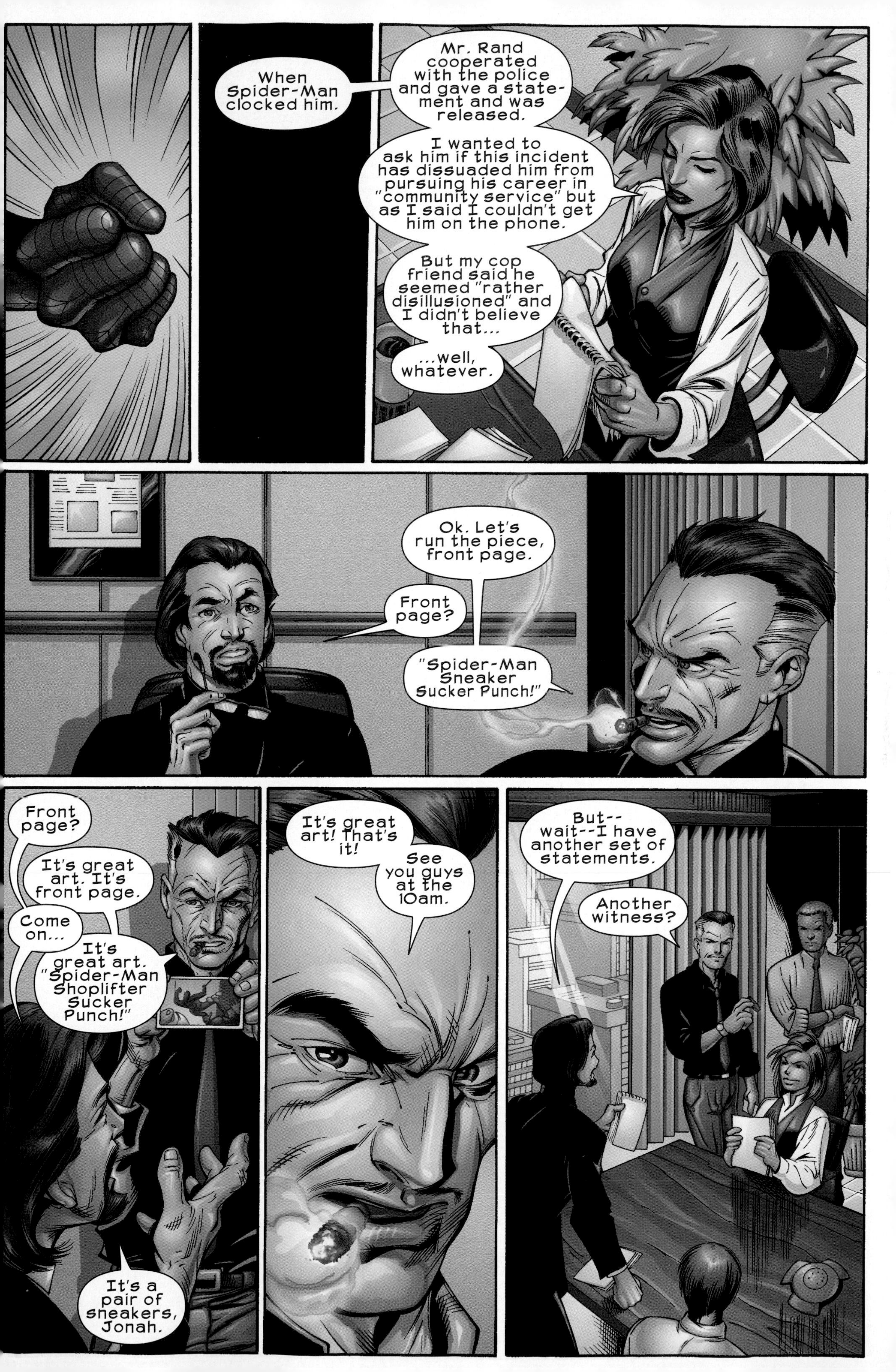
When Spider-Man clocked him.
Mr. Rand cooperated with the police and gave a statement and was released.
I wanted to ask him if this incident has dissuaded him from pursuing his career in "community service" but as I said I couldn't get him on the phone.
But my cop friend said he seemed "rather disillusioned" and I didn't believe that...
...well, whatever.
Ok. Let's run the piece, front page.
Front page?
"Spider-Man Sneaker Sucker Punch!"
Front page?
It's great art. It's front page.
Come on...
It's great art. "Spider-Man Shoplifter Sucker Punch!"
It's a pair of sneakers, Jonah.
It's great art! That's it!
See you guys at the 10am.
But-- wait--I have another set of statements.
Another witness?

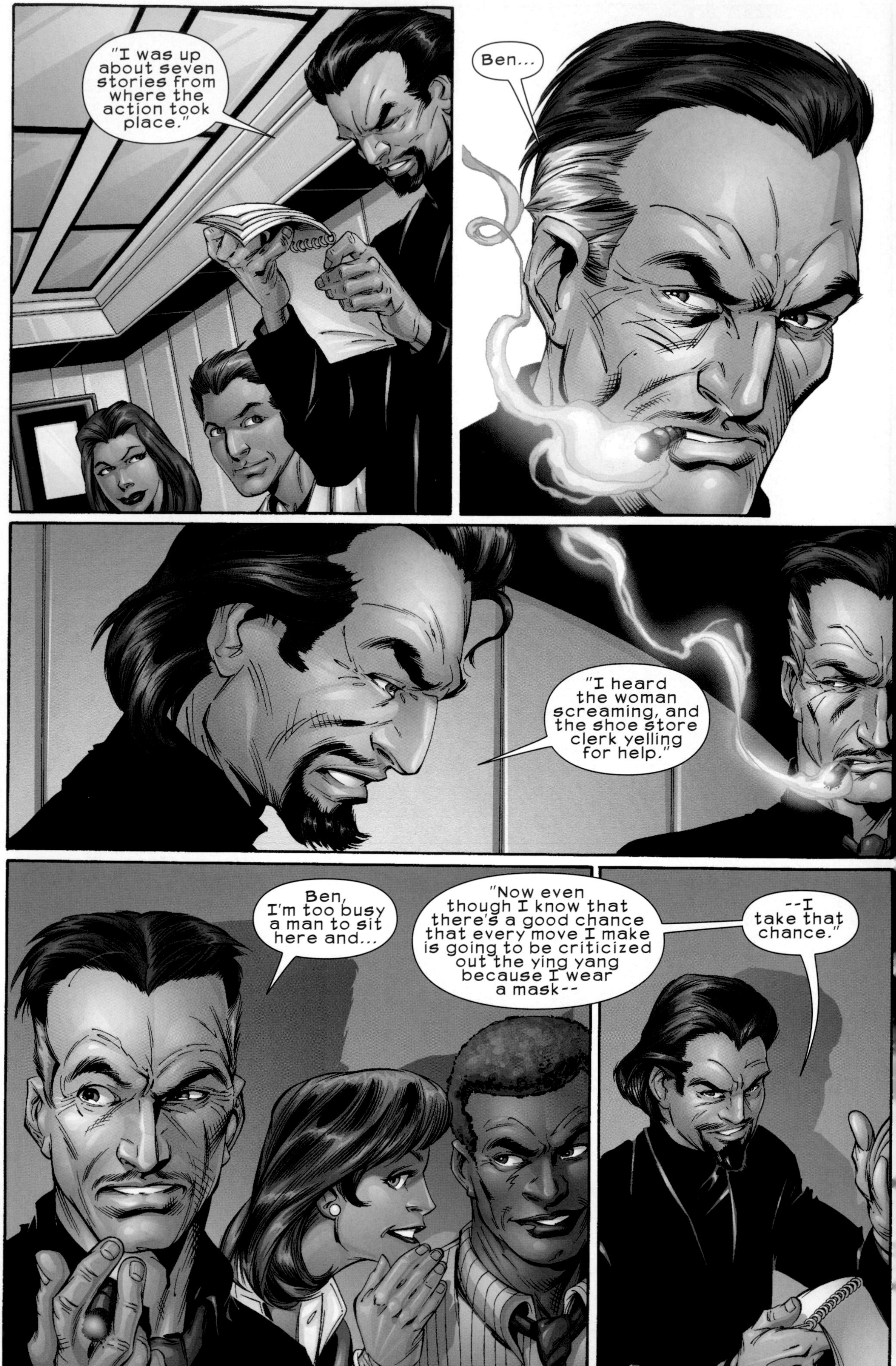

"I was up about seven stories from where the action took place."
Ben...
"I heard the woman screaming, and the shoe store clerk yelling for help."
Ben, I'm too busy a man to sit here and...
"Now even though I know that there's a good chance that every move I make is going to be criticized out the ying yang because I wear a mask--
--I take that chance."

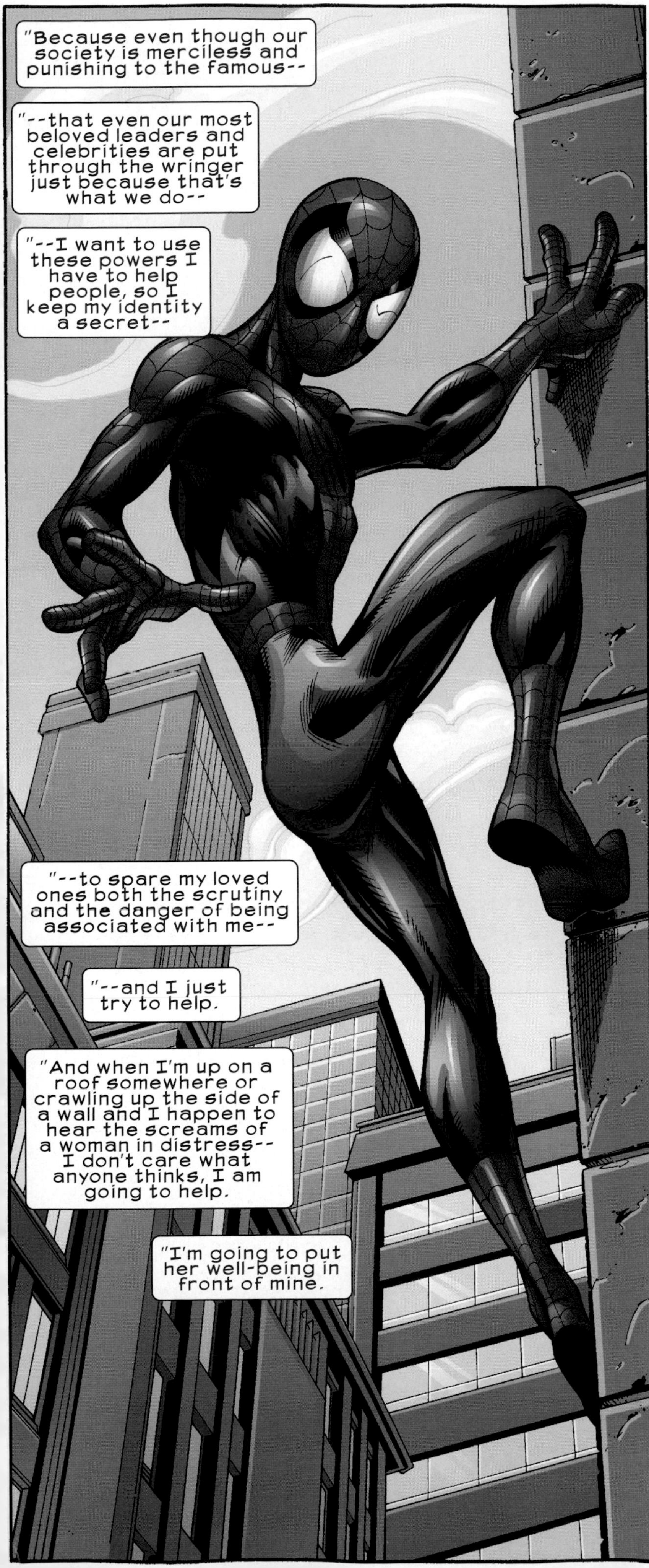
"Because even though our society is merciless and punishing to the famous--
"--that even our most beloved leaders and celebrities are put through the wringer just because that's what we do--
"--I want to use these powers I have to help people, so I keep my identity a secret--
"--to spare my loved ones both the scrutiny and the danger of being associated with me--
"--and I just try to help.
"And when I'm up on a roof somewhere or crawling up the side of a wall and I happen to hear the screams of a woman in distress-- I don't care what anyone thinks, I am going to help.
"I'm going to put her well-being in front of mine.

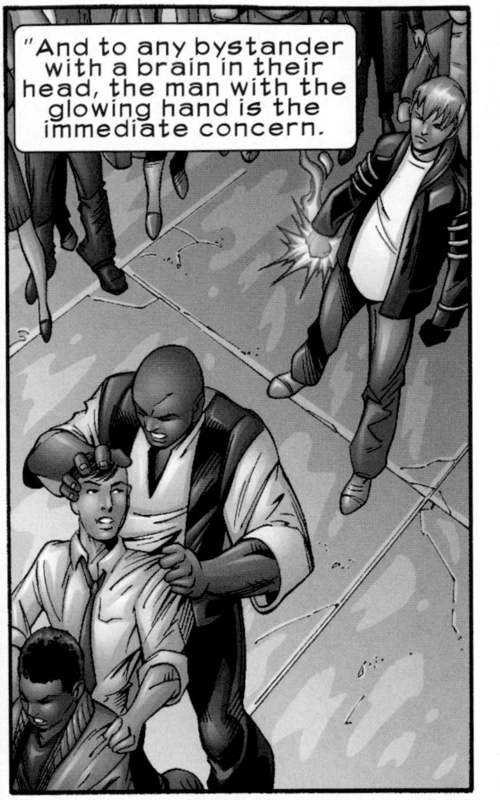
"And to any bystander with a brain in their head, the man with the glowing hand is the immediate concern.

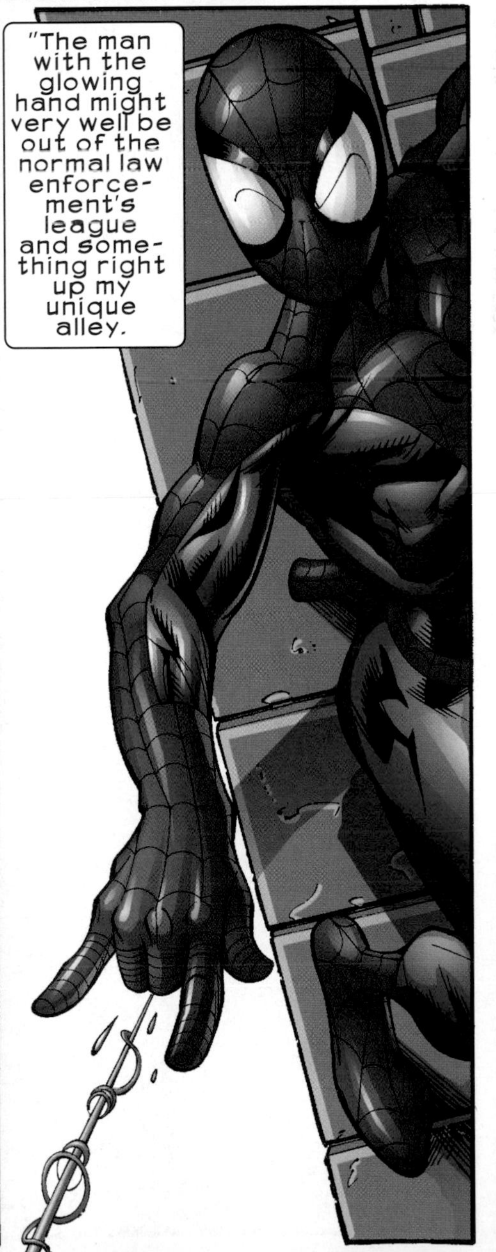
"The man with the glowing hand might very well be out of the normal law enforcement's league and something right up my unique alley.

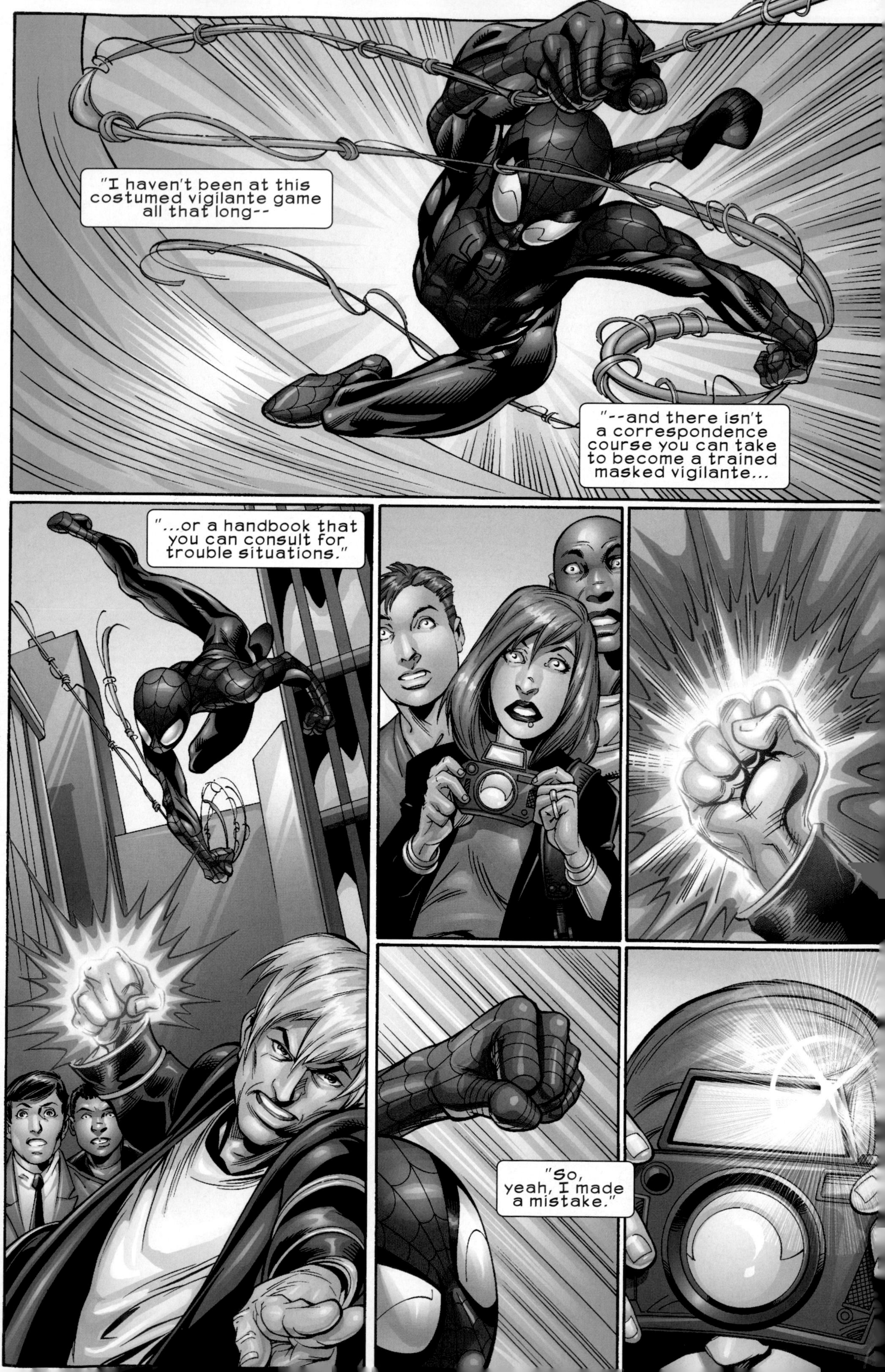

"I haven't been at this costumed vigilante game all that long--
"--and there isn't a correspondence course you can take to become a trained masked vigilante...
"...or a handbook that you can consult for trouble situations."
"So, yeah, I made a mistake."

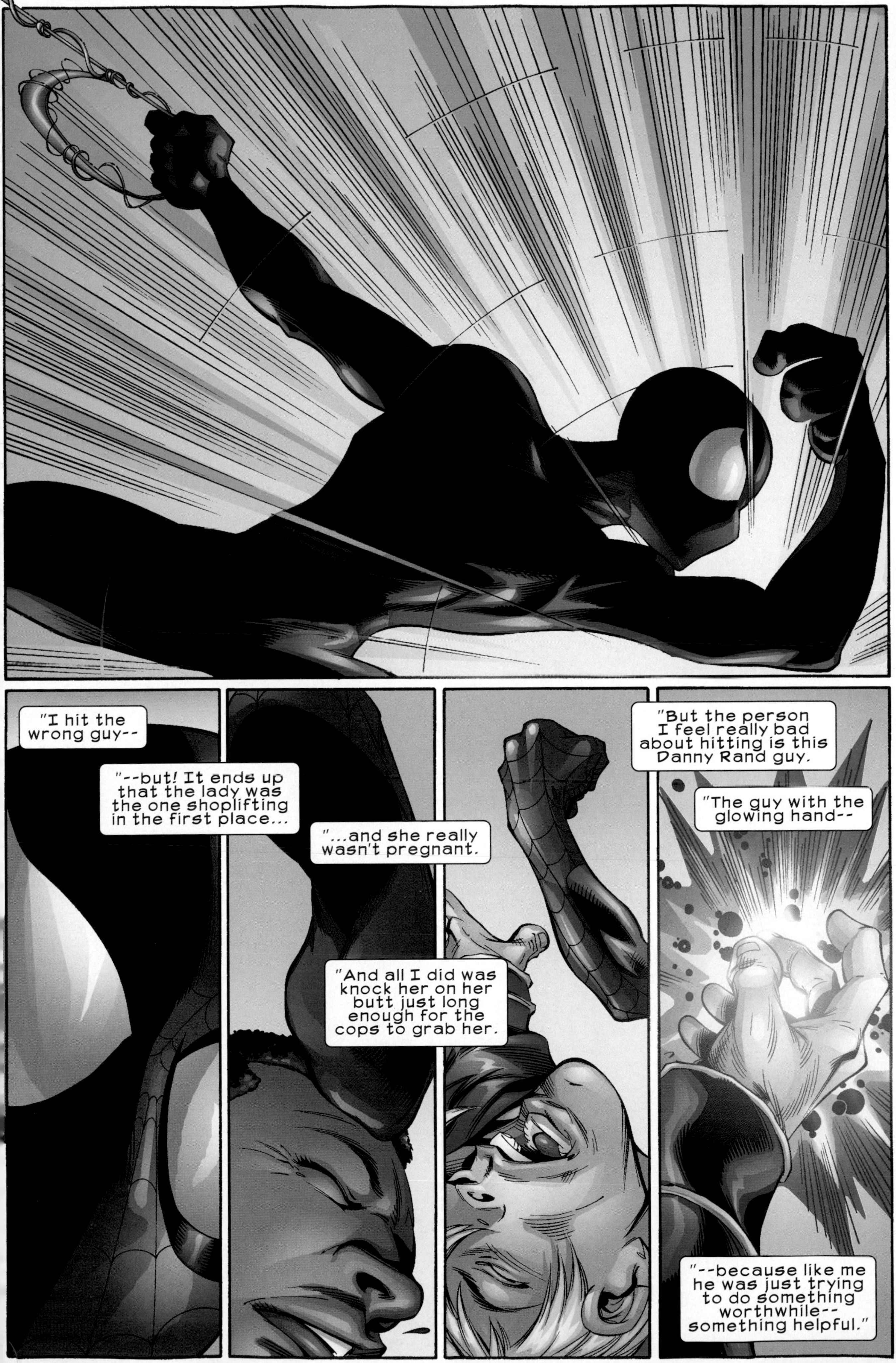
"I hit the wrong guy--
"--but! It ends up that the lady was the one shoplifting in the first place...
"...and she really wasn't pregnant.
"And all I did was knock her on her butt just long enough for the cops to grab her.
"But the person I feel really bad about hitting is this Danny Rand guy.
"The guy with the glowing hand--
"--because like me he was just trying to do something worthwhile--something helpful."

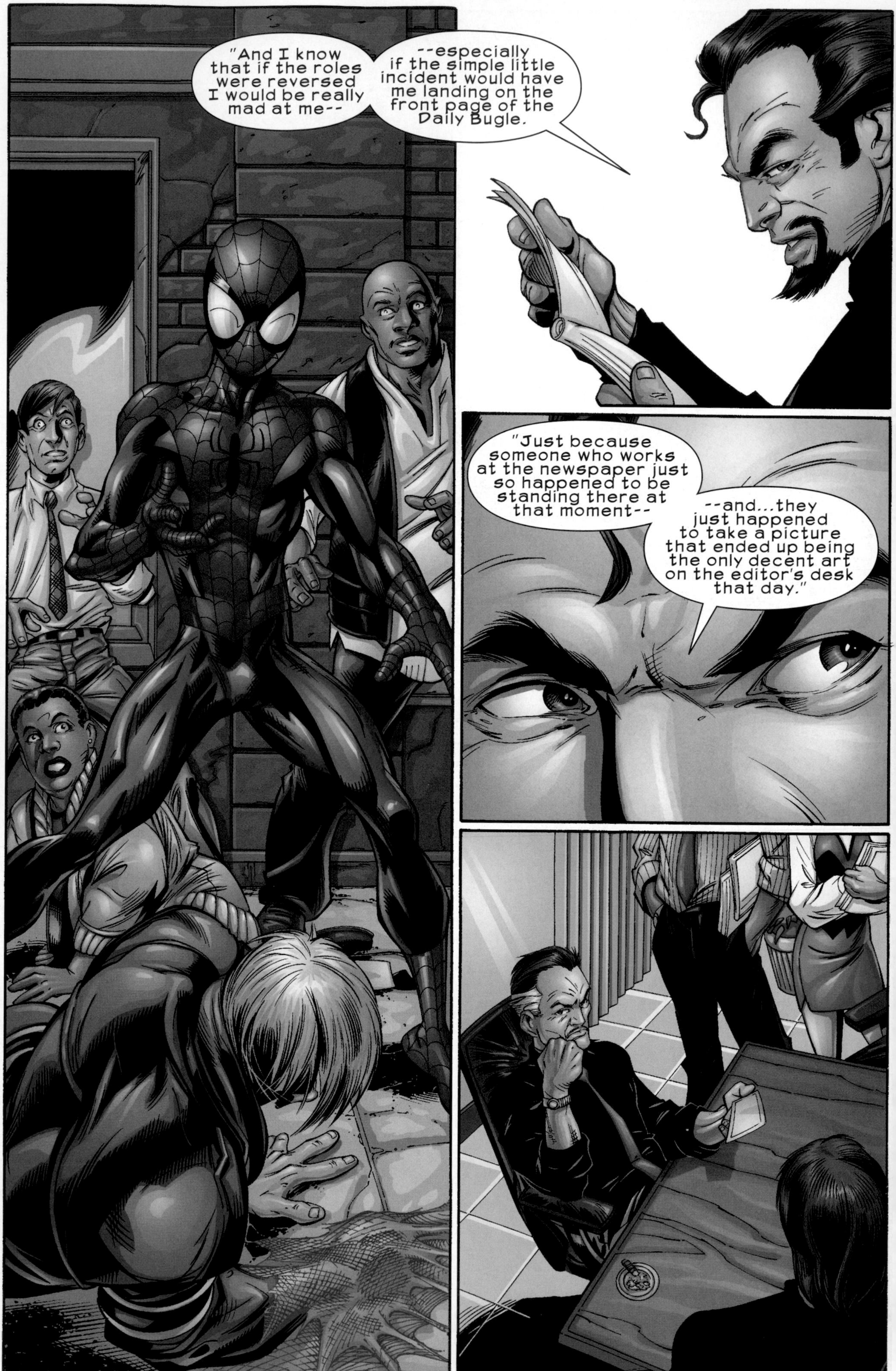
"And I know that if the roles were reversed I would be really mad at me--
--especially if the simple little incident would have me landing on the front page of the Daily Bugle.
"Just because someone who works at the newspaper just so happened to be standing there at that moment--
--and...they just happened to take a picture that ended up being the only decent art on the editor's desk that day."

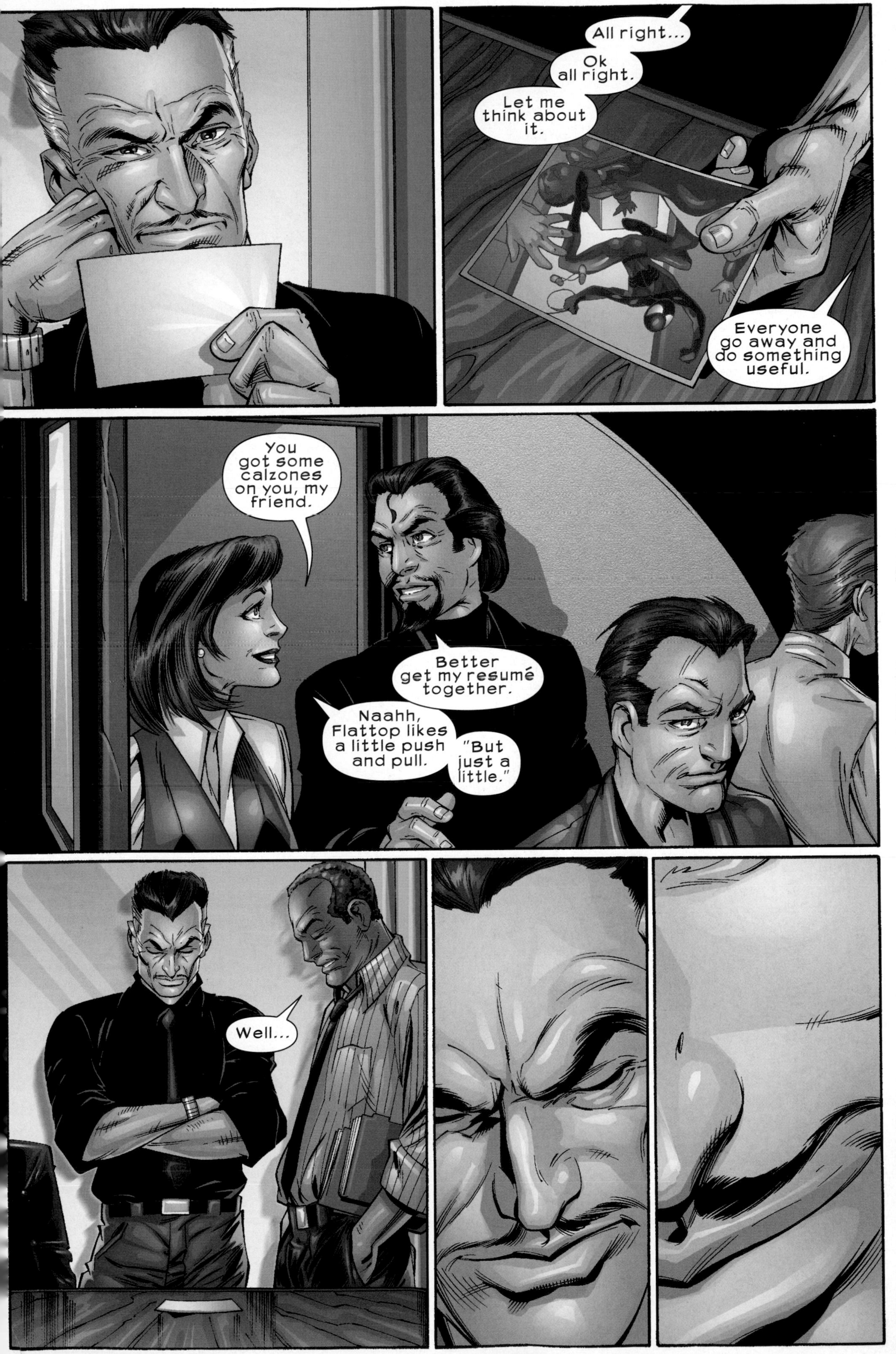
All right...
Ok all right.
Let me think about it.
Everyone go away and do something useful.
You got some calzones on you, my friend.
Better get my resumé together.
Naahh, Flattop likes a little push and pull.
"But just a little."
Well...

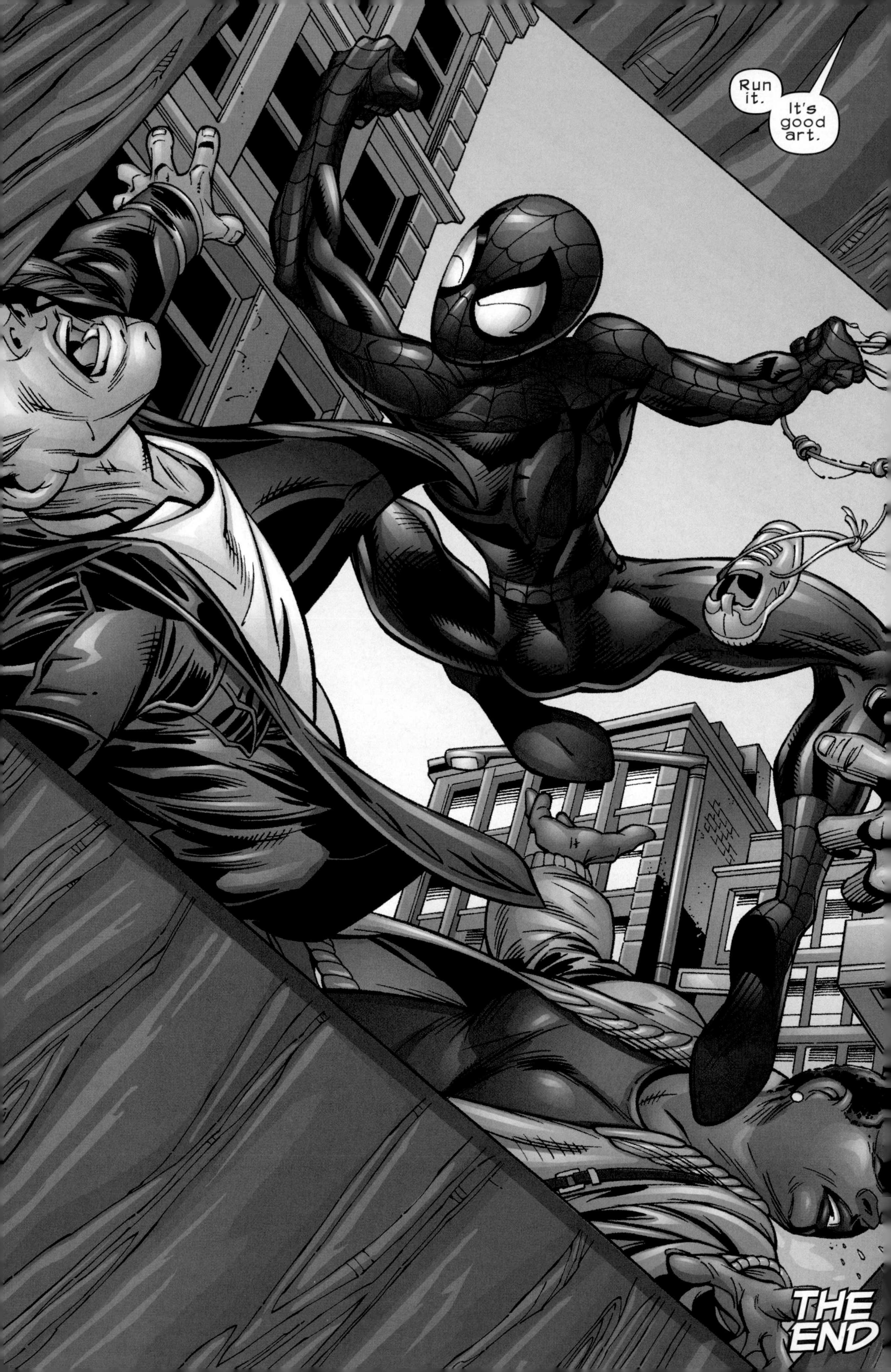
Run it.
It's good art.
THE END

BILL & BRIAN: A ONE ACT PLAY

BY BRIAN MICHAEL BENDIS

Brian, a thirty-something writer, is typing away in his basement studio. The phone rings. Brian looks at the clock. It's 5:30 in the morning.

BRIAN
Hello?

BILL
Brian, it's Bill Jemas.

BRIAN
Hey.

BILL
Very happy about where all the Ultimate titles are right now.

BRIAN
Yeah? Me, too.

BILL
Can you believe it? You're kicking ass.

BRIAN
I can't. No.

BILL
I have an idea. And I want to put it out there, and I want you to just let it sit out there.

BRIAN
OK.

BILL
You ready?

BRIAN
OK.

BILL
Venom.

BRIAN
Ugh. Venom sucks.

BILL
His costume is very cool.

BRIAN
His costume is cool. But he sucks. I hate the Secret Wars cosmic gobbity goo nonsense, what is that?

BILL
You should do an Ultimate Venom. You're exactly the guy to do it.

BRIAN
But I think Venom sucks.

BILL
That's why you're the perfect person to write him. If you can make him into something that would interest you, then you can convince all those people that agree with you that now he doesn't suck.

BRIAN
(pause)
I'll think about it.

BILL
Wouldn't it be cool if Eddie was a classmate, or someone from another school. Someone Peter used to be friends with. Or you know, if he was older, like a senior, or a college guy, someone for Peter to look up to. Like his parents used to be friends with Peter's parents.

BRIAN
(surprised)
...That's not a bad idea.

BILL
You know what would be very cool. If Venom came out of a mistake with Peter's webbing. Peter's father was trying to make Venom and he accidently made the webbing, or something—you can figure it out.

BRIAN
Actually, the father angle's a good angle, but not the webbing. You can't make the webbing into Venom because then every time he shoots a web or makes webbing, the audience will be thinking about Venom and his father. It'll take away from the story. Also, I like the little connection we have now with Peter and his dad and the webbing. I don't want to taint it with any super-villain crap. Way it should be is something really noble Peter's father was working on, and it accidently turned into Venom. Something noble turned into something horrible. And then his parents died soon after.

BILL
I like the webbing.

BRIAN
Trust me, the webbing is a bad idea. It causes more problems than we can solve.

BILL
Peter makes the webbing, but he doesn't know that he has made Venom.

BRIAN
It has to be something Peter's father was working on for Peter to look up to, to admire his father for even trying... like curing cancer or something.

BILL
Curing cancer is good.

BRIAN
Curing cancer! It'll tie into great power and great responsibility. You know how awesome it would be for Peter to find out his dad was trying to cure cancer...?

BILL
... But invented Venom instead.

BRIAN
And now Eddie is working on it.

BILL
Eddie has Venom.

BRIAN
But he doesn't know what it is. He thinks it's his legacy.

BILL
See, you're the guy to write Venom.

BRIAN
I hate Venom.

BILL
But you're the perfect guy for it. You just did it.

BRIAN
But I don't—

BILL
Oops, I have a meeting, gotta go, bye.

Brian looks at the phone, hangs up, sits and thinks.

BRIAN
A "Clone Saga" phone call is just three weeks away...

Hi Brian,

OK here goes, and this is me, so I have to give you the business end first. It would be great to get Venom started in the Ultimates because he is a hugely popular character that really has no place in what JMS is doing with *Amazing*. Kids really dig those Peter/Eddie and Spidey/Venom rivalries, and I could see Venom rolling around in your land. I'd also like to turn our licensees loose on Venom for toys and costumes and all that stuff.

And, because this is Ultimates (your baby now as much or more than it is mine — just think of this as a pitch/brainstorm).

Here are the threads that I'm trying to pull together.

What I was thinking is that the costume doesn't come from outer space, but is created by a scientific experiment. I'm thinking of a Frankenstein thing where the gist of the experiment is to bring the web fluid to life for two reasons — so that it can self-replicate and doesn't have to be refilled, and of course, because it could be a far superior material for the costume. But of course this goes way, way beyond what a high-school kid could possibly do in his basement.

So, enter Eddie the college kid. You know how in high school there were always a couple of guys from the local colleges who would sniff around the good-looking girls. At my school, for like three years running, the Prom Queens were going out with guys from Fordham and Montclair State. Charming and handsome enough for a high-school girl, but clearly *&^&^#ed in the head too much to appeal to a college girl.

What's fun for me is all the levels of intrigue.

I'm picturing Eddie sniffing around the girl of your choice — MJ, Gwen, Liz. Eddie tries to get to the girls by buddying up to Peter. Maybe, Peter and Eddie meet at the Bugle. Eddie strikes out with the college-age interns, so he worms his way into Peter's life to get at the high school babes.

Peter, honest as the day is long, has that night job as Spidey, so he has to be dishonest in that he doesn't tell Eddie what's going on, he just uses Eddie to get into the college lab. Eddie sees lots of what Peter is doing, but doesn't understand what's happening until the very end when, essentially, the costume attaches to Eddie and reveals all.

I also like this as the origin story for the black costume because the costume is really part of Peter much more than the alien could have been.

The love triangle, however we play it, would also be a blast so long as we choose a female who Peter either loves or wants to protect.

That's the general direction. And, as usual, I'm envisioning this being 80% high-school love triangle and soap opera and only 20% super stuff.

What do you think?

Bill

BEAT SHEET

BY BILL JEMAS

Hey Brian,

I would love to have you run at this. But I also have to put my publisher hat on and be clear and up front about one thing. The Eddie/Venom story should be a six-issue arc that revolves around Peter/Eddie, Spidey/Venom, and should make little or no reference to our ever-growing Ultimate continuity.

Joe and I don't agree on this by the way—he'd like to tie this back into the Green Goblin. But, Joe and I have agreed on one thing. When I know that I'm going to be inflexible on a certain point, then (rather than torturing everyone for two months and then pulling rank) I should just be clear from the outset.

So, the creative briefing here is that this story should focus on the main characters in the story and should have a beginning, middle and end. No Green Goblins, Doc Ocks or Kravens.

Beyond that the rest of this is springboard and brainstorm.

BEGINNING

Peter finds something wonderful and terrible in his father's notebooks. An experiment wherein the web fluid could be combined with animal DNA to give it "animated" qualities. Peter's father had dropped the experiment because it was too dangerous and was morally questionable (playing God etc.).

THE SUIT

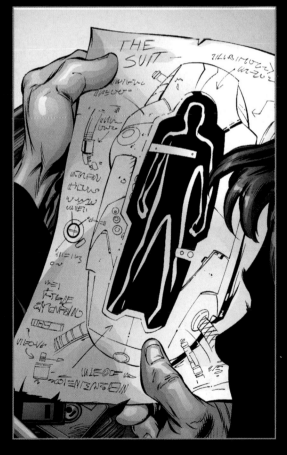

Peter feels his super-responsibility gives him super-authority to go beyond normal morals and goes on the hunt for the equipment he needs to make the organic fluid.

Eddie is an alienated/ lonely college sophomore. Nothing works for him; he lifts weights to look attractive to girls, but gets tongue-tied when a cutie asks him for help in the gym. He is very bright in class—but doesn't mix with his classmates. The key to this character for this purpose is that we all have to love/identify with him. He's very sweet, goes home to his parents' house for dinner. He's just sad and sweet.

Peter seeks out Eddie for access to the college lab.Eddie seeks out Peter for a path into the sweet land of high-school girls.

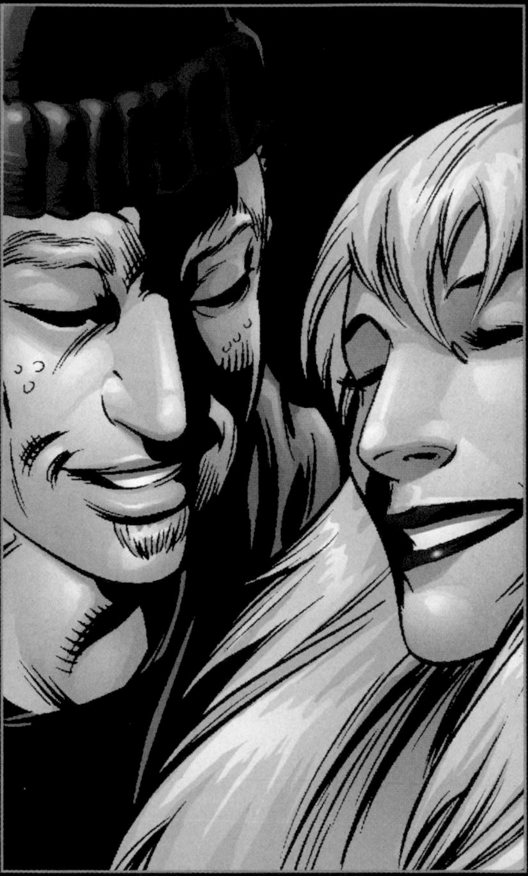

Peter and Eddie develop a happy and synergistic relationship, which will ultimately be undone by that secrecy and usury below the surface.

Eddie lets Peter into the college science world and the experiments start to work. Peter's secret is, of course, that he's Spidey and he's using Eddie for the costume. Things should go wrong between them when the experiment works. E.g., Peter has no choice but to run off with the costume, leaving Eddie to fail his class.

[Joe had this insane and wonderful image of the costume starting as a fetus – maybe the guys see it and maybe they don't. The costume/creature personality is of a spoiled, attention-wanting younger brother.]

Peter introduces Eddie to his friends, and they all like each other. But Eddie is not after Peter's friendship, he want to find love. And the love-triangle (With MJ or Gwen) breaks it all up.

END

The buddie movie goes bad.

Black Costume takes over Peter's life—you know that drill.

Eddie's relationship with the high-school girl falls apart—you know that drill too.

Peter dumps the costume, costume finds Eddie.

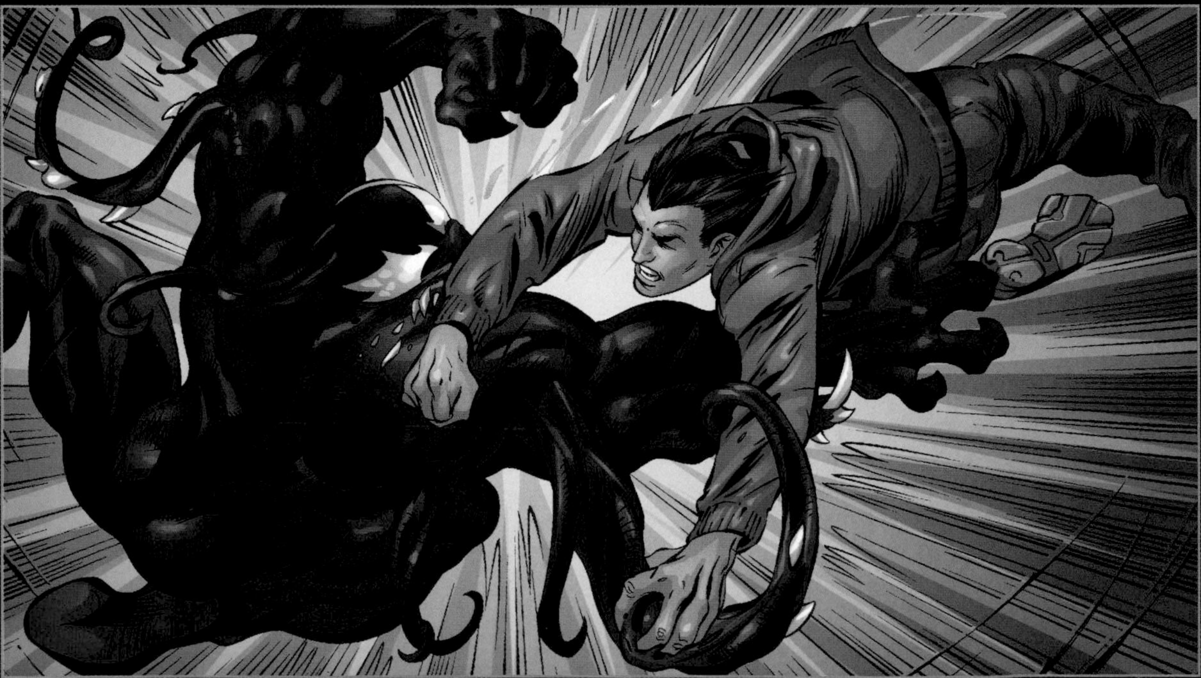

OUTLINE

BY BILL JEMAS

BEGINNING Books 1 and 2

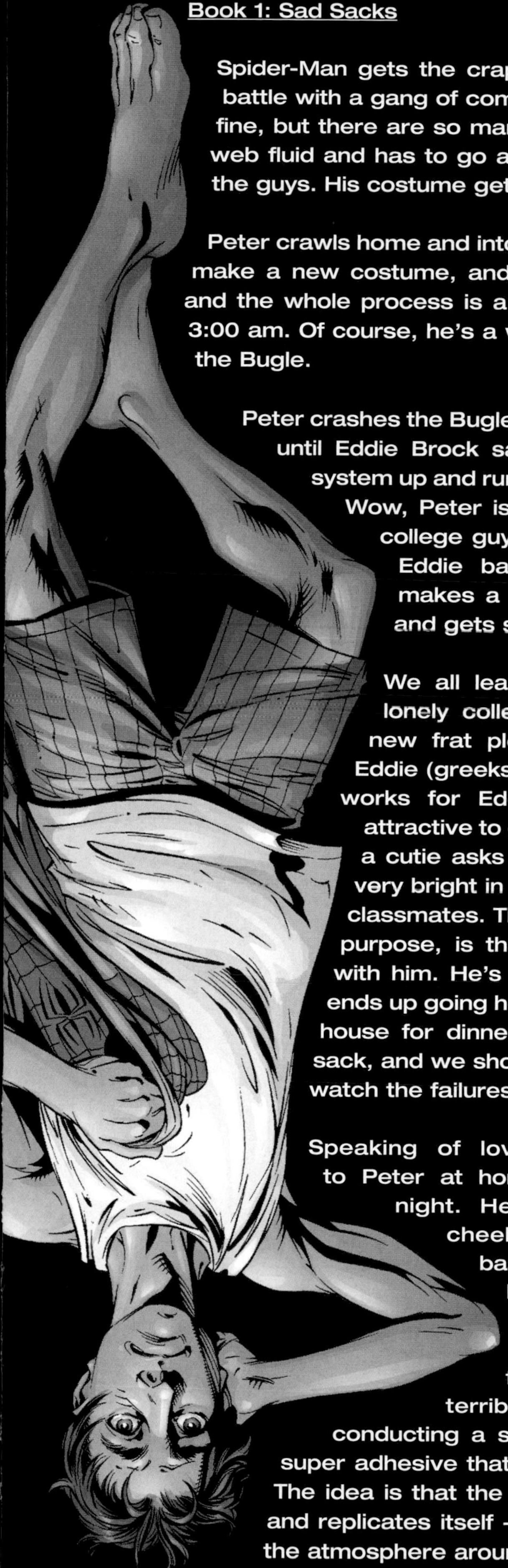

Book 1: Sad Sacks

Spider-Man gets the crap kicked out of him in a raging battle with a gang of common thugs. He starts out doing fine, but there are so many bad boys that he runs out of web fluid and has to go all hand-to-hand with the rest of the guys. His costume gets torn up and he gets pounded.

Peter crawls home and into the basement where he has to make a new costume, and back-up web fluid containers, and the whole process is a pain in the butt that lasts until 3:00 am. Of course, he's a wreck at school and a wreck at the Bugle.

Peter crashes the Bugle website, and JJJ goes ballistic, until Eddie Brock saves the day. Eddie gets the system up and running and covers Peter's tracks. Wow, Peter is very impressed with this cool college guy, and our readers get to follow Eddie back to his cubicle, where he makes a move on a cute college intern and gets slapped down..

We all learn that Eddie is an alienated/lonely college freshman. He lives with a new frat pledge who completely ignores Eddie (greeks don't mix with geeks). Nothing works for Eddie; he lifts weights to look attractive to girls, but gets tongue-tied when a cutie asks him for help in the gym. He is very bright in class - but doesn't mix with his classmates. The key to this character for this purpose, is that we all have to love/identify with him. He's very sweet, and very sad and ends up going home most nights to his parents' house for dinner. Eddie is a very lovable sad sack, and we should come to root for him as we watch the failures of his day-to-day life.

Speaking of lovable sad sacks. Pan back to Peter at home with Aunt May on Friday night. He gives her a peck on the cheek and heads down to the basement to study. Peter gets bored with schoolwork, and digs through a pile of his father's old notebooks. He finds something wonderful and terrible. Peter's father had been conducting a series of experiments with the super adhesive that Peter now uses for web fluid. The idea is that the fluid is alive on a cellular level and replicates itself - feeding off of the materials in the atmosphere around it.

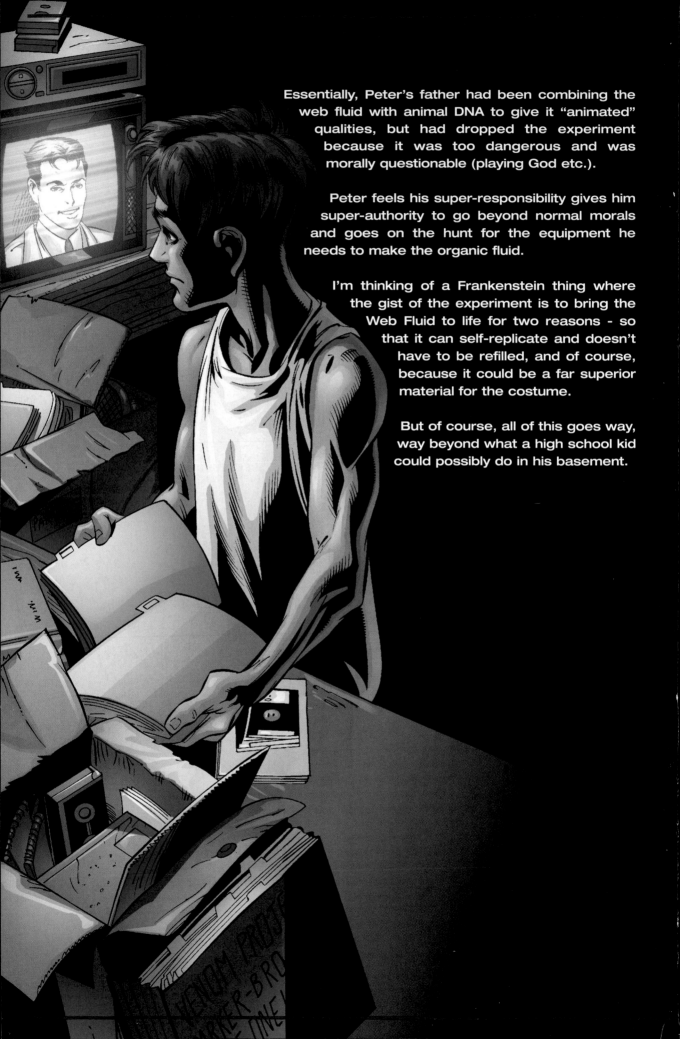

Essentially, Peter's father had been combining the web fluid with animal DNA to give it "animated" qualities, but had dropped the experiment because it was too dangerous and was morally questionable (playing God etc.).

Peter feels his super-responsibility gives him super-authority to go beyond normal morals and goes on the hunt for the equipment he needs to make the organic fluid.

I'm thinking of a Frankenstein thing where the gist of the experiment is to bring the Web Fluid to life for two reasons - so that it can self-replicate and doesn't have to be refilled, and of course, because it could be a far superior material for the costume.

But of course, all of this goes way, way beyond what a high school kid could possibly do in his basement.

Book 2: Symbiotic Relationship

Peter and Eddie start to hang out with each other. They are both good guys at heart, but on one level below the surface, they are using each other.

Peter uses Eddie to get access to college lab equipment. Peter shows Eddie his dad's notebooks, and suggests that they work together on the experiments as Eddie's freshman year biology project.

Eddie uses Peter to meet high-school girls. You know how in high school there were always a couple of guys from the local colleges who would sniff around the local girls. At my school, for like three years running, the Prom Queens were going out with guys from Fordham and Montclair State. Charming and handsome enough for an high school girl, but clearly *&^&^#ed in the head too much to appeal to a college girl.

And we layer in at least one more layer of intrigue.

Eddie goes hot and heavy after Gwen. She's too advanced for high-school boys, but too naïve to realize that Eddie is not particularly cool as college kids go. She also likes Eddie because her dad hates him and, well, because Eddie is head-over-heels in love with her and dotes on her every move. Peter introduces Eddie to his friends, and they all like each other. But Eddie is clearly using Peter as entrée into a new social life.

Peter may be honest as the day is long, but he does have that night job as Spidey. So he has to be dishonest in that he doesn't tell Eddie what's going on, he just uses Eddie to get into the college lab. Eddie is not nearly as smart as Peter, so he sees what Peter is doing, but doesn't fully understand what's happening until the very end.

THE BUDDIES Books 3 and 4

Book 3 – Buddies

Peter and Eddie develop a happy and synergistic relationship, which will ultimately be undone by that secrecy and usury below the surface. Peter's secret is, of course, that he is Spidey and he's using Eddie for the costume.

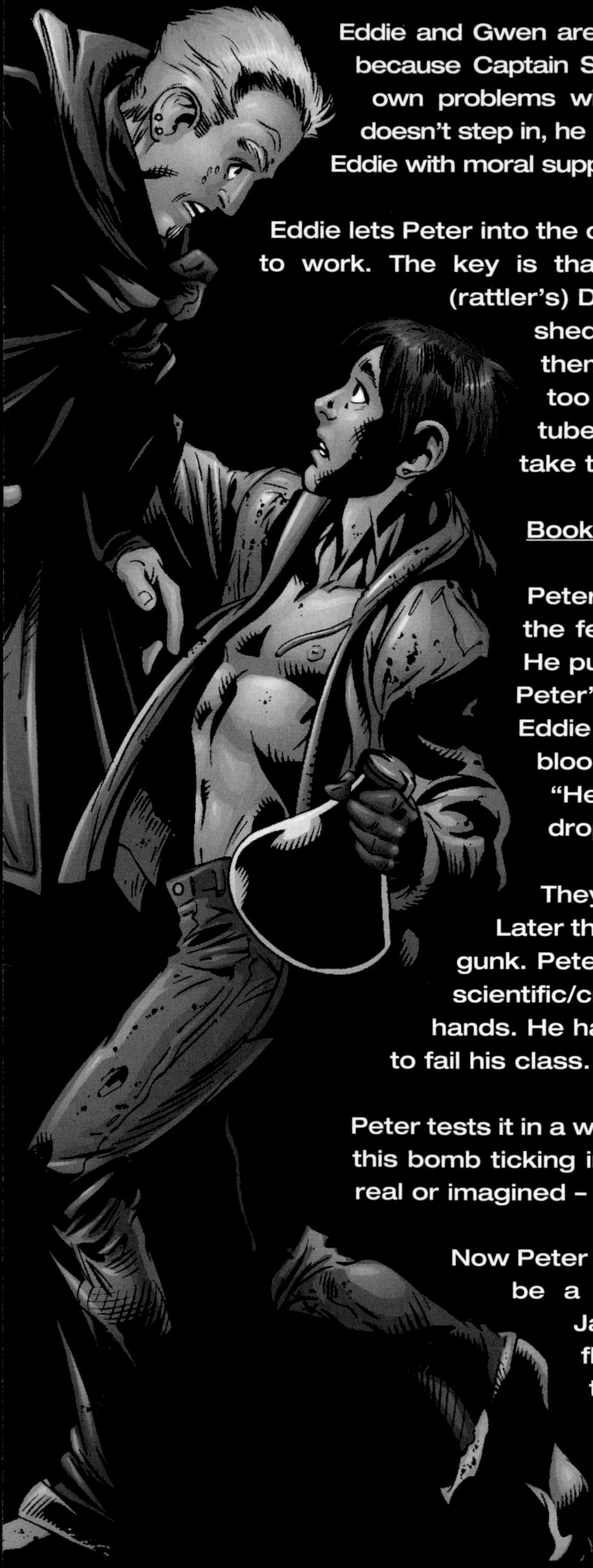

Eddie and Gwen are in love, but they have a Romeo and Juliet thing, because Captain Stacy can't stand Eddie. Moreover, Eddie has his own problems with Flash and Kong who rough Eddie up. Peter doesn't step in, he had his secret identity to protect, but he's there for Eddie with moral support.

Eddie lets Peter into the college science world and the experiments start to work. The key is that they use both human (Peter's) and snake (rattler's) DNA—you know how snakes constantly build and shed new skin. Things should go wrong between them when the experiment works. And it works all too well: not only does the fluid grow in the test tube (big freakin' test tube), but it actually begins to take the shape of a fetus.

Book 4 – Betrayal

Peter arrives at the lab early one morning to see that the fetus has grown to a child in a matter of hours. He pulls it out of the vat – and it liquefies right before Peter's horrified eyes. Then, two seconds later – Eddie shows up – with Peter's hands dripping black blood. Eddie has no idea what's up, so he says, "Hey cool, look at all of it – there was just a few drops yesterday."

They scoop up the stuff and put it back in the tube. Later that day, Peter sneaks out of the lab with all of the gunk. Peter doesn't want this thing circulating around the scientific/criminal community and getting into the wrong hands. He has no choice but to run off with it, leaving Eddie to fail his class.

Peter tests it in a web-shooter and it works great. But you still have this bomb ticking in the back of Peter's brain. Was the fluid fetus real or imagined – it couldn't have been alive – of course not.

Now Peter has the new fluid, and doesn't need Eddie. It will be a long, semi-scientific project, but, with Mary Jane's help, Peter learns to weave strands of fluid into a costume. We begin to lay the seed for the thrilling conclusion to the saga, as MJ and the costume and MJ and Eddie all get to know each other. Moreover, Eddie's relationship with Gwen falls apart, and Peter's staying out of it. On some level, he realizes that maybe Captain Stacy is right, a sixteen-

THE BLACK COSTUME BLAST Books 5 and 6

<u>Book 5 – The Clothes Make the Man</u>

Spider-Man does the town in his new black costume – now he's more super than ever. And every day he finds out new cool properties for the new cool costume.

This will be a carefree romp through black-costumed super powers. Peter finds that the costume generates its own webs, mends itself, and sometimes responds to Peter's mental commands.

While Peter is having a blast, Eddie is degenerating into a stalker. He's always hanging around the high-school, trying to get with Gwen. He's having trouble at the Bugle, and his roommate moves all the way out of the dorm room and into the fraternity.

At the end of Book 5, Spider-Man gets cornered by the police after stopping a crime. He's stuck in an alley (with a chopper overhead, and three police cars blocking his exit). Then the costume exhibits a spectacular quality – camouflage – it generates the pattern of the brick wall of the alley, effectively hiding Peter from the police.

<u>Book 6 – It's alive</u>

The costume has that famous life of its own. Each night, Peter goes to bed tired to the bone, after a full day of school and an early evening of crime stopping. As soon as he's asleep, the costume takes over, and goes out to continue the quest. Peter wakes more tired than he was when he fell asleep. And, he is constantly shocked to read in the Bugle about Spider-Man's exploits from the small hours of the morning.

Eddie gets fired from the Bugle, and has to move back home with his mom.

At the end of Book 6, Peter realizes what's going on and tries to abandon the costume. But the costume won't be going away easily.

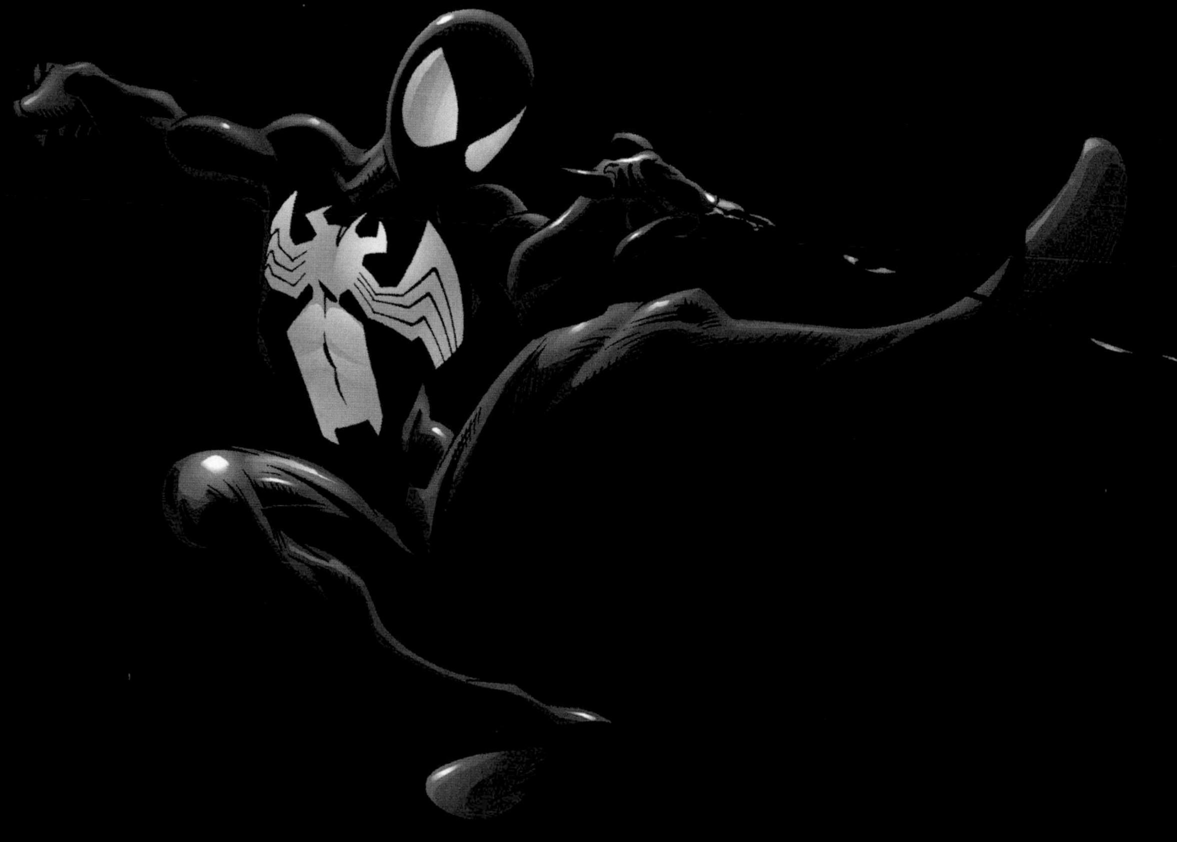

<u>Book 7 – Breaking Up is Hard to Do</u>

After Peter shuns the costume it finds its way to Eddie, who learns the entire "truth" of Peter's betrayal of both Eddie and the costume. In other words, the beauty of this whole story is the tangled web that Peter weaves when first he practices to deceive. He really does act badly toward Eddie and toward his father and to the costume. Our hero has a real flaw and it caused him true hardship.

Enter Venom. The symbiotic liquid is still a child looking for love. It senses the hole in Eddie's life, it finds much more comfort in its symbiotic relationship with Eddie—TA-DAA, ladies and gents, Venom!

<u>Book 8 – Battle.</u>

The costume even gives Eddie the ability to impersonate Peter. Eddie uses it to his advantage to go after Mary Jane. First in a weird and wired attempt to win her heart. But when she pushes Peter away—"what's gotten into you Peter?"—he turns into a full Venom and wants to kill her.

Battles and fun to follow.

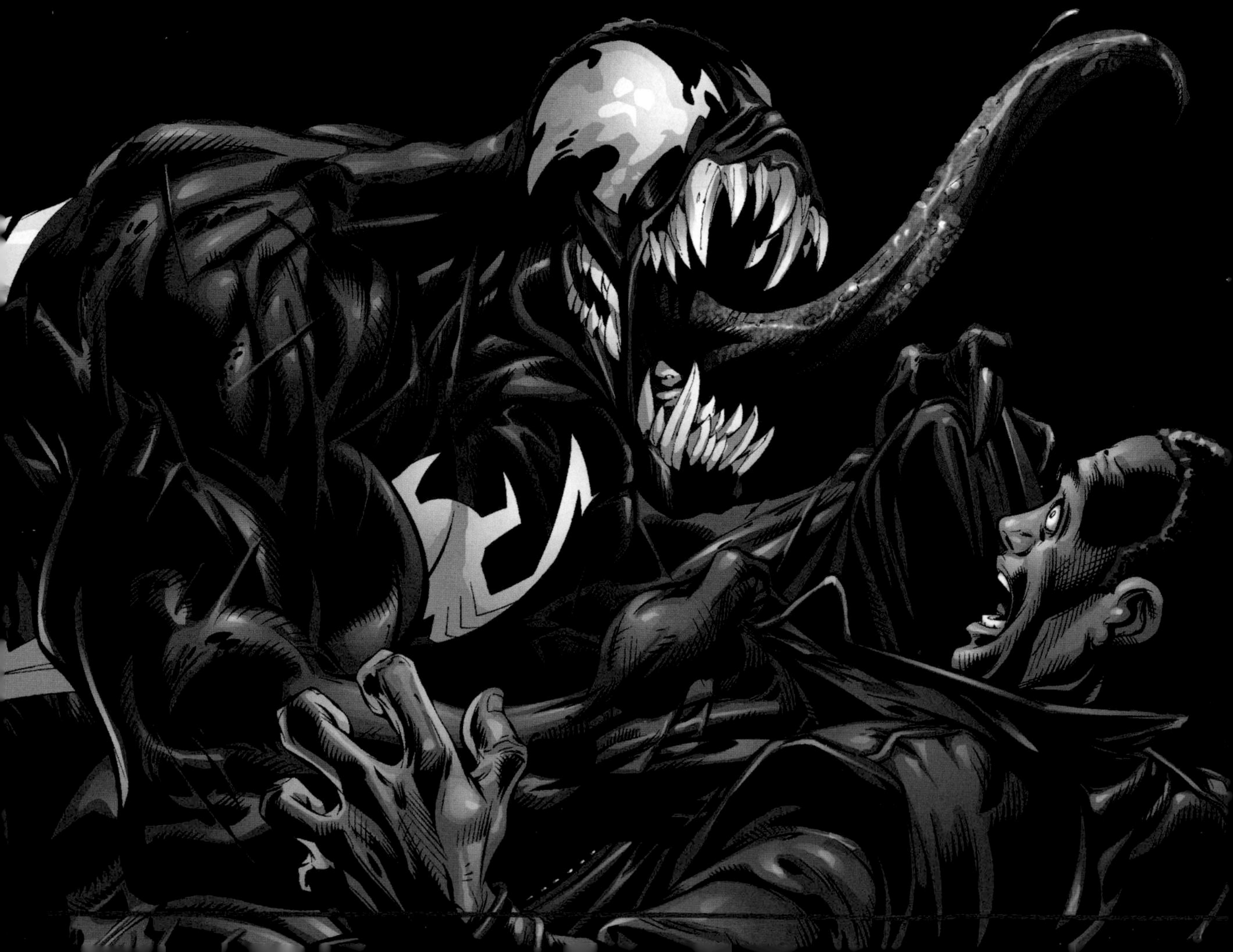

OUTLINE BY BRIAN MICHAEL BENDIS

VENOM ARC BY BENDIS

Issue 33: Peter finds a box of his father's belongings including an old videotape that takes him into his youth and to Eddie Brock. Peter goes to find Eddie, now in college. (Peter in five years?) Eddie shows Peter the bio invention both their fathers were working on. He calls it their "inheritance."

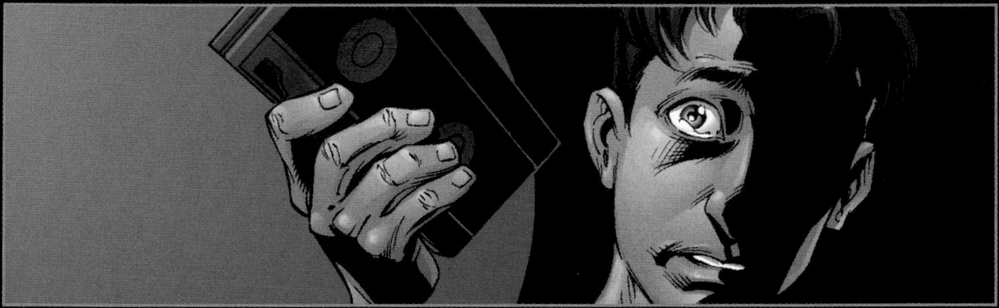

BILL JEMAS:
This introduction of Eddie is a flashback into newly made-up continuity. This is inconsistent with the fundamental creative briefing for the Ultimates.

Eddie should be a college student who also works at the Bugle, and Peter should seek him out for help - see below.

Issue 34: Peter and Eddie hang out. Become friends. Eddie is reliving high school like Rob Lowe in *St. Elmo's Fire*, hooking up with Gwen Stacy. They all become friends—maybe too quickly. But Peter can't stop thinking about this mysterious concoction of his father's invention.

Peter looks into his father's books and finds that his father was *this* close to finding a cure for cancer with this organic bio suit—but that the military wanted it as a bio weapon.

BJ:
CANCER-CURE BODY SUIT BIO WEAPON ??? This comes off as very contrived.

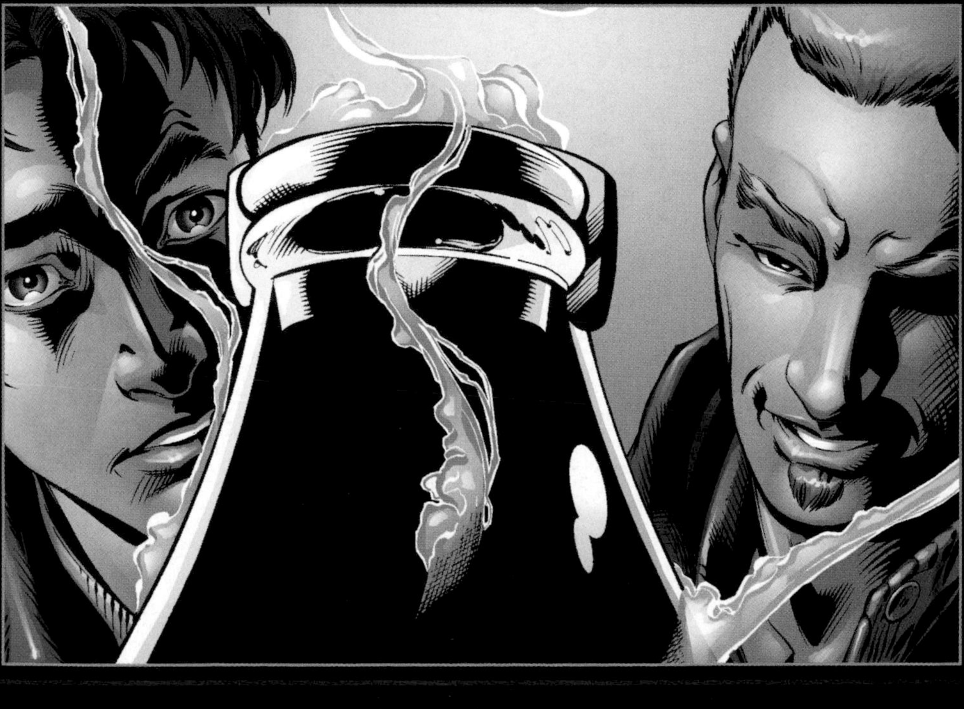

Peter meets Eddie
CANCER CURE BODY SUIT– bio weapon sticks to Peter's skin
Hi-jinx to follow

Something mysterious and bad happened around Peter and Eddie's parents' death because of this suit. Peter's dad learned the lesson that with great power, there must also come great responsibility.

JOE QUESADA:
Again, we are peeking at newly created back-story instead of watching a new story unfold. There is a big difference between typing "with great power, there must also come great responsibility" and telling a story that illustrates the point. This story doesn't have anything to do with that point. Let's talk about what the point of this story really is.

Spider-Man sneaks into the lab to examine the mixture only to have it inadvertently adhere to him. Into a powerful black Spider-Man costume.

BJ:
What we have now is Peter dealing with a series of unfortunate events. What should be driving the story forward are Peter's intentional decisions and actions, his steps and missteps.
Brian, I think you can do everything that you want to do, but in a much more organic framework.

1. Peter wants web fluid that doesn't run out and/or a more resilient costume.

2. He doesn't have the facilities/equipment he needs at home, so seeks out and uses Eddie to get it.

3. Eddie is a lonely geeky college kid who will use Peter to get back into the high-school world.

Are these two guys really friends, is there symbiosis? Or are they just mutual parasites? This is the core Black Costume/Venom theme.

OK, once you get going in this direction, you can certainly take some dips into father-father history, and play with sci-fi issues. I'm not crazy about that theme, but if you want to explore it, you can certainly do it. I just ask that you have the science unfold in a more orderly progression. For example you could build an entire issue of this series on the following:

We know that the fluid that Spider-Man uses in his web derives from a formula that Peter's father had developed when he was alive.

Dad could have been working on a formula to create a new living skin. You could mix the formula with the DNA of a burn victim, apply it to the area and create a new healthy skin.

Peter's dad was a chemist; Eddie's dad was a biologist – they had agreed to work together.

Was this symbiosis?

Well not really, because Eddie's dad was going to snatch the formula and sell it to the military as a body armor.

Peter's dad stops it –Eddie's dad gets killed.

I think that hits all the back-story points that you want to get to as well. I would request that if we go this direction, we do it as one self-contained issue, as opposed to clues mixed into the main story. In other words, it would be best to tell this whole back-story, let the reader know what happened, and watch Peter and Eddie figure it out. Of course, you might want to hold back the Eddie's dad death part as a reveal for everyone.

With respect to the creation of the Black Costume, there is so much more to do. I was thinking that rather than working in a college lab, they should "borrow" stuff from Eddie's college and bring it back to Peter's basement. Peter is justifying the theft by making the leap from great power and great responsibility to great personal privilege. Peter embraces the "power has its privileges" moral and makes some very bad decisions that really bite him in the ass.

With the above set up, we can use a lot of lab stuff that Joe had come up with. Including the black costume fetus growing in the big test-tube in Peter's office.

Also, with them working in Peter's basement, Peter can be doing most of the work while Eddie searches through old papers and pieces together the story of their fathers.

Finally, if they are working in Peter's basement, it is easy for Eddie and Gwen to run into each other. In fact, Peter can ask Eddie to keep Gwen busy and out of his hair as he works on the experiment.

JOE QUESADA:
Brian – I like 35-38, although it might work better as three issues. What I would suggest is a three-issue setup (including one whole issue dedicated to the dads) and a three-issue conclusion.

Issue 35: The black costume makes Spidey very powerful. It accentuates all his Spidey traits and powers. Peter is also amazed that he can physically feel his father's presence in the suit. (The suit was created using his father's DNA.) Almost the entire issue is a burst of Spidey action. Spidey doing good. Big action sequences. But the costume is also bringing out Spidey's darker side in a bigger way as well. He almost kills a bad guy but catches himself. Also, the costume is made from his father's DNA and the intoxication of being so close to his father is impossible to let go of...

Issue 36: Spidey does let go of the bio suit. He expels it. But even off his body it starts to haunt his psyche, it has attached itself to him. Mentally and physically. Peter lets it go. He is so creeped out that he warns Eddie to destroy the formulas and then stops returning Eddie's phone calls. Gwen and Eddie don't work out either. Peter and Gwen both cut him off making him feel like a loser again. Eddie left alone with the reactivated Venom is surprised to have it attached to him. He is Venom. And he is pissed.

Issue 37: Venom fights Spidey right on the football field at school. Venom wins because Peter is reluctant to fight—especially when he realizes it's Eddie and that Eddie knows he is Spider-Man. All the bio info is now a part of the Venom suit. The venom suit tells Eddie that Peter's dad is responsible for his own dad's death. Venom is going to kill Peter.

Issue 38: Spidey takes the fight to the skies. A rainy electrical storm. Spidey reluctantly destroys Venom. Eddie disappears with the suit. A shallow victory at best. Peter watches his father's video one more time, his father confessing how much he is looking forward to his son turning into a man.

"ORIGINS"

BY BRIAN MICHAEL BENDIS

E.S.U.

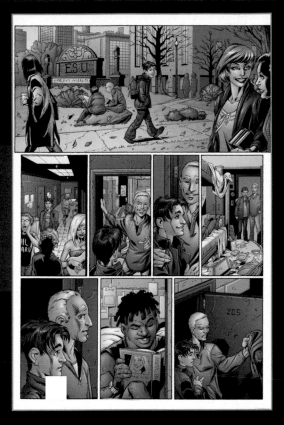

***ULTIMATE SPIDER-MAN* #33**
PAGE 16

1- Ext. Empire State University--
late day

Wide shot of the campus courtyard. Think NYU.

Peter Parker, his backpack over his shoulder, looks around campus with a beaming smile.
Aah, that first time on campus. It's exciting-- adult. It feels a little rebellious.

Peter is looking around amused-- he can't wait to get to college.

Interesting young people all over the place, a skateboarder careening his way to class, a couple of dreadlock girls in army pants playing hacky sack. Coffee everywhere.

PETER PARKER NARRATION
Oh man, I cannot wait to get to college.

Look at this-- College is people making important life decisions, self-discovery-- whoah... check her out.

Hobidooby!

2- Int. Empire State University dorms--same

Peter is walking down a crowded/borderline chaotic dorm hallway. He is walking away from us but he is turning back to see a hot young girl standing in her open dorm doorway strumming a guitar. Peter is momentarily in love with her.

PETER PARKER NARRATION
Oh my god--- this is how these people live?

How do they get any work done? eee--- what's that smell?

This entire place smells like a--- Whoah... check her out.

3- Peter is at the door, about to knock, when Eddie Brock swings open the door. He has a short buzz cut and a bad zoot hair growth under his upper lip. Eddie is all smiles-- very friendly. Very into this meeting. His enthusiasm keeps Peter a little quiet. Peter is still amused by it though.

EDDIE BROCK, JR.
Hey!!! There he is!

Look at you! You're all growed up!

4- Int. Eddie's Dorm room-- same.

In the doorway-- two shot. Eddie puts his arm around Peter, pulls him tight to his side in a manly way and brings him into his room. Peter is a little overwhelmed by Eddie but amused.

5- From behind the two of them. Eddie shows Peter his unbelievably small shoebox of a dorm room-- and he has a roommate.

A rasta-haired, pissed-off artist's type. They have bunk beds. There is crap everywhere, books, pizza boxes, beer cans, clothes. Science books, beakers, an easel, drawing pads. Brushes, posters, Patsy Walker bikini poster on the wall.

The roommate clearly doesn't like Eddie and doesn't even look up to smile at Peter. A crappy college roommate.

6- Same as three, but Peter is wincing. This is a horrible place to live. The reality of campus life.

    EDDIE BROCK, JR.
    Well it's not much...but, you know, it's not much.

7- Tight on the pissed off roommate reading in his bed. He doesn't even look up from his book when he mutters.

    ROOMMATE
    A little young for you, ain't he, Brock?

8- Eddie takes his arm off of Peter and growls to his off panel roommate.

Peter doesn't know what that crack means. Eddie's enthusiasm just deflates at the reminder of what a short end of the stick he drew in the roommate lottery.

    EDDIE BROCK, JR.
    Such an-- god!

    PETER PARKER
    Who is that?

    EDDIE BROCK, JR.
    That's the short end of the dorm room roommate stick.

    ROOMMATE
    Right back at ya.

    EDDIE BROCK, JR.
    Let's go get some coffee. Coffee?

PAGE 17

1- Int. STARBUCKS- late day
Peter and Eddie sit at a small table in front of a coffee shoppe window-- later day. They are talking quietly.

We can't actually show the STARBUCKS logo for legal reasons but make it look like your typical mainstream coffee franchise.

There's a smattering of people doing their coffee thing, reading, writing, talking.

    EDDIE BROCK, JR.
    ...astrophysics. So now I'm in the bio-engineering program.

    PETER PARKER
    Really, that's wow. That's going to be my major too.

    EDDIE BROCK, JR.
    Wow, aren't we two pieces of work.

    PETER PARKER
    What do you mean?

2- Over Peter's shoulder. Eddie plays with his coffee and laughs at his own observation.

EDDIE BROCK, JR.
Two little ghost chasers-- me and you.

Trying to impress our daddies.

3- Over Eddie's shoulder. Pete sips his Coke innocently and doesn't agree with Eddie's observation.

PETER PARKER
Well, I--

I read some of my dad's papers and I - I really believe in his work.

4- Similar to two-- Eddie waves off the perceived insult. He isn't trying to point a finger. He sees that Peter doesn't see his point.

EDDIE BROCK, JR.
No, I do too.

I mean at first I'm sure I was trying to-- I don't know-- relive my dad's... something. Right?

But I really do believe in what they were doing because, let me tell you...

If I didn't... bio is a crapload of reading to be into it for the wrong reason.

5- Two shot. Peter smiles and tries to bond with Eddie on this point, but Eddie waves him down. Eddie knows how much more college is than high school

PETER PARKER
Oh, yeah, I know--

EDDIE BROCK, JR.
No, no you don't.

No one prepares you for this workload.

They assign us three chapters a night. A hundred pages a day.

Plus you have to have at least one job.

Because Books-- Books alone are a fortune.

6- Eddie is counting all the craziness of his life on his fingers as he bitches to Peter.

EDDIE BROCK, JR.
And this city pretty much guarantees that you aren't going to be able to afford taking a girl out on a proper date unless you're one of those Wall Street guys...

...and who the hell wants to be one of those.

You got like a girlfriend or something?

PAGE 18

1- Peter's heart is on his sleeve; he slumps in his seat.

PETER PARKER
I did.

2- Eddie sips his coffee.

EDDIE BROCK, JR.
Did?

3- Peter starts to talk but he stops himself. It's too embarrassing.
4- Eddie wants to hear it.

EDDIE BROCK JR.
Come on. What happened?

5- Peter can't help but launch into it. His wounds are fresh and he still has the wind knocked out of him.

PETER PARKER
She just-- I just-- we broke up and it-- it just happened and I don't think it's sunk in yet.

But the thing is-- I really-- she's my best friend and I can't believe she'd just...

6- Eddie smiles at him. Slightly condescending-- he can't help it.

7- Peter looks away. Still wounded from the breakup.

8- Same as 6.

EDDIE BROCK, JR.
Man, high school.

Let me tell you something that I wish to God someone would have said to me...

All this stuff-- this stuff you're feeling... This girl that-- that girl this...

Five years from now--

Not fifty not a hundred--

Five years from now... you won't even remember her name.

Swear to God.

PAGE 19

1- Peter looks at him. These words are both shocking and a real eye opener.

EDDIE BROCK, JR.
This stuff, it's sooo important to you now... oh, the drama.

It only hurts this much now because you have nothing to compare it to.

It's all just training wheels, man. It all fades away.

2- Eddie points at Peter-- he means his words. Words to live by.

EDDIE BROCK, JR.
When real life starts-- when real life starts you'll know it.

Trust me.

Ah see, I know you think I'm full of it-- but it's true.

3- Peter shrugs.

PETER PARKER
I guess.

It just...

4- Eddie looks off-- smiling to himself.

EDDIE BROCK, JR.
If I could go back to high school.

Man, I would have played it all differently.

PETER PARKER
Like...

EDDIE BROCK, JR.
I just... would have sat back and not tried so hard.

5- Peter thinks about it. Wondering if he is trying too hard.

6- Eddie snaps out of it and bursts with false excitement. Gesturing towards Peter with a big smile.

EDDIE BROCK JR.
Man, look at you!

This is so off the scale weird.

7- Peter smiles at Eddie.

EDDIE BROCK, JR.
You're from, like, a lifetime ago.

And here you are.

PAGE 20

1- Eddie turns surprisingly dour, leaning forward, admitting this...

EDDIE BROCK, JR.
I think back then--

Sometimes it's--it's hard to even picture my mom's face. You know?

Sometimes it takes a while.

PETER PARKER
Yeah.

2- Peter looks at him and totally understands what he is saying. Peter gently pulls the videotape out of his knapsack and puts it on the table.

EDDIE BROCK, JR.
I look at the pictures and I go OK, that's them.

But sometimes I worry that I'm not remembering them right--

It's-- ugh-- it's hard to explain and I'm doing it badly.

3- Eddie doesn't know what it is and Peter did it so timidly it confuses him.

EDDIE BROCK, JR.
What's that?

4- Eddie picks up the tape as Peter gently explains himself.

PETER PARKER
It's a video of your parents.

It's all of us at a picnic. It's-- it's the reason I looked you up.

I thought you'd want a copy.

5- Eddie looks at it like it's the lost ark. His mouth drops.

> EDDIE BROCK, JR.
> Wow.

6- Peter smiles politely.

7- Eddie looks at Peter like a long lost brother.

> EDDIE BROCK, JR.
> That's about the nicest thing anyone has ever done for me.

8- Peter shrugs off the compliment modestly.

> PETER PARKER
> Well...

9- Eddie looks at him. He is deciding to show him something.

> EDDIE BROCK, JR.
> You know what?
>
> I have something to show you too.

10- Peter squints-- he doesn't know what this look is about.

PAGE 21

1- Ext. Empire State University/science center-- night
It's early evening on college campus. Very quiet, no one is around. A couple of lights are on and that's it.

The building sign in the foreground clearly reads: Reed Richards Science Center

2- Int. Science Center-- hallway
Tight on Eddie fiddling with the locks of a high tech laboratory door

3- Int. Science Center laboratory-- same
Eddie and Peter are standing in the doorway of a very dark lab. A couple of red and green machinery lights show us that there are working machines in the dark. Peter and Eddie silhouette in the doorway.

4- Same angle-- Eddie has turned on the light to show an amazing high tech display of modern equipment, very clean, very white. Peter is stunned by the huge, state of the art bio laboratory.

Pete is having a geek orgasm as Eddie gestures to the high ceiling in wonder. The back wall is a series of small metal freezer doors-- it almost looks like a morgue.

Every student has their own high tech freezer to keep their projects in, each one labeled or tagged, each one has a lock.

> PETER PARKER
> Hell yeah.
>
> This is-- this is not high school.

5- Eddie is sticking another key into a small metal freezer door with a lock on it. It does look like a morgue.

> EDDIE BROCK, JR.
> But that's not what I wanted to show you.
>
> This is what I want to show you.

6- Eddie is about to open the door, but he turns back and smiles at Peter. Peter might be nervous that he is being shown a dead body.

    EDDIE BROCK, JR.
    This, this is something...

7- Eddie opens the door and frozen air steams into the dry open air of the lab. It's dry ice steam. It surprises Peter but not Eddie.

8- The steam blocks Peter's view of what he is being shown. Peter squinting and waving the steam away from his face.

PAGE 22

1- Over Peter's shoulder. The steam is giving way. We see the beginning of some kind of black shape.

2- The steam clears. Peter squints to figure out what he is looking at.

3- Over Peter and Eddie's shoulder looking down at a bowl sized beaker style glass container. A round cup full of flat black liquid. Just flat black liquid.

4- The round beaker in the foreground. Eddie and Peter both lean down to look at it. Frost billowing.

Half of Eddie's face is warped in the container's reflection. Peter doesn't get it.

    PETER PARKER
    What is that?

    EDDIE BROCK, JR.
    It's our inheritance.

To be continued

VENOM DROWNS
BY BRIAN MICHAEL BENDIS

Brian Michael Bendis originally considered having Peter Parker destroy the Venom suit by drowning it. After rethinking the scene, he scrapped it in favor of Peter incinerating the suit. The following is Bendis' original rough cut.

PAGE 16

1:   INT. Peter digs in the basement storage.
2:   He pulls out a metal toolbox. Shot from behind Peter looking down at the red metal toolbox.
3:   He wraps the Venom jar in thick bubble wrap leftover from a computer part he ordered.
4:   Peter gently puts the bubble-wrapped jar in the box.
5:   Tight shot on Peter locking the box.
6:   Peter puts on his dirty hood again and sneaks out of the house.
7:   EXT. Atlantic Ocean/Manhattan pier. Night. Peter is at the end of the pier holding the box like he is about to scatter his father's ashes.
8:   Peter looks at it one more time.

PAGE 17

1:   Peter throws the toolbox as hard as he can.
2:   It lands hundreds of feet away.
3:   Peter recovers from the throw.
4:   The toolbox bobs in the water.
5:   Same, the toolbox sinks
6:   The toolbox is gone, bubbles pop up as the toolbox floats.
7:   It's gone.
8:   Peter is sad.

Ultimate Spider-Man #36, Pages 16-17, final story and art.

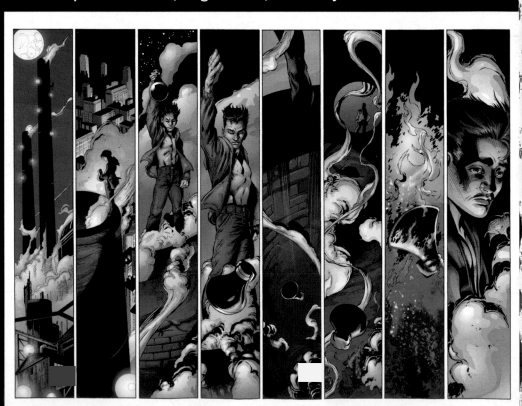

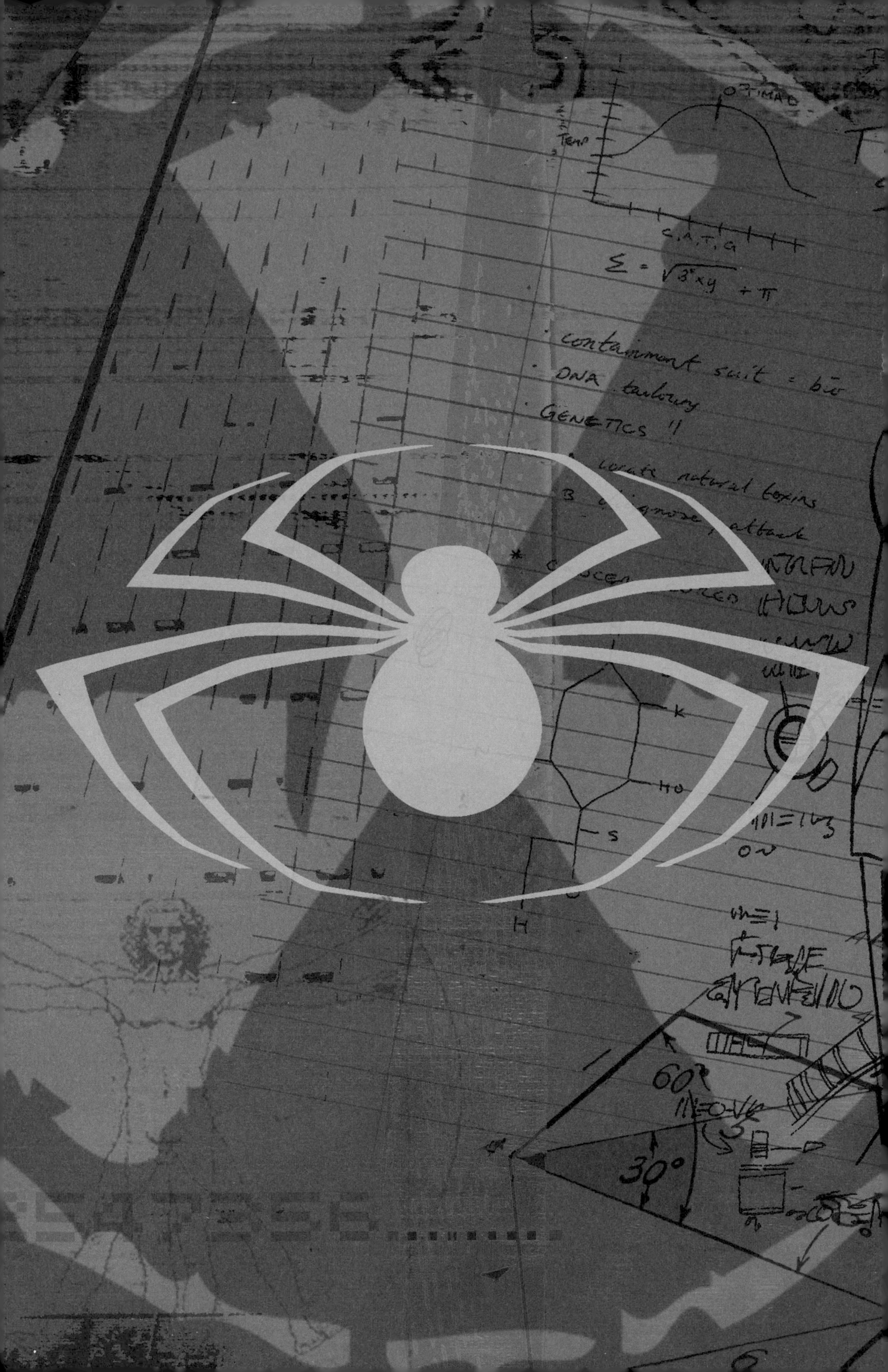
OPTIMAL
TEMP
C.A.T.G
containment suit = bio
DNA tailoring
GENETICS !!
locate natural toxins
diagnose, attack
60°
30°